A Guide Book of HARD TIMES TOKENS

Political Tokens and Store Cards 1832–1844

History • Values • Rarities

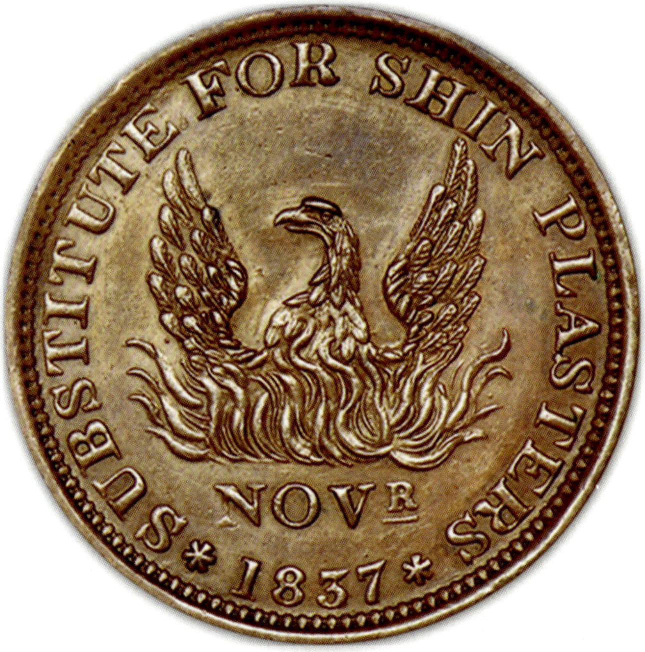

Q. David Bowers

Foreword by
Robert A. Schuman

Whitman Publishing, LLC
PUBLISHING SINCE 1934
www.whitman.com

A Guide Book of

HARD TIMES TOKENS

Whitman Publishing, LLC
PUBLISHING SINCE 1934
www.whitman.com

3101 Clairmont Road, Suite G, Atlanta, GA 30329

Correspondence concerning this book may be directed to the publisher, attn: Hard Times Tokens, at the address above.

ISBN: 079484295X
Printed in China

Disclaimer: Expert opinion should be sought in any significant numismatic purchase. This book is presented as a guide only. No warranty or representation of any kind is made concerning the completeness of the information presented. The author, a professional numismatist, regularly buys, sells, and sometimes holds certain of the items discussed in this book.

Caveat: The value estimates given are subject to variation and differences of opinion. Before making decisions to buy or sell, consult the latest information. Past performance of the rare coin market or any coin or series within that market is not necessarily an indication of future performance, as the future is unknown. Such factors as changing demand, popularity, grading interpretations, strength of the overall coin market, and economic conditions will continue to be influences.

Other books in The Official Red Book® series include: *A Guide Book of Franklin and Kennedy Half Dollars; A Guide Book of Double Eagle Gold Coins; A Guide Book of United States Type Coins; A Guide Book of Modern United States Proof Coin Sets; A Guide Book of Shield and Liberty Head Nickels; A Guide Book of Flying Eagle and Indian Head Cents; A Guide Book of Washington and State Quarters; A Guide Book of Buffalo and Jefferson Nickels; A Guide Book of Lincoln Cents; A Guide Book of United States Commemorative Coins; A Guide Book of United States Tokens and Medals; A Guide Book of Gold Dollars; A Guide Book of Peace Dollars; a Guide Book of Civil War Tokens;* and *A Guide Book of the Official Red Book of United States Coins.*

For a complete catalog of numismatic reference books, supplies, and storage products, visit Whitman Publishing online at www.whitman.com.

WCG™ Whitman® OCG™

Contents

Foreword *by Robert A. Schuman* iv

Preface vi

Chapter 1: Overview and Key to Using This Book 1

Chapter 2: A History of Collecting Hard Times Tokens 8

Chapter 3: The Prelude to the Hard Times 33

Chapter 4: The Bringer of the Hard Times 42

Chapter 5: Events of 1832 and 1833 55

Chapter 6: Events of 1834 to 1836 60

Chapter 7: Events of 1837 and 1838 69

Chapter 8: Events of 1839 to 1844 84

Chapter 9: Jackson Tokens of 1832 and 1833 91

Chapter 10: Political Tokens of 1834 to 1836 94

Chapter 11: Political Tokens of 1837 and 1838 103

Chapter 12: Political Tokens of 1840 119

Chapter 13: Hard Times Store Card Tokens 121

Chapter 14: Fantasy Hard Times Tokens 268

Appendix I: Selected Biographies 273

Appendix II: The Levick 1870 Study 281

Notes 287

Selected Bibliography 298

Credits and Acknowledgements 300

About the Author 301

Index of Low-to-Whitman Numbers 302

Index of Rulau-to-Whitman Numbers 306

Index 311

Foreword

In 1958, at the age of 13, I was offered and happily accepted a part-time job at Mason-Dixon Coin Exchange in Baltimore, Maryland, from owner Thomas P. Warfield. This was the beginning of my real introduction to coin collecting, and ultimately to numismatics. Fortuitously, at the shop I became interested in two books that would have significant impact on my numismatic interests and, in fact, on my life in general.

In 1958, *Penny Whimsy* (a ten-year revision of *Early American Cents* by William Sheldon) had just been published and released. Aside from providing superb technical, descriptive text of varieties—from which I learned to attribute large cents—the book, more importantly, instilled in me a sense of reverence for the pieces themselves, both as miniature works of art, and also as cherished historical artifacts.

In 1955, with much less fanfare, Charles V. Kappen produced a very attractive, full-size reprint of Lyman H. Low's 1900 magnum opus, *Hard Times Tokens*, along with half-tone reproductions of the famous Edgar H. Adams plates, circa 1915.

I became somewhat obsessed with both. I was allowed to attribute all large cents that came through the shop, which was a valuable experience. At the same time, I had intermittent opportunities to purchase Hard Times tokens, usually in Mint State, generally for $1 or $2 each. There was something about their clear historical context and physical similarity to large cents that was remarkably appealing. While my interest in and evolution as a collector of both series progressed, the next twelve years of my life were primarily occupied with college, medical school, an internship, and residency in Diagnostic Radiology in San Francisco.

Incidentally, during my senior year in medical school in 1971, I traveled to St. Louis for the Frank Masters sale of large cents. I had noticed in the partially plated catalog a cataloging error of great significance. An EF-40 1794, Head of 1793, large cent (my personal favorite type) had been called a Sheldon-*18b* with quite a few finer specimens known. Because of my prior experience with large cent attribution, it was clear to me that this was, instead, an *S-19b*, and quite possibly the finest in existence. I had no idea if anyone else had noticed this, and went to St. Louis to try to purchase it. As it turned out, of all the large cent experts and cherry-pickers out there, no one else had noticed this, and I bought it for $1,100.

I was immediately approached by a large group of collectors (Early American Coppers club members, as I later came to realize). Once I explained to them about the misattribution, they confirmed it and sheepishly admitted their oversight. I began receiving offers of twice what I paid, which was very flattering, but much more importantly, I was invited to join E.A.C. and attend their meeting. There I met many large cent luminaries who would become life-long friends, including Del Bland, Jack Beymer, Denis Loring, and others. This event also led to correspondences and subsequent friendships with C. Douglas Smith, John W. Adams, and Ted Naftzger. In a single weekend, I had become a large cent presence and had made friendships still strong to this day.

I mention this important but anecdotal story by way of introduction because I want to return to the Hard Times tokens which I have collected, loved, and studied for more than fifty years. I have been fortunate, being present when great specialized collections crossed the auction block, including the Stack's sale of the John J. Ford, Jr. Collection in 2004, their sale of the Collections of James E. Dice and M. Lamar Hicks in 2008, and two other sections of the Ford Collection of Hard Times tokens by Stacks Bowers Galleries in 2013. I have also gathered an extensive library of relevant auction catalogs dating back into the 19th century.

In 2010, I wrote a book, *The True Hard Times Tokens*, which concentrated on the earlier political issues, mainly centering on Andrew Jackson. This was very well received. However, it pales in comparison to the ground-breaking book you are about to read, written by the greatest numismatic author of all time, my good friend Q. David Bowers. I am honored and pleased that he asked me to write the foreword to his book.

The spontaneous origin of Hard Times tokens, the factors that led to their generation, the beginning of numismatic interest in them, their ascendance to the virtual pinnacle of numismatic desirability in the first few decades of the 20th century, and the continuing collector interest in them through the second half of the 20th century to the present are well documented by the author. The people responsible for these elements, both researchers and collectors, are also appropriately noted. In the past year, as the manuscript drew to a conclusion, I also shared with Dave my notes and observations.

However, even more importantly, Dave has, through extensive and meticulous work involving significant primary sources, discovered and described valuable information regarding the issues and the issuers behind these Hard Times tokens which is the real essence of the series. This information goes far beyond the scope and depth of anything previously published. With all due respect to Russell Rulau (whose early research in the 1960s, on merchants wrongly excluded by Low, was invaluable), his supposed definitive references are filled with non-token ephemera, inconsistent numbering, and sub-optimal photography. However, Russ's contributions had the great benefit that they publicized a series for which little modern information was otherwise available. Collectors of Hard Times tokens and potential collectors of Hard Times tokens needed a hero to appear to present a clear, complete, verified, carefully focused, and well-photographed listing of these important pieces. That hero is Q. David Bowers.

Dave has been interested in this subject for at least half a century, and the seeds for the emergence of this book have been germinating for nearly that long as well. For me, the essence of numismatics is the history, the people, and the stories behind the pieces. W. Elliot Woodward, in his 1884 sale of the Joseph N.T. Levick collection of tokens and store cards (perhaps the greatest of all time) wrote on page 11:

> Many of these cards and tokens are amongst the very rarest of all American issues, and if the word rare with its superlatives is thought to occur too frequently, let it be attributed to the fact mentioned, which every collector knows is perfectly correct. The 1804 dollar and the 1802 half dime are actually common in comparison with many of these pieces, and I confess, that apart from their money value, I regard them as much less interesting. These pieces and the political series, now so much neglected, are an epitome of the political and business history of the country, while the mint series is—money—that's all.

Dave Bowers, with virtually every book he has written, has had the almost unique ability to re-create the aura and the mystique of his subject matter in a way that captures the warmth, the nostalgia, and the joy that both collectors and historians feel when they immerse themselves in their own world of special treasures and thoughts. That same sensation emerges throughout this book, especially as one enters Dave's realm of Hard Times merchants. These pieces all represent human beings or groups of human beings who took the chance, the risk, and the leap of faith on the American entrepreneurial system approximately 175 years ago. I am sure there were sinners and saints among them, hoping to better their lot in life. Some failed almost immediately, and others were successful for decades. Of course, all have ultimately succumbed to human mortality. However, those relative few who chose to place their names on these small, metal discs that we now cherish have created for themselves a certain degree of immortality through that which we collect, and by our conscious collecting efforts we perpetuate and extend that immortality. The tokens about to be described are, in most cases, the only surviving remnants of the people that had them created and the hopes and dreams that lived within them when America was young.

I believe that, with this book, Dave Bowers has paid homage, finally, to the hundreds (if not thousands) of people who have been involved with these still fascinating pieces of history that have come to be known as Hard Times tokens. These people—issuers, researchers, students, and collectors—past and present, have long deserved a book of this caliber and stature to stand as a monument to them for what will hopefully be a future generation of interested historians and numismatists. Thank you once again, Dave Bowers, for casting light where, for so long, only shadow had existed.

Robert A. Schuman

Preface

If you're a longtime coin collector, as I am, you've probably read quite a few works by Q. David Bowers. After all, he's been writing in the field of numismatics since the 1950s, he published his first book (*Coins and Collectors*) in 1964, his list of titles has surpassed four dozen, and his articles and columns number in the thousands. *Yes, the thousands.* Dave's scope ranges from American colonial coins to modern-day Proofs, from ten-cent tokens to ten-million-dollar rarities. On top of that his prose is featured in various parts of the *Guide Book of United States Coins* (the hobby's best-selling "Red Book," with more than 23 million copies in print since 1946). So if you've been collecting coins, tokens, medals, or paper money for more than a year or two and you've never read a word of Bowers, I have good news and bad news. The good news is you're rarer than an 1804 dollar! The bad news is you're missing out on a full and complete hobby experience. Fortunately the solution is conveniently at hand.

I spoke with Mr. Q. David Bowers for the first time soon after I joined Whitman Publishing in December 2004. I was in the company's Atlanta headquarters and Dave was in Wolfeboro, New Hampshire, where he does most of his writing. At the time he was already Whitman's numismatic director. I had grown up, numismatically speaking, reading Bowers books and articles, so it was quite an honor for this recently minted numismatic publisher to be speaking with a legend as a colleague. "Call me Dave," he said. "Everybody does. If you insist on calling me 'Mr. Bowers,' I'll call you 'Mr. Tucker'!"

Dave and I have talked or emailed nearly every day since that first phone call. Over these ten years, we've worked on books ranging from 96-page monographs to 900-page encyclopedias. His productivity is amazing. One of the most frequent questions I hear from collectors is, "How does Dave Bowers write so many books?" The process is remarkable to observe. You've already read Robert Schuman's foreword to this book, which gives an experienced Hard Times token collector's perspective on the field and Dave's place in it. A *preface* is different from a foreword: it's the publisher's (sometimes the author's) place to make a statement about the book *as a book*. I'll use this opportunity to shed some light on how Dave Bowers does what he does.

First of all, he's been writing for more than 50 years. Perhaps *writing* isn't the best word; it's too constrictive, too narrow. Producing? Creating? What Dave does is multifaceted and immersive, more long-range than the simple physical act of sitting down at a desk and putting pen to paper (to use an old-fashioned expression). The bedrock of his system is the Bowers archives. Long before the Internet, Dave was compiling a personal library and research center of books, newspapers, magazine clippings and snippets, and other resources—anything and everything numismatic. He read and studied decades' worth of old periodicals, the likes of *Frank Leslie's Illustrated Newspaper*, and made note of everything relating to American coins, tokens, paper money, general and specific economic conditions, the intricacies of day-to-day bank operations, interesting financial-sector goings-on, Mint procedures, Treasury gossip, and more. (Again, this exercise was before Google searches, online book archives, and other modern conveniences. It has developed, or least strengthened, what I suspect is a photographic memory combined with instant recall.) In the mid-1950s, he began interviewing key figures in numismatics—B. Max Mehl, Abe Kosoff, Stephen Nagy, Robert Botsford, Mint directors from Rae Biester to date, and hundreds more, gaining knowledge that would have otherwise been lost forever. As technology has advanced, so has the Bowers research machine. Historical images that he earlier had to clip, photograph, or photocopy can now be scanned and saved digitally in high resolution. Instead of having to travel to faraway museums and archives, email and the Internet put him in a hundred places at once, with instant communications.

This brings up another important factor in how Dave Bowers works: collaboration. "To have a friend, you must be a friend," as the proverb goes. Over a career spanning decades, Dave Bowers has built a reputation as a researcher who generously shares information instead of jealously guarding it. His network has grown strong from this. Today, when a numismatist gets an email or phone call saying, "This is Dave. I'm working on a new book about [fill in the blank], and was wondering if you have any images, die varieties, new research, or other information to share?" the answer is nearly always an enthusiastic "Yes!" He knows all of the museum curators, all of the Treasury and Mint officers, all of the historians, the collectors, the dealers, the auctioneers, the researchers, archivists, and aficionados who make numismatics a vibrant and living American science. He goes out of his way to share his knowledge with them when they need help. In return they share their own specialized insight—and Dave absorbs and synthesizes it as only he can, to bring to you, his reader.

Another element of the Bowers method is a constant and never-resting spirit of inquiry that spans genres, disciplines, and fields. Dave is as curious a student of current Presidential dollars as he is of Massachusetts colonial silver and pre–Federal Reserve bank notes. He wrote a book on gold dollars minted from 1849 to 1889. He wrote another on State quarters that your kids can collect from pocket change today. Not to mention a massive study of pre-1916 American motion pictures . . . the definitive reference on automatic and coin-operated music machines . . . a monumental history of the California Gold Rush . . . an illustrated monograph on Art Nouveau artist Alphonse Mucha. . . . or an exploration of the American bison in popular culture. His subjects run up and down the Dewey Decimal System. The breadth and depth of Dave's intellectual curiosity and study bring to mind President John F. Kennedy's famous quote at a 1962 gathering of Nobel Prize winners: "I think this is the most extraordinary collection of talent, of human knowledge, that has ever been gathered together at the White House, with the possible exception of when Thomas Jefferson dined alone."

To define the man, add to these elements a genuinely engaging writing style; the ability to connect with and satisfy readers; a scientist's ability to rigorously test theories and fearlessly question conventional wisdom; a technician's grasp of information design and user interface; and an artist's knack of seeing the whole before the parts are assembled.

For the *Guide Book of Hard Times Tokens*, the foundation of Dave's manuscript was the research he'd been gathering for many years: biographies of die engravers, histories of issuing firms, and narratives about the political personalities involved; plus his observations on the market and collector activities, from several decades' perspective; and images gathered over the course of his career. He called upon friends and colleagues in the field. At Whitman our design team planned the book's look and feel, and our editorial staff worked with Dave to fine-tune the manuscript and marshal its million moving parts. Over the course of several months this huge project was given its legs to stand on, and it took off running. I can't think of another author who could have pulled it together in less than *years*, if it were possible at all.

At the same time, Dave was also actively working on manuscripts about obsolete paper money, Civil War tokens, 19th-century advertising shell cards, and several other topics. "I like to work on projects in parallel," he always tells me. When he gets bored with one he'll turn to another, which somehow charges his batteries so he can return to the first refreshed. A normal person would simply get tired, but the inimitable QDB is actually energized by work.

So there's some of my behind-the-scenes perspective on the Dean of American Numismatics. When ambitious young writers ask me, "How can I become the next Q. David Bowers?" the answer is simple. All it takes is an insatiable curiosity about the world, a steel-trap mind, the ability to connect a hundred different disciplines logically and with panache, a vast network of friendly collaborators whose respect hasn't been bought or beguiled but *earned*, and 50 years of experience. Start early. The encouraging news is that if you accomplish even one half of Bowers's output, you'll have earned a place in the numismatic history books.

Dennis Tucker
Atlanta, Georgia

1

Overview and Key to Using This Book

Overview

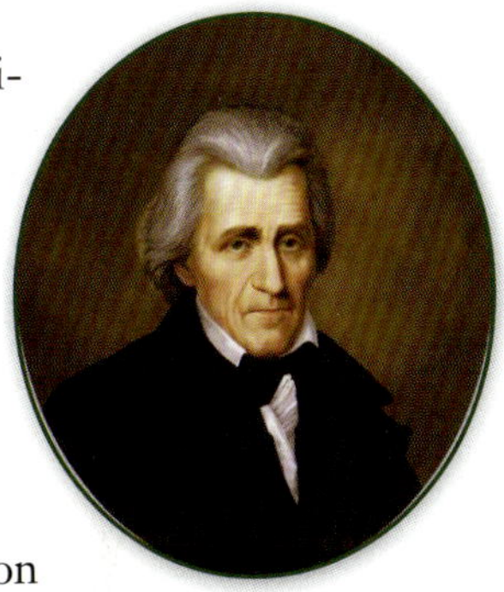

Andrew Jackson, president 1829–1837.

The controversial Bank of the United States went out of business in 1836, but debates for and against it continued for a long time. In brief, President Andrew Jackson and most other Democrats found that the institution, popularly called the "monster" by some, was an impediment to commerce in the form of unfair competition against hundreds of banks chartered by state legislatures. This situation formed the focus of Lyman H. Low's first scholarly work, which evolved to become the standard reference on Hard Times tokens.

Taking the opposing view were those who did not like Jackson and hoped to rally his opponents to strength in the election year of 1832. Several tokens were issued showcasing Jackson, inspiring Low to use this date, rather than 1834, in the 1899 expanded edition of his study, as the starting point for the Hard Times series. The scenario is given in the next chapter.

From 1832 until the onset of the Hard Times era with the Panic of 1837, copper cents were plentiful in circulation, but just about anything else of cent size passed at the same value as well. During this time many varieties of political tokens—as well as those with advertising (store cards)—were struck.

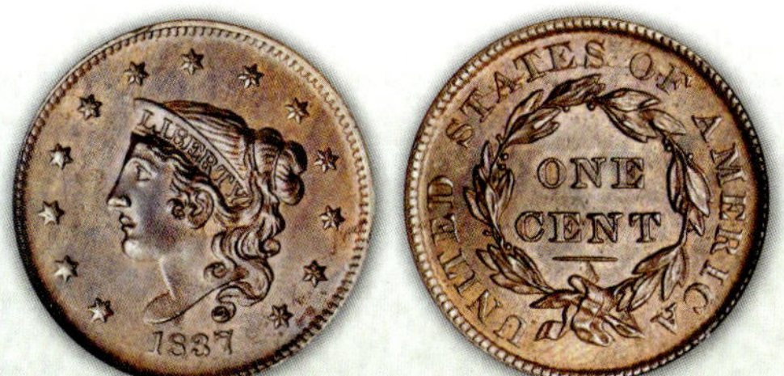

Federal cents such as this became scarce in 1837.

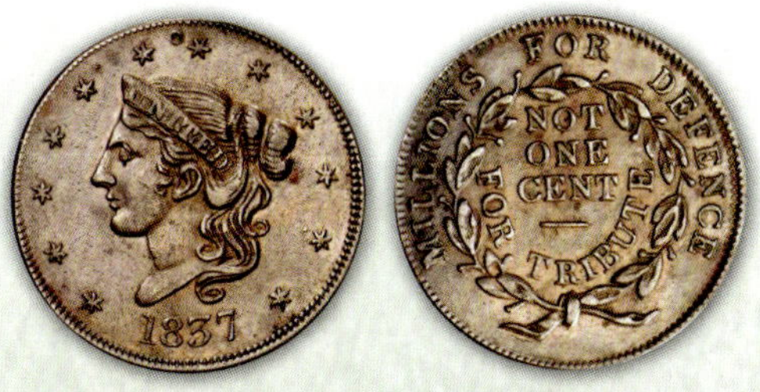

An 1837 privately minted Hard Times token in imitation of a federal cent, but with NOT ONE CENT on the reverse.

After the Panic began, federal cents disappeared, as noted. For the rest of the year and into 1838, privately minted copper tokens were effective substitutes. Later, more tokens were issued, but in much smaller quantities. Low's latest-dated token, thus defining his span of the series, is 1844. This is on a very rare copper token the size of a cent, with a Liberty Head on the obverse, dated that year and bearing on the reverse the advertisement of J. Cochran, a bell founder in Batavia, New York. This token was listed by Low in his 1906 supplement.

Hard Times tokens dated 1834 and later and with a political theme are mainly anti–Jackson and his successor, Martin Van Buren, and were issued by their detractors. Some pro–Jackson and Van Buren pieces were made as well. Jackson was president from March 4, 1829, until March 4, 1837. Van Buren, Jackson's second-term vice president, was president from 1837 to 1841. Both men were unmercifully lampooned on tokens, many of which are fascinating to study today.

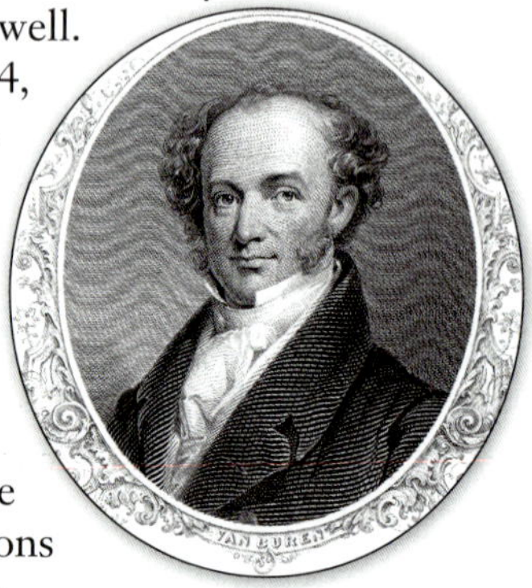

Martin Van Buren (Bureau of Engraving and Printing).

Other tokens made in quantity in 1837 are fairly close copies of official copper cents, with a Liberty Head on the obverse and wreath on the reverse, but with different inscriptions on the back, including NOT ONE CENT, the "NOT" often in small letters. These Liberty Head imitations prompted criticism and even legal actions and were mostly discontinued.

Hard Times tokens issued by merchants bear notices for more than 100 individuals and businesses offering goods and services. Some of these are quite pictorial, with images of an umbrella, boot, comb, or clock face, or other motifs. Other tokens were used as tickets for rides, such as one showing George Washington on horseback on the obverse and on the reverse a notation that the token was worth three cents' fare to Atwood's Rail Road Hotel, a stopping place of which little is known today.

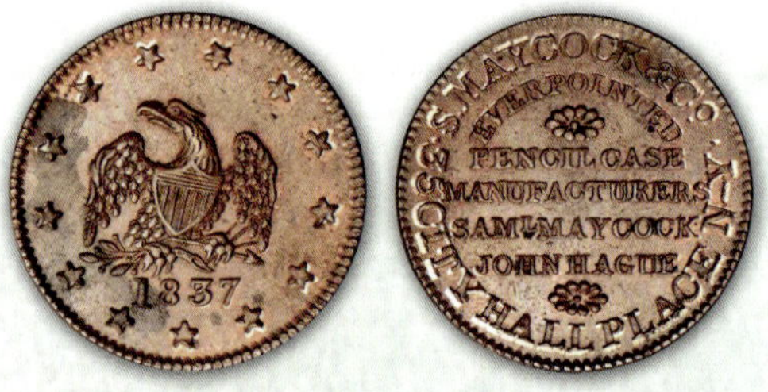

One of many different store cards issued by merchants from 1832 to 1844, defined as the Hard Times years.

Key to Using this Book

A Note on Quoted Material

Some quoted material has been lightly edited or rearranged, but in all instances the original meaning has been preserved. Common misspellings have been corrected. Footnotes, including in quoted material, are those of the author (QDB) unless specifically noted otherwise.

The Listings of Tokens

Which side to call the obverse and which to call the reverse? This has been debated, and there is no consistency. In January 1879 this was published in *The Coin Collector's Journal:*

> W.H.L., Syracuse, N. Y., asks: "What would be a safe rule to follow in determining the obverse and reverse of store-cards?" We answer: The purpose of a store-card is to advertise a storekeeper; very plainly, therefore, the side which gives prominence to the storekeeper's business or place of business, is the obverse of the token; the other side must then be the reverse. Sometimes the reverse of a store-card will bear some interesting or artistic device, but that is merely accidental and secondary to the storekeeper's purpose in issuing the token at first, and should not influence us in determining which is the obverse of the token itself.

This was Lyman H. Low's view as well. However, modern students of the series, including Russell Rulau, have often placed a side with the date and a portrait, such as 1837 Liberty Head, as the obverse. In the present text this has been followed in most instances. In other instances with inscriptions on both sides, the side with the name of the issuer is designated the obverse. If the issuer's name is on both sides and a date is on one side, the date side is chosen. The point is that the matter is highly subjective!

A typical entry is given below. This is for an 1837 Hard Times token designated as Whitman-11-260a.

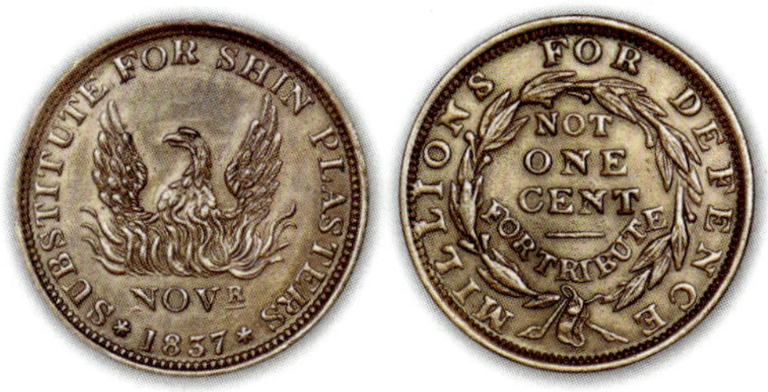

Hard Times token variety W-11-260a.

W-11-260a • 1837 Phoenix • Low-45; HT-56. R-1. 28 mm. Copper. Plain edge. Obverse with phoenix rising from flames, NOVr below. Around the border SUBSTITUTE FOR SHIN PLASTERS 1837. This represents the resumption of specie payments in New York City, a desirable substitute for shinplasters (paper notes of questionable value). Reverse with MILLIONS FOR DEFENCE around border. Berries below first L, first N and second E. Within wreath NOT / ONE / CENT / FOR TRIBUTE. Line below CENT.

The Whitman number is shorthand for cataloging, referencing, or other matters. Any example of this variety can be called W-11-260, and without further description it will be understood by everyone with access to the book. The prefix *11* refers to the chapter of this book in which the entry can be found. In the chapter on store cards, the Whitman number contains a prefix for the token's issuer and the state in which the token was issued.

Metals Used for Hard Times Tokens

As an example of metal identification, the lower-case letter at the end of W-11-260a refers to copper. Following the methodology used in several reference books on Civil War tokens, the metal letters for Hard Times tokens are:

a = copper
b = brass
e = white metal or pewter
f = silver
g = lead
j = German silver or Feuchtwanger's Composition

Most Hard Times tokens were struck in either copper or brass. Some were made in white metal or pewter, but not many as this metal was not durable in circulation.

Silver strikings were made for the numismatic trade as delicacies or rarities and were never intended for circulation. All are very rare.

Some Hard Times tokens were struck in lead, an unsatisfactory metal that often oxidized or deteriorated.

German silver, or Feuchtwanger's Composition, was used on quite a few varieties, especially those issued by Dr. Lewis Feuchtwanger.

Low and HT Numbers

Low numbers are cross-references to the same variety as listed by Lyman H. Low in his 1899 *Hard Times Tokens* book and its 1906 supplement. HT numbers refer to the numbers assigned by Russell Rulau in his *Standard Catalog of United States Tokens 1700–1900.*

In a few instances Low numbers are given in quotation marks, as Rulau: "Low-275." These refer to pseudo-Low numbers used by Rulau in the late 20th century and bear no relation to either the original Low numbers or Rulau's HT numbers. They are added for the convenience of readers who may have used them earlier.

Rarity Ratings

A letter and number such as R-1 or R-6 refers to the rarity rating of the token as approximated by collectors, dealers, and scholars over a period of time. As discoveries are made from time to time, and not all tokens in existence have been studied, these ratings are subject to change. Likely, many present entries rate certain tokens as rarer than they actually are. The rarity scale used is that devised by Dr. J. Hewitt Judd in 1959, an adaptation of Dr. William H. Sheldon's scale published in 1949:

R-1 = more than 1,250 known
R-2 = 501–1,250
R-3 = 201–500
R-4 = 76–200
R-5 = 31–75
Low R-6 = 21–30
High R-6 = 13–20
Low R-7 = 7–12
High R-7 = 4–6
R-8 = 2 or 3
R-9 = Unique; only 1 known

Diameter and Thickness of Hard Times Tokens

Diameters are expressed in millimeters. Hard Times tokens were struck in two ways:

Open collar: With no restraining circular collar to limit the spread of the planchet as it was struck in a coining press. The diameter of such tokens can vary. Within a given variety, one token might measure 28.5 mm, another 28.3 mm, another 28.6 mm. Such variations neither add nor subtract value.

Closed collar: Sometimes called close collar. A metal plate with a hole the size of the intended token was in the press. The inside of the hole, the collar, could be plain or it could have a series of tiny vertical or diagonal indentations for reeding. During the striking process the planchet spreads outward to the collar, which defines its diameter.

There were no standards or rules to determine the thickness or weight of a copper planchet. The lighter the weight, the more profitable the coinage would be, in the case of tokens intended to be passed out for the value of 1¢. Many copper Hard Times tokens are similar to the weight and diameter of federal cents, but there are many exceptions.

Edges of Hard Times Tokens

There are two main edge styles of Hard Times tokens: plain and reeded. Plain edges, produced either with open collar or closed collar, as described above, are by far the most often seen. Reeded edges were produced by a closed collar, also as described above. Most reeds or ridges are vertical, but a few varieties have diagonal reeds. Sometimes reeding is faint or partial.

Grading Hard Times Tokens

While no grading standards have been adopted for Hard Times tokens, the guidelines in the *Official American Numismatic Association Grading Standards* book (edited by Kenneth Bressett, narrative by Q. David Bowers), which relate to federal coins, have been adapted by most collectors and dealers. Grading is subjective, and one person's AU-55 might be another's MS-60. Tokens certified by the Numismatic Guaranty Corporation of America (NGC) or the Professional Coin Grading Service (PCGS) use the ANA numbers and have been popular in recent years.

Whereas federal cents of the Hard Times token period (1832–1844) all have the same general design—Liberty Head obverse and wreath reverse—there is no uniformity among Hard Times tokens. Accordingly, the indications of wear apply to features originally found—all lettering, a Liberty Head, a ship, or whatever—and how circulation gradually wore away the features.

The listing below is adapted by the author from the official ANA standards and used with the permission of the American Numismatic Association and Whitman Publishing.

MS-60 to 70 (Mint State) • In the lower Mint State grades, MS-60 and 61, some slight abrasions can be seen on the higher points of the motif (if there is one) or the high points on the letters. There will be some luster or mint frost in the fields. At the MS-63 level abrasions will be minimal. If the metal is copper, there may be traces of original mint red. An MS-65 token will have full luster and if in copper will be brown, red and brown, or full or nearly full mint red. Such coins are commonly abbreviated as MS-65BN, MS-65RB, or MS-65RD. Designations of red coloring are for original brightness, not for coins that have been cleaned. Most of the rarer Hard Times token varieties are in grades less than Mint State. The terms Uncirculated and Mint State are interchangeable, but with numbers attached the MS designation is used.

AU-50, 53, 55, 58 (About Uncirculated) • Friction is seen on the higher parts of a motif (if there is one), and more wear is seen on the legends. Friction and scattered marks are in the field, ranging from extensive at AU-50 to minimal at AU-58. Luster may be seen in protected areas, minimal at the AU-50 level, more visible at AU-58. At AU-58 the field may retain some luster as well. This is the ultimate grade for many Hard Times token varieties, including many at R-1 to R-3 levels, as they were not saved by numismatists at the time.

EF-40, 45 (Extremely Fine) • Wear is seen on the motif (if present) and on the lettering. Luster is minimal or nonexistent at EF-40.

VF-20, 30 (Very Fine) • Wear is more considerable than on the preceding, but all features such as elements of the motif (if present), ornaments, etc., are distinct. As a general rule, tokens at the Rarity-1 and 2 levels are usually sought in this grade or finer and not in lower grades.

F-12, 15 (Fine) • The details are fewer than on the preceding. F-15 shows slightly more detail. All lettering is readable.

VG-8, 10 (Very Good) • At this level a token shows considerable wear, and some lettering will be weak or, if not well defined in the die, may be missing. General features will all be distinct. The border is well defined in most areas. This and lower grades are desirable and highly sought in the case of rarities in which finer examples are impossible to find, or nearly so.

G-4, 6 (Good) • The token is well worn. The motif (if present) may be only in outline form. On many varieties the rim is faded into the field.

AG-3 (About Good) • Wear is more extensive than on the preceding, many of the letters or ornaments are missing, but the token is still readily identifiable as to variety.

Striking and Sharpness

Unlike federal cents, which were made to a standard and checked for quality, Hard Times tokens vary in the sharpness of details, both in the sharpness of the dies to begin with, and in the sharpness imparted during the striking process. Varieties with high-relief details on the obverse, such as the portrait of William H. Seward, Gulian C. Verplanck, or a Liberty Head, are often lightly struck on the highest points, lacking detail there and also on the corresponding part of the reverse. There was not enough metal to flow completely into the dies, thus the deepest recesses (which were to create the highest points on the tokens) were not filled.

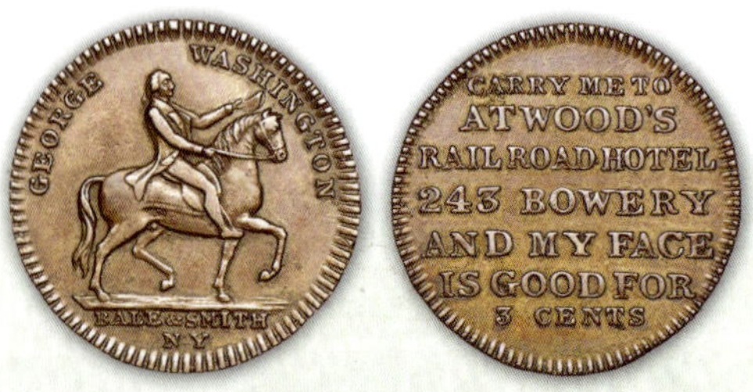

Hard Times token variety W-NY-200-11a by Bale & Smith of New York City, a well-struck issue. Atwood's Rail Road Hotel was next to a stop on the New York & Harlem Rail Road (which also issued Hard Times tokens).

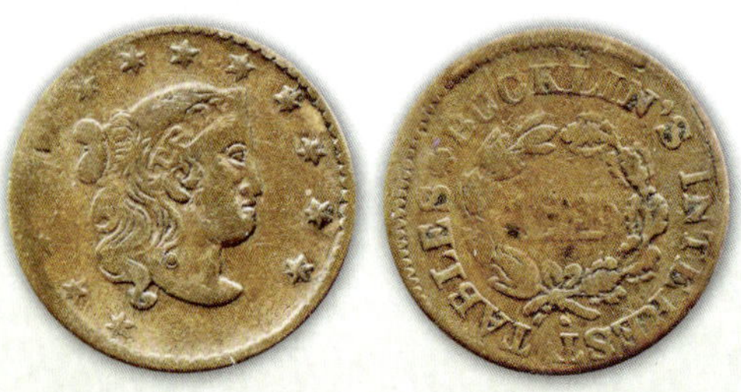

Hard Times token variety W-NY-1660-30a by a seemingly untalented die cutter named True who was in Albany, New York. The token was advertised by Isaac Bucklin who offered Interest Tables for sale. Rustically cut dies have a special numismatic appeal.

The dies made by Bale & Smith were nearly always sharply defined with excellent detail and were well struck. Several other firms turned out sharply defined tokens as well. In contrast the dies made by a Mr. True in Albany, New York, for certain merchants in Albany and nearby Troy were amateurishly cut, with poor detail and irregular features. The pair of dies made by Gustin & Blake of Chelsea, Vermont, had weak features at the outset. Tokens made by True and Gustin & Blake look well-worn even if they have had little circulation! Such rusticity adds to their numismatic desirability—just as "folk art" contributes to the value of certain amateurishly made art items.

Determining whether a token exists sharply struck can be best done by reviewing photographs or other illustrations. This will furnish a guide as to what can and cannot be found.

Planchet quality is usually very good for Hard Times tokens—with relatively few problems or flaws.

Market Availability

The overall availability of a given Hard Times token is directly proportional to its rarity. A token that is classified on the Rarity Scale as High R-7 or higher is usually desired by an advanced collector no matter what the grade of the token may be. An example is W-NY-080-10a (Low-161 and HT-211), issued by J. Cochran, a bell founder in Batavia, New York. There are only four known today. John J. Ford Jr., who formed the finest Hard Times token collection ever, had to settle for an example with part of the reverse lettering scraped off.

Condition rarity is another aspect to consider. There are many R-1 to R-3 tokens for which hundreds or more exist in grades of Very Fine to About Uncirculated, but in true Mint State they are rarities.

Over the years it has been a general rule for collectors to acquire as many different pieces as possible in Extremely Fine or About Uncirculated grades, which includes most of the varieties through Rarity-6, then to consider the rarer pieces on an individual basis.

While rarity and grade are important elements of value, *eye appeal* is vital as well. Most collectors agree that a pleasing VF-20 token is better to own than a discolored or unattractive EF-40. Accordingly, being patient when buying, and exercising connoisseurship, will pay dividends.

Auction Houses and Abbreviations

Many important sales of Hard Times tokens were handled by Stack's auction house, which had been in operation under that name since 1935. Stack's merged with American Numismatic Rarities in 2006, keeping the name *Stack's*. When the company merged with Bowers & Merena in 2010, Stack's became *Stack's Bowers Galleries*. Bowers & Merena is abbreviated in the auction listings in this book as *B&M*. Stack's Bowers Galleries is abbreviated in the auction listings in this book as *SBG*.

2

A History of Collecting Hard Times Tokens

The 1832 to 1844 Token-Issuing Era

The series known as Hard Times tokens is one of the most fascinating in American numismatics. No two tokens are alike, and each has a story—sometimes logical, sometimes improbable. The era covered in the numismatic definition invented by Lyman H. Low is 1832 to 1844. Any American token issued within this period is a candidate for inclusion. This time frame differs from the economic and historical view of the Hard Times era, which began with scattered problems in 1834, evolved into the Panic of 1837, and concluded with general recovery by the spring of 1843.

Low was a New York City professional numismatist who was considered to be in the front rank of scholars in the late 19th century. He wrote extensively and was an editor of the *American Journal of Numismatics.* Although he was not the first to chronicle tokens of the era, he became the most important.

The Beginning of Interest

An early numismatic mention of what were later called Hard Times tokens appeared in 1847 in an untitled commentary by C.P. Serrue in *Revue de la Numismatique Belge*, volume III, pp. 407–410, describing in French several different issues relating to the *grande crise financière*, including a Van Buren token, a tortoise and strongbox issue, and an Illustrious Predecessor token. Such pieces had little value at the time, and in America there were no numismatic journals, and no earlier numismatic mention of such tokens has been found.

Coin collecting became a very popular hobby in America a decade later in 1857 when many citizens lamented the end of the large copper "penny," a familiar sight since childhood. In that year the monthly *Historical Magazine* was launched. This publication carried wide-ranging information, mostly on American history, including many inquiries and features about rare coins. In the meantime, Jeremiah Colburn contributed articles about coins to the *Boston Evening Dispatch*, and teenaged Augustus B. Sage had a question and answer column in the *New-York Dispatch*. In March 1858, Sage and his friends organized the American Numismatic Society in his family's apartment upstairs at 121 Essex Street in New York City.

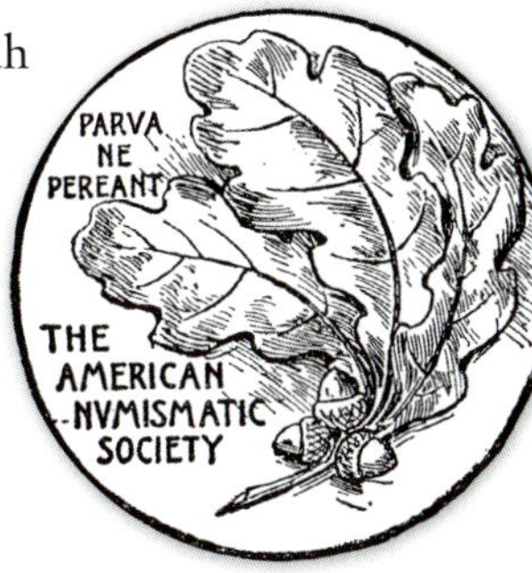

Seal later created for the American Numismatic Society and still used today.

In a reminiscence R.W. McLachlan told of his experiences in Canada when he began collecting coins in 1858:

> Of United States coins [in circulation] there were always present some of the large cents, a few colonials, an occasional Fugio and Nova Constellatio, and considerable numbers of the state issues of Connecticut, Vermont, and New Jersey; rarely a specimen from Massachusetts, New York, or Virginia turned up. Then there were always present a good sprinkling of Jacksonian and Hard Times tokens.[1]

In 1858 Charles I. Bushnell published *An Arrangement of Tradesmen's Cards, Political Tokens, also Election Medals, Medalets, &c. Current in the United States of America for the Last Sixty Years, Described from the Originals, Chiefly in the Collection of the Author*. All of this set the stage for a strong interest in tokens.

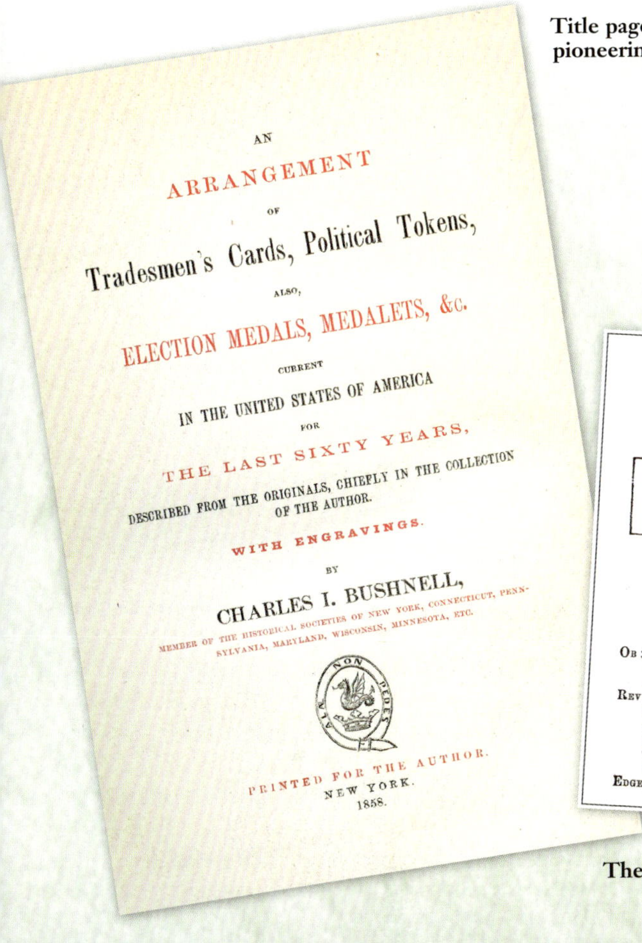

AN
ARRANGEMENT
OF
Tradesmen's Cards, Political Tokens,
ALSO,
ELECTION MEDALS, MEDALETS, &c.
CURRENT
IN THE UNITED STATES OF AMERICA
FOR
THE LAST SIXTY YEARS,
DESCRIBED FROM THE ORIGINALS, CHIEFLY IN THE COLLECTION OF THE AUTHOR.
WITH ENGRAVINGS.
BY
CHARLES I. BUSHNELL,
MEMBER OF THE HISTORICAL SOCIETIES OF NEW YORK, CONNECTICUT, PENNSYLVANIA, MARYLAND, WISCONSIN, MINNESOTA, ETC.
NON DEDES ALA
PRINTED FOR THE AUTHOR.
NEW YORK.
1858.

Title page of Charles I. Bushnell's pioneering 1858 book on tokens.

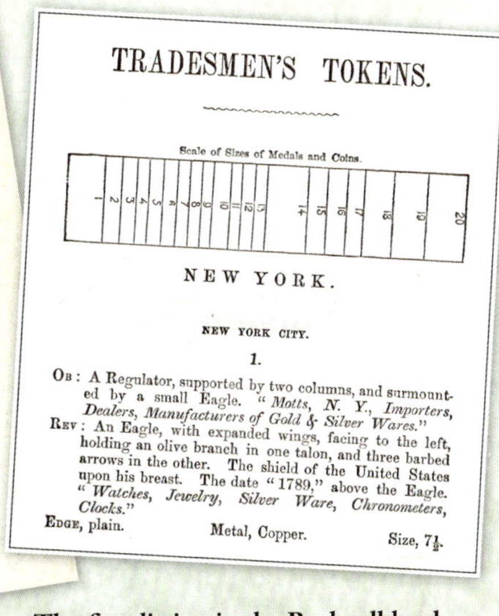

TRADESMEN'S TOKENS.

Scale of Sizes of Medals and Coins.

1 2 3 4 5 6 7 8 9 10 11 12 13 14 15 16 17 18 19 20

NEW YORK.

NEW YORK CITY.

1.

Ob: A Regulator, supported by two columns, and surmounted by a small Eagle. "*Motts, N. Y., Importers, Dealers, Manufacturers of Gold & Silver Wares.*"
Rev: An Eagle, with expanded wings, facing to the left, holding an olive branch in one talon, and three barbed arrows in the other. The shield of the United States upon his breast. The date "1789," above the Eagle. "*Watches, Jewelry, Silver Ware, Chronometers, Clocks.*"
Edge, plain. Metal, Copper. Size, 7½.

The first listing in the Bushnell book.

Charles I. Bushnell

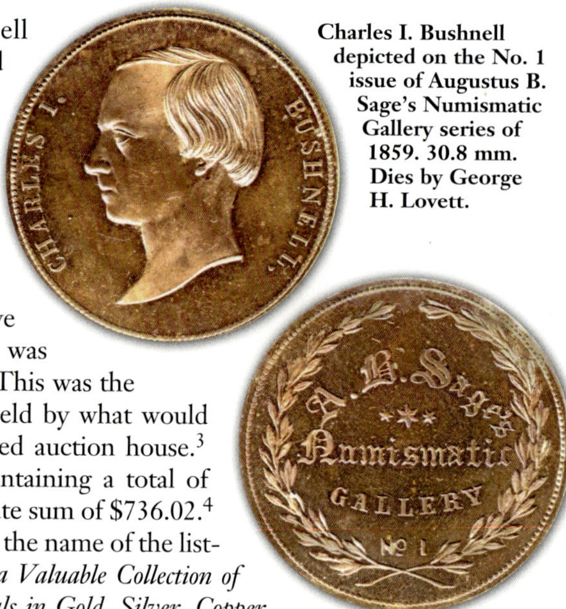

Charles I. Bushnell depicted on the No. 1 issue of Augustus B. Sage's Numismatic Gallery series of 1859. 30.8 mm. Dies by George H. Lovett.

Born on July 28, 1821,[2] Bushnell developed an interest in coins and history at an early age. He studied law and by the 1850s was a successful attorney in New York City. He carefully built a large and impressive collection.

On June 6, 1855, the collection of Peter (also known as Pierre) Flandin, a numismatist who had been active in New York City since the 1820s, was auctioned by Bangs, Brother & Co. This was the first truly notable numismatic sale held by what would be, in various forms, a very long-lived auction house.[3] The offering comprised 230 lots containing a total of 1,195 pieces, and sold for the aggregate sum of $736.02.[4] Flandin's name was not mentioned in the name of the listing, which was entitled *Catalogue of a Valuable Collection of American and Foreign Coins and Medals in Gold, Silver, Copper and Bronze.*

In the absence of having a staff numismatist, Bangs, Brother & Co. probably called upon someone in the New York City area to do the cataloging. It is possible that Charles I. Bushnell was the individual to assist them in this regard. It is known that Bushnell attended and bought in the sale, and he owned the dies for at least one item sold, Lot 159 (described as "Medal given by the City of New York to the Mexican Volunteers").[5]

In that era, using methodology no doubt derived from his legal background, he carefully searched records in an effort to learn how and where certain colonial and state coins were minted. Tokens formed the focus of much of his attention, and by 1856 he had compiled a list of several hundred different varieties that had come under his view, forming the basis for his 1858 book. In the front of that text Bushnell told of delays and also gave a hint of more to come:

Advertisement

> This work has been ready for the press for more than two years, but the continued ill health of the author has prevented its previous publication. Additions have been made to it from time to time until it has assumed the form in which it is now submitted.
>
> The author will feel obliged for the use of any token, &c., not included in this arrangement, so that the same may be used by him in the preparation of a second edition, should the issue of such be hereafter determined upon.
>
> He would further say that he is now, and has been for several years past, engaged in the preparation of two other works connected with the Numismatology of this country, but of a more extensive and elaborate character. A vast amount of interesting and valuable material has been gathered together, and the result of his labors will be given to the public in due course of time.
>
> Any person possessing any information relative to American coins and medals will oblige the author by communicating with him.

To the misfortune of numismatists, there never was a second edition of his 1858 study. Sadder still, his extensive correspondence and research involving early issues, including the 1785–1885 copper pieces of Vermont, Connecticut, Massachusetts, New York, New Jersey, and Machin's Mills, were never published, although certain of his research notes were shared with others. In 1859 Montroville W. Dickeson in the *American Numismatical Manual,* used information from Bushnell, and in 1875 Sylvester S. Crosby published much from Bushnell in *The Early Coins of America.*

Bushnell did, however, publish *Crumbs for Antiquarians* (volume I), in 1854. This included a steel engraving of Bushnell by H.B. Hall and a collection of several essays on history, the only numismatic one being a reissue of *An Historical Account of the First Three Business Tokens Issued In The City of New York,* a pamphlet he had issued in 1859. The 1789-dated Mott token and the Talbot, Allum & Lee tokens of 1794 and 1795 are illustrated.

Bushnell was a private person, often kept his own counsel, and, for example, was not involved in the formation of the American Numismatic Society in New York in 1858. On February 13, 1868, Bushnell was elected to honorary membership in the renamed American Numismatic and Archaeological Society. However, he declined "for personal reasons."[6] Various comments published in later years indicated that Bushnell rarely showed or discussed his collection with other numismatists, nor did he seem to have any close friends in the hobby.

Nevertheless, his numismatic accomplishments were highly respected by his peers. In response to an inquiry, the editor of the newly established *American Journal of Numismatics* commented in the issue of July 1866: "The best collections in the country, in our opinion, are those of Joseph J. Mickley, Esq., Phila., Charles J. [*sic*] Bushnell, Esq., New York, and M.A. Stickney, Esq., Salem, Mass." At the sale of the Joseph J. Mickley Collection, cataloged by W. Elliot Woodward and sold over several days from October 28 to November 2, 1867, Bushnell was a major buyer, although for the majority of his purchases he did not bid under his own name, but bought as "Stephens"[7] and, possibly, under other designations. It was often the practice of well-known collectors to do this so as to draw attention away from themselves, lest others ride on their coattails and take advantage of their knowledge.[8] Levick was an especially qualified observer, as he was one of the leading exponents in the token field. In the *American Journal of Numismatics,* December 1868, Joseph N.T. Levick called Bushnell's collection of store cards one of the "most perfect" in the country.[9]

Bushnell's 1858 Study Engenders Interest

Interest in numismatics rose on every front. The Philadelphia Numismatic Society, which held its first meeting on New Year's Day 1858, grew rapidly. During its first year, the Society's membership totaled 25, to which 13 more were added in 1859. The leading lights in 1858 included John Bohlen, Arthur G. Coffin, Mark Wilkes Collet, M.D., Samuel H. Fulton, Montgomery L. Frederick, J. Ledyard Hodge, Joseph J. Mickley, Alfred Bates Taylor, and William S. Vaux. At one time Gulian C. Verplanck, a subject of Hard Times tokens, was an honorary member, as was erstwhile 1848 presidential candidate Lewis Cass, who was well known as an amateur historian.[10]

Bushnell's pioneering 1858 work, *An Arrangement of Tradesmen's Cards, Political Tokens, also Election Medals, Medalets, &c.,* was widely distributed and created a lot of attention. This served to dramatically increase collector interest in store cards. Hodge, who was at 611 Walnut Street in Philadelphia, engaged in correspondence with Richmond collector Robert Alonzo Brock, the corresponding secretary of the Virginia Historical Society. This letter mentions a popular token:

> No. 611 Walnut St.
> Dec. 1st, 1859
> R. Alonzo Brock, Esq.
>
> Dear Sir,
>
> I have delayed acknowledging your last two favors—expecting every day to do so—and be able to send with my answer a larger set of pieces than I do—However as they turn up rather slowly I have concluded to send what I have and forward by Adams Express of this day a package containing sixteen pieces, which I find cost altogether exactly $2. One of these is one of the Washington medallets you wanted, which I was unable to procure till the other day; the others are American tokens of various kinds.
>
> I send also a memorandum made by myself of a sale of a small collection of coins here some two or three weeks ago, which will serve somewhat as a guide for you.[11] We are all now in an excitement about a sale of a very fine collection to take place here the 20th of this month.[12] It is remarkable more for the quality and variety of the pieces than their number, and is probably the *best* collection offered for sale for a long time. I will send you a catalogue next week when they come out, and if you desire to purchase any will be glad to bid for you at such prices as you may fix. After the sale a few *priced* catalogues will be issued at I believe 50 cts. each. If you wish one please inform me.
>
> I enclose also one of the circulars issued by our Committee asking for information regarding our proposed works. We intend getting up the volume on store cards, tokens etc., first leaving the one on Medals till afterwards. If you have any pieces not mentioned in the Bushnell work, we would like to have rubbings and descriptions. Probably before answering, you had better wait for the catalogue of this coming sale which will contain over 400 varieties of store cards, many of them not in Bushnell, and the owner has allowed us to take descriptions of all not in our own collections, so we will want no descriptions of any piece in that Catalogue.

62 TRADESMEN'S TOKENS.

VIRGINIA.

RICHMOND.

1.

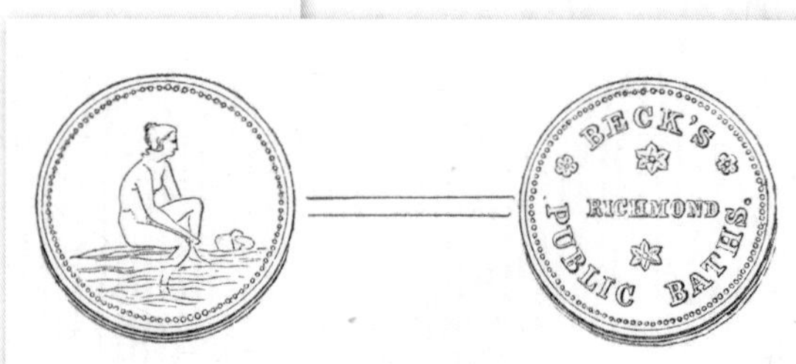

OB: A Female bathing.
REV: "*Beck's Public Baths, Richmond.*"
EDGE, plain. Metal, copper. Size, 8.

Bushnell's 1858 description and illustration of the Beck's Public Baths token.

As regards the privilege of corresponding members of our Society, they are I believe mentioned in the Constitution etc. which you have, and have the right to attend meetings when in town, privilege of the room, etc.[13] I would be glad to propose your name if you desire it.

Can you procure any more of the card you sent me "Beck's Public Baths"? I will take any you can get with pleasure, as I have three or four friends here who want them.

Yours very truly,
J. Ledyard Hodge

As an early project of the newly-formed Society, three members were named to a committee to create a reference or check list of advertising tokens as mentioned in Hodge's letter. In early 1860, Mark W. Collet (a medical doctor who later lost his life in the Civil War), Hodge, and Alfred B. Taylor[14] created a 16-page quarto work describing 423 pieces, *titled Catalogue of American Store Cards &c., With Space for Marking the Condition, Price, Rarity, &c., of Each Piece, Designed for the Use and Convenience of Collectors.* The booklets were distributed by Philadelphia dealer Edward D. Cogan. Apparently, they ventured in territory beyond their collective expertise, as the study, begun in 1858, was viewed as useless. Little was heard of it in later years, and none but the most dedicated student of tokens was apt to seek a copy.

In 1861 a widely-distributed book by W.C. Prime, *Coins, Medals and Seals*, included scattered listing of tokens which were later incorporated into the Hard Times series. All listings in the early times included 1832 to 1844 pieces among tokens and political memorabilia in general, without noting their Hard Times provenance.

W. Elliot Woodward

In 1860, W. Elliot Woodward, who operated an apothecary shop, lending library, coin dealership, and second-hand goods store in Roxbury, a suburb of Boston, published his first auction catalog. His success was immediate, and by 1863 he was widely respected by collectors and dealers alike. Woodward was intellectually inclined: he was well-versed in American history, the possessor of a large reference library, and a facile writer. In ensuing decades he stood above his contemporaries from the aspect of scholarly descriptions.

The Mt. Pleasant Apothecary Store and his business of selling books, antiques, and second-hand goods seem to have generated a sufficient revenue stream to permit him to buy major collections outright. It also allowed him to indulge in creating catalogs that were crafted with something above and beyond an orientation for profit. He spent much time detailing various tokens and medals which were otherwise considered obscure, along with other things of low value, simply for the pleasure of sharing his information with others. A commentary in the *American Journal of Numismatics* (first published in 1866) called him "the lion of the day."

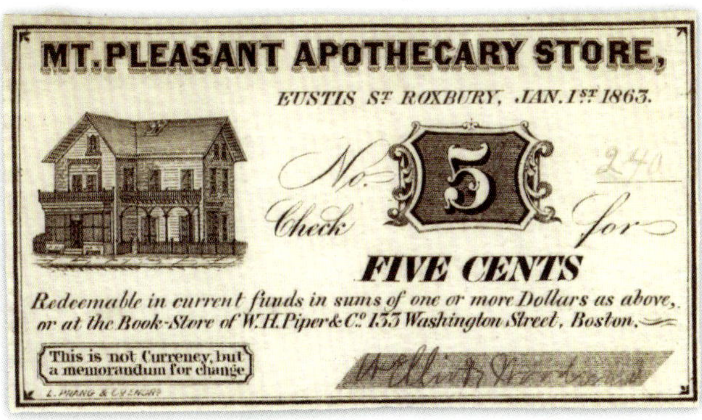

A five-cent scrip note issued and signed in 1863 by W. Elliot Woodward for this Mt. Pleasant Apothecary Store, a beehive of numismatic activity in addition to the pharmacy trade.

It was his practice to pay cash for collections and other property and then to offer them at auction, stating he was the owner. Woodward's sale of April 28 to May 1, 1863, included items he had acquired from the Henry M. Brooks, Jeremiah Colburn, Rev. J.M. Finotti, Dr. Edward M. Field, and Dr. Augustine Shurtleff collections. Among the diverse items offered were many tokens that today are incorporated into the Hard Times series. It was not unusual for such pieces to sell for as low as 5¢ to 10¢. Despite the low monetary value of his offerings, Woodward not only published a catalog describing such pieces individually but after the sale issued another version which printed the prices achieved. One can only speculate that this was one of countless instances in which he listed many such tokens as a service to numismatics—not for profit.

Sample entries are given here, preceded by the lot number in the sale. The number at the end, such as 18, gives the diameter in sixteenths of an inch. Thus, 18 is eighteen-sixteenths of an inch, or an inch and two-sixteenths. The price brought at the sale is given in brackets at the end:

> 1296. Anderson, Henry, books and shoes, N.Y., copper, 17. [5¢]
>
> 1298. Adams, John J., Taunton, Mass., copper, very fine, 18. [5¢]
>
> 1332. Benedict & Burnham, Waterbury, Ct., copper, 17. [15¢]
>
> 1338. Bucklin's Int. Tables, 1835 (T under date) copper, fine, scarce, 16. [10¢]
>
> 1343. Bucklin's Book-Keeping, "Showing at one view the exact state of your business," &c.; rev. Bucklin's Int. Tables; copper, extremely rare, 18. [5¢]
>
> 1372. Duseaman, T., butcher, Belleville, copper, rare 16. [12¢]
>
> 1399. East Boston, 1837; rev. "Maverick Coach, 1837," German silver, very fine and rare, 12. [13¢]
>
> 1458. Gustin and Blake, Chelsea, Vt., copper, rare, 18. [40¢]
>
> 1582. March, Nath'l, Portsmouth, N.J., copper, 17. [12¢]
>
> 1626. New York & Harlaem R.R. Co.; by Bale & Smith; German silver, fine, 11. [25¢]
>
> 1695. Seaman, T.D., Belleville; rev. a cow, "A Friend to the Constitution," copper, fine and rare, 17. [75¢]
>
> 1733. Smith's Clock Establishment, hand pointing to figure 10, copper, rare variety, 18. [15¢]

Many other such tokens were described in further catalogs by Woodward, Edward Cogan, and others. By 1867 the term *Hard Times tokens* was in use, and it was used in Woodward's sale of April 1867. However, the designation was mainly applied to issues of 1837, often called "Jackson cents."

J.N.T. Levick and Henry Davenport

Joseph N.T. Levick, who lived in Philadelphia in the 1850s and moved to New York City in 1860 (see his biography in appendix I), was one of the most active collectors of tokens, including those of the Hard Times era, in the 1850s through the 1880s. In the *American Journal of Numismatics*, April 1870, Levick's article, "Description of the 'Hard Times Tokens' of '37," described in detail 56 numbered varieties of this year. These are given in their entirety in appendix II of this book. Among his descriptions this entry is especially significant, describing a token of which several examples were sold at Woodward's McCoy sale:

> 9. Obv. and Rev.: Same as 8, with the exception of being another pair of dies. The marked difference between 7 and 8 and 9 is in the word "Financiering" instead of "Experiment." The difference between 8 and 9 is somewhat difficult to point out, but in comparing the two together can be readily seen. In 8 the donkey's right ear points in the direction of the second L in "Illustrious"; the letter I in "I follow" comes almost under the space between L and U in "Illustrious." In 9 the donkey's ear is under the first L of "Illustrious"; "I" in "I follow", under second L in "Illustrious."
>
> Of 8 or 9 there exists a piece struck in silver, which, it is said, was originally from the "Davenport" Collection, was sold at the "McCoy" Sale to F.I. Illsley for $8.50, and resold in Woodward's Fifth Semi-Annual Sale for $7 to John Bailey.

The McCoy sale featured many tokens that were once in the collection of Henry Davenport, a collector known for having tokens struck for his own collection. In fact, the catalog for the McCoy sale contained items Woodward had purchased from multiple sources, as did all of Woodward's other offerings of the era. Some sellers were mentioned on the title page; others were not. In the McCoy sale some offerings came from Jeremiah Colburn. These are two rarities:

> **2302.** The next two pieces in silver are both originals, struck for Mr. Davenport; for many years in his collection, more recently from the collection of Mr. Colburn. Ship full-rigged, "Webster, Credit, Current;" rev. ship struck by lightning, "Van Buren, Metallic, Current;" silver, proof, unique. [sold for $10.00]
>
> **2303.** Tortoise with safe; rev. jackass running, "I follow," &c.; silver, proof, unique. [$8.50]

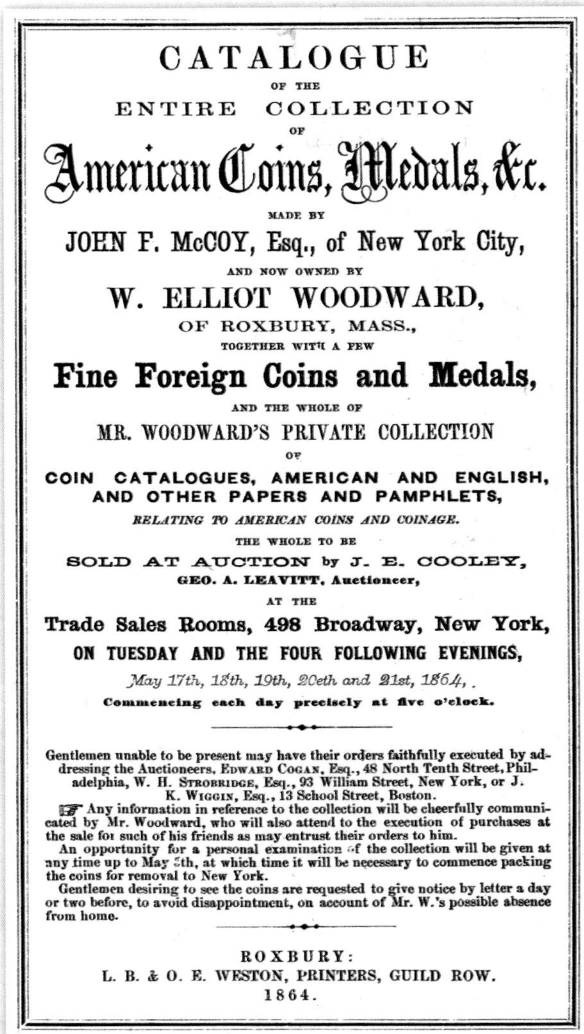
CATALOGUE
OF THE
ENTIRE COLLECTION
OF
American Coins, Medals, &c.
MADE BY
JOHN F. McCOY, Esq., of New York City,
AND NOW OWNED BY
W. ELLIOT WOODWARD,
OF ROXBURY, MASS.,
TOGETHER WITH A FEW
Fine Foreign Coins and Medals,
AND THE WHOLE OF
MR. WOODWARD'S PRIVATE COLLECTION
OF
COIN CATALOGUES, AMERICAN AND ENGLISH, AND OTHER PAPERS AND PAMPHLETS,
RELATING TO AMERICAN COINS AND COINAGE.
THE WHOLE TO BE
SOLD AT AUCTION by J. E. COOLEY,
GEO. A. LEAVITT, Auctioneer,
AT THE
Trade Sales Rooms, 498 Broadway, New York,
ON TUESDAY AND THE FOUR FOLLOWING EVENINGS,
May 17th, 18th, 19th, 20eth and 21st, 1864,
Commencing each day precisely at five o'clock.

Gentlemen unable to be present may have their orders faithfully executed by addressing the Auctioneers, Edward Cogan, Esq., 48 North Tenth Street, Philadelphia, W. H. Strobridge, Esq., 93 William Street, New York, or J. K. Wiggin, Esq., 13 School Street, Boston.

☞ Any information in reference to the collection will be cheerfully communicated by Mr. Woodward, who will also attend to the execution of purchases at the sale for such of his friends as may entrust their orders to him.

An opportunity for a personal examination of the collection will be given at any time up to May 5th, at which time it will be necessary to commence packing the coins for removal to New York.

Gentlemen desiring to see the coins are requested to give notice by letter a day or two before, to avoid disappointment, on account of Mr. W.'s possible absence from home.

ROXBURY:
L. B. & O. E. WESTON, PRINTERS, GUILD ROW.
1864.

Title page of W. Elliot Woodward's sale of the McCoy Collection sold in 1864.

Woodward's 46th Sale, April 1882

From April 19 to 21, 1882, W. Elliot Woodward offered many items at auction in his 46th Sale catalog titled *The Numismatic Collections of Frank Dietrich of Harrisburg, Penn., and S.H. Morgan of Louisville, Kentucky*. This catalog included an extensive discussion of Hard Times tokens, one of the earliest narratives encountered by the writer, and the first photographs of such tokens. In its summary of the sale the *American Journal of Numismatics* included this:

> A marked feature of the sale was a large selection of the Hard Times tokens of 1837. They were mostly in very fine condition and brought from 15 cents to $2.87 each. These tokens were illustrated by two very fine heliotype plates which give to the catalogue a peculiar value for reference as we are not aware that any of the pieces have ever before been pictured. Three of the Belleville tokens sold for $6.40.

By way of comparison the review also noted: "A nearly complete line of Proof sets 1859 to 1880 sold for from $4.00 to $7.20; set of pattern trade dollars, 1873, Proof, six pieces $24.25."

The two plates were all of common varieties, most showed light wear, one was holed, and another had part of the reverse inscription tooled away. Considering the expense of making the plates and the nominal prices achieved, characteristically, Woodward provided them for the good of numismatics. Often he would include in his sales detailed

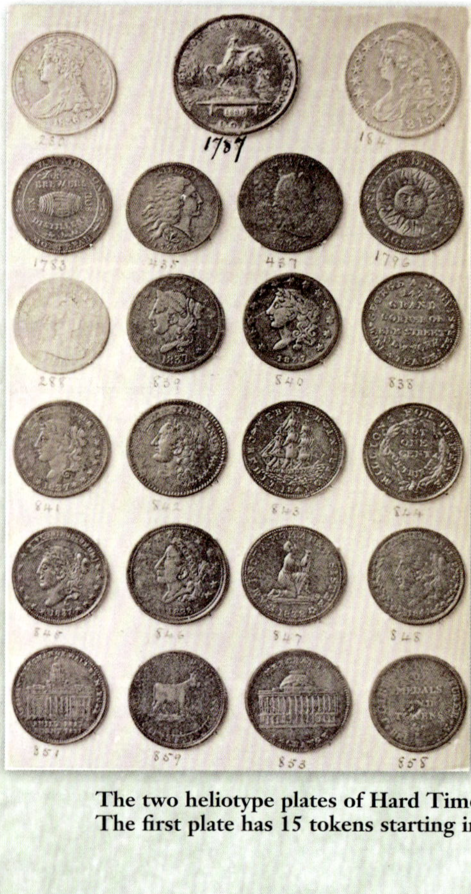

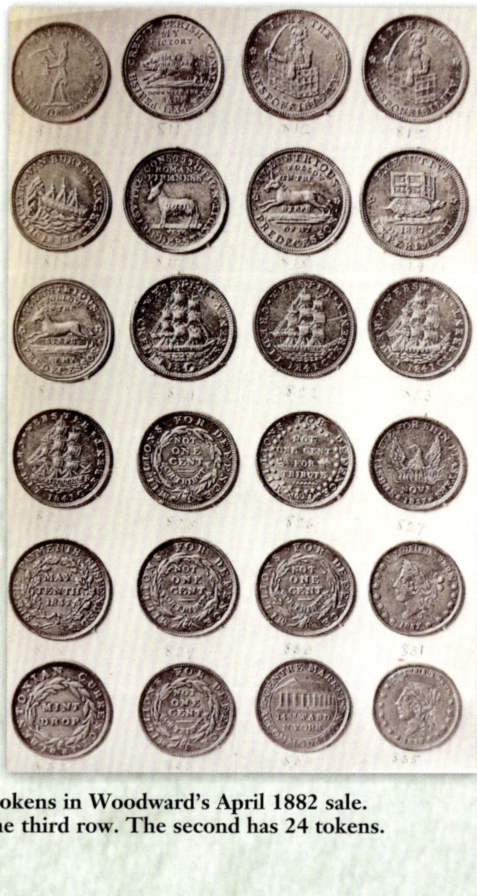

The two heliotype plates of Hard Times tokens in Woodward's April 1882 sale. The first plate has 15 tokens starting in the third row. The second has 24 tokens.

discussions of interesting tokens and medals of relatively little value. Concerning the tokens, his commentary included this, ending with the rationale for the photographs:

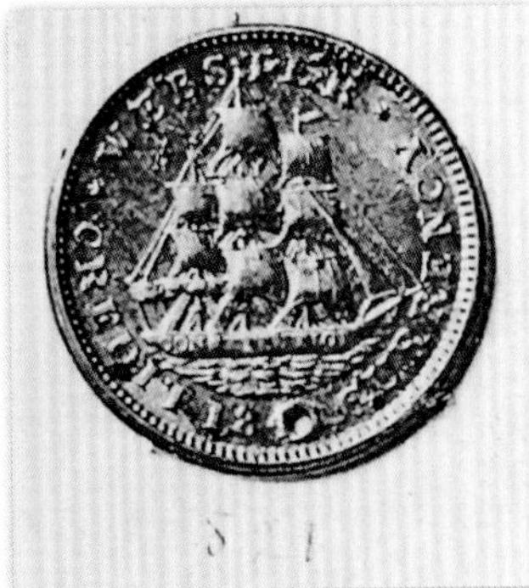

Detail from the second plate showing a holed example of a common issue.

> The series, marking as it does an important period in the financial history of the United States, is very interesting and heretofore has not attracted the degree of attention that it merits. Many persons whose memory extends back to the period, especially if residents of New England, will remember that these Jackson cents, as they were then called, formed no inconsiderable portion of the currency of the time. They as well as store cards passed freely and, owing to the dearth of small change, were really a great convenience to the trading community.
>
> As to the origin of these pieces, I am not aware that anything has been written, and it may be worthwhile to record some facts. In conversation not long since with an aged gentleman who still survives, he informed me that he was at the time of their issue a member of a company which, reorganized, became the Scovill Manufacturing Company of Waterbury, Connecticut; then in its infancy, found profitable employment in the manufacture of these tokens, of which they made hundreds of thousands, comprising most if not all of the varieties now known.
>
> When the business had gone on for years and grown into large proportions the United States authorities stepped in and either prosecuted the makers or threatened prosecution, but suspended proceedings in consideration of an agreement that the manufacture should be discontinued and all existing dies destroyed. This agreement was faithfully carried out, and every die was defaced.
>
> The company re-formed, and its successors also made most of the private store cards of old red cent size up to quite a recent period. I was informed by the engraver of the establishment that all the old dies—several hundred in number—were destroyed by the fire which so seriously damaged the works about a year ago.
>
> As few if any of these pieces were ever pictured, I have thought it advisable to illustrate them in this catalogue, an edition of which, fifty in number, have been printed with two heliotype plates, one of which is mainly devoted to this series. . . .

The Bushnell Sale, June 1882

Charles I. Bushnell died on September 17, 1880. In time, Bushnell's collection was offered intact by his son for $10,000, a sum that was not reached. The highest tender received was from Lorin G. Parmelee, a Boston bean baker whose collection of regular-issue United States coins was considered the finest in America He purchased it for about $8,000. Parmelee selected Samuel Hudson Chapman and Henry Chapman, said to have been nephews of Bushnell, to conduct a public auction sale of the remainder. This was much to the dismay of other older and, presumably, wiser dealers, who viewed the Chapmans as brash upstarts. The Bushnell holding was well known for its size and value, but few knew anything about its contents. The collection was auctioned in June 1882.

The Bushnell Collection contained an unremarkable listing of Hard Times tokens except for a select three:

2169. Quarter dollar. Eagle bearing U.S. Shield, holding an olive branch in right talon and three arrows in left; AMERICAN SILVER, above. Rev. TOKEN 25 CENTS, 1837; border on obv. beaded; edge plain. Silver. Extremely Fine. Unique and unpublished. Size 17. This piece is the work of the period.

The above token was issued by Lewis Feuchtwanger in New York City in 1839 and is made of Feuchtwanger's Composition, a German silver alloy.

2202. Same obverse as preceding [lot 2201]. Rev. same but has E in ONE instead of F as above; wreath composed of thirty-eight leaves and seventeen berries. Bronze. Proof. Unique and unpublished.

2208. Head of Liberty laureated to left; wreath of vine leaves; 7 stars in front and 6 behind; "E Pluribus Unum," in field above. Rev. "MILLIONS FOR DEFENCE NOT ONE CENT FOR TRIBUTE." Laurel branch (with ribbon at stem) composed of thirty leaves and twelve berries. The end does not meet the stem. Bronze. Proof. Unique and unpublished.

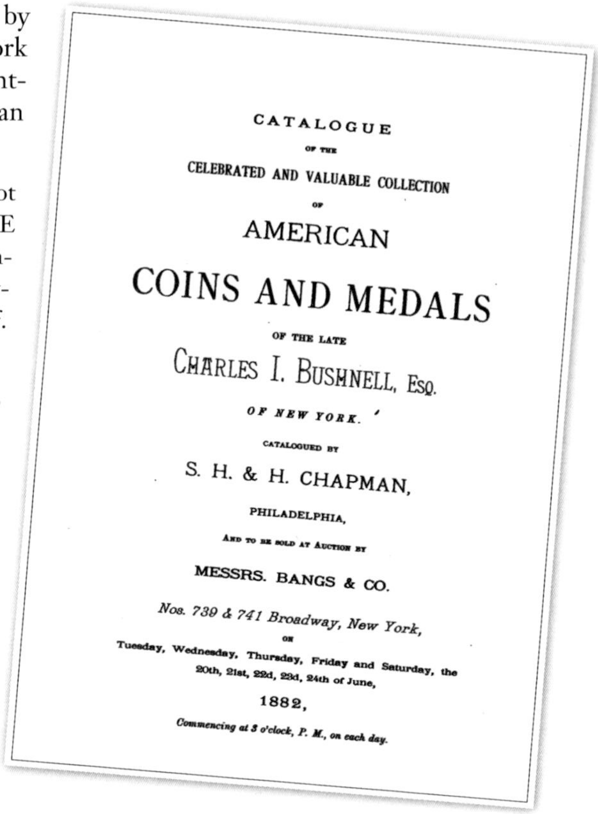
CATALOGUE

OF THE

CELEBRATED AND VALUABLE COLLECTION

OF

AMERICAN

COINS AND MEDALS

OF THE LATE

CHARLES I. BUSHNELL, ESQ.

OF NEW YORK.

CATALOGUED BY

S. H. & H. CHAPMAN,

PHILADELPHIA,

AND TO BE SOLD AT AUCTION BY

MESSRS. BANGS & CO.

Nos. 739 & 741 Broadway, New York,

ON

Tuesday, Wednesday, Thursday, Friday and Saturday, the 20th, 21st, 22d, 23d, 24th of June,

1882,

Commencing at 3 o'clock, P. M., on each day.

Title page of the Charles I. Bushnell Collection sale catalog, 1882.

The above two are fantasy pieces made by an unknown person, perhaps to the order of J.N.T. Levick. These are usually seen with artificial wear and in any event are not known today in unimpaired Proof format. The sale of these two from the Bushnell Collection led Lyman H. Low to later attribute these and other fantasies to Bushnell's authorship. No supporting evidence of such a connection has ever been made, and it is virtually certain that he was not involved in any way. See chapter 14 for more information.

Woodward's Sale of the Levick Collection 1884

From May 26 to 29, 1884, W. Elliot Woodward offered for sale the collection of Joseph N.T. Levick, the most comprehensive listing of Hard Times tokens up to that time. The Hard Times tokens were listed in accordance with Levick's study in the April 1870 issue of the *American Journal of Numismatics.* The sale was concluded with an offering of seven fantasy pieces, but with no information given as to their origin.

In the catalog Woodward, discussing the series, noted that Henry Davenport had caused certain rare Hard Times tokens to be struck for his cabinet in *1837*, the original year of

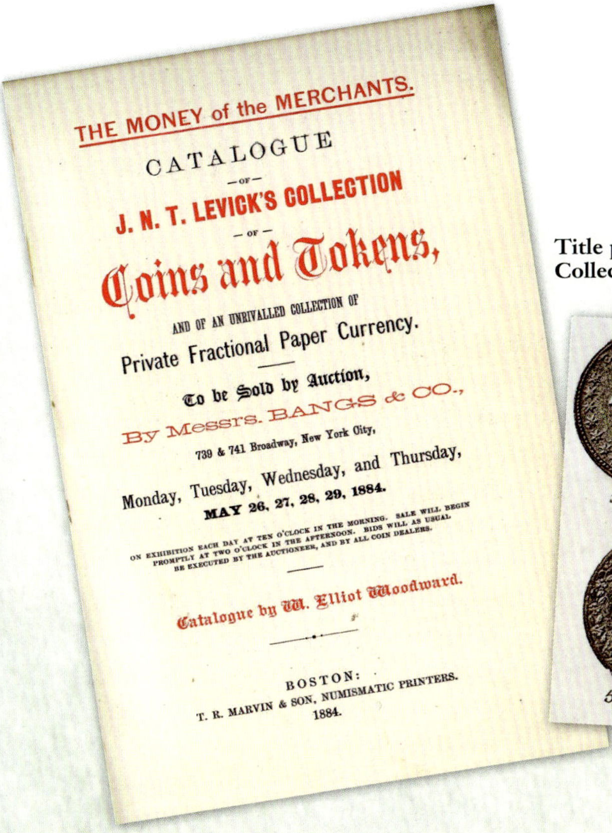

THE MONEY of the MERCHANTS.

CATALOGUE

—OF—

J. N. T. LEVICK'S COLLECTION

—OF—

Coins and Tokens,

AND OF AN UNRIVALLED COLLECTION OF

Private Fractional Paper Currency.

To be Sold by Auction,

By Messrs. BANGS & CO.,

739 & 741 Broadway, New York City,

Monday, Tuesday, Wednesday, and Thursday,

MAY 26, 27, 28, 29, 1884.

ON EXHIBITION EACH DAY AT TEN O'CLOCK IN THE MORNING. SALE WILL BEGIN PROMPTLY AT TWO O'CLOCK IN THE AFTERNOON. BIDS WILL AS USUAL BE EXECUTED BY THE AUCTIONEER, AND BY ALL COIN DEALERS.

Catalogue by W. Elliot Woodward.

BOSTON:
T. R. MARVIN & SON, NUMISMATIC PRINTERS.
1884.

Title page of the Levick Collection sale catalog.

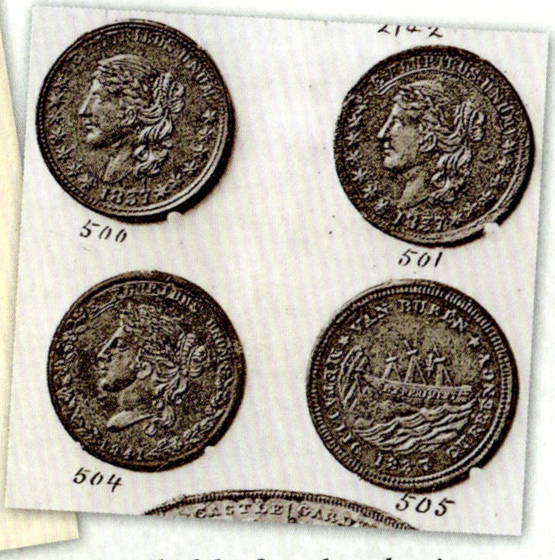

Detail of the first plate showing several fantasy Hard Times tokens.

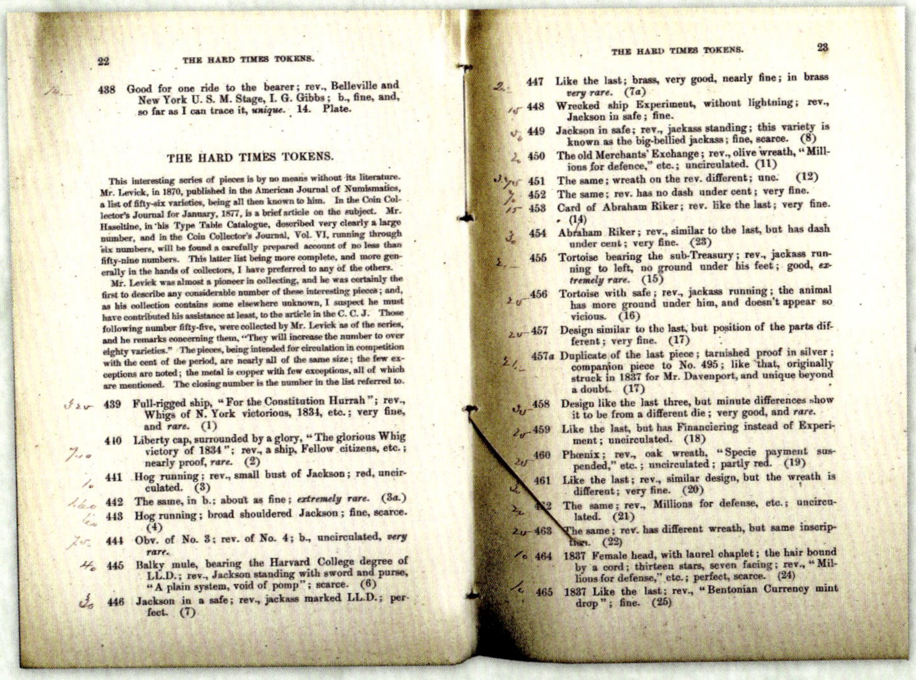

22 THE HARD TIMES TOKENS.

438 Good for one ride to the bearer; rev., Belleville and New York U. S. M. Stage, I. G. Gibbs; b., fine, and, so far as I can trace it, *unique*. 14. Plate.

THE HARD TIMES TOKENS.

This interesting series of pieces is by no means without its literature. Mr. Levick, in 1870, published in the American Journal of Numismatics, a list of fifty-six varieties, being all then known to him. In the Coin Collector's Journal for January, 1877, is a brief article on the subject. Mr. Haseltine, in his Type Table Catalogue, described very clearly a large number, and in the Coin Collector's Journal, Vol. VI, running through six numbers, will be found a carefully prepared account of no less than fifty-nine numbers. This latter list being more complete, and more generally in the hands of collectors, I have preferred to any of the others.

Mr. Levick was almost a pioneer in collecting, and he was certainly the first to describe any considerable number of these interesting pieces; and, as his collection contains some elsewhere unknown, I suspect he must have contributed his assistance at least, to the article in the C. C. J. Those following number fifty-five, were collected by Mr. Levick as of the series, and he remarks concerning them, "They will increase the number to over eighty varieties." The pieces, being intended for circulation in competition with the cent of the period, are nearly all of the same size; the few exceptions are noted; the metal is copper with few exceptions, all of which are mentioned. The closing number is the number in the list referred to.

439 Full-rigged ship, "For the Constitution Hurrah"; rev., Whigs of N. York victorious, 1834, etc.; very fine, and *rare*. (1)

440 Liberty cap, surrounded by a glory, "The glorious Whig victory of 1834"; rev., a ship, Fellow citizens, etc.; nearly proof, *rare*. (2)

441 Hog running; rev., small bust of Jackson; red, uncirculated. (3)

442 The same, in b.; about as fine; *extremely rare*. (3*a*.)

443 Hog running; broad shouldered Jackson; fine, scarce. (4)

444 Obv. of No. 3; rev. of No. 4; b., uncirculated, *very rare*.

445 Balky mule, bearing the Harvard College degree of LL.D.; rev., Jackson standing with sword and purse, "A plain system, void of pomp"; scarce. (6)

446 Jackson in a safe; rev., jackass marked LL.D.; perfect. (7)

THE HARD TIMES TOKENS. 23

447 Like the last; brass, very good, nearly fine; in brass *very rare*. (7*a*)

448 Wrecked ship Experiment, without lightning; rev., Jackson in safe; fine.

449 Jackson in safe; rev., jackass standing; this variety is known as the big-bellied jackass; fine, scarce. (8)

450 The old Merchants' Exchange; rev., olive wreath, "Millions for defence," etc.; uncirculated. (11)

451 The same; wreath on the rev. different; unc. (12)

452 The same; rev. has no dash under cent; very fine.

453 Card of Abraham Riker; rev. like the last; very fine. (14)

454 Abraham Riker; rev., similar to the last, but has dash under cent; very fine. (23)

455 Tortoise bearing the sub-Treasury; rev., jackass running to left, no ground under his feet; good, *extremely rare*. (15)

456 Tortoise with safe; rev., jackass running; the animal has more ground under him, and doesn't appear so vicious. (16)

457 Design similar to the last, but position of the parts different; very fine. (17)

457*a* Duplicate of the last piece; tarnished proof in silver; companion piece to No. 495; like that, originally struck in 1837 for Mr. Davenport, and unique beyond a doubt. (17)

458 Design like the last three, but minute differences show it to be from a different die; very good, and *rare*.

459 Like the last, but has Financiering instead of Experiment; uncirculated. (18)

460 Phœnix; rev., oak wreath, "Specie payment suspended," etc.; uncirculated; partly red. (19)

461 Like the last; rev., similar design, but the wreath is different; very fine. (20)

462 The same; rev., Millions for defense, etc.; uncirculated. (21)

463 The same; rev. has different wreath, but same inscription. (22)

464 1837 Female head, with laurel chaplet; the hair bound by a cord; thirteen stars, seven facing; rev., "Millions for defense," etc.; perfect, scarce. (24)

465 1837 Like the last; rev., "Bentonian Currency mint drop"; fine. (25)

Two pages from the Hard Times token listings of the Levick Collection.

issue. Davenport had been a collector since about 1830.[15] The Davenport numismatic delicacies are not to be confused with what a later generation of collectors called "Bushnell pieces" or, per Russell Rulau, "Bushnell fantasies," although it is likely that Bushnell was not connected with them in any way. The fantasies were made from antedated dies to the order of someone who wanted to create deceptive rarities. Most were acid-etched or distressed to give the appearance of having been used in circulation. The 1884 Levick sale included seven of the fantasies and Thomas L. Elder's 1907 sale of much Levick material, a year before Levick's passing, included nine. Consequently, *Levick fantasies* would seem to be an appropriate designation for the forgeries. A listing is given in chapter 14.

Lyman H. Low in 1886

Today the name of Lyman H. Low stands tall in the field of Hard Times tokens. By the time he got involved in the specialty in the 1880s others such as Levick and Woodward had already done much to popularize the series, but Low's contributions to the study of Hard Times tokens are invaluable. Appendix I includes the biographies of Levick and Low.

By 1886 Low was one of the most active coin dealers in New York City, the center of the coin-selling business at the time. In the city a half-dozen or more other dealers had shops, attended auctions, and added to the dynamism of the hobby. At the time, in a rapid period of growth, auctions of rare coins, mainly in New York, were held on the average of about once a week. The metropolis was home to the American Numismatic and Archaeological Society (formed in 1864, heir to the interests of the American Numismatic Society that had been active in 1858 and 1859). The Society had published the *American Journal of Numismatics*—the official publication for recording new discoveries, reporting on auctions, and publishing feature articles—since 1866. In 1907 it changed its name to that of its predecessor, the American Numismatic Society. In 1908 the Society moved into its beautiful new building on Audubon Terrace, Broadway

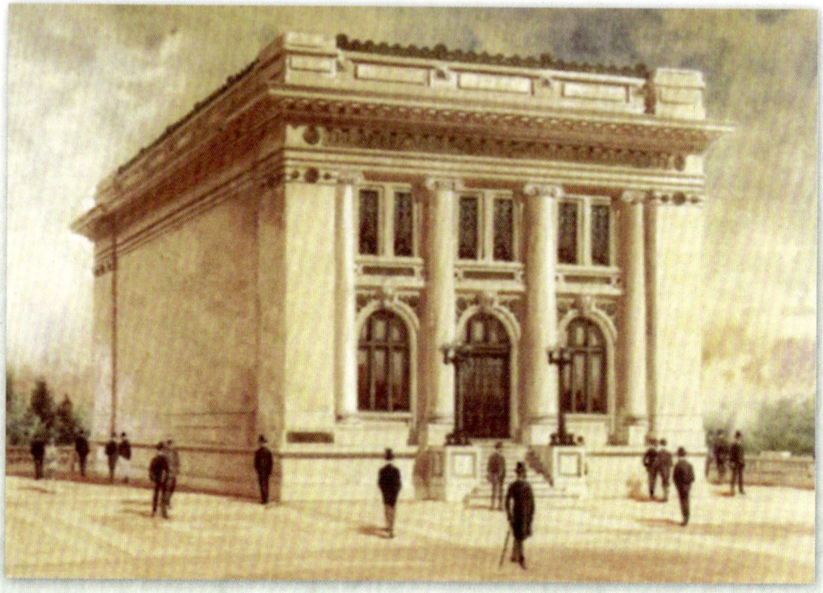

The beautiful American Numismatic Society building opened in 1908. For many years this facility, with its comprehensive library and reference collection, was the epicenter of numismatic research in the United States.

between 155th and 156th streets. This was made possible by the gift of Archer Huntington, scion of a railroad-building family.

Low had been a dealer with the firm of B. Westermann & Co. since 1883. Located at 838 Broadway, he dealt in coins, medals, tokens, and numismatic books. By 1886 Low was on his own, dealing in coins and contributing articles to *The Stamp and Coin Gazette*, published in Altoona, Pennsylvania. At that time he had an office at 853 Broadway.

In 1886 Low published the first stand-alone study of tokens of this era, 18 pages in length, titled *Descriptive Catalogue of Hard Times Tokens Issued for and Against the United States Bank, and with Reference to the Financial Troubles of 1834–1841.* Copies were offered for 25¢, with orders to be sent to the author at his Broadway address. The study was a priced listing of tokens he had available for sale. As the title indicated, it emphasized political pieces. Many store cards awaited a future listing.

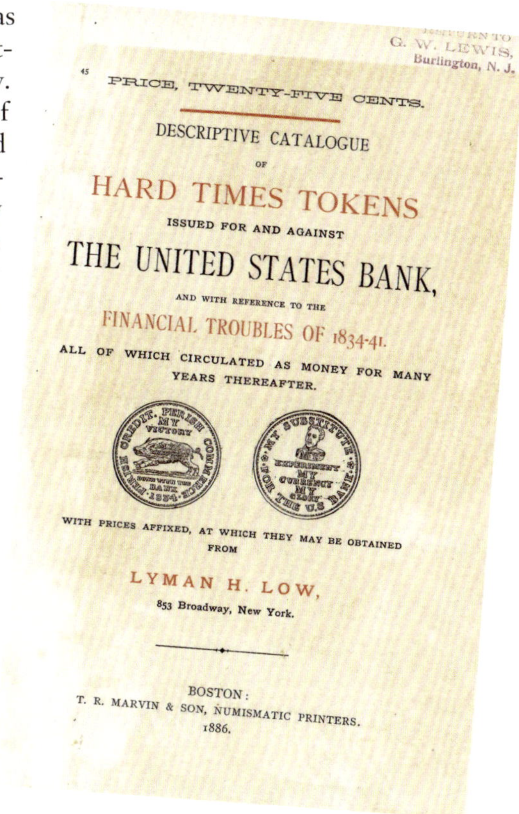

G. W. LEWIS,
Burlington, N. J.

45

PRICE, TWENTY-FIVE CENTS.

DESCRIPTIVE CATALOGUE

OF

HARD TIMES TOKENS

ISSUED FOR AND AGAINST

THE UNITED STATES BANK,

AND WITH REFERENCE TO THE

FINANCIAL TROUBLES OF 1834-41.

ALL OF WHICH CIRCULATED AS MONEY FOR MANY YEARS THEREAFTER.

WITH PRICES AFFIXED, AT WHICH THEY MAY BE OBTAINED FROM

LYMAN H. LOW,

853 Broadway, New York.

BOSTON:
T. R. MARVIN & SON, NUMISMATIC PRINTERS.
1886.

The cover of Lyman H. Low's 1886 study.

In April 1887, Low's "Numismatic Notes" column began in the *American Journal of Numismatics.* On September 1 of that year he joined the staff of the Scott Stamp & Coin Co., 721 Broadway, which was primarily a retailer of inexpensive items to amateur collectors. However, he may also have been involved with the firm's magazine, *The Coin Collector's Journal*, earlier edited by David U. Proskey, which had excellent content and was well respected. Scott also published several editions in its *Standard Catalogue* series, which was obviously created by people other than Proskey and Low, for the information was often inaccurate, and there was hardly any narrative.

Not content to stop, Low spent the next 12 years gathering more information, especially about tokens issued by merchants during the Hard Times era. He was fortunate in that some issuers were still living and could be interviewed, and for many others he tracked down descendants. As a result he learned much that would have otherwise been lost to a later generation.

Low's Expanded Study

In July 1898 in the *American Journal of Numismatics*, Low began his second and more extensive serialization of this series, complete with many important historical notes, a *tour de force* of research based on information gathered since the 1880s. In 1899 he published *Hard Times Tokens. An Arrangement of Jackson Cents Issued for and Against the United States Bank.* This comprised 65 pages, including engraved illustrations. This work, nearly always cited simply as *Hard Times Tokens,* became the standard reference.

Until then, Bushnell's 1858 list of store cards, the auction catalogs of Woodward and others, and further offerings were a mixed bag with tokens from various eras—the only exception being found in the description of Jackson-related political Hard Times tokens, which Low furnished in 1886. Now in 1899, the combined political and store card tokens of the 1830s and early 1840s could be defined—although the title of his new study did not reflect store cards. Collectors could build "want lists" and seek specific pieces.

The Hard Times tokens described by Low were mostly viewed as *monetary substitutes*—pieces that passed as money, usually at the value of 1¢. However, the arrangement was a mixed bag with political tokens added in—such as pieces relating to Gulian C. Verplanck, William Seward, and Martin Van Buren that never were used in circulation.

Low arranged the tokens featuring first most of the political and financial motifs, which were followed by store cards arranged by date and then a hard-to-follow miscellany. No. 161 was of J. Cochran, bell founder; No. 162 a political token of Van Buren; No. 163 of Howell Works Gardens in New Jersey; and No. 164 with the advertisement of H.M. & E.I. Richards on one side and that of S.B. Schenck on the other. Engravings were sprinkled throughout the text. At the end he provided a rarity guide and useful index.

In this book 164 different die combinations were each given a number, and information was provided as to the metals in which such a token was made. Most were copper, but some numbers described copper as well as brass pieces, and some others had German silver, including the variation known as Feuchtwanger's Composition.

Lyman H. Low attributed to Charles I. Bushnell certain rarities he did not understand. In Low's description of Low-50, known today to be an American Silver token issued by Lewis Feuchtwanger, he stated this:

> I purchased the piece for a collector who still retains it; no other is known to me, and I have no hesitancy in stating that my conclusions are, that it is unique and was struck from dies made by Bushnell's order. I hold a similar unfavorable opinion of Nos. 24, 25, 26, 27, 41, 42 and 43, but in these latter I think a partner was admitted, and a very limited number of each was struck, but probably only single specimens in silver.

In reality, Bushnell is not known to have made any restrikes, fantasies, or other pieces associated with the Hard Times series. Low's Bushnell comment evolved into supposed

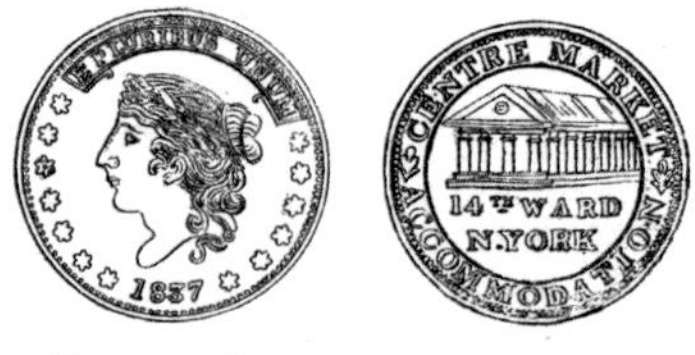

110. *Obv.* Same as No. 34. *Rev.* CENTRE MARKET above, and → ACCOMMODATION ← below. Front and side view of a building with columns. Below, 14TH WARD | N. YORK all within a circle. Borders 4. Edge 1. Metal Æ. Size 28.

The crossbar of A in WARD is incomplete on the reverse of this variety, but it is perfect on the following.

The name of the individual who founded this Market has not been learned. In March, 1897, the property owners on Centre Street, in the vicinity of this old Market, took steps to secure legislation to erect a municipal building on the site it had so long occupied, which however has not yet materialized.

Low's entry for the Centre Market token, one of relatively few illustrations in the book.

fact, and Russell Rulau and many others have called these Bushnell pieces, as I did until I learned differently. See chapter 14.

A second edition was published in 1900, as the supply of 1899 copies had become exhausted. In 1909 he wrote to clients, advising them: "My edition of *Hard Times Tokens* is long out of print, and it will be quite difficult for you to obtain a copy. Sometimes they come up in auction sales."

Benjamin P. Wright

In the meantime, in January 1898 *The Numismatist* commenced with the first installment of an article, "The American Store or Business Cards," by Dr. Benjamin P. Wright. This study discussed tokens issued from the 18th century onward, beginning with a series of about a dozen listings, which was designated "A," and continuing with the letter B series. The alphabetical order made it easy to find given pieces but not to identify them by era of issue. This was difficult unless they bore a date. The Wright study was continued in further installments, and, in time, it would be recognized as one of the most important contributions to the study of the subject.

As a result of the popularity of Low's *Hard Times Tokens* book and Wright's extensive study, tokens of all eras became very popular, as were colonial coins, encased postage stamps, and medals. Studying tokens and other unusual issues captured the attention and imagination of numismatists of the day, particularly those with an intellectual turn of mind. However, there were no price guides available for any coins, tokens, medals, or bank notes, and no grading standards had been established. This situation added to the challenge of collecting.

Once bitten by the "coin bug," as some called it, most remained in the hobby for many years. At the time no more than a dozen people collected Morgan silver dollars by date and mint, while probably 500 to 1,000 or more were seriously interested in tokens and medals. This seems almost unbelievable to contemplate today! Nevertheless, there were many thousands of casual collectors who were interested in 19th-century copper and silver coinage.

Low Lists More Varieties

In 1906 Lyman H. Low published a supplement to his book in the *American Journal of Numismatics*, introduced with this comment:

> Since the publication of the *Descriptive Catalogue of Hard Times Tokens* in the *Journal* in 1899, a greatly increased interest in the series has arisen; and there is also an evident desire on the part of collectors to obtain the rarer numbers in order to complete the sets in their cabinets. As I have not only gathered some additional information concerning those already described, but have also discovered a few new varieties, and some errors in description have come to my knowledge, the material now in hand seems sufficient to justify the publication of a supplement. . . .

Low added a comment that if tokens were considered only for their designs, interest in them would not be sustained. It is the history behind them that contributes to their fascination and the desire to collect them. The supplement offered expanded numbers to include 165 through 183.

Others continued Low's work. In 1910 William Forrester Dunham published a simplified guide to the varieties with an index and many engraved illustrations. Not long afterward, Edgar H. Adams, who was one of the most prolific writers and researchers of his era, issued a set of photographic plates showing the series. In October 1911, the *American Journal of Numismatics* provided this updated view:

What Next?

> Coin collecting has its fads and fashions as well as other lines. A while ago encased postage stamps were sought; then private gold; next the regular gold series in general and mint-marks on silver coins began to attract attention. Thus, first one series, and then another steps into the lime-light. Sometimes a series drops out of public notice for a while, but, like some fad in a dress, having performed its cycle of partial oblivion, it revives and comes again into its own.
>
> Just now the Hard-times Tokens seem to be the rage, and everyone appears to be seeking them; the auction sales are full of them, and the first question one collector asks another is whether he has any of these to sell. What will come next? Will the American store card be in demand again? It certainly is high time that some attention be once more given to this interesting series. A noticeable tendency of all revivals is that better and better specimens are sought for the ordinary pieces which satisfied the collector of a few decades ago do not tempt one to-day. The wonder of it is, where do all the specimens come from, when a series is extensively collected? One cannot breed them as dogs are bred, when some new or long-forgotten kind is demanded to supply the fashion of the day!

Edgar H. Adams continued his interest and research in Hard Times tokens, and in a column in *The Numismatist* he occasionally told of new varieties, or the history of those already known.

The 1914 A.N.A. Convention

From August 22 to 26, 1914, the annual convention of the American Numismatic Association was held at the Auditorium of the Springfield Municipal Group in Springfield, Massachusetts. Lyman H. Low had announced he would be there to deliver a talk on Hard Times tokens, but begged off by writing this to president Frank G. Duffield: "I very much regret finding it impossible to reasonably condense what I have prepared on the subject of Hard Times tokens to read within the prescribed limit as indicated in the official program."

Apparently miffed at the short time allotted to him, Low did not attend—although the venue was an easy train ride from New Rochelle, New York, his home in recent years. No matter, this series of Hard Times tokens was featured in exhibits at the show, per these reports published in *The Numismatist* in October:

> *Robert Bird*, Canton, Mass.—An extremely fine set of Hard Times Tokens, in all numbering 140 pieces, including many of the rarities, among which may be mentioned excessively fine [Low] Nos. 11, 13, 15 and 16. One of the best known No. 17s, which is uncirculated, with some red. Splendid Nos. 21, 22 and 23, and a very fine No. 57. A No. 77 shown by Mr. Bird is undoubtedly one of the best in existence. He also showed an excessively fine No. 87, which is in a fine state of preservation. This is the well-known Boutwell token of Troy, N. Y. He also showed a very fine No. 105; and extremely fine Nos. 114 and 118. His set of Smith tokens was also very fine, and included all the varieties of this set; Nos. 141, 142 and 145, were as fine as could possibly be obtained. The No. 156 was very fine, and he showed, in uncirculated condition, Nos. 171 and 175.

Frank H. Shumway, Boston, Mass.—Mr. Shumway showed only his collection of Hard Times Tokens, which was an extremely fine and comprehensive one, and included many of the rarities. The collection as a whole was noted for the superb state of preservation. In this collection No. 72, the Brigham token, which is rare in almost any condition, is shown in almost perfect condition, containing much of the original red and being undoubtedly the best specimen of this variety known. The No. 105 undoubtedly also is the finest specimen of this variety known, being in mint condition and containing nearly all of the original red. The No. 118 of the Feuchtwanger series, so far as known, is the best specimen extant, it being in practically uncirculated condition. Mr. Shumway showed a very fine and uncirculated series of the Smith tokens, two fine specimens of the Sweet tokens, Nos. 140–141; fine specimens of No. 150 and No. 162. The collection was also remarkable as showing both specimens of the Gustin & Blake tokens, Nos. 175 and 176, in splendid condition. All of these tokens are very rare, and it is not often that a collection shows both of these varieties. Mr. Shumway obtained these two specimens by order from a member of the Gustin family. He also showed No. 181 in uncirculated condition. In this collection also were shown three specimens, in silver, brass, and copper, of the medal issued by the Boston Numismatic Association in 1875.

The 1920s Onward

Edgar H. Adams continued to spend time and effort studying the earlier works of Wright and Low and adding his own discoveries. The result was a 75-page book published in 1920, *United States Store Cards. A List of Merchants' Advertising Checks, Restaurant Checks, and Kindred Pieces Issued from 1789 up to Recent Years, Including Many of the Tokens Which Passed as Money and Known as Hard Times Tokens.* This was well received, and Adams numbers were used by specialists for many years afterward.

In 1924 the Guttag Brothers, well-financed rare coin dealers, published *Hard Times Tokens*, a reissue of Low's study, copies of which had become scarce. The Guttags were in the securities business and were riding high (but they failed during the Depression).

Into the Depression years of the early 1930s, interest in numismatics remained strong, although prices of rarities weakened. This changed dramatically in 1934 with the publication, by Wayte Raymond, of the *Standard Catalogue of United States Coins.* Listing market prices plus mintage figures, it was issued in 18 editions through 1958. The *Catalogue* became a useful

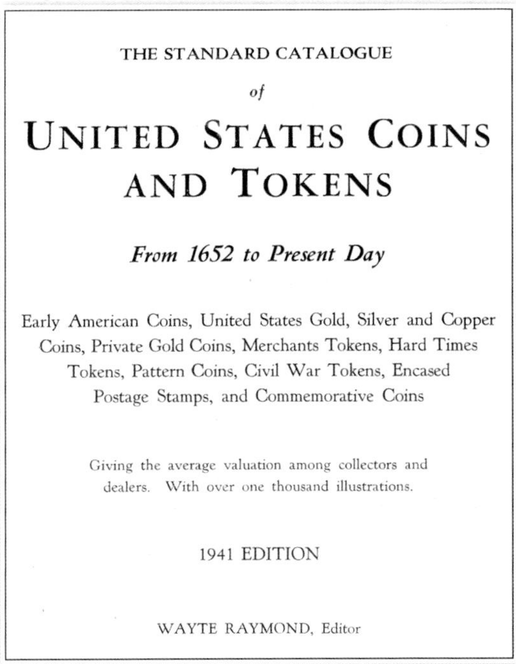
THE STANDARD CATALOGUE

of

UNITED STATES COINS AND TOKENS

From 1652 to Present Day

Early American Coins, United States Gold, Silver and Copper Coins, Private Gold Coins, Merchants Tokens, Hard Times Tokens, Pattern Coins, Civil War Tokens, Encased Postage Stamps, and Commemorative Coins

Giving the average valuation among collectors and dealers. With over one thousand illustrations.

1941 EDITION

WAYTE RAYMOND, Editor

Title page of Wayte Raymond's 1941 *Standard Catalogue*. Ever seeking to educate his readers, Raymond devoted many pages to tokens in addition to the usual federal series.

reference for information that earlier required a lot of effort to obtain. Raymond enjoyed Hard Times tokens, was an avid collector of them, and devoted many pages to the series in the 1940 and 1941 editions of his book.

Raymond also marketed a line of attractive cardboard album pages with clear acetate covering to protect the coins, which could be viewed from either side. *Penny boards* were launched by J.K. Post of Neenah, Wisconsin. The rights to these were acquired by what is today known as Whitman Publishing, a firm that in 1946 issued the first of many annual editions of *A Guide Book of United States Coins.*

The *Standard Catalogue*, album pages, and coin folders introduced a dynamism into coin collecting, with the curious result that, deep into the economic Depression, numismatics was more active than ever, and prices rose steadily! There was more to come: in 1935 there was great excitement regarding new commemorative coins. An issue of 10,000 coins to observe the 150th anniversary of the founding of Hudson, New York, was made available to collectors for $1 per coin. Due to a miscalculation, the official distributor of the coins, the First National Bank of Hudson, thought there would be little demand—and wholesaled most of them to Julius Guttag, a rare coin dealer. Demand proved to be intense, and in the aftermarket the coins sold for $6 or more each. The rush was on as many more commemoratives were issued in 1935 and 1936. The *Numismatic Scrapbook Magazine*, a monthly that made its debut in 1935, added fuel to the market fire. The population of numismatists in America multiplied!

After the commemorative boom and other excitement, hobbyists explored areas beyond federal coins, and tokens received much attention. In *The Numismatist*, January 1940, Alfred Z. Reed, a New York City specialist and advisor for Raymond's *Standard Catalogue*, contributed "Guide to Hard Times Tokens." The commentary began with "The rapidly reviving interest in Low's series of Hard Times tokens between 1832 and 1844 is gratifying to older collectors." With a sense of humor, Reed ended his discussion with a little poem intended to help readers remember how to identify die varieties—and also to help interest their wives in the hobby. Lots of fun! Reed's article is reproduced here:

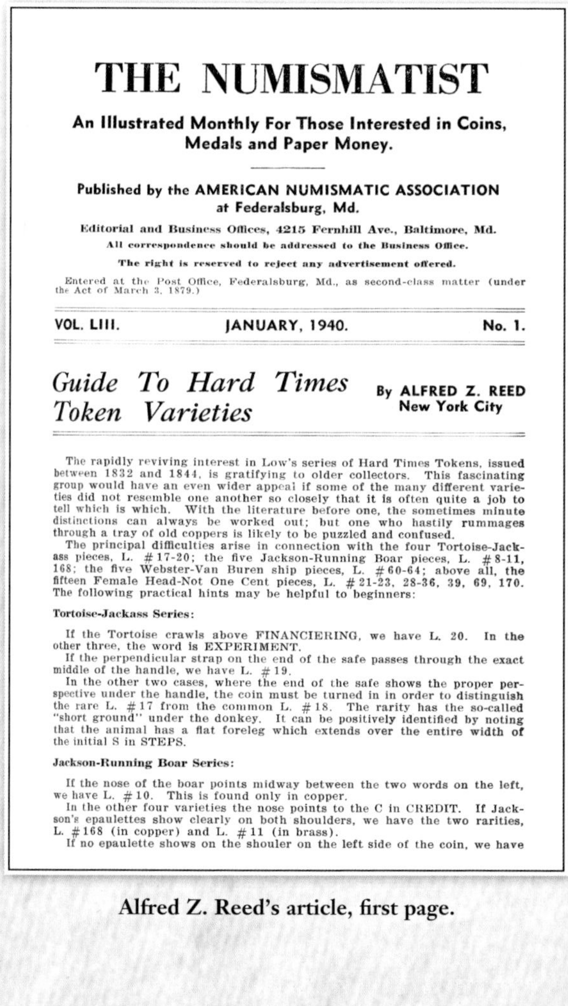

THE NUMISMATIST

An Illustrated Monthly For Those Interested in Coins, Medals and Paper Money.

Published by the AMERICAN NUMISMATIC ASSOCIATION at Federalsburg, Md.

Editorial and Business Offices, 4215 Fernhill Ave., Baltimore, Md.

All correspondence should be addressed to the Business Office.

The right is reserved to reject any advertisement offered.

Entered at the Post Office, Federalsburg, Md., as second-class matter (under the Act of March 3, 1879.)

VOL. LIII. JANUARY, 1940. No. 1.

Guide To Hard Times Token Varieties

By ALFRED Z. REED
New York City

The rapidly reviving interest in Low's series of Hard Times Tokens, issued between 1832 and 1844, is gratifying to older collectors. This fascinating group would have an even wider appeal if some of the many different varieties did not resemble one another so closely that it is often quite a job to tell which is which. With the literature before one, the sometimes minute distinctions can always be worked out; but one who hastily rummages through a tray of old coppers is likely to be puzzled and confused.

The principal difficulties arise in connection with the four Tortoise-Jackass pieces, L. #17-20; the five Jackson-Running Boar pieces, L. #8-11, 168; the five Webster-Van Buren ship pieces, L. #60-64; above all, the fifteen Female Head-Not One Cent pieces, L. #21-23, 28-36, 39, 69, 170. The following practical hints may be helpful to beginners:

Tortoise-Jackass Series:

If the Tortoise crawls above FINANCIERING, we have L. 20. In the other three, the word is EXPERIMENT.

If the perpendicular strap on the end of the safe passes through the exact middle of the handle, we have L. #19.

In the other two cases, where the end of the safe shows the proper perspective under the handle, the coin must be turned in in order to distinguish the rare L. #17 from the common L. #18. The rarity has the so-called "short ground" under the donkey. It can be positively identified by noting that the animal has a flat foreleg which extends over the entire width of the initial S in STEPS.

Jackson-Running Boar Series:

If the nose of the boar points midway between the two words on the left, we have L. #10. This is found only in copper.

In the other four varieties the nose points to the C in CREDIT. If Jackson's epaulettes show clearly on both shoulders, we have the two rarities, L. #168 (in copper) and L. #11 (in brass).

If no epaulette shows on the shouler on the left side of the coin, we have

Alfred Z. Reed's article, first page.

L. #8 (in copper) or L. #19 (in brass, silvered before striking, and on a thin flan). There is also a variety struck in brass not silvered, on a flan of about the usual thickness, to which Hewitt, in his "Hard Times Tokens," 1933 edition, gives the number 8-A.

Webster-Van Buren Ship Series:

Start with the VAN BUREN side. If the word to the right is CURRENT, we have L. #62. If the word is CURRENCY, and, as on the preceding, there are lightning flashes in the field, we have either the common L. #60 (straight deck), or the rare L. #61 (curved deck). A plain field denotes the original die. This was combined with two WEBSTER obverses. On L. #63, as on all the other Websters, only a single sail is set on the mast to the left. L. #64 shows two sails here, not to mention a jib on the right.

Female Head-Not One Cent Series:

Thirteen of the fifteen are dated 1837, and the NOT ONE CENT is surrounded by a wreath. The two exceptions, L. #39, with stars in place of wreath, and L. #69, dated 1841, present no difficulties. Both are products of the Scovill firm, of which more anon, and are quite common.

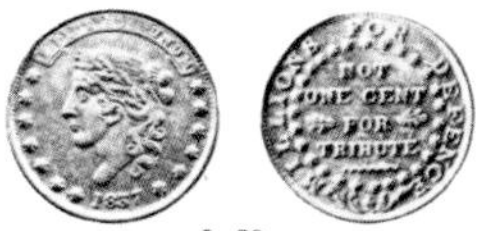

L. 39.

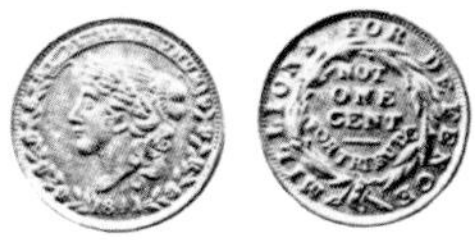

L. 69.

Three of the thirteen 1837-wreath pieces show only stars above the head. L. #23 has only twelve stars, but is more quickly identified as the only head of the series which wears a coronet. L. #21 and 22, with the usual chaplet, are distinguished from one another by the presence, on L. #22, of two extra small stars on each side of the date. All three pieces are scarce but not rare.

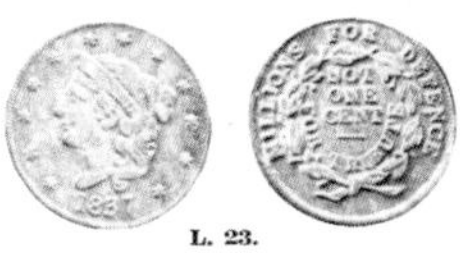

L. 23.

Four of the pieces show E PLURIBUS UNUM, but are distinguished from the commoner Scovill group by having much larger dates. L. #29 is readily recognized by its crudity, its peculiar border, and the apparently worn spot (really due to defect in design) which always appears on the reverse

Alfred Z. Reed's article, second page.

L. #28 is distinguished from the commoner L. #30 by the fact that L. #28 is the only one of the series having six stars on the left side. It is really easier, however, to note that L. #28 has on the reverse the usual dash below the word CENT, while L. #30 is the only one of the entire group which omits this. Before dismissing your L. #28, however, make sure that it has six outside berries. If it has only five, it is the exceedingly rare L. #170.

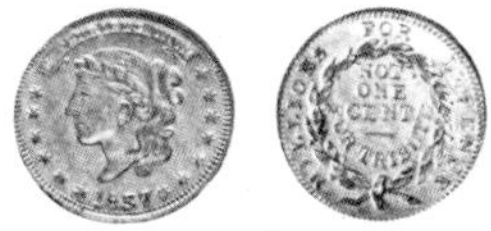

L. 28.

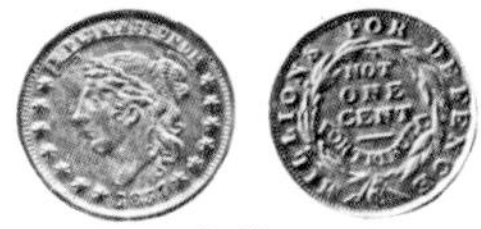

L. 33.

A small 1837 on an E PLURIBUS UNUM-wreath piece immediately identifies it as one of six (L. #31-36) manufactured, with many others, by the Scovill firm of Waterbury, Connecticut. At this point, however, the beginner's real troubles begin. He should start by examining the word DEFENCE on the other side to see whether there is a berry opposite the first E; or whether there is a berry opposite the second E; or whether there is

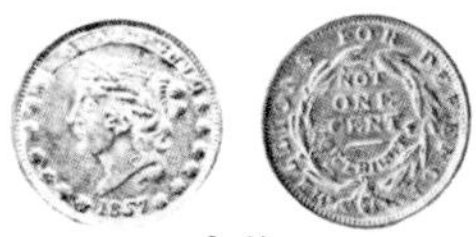

L. 31.

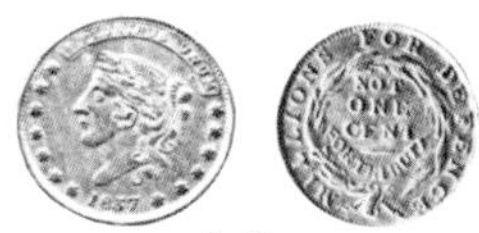

L. 36.

no berry opposite any letter in this word, but something intended to be a berry (though not very convincing) inside the wreath, near the E in TRIBUTE. After he has learned to differentiate, by their berries, these three significant E's, he can then readily assign the six Low numbers by crooning the following inspired verses:

Alfred Z. Reed's article, third page.

6 THE NUMISMATIST, January, 1940

The number first crooned is the commonest of the lot; the next two are the least common, but none of the six are rarities.

THE CHANT OF THE SIX SCOVILLS.

Second E is 33,
Inside E is 36,
But first E will the number fix
Only if a stem keeps the berry alive;
This is the retouched 35.
The other three are identified
By what we find on the other side.
A scroll ending N instead of U
On a first-E piece means 32.
First-E, scroll-U, and as always before,
Lowest curl turns left, is 34.
But if curl turns right, our job is done;
We know right away we have 31.

Memorize at once this charming ditty! If you have a wife who can set it to music, so much the better. It wil lhelp you to remember it, and she will become actively interested in your hobby.

The humorous conclusion to Reed's article.

Donald M. Miller

Wayte Raymond was joined in the pursuit of Hard Times tokens by F.C.C. Boyd, John J. Ford Jr., and Donald M. Miller, among others. By the early 1950s the demand for scarce and rare varieties was intense. A memorable highlight was the 45th sale of the New Netherlands Coin Co., April 22, 1955, which was held in a gallery off of the roof garden at the top of the New Weston Hotel in New York City. I was among those in attendance. Don Miller warmed up by fraternizing in the adjacent bar before the sale. In a somewhat lubricated state he took a $500 bill from his jacket and passed it around so that others could see the unusual denomination. Then it disappeared, much to his consternation and anger.

John Ford, who with Charles M. Wormser conducted New Netherlands, was present. During this time, and into the early 1960s, New Netherlands was the premier auction house for offering tokens and medals. The scholarship of Ford with the assistance of Walter Breen had no equals in the field at the time. Shortly after Miller's bill disappeared, Ford engaged him in a heated argument as to who had the "right" to bid on a certain Jackson token described as Low No. 1. Both men wanted the token, and both could afford any price it brought. Soon, there was a scuffle, and Miller grabbed Ford and pushed him to the railing of the roof garden and tried to heave him over the edge. I and two or three others rushed to the rescue and pulled Don away. Matters calmed down, and the sale opened as planned. Miller and Ford remained enemies for the rest of their lives.

By that time Don Miller was a consummate student of Hard Times tokens.[16] He purchased several intact collections of these tokens, as well as of Civil War tokens. One collection, formed by Dr. Mark W. Collet, who was killed in the Civil War, had been off the market for generations. Another was formed by George Hetrich, who was well known for his work with Civil War tokens, but who had a large cabinet of Hard Times tokens as well. Miller purchased the collection of Dr. Angus C. Black and auctioned off the duplicates within Black's collection. He acquired the Hard Times token collection of Brooklyn dealer Joseph Barnet, culled unwanted pieces, and sold them.

Among Miller's more curious purchases were certain tokens from B. Max Mehl, who offered the William Forrester Dunham Collection for sale to mail bids on June 3, 1941. Beginning in 1939, Mehl had privately offered selected items from the Dunham Collection to certain of his important clients, including John Work Garrett (Baltimore), Amon Carter (Fort Worth), and Charles Williams (Cincinnati), among others. The net result was that by June 3 many of the prizes had already been sold—but this information was kept hush-hush.[17] As if this did not lend enough complication to anyone wanting to find out today what *really* happened with the Dunham sale, in many instances duplicates of some pieces, including in particular the listed Hard Times tokens, were sold to different buyers, each of whom believed he had purchased *the Dunham specimen* of a given coin.[18] Many of the Hard Times tokens listed in the catalog were purchased by Miller, who was chagrined to later learn that some of the same "rarities" had been bought by someone else as well—Dunham had many duplicates! As to the pieces that had already been sold to Miller and others, Mehl topped any later bids with fictitious figures he published as "prices realized." This was puzzling to those who read the list of prices realized and knew they had bought some for less, but the matter was never openly discussed. There was no consignor or estate for Mehl to deal with as Dunham was no longer living. Mehl owned the collection, and no one was the wiser.

Another unusual Miller situation involved the magnificent collection of George L. Tilden, formed in the early 20th century. It included 160 different Low numbers. Miller obtained the collection intact, pulled out six pieces he needed, and consigned the spectacular remainder to Kenneth C. Rendell—then a teenaged dealer and, since, a close friend of mine. Rendell published a 16-page catalog of the Tilden pieces in 1958. The curious part is that Miller did not upgrade tokens he already had. If Tilden's was finer he let it go!

In 1962, Empire Coin Co., of which I was co-owner with Jim Ruddy, published Don's book, *A Catalogue of U.S. Store Cards or Merchants Tokens. The Money of the Merchants. A Part of the Unofficial Coinage of the U.S.*, an updating and expansion of the 1920 study by Edgar H. Adams. After this point, his acquisitions became fewer. Gradually, he stopped collecting coins and turned his interest to other areas, including old-time advertising tin containers and country store items. I eventually acquired his Hard Times token collection and sold it to Don Partrick. John J. Ford was the intermediary. Later I learned that Ford secretly kept a few of Miller's pieces that he needed.

In an article he wrote for the *Journal of the Civil War Token Society*, Spring 1996 issue, "The Disposition of Major Civil War Token Collections," Dr. George J. Fuld noted that, after Dr. George Hetrich died in 1928, his collection of Civil War tokens remained in his family until about 1954, when Pennypacker—a Reading, Pennsylvania, auction house—offered these, as well as his collections of Hard Times tokens and Pennsylvania tokens.

These three collections were offered only as three lots and occupied less than half a page in the small catalog. Word of the sale, with only a week or two notice, aroused the interest of several bidding groups. The late Donald Miller represented himself and Barney Sipos, a neighbor. A bidding group of Tom Warfield of Baltimore, Ben Douglas of Washington, and Melvin Fuld was formed. Several New York dealers made a group, but were really not serious contenders.

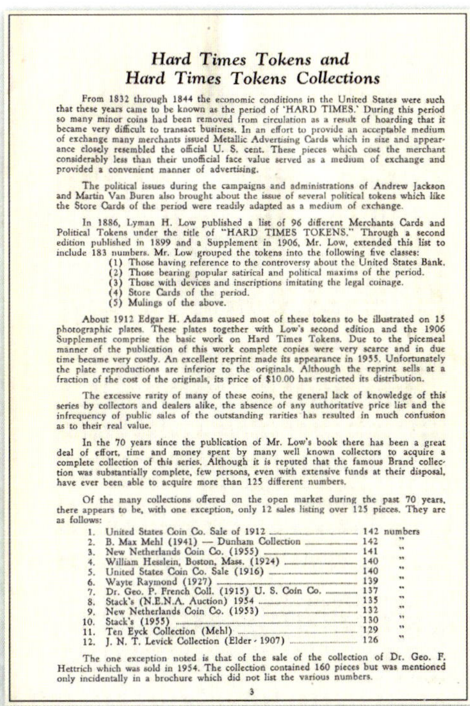

Hard Times Tokens and Hard Times Tokens Collections

From 1832 through 1844 the economic conditions in the United States were such that these years came to be known as the period of 'HARD TIMES.' During this period so many minor coins had been removed from circulation as a result of hoarding that it became very difficult to transact business. In an effort to provide an acceptable medium of exchange many merchants issued Metallic Advertising Cards which in size and appearance closely resembled the official U. S. cent. These pieces which cost the merchant considerably less than their unofficial face value served as a medium of exchange and provided a convenient manner of advertising.

The political issues during the campaigns and administrations of Andrew Jackson and Martin Van Buren also brought about the issue of several political tokens which like the Store Cards of the period were readily adapted as a medium of exchange.

In 1886, Lyman H. Low published a list of 96 different Merchants Cards and Political Tokens under the title of "HARD TIMES TOKENS." Through a second edition published in 1899 and a Supplement in 1906, Mr. Low, extended this list to include 183 numbers. Mr. Low grouped the tokens into the following five classes:

(1) Those having reference to the controversy about the United States Bank.
(2) Those bearing popular satirical and political maxims of the period.
(3) Those with devices and inscriptions imitating the legal coinage.
(4) Store Cards of the period.
(5) Mulings of the above.

About 1912 Edgar H. Adams caused most of these tokens to be illustrated on 15 photographic plates. These plates together with Low's second edition and the 1906 Supplement comprise the basic work on Hard Times Tokens. Due to the picemeal manner of the publication of this work complete copies were very scarce and in due time became very costly. An excellent reprint made its appearance in 1955. Unfortunately the plate reproductions are inferior to the originals. Although the reprint sells at a fraction of the cost of the originals, its price of $10.00 has restricted its distribution.

The excessive rarity of many of these coins, the general lack of knowledge of this series by collectors and dealers alike, the absence of any authoritative price list and the infrequency of public sales of the outstanding rarities has resulted in much confusion as to their real value.

In the 70 years since the publication of Mr. Low's book there has been a great deal of effort, time and money spent by many well known collectors to acquire a complete collection of this series. Although it is reputed that the famous Brand collection was substantially complete, few persons, even with extensive funds at their disposal, have ever been able to acquire more than 125 different numbers.

Of the many collections offered on the open market during the past 70 years, there appears to be, with one exception, only 12 sales listing over 125 pieces. They are as follows:

1. United States Coin Co. Sale of 1912 .... 142 numbers
2. B. Max Mehl (1941) — Dunham Collection .... 142 "
3. New Netherlands Coin Co. (1955) .... 141 "
4. William Hesslein, Boston, Mass. (1924) .... 140 "
5. United States Coin Co. Sale (1916) .... 140 "
6. Wayte Raymond (1927) .... 139 "
7. Dr. Geo. P. French Coll. (1915) U. S. Coin Co. .... 137 "
8. Stack's (N.E.N.A. Auction) 1954 .... 135 "
9. New Netherlands Coin Co. (1953) .... 132 "
10. Stack's (1955) .... 130 "
11. Ten Eyck Collection (Mehl) .... 129 "
12. J. N. T. Levick Collection (Elder - 1907) .... 126 "

The one exception noted is that of the sale of the collection of Dr. Geo. F. Hettrich which was sold in 1954. The collection contained 160 pieces but was mentioned only incidentally in a brochure which did not list the various numbers.

3

Donald M. Miller wrote this essay for page 3 of Kenneth Rendell's 1958 catalog of the Tilden Collection.

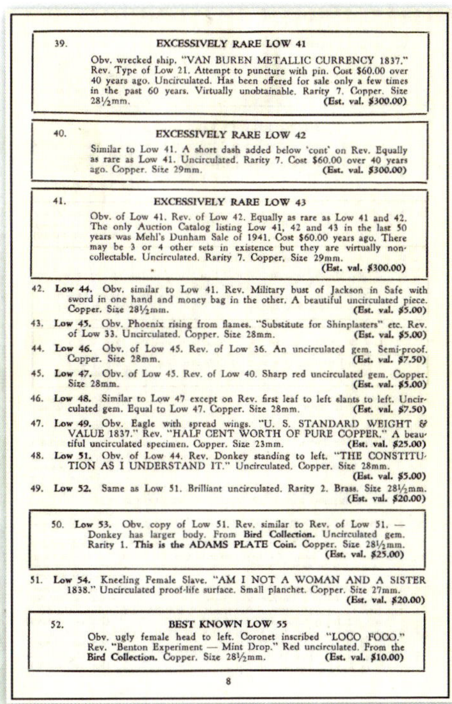

39. **EXCESSIVELY RARE LOW 41**
Obv. wrecked ship. "VAN BUREN METALLIC CURRENCY 1837." Rev. Type of Low 21. Attempt to puncture with pin. Cost $60.00 over 40 years ago. Uncirculated. Has been offered for sale only a few times in the past 60 years. Virtually unobtainable. Rarity 7. Copper. Size 28½mm. **(Est. val. $300.00)**

40. **EXCESSIVELY RARE LOW 42**
Similar to Low 41. A short dash added below 'cont' on Rev. Equally as rare as Low 41. Uncirculated. Rarity 7. Cost $60.00 over 40 years ago. Copper. Size 29mm. **(Est. val. $300.00)**

41. **EXCESSIVELY RARE LOW 43**
Obv. of Low 41. Rev. of Low 42. Equally as rare as Low 41 and 42. The only Auction Catalog listing Low 41, 42 and 43 in the last 50 years was Mehl's Dunham Sale of 1941. Cost $60.00 years ago. There may be 3 or 4 other sets in existence but they are virtually noncollectable. Uncirculated. Rarity 7. Copper. Size 29mm. **(Est. val. $300.00)**

42. **Low 44.** Obv. similar to Low 41. Rev. Military bust of Jackson in Safe with sword in one hand and money bag in the other. A beautiful uncirculated piece. Copper. Size 28½mm. **(Est. val. $5.00)**

43. **Low 45.** Obv. Phoenix rising from flames. "Substitute for Shinplasters" etc. Rev. of Low 33. Uncirculated. Copper. Size 28mm. **(Est. val. $5.00)**

44. **Low 46.** Obv. of Low 45. Rev. of Low 36. An uncirculated gem. Semi-proof. Copper. Size 28mm. **(Est. val. $7.50)**

45. **Low 47.** Obv. of Low 45. Rev. of Low 40. Sharp red uncirculated gem. Copper. Size 28mm. **(Est. val. $5.00)**

46. **Low 48.** Similar to Low 47 except on Rev. first leaf to left slants to left. Uncirculated gem. Equal to Low 47. Copper. Size 28mm. **(Est. val. $7.50)**

47. **Low 49.** Obv. Eagle with spread wings. "U. S. STANDARD WEIGHT & VALUE 1837." Rev. "HALF CENT WORTH OF PURE COPPER." A beautiful uncirculated specimen. Copper. Size 23mm. **(Est. val. $25.00)**

48. **Low 51.** Obv. of Low 44. Rev. Donkey standing to left. "THE CONSTITUTION AS I UNDERSTAND IT." Uncirculated. Copper. Size 28mm. **(Est. val. $5.00)**

49. **Low 52.** Same as Low 51. Brilliant uncirculated. Rarity 2. Brass. Size 28½mm. **(Est. val. $20.00)**

50. **Low 53.** Obv. copy of Low 51. Rev. similar to Rev. of Low 51. — Donkey has larger body. From **Bird Collection.** Uncirculated gem. Rarity 1. **This is the ADAMS PLATE Coin.** Copper. Size 28½mm. **(Est. val. $25.00)**

51. **Low 54.** Kneeling Female Slave. "AM I NOT A WOMAN AND A SISTER 1838." Uncirculated proof-life surface. Small planchet. Copper. Size 27mm. **(Est. val. $20.00)**

52. **BEST KNOWN LOW 55**
Obv. ugly female head to left. Coronet inscribed "LOCO FOCO." Rev. "Benton Experiment — Mint Drop." Red uncirculated. From the **Bird Collection.** Copper. Size 28½mm. **(Est. val. $10.00)**

8

Page 8 from the Tilden Collection catalog. The market prices are generally dozens of times higher today.

Miller and Sipos bought all three lots, with the Warfield group being the underbidder on all three. Sipos acquired the Civil War collection of some 5,500 pieces. Miller nearly completed his Hard Times collection with the rare additions from Hetrich. All in all, the three groups sold for about $10,000 and today if reoffered would closely approach seven figures.

Changes of the 1960s

The "old era" of numismatics changed in 1960 when *Coin World* was first published and the 1960 Small Date Lincoln cent became a nationwide sensation in print and on television. A $50 face value bag of such coins readily sold for $12,000! Buying coins for investment became the priority of the day, and studying and enjoying coins for their history and romance took a back seat. Then came the widespread use of numerical grading, the development of calling the hobby an *industry*, the introduction of certified grading, and more. Hard Times tokens, colonials, medals, early American coins by die varieties, and other series which required an appreciation of history and a keen intelligence became niches, the purview of specialized societies. This has been just fine for most enthusiasts. In the meantime, hundreds of thousands of collectors pursued silver dollars, commemoratives, gold coins, and other items available in large quantities.

In contrast to this, on November 19, 1960, the Token and Medal Society was organized. Soon, it began publication of the *Token and Medal Society Journal*, a repository of much useful information, including some on Hard Times tokens.

Russell Rulau

In the late 20th century Russell Rulau developed an intense interest in the Hard Times series, and he published a series of monographs, beginning in 1980. He dropped Lyman H. Low's numbers but still used the Low designation, giving new and added numbers. He more than doubled the varieties listed by the original author in 1899. For a long time, including in articles in *The Numismatist* and the *Token and Medal Society Journal*, various authors illustrated and described tokens of the 1832 to 1844 era that should have been in the original Low work, but were overlooked.

These Hard Times token monographs were succeeded by Rulau's large reference book, *Standard Catalog of United States Tokens 1700–1900*, which dropped Lyman H. Low's 1899 numbers as well as many of his own new Low numbers of the 1980s. The resulting "HT" numbers, without cross reference to the 1899 designations, were not in strict numerical sequence. This made the book a bit confusing in some aspects, but bold subheads and many illustrations helped.

The *Standard Catalog*—the latest edition of which, the fourth, was published in 2004—grouped the tokens more logically than did Lyman H. Low. All of the

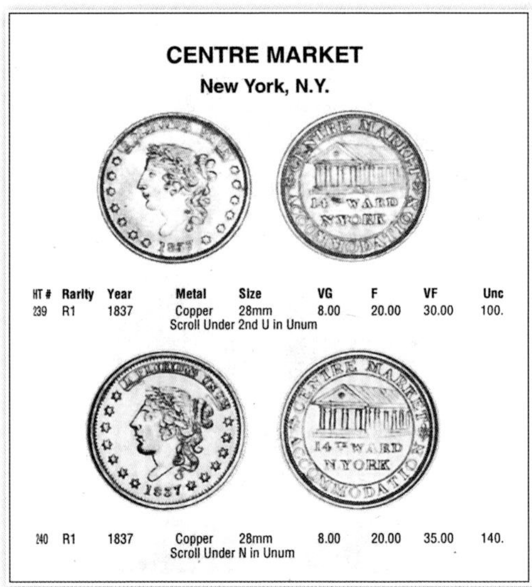
CENTRE MARKET

New York, N.Y.

HT #	Rarity	Year	Metal	Size	VG	F	VF	Unc
239	R1	1837	Copper	28mm	8.00	20.00	30.00	100.
			Scroll Under 2nd U in Unum					
240	R1	1837	Copper	28mm	8.00	20.00	35.00	140.
			Scroll Under N in Unum					

Listings for the Centre Market token in the 4th (2004) edition of the popular *Standard Catalog of United States Tokens 1700–1900* by Russell Rulau.

political issues—Jackson, Van Buren, Webster, suspension of specie payments, etc.—were in the first part of his listing, then the store cards alphabetically by state and town in the last part. He also added many counterstamped coins and other pieces not viewed by some collectors as part of the token series, which were thus confusing to contemplate. Some traditionalists such as Robert A. Schuman stayed with the old numbering system. Others, such as the late Stephen L. Tanenbaum, embraced the new.

No matter, Russell Rulau's immense catalog was and still is widely distributed, and it did much to increase interest in *exonumia*—a word he coined to describe numismatic specialties outside of federal coinage. His numbering system, minus the counterstamps and non-tokens, is useful today for keeping Hard Times tokens in approximate order and is cross-referenced in the present book.

In Later Times

Selections of Hard Times tokens from the John J. Ford, Jr. Collection were offered at auction by Stack's in 2004 and Stack's Bowers Galleries in 2013.[19] Ford had collected in secret for many years and, through private transactions with their widows, had obtained what he desired and at the price he wanted to pay the estate coins, tokens, medals, and paper money formed by Wayte Raymond and F.C.C. Boyd. Certain issues that interested him, such as the Carry Me to Atwood's Rail Road Hotel, New York & Harlem Rail Road, William H. Seward, Gulian C. Verplanck, and other Hard Times tokens he acquired in multiples—often having five or more of issues that were viewed as rare or very rare.

His collection was unofficially augmented when I purchased the Hard Times token collection of Donald M. Miller intact and offered it to Donald G. Partrick, a dedicated collector and connoisseur who lived on Long Island, New York. Ford requested to study and examine the collection for research purposes and then turn it over to the buyer, and this was done with the buyer's consent. When it arrived it was discovered that certain pieces had disappeared and others had been switched. After his estate was sold—nothing was held back by his heirs—a vast treasure trove of Hard Times tokens became available. In time these will disappear back into private collections, leaving a future generation of enthusiasts wishing they had been on the scene in 2004 and 2013.

Another stellar auction took place in June 2008 when Stack's offered the collections of James E. Dice and M. Lamar Hicks.[20] After

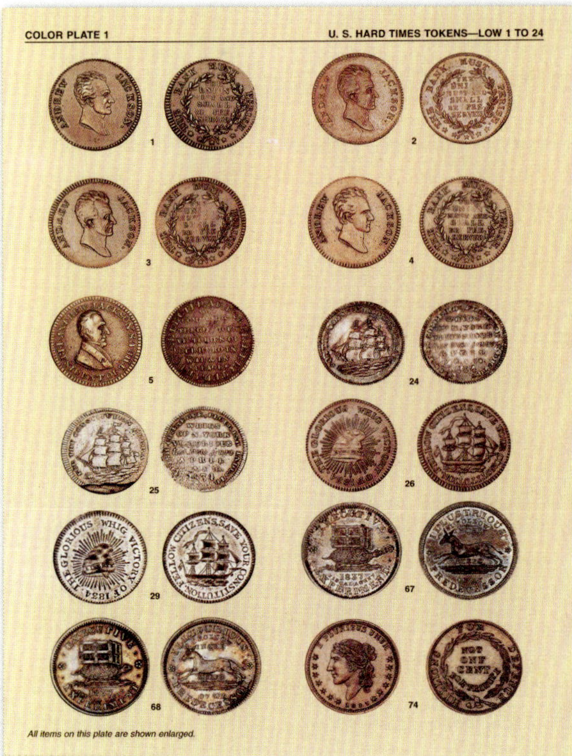

The first of several color plate pages in the 2004 sale of the John J. Ford Jr. Hard Times tokens by Stack's.

collecting independently, the two doctors decided in 1980 to combine their collections and strive to obtain one of each different variety described by Lyman H. Low and, later, to add many listed by Russell Rulau. With a generous measure of connoisseurship and effort, they succeeded admirably, aided considerably by purchases in the Ford sale of 2004. The sale, cataloged by Michael Hodder, attracted wide attention, and many records were set.

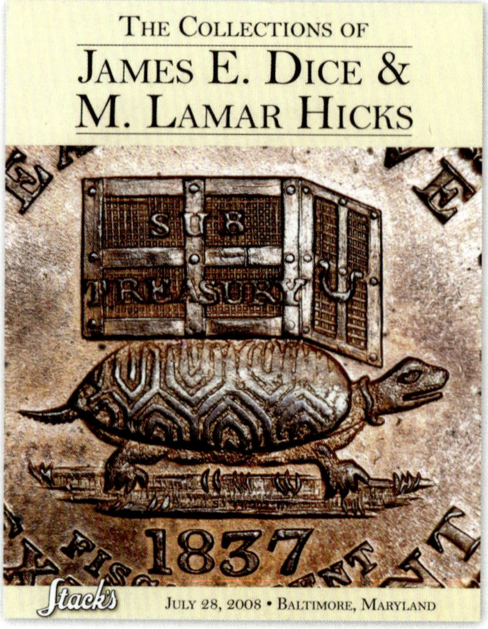

Cover of the catalog showcasing the Collections of James E. Dice and M. Lamar Hicks.

In 2010 Robert A. ("Bob") Schuman wrote and published *The True Hard Times Tokens*, an informative text that focused on the history and background of the political issues of Jackson and others. Illustrations of tokens from Bob's magnificent collection were used. For the present text, Bob was the most important research associate in addition to writing the foreword. His numismatic interest dates back a long time and, like the course followed by many other old-timers, has included multiple disciplines over the years. At one time he was a leading exponent in the field of early copper cents.

Reflective of the position of Hard Times tokens in the numismatic spectrum, the specialty in many ways remains as it has been since the early 1960s. Federal coins have dominated the marketplace, with a momentum accelerated by the formation of the Professional Coin Grading Service (PCGS) in 1985 and the Numismatic Guaranty Corporation of America (NGC) in 1987. This has made it possible for newcomers and others to spend large sums and build collections quickly without having an in-depth knowledge or appreciation of the pieces they acquire. There are, of course, many exceptions. Somewhat illogically, dates and mintmarks of modern coins that are very common in grades such as MS-65 can bring many thousands of dollars if certified by PCGS or NGC as MS-69 or MS-70.

Specialties that require a combination of intellectual curiosity, familiarity with history, and careful study have become niches. This is probably all for the best. While, for example, a specimen of an 1804 silver dollar with 15 known will readily sell into the millions of dollars (I've auctioned a number of such at record prices amid much excitement), a Hard Times token, early medal, or colonial copper with 15 known might be worth in the low thousands of dollars, but not much more. Among Hard Times tokens many of the more popular varieties still cost only in the tens of dollars. This makes it possible for many people to build nice collections even though they may not be of great financial means. While grade is important in most numismatic disciplines, most specialists would rather have a cabinet of, say, 50 different tokens, bank notes, or the like than just two or three ultra-grade pieces that cost the same amount of money.

There is another benefit to this situation: specialists who appreciate a series and build a collection over a period of time tend to stay with numismatics for a long time, to build friendships, and make the hobby an integral part of their lives. Almost everyone I knew as a token specialist in the 1950s and 1960s is still with numismatics if they are still living.

3

The Prelude to the Hard Times

Good Economic Times

By 1832, the first year in the Hard Times token era as defined by Lyman H. Low, America was in a growth pattern. Basic transportation of bulk goods was by steamboats on inland rivers, by canal boats and barges, and by ships on the sea. The Erie Canal, commenced in 1817 and officially opened with a grand ceremony on October 26, 1825, connected the Hudson River with Lake Erie and spurred industry and commerce in the Great Lakes district.

The future seemed bright, and it was envisioned that eventually travel by canal would be possible through several routes from the Atlantic coast to the Mississippi River, with certain locks in higher areas. Along the Atlantic seaboard the most active ports were Boston, New York, Philadelphia, Baltimore, Charleston, and Savannah. On the Gulf of Mexico the port of New Orleans was the entry to the Mississippi River basin and the Midwest. On land, passenger coaches on regular schedules connected many towns and cities. Freight was hauled by wagons and also shipped on river boats.

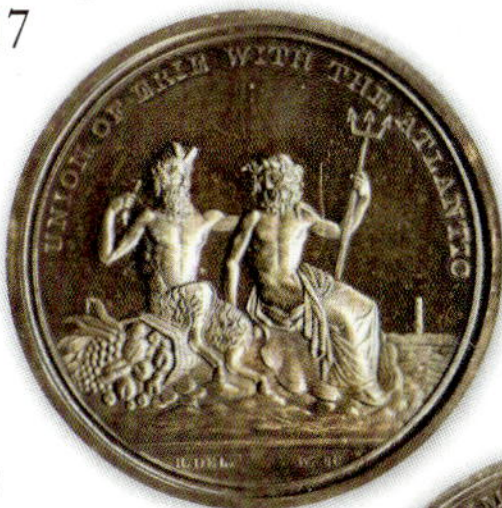

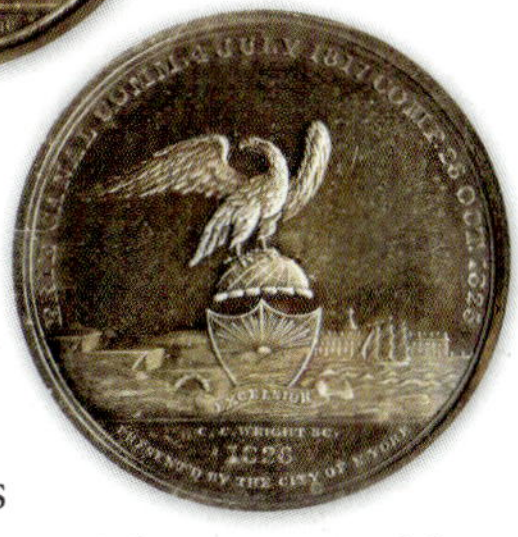

The opening of the Erie Canal furnished the occasion for the issuance of this silver medal from dies engraved by Charles Cushing Wright.

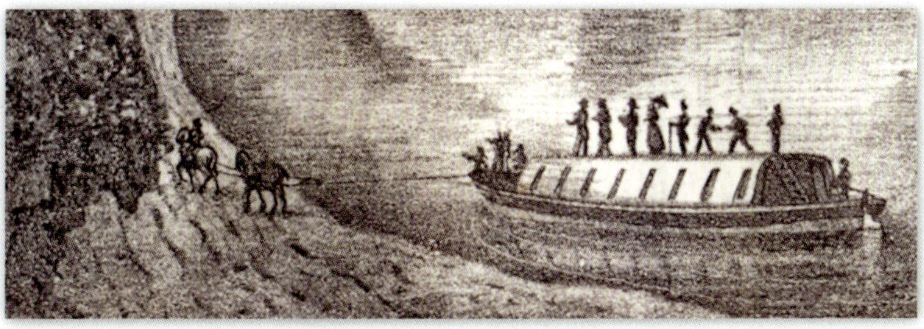

Passengers on the top deck of a boat on the Erie Canal.

In 1828 construction began on the Baltimore & Ohio Railroad, heralding a new era of transportation. Rails were laid that soon linked the bustling seaport of Baltimore to the American West, this being the land beyond the Allegheny Mountains. This project opened up the territory to settlement and in the next decade engended great growth. By 1832 there was great excitement as new companies were being formed, stock sold, and great expansion envisioned.

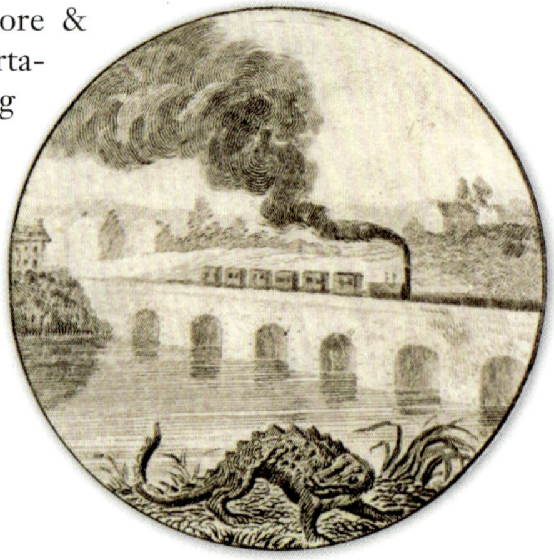

Railroads, starting to gain momentum as the growth industry of the era, were popular motifs on bank notes. This illustration is from a $4 note of the Bank of Florida in Tallahassee. The same motif but without alligator was used on banks in the North.

Federal Coins

The Philadelphia Mint, opened in 1792, provided federal coinage. In 1832 current denominations included the half cent, cent, half dime, dime, quarter dollar, half dollar, and gold $2.50 and $5 pieces. The coinage of silver dollars and $10 gold eagles had been suspended in 1804 as many if not most were shipped overseas in international commerce, thwarting the government's intention of making such pieces common in domestic commerce.

The price of gold rose on international markets, beginning in 1820, creating the unusual situation that it cost more than $5 in gold metal to produce the highest denomination coin of the country, the half eagle. Accordingly, those in circulation were snapped up by speculators and others and disappeared without a single example to be seen in the channels of commerce. Mintage continued, however, as they were necessary for foreign exchange. A merchant or bank in England, France, or another location preferred gold coins to paper money, and $5 issues were received there, not at face value but at slightly more, based on the actual value of the metal. All were satisfied. Silver and gold coins were called *specie* in various public and other accounts. This term was confusing to authors of the era and to the general public, and it was often misused to include copper coins.

Taking the place of gold coins in American commerce from 1820 through the early 1830s were silver coins, the highest denomination being the half dollar. These were produced in quantity. In the meantime, state-chartered banks turned out thousands of varieties of bills, mainly of the denominations $1, $2, $3, $5, and $10. Higher denominations were produced as well, including $20, $50, and $100, interspersed with a few banks issuing $500 and $1,000.

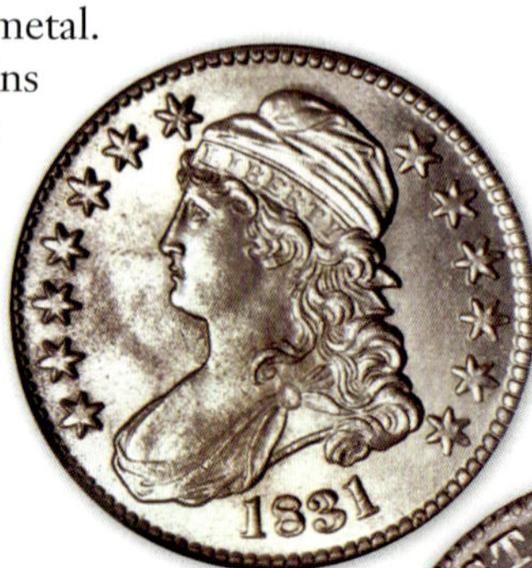

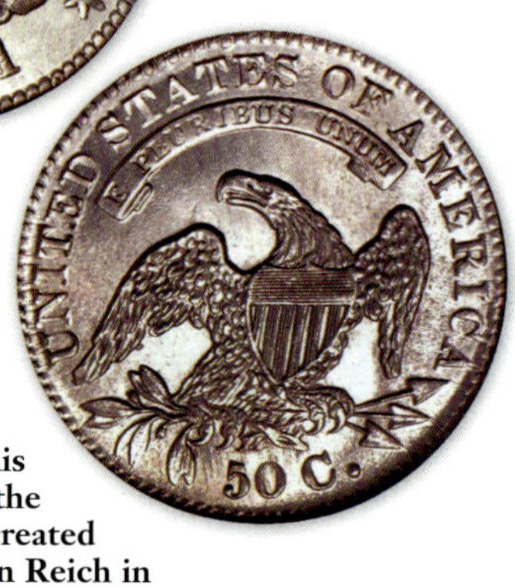

In the 1820s and early 1830s the silver half dollar was the largest-denomination coin seen in circulation in the United States. This 1831 half dollar is of the Capped Bust design created by Mint engraver John Reich in 1807 and in use since that time.

Banks and Paper Money

The Continental Congress had issued paper money from 1775 to 1779. These notes were payable in Spanish milled silver dollars or eight-real pieces. However, as young America had little in the way of assets, they could not be redeemed at par. Finally, by 1790 it took $40 in paper notes to buy one such silver dollar.

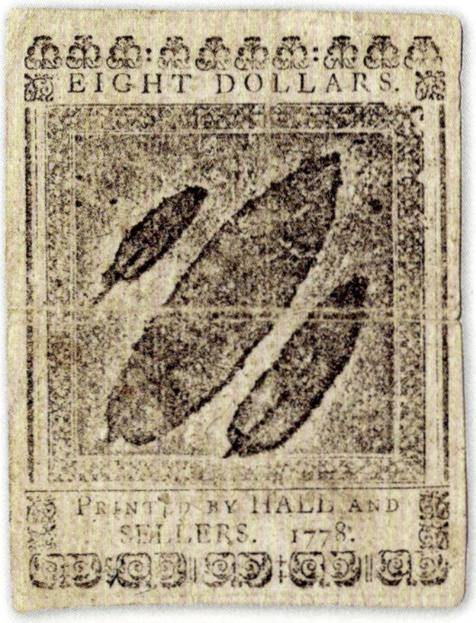

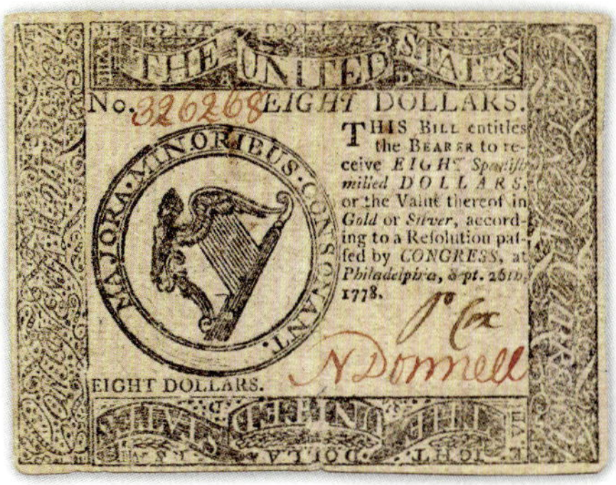

Continental Currency
$1 note issued in 1778.

After that time, as commerce expanded it fell to the state legislatures to award bank charters to groups of individuals. Had the federal government issued its own notes they probably would have been rejected, based on the poor reputation of the Continental notes. Although regulations varied, a typical provision was that a bank could issue paper bills up to the amount of its paid-in capital. Accordingly, if a bank was chartered for $100,000 it could order that amount of currency from a bank-note engraving and printing company.

Banks made their profits by loaning money. Accordingly, it was good policy to keep only a limited amount of specie on hand to redeem bills as they came in and to engage in other over-the-counter transactions—say $10,000 to $15,000 in such coins. Under normal banking and economic practice this reserve would be sufficient. However, if a bank had financial difficulties or rumors suggested that it might fail, a *run* would occur and far more bills would be presented than could be redeemed on short notice. In some instances such runs caused banks to fail. Most of the banks were well managed and had no problems. However, the scenario was punctuated by stories of banks that had to suspend specie payments for a time or close their doors.

Although no reliable data exists, it was estimated that in 1830 silver and gold coins in circulation or held by banks and citizens totaled $19,800,000, and the face value of current paper money amounted to $44,800,000, or a ratio of $100 in precious-metal coins to $226 in bills.[1]

On September 14, 1833, *Niles' Weekly Register*, using information from the *National Intelligencer*, gave this review of all banks ever formed in the states mentioned, and their current status:

Banks in the United States

Alabama, 7 banks, 2 failed.

Connecticut, 31 banks, 1 fraudulent, 4 failed.

Delaware, 8 banks.

District of Columbia, 15 banks, 2 closed, 3 failed.

Georgia, 19 banks, 1 closed, 10 failed.

Louisiana, 15 banks, 3 failed.

Maine, 36 banks, 5 closed, 5 failed.

Maryland, 31 banks, 5 closed, 4 failed.

Massachusetts, 118 banks, 4 closed, 1 fraudulent, 12 failed.
Michigan, 4 banks, 2 failed.
Mississippi, 4 banks.
New Hampshire, 24 banks, 1 failed.
New Jersey, 34 banks, 9 failed.
New York, 111 banks, 7 fraudulent, 22 failed.
North Carolina, 8 banks, 1 failed.
Ohio, 42 banks, 2 closed, 19 failed.
Pennsylvania, 70 banks, 3 closed, 1 fraudulent, 15 failed.
Rhode Island, 63 banks, 3 fraudulent, 2 failed.
South Carolina, 12 banks, 2 failed.
Tennessee, 9 banks, 2 failed.
Vermont, 20 banks, 3 failed.
Virginia, 24 banks, 1 closed, 2 failed.
Total: 705 banks, 23 closed, 13 fraudulent, 123 failed.

Editor Hezekiah Niles added this comment:

> The preceding list, though it may be, in the main, pretty nearly correct, has some errors. For instance, the New York *Commercial Advertiser* says the present total of banks in that state does not exceed 80 and that only 8 of those which were incorporated had broken—the names of which are given.
>
> The public losses, because of the failure of the 123 banks stated—perhaps really 200, if those of Kentucky, &c. were counted, must have amounted to not much less than $20,000,000—out of which, perhaps, the brokers and other dealers in bank notes made more than $5,000,000.

Important, but not stated, was the fact that most failures were of earlier times. In the early 1830s the banking community was doing very well! Still, the preceding gives a nice synopsis of history. *Niles' Register*, also known as *Niles' Weekly Register*, published in Baltimore, was distributed nationally and remained one of the most important sources of political, financial, and other news into the 1840s. In the 1830s the title was changed to *Niles' National Register*.

The First Bank of the United States

The First Bank of the United States was chartered in 1791 for a term of 20 years, subject to renewal in 1811. Most of its stockholders were individuals and companies. The federal government had a minority interest. It was not the official bank for the United States of America. The Treasury Department took that position. However, many people, especially foreigners, were not aware that it was largely owned by stockholders.

Headquartered in Philadelphia, the Bank of the United States had branches in major cities. It issued paper money that was readily accepted at par or face value everywhere.

In contrast, the more numerous state-chartered banks mainly traded in limited areas, and a $10 note issued in Philadelphia would be received at a slight discount at a distant place such as Portland, Maine. Further, although most banks were well financed and operated, the occasional failures generated a mistrust in paper money in general. In contrast, Bank of the United States bills were thought to be good by everyone. This caused bitterness on the part of the officers, directors, and stockholders of the state-chartered banks, who thought it was unfair competition. This was a powerful force, as most of the state-chartered banks had prominent citizens, including politicians, as their stockholders.

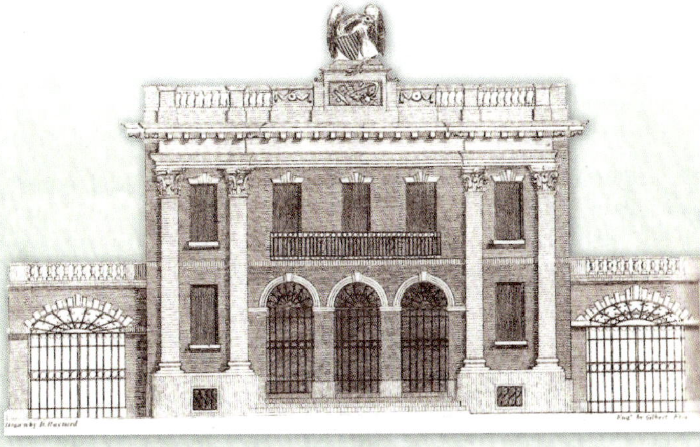

The Boston branch of the First Bank of the United States as it appeared at the turn of the 19th century.

As the charter renewal date of 1811 approached, resentment toward it built in different state legislatures. Senators and representatives were aware that its status was viewed as unfair. The charter was not renewed.

Uncertain Times

In the last few years of the bank's existence the economy experienced difficulties related to maritime commerce. Ships of the British Navy were intercepting American commercial vessels, boarding them, and taking captive any sailors who had been born in England. The British did not recognize the American concept of naturalized citizens. The French, at war with England, interfered with maritime commerce as well. With Thomas Jefferson as president, Congress, in 1807, passed the Embargo Act, which prohibited American ships from sailing to distant ports. This proved to be a great hardship on coastal towns on the Gulf of Mexico and along the East Coast. It also produced a chill in certain of the inland areas that depended on imports and exports. In 1809 the Non Intercourse Act took its place, slightly lessening the regulation, but distress continued. There were many evasions, such as claiming that a coastwise ship had been blown off course and ended up in the Caribbean.

Adding to the problem with Britain was British support through Canada of Indian raids on American communities. When such incidents occurred they were given great press coverage.

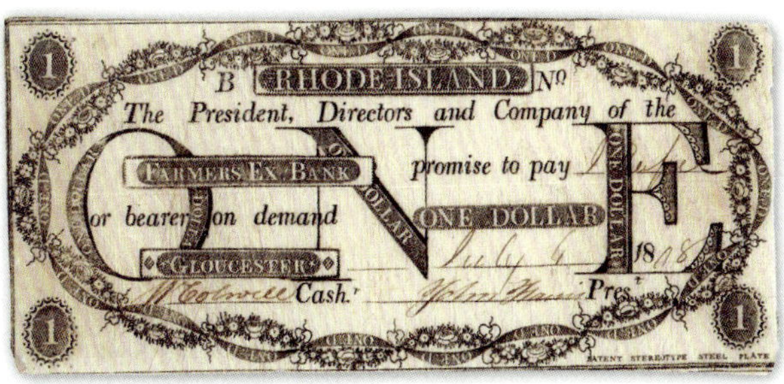

The Farmers Exchange Bank of Gloucester, Rhode Island, was a fraudulent operation conducted by Andrew Dexter. Its worthless bills contributed to the wariness of citizens toward notes issued by state-chartered banks.

The formation of new businesses slowed and several banks failed, including some fraudulently operated ones such as the Farmers Exchange Bank of Gloucester, Rhode Island, and the Hillsborough Bank of Amherst, New Hampshire. When the Bank of the United States closed its doors at its charter expiration in 1811 there was great concern as to the worth of the bills of other institutions. Most larger newspapers ran continuous dispatches alerting the public to new varieties of counterfeit bills.

In an attempt to restore maritime commerce, Congress declared war against Great Britain on June 18, 1812.

British forces engaged American troops on several different fronts, including along the border with Upper Canada, and in naval battles on Lake Erie and Lake Champlain. Extensive engagements were fought in the Atlantic, not only by Navy ships, but by many privateers who secured *letters of marque*, which entitled them to send their own armed vessels out to sea to capture whatever British merchant ships they could find and keep most of the value of the cargoes. In Portsmouth, New Hampshire, for example, several men established fortunes by doing this. In the ocean the USS *Constitution* engaged, captured, and burned the HMS *Guerriere*—the first American naval victory of the war.

Troops invaded Washington and burned the Capitol, President's House (or President's Mansion; it was not generally known as the White House until years later), and other government buildings. The British then headed to Baltimore, an even greater prize, as it was one of America's largest commercial centers. On August 27, 1814, the banks in Baltimore suspended specie payments. These were parlous times.

A battle between British and American troops had taken place three days earlier at Bladensburg, Maryland. There was a ripple effect of confidence, and on August 30 the banks in Philadelphia suspended specie payments, followed by those in New York City on September 1. This was the first widespread suspension of specie payments during the state-chartered banking era, except in the case of certain bank failures which caused regional difficulties. However, the failed bombardment of Fort McHenry, with the Star Spangled Banner still waving on the morning after, put an end to the British plans, and Baltimore was spared.

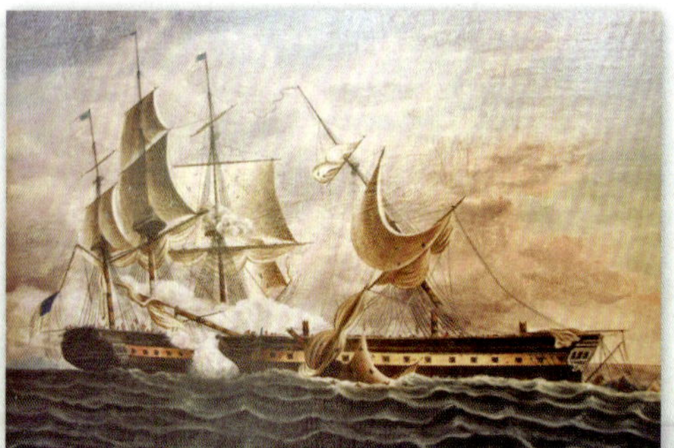

The USS *Constitution*, later nicknamed "Old Ironsides," versus the HMS *Guerriere* at sea. (Engraved by C. Tiebout after a painting by T. Birch; entered according to an Act of Congress the 18th day of August 1813 by James Webster of the State of Pennsylvania.)

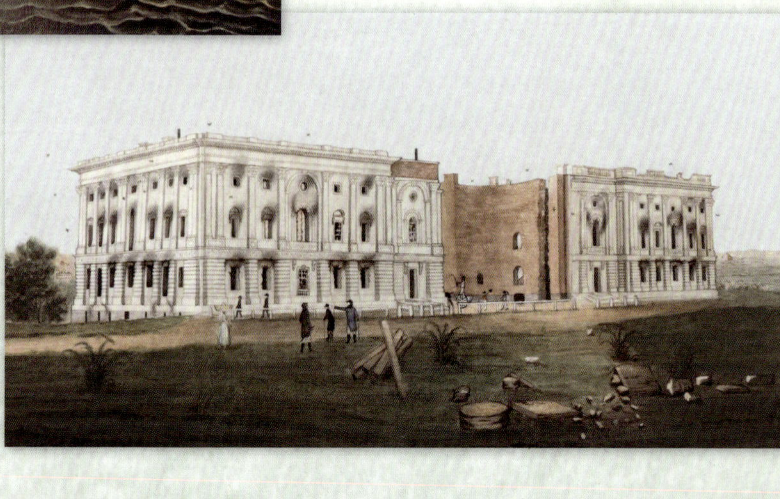

The United States Capitol after the British invasion of Washington.

In the meantime, some banks continued to suspend redemption of their notes. This caused more distrust on the part of the public. Silver and gold coins became scarce in circulation, and those in the hands of banks, specie brokers, and speculators were available only by paying a premium in bank notes. In Connecticut in October 1814, it cost an 11 percent premium, payable in paper money of sound banks, to acquire specie. Exchange rates varied constantly, not only by date but by location. Thus, a Spanish-American dollar might trade at one value in New York City on a given day and a few cents higher or lower in Boston or Charleston. A later writer on the subject noted that during the war the premium on specie varied from 5 percent to 21-1/2 percent in Baltimore and 2 percent to 16 percent in New York City.[2]

Great Britain vanquished the French army in 1814, and Napoleon Bonaparte, their leader, went into exile. The British stopped kidnapping American sailors. After the British went home in late summer of 1814, Great Britain and the United States realized the war had resulted in a stalemate, more or less, with little benefit to either country.

The war officially ended when British and American envoys signed the Treaty of Ghent, in neutral Belgium, on December 24, 1814. News of this did not reach America until well into January. In the meantime, on January 8, 1815, the Battle of New Orleans was fought, with General Andrew Jackson leading 5,000 American troops to overwhelming victory against 7,500 opponents. The Americans had 13 dead and 1,262 wounded, while the British counted 291 dead and 2,037 casualties. Jackson became an instant hero.

In February, news of peace circulated throughout the United States. It was expected that maritime shipping would resume full force, now with more ships than had been available before, and that commerce would return to normal conditions. To the surprise of nearly everyone, this did not happen.

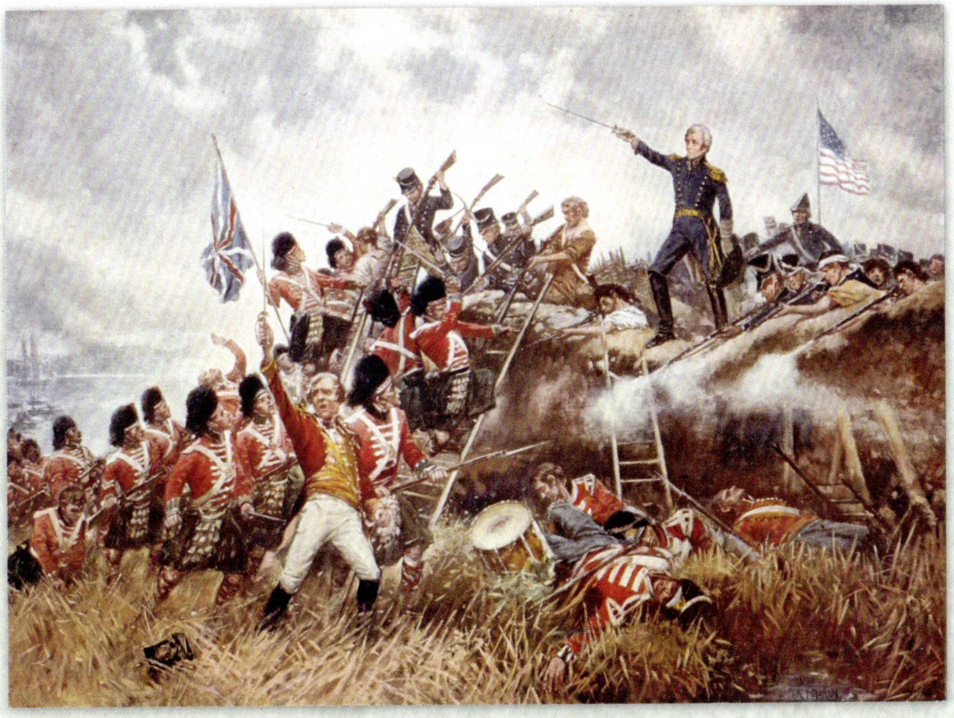

Scene at the Battle of New Orleans (Edward Percy Moran, Library of Congress).

The monetary system continued to be distressed. In July 1815, the premium of gold and silver coins in relation to bills of a good bank rose to 15 percent.[3] There were no coins in circulation. Towns, banks, turnpikes, factories, and other entities had local printers turn out paper scrip notes and certificates of fractional amounts, from a cent up to a half dollar. These notes were in addition to regular denominations such as $1, $2, $3, and $5.

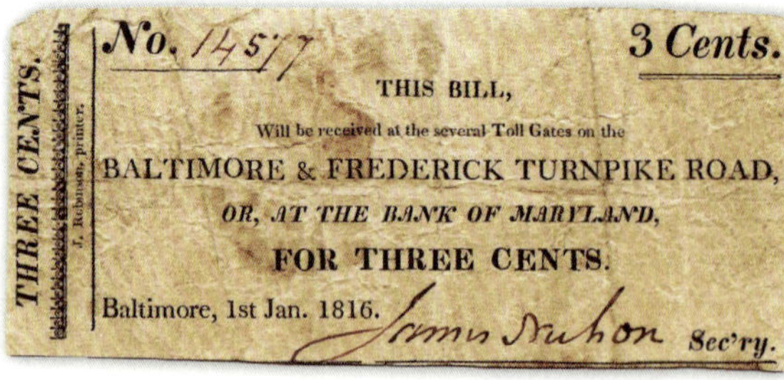

Scrip note for three cents issued by the Baltimore & Frederick Turnpike during the monetary crisis of 1815–1816.

The Second Bank of the United States

Many citizens, including congressional leaders, thought that if a new Bank of the United States could be launched, normal monetary conditions would be restored. This would also help curb some of the abuses that had arisen with state chartered banks, certain of which conducted business with a minimum of assets and had poor management.[4] A 20-year charter for the (Second) Bank of the United States was given by Congress in 1816. Good times were in the offing. The stock, mostly bought by private citizens and commercial interests, was felt to have great investment potential. Enthusiasm continued, and by May 1817, "Stock of this bank, for 65 dollars paid, has been selling at $100 a share."[5] Then in July: "The Bank of the United States has declared a dividend of *four per cent* on the stock . . . and are said to have a *surplus* of profits of about $200,000 more."[6]

Matters improved, coins were once again seen in circulation—although there were scattered regions in which the economy continued to have problems. It was not at all certain that the latest iteration of the Bank of the United States was the cause of the improvement, but certainly it had a positive effect. With this new era of looming prosperity, state-chartered banks enjoyed good business as well. However, it wasn't long before the Bank of the United States was accused of unfair competition.

Hezekiah Niles, editor of *Niles' Weekly Register*, turned sour on the bank, and in 1818 many condemnatory articles were published concerning it. Directorships were:

> too often bargained for, like *hogs* are bought in the market—*"If you'll give that, I'll give this."* . . . I am convinced, by *casting together* some things that are notorious, that three-fourths of the stock of the Bank of the United States was originally taken by less than 100 persons. . . .[7]

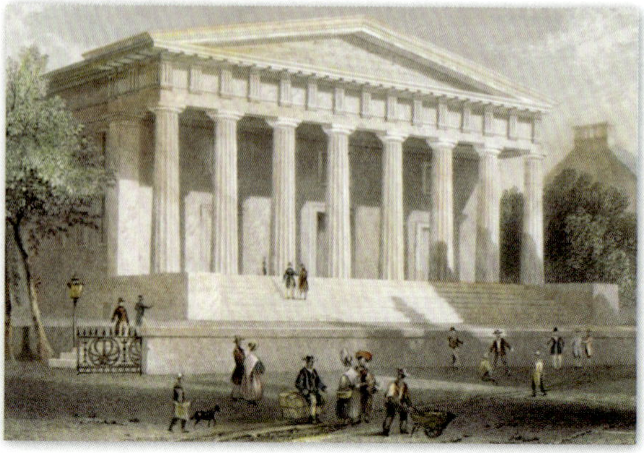

Second Bank of the United States headquarters in Philadelphia (Bartlett, *American Views,* 1829).

A caper was being practiced, Niles suggested, by certain stockholders pledging their now-appreciated shares against their original stock subscriptions, which still had not been paid for. The balance sheet of the Bank of July 1, 1817, showed that of $28,000,000 in assets, not even $2,500,000 was in specie. Most of this figure consisted of stock subscriptions to state-chartered banks.[8] Moreover, according to Niles, many published *prices current* listing values for the bank's stock were grossly inflated, as no quantity of shares could be sold for such prices. Seemingly, the second Bank of the United States was off to a rocky start.

Although domestic commerce and banking remained fairly stable, on international markets the price of gold rose. Accordingly, $2.50 or $5 gold pieces served as bullion coins and were mostly shipped overseas where they were received based on their gold content rather than their denomination.

The Bank of the United States went through difficulties for the next several years, but gained in strength when Langdon Cheves was named as president. In 1822 he submitted his resignation, his duty done. In Philadelphia, Nicholas Biddle became president in January 1823, after which time the fortunes of the Bank improved further. Not long after Biddle's entry, the Bank of the United States achieved a measure of strength, criticism subsided further (but never went away), and it took its place as an important and stabilizing factor in American commerce.

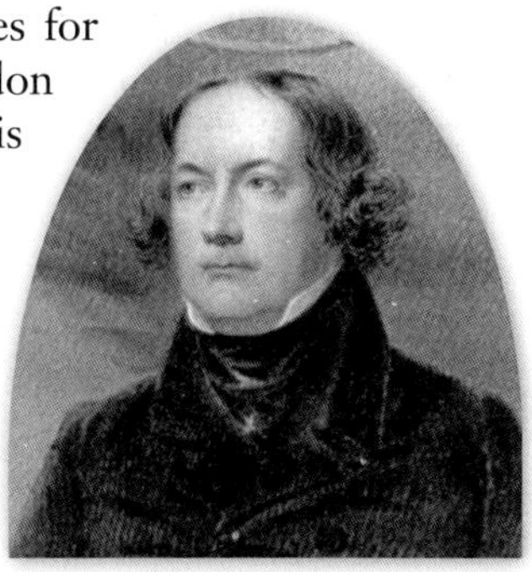

Nicholas Biddle.

Still, the existence of the institution continued to be resented by state-chartered banks, as the Bank of the United States often sought to restrict their enterprise by unfair, but legal, tactics. A typical caper included agents of the Bank of the United States presenting a small bank with a large quantity of its notes and demanding immediate redemption in specie. They also refused to accept notes of smaller banks at Bank of the United States branches, even though the bills of the Bank were rated as sound and readily accepted by other banks and merchants. The "monster" deserved its moniker for such activities. Although, to be fair, many state banks and exchange brokers engaged in similar shenanigans with paper money. It is just that the Bank of the United States was supposed to represent the epitome of rectitude, a model institution.

While most of the "Office of Discount and Deposit" branches of the Bank of the United States opened in 1817, others opened as late as 1830. The home office in Philadelphia and branches, locations, and dates of activity are:

> *Opened in 1817:* Philadelphia, Pennsylvania • Augusta, Georgia (discontinued in the same year). • Baltimore, Maryland • Boston, Massachusetts • Charleston, South Carolina • Chillicothe, Ohio (closed in 1825).[9] • Cincinnati, Ohio (closed in 1820, reopened in 1825) • Fayetteville, North Carolina • Middletown, Connecticut (moved to Hartford in 1824). • Lexington, Kentucky • Louisville, Kentucky • New Orleans, Louisiana • New York City, New York • Norfolk, Virginia • Pittsburgh, Pennsylvania • Portsmouth, New Hampshire • Providence, Rhode Island • Richmond, Virginia • Savannah, Georgia • Washington, D.C.
>
> *Opened in 1824:* Hartford, Connecticut (relocation of the Middletown, Connecticut branch opened in 1817).
>
> *Opened in 1826:* Mobile, Alabama • Nashville, Tennessee • Portland, Maine • Buffalo, New York • Utica, New York
>
> *Opened in 1829:* St. Louis, Missouri • Burlington, Vermont
>
> *Opened in 1830:* Natchez, Mississippi[10]

4

THE BRINGER OF THE HARD TIMES

Andrew Jackson

Andrew Jackson, the most prominent of the Hard Times token subjects, was born in Waxhaw, North Carolina, on March 15, 1767, the son of Andrew and Elizabeth Hutchinson Jackson. His education was intermittent, causing many later critics to call him illiterate. Regardless, he read law for about two years, and then entered practice in Tennessee, where he was viewed as very competent. He became well-to-do and built a mansion, Hermitage, near Nashville, where he was a slave owner. He was a ready debater and quickly rose to challenges. In a duel with a man who had insulted his wife, Jackson was the winner. In 1796 and 1797 Jackson served as a congressman, then as a senator for the next two years, followed by a judicial position on the Tennessee Supreme Court until 1804.

After the War of 1812 he became known as the "Hero of New Orleans." Because of his toughness, "Old Hickory" was another popular name for him. While some admired that toughness, it was less than admirable in some instances.

Information was found to the effect that Spain and Great Britain were aiding and abetting the Indians against Americans. In December 1817, President James Monroe directed him to go to Georgia to head an attack on Seminole and Creek Indians and to prevent Spanish-owned Florida from becoming a haven for escaped slaves—the latter instruction being given in a commission which seemed to suggest Jackson should take over the territory. With extreme cruelty Jackson, claiming self-defense as an excuse for his actions, killed men, women, and children. This precipitated international censure, but in time the uproar over the matter became subdued. The Spanish governor was ousted. Jackson was appointed governor of the Florida Territory in 1821. He later served as a United States senator.

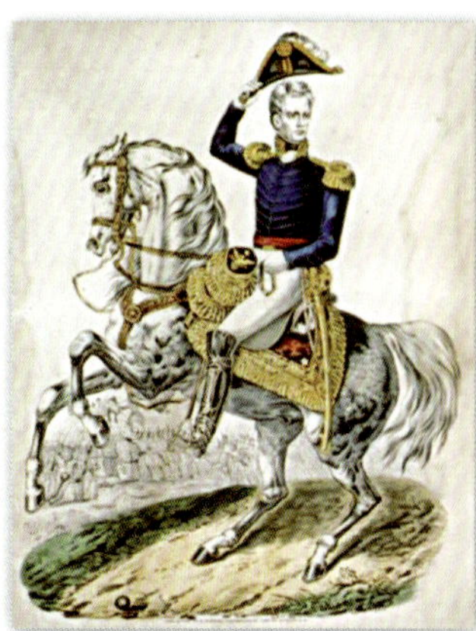

The Hero of New Orleans (Nathaniel Currier lithograph).

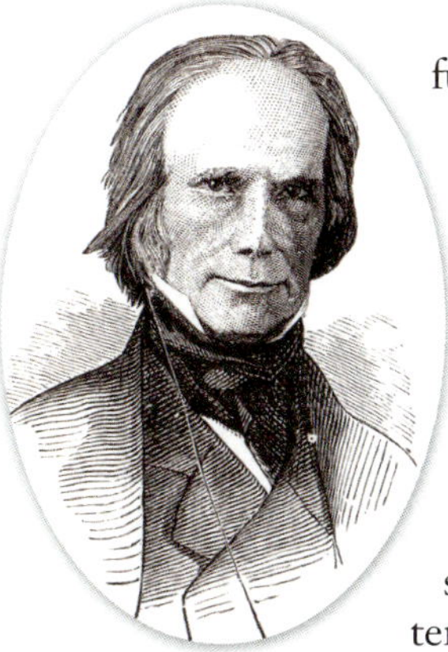

Henry Clay was a formidable adversary to Andrew Jackson during the 1820s and 1830s.

In 1824 the Democratic-Republican Party was the only fully functioning party. It became split, and four men were nominated for the presidency: Jackson, John Quincy Adams, William H. Crawford, and Henry Clay. Jackson and Adams shared the same running mate, John C. Calhoun of South Carolina.

Voting took place from Tuesday, October 6, to Thursday, December 2. Jackson, with 157,271 popular and 99 Electoral College votes, seemed to be the winner. Adams was the runner-up with 113,122 popular and 84 Electoral College votes, and Crawford and Clay trailed far behind with 40,856 and 41, and 47,531 and 37, respectively. Because Jackson did not have a plurality of Electoral College votes, the matter was sent to the House of Representatives. On February 9, 1825, Adams was declared the winner in what became known as the "Corrupt Bargain", said to have been engineered by men of wealth in the East. In what appeared to be a quid pro quo, Clay was named secretary of State—a position which was considered to be a stepping stone to the presidency.

Jackson backers went on to form the Democratic Party, while adherents of John Quincy Adams and Henry Clay organized the National Republican Party, which in the early 1830s became known as the Whig Party. After the election, the defeated Jackson had mixed reviews. Some admired him as the Hero of New Orleans and felt sorry for him as a victim of political intrigue. Others remembered his lead in killing Indians and felt that such a man was not fit to hold the highest office. Jackson spent much time at Hermitage, which, by that time, was a farm hundreds of acres in size tended to by slaves.

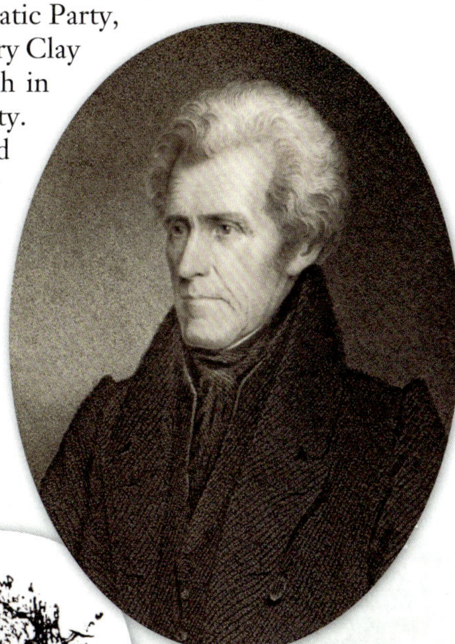

Andrew Jackson as engraved by James B. Longacre (*National Portrait Gallery of Distinguished Americans*, 1837).

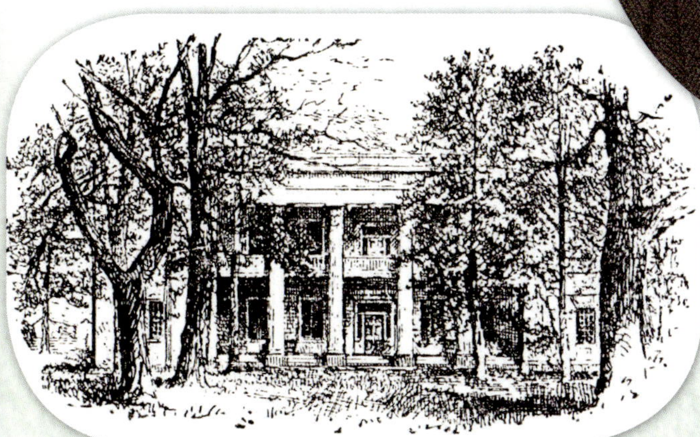

Andrew Jackson's Hermitage plantation mansion near Nashville.

The American System

Many manufacturing businesses, especially in the North, were hurt or even idled by large quantities of imports from abroad, from England in particular but also France, Russia, the German states, and elsewhere. Newspapers of the 1820s were filled with announcements of clothing, jewelry, household goods, and other items arriving in port and available for sale at bargain prices.

The Tariff of 1828 was signed by President John Quincy Adams on May 19, 1828, well before the presidential election of that year. The tariff placed a high charge on imported goods and led to great prosperity in succeeding years, into the Jackson administration. This policy became known as the *American System*. It had several side effects.

For one, the export of specie, especially gold coins, slowed as fewer payments were being made abroad for merchandise. This did not release any gold coins into domestic circulation, because they were still trading at a higher value than their denomination. The premium on U.S. gold coins if purchased with silver coins varied from 4-1/2 percent to 6-1/2 percent.[1]

More dramatically, the legislation severely dampened imports from England, a country that was the South's best customer for cotton, which went to supply the mills of Manchester and other industrial cities. In the South many called it the Tariff of Abominations. The reaction was intense, particularly on the part of Senator John C. Calhoun and the delegation from South Carolina. On June 14, *Niles' Weekly Register* began an article with: "Half Mast! The flags of some of the vessels lying at Charleston, S.C. were hoisted half mast, when news of the passage of the tariff law was received."

This led to several decades of sharp debates in Congress, South Carolina opposing the policies of the North and threatening withdrawal from the Union. It was the stance of Calhoun and others that individual states should regulate tariffs to benefit citizens of that state, and that the United States government should not. This was called the "states' rights" movement and was a strong factor in the tensions leading up to the Civil War. In 1832 South Carolina caused the *nullification crisis* when it contended the tariff was illegal and would not be followed. The tariff rift that started in 1828 and the increasing favor in the North for the nationwide abolition of slavery were the two most important factors leading to the Civil War in 1861.

In 1828, when the Bank of the United States was going strong, there was widespread fear concerning the worth of paper bills issued by certain *other* banks. While most institutions were solidly financed, there were enough exceptions to stir fear. Dozens of banks were experiencing difficulties, and although they were but a small fraction of the industry, reports about them engendered widespread concern. A report made to the North Carolina State Legislature in this year revealed that the Bank of Cape Fear and the Bank of New Bern had no specie backing. Both were chartered in 1804, under the law that the capital stock be paid for in gold or silver. No gold or silver was ever paid. Several years later, each boasted a capital of $800,000, still with no gold or silver paid in. These banks issued more than $3,000,000 in paper notes, based upon no backing at all, but returning to the banks' investors "something like $200,000 annually."[2]

In the meantime the tariff brought unprecedented prosperity to the North. In June 1831 the *Portland Advertiser* told this:

> Boston has given us a powerful, and we may say without exaggeration, a splendid illustration of the excellence of the American system. Her trade before the tariff of '28, and for some time after, (till the country was invigorated by new protecting duties),

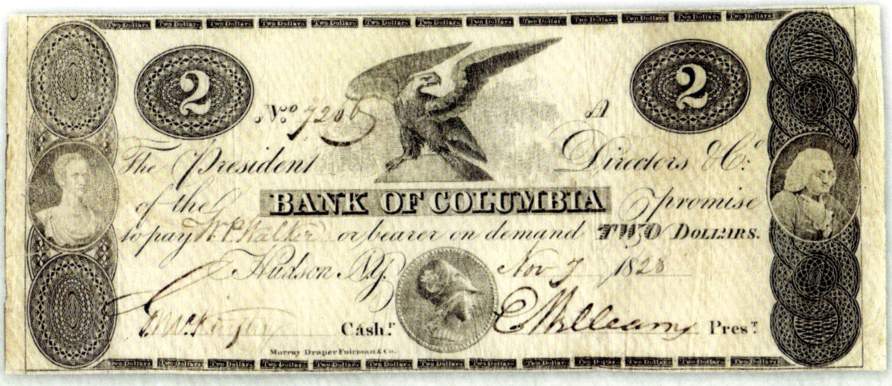

The Bank of Columbia was chartered by the state of New York in 1792, one of the earliest such institutions in America. With a stated capital of $160,000, it opened for business. By 1828, when this $2 note was issued, the bank was having great difficulty, although the recipient of such a bill would have no way of knowing this unless he was aware of bank reports. The Bank of Columbia failed in 1829, and its notes became worthless. In contrast Bank of the United States bills were redeemable at par everywhere.

was drooping. Her stores and shops and houses were untenanted. Real estate decreased in value; mechanics were out of employ; and even misery was lifting up its visage.

Now the tariff of '28 is under full wing. An impulse like that of an electric battery is given to trade. Our Eastern traders who had purchased goods there this season tell us old Babylon was not more noisy. Nothing but bustle, bustle,—or to use the expressive language of the day (which is always best in matters of this sort) "they are making money hand over fist." All our cities and large towns, certainly, are in a state of wonderful prosperity. . . .

The Election of 1828

In the presidential contest of 1828, Andrew Jackson on the Democratic ticket challenged John Quincy Adams, as he had in 1824. John C. Calhoun, who had served as vice president under Adams, joined Jackson on the 1828 ticket. Both were Southerners. Their supporters called themselves Democrats. Throughout the summer, and into the autumn of 1828, each side accused the other of misdeeds, immorality, and bad practice.

The Adams contingent seized on the marriage of Jackson to his wife Rachel in 1791. She and her groom thought she was legally divorced from another man, but that was not the case They simply had a second ceremony once the papers were in order. Charles Hammond, owner of the *Cincinnati Gazette*, saw it differently: "Ought a convicted adulteress and her paramour husband be placed in the highest offices of this free and Christian land?" This was an era in which, to be successful, most politicians had to be Anglo-Saxons and church-attending Christians. Jackson blamed Adams and his fellow campaigners heartily for the vile things they had said about his wife.

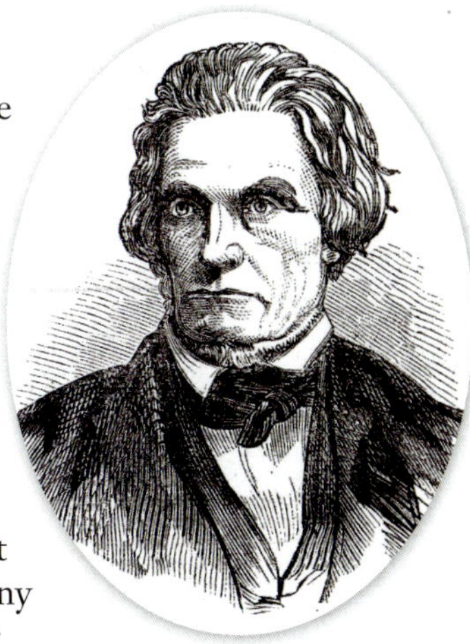

Senator John C. Calhoun of South Carolina was an outspoken critic of the Tariff of 1828 and espoused states' rights over those of the federal government. He was vice president to Jackson in the successful presidential campaign of 1828.

Printed circulars showcased Jackson's massacres of innocent Indians and his execution of soldiers who deserted, which was, indeed, a large blot on the Jackson escutcheon, as well as on the history of our nation. He was known for his ruthlessness, fine in the Battle of New Orleans, but not so fine in certain other scenarios.

Adams, son of a president and from a well-respected New England family, had fewer skeletons to be found in his closet. However, there was a nasty situation when, while serving as minister to Russia, he turned over young girls to Czar Alexander to satisfy the potentate's sexual desires. He was also accused of misusing federal funds to buy gaming equipment for the President's House—a billiard table and chess set, as it turned out. Even with these offenses, his bill was much cleaner than was Jackson's. Such was politics.

Rachel Jackson suffered pains throughout the year, became ill, and died on December 22, 1828. The Rachel–Andrew Jackson wedding story did not die. It would surface again in the campaign of 1832, then mostly spread by Henry Clay.

This time around, despite a torrent of invective against him, Jackson won the election. On March 4, 1829, he was inaugurated and went to the President's House. On the day of the inauguration the doors to the President's House were thrown open to just about everyone, including ragtag elements and those in muddy boots who stood on upholstered chairs to get a better view.

Jackson was widely disliked by many in traditional Washington politics and society, as well as being detested by abolitionists, who reviled him for owning slaves. He was considered by his detractors to be a brilliant strategist, but not well educated—indeed somewhat illiterate—and lacking social graces. Jackson was the first occupant of the White House (as it was later called) to be born in a log cabin—an appeal that was used by others in later elections to win the popular vote. Former presidents were mostly of the gentry, with four out of six coming from Virginia. While Jackson, too, owned a plantation, had slaves, and was a man of wealth, this did not define his public image. He did not emphasize these characteristics and was never a part of "high society." Instead he was the Hero of New Orleans, a common man, a citizen with bonds which many voters could identify with.

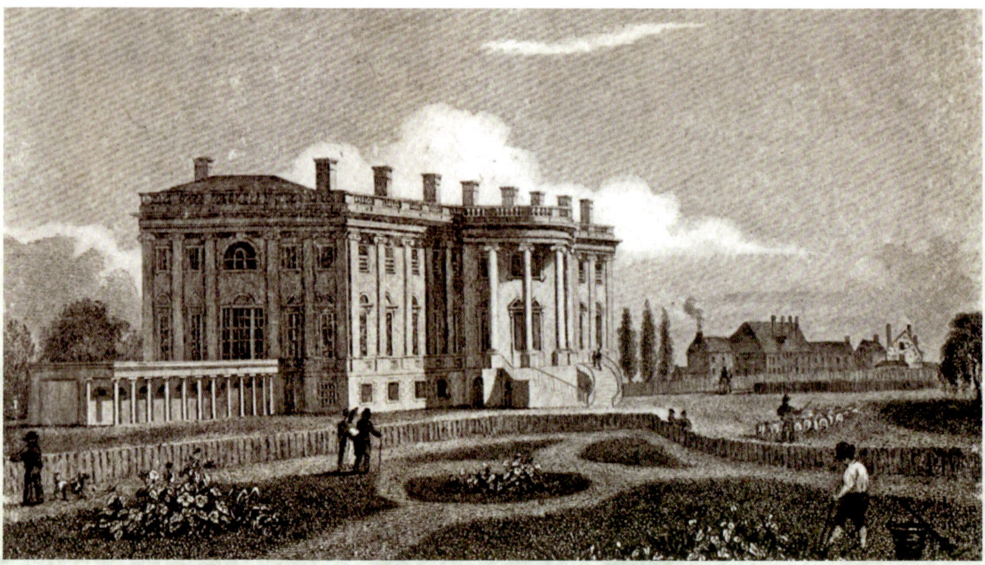

The President's House, as it was popularly called, as shown early in the Jackson administration (Hinton, Simpkin & Marshall, 1831).

Isaac Hill vs. the Portsmouth Branch

An omen of the upcoming Bank of the United States controversy arose from the relationships Jackson formed early in his presidency. Isaac Hill, a well-known New Hampshire banker (until recently the president of the Merrimack County Bank in Concord, *the* best politically connected bank in the capital city), and a prominent state political figure, was a close friend of the new president.[3] In the election of 1828, Hill led the Jacksonians to victory in the Granite State. Hill was appointed as second comptroller of the Treasury Department. In that position he sought to transfer the account that the United States Pension Agency had with the Portsmouth branch of the Bank of the United States to the Merrimack County Bank in Concord, to which he still had close ties. A large infusion from the Pension Agency would certainly be an impressive addition to its deposits and no doubt would help attract other business to the Bank as well. This would be an ideal way to reduce the aura of exceptionalism that the Bank of the United States had with the public and give some prestige to his state-chartered bank. It would also please the officers and stockholders of other banks in New Hampshire, many of whom were well-connected politically. In contrast, there was little support of state politicians for the Bank of the United States.

Jackson had another strong friend and ally in Senator Levi Woodbury, also from New Hampshire, who would rise in his administration through two Cabinet positions (in May 1831 Woodbury was appointed by Jackson as secretary of the Navy, a post he held until 1834; on June 27, 1834 he was appointed secretary of the Treasury). Hill enlisted Woodbury in his effort to move the funds. Hill tapped many others in an effort to oust Jeremiah Mason, president of the Portsmouth branch. This would, in a small way, discredit the entire infrastructure of the Bank of the United States.

On June 17, 1829, a petition signed by 56 citizens of Portsmouth, including many of the most influential business and political figures, was sent to Nicholas Biddle, the president of the Bank of the United States, and the bank's directors. The document alleged that the Portsmouth branch had been conducted in a manner "partial, harsh, novel, and injurious to the interest of the bank," and that Mason was specifically responsible for the untenable situation. The petitioners sought removal of Mason and the entire board of directors and requested their replacement with people who were aware of the business necessities of Portsmouth and were "disposed to dispense the favors of the Bank impartially."

On June 27, 1829, Woodbury wrote a letter marked "Confidential" to Samuel D. Ingham, Jackson's secretary of the Treasury, endorsing the action of the petitioners. He added the telling comment that Jeremiah Mason "is a particular friend of Mr. [Daniel] Webster," who was said to have been instrumental in securing the position for him. Webster was one of the main detractors of Jackson, a political archenemy. Along with Henry Clay, Webster objected to just about everything Jackson and his administration did.

The campaign ramped up with more requests to toss Mason and his crew out. Another petition charged that the Portsmouth branch had refused small, safe loans to established businessmen in Portsmouth, while large and risky loans had been made to favored out-of-state parties. In yet another of many messages, Hill advised that he had reliable information that Jeremiah Mason was "unaccommodating to pensioners," and that he made large loans to his brother-in-law in Boston, "while refusing to accommodate our merchants with two or three thousand dollars, and this, too, on the very best paper."

On August 3, 1829, Secretary of War John H. Eaton (of Eaton's wife Peggy more will be said) wrote to Jeremiah Mason, taking direct action in accordance with the implied wishes of Isaac Hill. Eaton advised Mason that "it has been found necessary" to move the Pension Agency from under his control in Portsmouth to a new location in

Concord, and that a pension agent has been appointed to reside in Concord. Mason was requested to deliver to the new agent all the books, papers, and *money* belonging to the Pension Agency. This transfer of federal funds to a state-chartered bank increased the likelihood of other state-chartered banks taking future government contracts.

Nicholas Biddle visited Portsmouth, interviewed Mason, and reported that the charges were "entirely groundless." Mason gained a vote of confidence and was reelected president of the branch. The battle lines were now drawn.

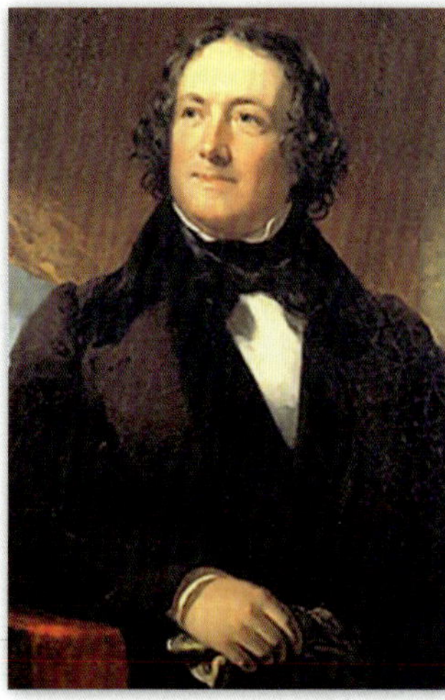

Portrait of Nicholas Biddle by William Inman.

The contrast between the two camps was indeed stark. Nicholas Biddle, the president of the Bank of the United States, was born to a wealthy family, attended Princeton (remarkably graduating at the age of 15), had widely traveled throughout Europe, and had a literary bent, having written the first important account of the 1804–1806 Lewis & Clark Expedition. As a scion and at the top of Philadelphia society, his aristocracy was neither understood nor appreciated by the typical American citizen who read about the "Bank war." Perhaps no one was more primed to find himself in opposition to Jackson, the populist president.

Jackson vs. the Bank of the United States

In his first annual message to the House and Senate, December 7, 1829, this manifesto was included:

> The charter of the Bank of the United States expires in 1836, and its stockholders will most probably apply for a renewal of their privileges. In order to avoid the evils resulting from the precipitancy in a measure involving such important principles, and such deep pecuniary interests, I feel that I cannot, in justice to the parties interested, too soon present it to the deliberate consideration of the legislature and the people.
>
> Both the constitutionality and the expediency of the law are well questioned by a large portion of our fellow citizens; and it must be admitted by all, that it has failed in the great end of establishing a uniform and sound currency.[4]
>
> Under these circumstances, if such an institution is deemed essential to the fiscal operations of the government, I submit to the wisdom of the legislature, whether a national one founded upon the credit of the government and its revenues, might not be devised, which would avoid all constitutional difficulties; and, at the same time, secure all the advantages to the government and country that were expected to result from the present bank.[5]

Jackson's second annual message to Congress, delivered on December 6, 1830, reiterated his animus toward the Bank:

> The importance of the principles involved in the inquiry whether it will be proper to recharter the Bank of the United States requires that I should again call the attention of Congress to the subject. Nothing has occurred to lessen in any degree the dangers which many of our citizens apprehend from that institution as at present organized.

> In the spirit of improvement and compromise which distinguishes our country and its institutions it becomes us to inquire whether it be not possible to secure the advantages afforded by the present bank through an agency of the Bank of the United States so modified in its principles and structure so as to obviate constitutional and other objections.
>
> It is thought practicable to organize such a bank with the necessary officers as a branch of the Treasury Department, based upon the public and individual deposits, without power to make loans or purchase property, which shall remit the funds of the government, and the expense of which may be paid, if thought advisable, by allowing its officers to sell bills of exchange to private individuals at a moderate premium.
>
> Not being a corporate body, having no stockholders, debtors, or property, and but few officers, it would not be obnoxious to the constitutional challenges which are urged against the present bank; and having no means to operate on the hopes, fears, or interests of large masses of the community, it would be shorn of the influence which makes that bank formidable.[6]
>
> The states would be strengthened by having in their hands the means of furnishing the local paper currency through their own banks, while the Bank of the United States [the *new* bank proposed by Jackson, not the existing bank], though issuing no paper, would check the issues of the state banks by taking their notes in deposit and for exchange only so long as they continue to be redeemed with specie. In times of public emergency the capacities of such an institution might be enlarged by legislative provisions.[7]

In 1831 Henry Clay, leader of the opposition, joined by Daniel Webster, championed the renewal of the Bank of the United States charter as fervently as Jackson and the Democrats opposed it. Clay had a vested interest: he was an attorney for the Bank and was on a retainer. Mason, seemingly tired of the controversy, resigned his post as branch bank president in May 1831.

The Indian Removal Act

For generations the Cherokee Indians had lived in their country—a territory which, at the time white men arrived from Europe, encompassed much of what later became Georgia and the Carolinas. Everything changed in the 1820s. Gold was discovered in the region, and there was a rush to settle the territory. In 1829 President Jackson endorsed the idea of evicting the natives. On May 28, 1830, the Indian Removal Act became law.

On July 17, 1830, *Niles' Register* included this:

> *Gold mines in Georgia and the Cherokee Nation.* We were yesterday shown a phial full of gold from these mines, of a beautiful color, with various specimens of the stones and sand in which this precious mineral is found. When the cry of "gold mines" was first sounded among us, no person dreamed, not even the most sanguine, of the extent and quantity of the mineral which existed in the country, and most were disposed to regard the whole subject as a matter of ridicule. But we are assured by a gentleman who has had the best opportunities of knowing that for some time past, (until very recently, when the Cherokee mines were abandoned pro tem).
>
> By order of the government gold has been obtained there and in the county of Habersham (Georgia) at the rate of a million and a half of dollars per annum. Single pieces have been found which were worth $75 or $80 each. The following facts are furnished us by the gentleman above mentioned. . . .

Adventurers by the countless thousands came from all directions to settle in the Cherokee Nation and stake their claims. The Indians who had lived there for generations were forcibly torn from their homes and transported to the Midwest in the tragic *Trail of Tears*. Jackson steadfastly maintained that Indians were a sub-species of humans incapable of being integrated into white society—forever a blot on his character and administration.

Peggy O'Neale

In the usual course of events, the mélange of sex, lies, accusations, and political mudslinging that surrounded Peggy Eaton—formerly Timberlake, née O'Neale—would be out of place in a text devoted to numismatics. However, in the nation's capital, the miasma of gossip which settled on Miss O'Neale changed the course of American history. It was directly responsible for the ascension of Martin Van Buren to the presidency at the end of Andrew Jackson's term—thus securing Van Buren's position as the subject of so many Hard Times tokens. It was a disagreement over the actions of Peggy O'Neale which separated the interests of President Jackson and his first vice president, John C. Calhoun, who would have otherwise found himself the second president of the Hard Times.

Central to the drama was the account of the actions of Margaret O'Neale Eaton, known to many as Peg or Peggy, born on December 3, 1799. Margaret's parents, Mr. and Mrs. William O'Neale, owned the Franklin House, a popular Washington tavern and hotel on I Street, which was frequented by many important officials and was a stop for many stage coaches.[8] Mr. and Mrs. O'Neale were warm hosts and offered a home away from home for countless senators, representatives, and other politicians, including diplomats from abroad. In 1824, when Marquis de Lafayette, French hero of the American Revolution, visited the United States as "the Nation's Guest" (per Congress), among his many stops was a stay at the Franklin House.

The facility was described in an advertisement in the *Daily National Intelligencer*, December 6, 1816:

> Franklin House, City of Washington: The proprietor begs leave to inform his friend and the public in general that he has fitted the Tavern handsomely, also has put in complete order his two Boarding Houses adjoining the Franklin, where ladies and gentlemen will be accommodated in the best manner.
>
> Passengers will be carried to and from the steam boat gratis. Three stages daily to Baltimore, seats or whole stages taken at the Franklin.
>
> *Wm. O'Neale.*

Bright, slender, blue-eyed, and with flowing hair, the celebrated Peggy flirted with and enjoyed the company of many men—sometimes intimately, it was alleged! When she was 12 she gave a dance recital for First Lady Dolley Madison. When she was 14 or 15 a paramour she spurned, apparently not her first, committed suicide. At age 15 she attempted to elope with Major Francis Smith Belton, an aide to General Winfield Scott, by climbing out a window at night, but she tipped a flower pot that crashed and broke, alerting her father. Then she fell in love with another man, Captain Richard R. Root, but it didn't last. At age 17, in 1816, she married John Bowie Timberlake, age 39, a purser in the Navy. In time the couple had three children. The family lived at the Franklin House in special quarters.

In the meantime, in 1818, two years into her marriage, Peggy met John Henry Eaton, a widower, age 28, newly elected as a senator from Tennessee. Seemingly, the two carried on a lengthy affair. Or did they? When Jackson came to Washington in December

1823 as the junior senator from Tennessee, he stayed at the Franklin House and became a close friend of the O'Neale family. He grew fond of Margaret and her husband. John Timberlake, however, died in April 1828 in the Mediterranean Sea while on a four-year voyage aboard the USS *Constitution*. The circumstances of his passing were controversial. Did he commit suicide because of his wife's disloyalty? Or did he end his life over his mishandling of Navy funds, as seemed more likely to be the case?

Peggy, nearly always referred to in print as Margaret, married Senator Eaton in a candlelight ceremony on New Year's Day, 1829, just before the start of the Jackson administration. The story spread that Eaton would be appointed to the new Cabinet. The rumor mill turned relentlessly.

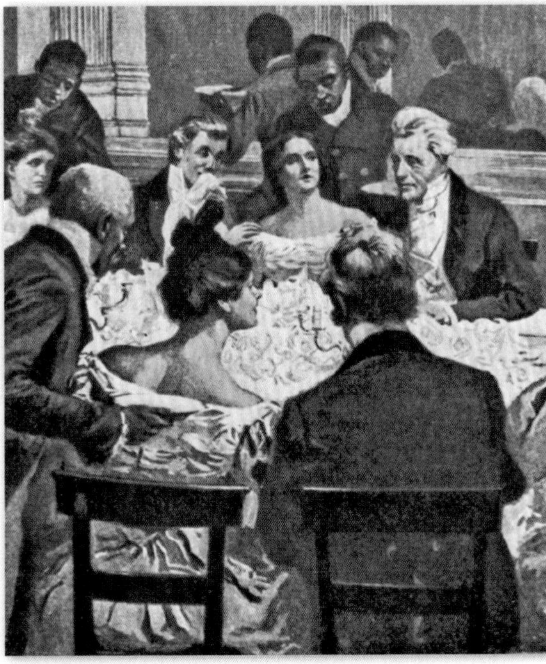

"President Jackson and Peggy O'Neale Eaton at the Banquet Given in Her Honor by the President." (Painting reproduced in *Autobiography of Peggy Eaton*, from *The Ladies' Home Companion*.)

Reverend Ely and President Jackson

Reverend John N. Campbell, pastor of the Presbyterian church in Washington that Mr. and Mrs. Jackson attended, wanted to inform Jackson about the "real" Peggy, but hesitated to do so. Instead, he communicated information to Reverend Ezra Stiles Ely in Philadelphia, who had attended the inauguration. Ely wrote to the president on March 18, detailing all he had heard from Campbell.

The accusations were many: Peggy had had a bad reputation since girlhood; a resident of the hotel knew her to be dissolute; and the ladies of the city would not speak to her. More grievously, he lambasted her with rumors designed to discredit her current husband: Peggy instructed the servants to call the children that she had had while married to Timberlake by the last name of Eaton, because Eaton was their father; she had had an abortion when Mr. Timberlake had been away for a year; and Major Eaton and Mrs. Timberlake had traveled together and registered in hotels as man and wife. True or false in whole or part, these allegations reflect the gossip at the outset of the Jackson administration.

Jackson sent this forceful reply to Ely:

> Washington, March 23, 1829
>
> Dear Sir: Your confidential letter of the 18th instant has been received in the same spirit of kindness and friendship with which it was written.
>
> I must here be permitted to remark that I sincerely regret you did not personally name this subject to me before you left Washington, as I could, in that event, have apprised you of the great exertions made by Clay and his partisans, here and elsewhere,

to destroy the character of Mrs. Eaton by the foulest and basest means, so that a deep and lasting wrong might be inflicted on her husband. I could have given you information that would at least have put you on your guard with respect to anonymous letters containing slanderous insinuations against female character. If such evidence as this is to be received, I ask where is the guarantee for female character, however moral—however *virtuous?*

To show you how much you have been imposed upon, and how much Mrs. E. has been slandered, I am warranted in the positive contradiction of the very first charge made against her—"that she was in ill-fame before Mr. Eaton ever saw her"—from the united testimony of the Hon. John Shea, Dr. Hogg, and others who boarded with Mr. O'Neale, long before Mr. Eaton was a member of Congress. If you feel yourself at liberty to give the names of those secret traducers of female reputation, I entertain no doubt but they will be exposed and consigned to public odium, which should ever be the lot of those whose morbid appetite delights in defamation and slander. . . .

One observation on the Bank conversation. The place where the remark was made is sufficient evidence, to my mind, that it emanated from Clay or his satellites, with a view of completing what he had *here* begun. I am fully warranted in charging Mr. Clay with circulating these slanderous reports, from information derived from a very intelligent lady who met Mr. Clay and his wife on her way to this city. This lady says Mr. and Mrs. Clay spoke in the strongest and most unmeasured terms of Mrs. Eaton. She inquired of them to know upon what grounds these charges rested. "*Rumor, mere rumor,*" was the answer. So far from this attempt to injure Mrs. Eaton on the part of these personages having the effect intended, the lady, as soon as she arrived, sought to become acquainted with her and Mr. Eaton. . . .

It is due to me to be made acquainted with the names of those Bank directors who have dared to throw an imputation on the memory of my departed wife. Men who can be base enough to speak thus of the dead, are not too good *secretly* to slander the living; and they deserve, and no doubt will receive, the scorn of all good men. Mr. Eaton has been known to me for twenty years. His character heretofore, for honesty and morality, has been unblemished; and am I now, for the first time, to change my opinion of him, because of the slanders of this city? We know *here* that none are spared. . . .

I became acquainted with Major O'Neale in this city before Congress ever sat in it. I never saw him again until 1819, when I visited his house to pay my respects to Mr. Eaton, who in December preceding took his seat in the Senate for the first time. In 1823 I again visited the city in the character of Senator from Tennessee, and took lodging with Mr. Eaton at Major O'Neale's, when and where I became acquainted with Mr. and Mrs. Timberlake. I was there when Mr. Timberlake left this country for the Mediterranean, and was present when he took leave of his wife, children, and family. He parted with them in the most affectionate manner, as he did also with myself and Mr. Eaton. Between him and the latter gentleman there appeared to be nothing but friendship and confidence from the first time I saw them at Major O'Neale's, until the day of his departure.

From the situation and proximity of the rooms we occupied, there could not have been any illicit intercourse between Mr. Eaton and Mrs. Timberlake without my having some knowledge of it; and I assure you, sir, that I saw nothing, heard nothing which was calculated to excite even the slightest suspicion. Shortly after Mr. Timberlake left Washington for the Mediterranean, I was told in great confidence that it was rumored in the city that Mr. Eaton and Mrs. Timberlake were too intimate. I met it, as I meet all slanders, with a prompt denial, and inquired from what source this rumor came, and found it originated with a female, against whom there was as much said as is now said against Mrs. Eaton. This report came to the ear of Mrs. Jackson through the same channel; but to the day of her death she believed it to be a base slander, as I do at this day. As to what servants may have said about her telling them not to call her children Timberlake, but Eaton, it is a matter of regret to me that you have named it. My dear sir, if the tales of servants, who become offended by being dismissed, are to be believed, what security has your dear wife for her virtuous character, or that of any other lady?

It is reported that Mr. Timberlake declared he would never again return to this country, in consequence of Mr. Eaton having seduced his wife. How can such a tale as this be reconciled with the following facts? While now writing, I turn my eyes to the mantel-piece, where I behold a present sent me by Mr. Timberlake of a Turkish pipe, about three weeks before his death, and presented through Mr. Eaton, whom in his letter he calls his friend. Now, sir, could this be so, if he did really believe Mr. Eaton had injured him, or wronged him? No, I am sure you will say it is impossible. . . .

Your friend, Andrew Jackson[9]

The Petticoat Affair

In March Eaton was appointed as secretary of war in Jackson's Cabinet. The new Mrs. Eaton was ostracized by the wives of other Cabinet members and officials, who shunned her at functions, such as receptions and gala balls. Floride Calhoun, wife of the vice president, was particularly vehement in her condemnation. In the midst of this scenario, Secretary of State Martin Van Buren continued to staunchly defend Peggy, including at social functions. As a widower, Van Buren faced little pressure from the women whom Henry Clay and others enlisted to enforce Mrs. Eaton's ostracism. This state of events escalated into a scandal some called the "Petticoat Affair."[10]

In early 1831 Jackson broke with his vice president because of this, and he also developed disagreements with Cabinet members appointed through Calhoun's recommendations. The two men ceased their friendship. John H. Eaton, remaining loyal to the president, resigned as secretary of war on April 7, and Martin Van Buren resigned on the 11th of the same month, giving Jackson the opportunity to make other changes. Cabinet members John M. Berrien, John Branch, and Samuel D. Ingham were shown the door. Onlookers were in shock. Nothing like this had ever happened before.

Jackson then relied on unofficial advisors and created the "Kitchen Cabinet," so called by his opponents because they were said to meet in the presidential kitchen. These men served in addition to his regular cabinet, called the "Parlor Cabinet" by some. Writer and editor Amos Kendall was the most important cook in the Kitchen Cabinet, and the president relied deeply on his advice.[11] Others in the metaphoric kitchen included Kentucky newspaper editor Francis Preston Blair, long-time associate John Overton, personal secretary and adopted son Andrew Jackson Donelson, erstwhile New Hampshire banker Isaac Hill, Martin Van Buren, and former military officer William B. Lewis. In the meantime multiple modern historians have written that there was a popular toast at Washington functions, "Here's to the next Cabinet—may they all be bachelors or else leave their wives at home."[12]

Some considered Secretary Van Buren's defense of Peggy a political ploy. Onlookers, especially among Jackson's enemies, viewed Van Buren as obsequious and self-serving. Nonetheless, his influence in Jackson's administration was undeniable. He left Washington when he was appointed minister to Great Britain, the most important ambassadorial posting, after which he became a candidate for the vice presidency in 1832.

It is not unreasonable to join other historians who have suggested that if it hadn't been for Peggy, Vice President John C. Calhoun would have ridden on Jackson's coattails to become president in 1836 and, thus, a familiar figure on Hard Times tokens.

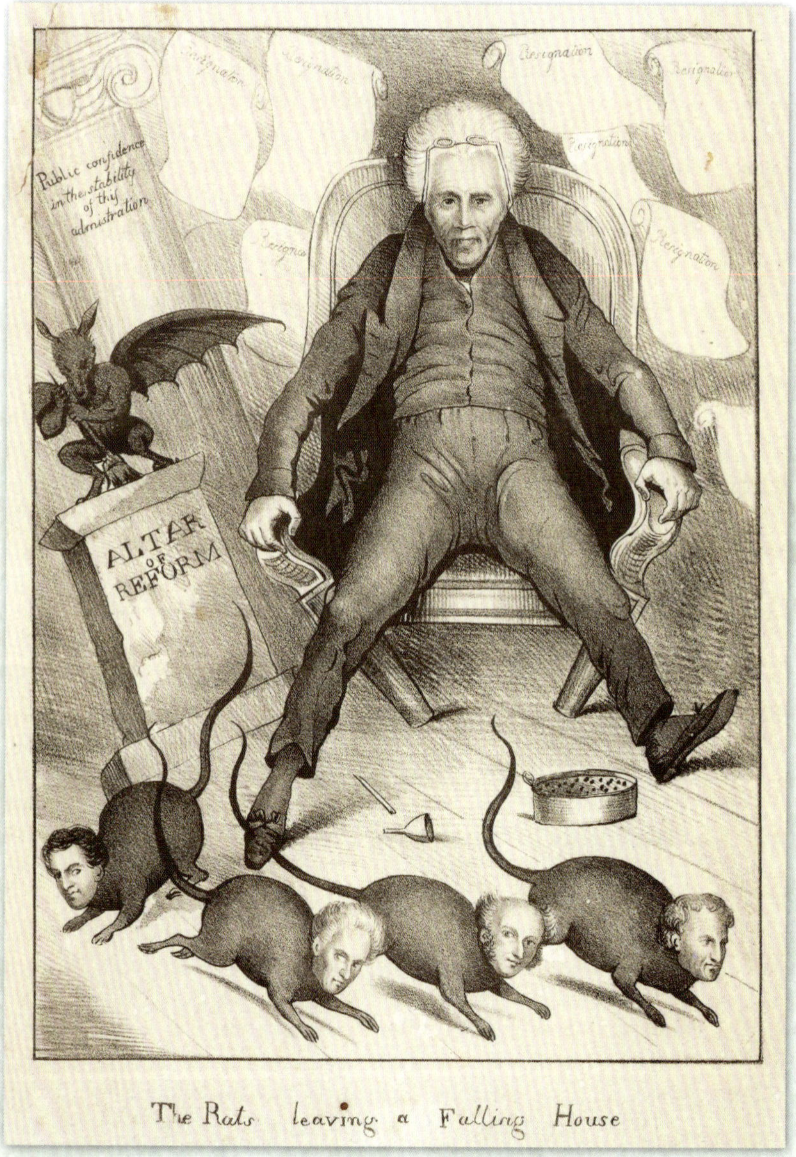

War Department secretary John H. Eaton, naval secretary John Branch, State secretary Martin Van Buren, and Treasury secretary Samuel D. Ingham are shown as scurrying rats, abandoning President Jackson under a shower of resignations. Jackson's foot pins Van Buren's tail to the ground.

5

Events of 1832 and 1833

The Vote to Renew the Charter

The renewal of the Bank of the United States charter came up before Congress in the summer of 1832, early in the start of what Lyman H. Low defined as the Hard Times era. The bank would be the focal point of many anti-Jackson tokens in the next several years. Battle lines were drawn with Jackson and his supporters on one side and his opponents, including Daniel Webster and Henry Clay, on the other. Clay, on retainer from the Bank, encouraged Congress to bring the matter of renewal to an early resolution, to forestall any future actions by Jackson against it.

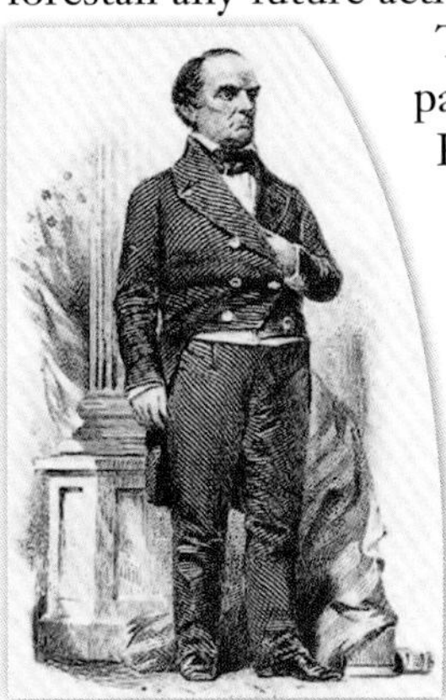

Daniel Webster was a constant foe of Jackson's and criticized nearly everything his administration did or tried to do. This engraving of him appeared on a note of the Webster Bank of Boston, Massachusetts.

The bill was determined in the Senate on June 11, 1832, and was passed by a vote of 28 to 20. It was voted upon in the House of Representatives on July 3 and was passed 109 to 76. It was then sent to President Jackson for his signature, and was returned to Congress on July 4th, marked "Vetoed."

In a message prepared with the particular assistance of Amos Kendall, along with Roger B. Taney, Levi Woodbury, and Andrew J. Donelson, Jackson termed the Bank a monopoly against the interests of the common people. It was stated that the institution had these unsatisfactory aspects, among others:

1. Bank stock valued at $8 million is held by foreigners. If the bank were to be rechartered, the stock would increase in value 20% to 30%, thus making this a gift to foreigners, without the slightest advantage accruing to American citizens.

2. If it is granted that the Bank is a monopoly, then a fair price, such as $17,000,000, should be charged for it, instead of the $200,000 annual the government would receive under its current arrangement as an interested party.

3. The Bank of the United States charter excludes any national competition. Other private interests have offered to take a charter on terms more favorable to the United States than offered by the Bank.
4. The Bank of the United States extends more favorable terms to its branches than to general citizens. As an example, the St. Louis Branch can readily have its notes accepted anywhere at par, whereas a merchant in St. Louis has no such possibility and must offer his paper at a discount outside of the city.
5. Bank stock held by foreigners cannot be taxed, thus depriving the government of revenue and giving foreign-held stock a value 10% to 15% higher than the stock held by American citizens.
6. As states can tax only the amount of stock held by its own citizens in the state, and as most stock is held by out-of-state people, branches can operate within a state on a favorable tax advantage.
7. Of the 25 directors, five are appointed by the government and the rest by stockholders who are required to be American citizens. The rechartering of the Bank would accelerate the flow of stock into foreign hands, eventually giving the reduced number of Americans the power to vote 20 directors, even though these Americans might eventually own only a small amount of stock, and would "be able to re-elect themselves from year to year, and who will wield a power dangerous to the institutions of the country."
8. If most of the stock goes to foreign interests in a given country, and we go to war with that country, "all the operations of the Bank within would be in aid of the hostile fleets and enemies without."[1]

Jackson's statement went on to discuss his view of the constitutionality of the Bank of the United States, which had been questioned: "Each public officer who takes an oath to support the Constitution, swears that he will support it *as he understands it*, and not as it is understood by others." This comment, taking the form of, "The Constitution as I understand it," was later used for an inscription on Hard Times tokens. The "others" whose opinion Jackson was unimpressed by were the justices of the Supreme Court. After the same fashion is the Jackson comment: "The opinion of the judges has no more authority over Congress than the opinion of Congress has over the judges, the president is independent of both."

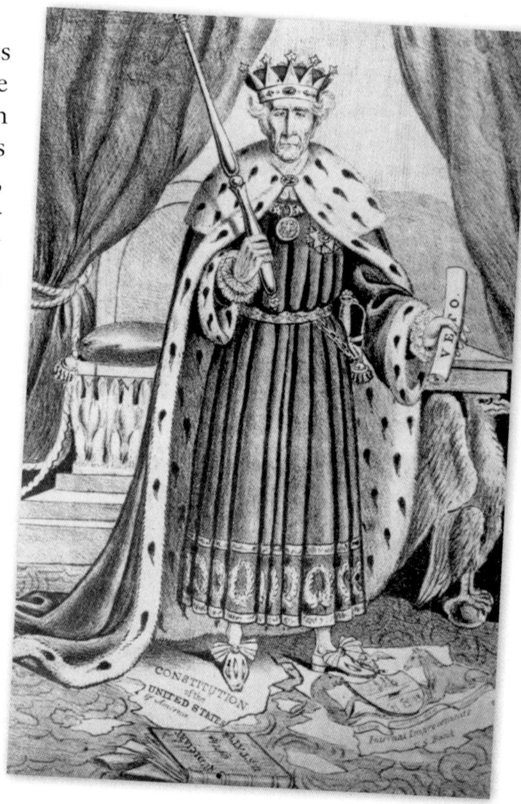

Jackson, veto in hand and stepping on the Constitution, satirized as "King Andrew."

The Presidential Election of 1832

After Jackson's veto of the Bank-charter renewal, sides were polarized for the presidential election of 1832. On one side was Jackson and on the other side Henry Clay, a vehement long-time adversary. Clay was backed by president Nicholas Biddle and other officers of the Bank of the United States, who held him on a retainer compensation. Each candidate enlisted friendly legislators to make tedious speeches, complete with personal attacks and accusations of dishonest and dishonorable actions—a scenario that continued up to the adjournment of Congress at 6 a.m. on July 16.

The popular press became involved, predicting either the salvation of America with the "monster" gone, or, alternatively, its financial ruin if the charter veto was not challenged, depending upon the political orientation of the editor. Many if not most readers were thoroughly confused. Much was in disorder, and the appointment of Jackson's Kitchen Cabinet in opposition with his regular Cabinet further confused observers.

About mid-August, President Jackson and a small entourage left Washington to visit the Hermitage, Jackson's home in Tennessee. According to a later account, Jackson made a point of paying his expenses in gold coins along the way. "No more paper money, you see, fellow citizens, if I can only put down this Nicholas Biddle and his *monster* bank," he was quoted as saying by his biographer, decades later.[2] If he had a purse full of gold coins this was very unusual—for such had not circulated at par since 1820, as it cost more than face value to produce them. If he did have gold coins, then he paid a small premium to acquire them, and when spending them he probably obtained a value higher than the denomination. Likely, the quote was imaginative.[3]

As the election approached, each party was confident of success. In November the results were more one-sided than the most optimistic supporters of Jackson and his vice-presidential companion Martin Van Buren could have imagined.[4] After the popular vote was tallied (687,502 for Jackson, 530,189 for his opponent), the Electoral College returned 219 of its possible 288 votes for Jackson, leaving Henry Clay a miserable (indeed embarrassing) 49, with a few remaining scattered votes going to regional favorites.

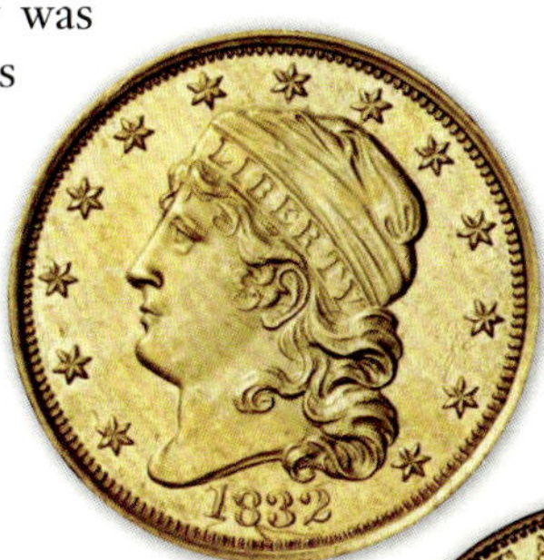

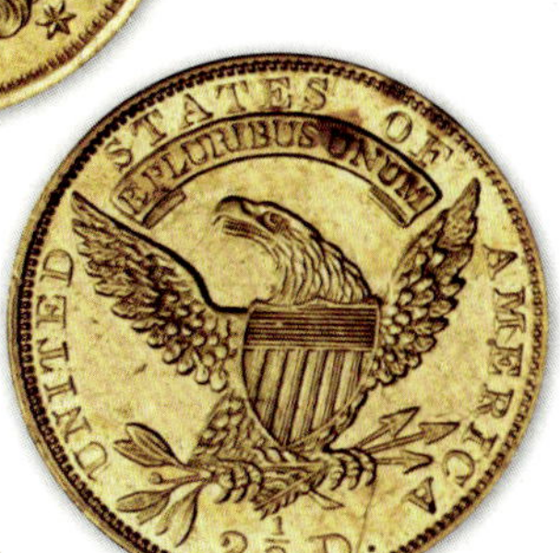

A $2.50 quarter eagle of 1832. Gold coins cost more than face value to produce at the time and were not used for general circulation. Instead, they traded at a premium at exchange offices and bullion dealers.

Not only had Clay suffered a disastrous defeat, the Bank of the United States was dead for all practical purposes. What to do? Perhaps in jest and perhaps not, in Washington, the *Globe* reported that certain influential members of the defeated party were prompting "the minions of the Bank to save the institution by the only expedient that could save it—the assassination of the president."[5] Rumors abounded, and it was stated that the Bank had $50,000 to give to any man who would render to the future of America such a service. As was the case with Peggy Eaton, facts were scarce.

"Pet Banks"

In an effort to cripple the Bank, whose charter was still in effect—and would remain so until 1836—Jackson ordered that future federal deposits would be given to various state-chartered institutions instead of being sent to a branch of the Bank of the United States. This change was to take place beginning on October 1, 1833,

> or sooner, provided the necessary arrangements with the state banks can be made. The President thinks that the state banks ought immediately to be employed in the collection and disbursement of public revenue, and the funds now in the Bank of the United States drawn out with all convenient dispatch. [6]

These state institutions were officially called "deposite [*sic*] banks," but popularly referred to as "pet banks," a term which became popular in news accounts beginning in the autumn of 1833. The amount to be deposited in the banks of each state was based upon the number of Electoral College votes of that particular state.[7] Jackson started by selecting seven banks. By the end of the year there were 22 such "pets."

In his fifth annual message to Congress, December 3, 1833, Jackson discussed the shifting of funds, noting that he had instructed the secretary of the Treasury to take appropriate action (through an order by the secretary of the Treasury, September 26, 1833).[8] Further:

> The near approach of the day on which the charter will expire, as well as the conduct of the bank, appeared to me to call for this measure upon the high considerations of public interest and public duty.
>
> The extent of its misconduct, however, although known to be great, was not at that time fully developed by proof. It was not until late in the month of August that I received from the government directors [five on the board of 25] an official report establishing beyond question that this great and powerful institution had been actively engaged in attempting to influence the elections of public officers by means of its money, and that, in violation of the express provisions of its charter, it had by formal resolution placed its funds at the disposition of its president [Biddle] to be employed in sustaining the political power of the bank. . . .

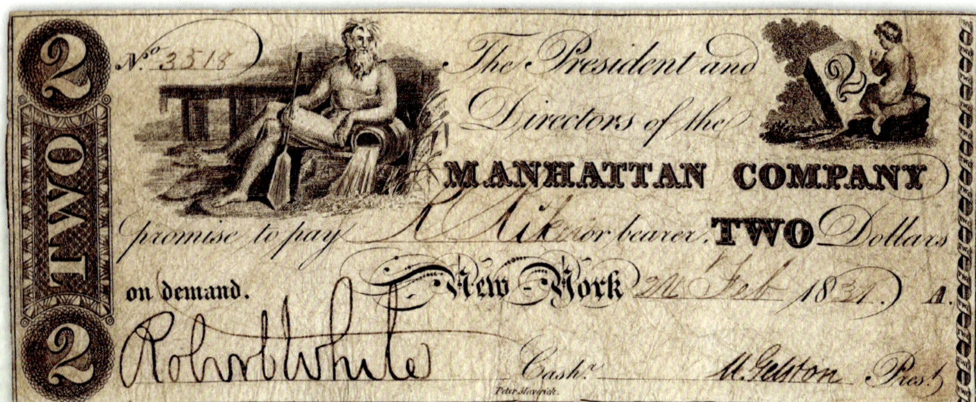

The Manhattan Company of New York City was one of the earliest pet banks.

Biddle's feelings were summarized in a letter he sent on February 21, 1834, to Joseph Hopkinson, judge of the U.S. Court in the District of Pennsylvania:

> I have to thank you for your letters, all very interesting & very welcome. The last only requires any answer & that I will give very explicitly. You may rely upon it that the Bank has taken its final course and that it will be neither frightened nor cajoled from its duty by any small driveling about relief to the country. All that you have heard on that subject from New York is wholly without foundation. The relief, to be useful or permanent, must come from Congress & from Congress alone.
>
> If that body will do its duty, relief will come — if not, the Bank feels no vocation to redress the wrongs inflicted by these miserable people. Rely upon that. This worthy President thinks that because he has scalped Indians and imprisoned judges, he is to have his way with the Bank. He is mistaken — and he may as well send at once and engage lodgings in Arabia. . . .[9]

Pet banks, no matter how solid they were, became the center of problems. In Philadelphia the government paid Navy sailors in notes from the Girard Bank, a pet, instead of, as before, bills of the Bank of the United States. In distant ports sailors would have problems spending the Girard notes at par, so they exchanged them at the Bank of the United States. Similar issues erupted elsewhere when the government paid its obligations in bills issued by the pets.

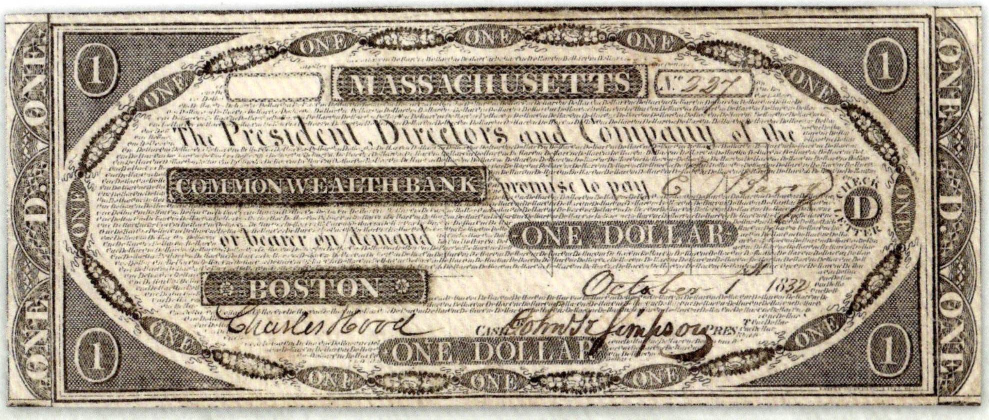

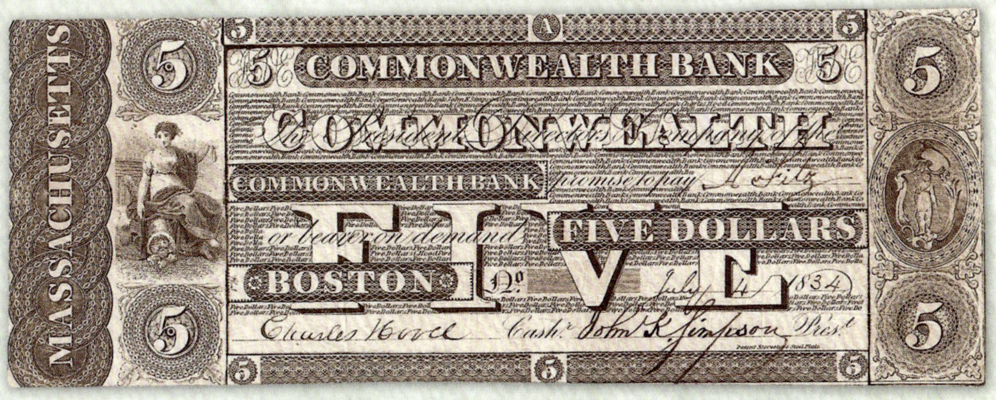

The Commonwealth Bank of Boston, a pet bank, issued these notes. It failed in 1838.

6

Events of 1834 to 1836

Jackson Censured

There was a general expansion of commerce during this period.[1] On January 1, 1834, about $200,000,000 was employed in banking capital and about $95,000,000 was in circulation as bank bills. Gold coins were not seen in domestic commerce, nor had they been since 1830. No silver dollars had been struck since 1804. Half dollars were filling the need for specie, as they were plentiful in general trade, bank holdings, and elsewhere. Most cash business was conducted by bank notes. While there were scattered exceptions, most banks were in solid financial condition.

Politics continued to be polarized. The typical citizen continued to be either pro–Jackson and his actions toward the Bank of the United States, or anti–Jackson and his veto of the bank's charter renewal. Both opinions were reflected in satirical prints, including faux bank notes. Jackson's Cabinet was again functional, now that Peggy Eaton was old news, but historians generally agree that certain of his choices were ineffective men.

On March 28, 1834, the United States Senate censured President Jackson for removing the government's deposits from the Bank of the United States. Jackson protested, and on April 15, 1834, sent a document in reply to the Senate.[2] This stated:

> The ambition which leads me on is an anxious desire and a fixed determination to return to the people unimpaired the sacred trust they have confided to my charge; to heal the wounds of the Constitution and preserve it from further violation; to persuade my countrymen, so far as I may, that it is not in a splendid government supported by powerful monopolies and aristocratical establishments that they will find happiness or their liberties protection, but in a plain system, void of pomp, protecting all and granting favors to none, dispensing its blessings, like the dews of Heaven, unseen and unfelt save in the freshness and beauty they contribute to produce. It is such a government that the genius of the people requires; such one only under which our states may remain for ages to come united, prosperous, and free.

From this, "a plain system, void of pomp" was taken up by Jackson's detractors and used on a die that struck tokens.

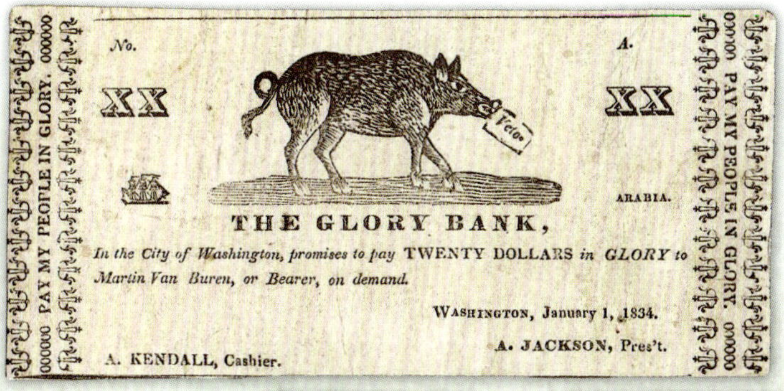

A satirical note relating to Jackson's veto. Boars and hogs appeared on many comic notes and tokens of this era.

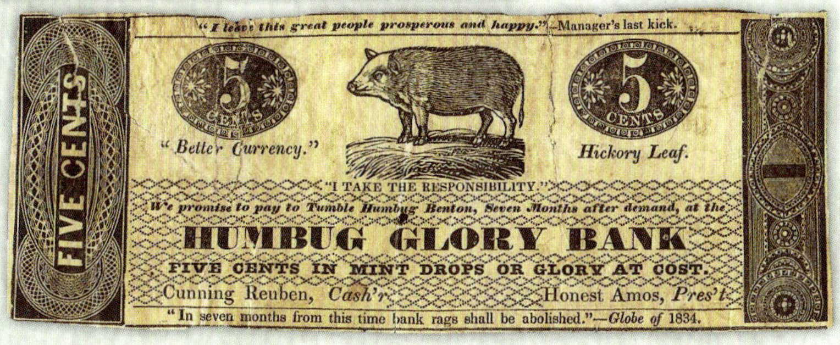

Another satirical note with related themes.

Years later, in 1837, the "Expunging Resolution," hotly debated, would result in the censure being officially removed from Senate records. This occurred primarily through the efforts of Senator Thomas Hart Benton. A further salvo against the Bank of the United States was included in Jackson's sixth annual message to Congress, December 1, 1834.[3]

The Coinage Act of June 28, 1834

Although gold coins had been minted in quantity since 1795, by 1834 most had been melted or exported. Of all coined—about $10 million face value in all—probably not even one million dollars remained in the country, and all of that was held by banks and speculators.[4] Changing the course of this was Senator Thomas Hart Benton (1782–1858) of Missouri, who served five terms in that office, from 1821 to 1851, becoming a powerful figure. He was an advocate of western expansion, later called *manifest destiny* (the idea that it was the right of the white men to occupy the territory of Native Americans) and *hard money*—gold and silver coins, not bank notes.[5] His nickname was "Old Bullion."

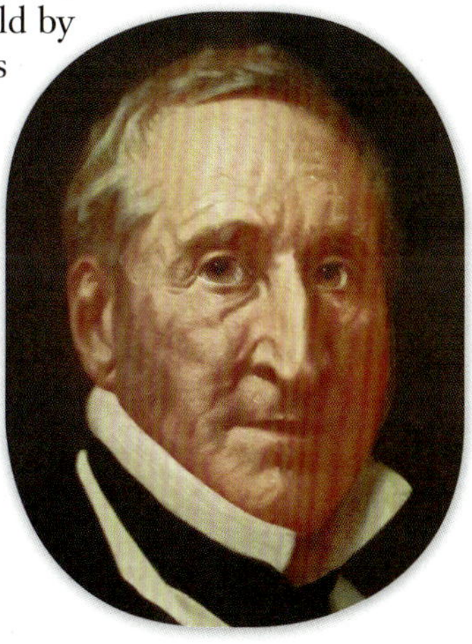

Senator Thomas Hart Benton of Missouri, a staunch advocate of silver and gold coins.

In earlier times he had served in the military under Jackson. The two men had some fights and sharp differences. However, after Jackson lost the 1824 election to John Quincy Adams, Benton and Jackson became strong allies. When Jackson became president in 1829, Benton was the senatorial leader of the Democratic-Republican Party (which later became the Democratic Party). When Jackson launched his anti–Bank of the

United States campaign, Benton was a strong supporter. It was Benton who led the expungement campaign that in 1837 removed Jackson's censure from the official records.

To the advantage of the Democrats, Benton was a superb orator and had no problem taking on and sometimes besting Daniel Webster and Henry Clay. Benton also faced John C. Calhoun, when the latter became alienated from the president.

In 1834 Benton led the effort to restore gold coins to domestic circulation. The Democrats believed this would tighten credit and create a more sound financial system. In contrast the Whigs were for liberal use of paper money to ease and facilitate credit. The expedient was simple enough: to reduce the authorized weight slightly so that it would be unprofitable to melt them. The Act of June 28, 1834, was the result. It received the general support of both parties, although Daniel Webster succeeded in removing a provision to introduce a new denomination, the gold dollar.

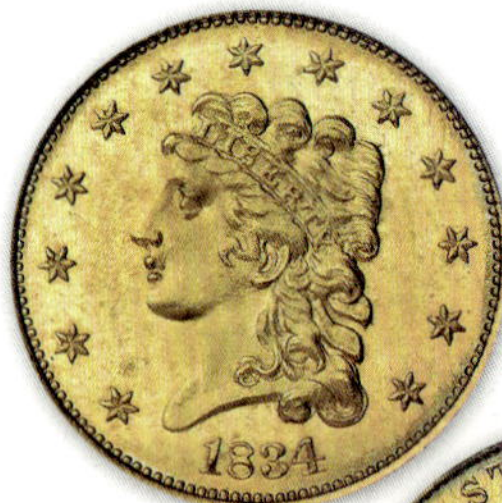

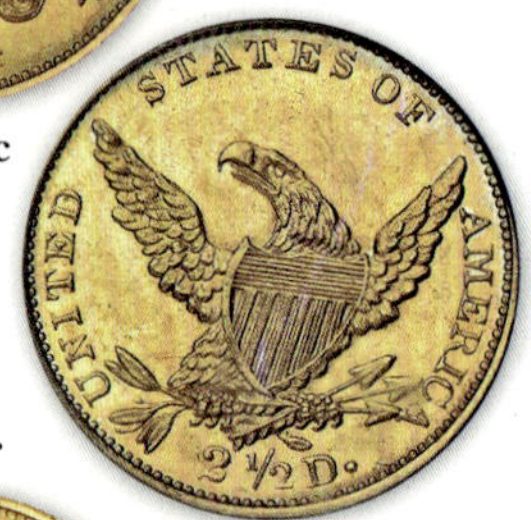

The new Classic Head $2.50 gold quarter eagle of 1834 designed by Chief Engraver William Kneass.

The legislation became effective on August 1. There were detractors, as might be expected—one complaint predicted that banks would hoard gold and pay out paper instead, unless strong demands were made. However, the bill was a success. By autumn new quarter eagles and half eagles appeared in circulation, which were of the Classic Head design by William Kneass, chief engraver at the Mint. In 1838 $10 gold eagles were made for the first time. Gold coins were seen in circulation and were easily obtainable at banks for the remainder of the Hard Times era, indeed until late 1861, when the uncertainty of the outcome of the Civil War prompted hoarding.

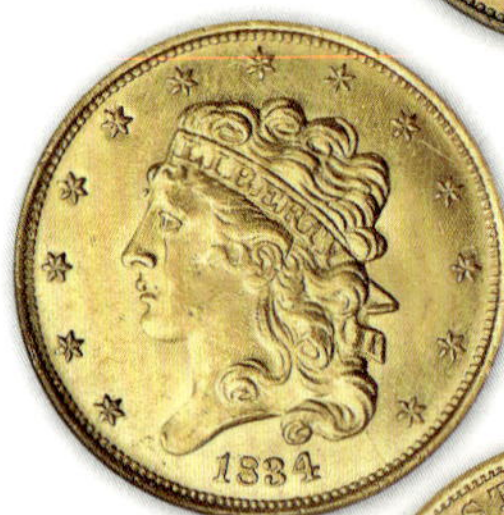

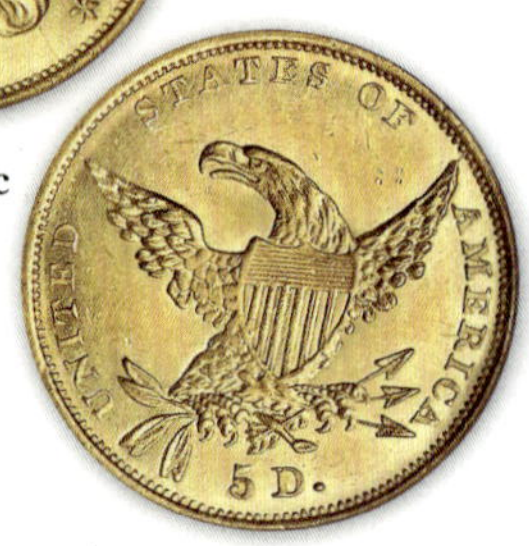

The new Classic Head half eagle of 1834.

The new coins were called "Benton's mint drops" by some, and some specie dealers and exchange brokers advertised under this name to buy and sell them.[6] "Bentonian currency" was another term.

Years later a report of American gold coinage given at the International Monetary Conference, 1878, gave this view of the 1834 legislation:

> The good effects of the bill were immediately seen. Gold began to flow into the country through all the channels of commerce; old chests gave up their hoards;[7] the mint was busy: and in a few months, and as if by magic, a currency banished from the country for 30 years, overspread the land, and gave joy and confidence to all the pursuits of industry. But this joy was not universal.
>
> A large interest connected with the Bank of the United States, and its subsidiary and subaltern institutions, and the whole paper system, vehemently opposed it; and spared neither pains nor expense to check its circulation, and to bring odium upon its supporters. . . .[8]

Presciently, *Niles' Register* printed this on December 20, 1834:

> Motions have been made in Congress to inquire into the expediency of establishing branches of the Mint of the United States in North Carolina, and at New York, and New Orleans, and, we think, at one or two other places. It is important, in our belief, if (as seems expected by some) the gold and silver coinage is to be a large one, that it should all be performed at one place, as well to insure certainty of the value of the coins, and to reduce the expenses of coinage—one director, treasurer, assayer, &c. will do the business better than a dozen of each, and at much less cost.

Congress disagreed, and branch mints were constructed at New Orleans, Louisiana; Dahlonega, Georgia; and Charlotte, North Carolina. Although there was no significant mining of gold anywhere near New Orleans, the city was the gateway to the Mississippi River Basin and received large quantities of foreign silver and gold coins that could be melted to created federal coinage. Dahlonega and Charlotte were in gold-mining districts, now thriving as most of the Cherokees had been brutally removed to the West in the Trail of Tears—an action which joins the Fugitive Slave Act and the Dred Scott decision as one of the largest stains on the Star-Spangled Banner.

Meanwhile, on December 26, 1833, Henry Clay delivered a lengthy speech addressed to Jackson before the Senate, outlining the evils of the present administration, especially the transferal of federal funds to the pet banks, concluding with:

> We behold the usual incidents of approaching tyranny. The land is filled with spies and informers; and detraction and denunciation are the orders of the day. People, especially official incumbents in this place, no longer dare speak in the fearless tones of manly freemen, but in the cautious whispers of trembling slaves. The premonitory symptoms of despotism are upon us; and if Congress do not apply an instantaneous and effective remedy, the fatal collapse will soon on, and we shall die—ignobly die! Base, mean and abject slaves—the scorn and contempt of mankind—unpitied, unwept, unmourned!

Concern for the Economy

The continuing transfer of federal deposits from the Bank of the United States to "pet" banks provoked extreme criticism in certain areas. In many towns and cities mass meetings were held to protest the action. At the same time, there was a contraction of business and the economy. *Niles' Weekly Register* and certain other journals, some of which had criticized the Bank of the United States in earlier times, now printed many virulent anti-Jackson commentaries, blaming the state of business on the Bank situation. Discounts on the notes of various state-chartered bank notes were emphasized, although such had been the practice for a long time.

Mr. Noah, editor of the New York *Evening Star*, commented:

> We have frequently been asked, "Does the president know anything of public opinion—does he read the newspapers?"
>
> His engagements, we think, are so pressing, that he has no time to read himself, but we are told that one of his family reads the papers to him, but only such papers and extracts as his particular friends are desirous he should read, and he is struck by the singular coincidence of public opinion that certain journals in New Hampshire, Boston, New York, Philadelphia and Cincinnati, should so exactly agree in opinion as to his measures, when that opinion has been manufactured by the kitchen cabinet at Washington, and sent to those very papers for publication. It is thus that we are now governed—and so much for this manufacture of public opinion.[9]

Such comments did not seem to have much effect on Jackson's popularity with the general population.

Try as they might, Henry Clay, Daniel Webster, and other Jackson opponents, now under the new banner of the Whig Party, could not sway much public opinion against the president, or his stand on the Bank of the United States. In many states, prominent bankers and many politicians continued to consider the "monster" bank inimical to their own interests, even if the typical merchant felt differently. The bank itself continued to do well financially.

On February 5, it was Daniel Webster's turn to deliver a long anti-Jackson speech to the Senate. The removal of deposits from the Bank of the United States was the source of most of the problems affecting the country, he claimed. Webster asserted, once again, that Jackson was oblivious to reality. Both of these sentiments were eventually inscribed on Hard Times tokens.

There was very little true understanding of the American monetary system by newspaper editors, members of Congress, and the general public. This contributed to a vast proliferation of newspaper articles, political speeches, and more—often contradictory.

The Elections of 1834

Beginning in early 1834, there were many mid-term elections of state and local officials. This set the scene for several varieties of copper and brass tokens, some picturing Jackson, others with different messages, reflecting hopes, policies, and contentions of the 1832 presidential election, the veto of the Bank charter, the 1834 mid-term elections, and more—today, all a part of the Hard Times series. In January a mass meeting of merchants was held in Boston, after which a petition was sent to Congress urging the prompt restoration of deposits to the Bank of the United States. There was a chill in the commerce of Eastern cities.

The discounting of the paper money issued by state-chartered banks, including some of the pets, was adding to the problem. Bank of the United States bills readily circulated at par.

In the first two weeks of April, far more than 100 businesses failed in New York City alone. As in Boston and numerous other cities, many merchants (including some who issued store cards as part of the Hard Times series) placed the blame on Jackson. The corollary effect was that, in elections held in the second week of that month, the Whig Party made gains in the states of Connecticut and New York. The city papers proclaimed the event, as shown in this entry from the *New York Courier & Enquirer*, April 11: "We subjoin the result of the election, as far as ascertained, and it will be perceived that we have indeed achieved a GLORIOUS VICTORY." In New York City, to commemorate the occasion, engraver Robert Lovett created a token with this inscription:

> FLOURISH COMMERCE, FLOURISH INDUSTRY, WHIGS OF N. YORK VICTORIOUS. *Les trois jours* [the three days] APRIL 8. 9. & 10. 1834.

This token with its positive inscription was complemented by an anti-Jackson token by another (unknown) engraver showing a boar inscribed MY THIRD HEAT, probably a reference to Jackson running for the presidency three times—losing in 1824 and successful in 1828 and 1832. Below was DOWN WITH THE BANK. Around the border was the inscription describing what Jackson was doing, in contrary to the Whigs' success: PERISH CREDIT. PERISH COMMERCE. 1834.

Continuing Events

On January 8, 1835, the United States public debt was officially registered as zero dollars, the first and only time in the history of our country. The Treasury had a surplus that year and returned money to each state. This resulted from a combination of two main factors. The first component of this increase, revenue from the Tariff Act of 1828, added to federal coffers while at the same time continuing to fuel prosperity in most manufacturing specialties.

The second main element of this prosperity had to do with speculation in Western lands, those on the far side of Pennsylvania. Settlements that are now in Ohio, in Indiana, in Illinois, and along the Mississippi River grew by leaps and bounds. Acreage was inexpensive, and it could be paid for in bills of state-chartered banks, some of which were not particularly sound. Parcels of land changed hands left and right, at ever-advancing prices, creating a lot of wealth on paper, plus some real wealth also. Everything was rosy, crows became swans, and in 1835 the federal government declared a surplus! Money was returned to each of the states, a circumstance unprecedented before and never equaled again.

Westward expansion boomed. *The American Almanac* reported that as of January 1, 1835, there were 2,867 miles of completed canals and approximately 1,600 miles of completed railroad track. The rail lines were in the ascendancy, and in the next several decades all but a few canals would close. In oceanic commercial shipping, sailing vessels were dominant, and just 60,000 tons (of 2,350,000 total) of shipping were by steam. Railroad bonds and other securities became hot tickets for investors. On October 20, 1835, the Texas Revolution began at the Battle of Gonzalez when Mexican soldiers were challenged by a group of local armed men. On March 6, 1836, after 188 men defended themselves against an 11-day siege, the Alamo in San Antonio fell to 4,000 troops under the command of General Santa Anna, president of Mexico. Among the dead, the names of William B. Travis, James Bowie, and Davy Crockett would live in history. The Republic of Texas, an independent nation, was founded later in the year, with Sam Houston serving as president.

In the East, on December 16 and 17, 1835, a massive fire in lower Manhattan destroyed more than 500 buildings, including the New York stock exchange and nearly all of the financial district. The Merchants' Exchange, one of the most prominent features in the city, was reduced to ashes and was subsequently memorialized on tokens.

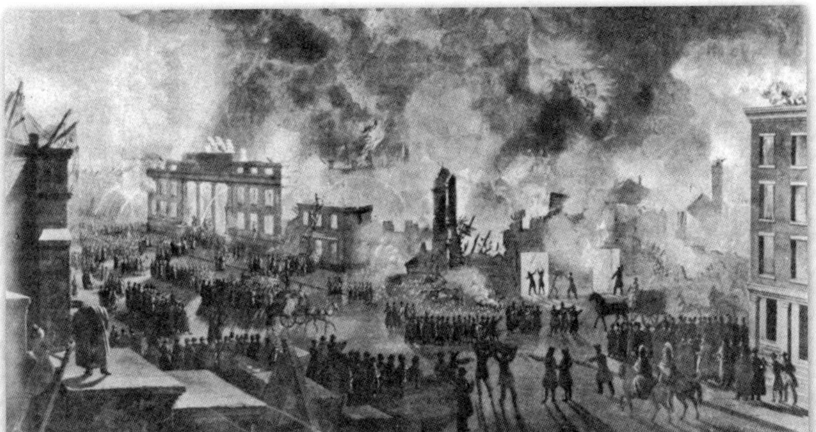

On December 16 and 17, 1835, much of the commercial district in lower Manhattan was destroyed by fire. This perspective is from a high story in the Bank of North America at the corner of Wall and William streets.

The Specie Circular

However exciting the boom in Western real-estate seemed, there was trouble in the Western paradise, and, if left unchecked, there were certain to be problems on a national scale. On July 11, 1836, Andrew Jackson issued his *Specie Circular*, a document stating that henceforth federal lands had to be paid for in gold and silver coins, not in paper. An exception allowed homesteaders to purchase land with bank notes. The text began:

> In consequence of complaints which have been made of frauds, speculations, and monopolies, in the purchase of public lands, and the aid which is said to be given to effect these objects by excessive bank credits, and dangerous, if not partial, facilities through bank drafts and bank deposites, and the general evil influence like to result in the public interests, and especially the safety of the great amount of money in the Treasury, and the sound condition of the currency of the country from the further exchange of the national domain in this manner, and chiefly for bank credits and paper money, the President of the United States has given directions, and you are hereby instructed, after the 15th day of August next, to receive in payment of public lands nothing except what is directed by the existing lays, namely, gold and silver, and, in the proper cases, Virginia land scrip; provided, that till the 15th of December next, the same indulgences heretofore extended as to the kind of money received, may be continued for any quantity of land not exceeding three hundred and twenty acres to each purchaser who is an actual settler, or bona fide resident in the state where sales are made. . . .

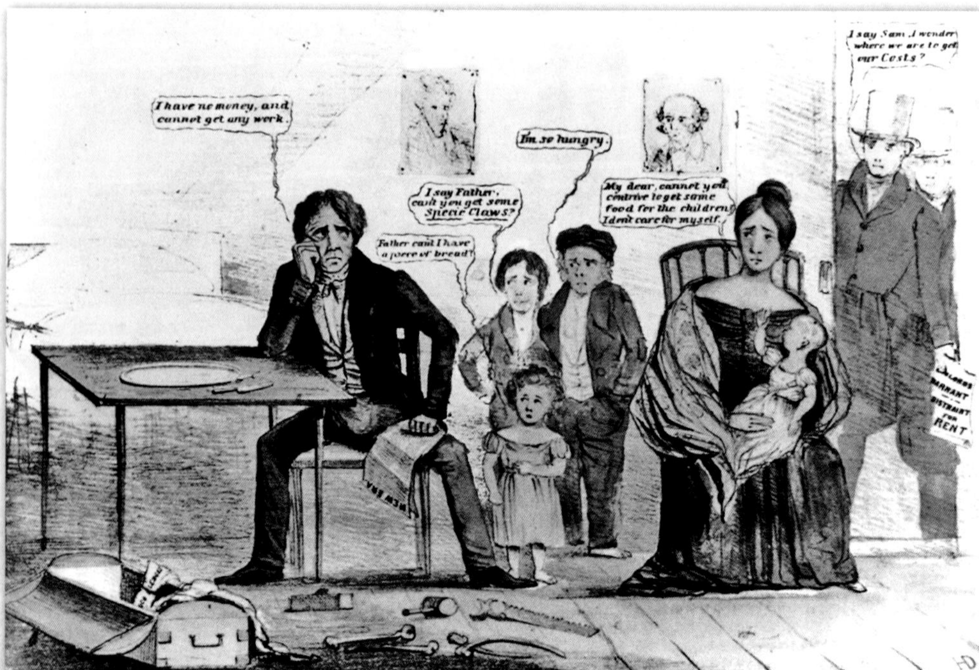

This punning "Specie Claws" cartoon has it that because of Jackon's hard-money policies, father is out of work, and the family is hungry.

While speculation slowed down rapidly, technology was advancing on many fronts. At the Philadelphia Mint, in 1836, steam power was used for the first time to run coinage presses. Die-making became more standardized and mechanical with less hand work. Railroads, the growth industry of the decade, were expanding in many directions. There was a growing interest in the domestic breeding of silkworms and the production of silk fabric, especially in New England, where incentives were provided to set up in the industry. In textile mills, mostly for cotton, a young boy or girl could tend four or more spinning looms (there were no child labor laws). In New York City, a newspaper reported that the typical lawyer earned $300 or more per year, while mechanics took home double that amount, but it was more fashionable to be a lawyer.

Requiem for the Bank

At the time of its closing, Bank of the United States stock was worth a premium of more than 15 percent, and the stock in the Bank owned by the United States was paid back to it in full, so that the United States received a premium in addition to the previous regular dividends. Consequently, the United States made money on its stock, and did not lose a dollar of the money deposited in the Bank. The moribund institution fulfilled all its obligations to the government, redeemed all its circulating notes at par, paid all its private depositors, and went out of existence with a clean record.

The impending closing spurred many entrepreneurs to apply for and receive state charters for banks. These opened, issued a lot of paper money of varying worth, and added strength to the uncertain economy.

As the Bank of the United States was winding down, the bank's president, Philadelphia socialite and scion, Nicholas Biddle, would soon be unemployed. The Pennsylvania State Legislature came to the rescue, and on February 18, 1836, a 30-year charter was granted to the United States Bank *of Pennsylvania.* Some capital was transferred from the old Bank of the United States, and new shares were sold, resulting in a capitalization of $35,000,000—an incredible sum for a state-chartered bank.

Biddle and his associates, if not acting fraudulently, certainly misled the public by leaving "of Pennsylvania" off of its paper money. They created the illusion that the old bank had somehow revived!

In 1836, the new bank made heavy loans to borrowers who provided stocks in private companies as collateral. There was rampant speculation in stocks, and Biddle and his associates were all too happy to provide money to those who wanted to play in the game. The new bank engaged in unwise speculations, lost in the market for cotton futures, and quietly moved gold and silver coins from one account to another to give the appearance of profitability. The bank went into liquidation in 1841. Debate raged as to whether Biddle was a fraudster or was a victim of circumstances beyond his control.

The Election of 1836

Contemplating the presidential election of November 8, 1836, Jackson opted for retirement, and Vice President Martin Van Buren ran on the Democratic ticket against four Whigs: William Henry Harrison, Hugh Lawson White, Willie Person Magnum, and Daniel Webster. This curious and unprecedented running of four men from the same party was intended to allow each to become the winner in a particular part of the nation, collectively garnering enough votes that Van Buren would lack a majority. The decision would then be up to the House of Representatives, whose members would choose a Whig. The strategy failed, as Van Buren won a majority of the popular votes and took the Electoral College votes by a landslide. Van Buren pledged to follow in the footsteps of his "illustrious predecessor," a catchphrase that in 1837 would reappear on copper Hard Times tokens depicting a jackass. At this early time the jackass (donkey) was not the emblem of the Democratic Party. That would come much later.

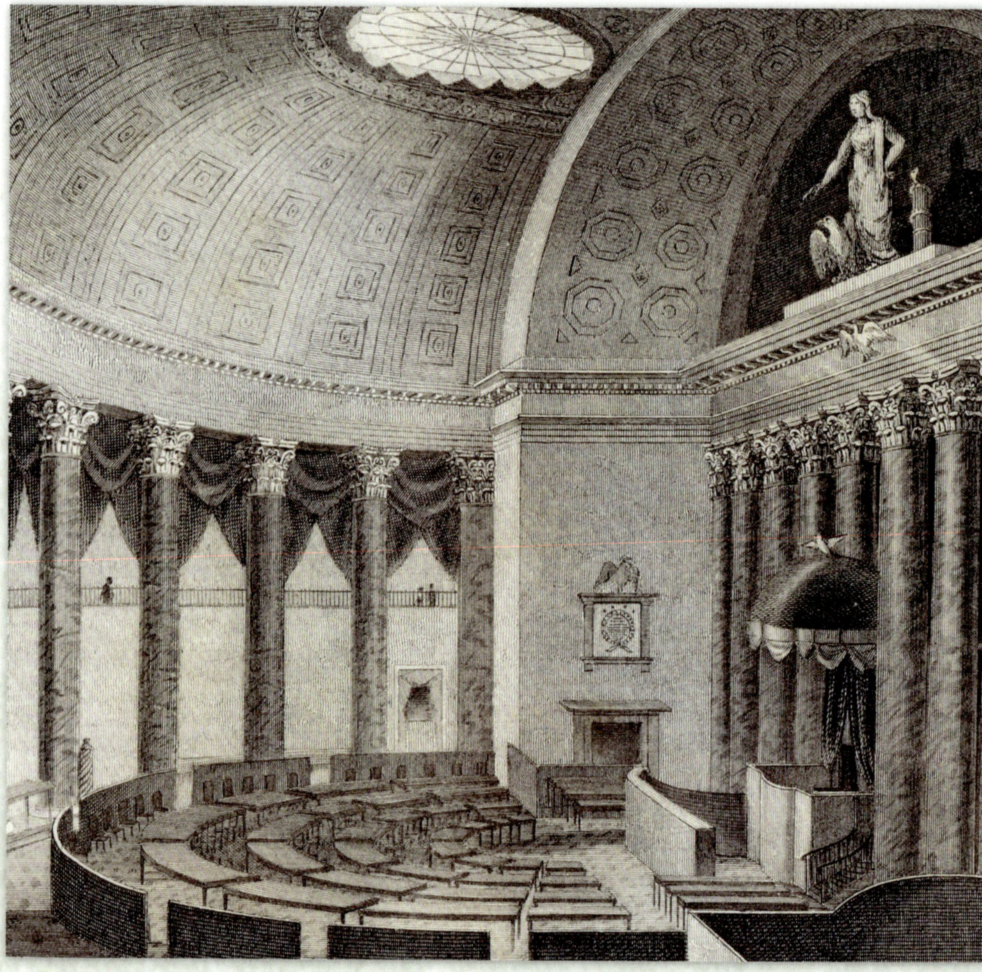

The chamber of the House of Representatives in the Capitol.

7

Events of 1837 and 1838

The American Scene in 1837

Leading transcendentalist Henry David Thoreau graduated from Harvard in 1837, characteristically suggesting that man should not work for six days and rest on the seventh, but rather should work one day and leave six free for the "sublime revelations of nature." In Cincinnati, Procter & Gamble was founded, and in New York City, Tiffany & Co. began business. Samuel F.B. Morse demonstrated his magnetic telegraph and sought a patent on it. The first ships to cross the ocean entirely under steam power completed the trip from England together on April 23, 1838; one, the SS *Sirius*, taking 19 days from London, and the other, SS *Great Western*, 15 days out of Bristol.

Financial Distress

All remained well in most sectors of the American economic scene until early 1837, when there was a chill in certain parts of the market. The Flour Riot broke out in New York City, caused by reactions to poverty and the rising cost of flour—which had doubled in price! Conditions in the city had been unsettled for some time.

On March 4, President Van Buren was inaugurated in the midst of these troubles. Andrew Jackson went back to the Hermitage. Problems continued. On April 3 the New York *Journal of Commerce* published this:

> The past week will long be remembered by our merchants as a season of trial and difficulty such as before has not been experienced for many years. It will be remembered also, we trust, as the crisis of the great financial troubles which have been gathering for more than a year past, from the combined influence of speculation, the surplus revenue, bad government, etc.
>
> The first three days of the week were indeed gloomy; a number of failures occurred, chiefly however of houses essentially sound, but which were unable to sustain themselves under the tremendous money pressure which existed; and what was worse than all, in some of its bearings, confidence, that essential element of credit, appeared for panic makers, croakers, and assassins of credit, and well did they

> improve the opportunity afforded them. We could mention a dozen of our largest and best houses who were reported among the fallen, but who still survive unharmed.
>
> The temporary suspension of payments by Messrs. E.M. Morgan & Co. who were agents for 20 or 30 country banks, gave opportunity by the enemies of such institutions to propagate suspicions concerning them; and all these troubles were aggravated, we will not say wantonly aggravated, by a portion of the press. Thus things were proceeding, when by a concerted movement between the United States Bank and our local institutions, measures were adopted for the relief of the community, and from that moment the state of the money market has been evidently improving.
>
> During the three last days of the week we did not hear of a single failure.—Stocks which had been rapidly declining, began to rally—and confidence, though still scarce, was perceptibly gaining ground. We feel assured that these encouraging indications will continue and increase, until the money market shall recover its usual healthy condition. Perfect restoration is not, however, to be expected in a day; the disease was too deeply seated, and some of the exciting causes still remain. . . .
>
> The result of the whole matter, instead of destroying confidence, ought to increase it.—confidence, we mean, in the general soundness of the business community of New York, and their ability, under any supposable circumstances, to meet their engagements. We can say without fear of contradiction, that there is no other mercantile body, equally numerous, in the world, which could have met such a storm, with so few disasters. And as to the banks, there has not been a single failure, far or near. This speaks well for their condition since to them also, as well as to the merchants, the ordeal has been severe. We think it is now time for people to "thank God and take courage."
>
> Down with the panic makers, and down with the prevalent distrust. The resources of the country are vast, and no financial embarrassments, in time of peace, can be more than temporary. A bright sun will soon dispel the remaining darkness, and days of prosperity and glory will be ours. In the meantime we shall have learned lessons of wisdom which experience alone can teach, and which will tend greatly to restrain speculation in times to come. What we learn from our fathers we soon forget; but what we learn by experience, we are apt to remember. Nobody, says Dr. Johnson, ever forgot the man that kicked his shins.

On April 25 a large meeting of New York City merchants was held at Masonic Hall to hear the report of a committee charged with forming a delegation to go to Washington and lay before President Van Buren their concern about worsening economic conditions. It had been hoped that dozens of people would make the trip, but when a sign-up took place there were just 15 names. This number was reduced to just nine at departure, as others said commitment prevented their attendance. The group reached Washington and put up at Gadsby's Hotel, not far from the President's House.[1]

Isaac Hone, chairman, sent a note to the president the next morning, requesting an interview. Van Buren replied quickly:

> Sir: I have received your letter, informing me that a committee had been appointed by a meeting of the merchants of New York, for the purpose of addressing me upon the present distressed condition of that city, and requesting an audience at as early an hour as my convenience will admit.
>
> I will receive the committee at two o'clock today, and will, at that, or at any other time more agreeable to them, be pleased to receive any communication which they may desire to present to me. To avoid the misapprehensions to which oral communications

> are liable, and also to avoid the errors which, with the best intentions, are so apt to occur, on both sides, in giving accounts of such interviews, I think it most proper that the representation of the committee be made in writing. In that form, I shall be happy to receive it, and when so received, it shall be respectfully considered, and answered in the same manner. I am, sir, very respectfully, your ob't serv't,
>
> *M. Van Buren*

Hone was received at the appointed hour. With Van Buren were the secretary of State and the secretary of the Treasury. As requested, the merchants had written their petition. It told of the distress of merchants, banks, and the community in general, laying the problem on Jackson's 1836 *Specie Circular*, which required that many debts be paid in gold and silver coins. This had the effect of making credit very tight and forcing some bondholders to the wall, which in turn affected business in general.

Hone read the petition aloud, which began:

> *To Martin Van Buren, president of the U. States:*
>
> Sir: We have the honor of informing you that a very numerous meeting of the merchants of New York was held on the 25th of April, for the purpose of considering the present distressed condition of the city, and deliberating upon the means of relief. It was called by more than three hundred firms, and attended by a large proportion of those merchants who are connected with the internal trade of the country, and who have an especial and direct interest in the state of domestic exchanges.
>
> A committee was appointed to repair to Washington, and remonstrate with the executive against the continuance of the Specie Circular, and to urge its immediate repeal; also, to ask that instructions may be given to prevent the commencing of suits in any of the collection districts, upon unpaid bonds, until after the first day of January next: and to urge upon the executive the propriety of calling an extra session of Congress at as early a day as possible. . . .
>
> We fully appreciate the respect which is due to our chief magistrate, and disclaim every attention inconsistent with that feeling; but we speak in behalf of a community which trembles upon the brink of ruin, which deems itself an adequate judge of all questions connected with the trade and currency of the country, and believes that the policy adopted by the recent administration, and sustained by the present, is founded in error, and threatens the destruction of every department of industry.
>
> Our merchants, manufacturers and mechanics have repeatedly predicted the fatal issue of that policy. "What was prophecy, has now become history," and the reality far exceeds our most gloomy apprehensions. Under a deep impression of the propriety of confining our declarations within moderate limits, we affirm that the value of our real estate has, within the last six months, depreciated more than forty millions: that within the last two months, there have been more than two hundred and fifty failures of houses engaged in extensive business: that within the same period, a decline of twenty millions of dollars has occurred in our local stocks, including those rail road and canal incorporations, which, though chartered in other states depend chiefly upon New York for their sale; that the immense amount of merchandise in our ware houses has within the same period fallen in value at least thirty per cent; that within a few weeks not less than twenty thousand individuals, depending upon their daily labor for their daily bread, have been discharged by their employers, because the means of retaining them were exhausted—and that a complete blight has fallen upon a community heretofore so active, enterprising and prosperous.— The error of our

> rulers has produced a wider desolation than the pestilence which depopulated our streets, or the conflagration which laid them in ashes.
>
> We believe that it is unjust to attribute these evils to any excessive development of mercantile enterprise, and that they really flow from that unwise system which aimed at the substitution of metallic for a paper currency—the system which gave the first shock to the fabric of our commercial prosperity by removing the public deposites from the United States Bank, which weakened every part of the edifice by the destruction of that useful and efficient institution, and now threatens to crumble it into a mass of ruins under the operations of the Specie Circular, which withdrew the gold and silver of the country from the channels in which it could be profitably employed. . . .[2]

Matters did not improve, and meetings held in Baltimore, Philadelphia, and elsewhere brought the same information to the fore: the requirement that only gold and silver could be used to pay certain bonds and obligations was creating a huge problem. In comparison, the days of bank notes being used for nearly all obligations, including paying debts to the government, were prosperous.

This new necessity for coin engendered a fear that if holders of bills wanted to exchange them for gold and silver coins, easily available at banks, there might not be enough to go around. This of course was true—as banks put their assets to work by making loans and financing transactions. Gold and silver coins were kept on hand only to the extent of making normal daily exchanges in business. Such coins were only a tiny fraction of a bank's total paper money in circulation.

If a rumor spread that a bank was in financial trouble there would be a run on it when holders of bills demanded coins. Banks then had two choices: to suspend paying out specie (silver and gold coins) or to close their doors. By 1837 this scenario had been played out many times in cities across the country.

In May 1837, more and more holders of bank notes turned them in for coins—to wait out what might be an impending economic problem. Continuing unemployment, insolvencies, and other negative news exacerbated public fear.

Suspension of Specie Payments

The New York *Journal of Commerce* reported this on May 10:

> *The city—two o'clock.* The suspension of specie payments by the banks, has, as might be expected, created a considerable sensation throughout the city. To the reflecting and intelligent part of the community, it is however a matter neither of astonishment or alarm; and even amongst that class of persons who must be supposed to know less about the causes which have produced it, it has not occasioned as much excitement as might have been expected.
>
> Up to this hour not the slightest ebullition of popular violence has been exhibited, nor is anything of the kind expected, but the city authorities have nevertheless prudently made ample preparation to meet the evil if it should come. They have a large body of troops under arms, besides all the police and watch force of the city, ready to act at a moment's notice. As yet there is no symptom that their services are likely to be required.
>
> The three banks which were not parties to the notice of suspension which we published this morning, have since come into the measure. None of the banks have paid specie to-day.

The *Baltimore American* printed this on May 12:

> At half past nine o'clock last night we received the following proceedings of the officers of the several banks in Baltimore, by which it will be seen that they have determined to suspend specie payments. The resolution takes effect forthwith. In closing this paragraph we cannot do better than quote the language of the *New York Commercial*, in speaking of the same measure in that city, "that our citizens, one and all, be exhorted to avoid excitement, and to conduct themselves with all possible forbearance towards the banks, and towards each other.
>
> "The banks are beyond all doubt perfectly solvent. Their notes are worth just as much to-day as they were yesterday. They will go just as far in the discharge of liabilities, and in the purchase of goods and provisions. Let no man, therefore, sacrifice his paper, or indulge apprehensions as to his funds in deposite. The bills of our banks will still be the 'current money' of the city, and will answer all the necessary purposes of the community."

Pet Banks Affected

To the dismay of the Van Buren administration and the Treasury Department, the pet banks suspended specie payments as well. This was not supposed to happen. On May 17 Secretary of the Treasury Levi Woodbury sent this notice to the cashiers of the banks:

> **Circular to Deposit Banks**
>
> Sir:
>
> As the painful information has reached this department through the public press, that your bank has suspended specie payments, the object of this letter is to learn, officially, if that fact has happened; and to receive such explanations concerning the reasons for it, and the future course of your business, as it will be apparent are so important for this department to know, under the existing liabilities and relations between you and the government.
>
> While, on the one hand, it is deemed proper that such indulgences should be granted by this department to its former fiscal agents, as they may request consistently with the laws and with the present state of the treasury; it must be apparent, on the other hand, that nothing can be granted which is likely to endanger the safety of the public funds, and other important public interests.
>
> The imperative provisions of the act of June, 1836, make it the duty of this department to discontinue ordering any further sums of public money to be placed with the deposit bank, after suspending specie payments. And hence, you are notified, that no more can be thus deposited in your institution, provided such a failure to redeem your notes has actually occurred.
>
> It is also made my duty, as soon as practicable, to select other depositories, and place with them the money of the United States in your possession, as well as the accruing revenue; but the department will endeavor to draw out the funds in your hands by warrants and transfers, reasonable in their amount, and in the periods of their payment. Such warrants and transfers, it is trusted, you will at all times be anxious and able to meet, in a manner satisfactory to all concerned; not only with a view to fulfill faithfully your contract, and relieve the treasury and its creditors from embarrassment and losses, but to exonerate yourselves and sureties from consequences equally injurious, inevitable and unpleasant.

I trust, further, that you will continue to regard it your duty, while any public money remains in your possession, to forward, regularly, all the returns and statements which are required by your agreement—the mutual advantages from doing which, cannot fail to be obvious.

The department will also feel much obliged, if you will furnish, as early as practicable, replies to the two following inquiries, in order that it may be in possession of such intelligence from you, in an authentic form, as will be useful to the community and the states, and very material for regulating properly the future measures of the treasury. Those inquiries are:

1st. Whether you expect to resume specie payments soon, and what mode you propose to take fully and reasonably to indemnify, secure, and satisfy the government and the public creditors for any breach of your agreement and bond?

2d. Whether, if you do not expect to resume specie payments soon, any particular time for it hereafter has been yet decided on, and what special efforts or arrangements you intend to make for that very important object?

I am, very respectfully, your obedient servant.
Levi Woodbury,
Sec'y of the Treasury

The Panic of 1837

Thus began what history records as the Panic of 1837. Silver and gold coins disappeared from commercial channels and went into the hands of citizens who, distrustful of paper money, hoarded specie for security. Speculators, banks, exchange offices, and specie brokers did likewise. Coins were available, but only at a premium in terms of bills, even those from banks that were viewed as solid. The banks themselves had abundant specie in terms of traditional reserves, but not nearly enough to redeem even a large percentage of their outstanding bills.

Soon, even federal copper one-cent pieces became scarce. Even if this had not happened, there were not nearly enough in circulation to take the place of gold and silver coins. Banks issued still more bills in order to facilitate commerce. Included were some of such odd denominations as $1.25, $1.50, and $1.75 to help with transactions in fractional parts of a dollar.

The months after May were very distressful. In domino-like effect, many weak banks collapsed, thousands of businesses and shops closed their doors forever, and millions of citizens saw true hard times as they lost their employment or suffered reduced wages.

Copper Tokens as Money

In 1837 the small change in circulation was dominated by copper cents struck at the Philadelphia Mint. These had been made continuously since 1793, with the solitary exception of 1815, when copper stock was scarce. Whereas the coinage of silver and gold was mainly done to accommodate the needs of depositors of such metal, and a small charge was levied, the production of cents and the less-popular half cents returned a profit to the Mint—the difference between metal cost and face value. Because of this, regardless of economic conditions, the pace of cent production remained strong throughout the years.

In addition to federal coins, many foreign copper coins were seen in circulation, although they had no legal-tender value. Copper coins issued by Vermont, Connecticut,

New York, New Jersey, and Massachusetts in the 1785 to 1788 era were often seen, as were many tokens issued by merchants. By that time, quite a few commercial enterprises had issued tokens. Some of those, such as tokens issued by Walsh's General Store in Lansingburgh, New York, depicted Lafayette. Others bore inscriptions on both sides. Some were smaller, such as the "Carry Me to Atwood's Rail Road Hotel" denominated as three cents and useful as a ticket on a horse-drawn coach. Octagonal tokens of even smaller size served as tickets to ride on the New York & Harlem Railroad, which opened in the early 1830s.

The merchants' tokens that can be attributed to the 1832 to 1836 years form the foundation of the collection listed by Lyman H. Low as Hard Times issues.

Copper "Not One Cent" Tokens

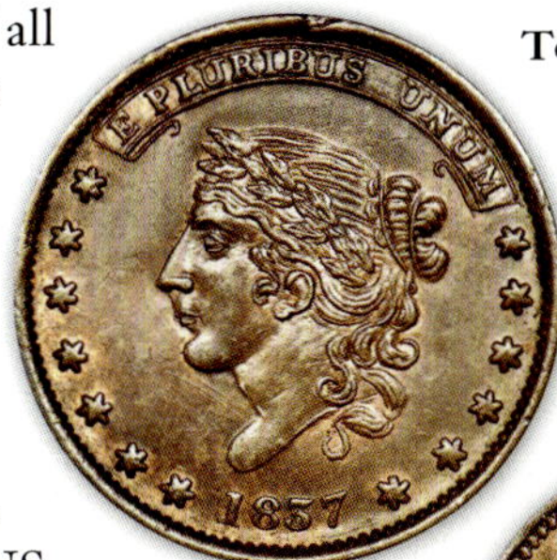

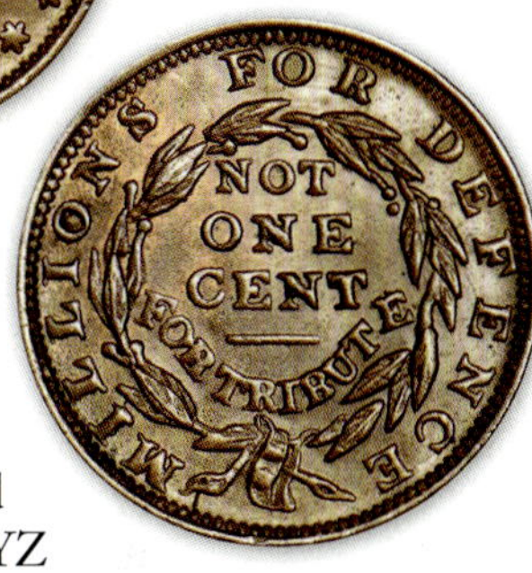

Tokens of the NOT ONE CENT type with Liberty Head obverse too closely resembled federal cents, it was said (W-11-140a, Low-33).

The Panic of 1837 and its shortage of all coins, including copper cents, formed an unprecedented opportunity for private individuals, including J.M.L. & W.H. Scovill, button manufacturers of Waterbury, Connecticut, to turn out a flood of cent-size tokens. Many featured a Liberty Head on the obverse, in imitation of federal cents, and on the reverse an inscription such as MILLIONS FOR DEFENCE, NOT ONE CENT FOR TRIBUTE. "NOT ONE CENT" was typically in the center, within a wreath, with "NOT" in much smaller letters. This sentiment arose in 1797 and 1798 during the John Adams administration. French foreign minister Talleyrand stated that attacks on American shipping would be stopped if payments were made. This was part of the so-called XYZ Affair, in which the names of certain French officials were replaced by these code letters. South Carolina congressman Robert Goodloe Harper proposed a toast that became a rallying cry in America, "Millions for defence, not one cent for tribute."[3] This phrase was later echoed when Barbary pirates in the Mediterranean Sea demanded money for the safety of American ships.

These tokens were sold at varying rates, from about $8 to $9 per thousand, to storekeepers and others who passed them out at the value of 1¢ when making change. By autumn, problems arose. Many newspaper accounts, letters, and other exchanges found the coins to be deceptive.

On October 18, 1837, the *Columbian Register*, published in New Haven, said this:

Not One Cent

> It will be seen that the New-York papers have denounced the iniquity of manufacturing and circulating Waterbury and other base coin. There was no call for copper coin, there having been an abundance of it in circulation from time immemorial. The spurious coin is not worth more than half the amount it is offered for. Almost every poor person must now lose a few pence, in consequence of the criminal conduct of manufacturers who dare not avow themselves as the authors of the mischief.

> We understand that bills purporting to be one dollar notes on some of the eastern banks, without the signature of president or cashier, have been palmed off in the hurry of businesses on the unsuspecting. Rumors unfavorable to the Lafayette Bank, Boston, are in circulation. We hope the days of small bank bills of any description will soon come to a close.

The *Columbian Register* told more about the pesky tokens on October 28:

> **Not One Cent**
>
> *Not one cent* is a part of a fraudulent inscription upon a base coin manufactured at certain button factories in New Haven County. Since the moneyed operations of Nicholas Biddle and the English bankers, the button business has declined. The machinery used in cutting and stamping buttons can conveniently be appropriated to the purposes of the mint. A coin, having the appearance of copper, with a head and other insignia of a cent, of the same size and finish, in all respects resembling that coin with the exception of the word *not* obscurely overshadowed by a wreath, and immediately preceding the words *one cent*, has been manufactured in great quantities; about two hundred gross at one factory, and three hundred at another, per day. They are sold by the manufacturers, at 100 for 90 good cents, and sent abroad to New-York and elsewhere by the ton.
>
> This coin is composed of about 40 per cent copper, and 60 per cent of some cheaper metal, yielding a profit of about 50 per cent. Agents are employed to give it circulation. Many kegs are said to have been disposed of at the military review at Cheshire [Connecticut].
>
> These manufacturers are prime Whigs; the noisy advocates of a United States Bank as a regulator of the currency. They erect splendid houses and fatten on the labor of industrious men, women, and children, whom they hold in a state of slavish dependence, and attempt to rule with that imperious sway imparted only by a direct dominion over

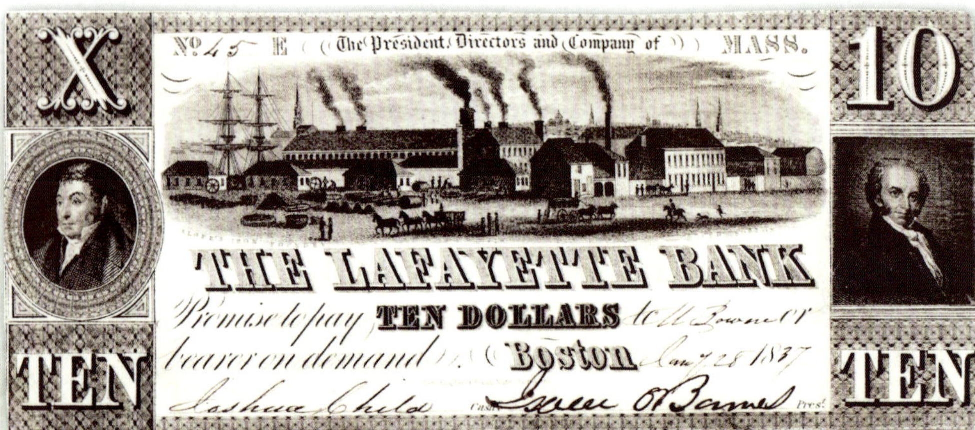

In 1837 rumors swirled concerning the Lafayette Bank of Boston, a relatively new institution that opened its doors on July 13, 1835, with a stated capital of $150,000. The worries were well founded for a committee of the State Legislature reported on February 2, 1838, that most capital had never been paid in, the books were in disarray with ledger pages missing, and vastly more notes had been issued than had been stated. By that time the bills were worthless. The vignette shows Alger's Iron Foundry in South Boston.

> their daily bread, willing by base means to be enrolled in heartless aristocracy of wealth. In all civilized governments, debasing the coin has been esteemed a high offence against public policy, and public morals. Its moral degradation consists in the acquisition of money by *fraud*, aggravated in this case by the certainty that the loss will at last fall on small dealers and the poorer classes of society.
>
> Counterfeiting is made severely penal, yet the principle involved in this manufacture is the same that makes counterfeit money. Whether this be an offence against the enactments of the criminal code, the lawyers and judges have not determined. Honesty and common sense declare, there should be no difference in the consequences, where the motif has the same corruption. Yet these haughty manufacturers would feel indignant, should they be charged with counterfeiting—perhaps more from the infamy of the punishment than the infamy of the principle. The loafer that passes a counterfeit dollar is convicted, and sent to the State Prison, while these affluent speculators on public credulity by means involving equal turpitude, pass by with their splendid equipage and spurn their degraded brother. . . .
>
> The pride of these ardent Whig leaders would be wounded, if they should be detected in using false weights and measures, by which they gained sixty cents out of every hundred of the pork, or cheese, or grain they bought or sold. Yet this traffic is based on the same principle. It is not the weakness of an infirm nature that commits this offence, like *manslaughter or adultery*—but cool, well matured close calculating fraud—like forgery. Yet these are honorable men, clad in purple and fine linen; they exhibit themselves in the market place, with a sovereign contempt for the operatives, and superciliously, at the corners, speak of the ignorant multitude. . . .This is but one specimen of the speculating propensity of the aristocracy of wealth, and is a practical illustration of the spirit of the times.
>
> Making haste to be rich by any, and all means; it is this object that combines the efforts of the cunning and unprincipled, to establish a stupendous system of credit, rag money incorporations, and the whole machinery and organization by which wealth can be accumulated, by the dishonest few at the expense of the honest and unsuspecting many. Avarice, villainy, and the lust of dominion, lie at the foundation.

In New Hampshire on November 11 the *Portsmouth Journal of Literature and Politics* told how merchants could make a lot more than a fraction of a cent by giving out quantities of tokens in a single transaction:

> They have at the present time in New York City a plentiful supply of metallic currency. The button factories have been induced by the scarcity of change to turn their attention to the manufacture of copper tokens which pass for cents. They are sold by wholesale to the traders at eight dollars a thousand, and the grocers will now change a five-dollar bill for a cent's worth of tobacco, turning out 499 coppers in change.

In Baltimore, the *Sun* printed this on December 2:

> The attempt to put into circulation a spurious copper coinage sufficiently like cents in the general appearance to be taken by the unwary as genuine, has very properly received a prompt check from the officers of the government, who are on the alert to discover and punish every person who knowingly assists in giving them currency. We therefore caution our fellow citizens to look with care at each piece of copper coin that may be offered them, as by inattention, they may receive and pay them away again, which may involve them in an unpleasant difficulty.

The spurious coins, which are offered in so great quantity as to leave no doubt that the object of the makers was to circulate them as currency, have on one side, in a circle near the edge, the words "MILLIONS FOR DEFENCE," and in the centre "NOT ONE CENT FOR TRIBUTE"—the other side is in the general appearance much like a cent, although it is in some respects different.—*Gazette.*

We are equally pleased with our neighbor, the *Gazette*, that the officers of the government are on the alert to discover and punish the persons engaged in putting this spurious coin in circulation. We are in favor of putting down every violation of the laws. But it is curious to see how prompt the *Gazette* comes out against these coppers, when it has, during the past season, repeatedly urged the issue of shinplasters by banks and companies, of a less denomination than five dollars, which is strictly forbidden by the laws of the state. It would seem the editor thinks there is a mighty difference between shinplaster and copper frauds! For our part we cannot discover why one should be tolerated any sooner than the other. We look upon them all as belonging to the same school, and should like to see every individual engaged in issuing shinplasters and spurious copper coins, equally punished to the fullest extent of the law.

Shinplasters was a popular derisive term for paper money that dated back to colonial times. It was said that certain bills were not worth anything as money, but with starch added could be dampened and applied as a poultice to hurt shins. One cent-size Hard Times token has the inscription, SUBSTITUTE FOR SHIN PLASTERS.

Legal action against the Scovills put a damper on the production of cent-design imitations, and it is likely that production ceased about that time. In September 1838, a legal action was filed against the partners. However, no convictions were ever obtained, and in time the matter was forgotten.

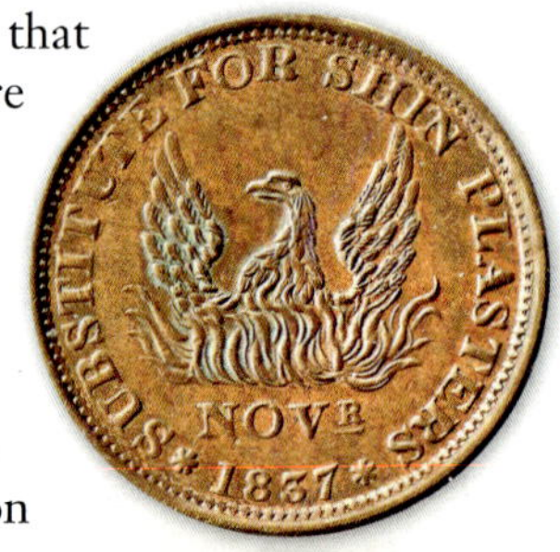

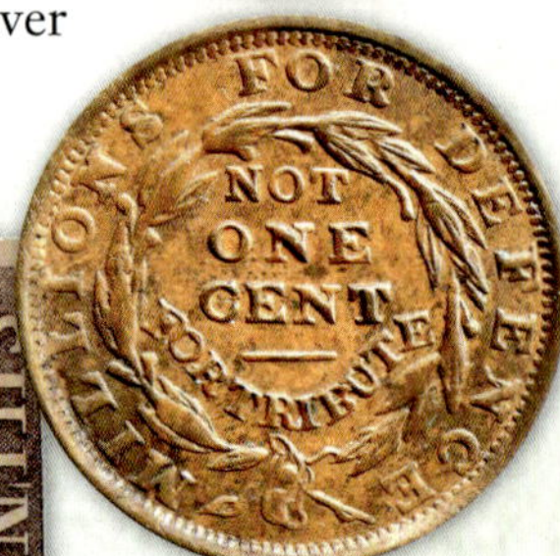

This SUBSTITUTE FOR SHIN PLASTERS token with the controversial NOT ONE CENT reverse was made to the extent of several hundred thousand pieces (W-11-260a, Low-45).

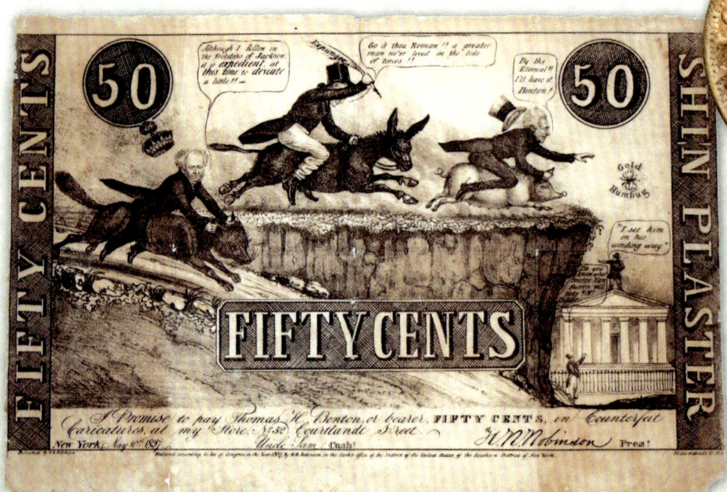

A satirical shinplaster note published in 1837 by H.R. Robinson, New York City, who issued a variety of bills with commentary on the financial and political turmoil of the time. These were for sale at 52 Courtlandt Street, 11-1/2 Wall Street, and 38 Chatham Street and were very popular in their time.

Other Tokens of 1837

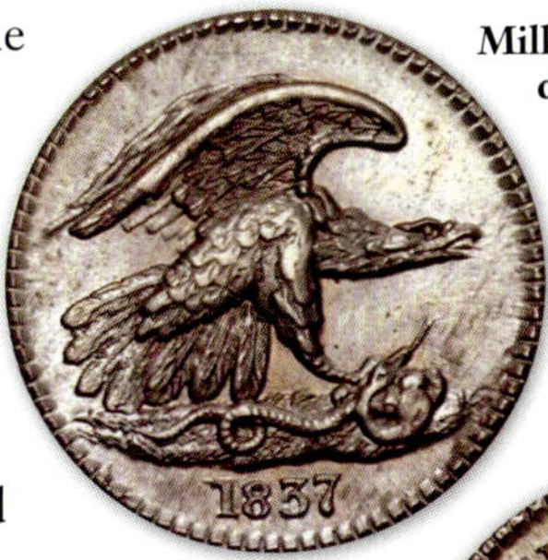

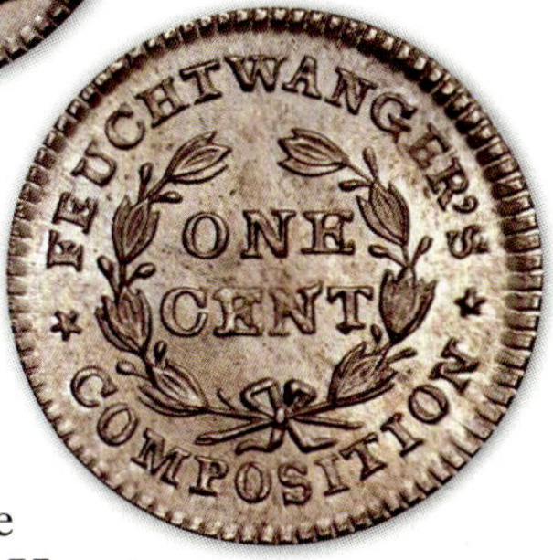

Millions of small-diameter (18.5 mm) Feuchtwanger cents were circulated in 1837. (W-NY-480 Dies 6-I, Low-120, the most often seen variety.)

In 1837 many merchants signed with the Scovills and other coiners, purchasing large quantities of cent-size copper tokens with a date and Liberty Head on the obverse and an advertising message, sometimes with an icon such as an umbrella or boot, on the reverse. These were circulated widely and attracted unfavorable attention from the press and letter-writers.

Most prominent among token issuers was Dr. Lewis Feuchtwanger, who came from Bavaria and, earlier in the decade, set up a pharmacy stocking drugs imported from the German states—attractive to many German immigrants in the city. He also compounded patent medicines. His most important product was Feuchtwanger's Composition, an alloy of the class of German silver, useful for table ware, utensils, beer pumps, and other metal implements. He exhibited at the annual fairs of the American Institute and consistently earned awards. In 1837 he had Bale & Smith prepare dies and strike small tokens in his composition—these were about dime-size and had reeded edges. On the obverse an eagle killing a rattlesnake was depicted, and on the reverse around the border was FEUCHTWANGER'S COMPOSITION and within a wreath, ONE / CENT. These were made in large quantities, probably into the millions, from multiple die pairs. With the endorsement of Senator Thomas Hart Benton, he petitioned Congress to adopt his alloy for regular cent coinage, and he provided samples for the various legislators. However, the director of the Mint rejected the idea in 1838, and the proposal died.

The Sub-Treasury Bill

Unfortunately for supporters of Jackson's pet banks—and to the delight of the Whig Party—many of the dozens of pet banks (more than 90 in number) had severe problems. In step with other banks, most did not have enough specie to redeem their bills in gold and silver. One, the Bank of Michigan, based in Detroit, used deposited federal funds to loan to speculative ventures and failed. Even Andrew Jackson in retirement at the Hermitage was dismayed at the turn of events.

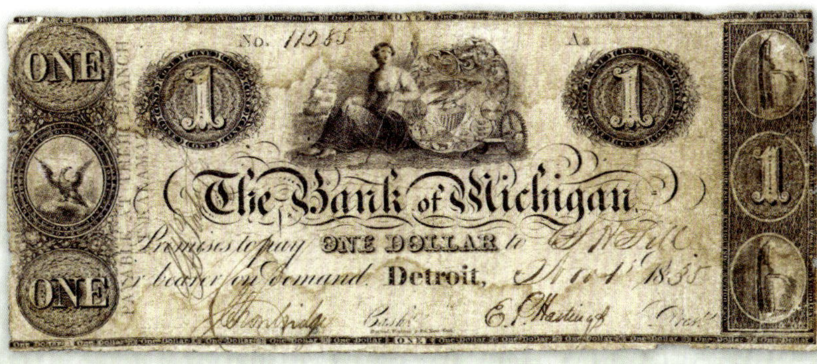

The Bank of Michigan in Detroit was a favored pet bank that went wrong. The officers used deposited federal funds to engage in speculation, and the bank failed.

In September 1837 the "Report of the Secretary of the Treasury" named these *banks of deposite* (pet banks) that had been in business in 1836, nearly all with this status discontinued:

Banks of Deposite

Alabama: Branch Bank of Alabama, Mobile

Connecticut: Quinebaug Bank, Norwich • Farmers and Mechanics Bank, Hartford • Mechanics Bank, New Haven

Delaware: Bank of Wilmington and Brandywine, Wilmington, Bank of Delaware

District of Columbia: Bank of the Metropolis

Georgia: Bank of Augusta • Planters Bank of the State of Georgia, Savannah • Insurance Bank of Columbus

Illinois: Bank of Illinois at Shawneetown

Indiana: State Bank of Indiana, Indianapolis

Kentucky: Bank of Kentucky and branches • Northern Bank of Kentucky, at Lexington, and branch at Louisville • Louisville Savings Institution

Louisiana: Union Bank of Louisiana, and branches, New Orleans • Commercial Bank, New Orleans

Maine: Mercantile Bank, Bangor • Peoples Bank, Bangor • Maine Bank, Portland • Cumberland Bank, Portland • Granite Bank, Augusta • York Bank, Saco

Maryland: Union Bank of Maryland, Baltimore • Franklin Bank, Baltimore

Massachusetts: Merchants Bank, Boston • Commonwealth Bank, Boston • Franklin Bank, Boston • Hancock Bank, Boston • Phoenix Bank, Charlestown

Michigan: Bank of Michigan, Detroit • Farmers and Mechanics Bank of Detroit • Bank of River Raisin

Mississippi: Planters Bank of Mississippi and branches, Natchez • Agricultural Bank and branches, Natchez

Missouri: Agency of Commercial Bank of Cincinnati at St. Louis • Bank of the state of Missouri, St. Louis

New Hampshire: New Hampshire Bank, Portsmouth • Commercial Bank, Portsmouth • Portsmouth Bank, Portsmouth • Piscataqua Bank, Portsmouth • Merrimack County Bank, Concord (Isaac Hill's former bank) • Mechanics Bank, Concord

New Jersey: State Bank, Newark • Trenton Banking Company

New York: Mechanics and Farmers Bank, Albany • Brooklyn Bank • Manhattan Company, New York • Bank of America, New York • Mechanics Bank, New York • Seventh Ward Bank, New York • Lafayette Bank, New York • Phoenix Bank, New York • Leather Manufacturers Bank, New York • Tradesmens Bank, New York • Dry Dock Company, New York • Merchants Bank, New York • Union Bank, New York • Merchants Exchange Bank, New York • Brooklyn Bank, Brooklyn • Commercial Bank, Buffalo • Bank of Troy, Troy

North Carolina: Bank of the State of North Carolina, Raleigh

Ohio: Clinton Bank of Columbus • Franklin Bank of Columbus • Bank of Chillicothe • Franklin Bank, Cincinnati • Commercial Bank, Cincinnati • Bank of Zanesville • Bank of Wooster • Commercial Bank of Lake Erie, at Cleveland • Bank of Cleveland

Pennsylvania: Girard Bank, Philadelphia • Moyamensing Bank, Philadelphia • Merchants and Manufacturers Bank, Pittsburgh

Rhode Island: Arcade Bank, Providence • Rhode Island Union Bank, Newport

South Carolina: Planters and Mechanics Bank, Charleston • Bank of Charleston

Tennessee: Union Bank of Tennessee, Nashville • Planters Bank and branches, Nashville

Vermont: Bank of Burlington • Bank of Windsor, Windsor

Virginia: Bank of Virginia, Richmond • Farmers Bank of Virginia, Richmond

In a message to Congress on September 5, 1837, President Martin Van Buren proposed establishing Sub-Treasury offices in cities to receive and hold federal funds, which were then in pet banks. By that time, paper money in circulation included many bills that were completely worthless, some issued by fictitious banks. While Sub-Treasuries would not replace the defunct Bank of the United States, it was thought that they would help restore public confidence.

The Sub-Treasury Bill was introduced in the Senate in October, made its way through two different sessions of Congress, and became law in June 1839 as the Independent Treasury Act. Sub-Treasury branches were proposed for New York City, Boston, Philadelphia, St. Louis, Charleston, and Washington. Certain provisions of the bill were repealed in 1841. The slow movement of funds from pet banks to Sub-Treasury offices was lampooned by tokens showing a tortoise with a strongbox on its back.

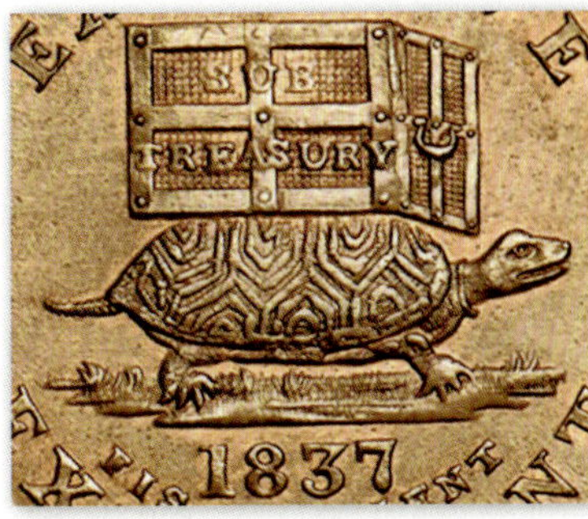

Detail of a token satirizing the expected slow movement of federal funds from pet banks to Sub-Treasury offices (W-11-520a, Low-18).

This satirical cartoon by H.R. Robinson, "Sub-Treasury System, or Office Holders Elysium," suggests that the plan benefited politicians.

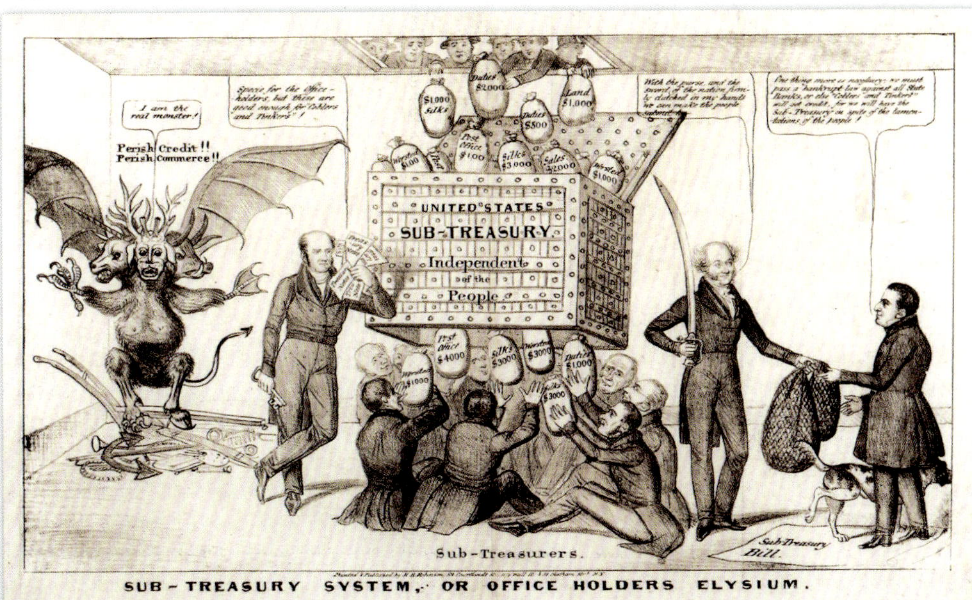

About this time, many varieties of tokens were issued with one side dated 1837 showing a ship named *Experiment* wrecked on a rocky shore, with VAN BUREN / METALLIC CURRENCY around the border. The experiment was Van Buren's continuing of Jackson's and Benton's policy that gold and silver coins—hard money—was preferable to paper money, even though it restricted credit. The other side shows the fully rigged frigate, the USS *Constitution*, sails billowed with WEBSTER above and CREDIT 1841 CURRENT below. Webster, of course, was a die-hard advocate of paper money and easy credit. As to 1841, on March 4 of that coming year, there would be a new president, Webster perhaps.

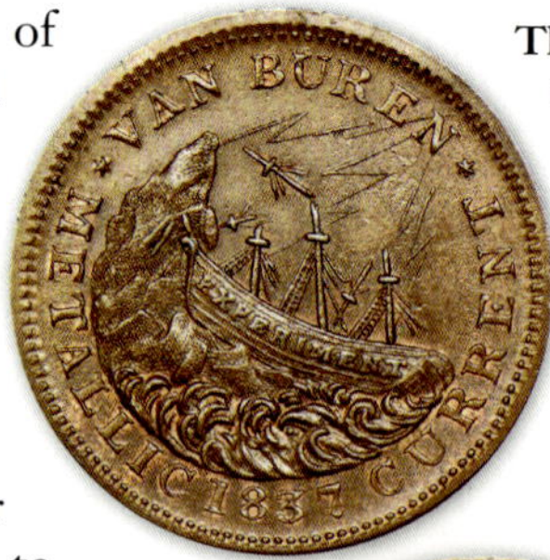

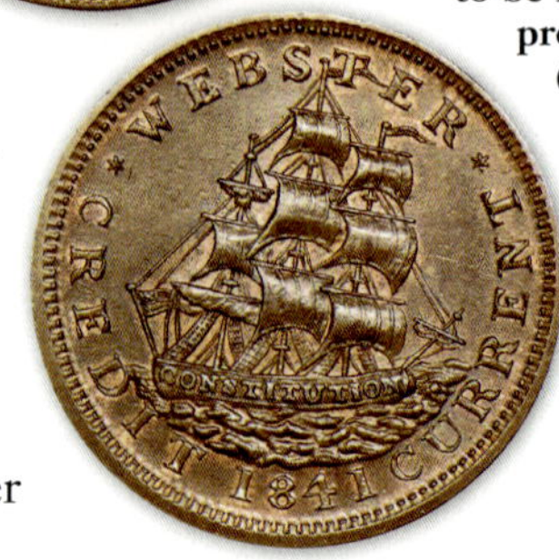

This token, issued in 1837, depicts Van Buren's insistence on metal coins represented as an allegorical ship, *Experiment*, being wrecked on a rocky shore. The ship *Constitution* on the reverse predicts smooth sailing if Webster were to be inaugurated as president in 1841 (W-11-630a, Low-62).

The allegories on political Hard Times tokens invite investigation as to the full meaning of the inscriptions and motifs. It may be relevant to note that on Thursday, September 9, 1830, the *Boston Commercial Gazette* in "Old Ironsides Under the Hammer!!" reported that the USS *Constitution*, which was built in 1797 and had served with distinction in the War of 1812, was about to be scrapped. The late John B. Timberlake, husband of Margaret (Peggy) O'Neal, had once been purser. This planned destruction caused protests, Oliver Wendell Holmes's poem, "Old Ironsides," was published two days later, and the ship was saved. Today, in the Charleston Navy Yard near Boston, she is a national landmark and attraction. However, this destruction of the *Constitution* ship does not seem to be related to Jackson's later disregard of the Constitution document and the numerous Constitution mentions on tokens.

In November 1837, the Washington *Globe* commented on 1841-dated tokens being issued with mention of Webster, noting in part:

> Most of the coins referred to are stamped with political caricatures and other federal devices. An emission of them hails the inauguration of Daniel Webster as president in 1841, while others contain inscriptions insulting the late president of the United States. There really seems to be no bounds as to the limits of enterprise in the manufacture of spurious substitutes for money.[4]

Other News of the Time

In 1837, Phineas T. Barnum hoaxed more than 10,000 visitors to Niblo's Garden in New York City with his exhibition of Joice Heth, a frail "161-year-old" former slave who claimed to be the midwife who assisted in the delivery of baby George Washington in 1732. The New York & Harlem Railroad, which issued Hard Times tokens, extended its horsecar line to Harlem and developed the world's first steam-powered tram. On March 3, the number of Supreme Court justices was increased from seven to nine. Nathaniel Hawthorne's *Twice-Told Tales* was published and included a story about mint master John Hull giving as his daughter's dowry her weight in Pine Tree shillings. Farmland prices were depressed as a result of the *Specie Circular*, making homesteading more affordable. Michigan was admitted to the Union on January 26, 1837. Possibly more than any other state, Michigan was a haven for fraudulent "wildcat" banking and note-issuing operations.

By 1837 the so-called Underground Railroad was in operation and provided a method for slaves in the South to escape to the North or to Canada. Clandestine way stations were set up in 14 Northern states, but activities were greatest in Ohio, which serviced a stream of slaves coming up from Kentucky. In late 1837 thousands of cent-size copper tokens dated 1838 were released, showing a slave in chains kneeling and the inscription AM I NOT A WOMAN & A SISTER. Ironically, LIBERTY is at the center of the reverse.

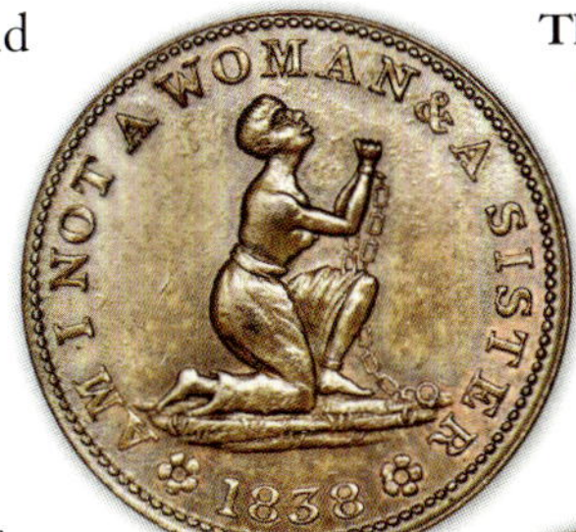

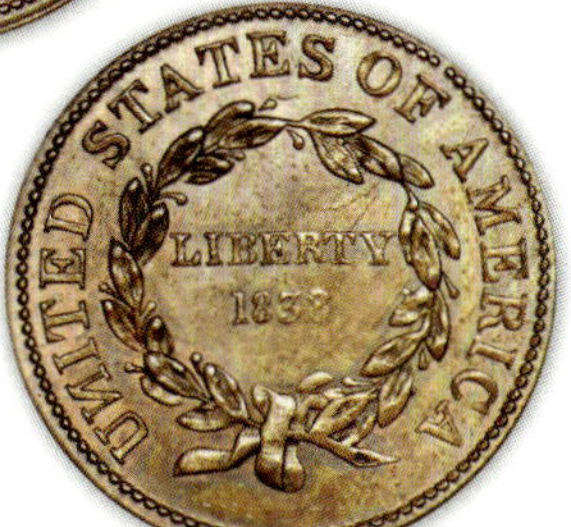

This Hard Times token was issued in quantity by the Anti-Slavery Office, No. 143 Nassau Street, New York City, beginning in autumn 1837 (W-11-720a, Low-54).

In 1837 and 1838 there was a flood of satirical "notes" lampooning Jackson, Van Buren, and other characters and events of the era. These were a combination of cartoons and wry humor.

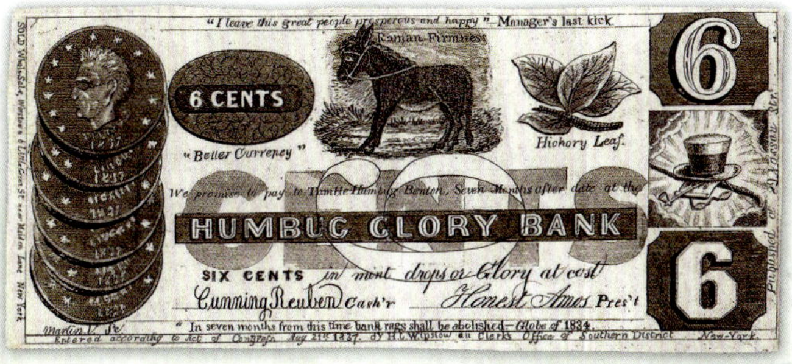

The Humbug Glory Bank note was issued in 1837 but referred to events of 1834 and illustrated tokens somewhat similar in appearance to earlier tokens.

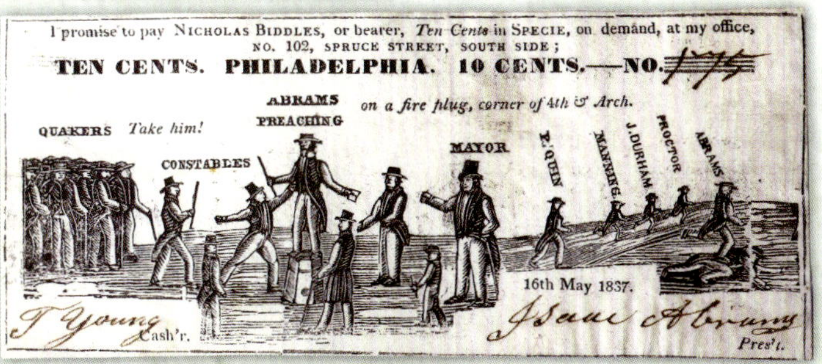

This comic note of 1837 mentions "Nicholas Biddles" in the headline.

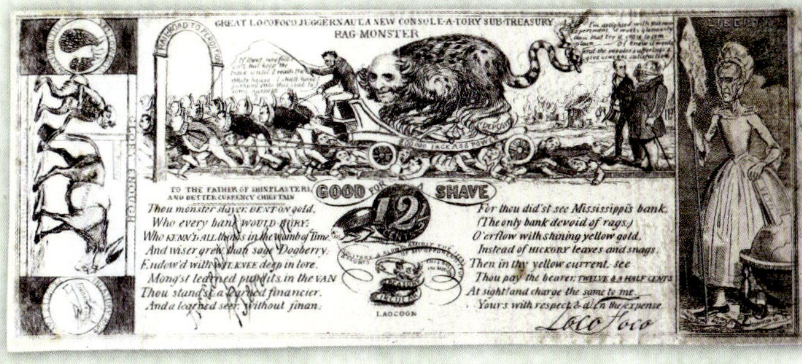

Van Buren sitting on money bags is hauling deposits on a wagon driven by Jackson, pulled by Loco Foco politicians. A poem begins with, "Thou monster slayer [reference to the Bank of the United States] bent on gold, Who every bank would bury. . . ."

8

Events of 1839 to 1844

Later Hard Times Tokens

The main era of Hard Times tokens, with *political* motifs and tokens the size of a copper cent, ended in 1838. By 1839 there were many federal cents back in circulation, and the making of tokens as monetary substitutes was no longer needed. Store cards of cent size continued to be made for advertising purposes.

Henry Clay, Daniel Webster, and the usual anti–Democratic Party politicians continued to combat President Martin Van Buren's proposal for Sub-Treasury offices and his backing, along with Senator Benton, of the use of specie in commerce.

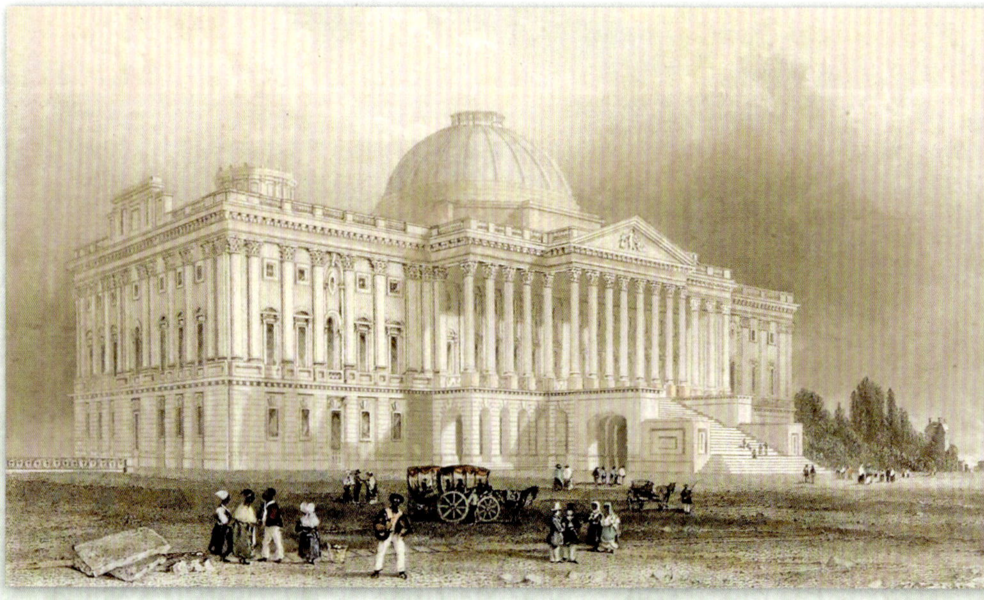

The Capitol in Washington as it appeared in 1839.

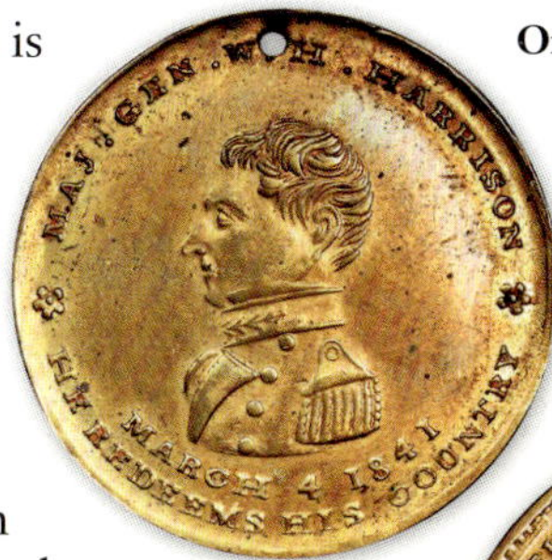

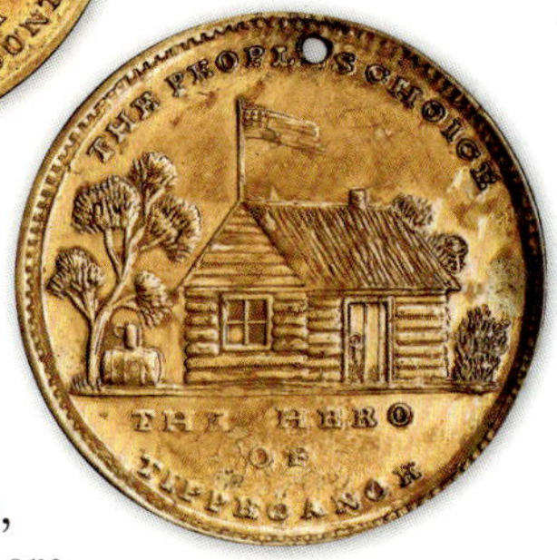

One of many 1840 campaign medals for William Henry Harrison (DeWitt WHH 1840-24. 29 mm).

From a numismatic viewpoint there is confusion about whether to include the presidential campaign tokens of 1840, which pitted incumbent Democrat Martin Van Buren against Whig challenger William Henry Harrison, in the Hard Times series. This campaign, handily won by Harrison, saw the issue of more tokens and medals than all earlier presidential contests combined. Lyman H. Low elected to include several campaign tokens, mostly holed for suspension, favoring Van Buren. The ones selected had reference to the Treasury or banking and, when seen, are usually worn—indicating they may have circulated.

Low completely ignored the presidential election of 1844, pitting Whig Henry Clay, certainly a key player in the earlier era of Jackson, against Democratic winner James Knox Polk, even though it fits within Low's Hard Times token period. In summary, of the presidential campaign tokens for 1840 and 1844, only a few were selected by Low for inclusion in his book. To expand that in the present text would cause confusion, so the present text stays with Low's choices.

As Lyman H. Low defined the Hard Times token era as from 1832 to 1844, later cent-size store cards fit comfortably within the series. Examples include the A. Loomis issues of Cleveland, some of which are dated 1843.

Twilight of the Hard Times Era

In 1839 Henry Clay, long-time aspirant to the White House, consulted advisors before making a speech urging moderation in the cause of abolition, the main point of difference between legislators from the North and South. When Clay, who hailed from Kentucky, a border state, was told that members of each major party were likely to be offended, he replied, "I trust the sentiments and opinions are correct; I had rather be right than be president."

The Hard Times era continued. Although most banks had resumed specie payments, there was a hiccup in 1839 when Philadelphia banks resumed suspension, a crisis that spread to the West and lasted in some areas until January 15, 1841.

There had been massive bank failures among state-chartered institutions in remote areas. In Michigan out of 40 banks, all but a handful failed. Some turned out to be fraudulent, but many legitimate banks held few assets, and these also failed. These were called "wildcat banks." Problems during the Hard Times era prompted many states to set up banking commissions, whereas prior to 1837 such authorities were few and far between.

Into the 1840s

According to the 1840 census, in 1839 the number of people employed in gold mining was 1,046, the amount of capital invested in the industry was $234,300, and the amount of gold extracted amounted to $529,500, of which Virginia produced $52,000, North Carolina $256,000, South Carolina $37,000, Georgia $122,000, Alabama $61,000, and Tennessee $1,500. During the same year, the amount deposited for coinage came to

$385,000, suggesting that about seven-tenths of the annual production of gold from 1839 was converted into United States coins. Of course, much gold for coinage came from other sources—mostly from the melting of foreign issues.

New York City, in the 1840 census, was listed as having 312,000 inhabitants, a sharp increase from 124,000 in 1820. Most of upper and mid-Manhattan was farmland and woods. Some 90 percent of Americans lived in rural areas. Most citizens stayed at home, and it was not unusual to find an octogenarian who had never traveled beyond the limits of his or her state. The national population amounted to 17,069,453.

The number of banks in the United States reporting to the secretary of the Treasury was 661 in 1840 or, counting individual branches of banks, 901. These banks had outstanding loans in the amount of $462 million and possessed specie (silver and gold coin) in the sum of $33.1 million. Capital stood at $358.4 million, and notes of the banks in circulation amounted to $106.9 million. Although various states had regulations affecting the issuance of paper money by banks, in practice many financial institutions were poorly capitalized, had few real assets, and emitted paper money in issues which the banks could not redeem in their entirety. In 1840 the effects of the Panic of 1837 were still being felt, and, although recovery was underway, many areas of business and finance were uncertain.

In 1840 Martin Van Buren threw his hat in the ring for the November election, seeking a second term, but the continuing poor economy was his downfall. Unsurprisingly, his proud accomplishments, among which was the "removal of whole Indian nations," were not enough to counter the public's dissatisfaction.[1] He was bested by William Henry Harrison, the hero of the Battle of Tippecanoe, who, with

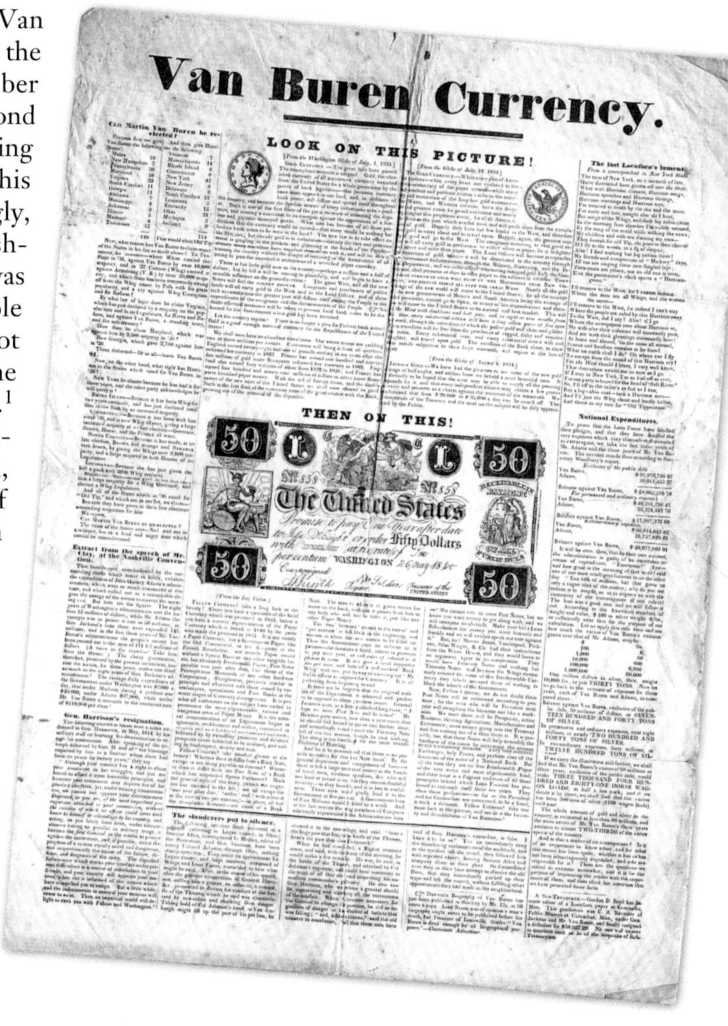
Van Buren Currency.

LOOK ON THIS PICTURE!

THEN ON THIS!

An anti–Van Buren broadside issued by his opponents during the presidential election campaign of 1840.

his running mate John Tyler, used the slogan "Tippecanoe and Tyler too." At his inaugural ceremony on March 4, Harrison caught a cold. His condition worsened, and he died on April 4. Tyler became president and continued in the office for the next four years. The three leading social issues were slavery, first and foremost; temperance; and, trailing by a distance, women's rights. Regarding temperance, there were many societies, hotels, restaurants, and publications that catered to advocates of this philosophy. *Saloon* was a popular word referring to a nice parlor or gathering place, not particularly to the serving of alcohol; oysters were the most popular "fancy" dish of the era, and were served in many styles: accordingly, oyster saloons, temperance saloons, and other businesses were popular. One issuer of Hard Times tokens even advertised his bowling saloon.

The decennial census revealed these statistics: white persons in the United States: 7,249,266 males, 6,939,842 females; free colored persons: 186,467 males, 199,778 females; and slaves: 1,246,408 males (of whom 422,599 were under 10 years of age), 1,240,805 females (of whom 421,470 were under 10).

Following the trend of the 1830s, the funds of the United States, as shown by a surplus in the Treasury, continued to build up. On January 1, 1841, the amount of excess funds stood at $13,500,000, up sharply from $5.2 million a year earlier. By January 1, 1842, the amount increased to $20.6 million. These were the days of intended fiscal responsibility, a posture which, over the coming decades, would furnish great strength to the government and the American System of commerce and trade. While political campaigns of the 1840s were often free-swinging and irresponsible as they would be, the well-managed Treasury Department held its own while commercial interests, although improving, were still feeling the impact of the Panic of 1837.

In early 1841, many banks that had not done so earlier resumed specie payments. Sometimes this was done by offering to exchange bills not at par but at a discount ranging up to about five percent. Resumption was premature in some instances, and scattered suspensions took place later. The true nature of Nicholas Biddle's Bank of the United States of Pennsylvania was becoming known, and its suspension and difficulties affected other banks, particularly in Philadelphia.

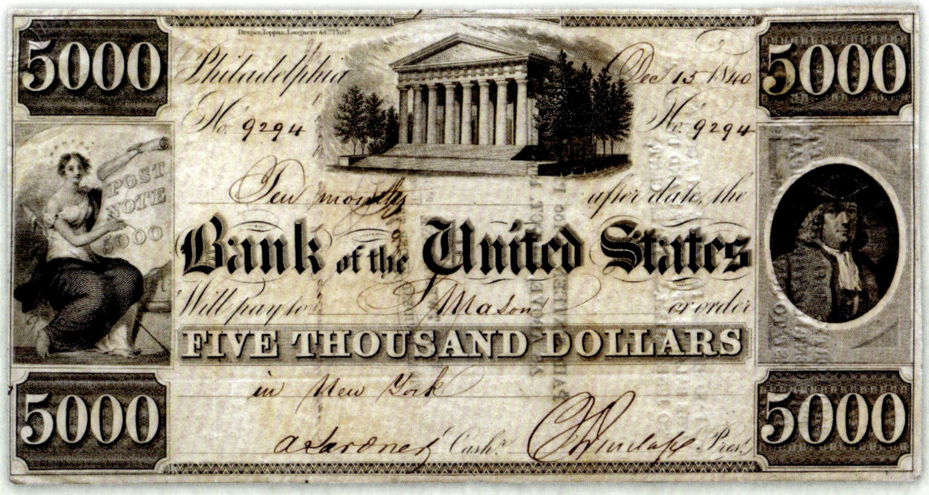

A $5,000 note issued by Nicholas Biddle's Bank of the United States of Pennsylvania, with "of Pennsylvania" omitted and showing the former home of the Bank of the United States, with which this new bank had no connection! The bank collapsed and Biddle later died in disgrace.

On June 12, 1841, an act calling for a fiscal bank of the United States was introduced in the Senate and was passed by both houses, but it was vetoed by President Tyler. His entire cabinet, with the exception of Secretary of State Daniel Webster, resigned in protest over the president's action.[2] The idea of satirizing or popularizing such actions on copper cent-sized tokens had long since passed. On December 21, 1841, Walter Forward, secretary of the Treasury, successor in the post to Thomas Ewing (who earlier in the year had succeeded Levi Woodbury, but who resigned on September 11) forwarded his annual Treasury Department statement to Congress.[3] He noted that business conditions were very slow and that there were many problems. Concerning money in circulation, he observed that notes of even the most sound banks were not tradable at par at any distance from where they were issued. He proposed that a federal currency be issued that would be used throughout the Union.

In 1842 problems with specie payment resumption continued in scattered areas, mostly in Pennsylvania and westward, where expansion of settlements continued. The Oregon Trail was mapped by U.S. Army lieutenant John Charles Frémont, age 29, who had eloped the previous year with Jessie Benton, the 16-year-old daughter of Thomas Hart Benton.[4] This survey initiated *Oregon fever*. Hundreds of adventurers and families headed in that direction, later swelling to thousands, usually starting from Independence, Missouri.

In Massachusetts, children *under* the age of 12 were limited to working no more than 10 hours per day, but there were no such restrictions on anyone older. Connecticut established the first system of public education in the United States. Elsewhere, few children, especially those in rural districts, had much in the way of formal education. Children were usually treated as chattel and could be assigned to others for apprenticeships and the like. Phineas T. Barnum, who purchased Scudder's Museum in New York, exhibited "Tom Thumb," a four-year-old midget (real name: Charles Sherwood Stratton), during this era. The recently invented camera caused a sensation on both sides of the Atlantic, and much experimenting was done—amongst other things, it was eventually used to record the depressing conditions of child laborers.

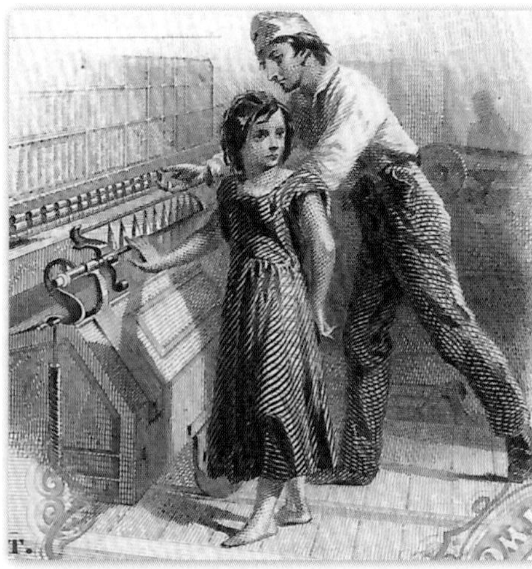

Children formed a large part of the labor force tending looms in textile mills in the 1840s. Often they worked ten hours a day. This vignette was used on a bank note. Public outcry against child labor did not gain much momentum until the early 20th century.

End of the Hard Times Era

John Quincy Adams, erstwhile president preceding Jackson, was back in Congress in 1843 and stated in an address to the House of Representatives, "If slavery must go by blood and war, let war come." Abolition remained the most divisive subject of the era. Samuel F.B. Morse received a $30,000 appropriation by Congress to facilitate the construction of an experimental telegraph line between Washington and Baltimore. At the time, news could travel only as fast as the speediest train, with the average of those travelling about 35 to 40 miles per hour.

In 1843 there were 4,442 miles of railroads in the United States, which are said to have cost at least $100,000,000 to build. The economy was in a revival mode, and into the spring of the year there was great optimism in manufacturing, banking, and other areas. The problem of specie payments had been largely resolved, most unsound banks had failed, and the stage was set for expansion. Most historians and economists agree that 1843 marked the end of the Hard Times era. An essay in *Niles' National Register*, August 26, 1843, titled "Business Review," included this:

> The papers of Boston, N. York, N. Orleans, and Philadelphia, as well as those upon all the interior thoroughfares of trade, indicate the gradual revival of trade, restoration of confidence, and the consequent relief of the people generally from a long agony of pecuniary sufferings, such as this country has seldom been subjected to. So prostrate indeed for a time, was every interest, so thoroughly shaken was the whole frame-work of credit, that it required much more than a national confidence —nothing but demonstration long maintained could replace the moneyed institutions of the country in the public estimation, or induce any but the most parsimonious use of the requisite facilities of trade.
>
> The public voice united with, or rather irresistibly controlled, legislation and compelled the country into an actual hard-money attitude. In that position we now are, or rather like the Indian's perpendicular, beyond it. The banks of three of the principal cities of the union, Boston, N.Y. and New Orleans, have now in their vaults in specie, $26,447,960, viz: New York, $12,589,103; Boston, $8,000,000; N. Orleans $5,858,857, vastly exceeding the amount of their circulation. The returns of the whole of the banks of the state of New York show an aggregate of specie in vault exceeding their aggregate circulation. We have no doubt the same in this moment [is] the case with the banks in Maryland and elsewhere also; and though this plethora it was generally supposed would be very transient, yet the time for expected re-action has gone on, and instead of re-action, hard money continues to accumulate notwithstanding the admitted revival of business.
>
> Merchants buy for cash, for the sake of getting the discount, and have to content themselves with that discount as their profit upon their sales. The whole people are learning to do a close business, buy what is actually wanting, and only what they have the means in hand to pay for. And what is the consequence? Most salutary. Business revives upon firm basis. Instead of running into debt, the people are running out of debt, both to Europeans, and to the money lenders of our own country. A wholesome and a comparatively happy condition of affairs is at hand. Stand by this course, maintain the interest of our own laboring men, and all will be well. . . .

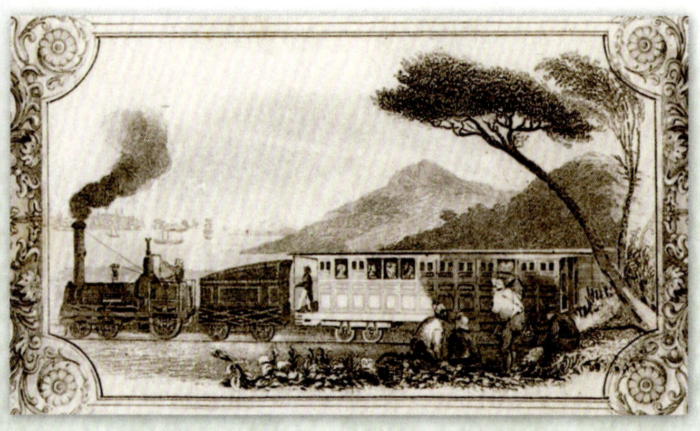

Railroads continued to be the primary growth business in America in 1844, just as they had been in 1832. This vignette is from a $100 note of the North River Banking Co., New York City, in the early 1840s.

On July 23, 1844, Chief Engraver Christian Gobrecht, primary designer of the Liberty Seated coins, died. While in office, Gobrecht did his work quietly and competently. He was succeeded on September 6, 1844, by James Barton Longacre, an accomplished engraver of illustration plates, including 24 published in the highly successful three-volume (or four in another edition) *The National Portrait Gallery of Distinguished Americans.* Longacre would serve until his death on January 1, 1869, and create many memorable coin designs.

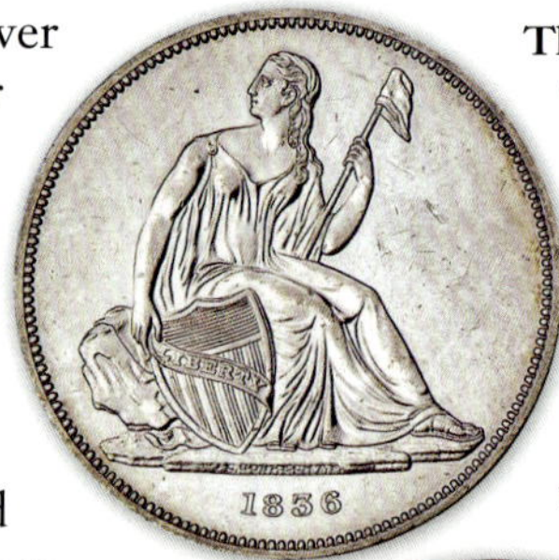

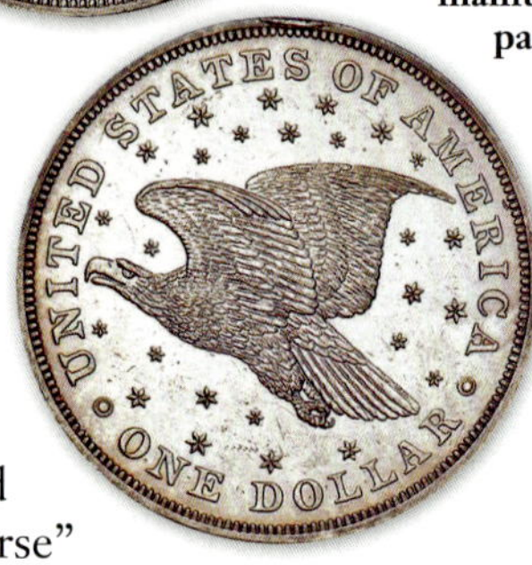

The Liberty Seated silver dollar of 1836, Christian Gobrecht's first major project when he was hired as an assistant engraver. After the death of Chief Engraver William Kneass in 1840, Gobrecht was appointed to that position, which he maintained until his passing in 1844.

In 1844 James Knox Polk, a relatively unknown figure, was nominated for the presidency by the Democrats, who were deadlocked in convention. Polk became the first "dark horse" candidate to run in a national election, which he did successfully, besting Henry Clay by 170 electoral votes to 105. The many tokens and medalets of the campaign were not noticed by Lyman H. Low in *Hard Times Tokens.* In Batavia, New York, J. Cochran, a bell founder, struck Liberty Head copper cent-size tokens, bringing down the curtain on the Hard Times era as defined by Low.

9

Jackson Tokens of 1832 and 1833

1832 and 1833

The Jackson tokens of the early Hard Times era have been numismatically famous for many years. In 1862's *An Arrangement of The Medals and Tokens Struck in Honor of the Presidents of the United States and of the Presidential Candidates From the Administration of John Adams to That of Abraham Lincoln, Inclusive*, Alfred H. Satterlee listed the Jackson tokens described below, but by types, not by die varieties. This was used as a standard reference for years later, supplementing Charles I. Bushnell's study of early store cards. Satterlee gave no narrative or historical notes.

The first tokens in the series have attracted particular attention over the years. Low described just one pair of dies. Carl Wurtzbach in "New Varieties of Hard Times Tokens," *The Numismatist*, March 1910, described, but did not illustrate, a second obverse variety. Later he described and illustrated all three. In the catalog of New Netherlands Coin Company's Sale No. 45, April 22, 1955, photographs of all three obverses caused a lot of excitement among those not familiar with Wurtzbach's efforts. The dies were by Wright & Bale, active from 1829 to 1833, and were probably made for the 1832 presidential campaign or in celebration of Jackson's subsequent victory. Typical examples are Fine to Extremely Fine, with some higher and lower. Some are holed.

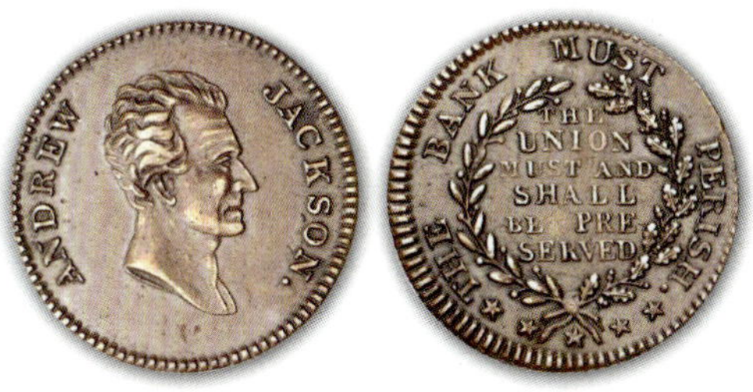

W-09-10a • Jackson Small Head • Low-1; HT-1. R-6. 27 mm. Copper. Diagonally reeded edge. This is the so-called "Small Head" variety as distinguished from the Scowling Head and the Aged Head issues. It is characterized by the first, third and fourth locks at the top of the head turning down and the mouth being equidistant between the nostril and the point of the chin. Elemental analysis of some shows slightly metallic variation, such as a trace of zinc, but all appear as copper. Ford (Stack's 2004) EF $10,350. Dice-Hicks (Stack's

2008) AU $14,950. Americana Sale (SBG 2010) AU-58 $10,350.

W-09-10b • Jackson • Low-166; HT-1A. High R-7. 27 mm. Brass. Low, who did not designate portrait differences, stated for Low-1: "Satterlee quotes it in brass in addition to copper and white metal, but I have never met with such or learned of it elsewhere." In the 1906 supplement he designated this as Low-166. In 2014 Robert A. Schuman reported that it was still unconfirmed. This reverse die was used with three obverses. The central description is from Jackson's 1830 Jefferson Day toast with John C. Calhoun present. Ford (Stack's 2004) Fine plus $4,600.

W-09-10f • Jackson • Low-167; HT-3A. Unverified. 27 mm. Silver. Low: "Extremely rare." In the 1906 supplement he designated this as Low-167. Probably does not exist. Rulau listed this as R-8 by "default" as he did with many unverified rarities. Neither Robert A. Schuman or H. Joseph Levine have ever heard of one.

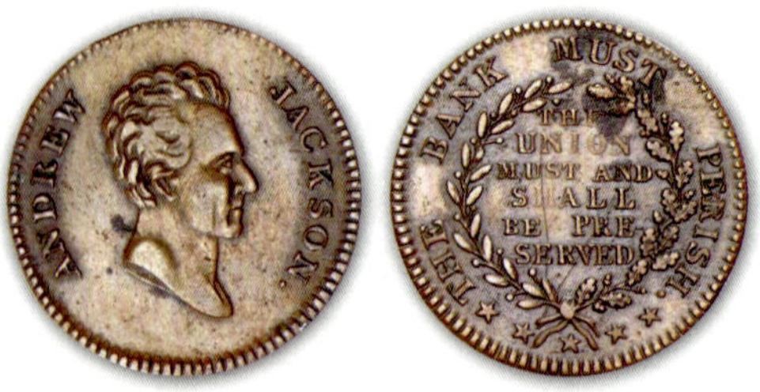

W-09-15a • Jackson Scowling Head • Low-1A; HT-2. R-8. 27 mm. Copper. Diagonally reeded edge. Three known. Ford (Stack's 2004) Choice VF $9,775 (later in Hayden's 2005 sale $13,750).

W-09-15e • Jackson Scowling Head • Low-165; HT-2A. R-7. 27 mm. White metal. Five known. One is slightly broadstruck and is of larger diameter than others in the series. In his 1906 supplement Low designated this as No. 165. Ford (Stack's 2004) VF-35 $37,375. Dice-Hicks (Stack's 2008) VF with the planchet cracked $6,000.

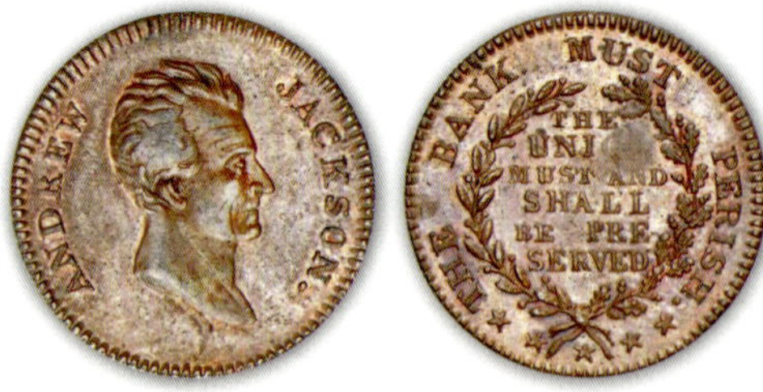

W-09-20a • Jackson Aged Head • Low-1B; HT-3. R-7. 27 mm. Copper. Diagonally reeded edge. All have weakness on the highest part of the portrait and on the corresponding area of the reverse, due to metal flow problems. Presidential Coin and Antique Co.: "Our exhaustive research of 20th century sales featuring Hard Times tokens has located 5 appearances of the Aged Head token and only two appearances of the Scowling head piece." Ford (Stack's 2004) VF-EF $5,175, Choice AU $40,250. Dice-Hicks (Stack's 2008) Choice gray-toned VF $13,800.

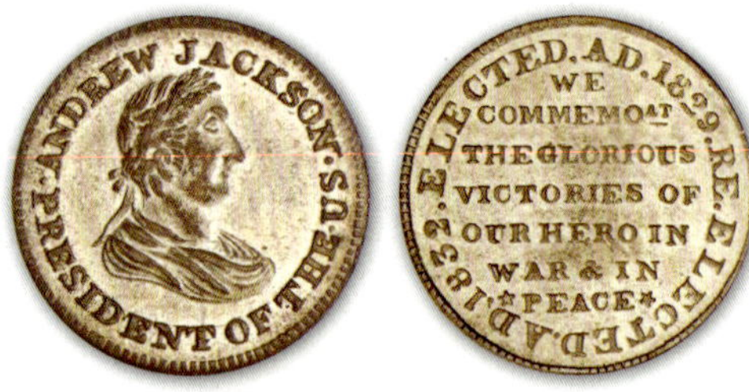

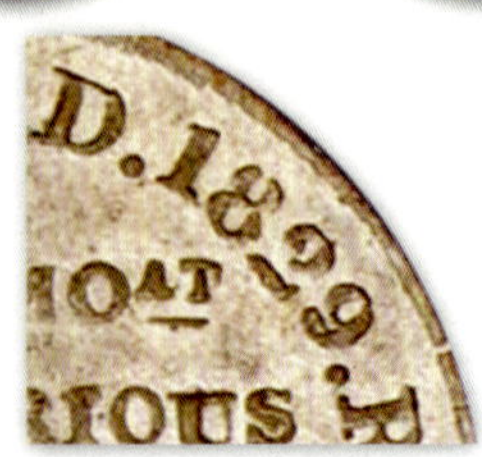

W-09-25b • Jackson in toga • Low-4; HT-6, copper HT-6B. R-2. 27 mm. Brass. Erroneous 1829 date; later corrected to 1828 (see following listings). Found silvered (as illustrated) and unsilvered. Typical grades are VF to AU. HT-6B in copper mentioned by Don Miller is unconfirmed and is probably a discolored brass piece. • VF-20 $250; EF-40 $400; AU-50 $750.

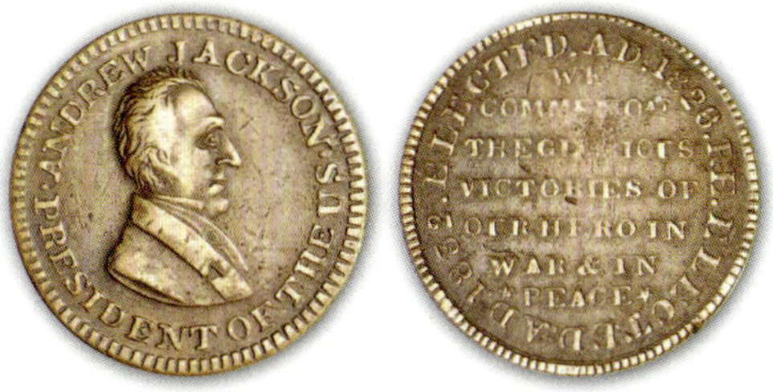

W-09-30b • Jackson in jacket, President of the U.S. • Low-2; HT-4. R-8. 27 mm. Brass. Reverse die corrected from the preceding, now reads 1828. One of the legendary great rarities in the series. The VF discovery example (illustrated) was in the Virgil Brand Collection to F.C.C. Boyd to John J. Ford Jr. and was sold in 2004 to Robert A. Schuman for $83,395. The other is Fine, holed and was sold by Stack's in September 1989 for $17,600.

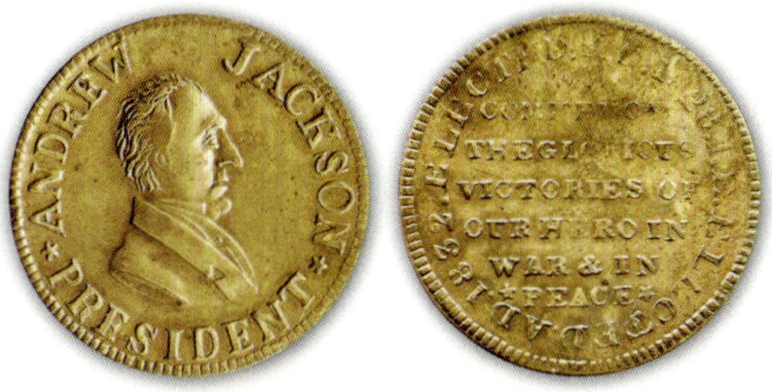

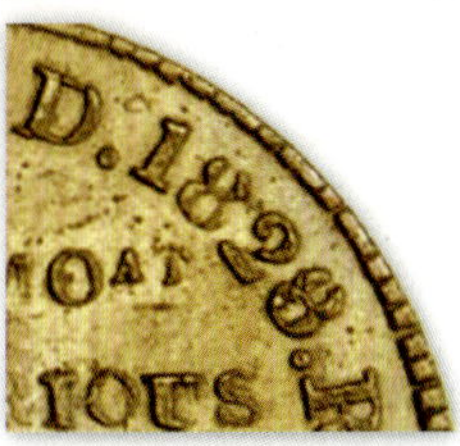

W-09-35b • Jackson in jacket, President • Low-3; HT-5. R-3. 27 mm. Brass. Corrected reverse die as preceding. Examples are easy enough to find. Typical grades range from VF to AU. • VF-20 $250; EF-40 $400; AU-50 $750.

W-09-40b PE • Jackson in uniform 1833, period after N • Low-5; HT-7A. R-9. 26 mm. Brass. Dies by Robert Lovett Sr. Plain edge caused by striking slightly off center. Bowers & Merena November 1997 lot 2016. Robert A. Schuman: "More likely a striking error than a true variety." Frank Ferland owns the clipped planchet token photographed by Edgar H. Adams in the early 20th century.

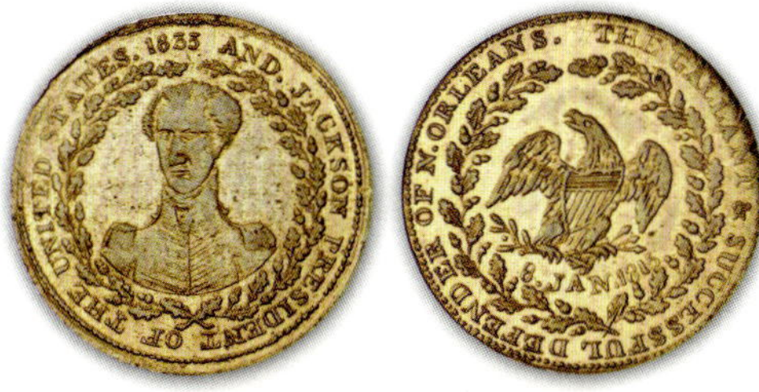

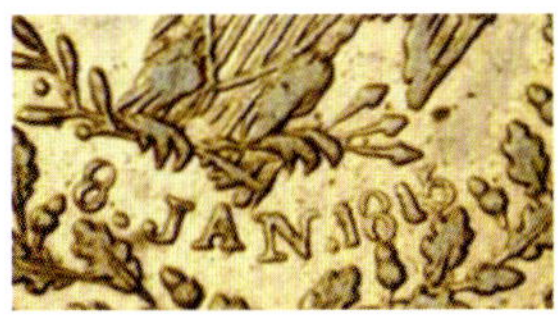

W-09-40b RE • Jackson in uniform 1833, period after N • Low-5; HT-7. R-5. 26 mm. Brass. Reverse with THE GALLANT & SUCCESSFUL DEFENDER OF N. ORLEANS. / 8. JAN. 1815. Diagonal as well as vertical edge reeding. The reeding is sometimes faintly defined. VF and EF are typical grades. Usually with some areas of light striking. • Fine-12 $150; VF-20 $350; EF-40 $700; AU-50 $1,000.

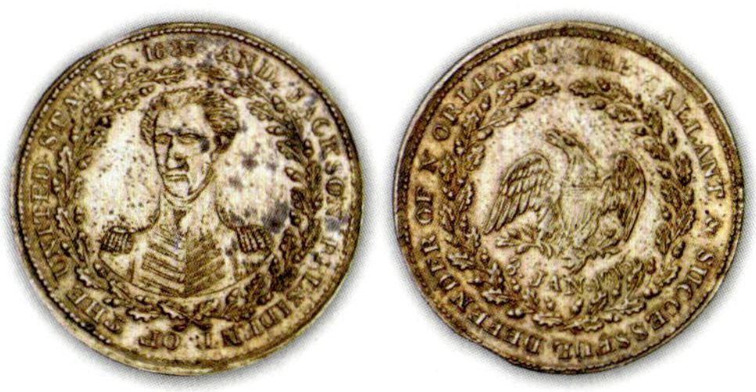

W-09-45b RE • Jackson in uniform 1833, no period after N • Low-5A; HT-8. R-6. 26 mm. Brass. Fine reeding on the edge, sometimes not well struck, giving a "plain edge" appearance. Obverse die as preceding. Reverse with no period after N in "N ORLEANS." Eagle with slightly smaller shield than on the foregoing. Dies by Robert Lovett Sr. Fine to EF are typical grades. Usually with some areas of light striking. • Fine-12 $175; VF-20 $400; EF-40 $800; AU-50 $1,250.

10

Political Tokens of 1834 to 1836

Whig Victory Tokens

The state and regional elections of 1834 resulted in many victories for the new Whig party, particularly in the East. This gave rise to the hope that the party would gain strength and place their candidate in the White House in 1836. To observe and further this enthusiasm, various tokens were issued with political inscriptions.

W-10-10b PE • Ship / Whigs of N. York • Low-6; HT-14A. R-5. 25 mm. Brass. Plain edge. Dies by George Lovett Sr. Obverse with FOR THE CONSTITUTION HURRA. Reverse with inscription FLOURISH COMMERCE, FLOURISH INDUSTRY around with center celebrating the GLORIOUS Whig victory at the three-day elections of New York, April 8 to 10, 1834 (*les trois jours*—seemingly an allusion to three memorable days in the French Revolution). The newly named Whig party envisioned this as the first step to a nationwide movement to counter the policies of Andrew Jackson. Usually seen in worn grades. See the following illustration for die characteristics.

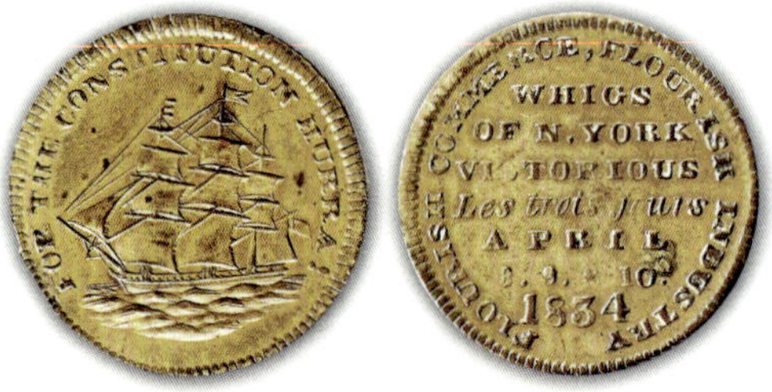

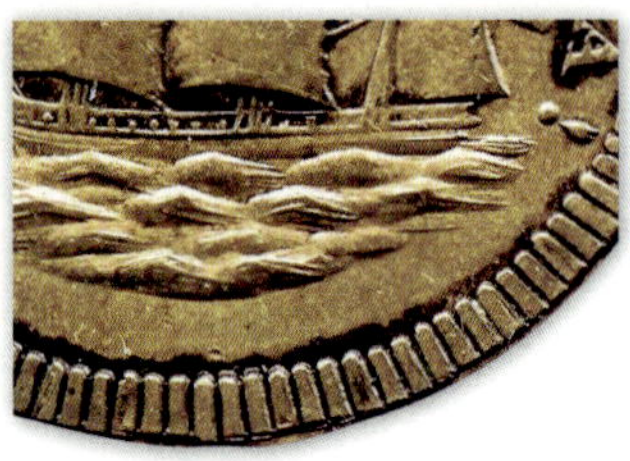

W-10-10b RE • Ship / Whigs of N. York • Low-6; HT-14. R-5. 25 mm. Brass. Diagonally reeded edge. Seen more often than the preceding. Usually found in worn grades. Detail view is from an example struck off center showing details of the irregular dentils in the die. • VF-20 $350; EF-40 $550; AU-50 $900.

W-10-10f RE • Dies as preceding • Rulau: "Low-6C"; HT-14C. R-8. 27 mm. Silver. Three known: One struck over an 1833, Capped Bust, quarter dollar, reeded edge from the quarter dollar, Tanenbaum Collection; overstrike on a quarter, Robert A. Schuman Collection; Fine, holed, ANS. HT-014C: Ford (Stack's 2004) Gem Unc $17,250.

W-10-10j RE • Dies as preceding • Rulau: "Low 6B"; HT-14B. R-9. 25 mm. German silver. Reeded edge. Unique. John J. Ford, Jr. Collection, with planchet damage.

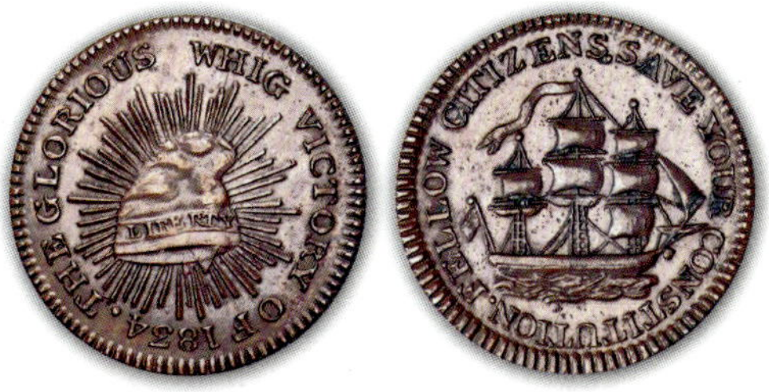

W-10-20a RE • Glorious Whig Victory, two long rays below H (WHIG) / Ship • Low-7; HT-15. R-6. 27 mm. Copper. Reeded edge. Obverse with Liberty cap surrounded with a glory of rays, THE GLORIOUS WHIG VICTORY OF 1834 around the border. (This motif was used by Christian Gobrecht in 1836 to make medals and pattern gold dollars.) "On copper examples, there is a long ray which points to the right upright of the U in GLORIOUS and a short ray which points to the center of the S. The ray that follows is slightly shorter and points to the space beyond the S. Additionally, there is a long ray which points to the right upright of the H in WHIG" (Presidential Coin and Antique Co.). Reverse with sailing ship and FELLOW CITIZENS, SAVE YOUR CONSTITUTION. Another token celebrating the Whig victories in certain Eastern elections in early 1834. Rulau mentions HT-15C, a late die state. Typical grades are VF to AU. • VF-20 $1,750; EF-40 $2,500; AU-50 $4,000.

W-10-30b PE • Glorious Whig Victory, different die / Ship • Low description ambiguous; HT-15E. R-8. 27 mm. Brass. Plain edge. Different obverse die from the preceding, same reverse die. "On the brass specimen there is again a long ray which points to the right upright of the U, but the ray that follows is of equal length and points to the center of the S. Additionally, there is a long ray which points slightly to the right of the right upright in the H of WHIG" (Presidential Coin and Antique Co.).

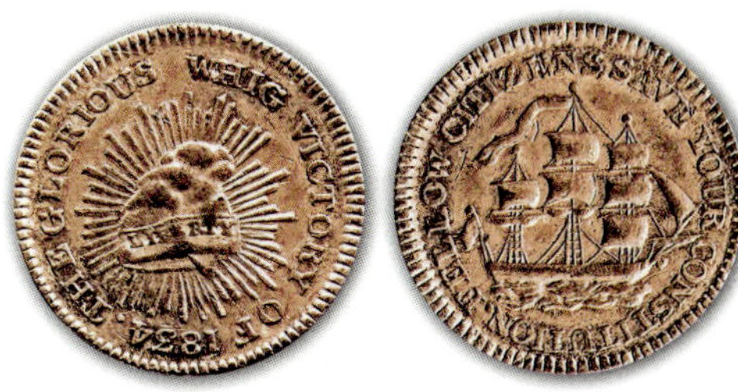

W-10-30e RE • Third obverse die / Ship • Low-7D; HT-15D. R-7. 27 mm. White metal. Reeded edge. "On white metal examples, there is also a long ray which points to the right upright of the U, but there follows two shorter rays which both point to areas under the S. Additionally, the long ray which points to the H in WHIG, points to the center of the H" (Presidential Coin and Antique Co.). Typical grades are EF and AU. Ford (Stack's 2004) Choice AU $8,338. Dice-Hicks (Stack's 2008) Unc $11,500. Hayden (2008) AU with stains $6,600.

1834 Seward and Verplanck Tokens

The New York State elections in 1834 furnished further subjects for several varieties of Hard Times tokens. None are more curious than those depicting William H. Seward and Gulian C. Verplanck. The Whig convention to nominate candidates for state governor and lieutenant governor opened in Utica on September 10. In the several preceding months there was speculation as to who would be chosen. During this time brass tokens were issued depicting William H. Seward and Gulian C. Verplanck.

When final balloting took place in Utica, Seward was the landslide winner with 119 delegate votes, trailed at a long distance by one for James Kent, one for Peter R. Livingston, and one for Verplanck. In November, Seward lost to the incumbent, Governor William L. Marcy, a Democrat and staunch supporter of Jackson.

WILLIAM H. SEWARD

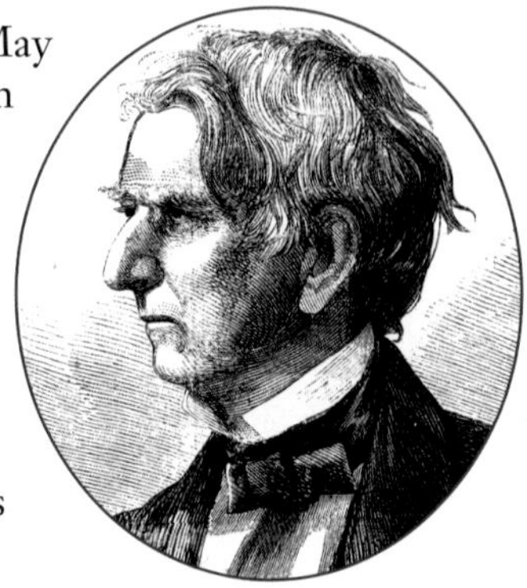

William H. Seward.

William H. Seward was born in Florida, New York, on May 16, 1801. He received his advanced education at Union College, studied law, and at age 21 was admitted to the bar. He became well known for his prowess in criminal cases. In 1830 he was elected to the New York Senate, where he took a stand in favor of the Bank of the United States during the great debate of the era. Cast as anti-Jackson he was a contender for the governor of New York in 1834 and handily took the Whig nomination, but failed in the November election. His Hard Times tokens memorialize that hope.

He tried again, and in 1838, as the Whig candidate, he won the governorship by a respectable majority of 10,000 votes. He served two terms, failed in his bid for a third, and returned to his law practice until the late 1840s. He reentered politics and spent the rest of his life in public service. In 1860 he was a contender for the Republican candidate for president, as was Salmon P. Chase. Lincoln was selected and later placed both men in his Cabinet, Seward as secretary of state, one of the most powerful positions. Among his accomplishments was persuading Great Britain, the largest export customer for Southern cotton, to remain neutral during the American Civil War and not side with the Confederacy.

He continued as secretary of state under President Andrew Johnson. In 1867 he negotiated the purchase of Alaska from Russia for $7,200,000, which his opponents called "Seward's Folly." He died in Auburn, New York, on October 10, 1872. His memory is still honored in that city.

W-10-110b • Seward (GOVnr at lower left) / Our Country die state 1 • Low-169; HT-29. High R-7 or R-8. 28 mm. Brass. (Also HT-29A; 27 mm; R-7.) Obverse with portrait of Seward facing left. WILLIAM. H. SEWARD. above; OUR NEXT GOVnr below, words inverted. Reverse with eagle, olive branch, and arrows, well detailed in the die. A FAITHFUL FRIEND. above; TO OUR COUNTRY. below. A distinctive die with FU (FAITHFUL) touching at the top, F RI E spacing in FRIEND, and other characteristics. The dentils are light in the die. This is the earliest state of the die later reworked. This is a muling of the obverse of Low-15 and the reverse of Low-16 (Verplanck token). Robert A. Schuman registers three examples: (1) EF, discovery piece, Lyman Low of March 1905, which may have inspired Low to add this variety in his 1906 supplement, but with a wildly low estimate of rarity; (2) AU, burnished, ex New Netherlands 43rd Sale 44 (1954) as EF, Gilbert Steinberg Sale I (Stack's 1989); (3) F-15, holed and plugged, Donald M. Miller Collection, Donald G. Partrick Collection.

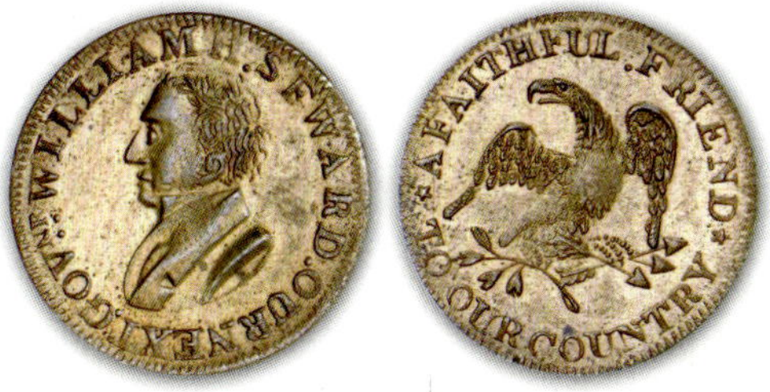

W-10-112b • Seward (GOVnr at lower left) / Our Country die state 2 • Low-15; HT-28. R-3. 27 mm. Brass. Plain edge. (Also HT-29; brass; 28 mm; R-7.) Obverse as preceding. Reverse Our Country die state 2. The preceding die was relapped or ground down slightly, removing certain of the lower-relief features including the period after COUNTRY. The leaves in the olive branch were reworked after relapping. The dentils were redone and are now bold. Typical grades are VF to AU, but scattered Mint State examples exist. • VF-20 $200; EF-40 $400; AU-50 $750; MS-63 $1,500.

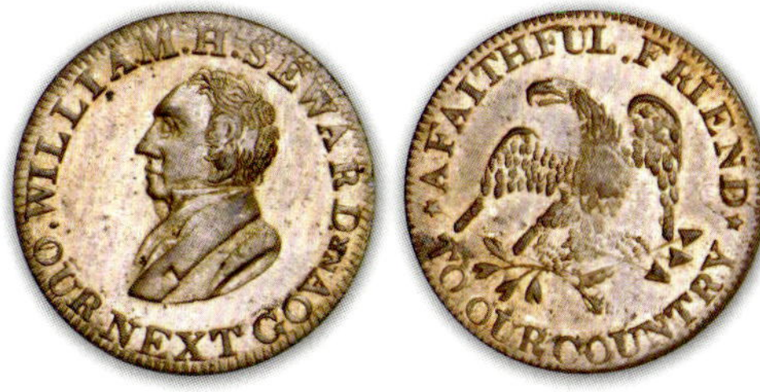

W-10-120b • Seward (GOVnr at lower right) / Our Country die state 3 • Low-13; HT-26. R-4. 27 mm. Brass. Plain edge. Usually seen unsilvered, but occasionally seen with silvering. Obverse with portrait, WILLIAM. H. SEWARD / OUR NEXT GOVnr [words oriented vertically]. The V in GOVnr is an inverted A complete with crossbar. Reverse Our Country die state 3 as described above. Typical grades are VF to AU, but scattered Mint State examples exist. • VF-20 $350; EF-40 $550; AU-50 $850; MS-63 $1,500.

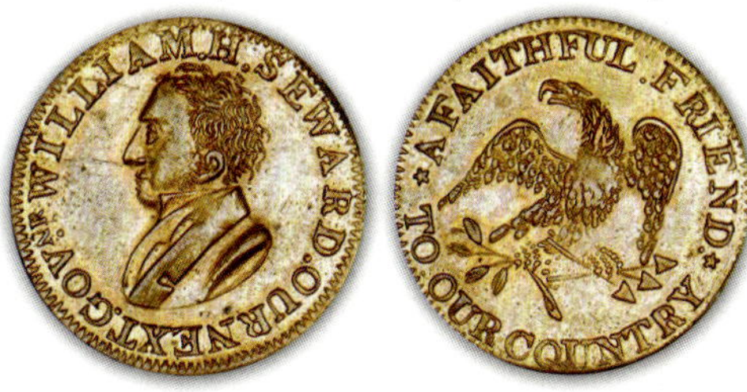

W-10-114b • Seward (GOVnr at lower left) / Our Country die state 3 • Low-15a or 169a; HT-29A. R-7. 27 mm. Brass. Plain edge. The reverse die was later relapped again, removing many details of the lower part of the eagle (definitive) and necessitating some slight reworking of the olive leaves. This is not on a small planchet as erroneously stated in the Dice-Hicks catalog. Dice-Hicks token illustrated. Hayden (2008) VF-30 $2,365.

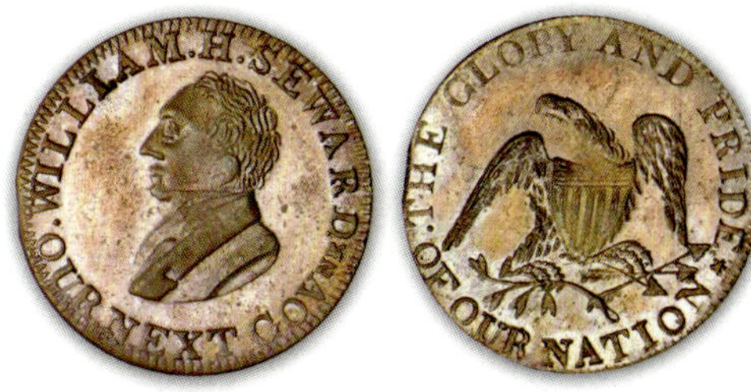

W-10-130b • Seward (GOVnr at lower right) / Our Nation • Low-14; HT-27. R-5. 27 mm. Brass. Plain edge. Found silvered (the majority) and unsilvered. Silvered is illustrated. Obverse die as preceding. Reverse with eagle with shield on its breast, olive branch, and arrows surrounded by THE GLORY AND PRIDE / OF OUR NATION. Typical grades are VF to AU, but scattered Mint State examples exist. • VF-20 $350; EF-40 $600; AU-50 $1,000; MS-63 $2,000.

Gulian C. Verplanck

Gulian Crommelin Verplanck was born in New York City on August 6, 1786, the son of Congressman Daniel C. Verplanck. He grew up in comfortable surroundings, with amenities of culture and education. He graduated from Columbia College in 1801, went on to study law, and, in 1807, was admitted to the bar. From 1820 to 1823 he was a member of the New York State Assembly.

During the 1830s he taught at the General Theological Seminary in New York City and was prominent in various civic and social circles, viewed as a man of letters and with a wide knowledge on many subjects. He was named as a regent of the University of the State of New York in 1826, and in 1858 he became vice chancellor there, a post he held for the rest of his life.

He was elected to Congress as a Democrat and served multiple consecutive terms from March 4, 1825, to March 3, 1833. He joined the rising group that became known as the Whig Party. In 1834 he was a candidate for the mayor of New York City and lost by a narrow margin, after which he sought but did not win the nomination for the governorship of the state, the occasion for the tokens issued with his name.

From 1838 to 1841 he was a state senator. In 1840 he supported Whig candidate William Henry Harrison, who bested the reelection effort of Martin Van Buren. Later, Verplanck went back to the Democratic Party. He held many civic offices in later life and was prominent in literary circles as an author of criticism, particularly for his condemnation of Washington Irving's humorous *Knickerbocker's History of New York*, told by the fictional Diedrich Knickerbocker. In 1846 his annotation of Shakespeare's works was well reviewed. Many other works could be mentioned.

Gulian C. Verplanck died at home in New York City on March 18, 1870. It can be said of him that he was well known there, but an unfamiliar name anywhere else—except among the literati!

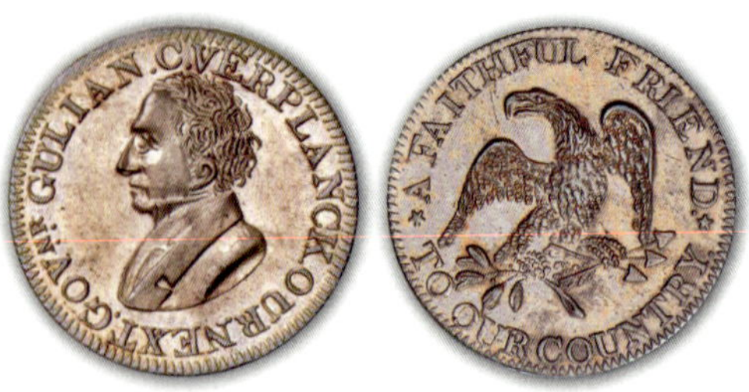

W-10-160b • Verplanck / Our Country die state 1 • Low-16; HT-30. R-2. 27 mm. Brass. Plain edge. (Also silvered brass; HT-30B; R-4). Obverse with portrait of *Seward*, GULIAN. C. VERPLANCK / OUR NEXT GOVnr [words inverted]. Reverse with Our Country die state 1 as described under W-10-110b. Russell Rulau gives a listing in copper and cites as his source the Mehl's 1941 Dunham catalog, considered unreliable in many aspects today; no copper striking has ever been verified. Typical grades are VF to AU, but scattered Mint State examples exist. • VF-20 $125; EF-40 $225; AU-50 $350; MS-63 $700.

It seems that the engraver had no likeness of Verplanck, so he used Seward's portrait on both! In an era before prints were widely used in newspapers, many recipients of the tokens probably didn't know the difference.

As Verplanck's fame as a Whig political candidate was fleeting, while that of Seward endured, his tokens were issued for just a short time, while Seward's were made in several varieties and for a longer time.

Low quoted a contemporary comment on the token from the *New York Times*, May 2, 1835:

> A few brief years will pass away, and with them almost every trace of the existence of the Whig party. That party, however, in the pride of its power and confidence of its success, adopted the same plan for perpetuating its name that has been adopted by kings and princes. The story of their accession and their continuance in power is told by the coins and medals circulated during their reigns. . . .
>
> We have in our possession a coin of the grand Whig emission of 1834. On

one side is an eagle, surrounded by the words "a faithful friend to our country," and on the other, an image surrounded by the words "Gulian C. Verplanck, our next Governor." It is made—most appropriately—of brass, symbolical of the modesty of the party by which it was issued. What a treasure will such a coin be to the antiquary a hundred years hence!—How will he pore over its image and superscription, and puzzle himself with most learned doubts as to its history and character!—At what epoch of the republic was it issued? What great event was it intended to commemorate, and who was the great man whose name, otherwise unrecorded—it has preserved for a hundred years? It speaks of Gulian C. Verplanck, "our next governor." He was probably the governor-elect. The people had chosen him, but he had not yet entered upon the duties of his office. . . .

Why should a coin be struck off with his name and head on it? In all other countries it is the possessor and not the heir to the throne whose effigy is stamped on the coin of the value [? realm]. In looking over the almost interminable list of governors of the different States, the name of Gulian C. Verplanck cannot be found. . . .

Most unfortunately, the coin bears no date, and for aught that appears to the contrary, it might have been issued anterior to the revolution. You cannot refer it to contemporary history, for the simple reason that you have no means of judging when it was issued. . . .

It is valuable because it is rare, and because from its most incomprehensible character, it will constantly call forth the discussions of antiquaries and virtuosi. It may be that in the wreck of matter of a hundred years, a few files of very old newspapers may survive. Possibly the very paper containing this article may chance to have a better fate than its brethren and furnish an addition to some collection of old and perhaps good for nothing trumpery.—Here then will be a key to unlock the mystery, and the *quid nuncs* of a hundred years hence will learn that in 1834, there flourished a mighty party called the great universal Whig party of the world, a party which lived and flourished on anticipation—celebrated victories which were to be won, but never were won, rejoiced over successes, which like the waters near the lips of Tantalus, were ever at hand but never reached; and struck medals in honor of governors who were never elected. . . .

We will mention by way of conclusion that the Verplanck Coinage of 1834 is becoming scarce. The pieces are at a premium, even now, the knowing ones among the Whigs having called in all they could possibly command.

1834 Running Boar Tokens

The inscription, "My third heat" probably refers to Jackson's third try at the presidency in 1832, having failed in 1824 and succeeded in 1828. "My victory" and "Down with the bank" refers to Jackson's achieving his goal of vanquishing the Bank of the United States.

"My substitute for the U.S bank" and "My experiment, my currency, my glory," are mockery of the not-so-successful experiment and his glory, sentiments negated by the obverse inscriptions.

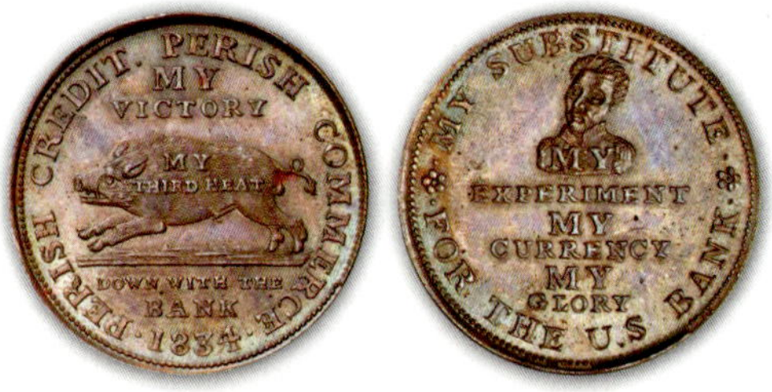

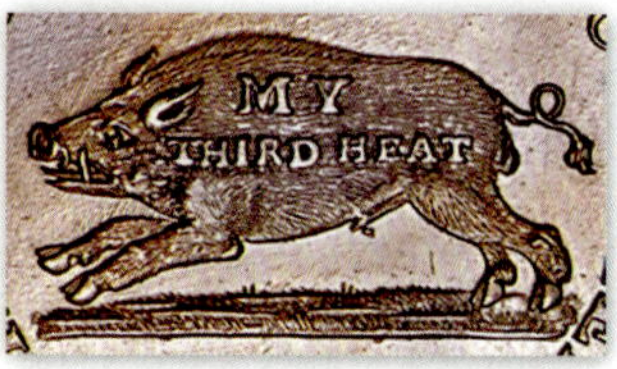

W-10-210a • Running Boar die 1 / Jackson Portrait die 1 • Low-8; HT-9. R-1. 28.5 mm. Copper. Thick, rounded plain edge. Obverse Running Boar die 1 with boar running left, *nose pointing directly at C,* MY / THIRD HEAT on his flank; MY VICTORY above; DOWN WITH THE / BANK below; PERISH CREDIT. PERISH COMMERCE 1834 around. Reverse Jackson Portrait die 1 with small portrait of Jackson above, *narrow* shoulders, MY lettered on portrait; EXPERIMENT / MY / CURRENCY / MY / GLORY below; around the border MY SUBSTITUTE / FOR THE U.S [no period] BANK. Easily available in grades from EF to Mint State. • VF-20 $30; EF-40 $60; AU-50 $100; MS-63 $300.

W-10-210b • Dies as preceding • Low-9; HT-10. R-2. 28.5 mm. Brass. Plain edge; thin, flat planchet. (Often seen silvered, HT-10A, R-3.) Easily available in grades from EF to Mint State. • VF-20 $75; EF-40 $150; AU-50 $250; MS-63 $500.

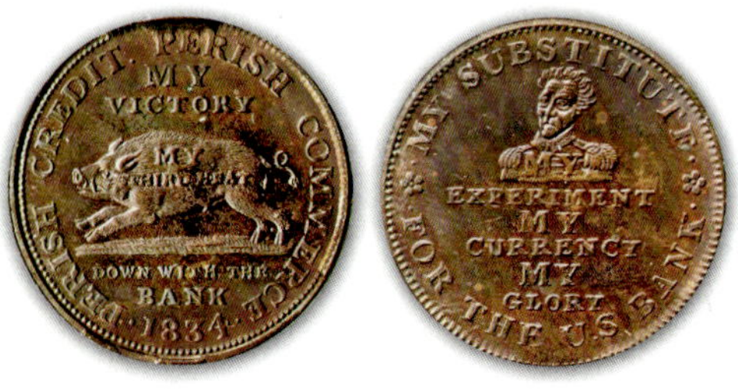

W-10-220a • Running Boar die 1 / Jackson Portrait die 2 • Low-168; HT-13. R-7. 28.5 mm. Copper. Thick, rounded plain edge. Four known. Ford 2004 EF burnished with pin pricks $16,100; resold in Dice-Hicks 2008 for $10,100. Obverse Running Boar die 1. Reverse Jackson Portrait die 2 with small portrait of Jackson above, *wide* shoulders, MY lettered on portrait; EXPERIMENT / MY / CURRENCY / MY / GLORY below; around the border MY SUBSTITUTE / FOR THE U.S [no period] BANK. Illustrated piece demonstrates a large and previously unrecorded cud die break from the tops of PER (PERISH) to the rim at 12 o'clock; this may have been a fatal break leading to the destruction of the die and the rarity of the tokens struck. This is Mint State, the finest known, ex Steve Tanenbaum, now in the Robert A. Schuman Collection.

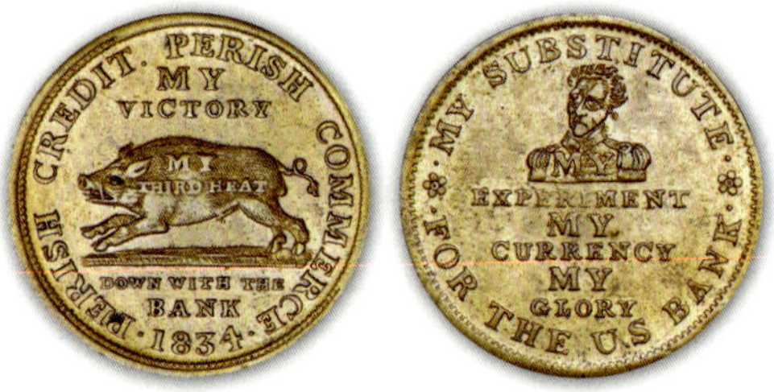

W-10-220b • Dies as preceding • Low-11; HT-12. R-5. 28.5 mm. Brass. Plain edge; thin, flat planchet. Often seen silvered. Typical grades are VF to AU. • VF-20 $400; EF-40 $650; AU-50 $1,000.

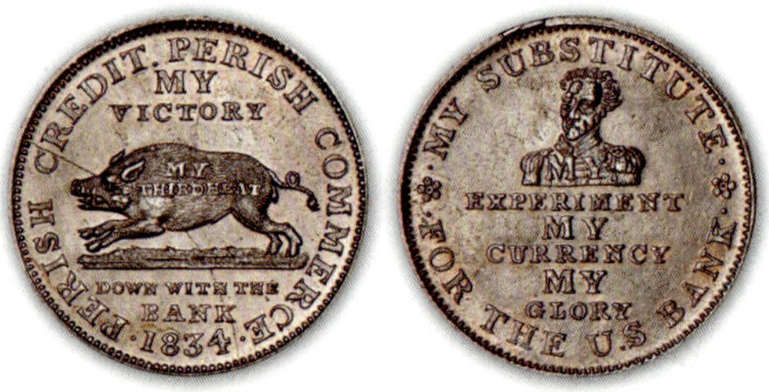

W-10-230a • Running Boar die 2 / Jackson Portrait die 2 • Low-10; HT-11. R-2. 28.5 mm. Copper. Plain edge. Obverse Running Boar die 2 with boar running left, *nose pointing between H and C,* MY / THIRD HEAT on his flank; MY VICTORY above; DOWN WITH THE / BANK below;

PERISH CREDIT. PERISH COMMERCE 1834 around. Reverse Jackson Portrait die 2. Exists with a perfect die and for many strikings with a crack on the obverse from the border at left between C and R, though the eye and shoulder of the boar, down through H (WITH) and K (BANK) to the border. Most examples seen have this crack, indicating that it occurred at an early time. Other die states exist. Typical grades are EF and AU with Mint State pieces being available but slightly scarce. • VF-20 \$35; EF-40 \$70; AU-50 \$125; MS-63 \$350.

Jackass with LL.D. Tokens 1834–1837

On the first token, the obverse shows Jackson holding a sword in one hand and a purse in another, calling out the warning that the same person should not control the military and the Treasury at the same time. "A plain system void of pomp" is a quotation from his message to the Senate, April 15, 1834, quoted in chapter six.

The reverse, dated 1834, satirizes him as a jackass with LL.D. on its flank, reflecting the derision of his foes when Harvard awarded him an honorary doctorate on June 26, 1833. Former President John Quincy Adams was invited to attend, but stated that "as an affectionate child of our Alma Mater, I would not be present to witness her disgrace in conferring her highest literary honors upon a barbarian who could not write a sentence of grammar and could hardly spell his own name."[1] Adams had long kept a detailed diary, in which numerous notations reflected his contempt of Jackson and his actions.

It also notes that he interpreted the Constitution "as I understand it." Some called Jackson stubborn and obstinate, but an admirer said he had "Roman firmness."

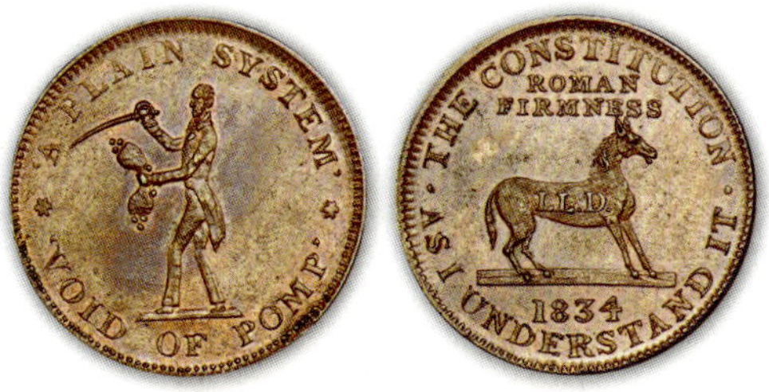

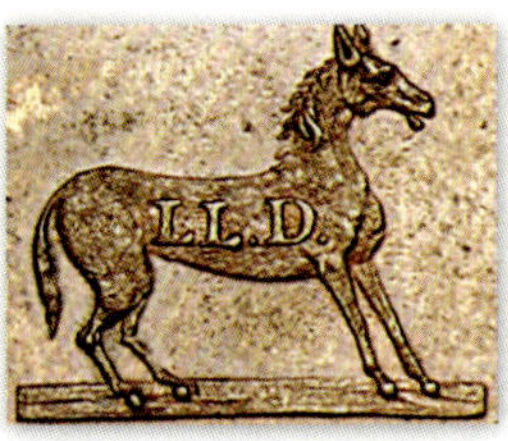

W-10-310a • A Plain System Void of Pomp / 1834 • Low-12; HT-25. R-1. 28.5 mm. Copper. Plain edge. Occasionally seen silvered. Based upon auction appearances this variety is somewhat scarcer than usually listed. Typical grades are VF to AU. • VF-20 \$35; EF-40 \$75; AU-50 \$200.

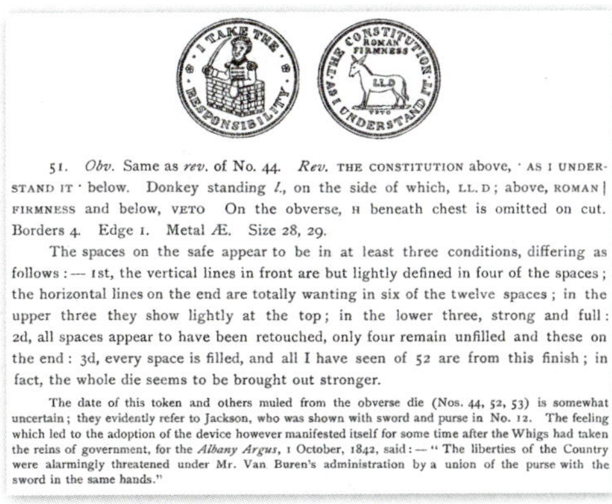

51. *Obv.* Same as *rev.* of No. 44. *Rev.* THE CONSTITUTION above, · AS I UNDERSTAND IT · below. Donkey standing *l.*, on the side of which, LL.D; above, ROMAN | FIRMNESS and below, VETO On the obverse, H beneath chest is omitted on cut. Borders 4. Edge 1. Metal Æ. Size 28, 29.

The spaces on the safe appear to be in at least three conditions, differing as follows: — 1st, the vertical lines in front are but lightly defined in four of the spaces; the horizontal lines on the end are totally wanting in six of the twelve spaces; in the upper three they show lightly at the top; in the lower three, strong and full: 2d, all spaces appear to have been retouched, only four remain unfilled and these on the end: 3d, every space is filled, and all I have seen of 52 are from this finish; in fact, the whole die seems to be brought out stronger.

The date of this token and others muled from the obverse die (Nos. 44, 52, 53) is somewhat uncertain; they evidently refer to Jackson, who was shown with sword and purse in No. 12. The feeling which led to the adoption of the device however manifested itself for some time after the Whigs had taken the reins of government, for the *Albany Argus*, 1 October, 1842, said: — "The liberties of the Country were alarmingly threatened under Mr. Van Buren's administration by a union of the purse with the sword in the same hands."

Low's description of Low-51.

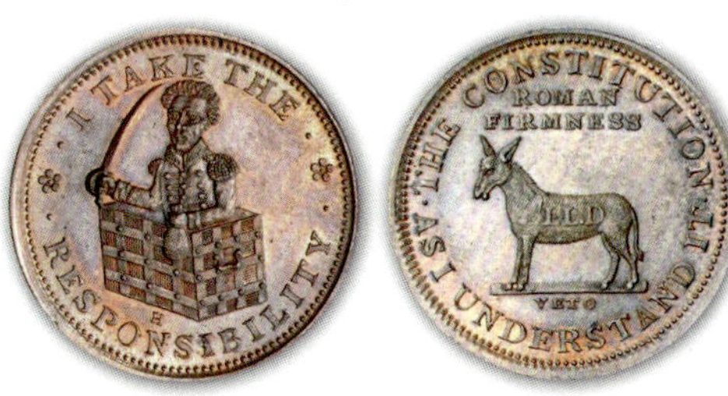

W-10-320a • I Take the Responsibility, H below safe • Low-51; HT-70. R-1. 28.5 mm. Copper. Plain edge. (Also gilt Low-171, HT-70A, R-3.) Reverse die with tip of right ear of jackass to left of F. Three obverse die states exist (see horizontal lines at the end of the safe). Common in AU and lower Mint State grades. • VF-20 $25; EF-40 $40; AU-50 $75; MS-63 $250.

W-10-320b • Dies as preceding • Low-52; HT-71. R-3. 28.5 mm. Brass. Plain edge. AU and lower-range Mint State pieces are about par for auction listings of pieces in fine collections. • VF-20 $70; EF-40 $110; AU-50 $175; MS-63 $400.

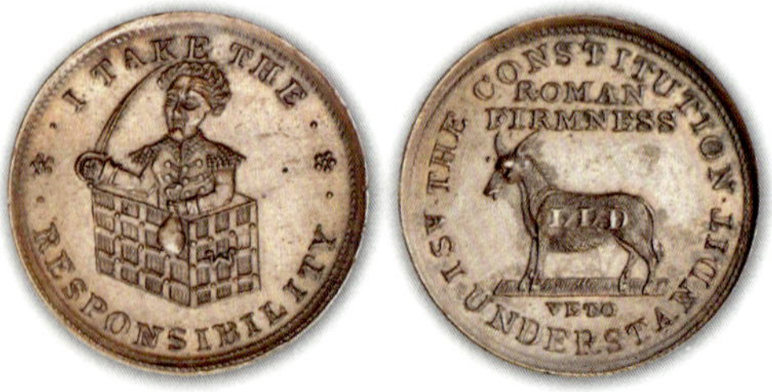

W-10-330a • I Take the Responsibility, no H below safe • Low-53; HT-72. R-2. 28.5 mm. Copper. Plain edge. Reverse from a different die with tip of right ear of jackass under F. The "fat bellied" jackass seen with high raised rims. Most are VF to AU, but Mint State coins are offered regularly. • VF-20 $35; EF-40 $90; AU-50 $225; MS-63 $500.

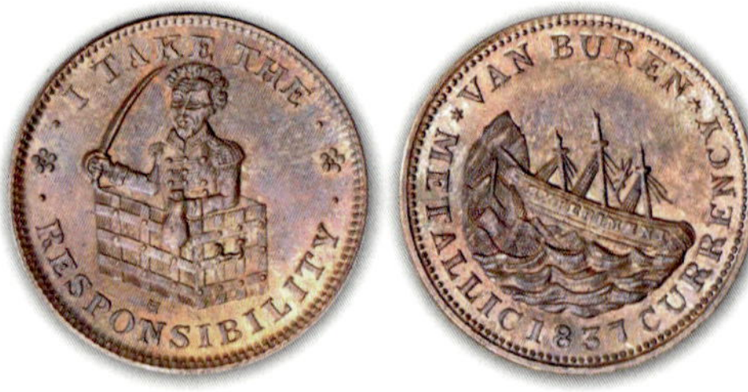

W-10-330a • I Take the Responsibility / 1837 Van Buren • Low-44; HT-69. R-1. 28.5 mm. Copper. Plain edge. Muling of Jackson die with H below safe with 1837 Van Buren die. Struck in 1837 or later. Three obverse die states are described by Low. AU and lower-range Mint State examples are usually found in leading collections. • VF-20 $25; EF-40 $40; AU-50 $75; MS-63 $250.

11

Political Tokens of 1837 and 1838

1837 Liberty Head "Not One Cent" Tokens

This class of tokens has a Liberty Head on the obverse with the date 1837 below. Surrounding are stars. The reverse has MILLIONS FOR DEFENCE and, within a wreath, NOT / ONE / CENT / FOR TRIBUTE. These resulted in allegations of counterfeiting and were likely discontinued by the end of the year. John J. Ford Jr. called tokens with this inscription "neutral specie substitutes."

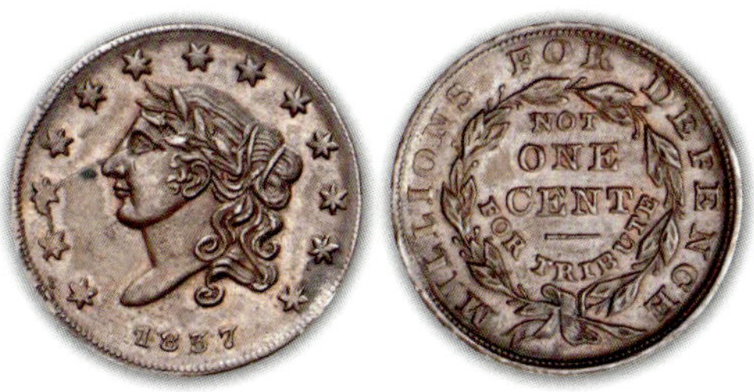

W-11-10a • 1837 13 stars • Low-21; HT-35. R-2. 27.2 mm. Copper. Plain edge. Obverse with distinctive head of Liberty with tiara of olive leaves. Typically seen with a prominent die crack from the bridge of the nose to star 3, to star 2, intermittently to border. Usually with significant wear. These circulated for a long time. VF and EF are typical grades found in advanced collections. • Fine-12 $35; VF-20 $80; EF-40 $250; AU-50 $500.

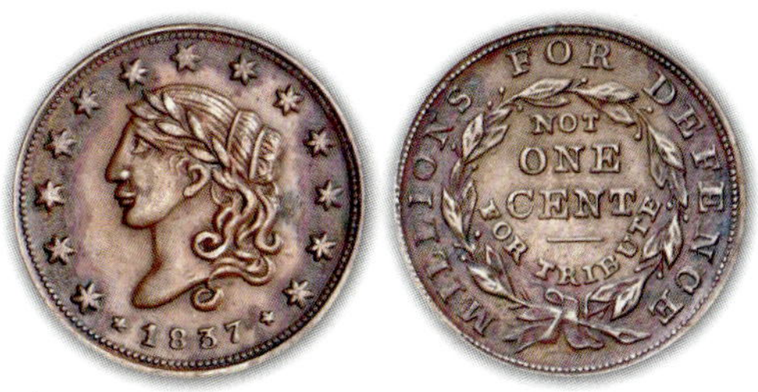

W-11-20a • 1837 15 stars • Low-22; HT-36. R-3. 27.5 mm. Copper. Plain edge. Obverse with tiara of olive leaves. Stars 1 and 15 are tiny. Reverse die as preceding. The Ford and Dice-Hicks tokens were in circulated grades. Most are Fine to VF, with EF being scarce and anything higher, rare. A poster example of a condition rarity. • Fine-12 $50; VF-20 $125; EF-40 $300; AU-50 $650.

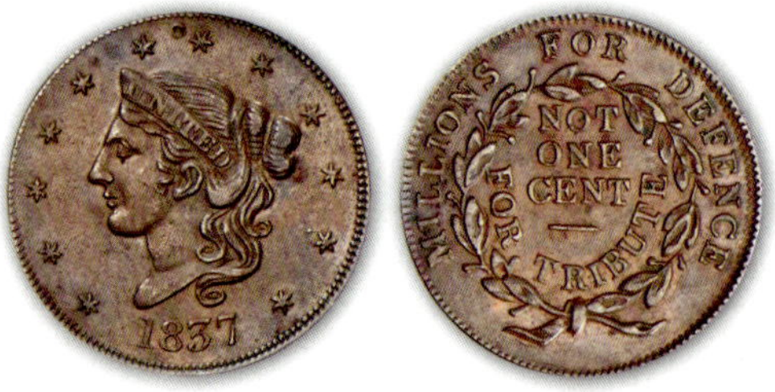

W-11-30a • 1837 12 stars UNITED tiara • Low-23; HT-37. R-4. 27.6 mm. Copper. Plain edge. Seen in worn grades. Obverse with tiara of olive leaves. UNITED is unique in the series. The Ford and Dice-Hicks tokens were in circulated grades. Ford's had an attempted puncture. Fine to VF with the occasional EF is about par for examples in leading collections. This is the scarcest of the tokens of this type, excepting numismatic strikes. • Fine-12 $90; VF-20 $250; EF-40 $550; AU-50 $900.

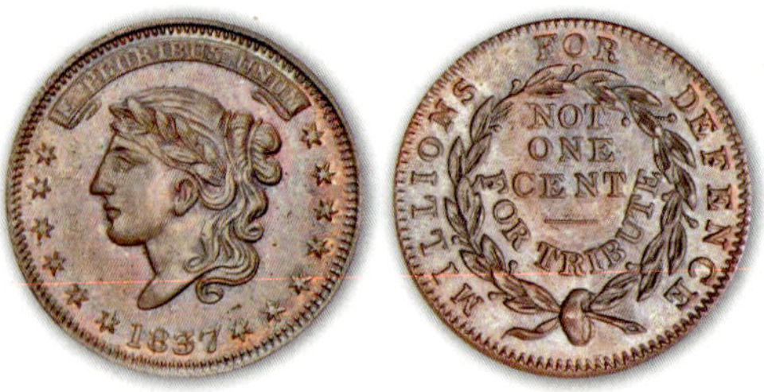

W-11-80a • 1837, stars 6x7, E PLURIBUS UNUM on scroll • Low-28; HT-42. R-1. 28 mm. Copper. Plain edge. Obverse with tiara of olive leaves, plain hair cords, E PLURIBUS UNUM on scroll above, 6 stars left, 7 stars right, medium 1837 date below. Reverse with continuous wreath, with short line below CENT, large space to each side of FOR at top of die; large berry directly below O. T (CENT) touches and slightly overlaps leaf. F (FOR) within wreath touches and slightly overlaps berry. Readily available in high grades. • VF-20 $35; EF-40 $65; AU-50 $110; MS-63 $275.

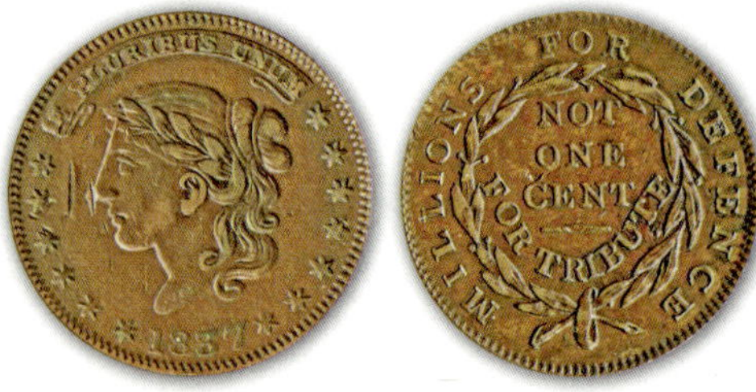

W-11-90a • 1837, stars 6x7, E PLURIBUS UNUM on scroll • Low-170; HT-43. R-8. 27 mm. Copper. Plain edge. Obverse die as preceding. Reverse with continuous wreath, with longer line below CENT, large space to each side of FOR; one berry directly below O. T (CENT) very close to leaf. Within wreath the other F (FOR) very close to berry; 5 berries inside wreath, 5 berries outside wreath. Rulau: Dies by John Gibbs. First published by Lyman Low in March 1905. Three known. Ford's AU sold for $27,000 in 2004.

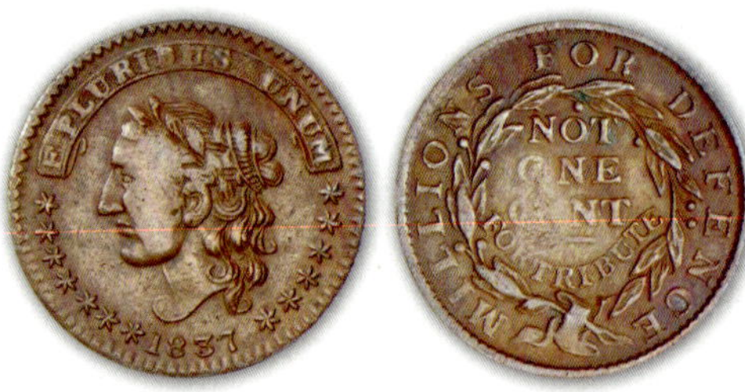

W-11-100a • 1837, stars 7x6, E PLURIBUS UNUM on scroll • Low-29; HT-44. R-3. 28 mm. Copper. Plain edge. Obverse with tiara of olive leaves, plain hair cords, E PLURIBUS UNUM on scroll above, leftmost leaf opposite UR, 7 stars left, 6 stars right, medium to small 1837 date below. Portrait somewhat crudely engraved and in high relief. This die was also used for W-NY-360-10a (Low-112). Reverse with wreath that ends close to ribbon but does not touch, with line below CENT, large space to each side of FOR; no berry directly below O. Two large berries opposite E. T (CENT) close to leaf. Within wreath the other F (FOR) touches edge of leaf. Always weak at the centers due to the high relief of the portrait. Rulau: Dies cut by James G. Moffett. Most grade VF or EF. AU examples are very elusive.

• Fine-12 $35; VF-20 $100; EF-40 $225; AU-50 $650.

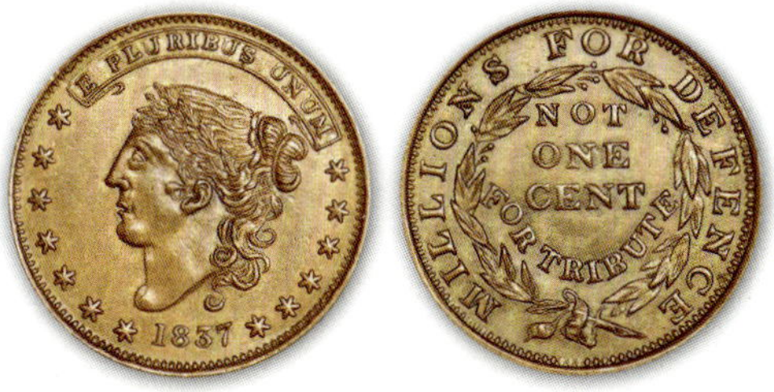

W-11-110a • 1837, stars 7x6, E PLURIBUS UNUM on scroll • Low-30; HT-45. R-2. 28 mm. Copper. Plain edge. Obverse with tiara of olive leaves, plain hair cords, E PLURIBUS UNUM on scroll above, right end of label close to hair bun, leftmost leaf opposite P, 7 stars left, 6 stars right, medium 1837 date below. Reverse with wreath that ends close to ribbon but does not touch, no line below CENT. Three berries on branch below O (FOR at top of die), two with disconnected stems. Inside wreath, F (FOR) touches leaf. Berries in wreath only from ONS FOR DE and not before or after. Seen with very high rims as on Low-65. Readily available in EF and AU grades. Rare in true Mint State. • VF-20 $40; EF-40 $75; AU-50 $200; MS-63 $450.

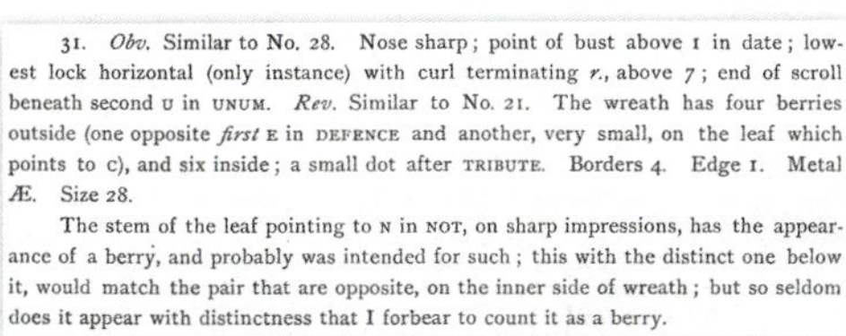

31. *Obv.* Similar to No. 28. Nose sharp; point of bust above 1 in date; lowest lock horizontal (only instance) with curl terminating *r.*, above 7; end of scroll beneath second U in UNUM. *Rev.* Similar to No. 21. The wreath has four berries outside (one opposite *first* E in DEFENCE and another, very small, on the leaf which points to C), and six inside; a small dot after TRIBUTE. Borders 4. Edge 1. Metal Æ. Size 28.

The stem of the leaf pointing to N in NOT, on sharp impressions, has the appearance of a berry, and probably was intended for such; this with the distinct one below it, would match the pair that are opposite, on the inner side of wreath; but so seldom does it appear with distinctness that I forbear to count it as a berry.

Lyman H. Low's description of Low-31 (W-11-120a).

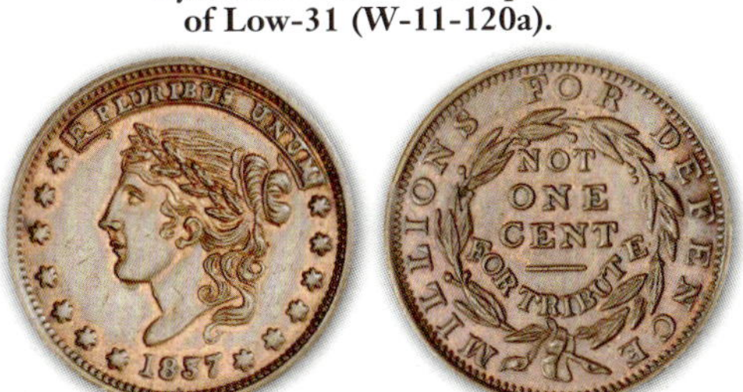

W-11-120a • 1837 Liberty Head, stars 7x6 irregularly aligned, E PLURIBUS UNUM on scroll • Low-31; HT-46, 46A, and 46R. R-1. 28 mm. Copper. Plain edge. Obverse with tiara of olive leaves, plain hair cords, highest leaf below L. This sturdy die was used on multiple tokens. In this variety, the 1837 date below appears with 3 crumbled and filled in, resembling 5 (occasionally causing excitement as a "new overdate"). Reverse with wreath that touches ribbon, line below CENT. Outside berries below first L, first N, and first E (no stem to last berry). Two inside berries, one of which is stemless, distant to right of E (ONE). EF to lower Mint State ranges are typical grades for leading collections. The die state with crumbled last digit is two or three times more common than the earlier state. Some were used as planchets for South American MITAD tokens. • VF-20 $30; EF-40 $45; AU-50 $75; MS-63 $250.

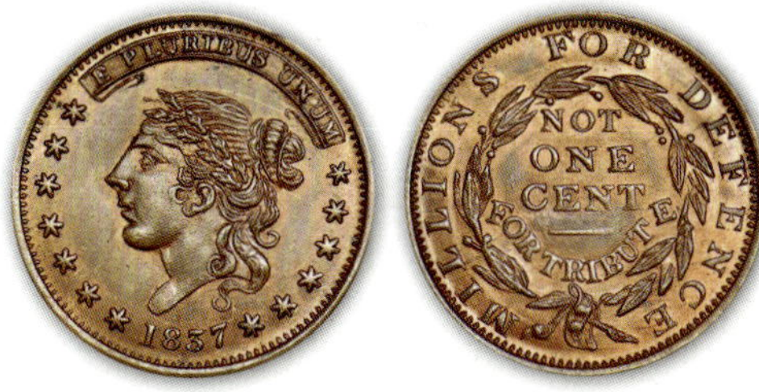

W-11-130a • 1837, stars 7x6, E PLURIBUS UNUM on scroll • Low-32; HT-47. R-1. 28 mm. Copper. Plain edge. Obverse with tiara of olive leaves, plain hair cords, E PLURIBUS UNUM on scroll above, tiny leftmost leaf (incomplete) opposite P, 7 stars left, 6 stars right, medium 1837 date below. Reverse die same as the preceding. EF and AU are typical high grades, punctuated by a few Mint State offerings. • VF-20 $30; EF-40 $45; AU-50 $75; MS-63 $250.

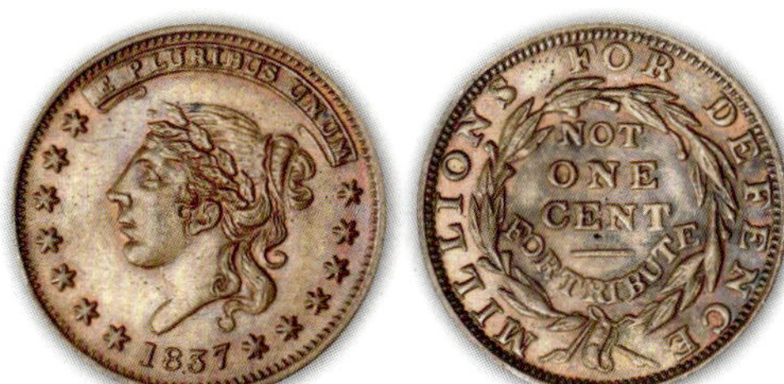

W-11-140a • 1837, stars 7x6, E PLURIBUS UNUM on scroll • Low-33; HT-48. R-1. 28 mm. Copper. Plain edge. Obverse with tiara of olive leaves, plain hair cords, E PLURIBUS UNUM on scroll above, tiny leftmost leaf (incomplete) opposite P, 7 stars left, 6 stars right, medium 1837 date below. Reverse with wreath that touches ribbon, line below CENT. Outside berries below first L, first N, and first E. Two inside berries, one of which is stemless, distant to right of E (ONE). EF and AU are typical high grades, although Mint State example are occasionally offered. • VF-20 $30; EF-40 $45; AU-50 $65; MS-63 $200.

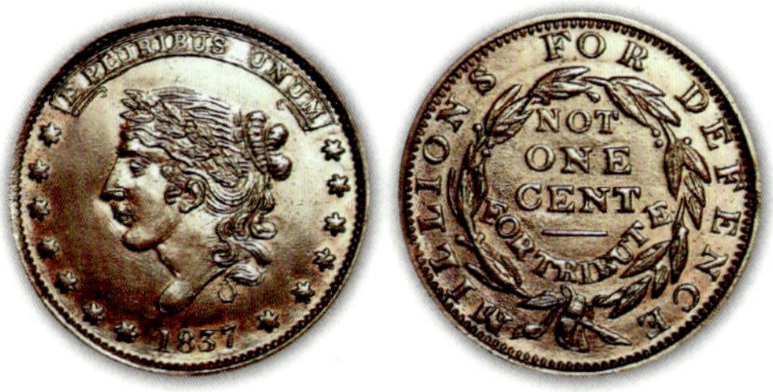

W-11-150a • 1837 Liberty Head, stars 7x6 irregularly aligned, E PLURIBUS UNUM on scroll • Low-34; HT-49. R-1. 28 mm. Copper. Plain edge. Obverse with tiara of olive leaves, plain hair cords, highest leaf below L. This sturdy die was used on multiple tokens. Reverse is the same as W-11-120 with wreath that touches ribbon, line below CENT. Outside berries below first L, first N, and first E (no stem to last berry). Two inside berries, one of which is stemless, distant to right of E (ONE). Again, EF and AU are typical high grades punctuated by a few Mint State offerings. • VF-20 $35; EF-40 $55; AU-50 $85; MS-63 $300.

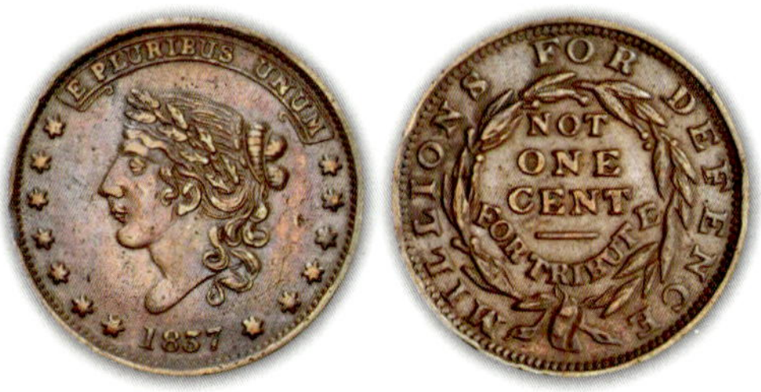

W-11-155a • 1837, stars 7x6 irregularly aligned, E PLURIBUS UNUM on scroll • Low-35; HT-50. R-3. 28 mm. Copper. Plain edge. Obverse die as preceding. Reverse is the same as preceding, but now with a curved stem added to the berry below the first E in DEFENCE. Same grade comment as for the preceding. • VF-20 $40; EF-40 $65; AU-50 $100; MS-63 $325.

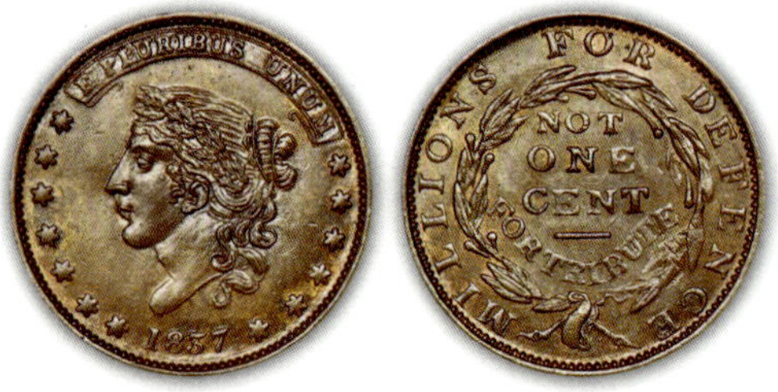

W-11-160a • 1837, stars 7x6 irregularly aligned, E PLURIBUS UNUM on scroll / Circle of stars • Low-36; HT-51. R-2. 28 mm. Copper. Plain edge. Obverse the same die as the preceding. Reverse with wreath with irregular end that is close to or touches ribbon, line below CENT. Outside berries below first L and first N. Berry with very long stem to right of T (CENT). Stem ends each with circular hole. AU and Mint State examples are available, with Mint State being par for most advanced collections. • VF-20 $35; EF-40 $55; AU-50 $85; MS-63 $300.

W-11-160b • Dies as preceding • Low-Unlisted; HT-Unlisted. R-9. 28 mm. Brass. Plain edge. Dice-Hicks ex Ford Collection, Mint State.

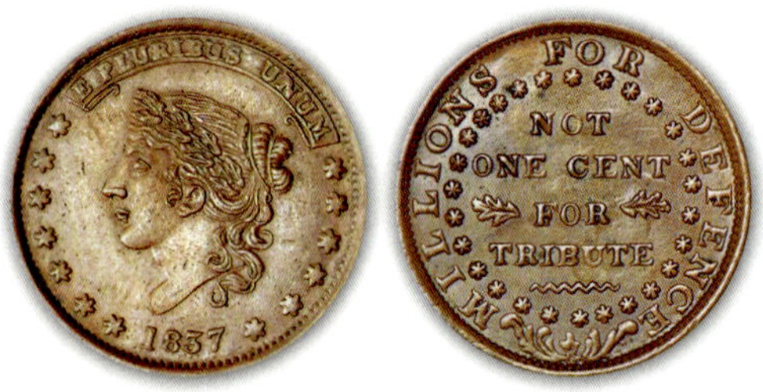

W-11-170a • 1837, stars 7x6 irregularly aligned, E PLURIBUS UNUM on scroll • Low-39; HT-52. R-2. 28 mm. Copper. Plain edge. Obverse the same die as the preceding. Reverse with MILLIONS FOR DEFENCE, ornament at bottom. Circle of stars enclose NOT / ONE CENT / FOR

/ TRIBUTE in straight lines plus ornaments. Lower–range Mint State coins are easy to find. • VF-20 $30; EF-40 $50; AU-50 $85; MS-63 $250.

Other "Not One Cent" Tokens

Some tokens made in 1837 are dated 1841, anticipating, several years in advance, that in 1840 any reelection bid of Van Buren would be defeated, and in 1841 Webster would be in the President's House. If successful, Webster would implement pro–paper money, defend the Constitution, and put other Whig policies in place.

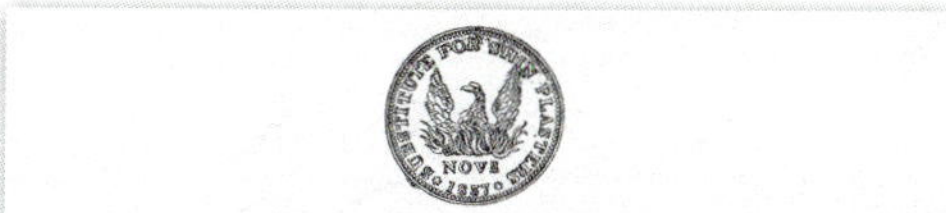

45. *Obv.* • SUBSTITUTE FOR SHIN PLASTERS • Phoenix rising from flames; beneath, NOV^R | 1837. *Rev.* Same as No. 33. Borders 4. Edge 1. Metal Æ. Size 28.

The last two figures of date show that portions have been recut.

"Shinplasters" have been referred to in the Introduction. The name was applied to bills of irresponsible banks and private parties. The device of the phoenix rising from flames seems to mean that the paper money was only fit to be burned, and that with its destruction new life would spring from its ashes. The date, November, 1837, is that of a convention held in New York on the 27th of that month, by representatives of leading banks in nineteen States, to fix a date for resumption. They met again the 16th of April, 1838, and decided to resume specie payments the 10th of May following, which was successfully accomplished after a suspension of exactly one year. (See No. 40.)

Lyman H. Low's description of Low-45.

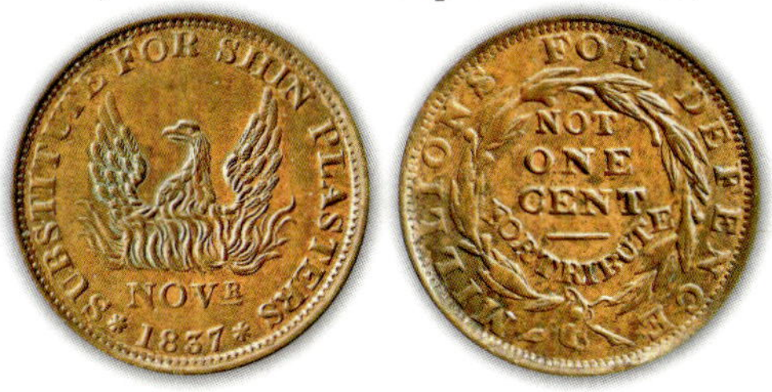

W-11-260a • 1837 Phoenix • Low-45; HT-56. R-1. 28 mm. Copper. Plain edge. Obverse with phoenix rising from flames, NOVr below. Around the border SUBSTITUTE FOR SHIN PLASTERS 1837. This represents the resumption of specie payments in New York City, a desirable substitute for shinplasters (paper notes of questionable value). Reverse with MILLIONS FOR DEFENCE around border. Berries below first L, first N and second E. Within wreath NOT / ONE / CENT / FOR TRIBUTE. Line below CENT. EF to lower-range Mint State examples are easy to find. • VF-20 $30; EF-40 $45; AU-50 $80; MS-63 $250.

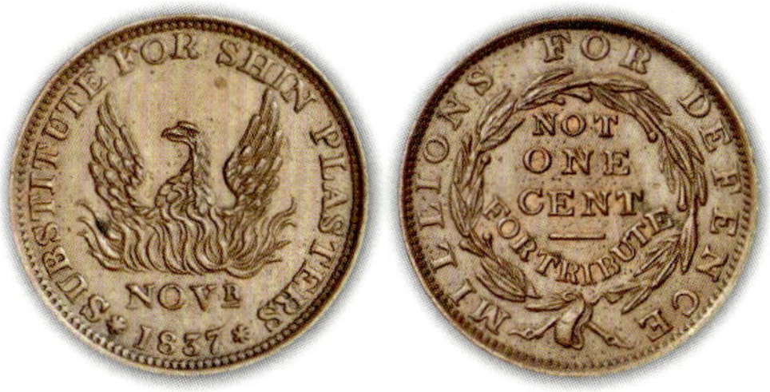

W-11-270a • 1837 Phoenix • Low-46; HT-57. R-2. 28 mm. Copper. Plain edge. Obverse die as preceding. Reverse with MILLIONS FOR DEFENCE around border. Berries below first L and first N. Within wreath NOT / ONE / CENT / FOR TRIBUTE. Line below CENT. Long stems to two berries at inside right. EF and AU are typical high grades. Mint State pieces are elusive. • VF-20 $30; EF-40 $45; AU-50 $80; MS-63 $250.

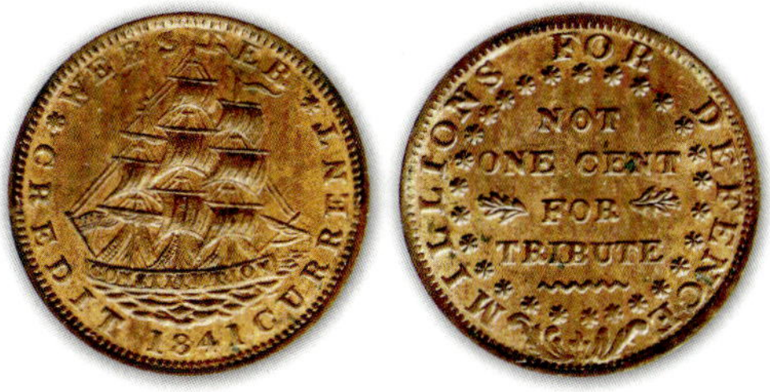

W-11-280a PE • 1841 Ship / Circle of stars • Low-58; HT-16. R-1. 28 mm. Copper. Plain edge. Obverse with ship *Constitution* under full sail, WEBSTER / CREDIT 1841 CURRENCY around border, suggesting that in 1841 if Webster were to become president the Constitution would not be compromised, as it allegedly was under the Jackson and Van Buren administrations. Reverse with MILLIONS FOR DEFENCE, ornament at bottom. Circle of stars enclose NOT / ONE CENT / FOR /

TRIBUTE in straight lines plus ornaments as also used on W-11-170. HT-16A reeded edge listed by Rulau. Readily available in AU and lower-range Mint State grades. Hayden 12/2008 VF-20 $484. • VF-20 $30; EF-40 $45; AU-50 $80; MS-63 $250.

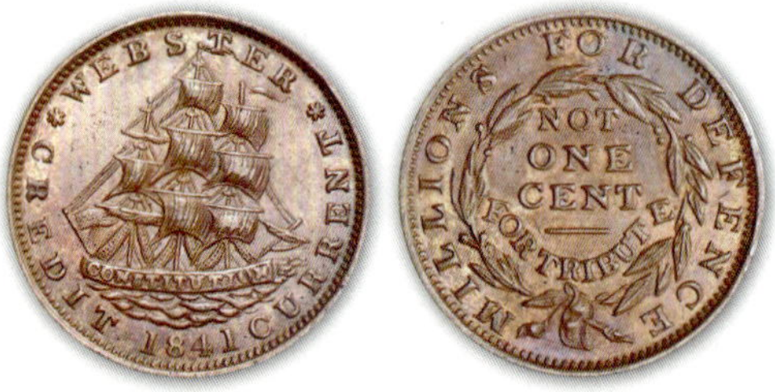

W-11-290a PE • 1841 Ship • Low-59; HT-17. R-1, but slightly less common than the preceding. 28 mm. Copper. Plain edge. Obverse as preceding. Reverse with wreath that touches ribbon, line below CENT. Outside berries below first L, first N, and first E. Two inside berries, one of which is stemless, distant to right of E (ONE). This die was used on several other tokens. Readily available in AU and lower-range Mint State grades. • VF-20 $35; EF-40 $50; AU-50 $90; MS-63 $275.

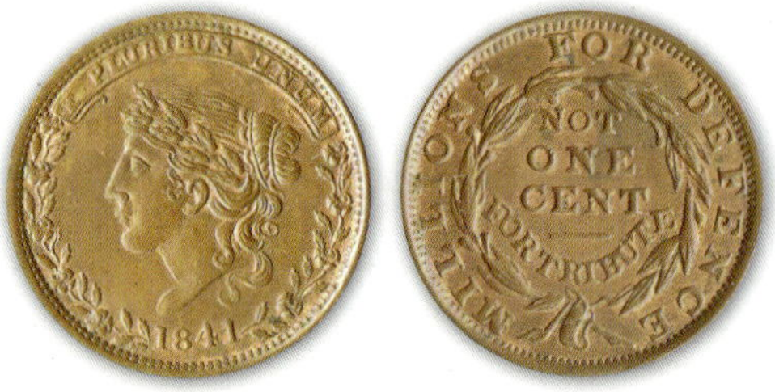

W-11-300a PE • 1841 Liberty Head • Low-69; HT-58. R-1. 28 mm. Copper. Plain edge. (Some silvered, HT-58A.) Obverse with Liberty head, E PLURIBUS UNUM on scroll above, wreath to each side, 1841 below, this date anticipating Van Buren to be defeated if he ran for reelection in 1840, after which a Whig would be in the President's House in 1841. This die was used on other tokens as well. Reverse as used on W-11-140 with berries below N, and first E. Two inside berries, one of which is stemless, distant to right of E (ONE). EF and AU are the usual high grades for this variety, with Mint State pieces being on the scarce side. • VF-20 $30; EF-40 $45; AU-50 $75; MS-63 $250.

"May Tenth 1837" Tokens

Faced with many bill-holders who demanded that their bills be exchanged for gold or silver coins, and with vault reserves not up to large-scale redemptions, banks in New York City stopped specie payments on May 10, 1837. Most of the banks were sound, but their capital was at work in loans and other business. Normally, only a small percentage of capital was kept idle in vaults. Word spread, and within a matter of days nearly all banks stopped payment. This ushered in a period of time in which coins could only be purchased at exchange houses and brokers by paying a premium in bank bills. Within a year, most banks resumed specie payments. Many others did not resume until later, and in the process many banks failed, and their notes became worthless.

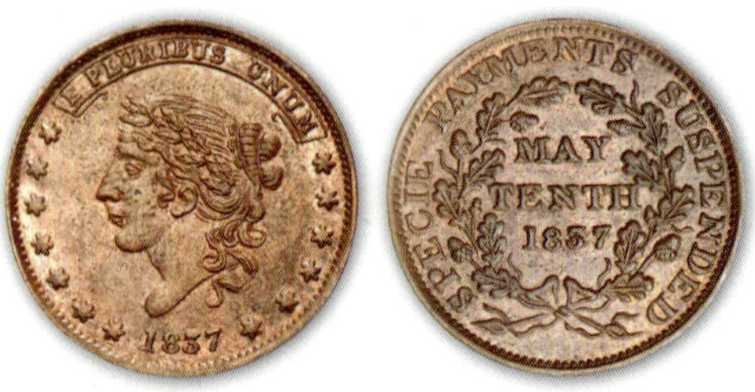

W-11-310a • 1837 Liberty Head, stars 7x6 irregularly aligned, E PLURIBUS UNUM on scroll • Low-40; HT-65. R-1. 28 mm. Copper. Plain edge. Obverse with tiara of olive leaves, plain hair cords, highest leaf below L. This sturdy die was used on multiple tokens. Reverse with SPECIE PAYMENTS SUSPENDED around border, oak wreath within, MAY / TENTH / 1837 at center. M (MAY) does not touch acorn. This token is dated on both sides. AU and lower-range Mint State examples are common. Some were used as planchets for South American MITAD tokens. • VF-20 $35; EF-40 $55; AU-50 $85; MS-63 $250.

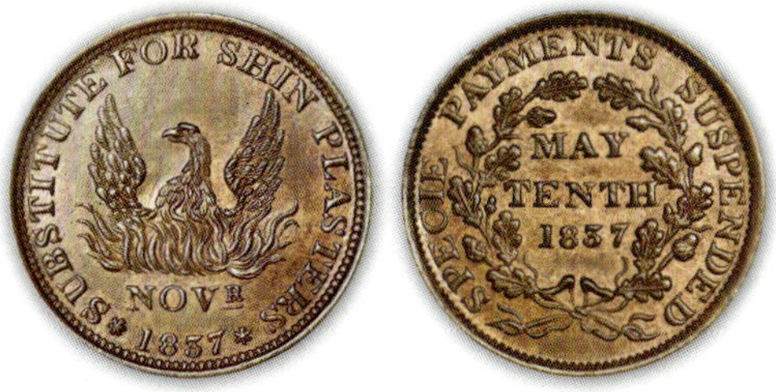

W-11-320a • 1837 Phoenix • Low-47; HT-66. R-1. 28 mm. Copper. Plain edge. (HT-66A medal-turn alignment.) Obverse with phoenix rising from flames, NOVr below. Around the border SUBSTITUTE FOR SHIN PLASTERS 1837. Reverse as preceding. AU and lower-range Mint State pieces are readily available. • VF-20 $25; EF-40 $45; AU-50 $75; MS-63 $225.

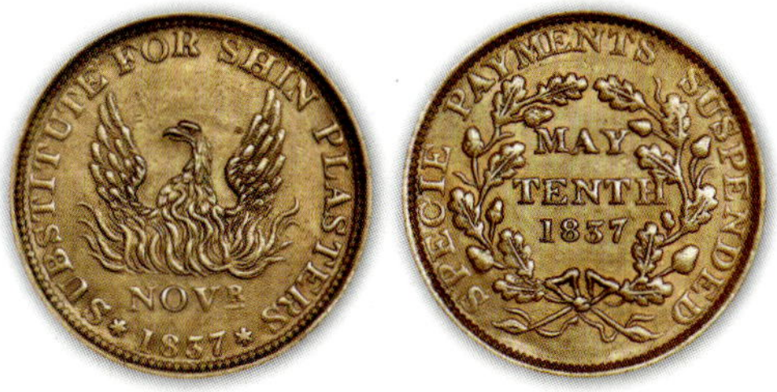

W-11-330a • 1837 Phoenix • Low-48; HT-67. R-1. 28 mm. Copper. Plain edge. Obverse as preceding. Reverse with SPECIE PAYMENTS SUSPENDED around border, oak wreath within, MAY / TENTH / 1837 at center. M (MAY) touches acorn; 1 in date slightly left of the upright of E (TENTH). This token is dated on both sides. AU and lower-range Mint State pieces are readily available. Crude contemporary counterfeits were made of this variety, such as the example appearing as lot 266 in Stack's sale of the Gilbert Steinberg Collection in 1989, where it brought $2,310, and another called G/VG sold in Hayden's 3/2002 sale for $4,620. • VF-20 $25; EF-40 $45; AU-50 $85; MS-63 $250.

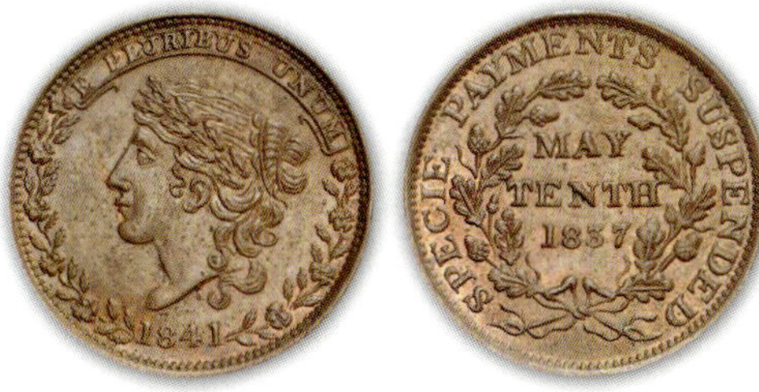

W-11-340a • 1841 Liberty Head • Low-67; HT-68. R-1. 28 mm. Copper. Plain edge. Obverse with Liberty head, E PLURIBUS UNUM on scroll above, wreath to each side, 1841 below. Reverse with SPECIE PAYMENTS SUSPENDED around border, oak wreath within, MAY / TENTH / 1837 at center. M (MAY) does not touch acorn, die used on W-11-310. Mint State examples are common in the context of the Hard Times series. • VF-20 $30; EF-40 $45; AU-50 $75; MS-63 $225.

"Mint Drop" Tokens

Mint drop, under other circumstances a type of mint candy, was a nickname for the new lighter-weight gold coins introduced by the Act of June 28, 1834, which was sponsored by Senator Thomas Hart Benton of Missouri, a hard-money advocate nicknamed "Old Bullion." Gold coins of heavier weight had not been seen in circulation since 1820. After 1834, much to the displeasure of anti-Jackson Whigs who wanted inflation and "cheap money," gold coins replaced some paper money in circulation.

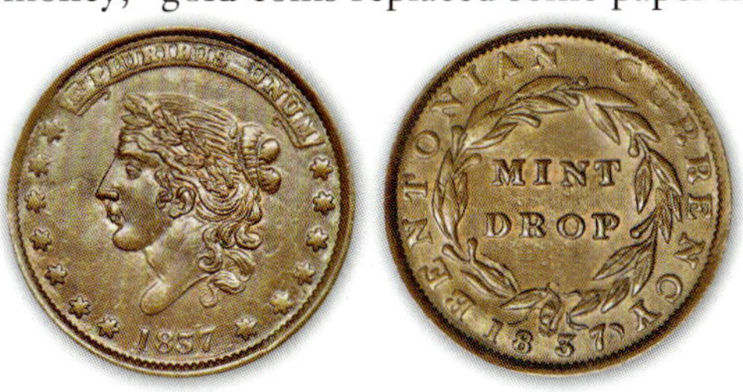

W-11-410a • 1837 Liberty Head, stars 7x6 irregularly aligned, E PLURIBUS UNUM on scroll • Low-37; HT-61. R-2. 28 mm. Copper. Plain edge. Obverse with tiara of olive leaves, plain hair cords, highest leaf below L. This sturdy die was used on multiple tokens. Reverse with

BENTONIAN CURRENCY 1837 around border, wreath, with MINT / DROP at the center. EF to Mint State grades are typical in advanced collections. • VF-20 $40; EF-40 $60; AU-50 $100; MS-63 $300.

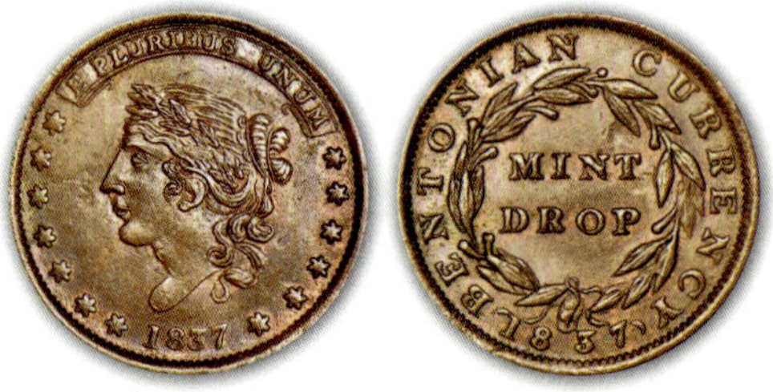

W-11-420a • 1837 Liberty Head, stars 7x6 irregularly aligned, E PLURIBUS UNUM on scroll • Low-38; HT-62. R-1. 28 mm. Copper. Plain edge. Obverse die as preceding. Reverse die as preceding plus the addition of a lune or cusp at the upper left of the 1 in 1837, giving it the appearance of an inverted L. EF to Mint State grades are typical in advanced collections. • VF-20 $30; EF-40 $50; AU-50 $85; MS-63 $250.

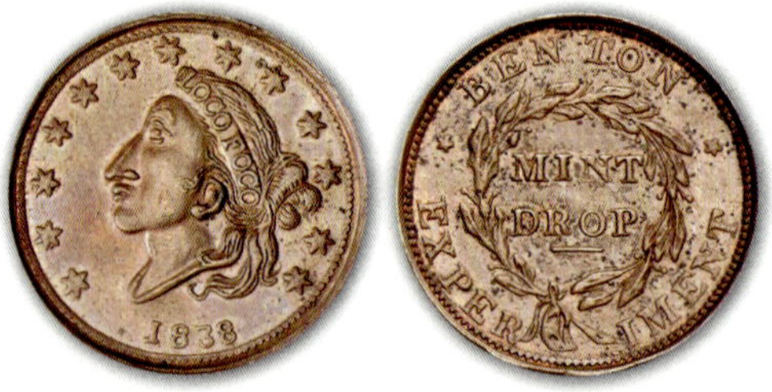

W-11-430a • 1838 Liberty Head, LOCO FOCO • Low-55; HT-63. R-1. 29 mm. Copper. Plain edge. Obverse with Liberty Head with LOCO FOCO on tiara, 13 stars surrounding. Reverse with BENTON above, a five-pointed star to each side, with EXPER [ribbon] IMENT below. Within a wreath MINT / DROP with line below DROP. These tokens have attracted a lot of numismatic attention over the years due to the inscription on the obverse and also the curious portrait. Examples in major collections are typically EF or AU with the occasional lower-range Mint State piece. • VF-20 $100; EF-40 $200; AU-50 $400; MS-63 $750.

History of the Tammany Society or Columbian Order, by E. Vail Blake, 1901, tells the origin of the Loco Foco term. The Wigwam was the headquarters of the Tammany Society. Self-igniting friction matches were called loco foco matches:

> **Loco Foco**
>
> One of the most singular cases of general misunderstanding, through the misapplication of a grotesque name to a very earnest and sincere party, is that which developed at the time of the formation of the "Equal Rights" association, which for years was called the "Loco Focos."
>
> This meaningless term was applied to certain dissenters in the Tammany Society through a mere incident which occurred at a meeting in the old Wigwam on Nassau street in 1835, under the following circumstances: On the 29th of October a meeting was called to assemble in Tammany Hall for the purpose of making certain nominations. The doors being open at seven in the evening, a great mass of the usual attendants rushed in and rapidly filled all the available space, but what was their surprise to find that they were not the first arrivals; the platform was already filled with those prepared to manage the meeting and secure the adoption of their own candidates.
>
> From the early comers in possession of the meeting, Isaac L. Varian was nominated as chairman, and without the question being properly put, he prepared to take his seat; when, from the floor of the house, the Equal Rights men nominated Joel Curtis for the chair. At the same time a broad banner was uplifted on which was the inscription, "Joel Curtis, the anti-monopolistic Chairman."

The confusion caused by this unexpected apparition was so great that Mr. Varian's effort to read the prearranged list of nominations was futile, so far as the hearing of the names was concerned. While the excitement was at its height, the Hall was suddenly immersed in darkness. Each of the factions present thought the opposition had planned this manoeuvre as a piece of fine strategy, and the incident has been so represented by some narrators; but, in fact, it was nothing of the kind, it was only the suddenly inspired trick of two young lads, one of whom was not more than fifteen years of age, and both of whom, now elderly men, are still living and not averse to telling the story.

At that time the gas-meter was located on the Frankfort Street side of the Hall, concealed from view by some decorative window drapery, but well known to these lads. When the lights were extinguished the Varian party got out of the Hall as quickly as possible, taking the rear egress by which they had entered, retreating to an adjoining tavern of much local celebrity, known as the "Pewter Mug," situated on Frankfort street, and there completed their nominations; while the Equal Rights party retained possession of the Hall, and in a very few moments, having produced [loco foco] matches from their pockets, and the janitor being found, they relit the gas, and the business for which they had assembled was proceeded with.

The next morning the term "Loco Foco" was spontaneously attached to the party holding the Hall, which name, for a long period, to the uninitiated, served to describe the whole Tammany Society.

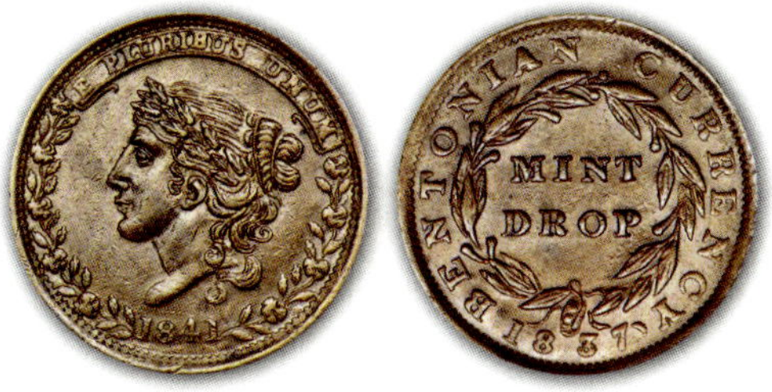

W-11-440a • 1841 Liberty Head • Low-68; HT-64; R-1. 28.5 mm. Copper. Plain edge. Obverse with Liberty head, E PLURIBUS UNUM on scroll above, wreath to each side. Reverse with BENTONIAN CURRENCY 1837 around border, wreath, with MINT / DROP at the center. A combination of two dies used earlier. VF and EF are the grades most often seen. Mint State tokens are rarities. • VF-20 $30; EF-40 $45; AU-50 $90; MS-63 $350.

"Illustrious Predecessor" Tokens

Regarding *illustrious predecessor*, this term seems to have been used by Martin Van Buren sometime between his election and inauguration, in reference to Jackson. "You, sir, have promised to tread in the steps of your illustrious predecessor," stated Senator Ambrose Sevier, of Arkansas, in a debate on public lands.[1] The term was hardly new at the time and had been applied to former presidents such as Jefferson in the past.

However, numismatic texts have generally attributed the phrase as originating from Martin Van Buren's inaugural speech on March 4, 1837: "In receiving from the people the sacred trust twice confided to my illustrious predecessor, in which he has discharged so faithfully and so well, I know that I cannot expect to perform the arduous task with equal ability and success."

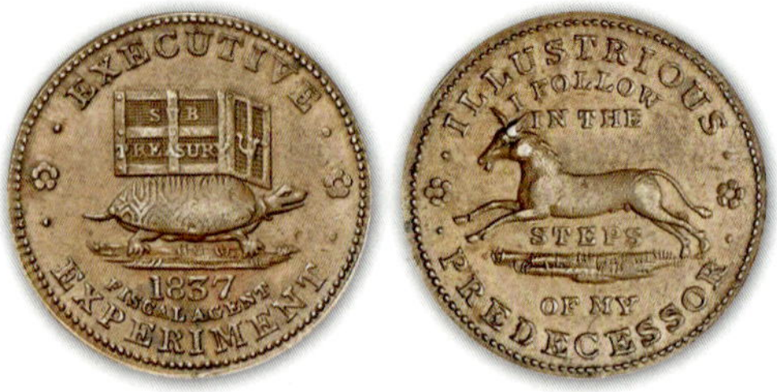

W-11-510a • Tortoise with safe die 1, EXECUTIVE EXPERIMENT (safe corner left of center of X) / Jackass die 1 • Low-17; HT-31. R-4. 28.5 mm. Copper. Plain edge. Obverse with a tortoise (diamondback terrapin) carrying a safe lettered SUB TREASURY, referring to the anticipated slow movement of federal funds to Sub-Treasury offices then under consideration in Congress. 1837 / FISCAL AGENT is below. 7 (1837) over E (AGENT). At the top and bottom borders, EXECUTIVE / EXPERIMENT. This refers to the continuing displeasure, of the opposing Whig Party, at Jackson followed by Van Buren taking charge of the movement and location of federal funds. The reverse has at the center a running jackass with the inscription above and below, I FOLLOW / IN THE / STEPS / OF MY, and at the top and bottom borders ILLUSTRIOUS / PREDECESSOR. The first S (STEPS) is *completely* under the foreleg of the jackass; the only die with this positioning. Typical grades are VF to AU. Mint State coins are elusive. • VF-20 $200; EF-40 $300; AU-50 $450; MS-63 $800.

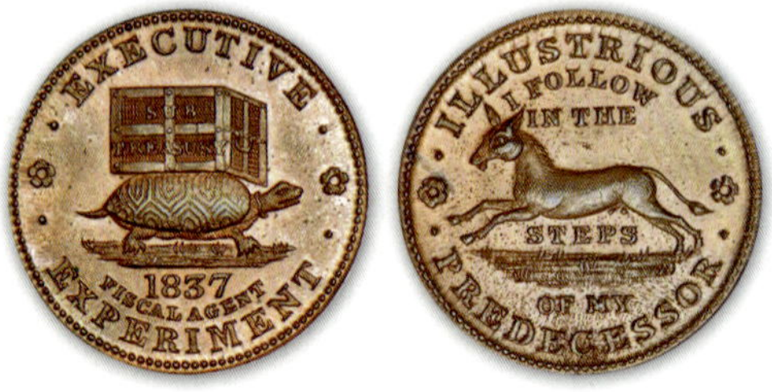

W-11-520a • Tortoise with safe die 1 / Jackass die 2 • Low-18; HT-32. R-1. 28.5 mm. Copper. Plain edge. Obverse as preceding. Reverse is a close copy of the preceding, but with many small differences. Note the position of the ear in relation to the first L (ILLUSTRIOUS), the shape of the tail, the relationship of the hooves to the ground, etc. Typical grades are VF to AU. One of these was used as a planchet for a South American MITAD token. • VF-20 $30; EF-40 $50; AU-50 $85; MS-63 $250.

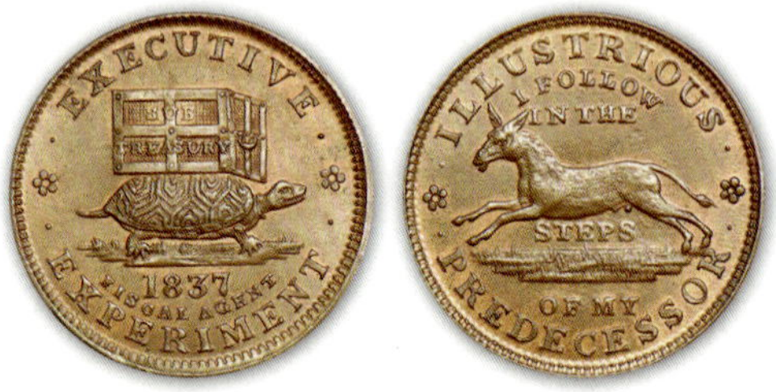

W-11-530a • Tortoise with safe die 2, EXECUTIVE EXPERIMENT (safe corner right of center of X) Jackass die 3 • Low-19; HT-33. R-1. 28.5 mm. Copper. Plain edge. Motifs as preceding, but from different dies. Obverse with corner of safe under right foot of X. 7 (1837) over E (AGENT). On the reverse the ear is close to second L (ILLUSTRIOUS), cinquefoils at left and right border are carefully formed, hindmost leg is very close to R, etc. Russell Rulau lists a variety as HT-A33 with dentils instead of beads, etc. It is thought that these, assigned R-5 status, are simply artifacts of striking and not from different dies.[2] Readily available in high grades. • VF-20 $25; EF-40 $45; AU-50 $75; MS-63 $225.

W-11-530f • Dies as preceding • Low-19; HT-33A. R-8. 28.5 mm. Silver. Plain edge. Low: "This piece was also struck in silver, it is said, for 'Capt. Davenport,' in 1837, concerning whom I have not been able to learn anything." The reference is to Henry Davenport, the numismatist (see earlier text). Three are believed to exist, each in Mint State. Ford (Stack's 2004) Unc $12,650, another Unc $27,600.

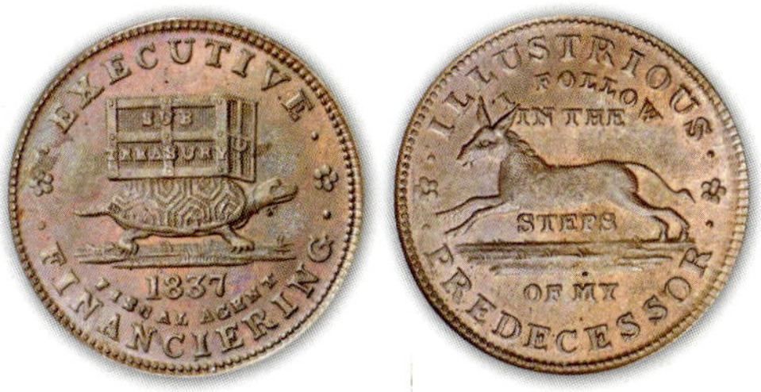

W-11-540a • Tortoise with safe die 3, EXECUTIVE FINANCIERING / Jackass die 4 • Low-20; HT-34. R-1. 28.5 mm. Copper. Plain edge. Obverse die with similar motifs as the preceding, but with EXECUTIVE / FINANCIERING at top and bottom borders. Reverse from a new die somewhat similar to the preceding but with differences. Note position of left ear and I (IN), O (FOLLOW) is over E (THE), etc. Easily available in AU and Mint State grades. South American MITAD tokens were struck over some of these. • VF-20 $30; EF-40 $45; AU-50 $75; MS-63 $225.

The term *executive financiering* arose from a paper which was circulated in mid-September 1837, and then read aloud in the Senate on September 23, 1837 by Senator John Pendleton King of Georgia, regarding the Sub-Treasury Bill. The speech is reported here in the third person:

> Mr. King, in conclusion, declared that he had found it necessary to take his stand against this progressive march of executive power and patronage in regard to the finances of the nation. The finances, he maintained, ought to be submitted to the Legislature—and that it became the Executive to consult and follow, not to lead.
>
> No country should live under executive financiering: and if, in this matter, said Mr. K., the present executive should tread in the footsteps of his predecessor I pledge my best endeavors to jostle him out.[3]

King went on to say, "If we did this we would have the fate of every other nation who submitted to executive financiering; we would first become a nation of beggars and then a nation of slaves."

1837 Van Buren / 1841 Webster Ship Tokens

These tokens are specifically anti-Martin Van Buren. The 1841 date anticipates Webster's presidency that year (although, as it developed, he did not run; it was William H. Harrison who challenged Van Buren in the 1840 election and went to the President's House in 1841).

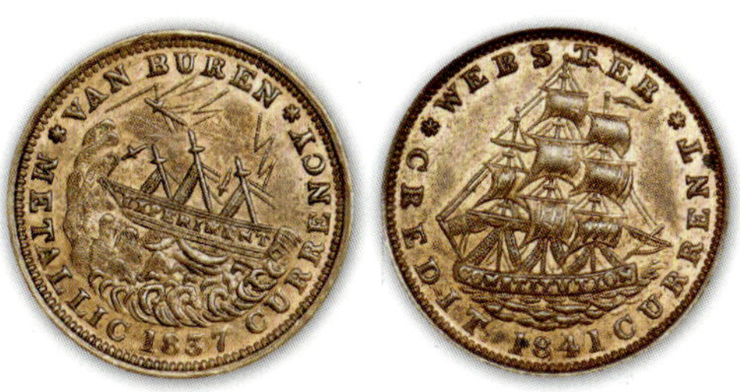

W-11-610a • Experiment die 1 CURRENCY / Constitution die 1 CURRENT • Low-60; HT-18. R-1. 28.3 mm. Copper. Plain edge. Obverse with ship *Experiment* wrecked on rocks, dismasted and with lightning bolts in the sky. VAN BUREN / METALLIC CURRENCY around the border. Reverse with ship *Constitution* under full sail. WEBSTER / CREDIT 1841 CURRENT around border. Reflecting that the Van Buren experiment with hard money and controlling federal funds was a disaster, and that if Webster were to become president in 1841 the Constitution would not be compromised. Readily available in AU and lower-range Mint State grades. • VF-20 $30; EF-40 $50; AU-50 $85; MS-63 $250.

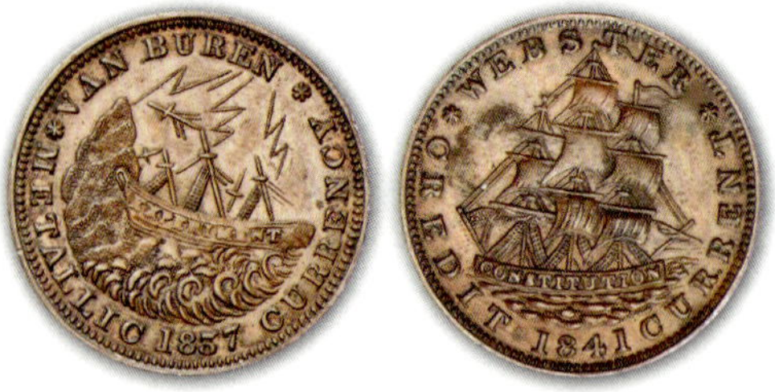

W-11-620a • Experiment die 2 CURRENCY / Constitution die 1 CURRENT • Low-61; HT-19. R-5. 28 mm. Copper. Plain edge. Obverse with same motifs as the preceding, but a different die. Border inscription reads VAN BUREN / METALLIC 1837 CURRENCY. Leftmost lightning bolt strikes right side of rock. Lightning bolts touch EN (BUREN). Reverse from the die as preceding. Typical grades are VF and EF with AU being elusive. Hayden (2004) MS-63 $1,650. • VF-20 $250; EF-40 $450; AU-50 $800.

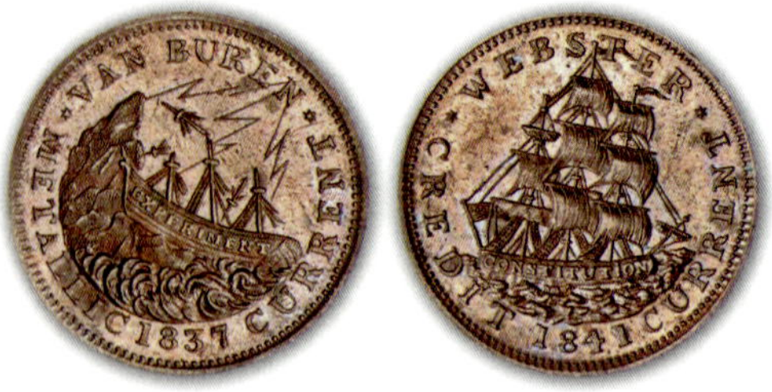

W-11-630a • Experiment die 3 CURRENT / Constitution die 2 CURRENT • Low-62; HT-20. R-1. 29 mm. Copper. Plain edge. Obverse motifs similar to the preceding but with slightly different details. Border inscription reads VAN BUREN / METALLIC 1841 CURRENT. Reverse with the same motifs as preceding, but a different die. Pennant ends below center of R (WEBSTER), ocean touched DI (CREDIT), etc. Some are struck from a rusted obverse die. EF to lower-range Mint State examples are easily available. • VF-20 $25; EF-40 $40; AU-50 $65; MS-63 $225.

W-11-630f • Dies as preceding • Low-62; HT-20A. R-7. 29 mm. Silver. Plain edge. Thought by Low to be unique. Probably made for Henry Davenport as stated by W. Elliot Woodward in his sale of the McCoy Collection in 1864. Today there are probably close to a dozen accounted for. Ford (Stack's 2004) Choice AU $8,625. Dice-Hicks (Stack's 2008) Unc $9,200.

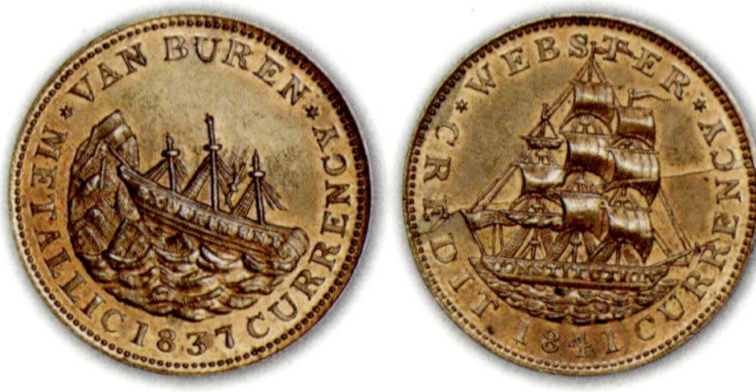

W-11-640a • Experiment die 3 CURRENCY / Constitution die 3 CURRENCY • Low-63; HT-21. R-2. 29 mm. Copper. Plain edge. Obverse with related motif of dismasted ship, no lightning in the sky. VAN BUREN / METALLIC 1837 CURRENCY around the border. Reverse with *Constitution* in the center, WEBSTER / CREDIT 1841 CURRENCY around border. Bisecting crack from E (CREDIT) to second C (CURRENCY) on all seen. AU and lower-range Mint State pieces are seen with frequency. • VF-20 $35; EF-40 $65; AU-50 $150; MS-63 $450.

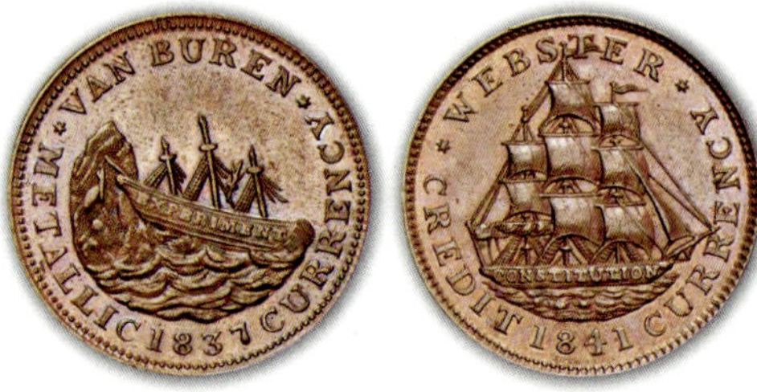

W-11-650a • Experiment die 3 CURRENCY / Constitution die 4 CURRENCY • Low-64; HT-22. R-1. 29.5 mm. Copper. Plain edge. Obverse die as preceding. Multiple die cracks are seen on some die states, often heavy. Reverse with *Constitution* at center, WEBSTER / CREDIT 1841 CURRENCY around, different die from the preceding, with changes in details. Pennant at upper right is farther from R (WEBSTER), CUR is farther from the water, etc. EF and AU grades are about the standard for this variety. True Mint State examples are rare. • VF-20 $25; EF-40 $40; AU-50 $65; MS-63 $225.

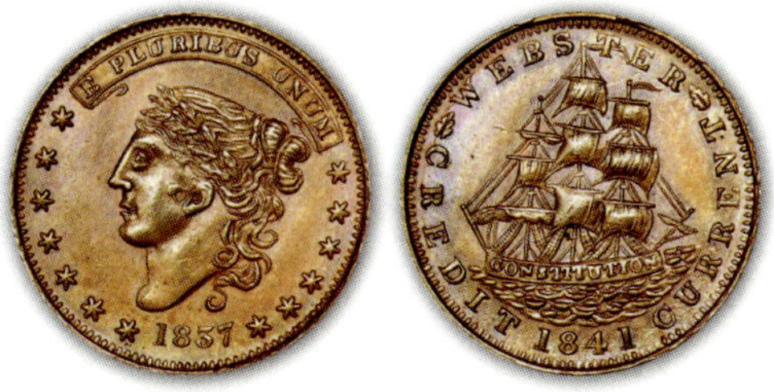

W-11-660a • 1837, stars 7x6, E PLURIBUS UNUM on scroll / Constitution die 5 CURRENCY • Low-65; HT-23. R-4. 28.3 mm. Copper. Plain edge. Obverse with tiara of olive leaves, plain hair cords, E PLURIBUS UNUM on scroll above, right end of label close to hair bun, leftmost leaf opposite P, 7 stars left, 6 stars right, medium 1837 date below. Also used on W-11-410. Reverse with *Constitution* at the center. WEBSTER above, CREDIT 1841 CURRENCY below. Different details, most noticeably with a leaf to each side of WEBSTER. Seen with very high rims as on Low-30. Most are in grades from VF to EF. AU examples are scarce and true Mint State tokens are rare. • VF-20 $120; EF-40 $200; AU-50 $300; MS-63 $700.

Other Hard Times Tokens of the Late 1830s

"Half Cent Worth of Pure Copper"

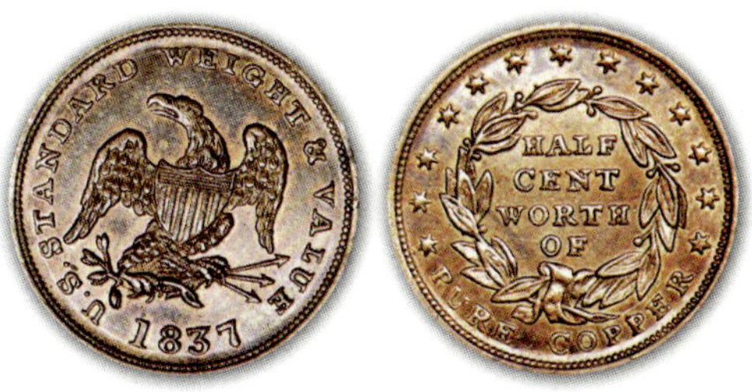

W-11-710a • 1837 Half Cent token • Low-49; HT-73. R-1. 23.5 mm. Copper. Plain edge. Obverse with eagle holding an olive branch and arrows, inspired by the motif on federal coins. Around the border is U.S. STANDARD WEIGHT & VALUE / 1837. Around the reverse border are 13 stars and PURE COPPER. Within a continuous wreath is HALF / CENT / WORTH / OF. In the 1930s Wayte Raymond included a space for this variety in half cent albums as no federal half cents were made this year. The *Guide Book of United States Coins* illustrates and lists the token among regular issues. As a result, examples in all grades have always been in strong demand. VF to EF and the occasional AU are about the standard in the marketplace, although at wide intervals a lower-range Mint State example is offered. • VF-20 $110; EF-40 $175; AU-50 $350; MS-63 $800.

"Am I Not a Woman & a Sister"

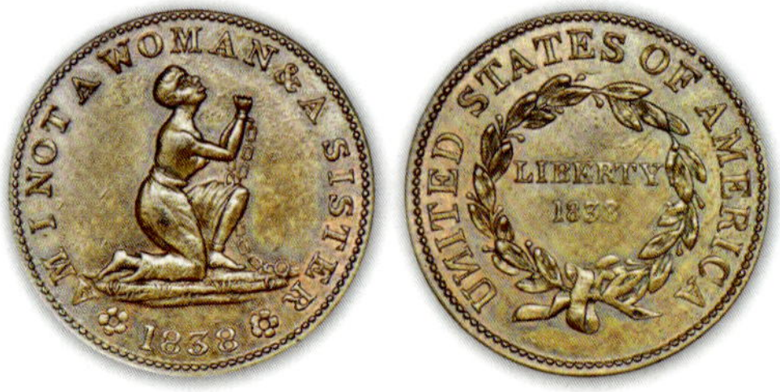

W-11-720a • 1838 Kneeling woman slave • Low-54; HT-81. R-1. 28.3 mm. Copper. Plain edge. (Also known on a 27 mm planchet; HT-81A; R-3.) Obverse with woman slave in chains, kneeling and facing to the right. Around the border is AM I NOT A WOMAN & A SISTER, with 1838 below. The reverse has UNITED STATES OF AMERICA around the border and a wreath that encloses LIBERTY / 1838, a punning inscription in view of the captivity of slaves. Typical grades are VF to EF and are very common. AU examples are scarce and true Mint State tokens are rare. • VF-20 $200; EF-40 $300; AU-50 $450; MS-63 $800.

The obverse legend, lettered on this token in 1838, had been used in London as early as 1787 by the Society for Effecting the Abolition of the Slave Trade. In the 1790s Birmingham makers of halfpenny tokens utilized the slogan, but with a male slave and "a man & a brother" inscription. "Am I Not a Woman and a Sister" (usually with "and" rather than "&" in print) was also used, but not as often. According to his memoir, in 1832 Boston preacher Timothy Gilbert "began to send out illustrations" that included a "poor slave, eyes looking toward heaven, and hands clasped, saying, 'Am I not a woman and a sister.' The platform began to resound with appeals, the pulpit sounded a trumpet which gave timely warning, and the church prepared for action."[4] At that time the fervor for abolition was intense among residents of Boston. In 1832 illustrations with this motif and inscription were published in *The Liberator*. By the late 1830s printed letter sheets were available with this inscription at the top.

On November 23, 1837, this advertisement appeared in *The Emancipator:*

> An artist in New Jersey has manufactured some anti-slavery copper medals, similar in appearance to new cents. They are nearly as heavy and are made of pure copper. On one side is a female slave in chains, in an imploring attitude, with the motto, 'Am I not a woman and a sister?' The execution is remarkably well done. On the reverse side is, in the center, the word 'LIBERTY,' surrounded by a wreath—and outside, in a circle, 'United States of America.' These medals can be had in any quantity at the Anti-Slavery Office, No. 143 Nassau Street, in any quantity at one dollar a hundred which merely covers the actual cost.
>
> It is proposed to make similar medals, with a man, kneeling in chains, with the motto, 'Am I not a man and a brother?' The price will be the same. The friends of liberty have it in their power now to put a medal into the hands of every person in the country, without cost, containing a sentiment of immense value. It is a tract that will not be destroyed. If it falls into the hands of the enemy of liberty he will 'read and circulate.' Orders are solicited from all parts of the country, post paid. Newspapers friendly to the cause of liberty are requested to copy this.[5]

In the *New-York Dispatch*, August 16, 1857, Augustus B. Sage, who conducted a column on coins, stated this: "*The Abolition Cent.*—On the front a Negress in chains, kneeling, surrounded by the words, "Am I not a Woman and a Sister;" underneath, the date, 1838. On the reverse, the word "Liberty' surrounded by a wreath, and the legend "United States of America"—the N being struck [as a backward N]."

These tokens are very common. More than any other Hard Times issue they have attracted the attention of historians, newspaper writers, and others without numismatic knowledge. An oft-mentioned, yet spurious, account said that these were used as secret passes for the Underground Railroad and had great rarity and value. This story in the *New York Tribune*, June 1900, describes the token and is typical:

> . . . The device is symbolical of the appeals that the Negroes were making to that sentiment of liberty in the North which afterward led to their freedom. Until the copper piece was unearthed by the Tipton youth it was not known that such a representation had survived the slavery days, and there are only few persons now in Indiana who remember the use to which such coins were put, and the magical effect that they had among those who were active in helping runaway slaves to a place of safety whenever they found their way to Indiana soil. Indeed, it was only the few who knew that such copper pieces were in existence, for not many of them were ever made, and these had no special significance except to those who understood their meaning and had bound themselves by solemn oaths to discharge every duty which their presentation placed upon those to whom they were sent.

"Am I Not a Man & a Brother"

This token was unknown to Low and escaped the notice of other scholars. The first known illustration of it, by Edgar H. Adams, is in June 1912, in *The Numismatist.* It has been conjectured that the token with the male figure was a pattern, and perhaps this is assumed because of its rarity. There is no foundation for this. All known examples show wear, indicating they circulated in their time.

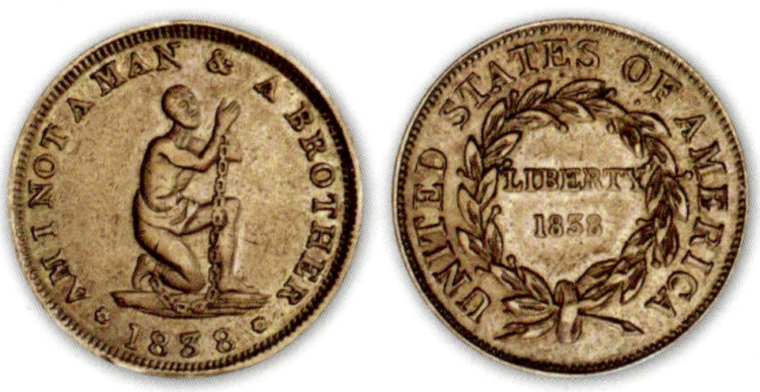

W-11-725a • 1838 Kneeling man slave • Low-54A; HT-82. R-8. 28 mm. Copper. Plain edge. The theme is similar to the preceding, except the slave is male and the obverse inscriptions reads AM I NOT A MAN & A BROTHER / 1838, following the male shown on a 19th-century British token. The reverse is similar in style to the preceding but is from a different die with variations in the details. Three examples are known, including the Ford token that sold for $71,875 in 2004 to Robert A. Schuman (illustrated). Two have been owned by the author, one sold to Eric P. Newman and the other to Donald G. Partrick from the Donald Miller Collection.

"A Friend to the Constitution"

The ship details are nearly identical with those on the 1841 Webster *Constitution* tokens; the dies are probably from the same hand. Both Lyman H. Low and Russell Rulau list this token under political issues. For convenience it is listed as such here. However, it probably would be better placed with the Gibbs tokens of Belleville. The A FRIEND TO THE CONSTITUTION die with a cow probably reflects that agricultural interests (also mentioned on the obverse) favored strict interpretation of the Constitution, unlike Jackson and Van Buren as viewed by their political adversaries.

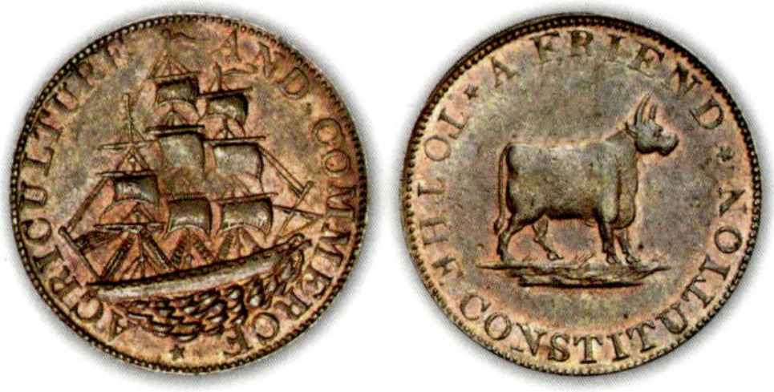

W-11-740a • Ship / Cow • Low-66; HT-24. R-2. 27.8 mm. Copper. Obverse with sailing ship, AGRICULTURE AND COMMERCE. Reverse with cow / A FRIEND TO THE CONSTITUTION. This is a muling of two dies made by John Gibbs of Belleville, New Jersey (see W-NJ-120). The ship die was probably made for use on a Canadian token, not located, but similar in style. VF and EF tokens are seen often, AU pieces on occasion, and true Mint State examples are very rare. In his auction sale of April 1861, in which on the cover he styled himself as "The Great Numismatist," Alfred S. Robinson listed one of these dateless tokens as a colonial issue. This token is typically seen from Fine to VF or EF. Any higher grade is rare. • Fine-12 $100; VF-20 $225; EF-40 $350; AU-50 $700.

12

Political Tokens of 1840

Van Buren Campaign tokens

The 1840 election contest between William Henry Harrison and Martin Van Buren generated more tokens and medalet varieties than all previous presidential campaigns combined. Lyman H. Low selected just three die combinations to include in his book—ones with mentions of banking or the Treasury. Accordingly, the present listing is limited just to these.

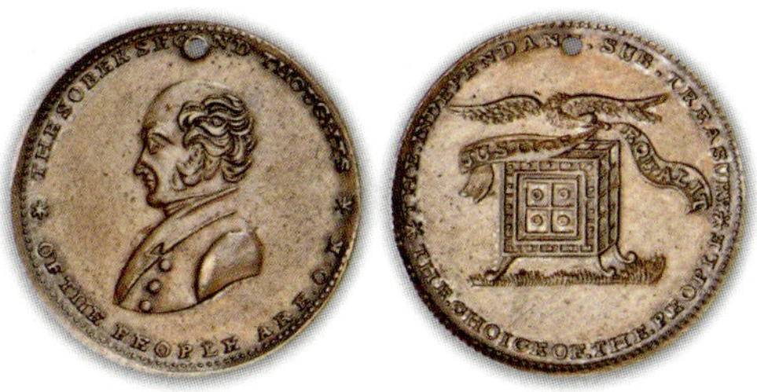

W-12-10a • Van Buren / Safe and eagle • Low-56; HT-75. R-2. 28.2 mm. Copper. Plain edge. Holed as issued. Seen in circulated grades. The obverse has a bust of Van Buren facing left. Around the border in small letters: THE SOBER SECOND THOUGHTS / OF THE PEOPLE ARE O.K. The reverse shows an eagle above a safe, holding a ribbon lettered JUSTICE EQUALIT [*sic*]. Around the border is THE. INDEPENDANT [*sic*]. SUB. TREASURY. Examples are plentiful and are usually seen in VF to AU grades. • VF-20 $85; EF-40 $150; AU-50 $300.

W-12-10b • Dies as preceding • Low-172; HT-75A. R-3. 28.2 mm. Brass. Plain edge. Holed as issued. (Some are silvered; HT-75-B; R-4.) Low mentioned a report of one in white metal which he was unable to confirm. Seen in circulated grades, with VF and EF being typical. • VF-20 $110; EF-40 $200; AU-50 $400.

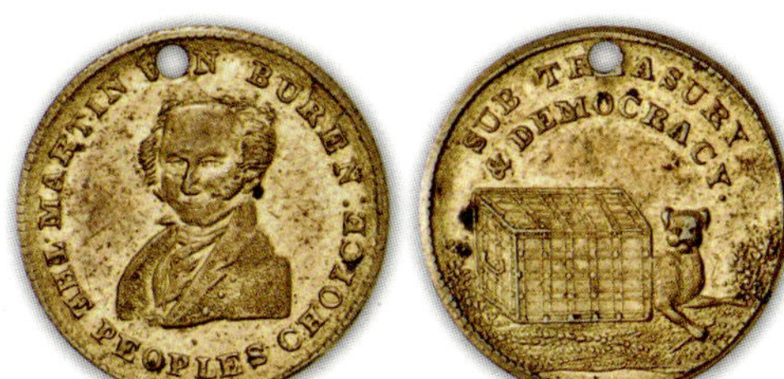

W-12-20b • Van Buren / Safe and dog • Low-57; HT-76. R-6. 22.5 mm. Brass. Plain edge. Holed as issued. Obverse with bust of Van Buren facing mostly forward to viewer's left. Around the border is

MARTIN VAN BUREN / THE PEOPLES CHOICE. On the reverse a dog guards a safe or strongbox. Above is SUB TREASURY / & DEMOCRACY. Most are in grades of VF and EF, frequently with problems. • VF-20 $2,000; EF-40 $3,000; AU-50 $4,500.

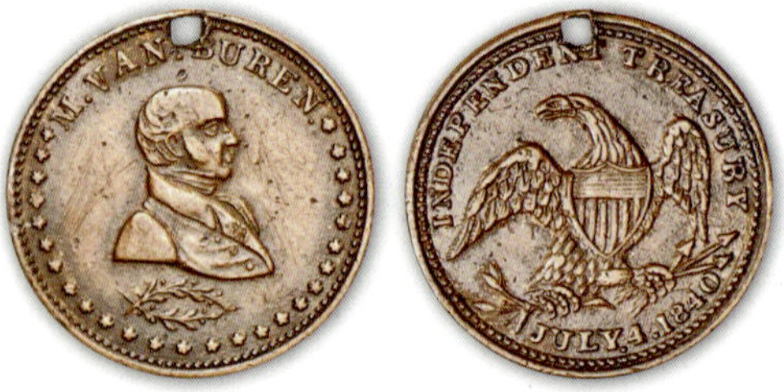

W-12-30a • Van Buren / Eagle • Low-162; HT-77. R-5. 23.7 mm. Copper. Plain edge. Holed as issued. (Some gilt; HT-77B; R-8.) Obverse with bust of Van Buren facing right, crossed laurel branches below (signifying a hoped-for victory). M. VAN. BUREN. above, 26 stars to the sides and below. Reverse with eagle in the style of federal coinage. INDEPENDENT above, JULY. 4. 1840 below. Fine and VF are typical grades. A properly graded AU is a rarity. • VF-20 $500; EF-40 $700; AU-50 $1,000.

W-12-30b • Dies as preceding • Low-183; HT-77A. R-7. 23.7 mm. Brass. Plain edge. Holed as issued. A number of pieces called Low-183 are actually Low-162 gilt before striking. Same grading comment as preceding. Ford (Stack's 2004) VF $237.75, Choice AU $2,350. • VF-20 $500; EF-40 $800; AU-50 $1,500.

13

Hard Times Store Card Tokens

Alabama Hard Times Tokens

E. & I. Bragaw
Mobile, AL / Newark, NJ
Hats and caps
W-NJ-200

(See E. & I. Bragaw, W-NJ-200.)

Hunt, Pynchon & Jackson
Mobile, AL
Hardware and cutlery
W-AL-040

The circumstances surrounding the token inscribed "Hunt, Pynchon & Jackson of Mobile Alabama, importers," remain a mystery. It is undated, and no information about the firm has been thus far located in directories or newspapers.

Russell Rulau states this:

> The partners were Jonathan Hunt, who appears in the 1830 and 1840 census reports, George A. Pynchon, who appears in the 1830 census, and someone named Jackson. The Jackson could be either of these men from the 1830 census; John H., Samuel or S.F. Jackson. Directory confirmation is lacking.

W-AL-040-10b • Low-Unlisted; HT-98. R-8. 27.3 mm. Silvered brass. This variety was missing from nearly all major sales. Ford (SBG 2013) MS-62 $11,162.

Stickney & Wilson
Montgomery, AL
Dry goods, groceries, etc.
W-AL-040

Henry G. Stickney and Joseph W. Wilson ordered brass tokens from the Scovill factory in Waterbury in 1835, per the latter firm's accounts.[1] Russell Rulau noted that only two pieces appeared at auction in the 20th century.

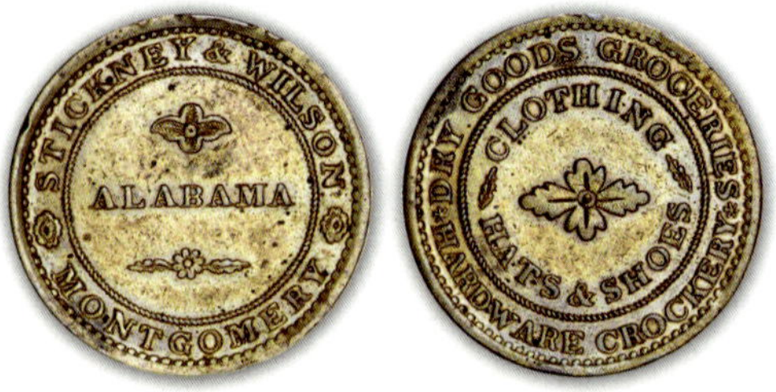

W-AL-060-10b • Low-Unlisted; HT-99. R-7. 27.3 mm. Brass. Reeded edge. Robert A. Schuman is aware of at least six pieces, and there may be others. Dice-Hicks (Stack's 2008) VF-EF $5,750. Ford (SBG 2013) AU-55 $7,637.50. Americana Sale (SBG 2013) AU-50 $4,700. Hayden (2013) VF-30 $8,000.

Connecticut Hard Times Tokens

Chamberlain, Woodruff & Scranton / Hotchkiss, Hall & Platts
Fair Haven, CT
Dry goods and groceries
W-CT-020

This token, mentioned in numismatics since the 19th century (in Benjamin Wright's "American Business Tokens," 1898, for example), is not dated and was not noticed by Lyman H. Low. Russell Rulau picked up the challenge of the enigmatic token and found most of the information given here.

The token has the advertisement of dry goods merchants Chamberlain, Woodruff & Scranton on one side—a partnership which was formed on January 1, 1836. The principals were Leonard Chamberlain, William E. Woodruff, and George H. Scranton. Horace Hotchkiss, a partner in the related firm mentioned below, provided $10,000 in cash to start this partnership. Accordingly, he was deeply involved in both enterprises.

The partnership of Hotchkiss, Hall & Platts, grocers, featured on the other side of the token, was formed three days later. The principals were Horace Rowe Hotchkiss, Edward E. Hall, and J. Curtiss Platts. Both firms were located in the Long Brick Store on Grand Street, at the east end of Fair-Haven Bridge in Fair Haven, Connecticut.

A notice in the *New Haven Daily Herald*, March 1, 1836, stated that the firm of Hotchkiss, Hall & Platts was being terminated. Chamberlain, Woodruff & Scranton was dissolved on July 25, 1837. The tokens were made by Scovill.

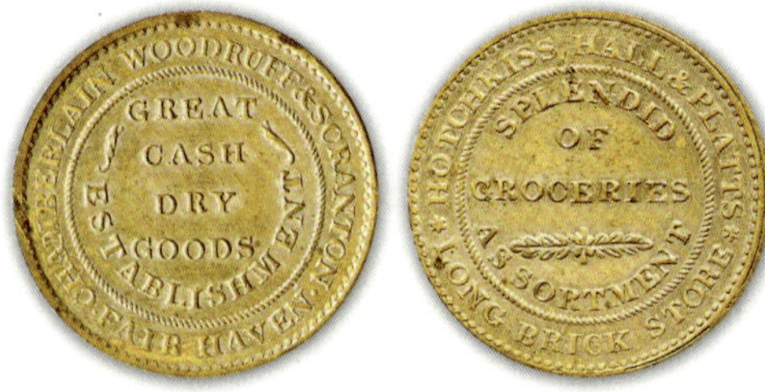

W-CT-020-10b PE • Low-Unlisted; HT-580. R-7. 29.8 mm. Brass. Some are silvered (HT-580B. R-7, illustrated). All are believed to be in brass despite the listing of HT-581 in copper. VF and EF are typical grades.

W-CT-020-10b RE • Low-Unlisted; HT-580A. R-5. 29.8 mm. Brass. (HT-580; silvered brass; R-7, per Steve Tanenbaum.) Litman Sale (Presidential Coin and Antique Co. 2003) silvered Unc $212.75. Ford (SBG 2013) AU-58 $282. VF and EF are typical grades. • Fine-12 $100; VF-20 $200; EF-40 $450; AU-50 $750.

D.W. Davenport
New Haven, CT
Variety store
W-CT-040

"Deodatus W. Davenport owned a tiny shop at 85 Chapel Street, New Haven, as early as 1836 and probably before that," Russell Rulau notes. By 1840 Davenport's address was 107 Chapel Street, possibly from renumbering and not an actual move. His token advertised combs, perfumery, baskets, toys, "general variety & fancy goods," and Hemmings genuine needles. Students at a nearby girls' school purchased many supplies there.

Rulau describes him as hunchbacked, somewhat eccentric, and a wearer of unusual clothes. He died in 1848 at age 50 and bequeathed the majority of his estate to the New Haven Orphan Asylum. His will stated, "As all my income has been derived from the savings of little children, it is right and my wish that it be returned to them."

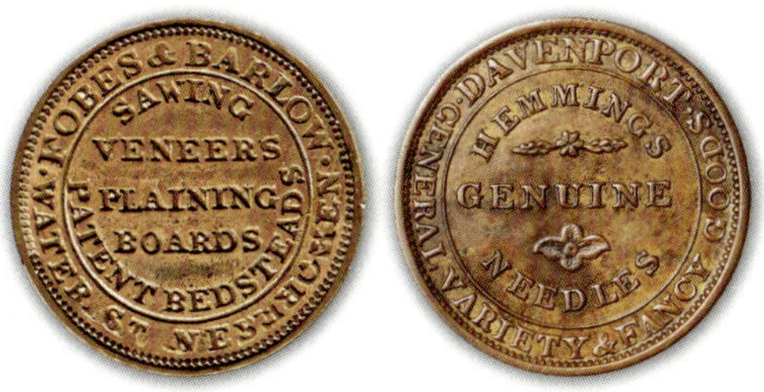

W-CT-040-10a • Rulau: "Low-305"; HT-101. R-5. 28 mm. Copper. Struck by Scovill. VF and EF are typical grades, but AU pieces are occasionally seen. • VF-20 $200; EF-40 $300; AU-50 $450.

Fobes & Barlow / New England Sash & Blind Manufactory
New Haven, CT
Sashes, doors, etc.
W-CT-060

Alpheus Fobes Jr., John M. Barlow, and Amos Hine formed the partnership of Fobes & Barlow on September 30, 1836, to make sashes, blinds, and doors. This was the successor firm to the New England Sash and Blind Manufactory—owned by Barlow, Hine, and one Elihu Atwater. This predecessor, located on Artisan Street, had been destroyed by fire on September 7. The loss was estimated at $20,000 to $25,000, and there was no insurance.[2] Fobes & Barlow revived the New England Sash and Blind Manufactory in premises on Water Street. In 1837 Fobes & Barlow established the Lewis & Beecher Co. in the same business.

Today one variety of the Fobes & Barlow token is recognized in the Rulau text. However, W. Elliot Woodward, a careful cataloger, offered lots 1452 and 1543 in his May and June 1863 sale, listing them as two different varieties of the token. They were not otherwise described. In his sale catalog of October 1877, S.K. Harzfeld described lot 730 as a brass impression from these dies.

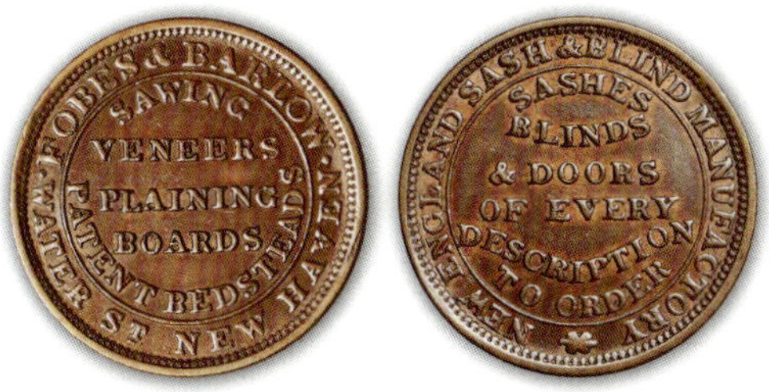

W-CT-060-10a • Rulau: "Low-291"; HT-102. R-2. 28.5 mm. Copper. Dies by Scovill. A brass example was reported in the 19th century but is not known or confirmed today. VF and EF are typical grades. • VF-20 $35; EF-40 $75; AU-50 $175.

Benedict & Burnham
Waterbury, CT
Metal products, including tokens
W-CT-080

Benedict & Burnham, which traced its beginnings to 1812, was a major force in the brass industry in Waterbury in the 19th century. During the War of 1812, Aaron Benedict, a former resident of Vermont who had served in the Revolution, bought scrap copper, set up a rolling mill in Waterbury, Connecticut, and turned out brass buttons for the government. In 1824 James Croft—by then a partner in the firm—went to England to purchase an improved rolling mill. This facilitated the increase of production. On February 2, 1829, Israel Coe became a partner, and the name was changed to Benedict & Coe. There were other partners and investors as well.

In 1832 Gordon Webster Burnham joined the partnership. After Israel Coe left, on February 14, 1834, the firm of Benedict & Burnham was formed—this is the name which appears on Hard Times tokens. The partners included Aaron Benedict, Gordon W. Burnham, Bennett Bronson, Henry Bronson, John De Forest, Samuel S. De Forest, and Alfred Platt.[3] The product line included buttons, kitchen utensils, door handles, furniture knobs, lamp accessories, and more. Most were of brass, but copper products were offered as well.

By 1840 the company had assets of more than $100,000. In that decade the telegraph was an exciting new industry, and the company was a major supplier of copper wire. On January 14, 1843, the firm incorporated as the Benedict & Burnham Manufacturing Co.[4] The company continued through various transitions until it failed in 1944.

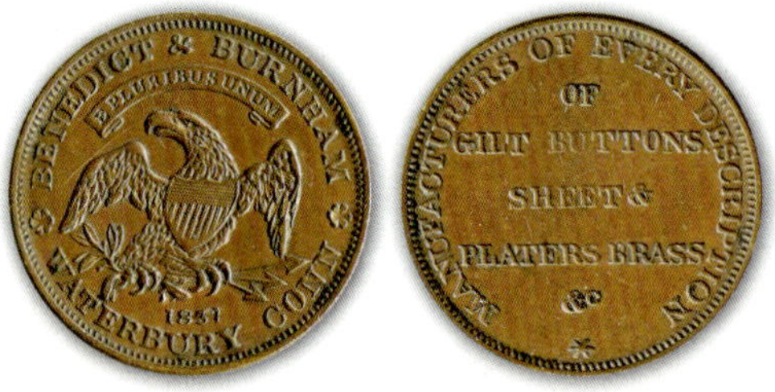

W-CT-080-10a • Low-109; HT-104. R-3. 27.5 mm. Copper. • VF-20 $70; EF-40 $150; AU-50 $250; MS-63 $500.

J.M.L. & W.H. Scovill
Waterbury, CT
Metal products including tokens
W-CT-100

The Scovill businesses can trace their beginning to 1802, when they were founded by a man called Abel Porter, and they continue in revised form today.[5] Of concern here is the partnership of J.M.L. and W.H. Scovill, which began in 1827. James Mitchell Lamson Scovill was born in Waterbury on September 4, 1789, and died May 15, 1857. His brother, William Henry Scovill, was born on July 27, 1796, and died on March 27, 1854.

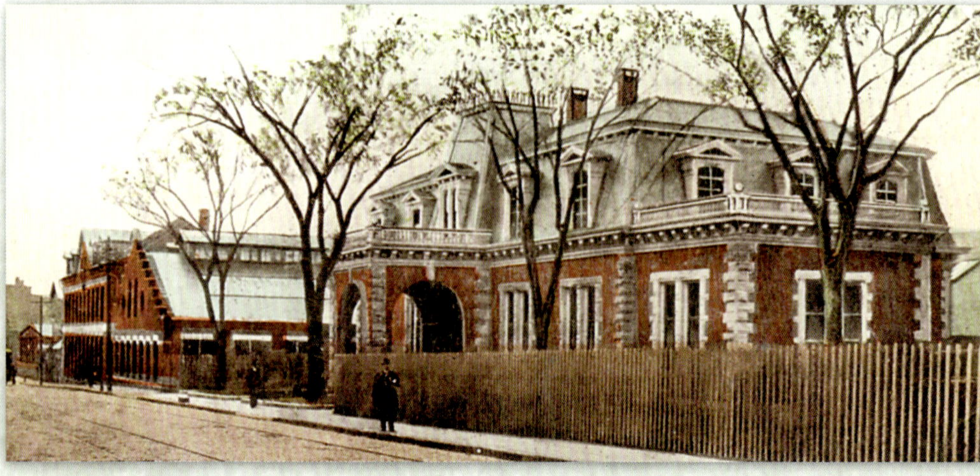

The factory of Benedict & Burnham as it appeared circa 1905.

In July 1829, William Eaves, a skilled die engraver from England, joined the company. By 1835 he was still the only such engraver on the staff. Buttons were the main product. On March 31, 1830, there was a major fire. Fortunately, the loss was insured through the Aetna Company in Hartford. This event may have inspired the image of the phoenix rising from ashes, later featured on the company's Hard Times token (although the same motif was used on political tokens).

In October 1830, at the American Institute Fair in New York City, the Scovills were awarded a "premium" for "various specimens of very superior gilt and plated buttons." This was a time before the Institute awarded medals.

In 1837 the Scovills turned out countless thousands of tokens with a Liberty Head on one side and on the other MILLIONS FOR DEFENCE BUT NOT ONE CENT FOR TRIBUTE, with NOT ONE CENT emphasized—until legal action was brought for counterfeiting in similitude to federal cents. It is likely that tokens with such text were not made after that year.[6]

In 1840 this partnership and several others joined to become Scovills & Co., which lasted until 1850. The Scovill Manufacturing Co. succeeded it and was a major producer of Civil War tokens.

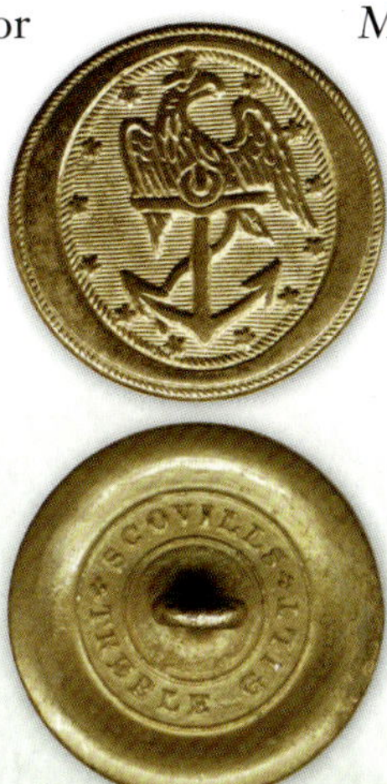

A gilt Navy button of the 1830s, with the Scovill imprint.

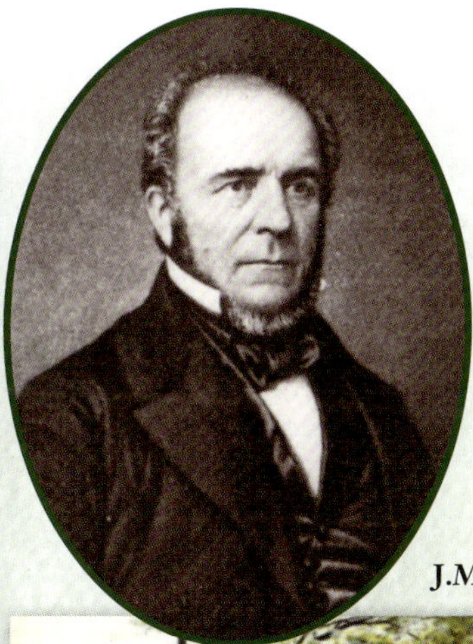

J.M.L. Scovill.

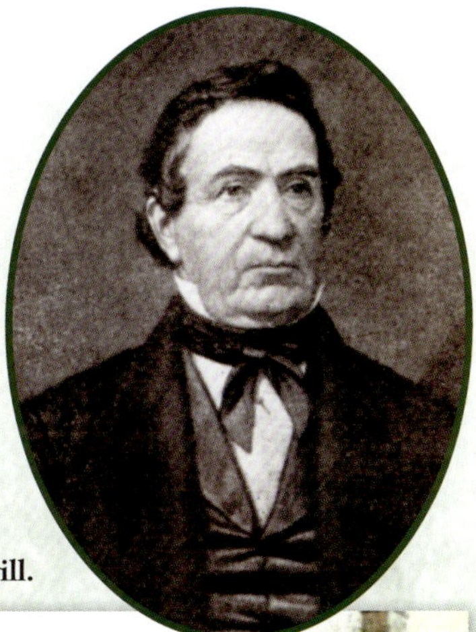

W.H. Scovill.

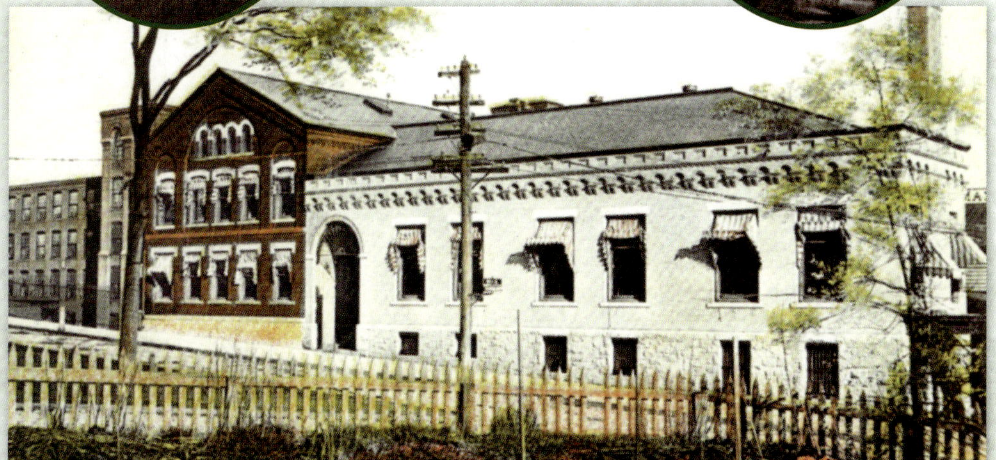

The Scovill factory as it appeared in the 1870s.

W. Elliot Woodward's sale of the J.N.T. Levick Collection, May 26 to 29, 1884, included lot 115, a medal from the 1830s that gave a capsule history of the firm and told of current products:

> [Medal with] view of the old factory of the Scovills at Waterbury, Conn. "Established 1804, enlarged 1812, burned down March 1830, rebuilt July, 1830"; rev., a wreath of oak leaves and acorns. "J.M.L. & W.H. Scoville [*sic*], Waterbury, Conn., manufacturers of naval, military, crest, fire, plain, gilt and plated, and all kinds of fancy buttons." Tin. Very Fine, indeed; *excessively rare, but one other known.* Size 29. Plate.

Woodward's sale catalog of April 27–29, 1886, included this preface to lot 1257, after which quantity groups were offered:

> About 30 years ago a number of gentlemen of New York, interested in numismatics, discovered at Waterbury, Conn., a large number of original dies of store cards and mercantile tokens. From these they obtained a number of impressions, struck in various metals, with which they supplied their own cabinets, and those of their friends. Mr. Levick then purchased the remainder, with the object of destroying, and thus rendering them scarce. In the purchase of the Levick Collection, the lot came into my hands. Very few of them have since been sold, and the entire stock is offered now, and the buyer will have a monopoly.
>
> They are all in beautiful Proof or bright Uncirculated condition, and the dies have all since been destroyed by fire, at the burning of the die room at the Scovill Co.'s factory. As no more exist, and none can be struck in the future, they must become very rare, as the number is inconsiderable. Nearly all are of old red cent size, and of the "Hard Times" period.

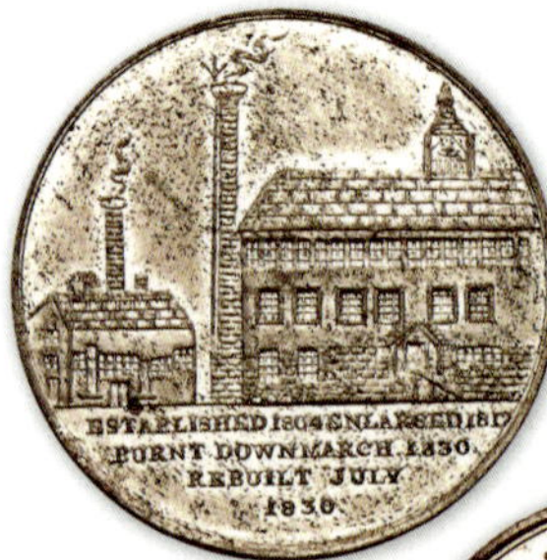

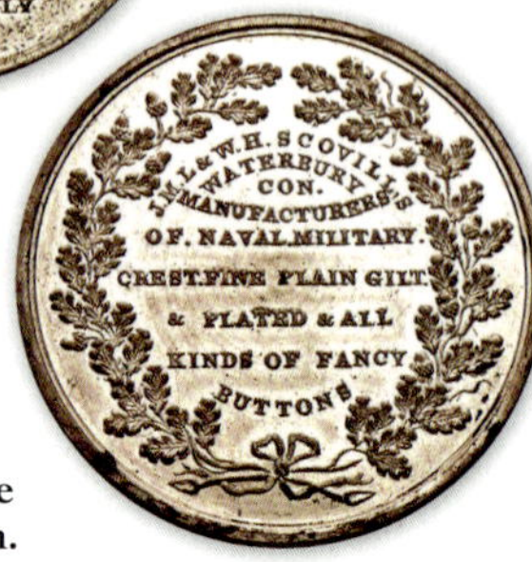

Scovill medal of 1830, white metal, 45.6 mm, showing the rebuilt works of that year. This is from the Ford Collection.

Today, numismatists consider these all to have been after the Hard Times era. Most were dated in the late 1840s into the 1850s and are described by Russell Rulau under the heading of Merchant Tokens 1845–1860.

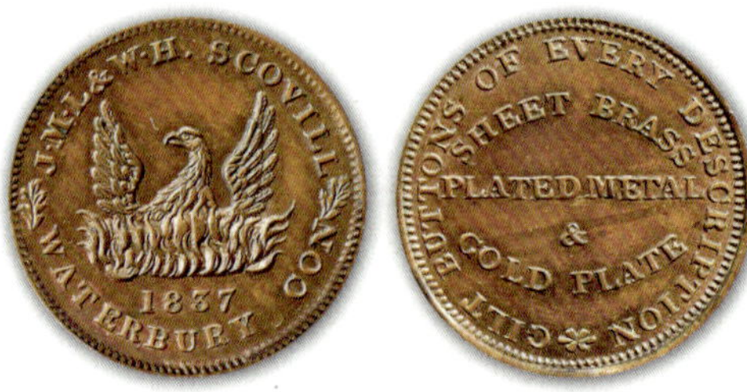

W-CT-100-10a • 1837 Phoenix • Low-130; HT-105. R-3. 28.5 mm. Copper. Plain edge. Top-drawer collections usually have an AU or lower-range Mint State example. • VF-20 $85; EF-40 $150; AU-50 $250; MS-63 $500.

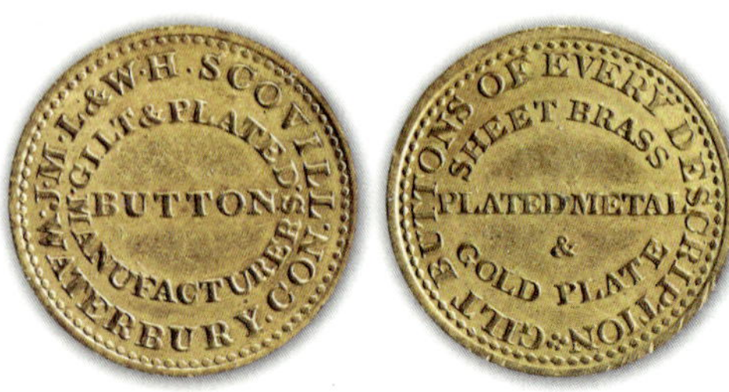

W-CT-100-15b • Lettering on both sides • Low-130A; HT-107. R-7. 26.8 mm. Brass. Reeded edge. • VF-20 $450; EF-40 $650; AU-50 $900; MS-63 $1,750.

Louisiana Hard Times Tokens

In *The Numismatist*, September 1911, under "Live American Numismatic Items," Edgar H. Adams mentioned several rare New Orleans tokens:

> Thanks are hereby tendered to Mr. Bauman L. Belden and, through him, to the American Numismatic Society, for the privilege of photographing some of the Hard Times tokens in the Society's collection. Among these were the excessively rare New Orleans pieces of J. Hall Walker and Walton, Walton, Walker & Co., and Nathan C. Folger, which are known to collectors respectively as Low Nos. 85, 106, and 121, and the unique Boutwell piece struck over a Spanish two-real silver piece, known as Low 174. The Society's collection of Hard Times tokens is an exceptionally fine one and includes some of the rarest of the series, such as Low 149 and 152, the Philadelphia shilling and fifty cent piece, struck in Feuchtwanger metal, and three varieties of the excessively rare tokens issued by Huckel, Burrows & Jennings of St. Louis, known as Low-102, 177, and 178. An inspection of this collection will afford much pleasure and some surprises to anyone interested in the series.

Daquin Brothers
New Orleans, LA
Bakers
W-LA-020

Louis D'Aquin was a baker in the 1820s and early 1830s. In the mid-1830s his business was known as Daquin Brothers and was at 36 New Levee Street, a location maintained into the early 1850s. They supplied bread to many customers, including the United States government.

All of the firm's tokens are of decagonal or 10-sided shape.

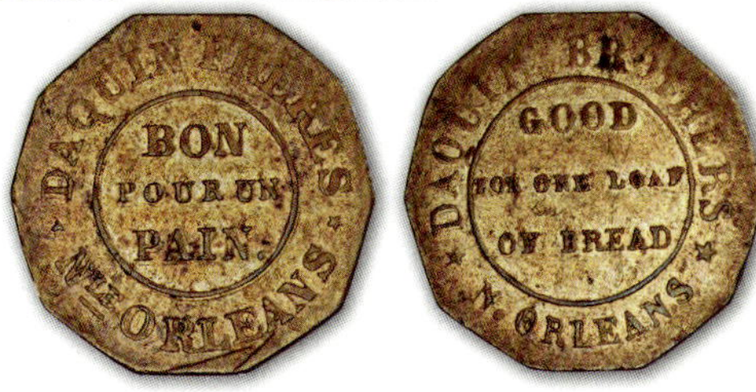

W-LA-020-10b • GOOD in single line, period after PAIN • Rulau: "Low-236"; HT-115. R-7. 23 mm. Brass. Rulau pairs this and the following variety under one HT-115 number. • VF-20 $1,350; EF-40 $2,350; AU-50 $3,000.

W-LA-020-10g • Dies as preceding • Low-Unlisted; HT-115. R-7. 23 mm. Lead.

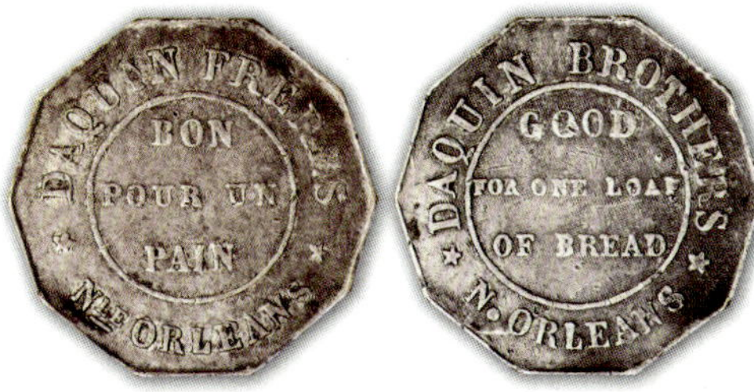

W-LA-020-15g • GOOD in single line, no period after PAIN • Rulau: "Low-236A"; HT-115A. R-7. 23 mm. Lead. One was in Scott & Co.'s sale of October 1877, lot 702: "Daquin Brothers, New Orleans, "Good For One Loaf of Bread," rev. the same in French. Scarce. Sold for $5. Dice-Hicks (Stack's 2008) F-VF $2,070. Ford (SBG 2013) EF $3,525.

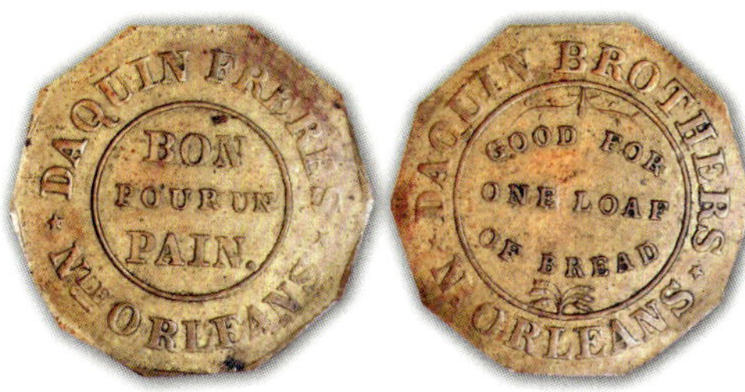

W-LA-020-20b • GOOD FOR in one line, period after PAIN • Rulau: "Low-237"; HT-116. R-6. 23 mm. Brass. Dice-Hicks (Stack's 2008) VF $633. Ford (SBG

2013) AU damaged $1,880. Ford (SBG 2013) MS-62 $3,818.75.

Nathan C. Folger
New Orleans, LA
Clothing and toys
W-LA-040

Nathan C. Folger was born in Hudson, New York, in April, 1810. He came to New Orleans on January 1, 1830, and set up in the business of wholesale clothing (including for slaves on plantations), dry goods, children's toys, and other products, all of which were imported by ship. On April 10, 1834, he married Madeline Godfrey of New Orleans. His large store at the corner of Customhouse and Old Levee streets was widely patronized and was especially known for its "plantation clothing." The business was continued by family members after the Hard Times era.

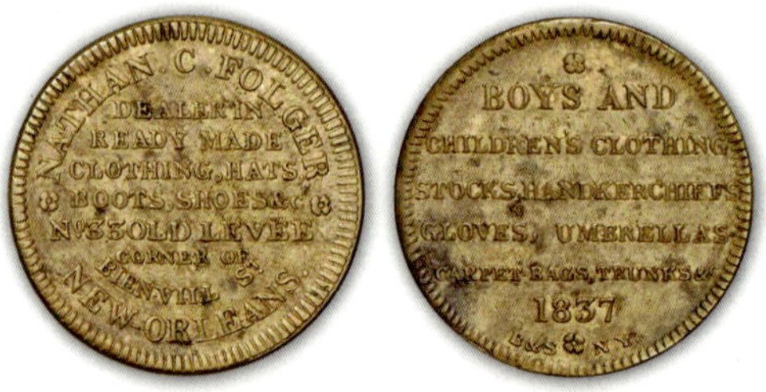

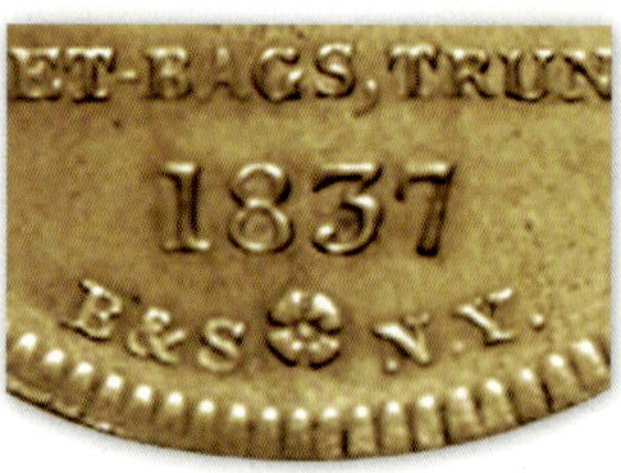

W-LA-040-10b • Low-121; HT-117. High R-7. 34 mm. Brass. One of the classic rarities in the Hard Times token series. Presidential Coin and Antique Co. recorded only three auction appearances in the 20th century, and each token had problems. Ford (Stack's 2004) AU $10,925. Dice-Hicks (Stack's 2008) EF $13,800.

Gasquet, Parish & Co.
New Orleans, LA
Dry goods
W-LA-060

William Gasquet, born in Avignon, France in 1799, emigrated with his father, Françoise Joseph de Gasquet, and his family to the Caribbean island of San Domingo. One night Joseph was awakened and told that the slaves the family owned were preparing to revolt, and that his family was in great danger. They left in a boat, were picked up by a fisherman, and were taken to Norfolk, Virginia. William grew up and married in Petersburg, Virginia, then went to New Orleans. In 1827 he set up in the dry goods business as W.A. Gasquet & Co. Soon afterward he made an arrangement to be the Southern depot for Parish, Marshall & Co., leading New York City merchants. Henry Parish, who had other mercantile interests in New York City, was his partner and financed the New Orleans branch, but remained in New York. By this time Parish was a wealthy man. The trade style was changed to Gasquet, Parish & Co. at 47 Chartres Street, the address on the firm's brass tokens. The business was very profitable to both partners. By the early 1840s it was at 18 Chartres Street. The firm owned real estate valued at $60,000, which was controlled by Parish.

Accounts vary as to when the firm closed. Court testimony of William A. Gasquet, years later in 1857, stated at one point that it closed in 1838 or 1839. Elsewhere in the testimony:

> I was in business in New Orleans from 1827 to about 1840. I was a partner of the decedent about eleven years; was on terms of intimate acquaintance with him.[7]

In 1842 the partners divided the assets of the company by lottery in a meeting held in New York. By 1857 Parish had been incapacitated for many years. Gasquet visited him occasionally when going to the city in the summer, the most recent time being 1855. Their relationship remained cordial, but in the later years Parish could only communicate with motions of his hands.

In the late 1830s Gasquet purchased a large tract of land on Camp and Saint Joseph streets. He became a developer and erected fine townhouses that were sold to wealthy buyers. The area became one of the city's most fashionable districts.

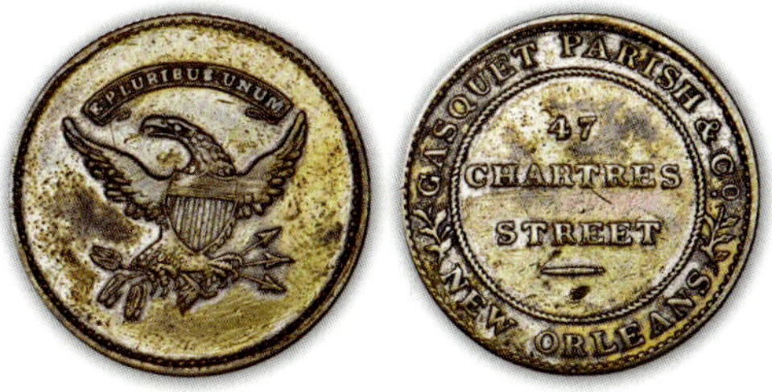

W-LA-060-20b • Rulau: "Low-344"; HT-118. R-7. 28 mm. Brass, usually lightly silvered. From Scott & Co.'s sale of October 1877, lot 703: "Gasquet Parish & Co., New Orleans, rev. spread eagle and shield, 'E Pluribus Unum,' Rare." Sold for $10, an extremely high price for the time. Woodward's 1884 sale of the Levick Collection had an example among other New Orleans token rarities. Dice-Hicks (Stack's 2008) VF $5,463. Ford (SBG 2013) EF-45 $3,055, Unc $4,700.

Henderson & Gaines
New Orleans, LA
Kitchen and household goods
W-LA-080

Russell Rulau writes that the firm of Henderson & Gaines was formed by William Henderson, born in New Hampshire circa 1808, and John G. Gaines, born there circa 1810. The firm sold china, small household furnishings, and other goods, mostly imported from England. Chinaware was the main specialty. Their ceramic plates and the related items on display at their store found a wide sale among the citizens and also sold in large quantities to the west, particularly to Texas. Their store was at 14 Canal Street. "Families, hotels, and steamboats supplied on the lowest cash terms."

On June 19, 1838, their premises were ravaged by fire. The blaze was thought to have been set by an arsonist. Several buildings, all owned by C. Paulding, were damaged or destroyed.[8] Later they were at 45 Canal Street.

During the occupation of New Orleans by Confederate forces, the firm "abetted treason." In August 1862, by which time the city had been repatriated into the Union, a committee of inquiry determined that the partnership had contributed $1,000 to the rebel cause, and fined the company $250 to go to aid the poor. The firm was dissolved in 1866 when Henderson retired. It was succeeded by Gaines & Relf.[9]

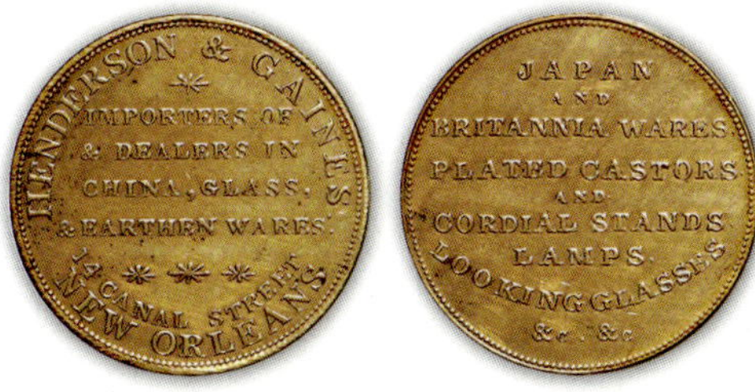

W-LA-080-20b • Rulau: "Low-254A"; HT-119. R-7. 33 mm. Brass. American Numismatic Society specimen illustrated. Low grades are usual. Dice-Hicks (Stack's 2008) VF $2,185. Ford (SBG 2013) VF with scratches $5,875, AU-58 $17,625.

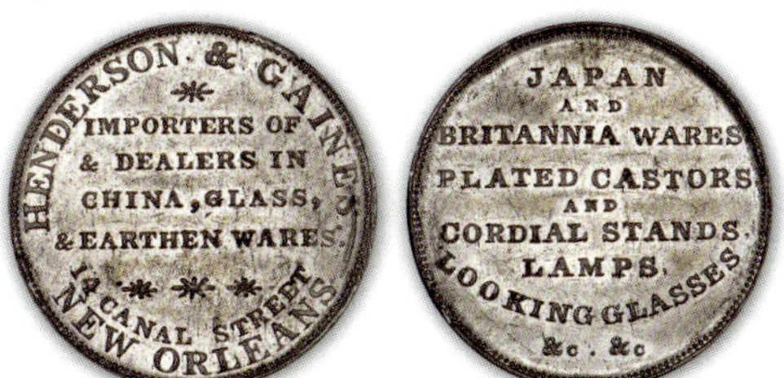

W-LA-080-20e • Rulau: "Low-254B"; HT-119A. R-9. 33 mm. White metal. Presidential Coin and Antique Co. Sale 74 (1995) AU $27.025, Dice-Hicks (Stack's 2008) Choice AU $18,400.

Henderson, Walton & Co.
New Orleans, LA
Ceramic ware
W-LA-100

Henderson, Walton & Co. advertised as importers of ceramics. Certain of its china plates and other goods were impressed "HENDERSON, WALTON & CO. / IMPORTERS / NEW ORLEANS." The company offered dining sets of several dozen or more pieces. Their clients were among the more well-to-do citizens of the city. The short-lived partnership did business from about 1834 to 1836.[10] Certain interests later went to Walton, Walker & Co. (see listing), with which H. Henderson was also involved.

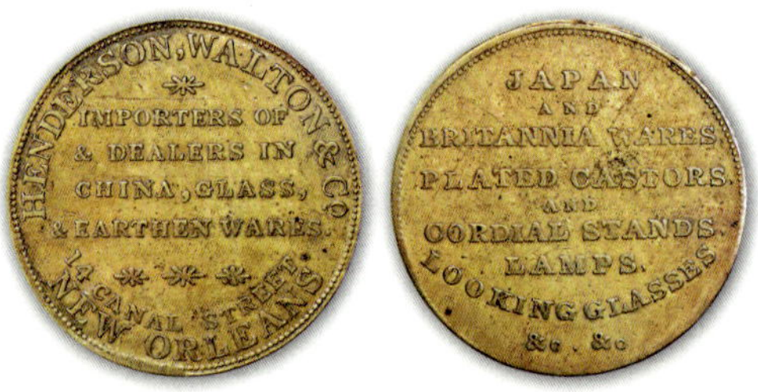

W-LA-100-10b • Rulau: "Low-254"; HT-120. R-7. 33 mm. Brass. From a sale cataloged by Emmanuel J. Attinelli and sold at Bangs & Co., January 1878, lot 242: "Henderson, Walton & Co. N.O. Brass. Fine and very rare." The token brought 50¢.[11] In Woodward's 1884 sale of the J.N.T. Levick Collection an example sold for the strong price of $11.25. Ford (SBG 2013) EF-45 $12,925.

J. Hall, Walker & Walton
New Orleans, LA
Hardware
W-LA-140

The firm of J. Hall, Walker & Walton was active in the 1830s as per the 1834 date on the token. Partner John Hall was born circa 1810 in Massachusetts. Their token was listed by Lyman H. Low in *Hard Times Tokens* in 1899, giving it an aura of desirability and value not shared with certain other New Orleans issuers who were not widely recognized until listed by Russell Rulau in the *Standard Catalog of United States Tokens 1700–1900.* Another firm, Irwin, Hall & Walton, was a separate entity in the same business at a later time.

W-LA-140-10b • Low-85; HT-121. High R-7. 33.6 mm. Brass. Virgil M. Brand had two. The silvered Mint State piece in the 2004 Ford Collection sale for sold $27,600 and reappeared in the Dice-Hicks sale in 2008, selling for $43,125. In the same sale a VG example sold for $8,625.

Part of the description from the Dice-Hicks sale describes this piece:

> Uncirculated. Plain edge. 170.1 gns. 33.6 mm. Struck coin turn. . . . Fairly sharp strike. Extremely rare: one of only two confirmed fully struck on both sides in brass, the other being the worn Low-85 that appeared in Joe Levine's sale of the Sara Hinckley Collection in 2006 (barely legible, it still sold for $6,500) and that can be found in the very next lot following this! There is one known fully struck on both sides in white metal (Ford: 158, the finest condition Hall Walker & Walton token of all seen). Virgil Brand had two Low-85's: one became Ford:157 but the history of the second is uncertain. It may have become Ford:158 or Hinckley:43 or it may still be unannounced. The Adams plate Low-85 appears to be a stunningly sharp specimen that is probably brass and is neither of the two Dice-Hicks pieces. It may be the second Brand token or a third fully struck brass Hall Walker & Walton token whose whereabouts may be guessed at. This present example is finer than the Hinckley piece, of course, and in the absence of any certain data on the condition of another we can unhesitatingly say this is the finest brass Low-85

Hall Walker & Walton token we have seen. This is only the fourth time in over 100 years that one of these great New Orleans token rarities has crossed the auction block, and interestingly, all four occurred in the past four years! This token was part of the special display of highlights from the Dice-Hicks Collection during the 2008 Long Beach, Baltimore and Phoenix mid-winter A.N.A. numismatic conventions. In 1834 New Orleans was the second most active port in America, after New York City. Ship chandlers were one-stop shopping centers to outfit sailing vessels and steamers with everything from hardware to bed sheets to, in some instances, food and provisions. A numismatic sub-specialty could be made of tokens issued by chandlers in these two cities. Ex our sale of the celebrated John J. Ford, Jr. Collection, Part IV (June 23, 2004, Lot 157); earlier, ex F.C.C. Boyd, New Netherlands Rare Coin Company, Horace Louis Philip Brand, Virgil M. Brand Collection.

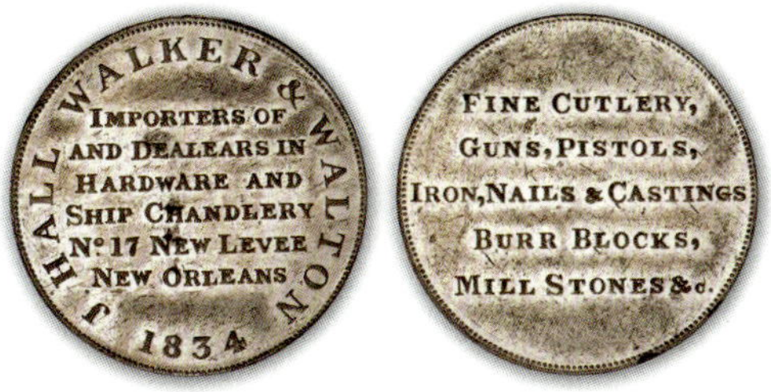

W-LA-140-10e • Rulau: "Low-85A"; HT-121A. R-9. 33.6 mm. White metal. Unique. Ford to Tanenbaum 2004.

Kohn, Daron & Co.
New Orleans, LA
Commission merchants
W-LA-160

In 1834 J. Kohn & Bordier were commission merchants at 28 Bienville Street. By 1838 Kohn, Daron & Co. was listed at the same address.[12] On March 2, 1840, petitions from Kohn, Daron & Co.—which were also sponsored by other merchants from New Orleans, Philadelphia, and New York City—were reviewed by Congress; they sought to have certain import tariffs rebated. The firm was bankrupt by March 1843, and its assets were disposed of by sheriff's sale to satisfy creditors.

W-LA-160-10b PE • Low-Unlisted; HT-431. R-8. 27 mm. Brass.

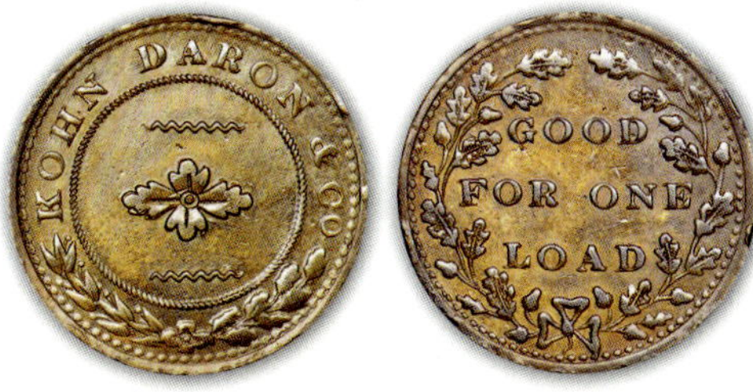

W-LA-160-10b RE • Low-Unlisted; HT-431A. R-7. 27 mm. Brass. Ford (SBG 2013) EF-45 $1,175, AU-55 $7,638. Americana Sale (SBG 2013) AU-55 $4,700.

John A. Merle & Co.
New Orleans, LA
Commission merchant
W-LA-180

John A. Merle was an importer, a commission agent, an agent in the sale of cotton, and also engaged in other commercial activities in the 1820s. In the 1830s, John A. Merle & Co. was located on Bienville Street, the address on the token. By the early 1840s, he moved to 30 Common Street. In the early 1820s, he was the New Orleans consul for Norway and Sweden. In 1842 he became consul for Switzerland. After that time his firm was known as Merle, Beyelle & Co. at 45 Old Levee Street.

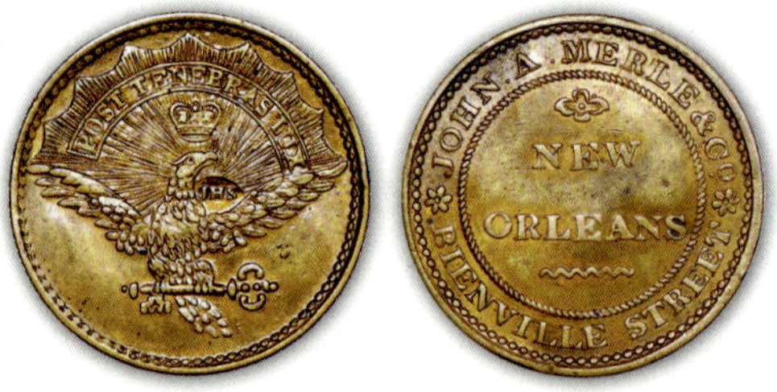

W-LA-180-10b • Rulau: "Low-264"; HT-122. R-5. 27 mm. Brass. The obverse has a spread-wing eagle with the motto POST TENEBRAS LUX above, signed with the initials JHS. The motto, "After darkness, light," a Calvinist motto, became the motto of the Protestant Reformation. Today it is the motto of several schools, the title of film, and is used elsewhere. The tokens were made by the Scovills in Waterbury. VF and EF are typical grades. Ford hoarded these; 2013 sale EF cleaned $329, EF-45 $646, AU-50 two at $764 each, AU-53 $2,350, AU-58 $1,410, prices lower than if they had been offered singly over a long period of time. Historically, market offerings have been occasional at best. Americana Sale (SBG 2013) AU-58 $1,057.50.

Puech, Bein & Co.
New Orleans, LA
Hardware
W-LA-200

By 1832, James Puech, who had been in the hardware business since 1823, partnered with John D. Bien to form Puech, Bein & Co. In that year they were at 24 Levee Street. Their token was listed by Low in 1899, after which it became highly sought.

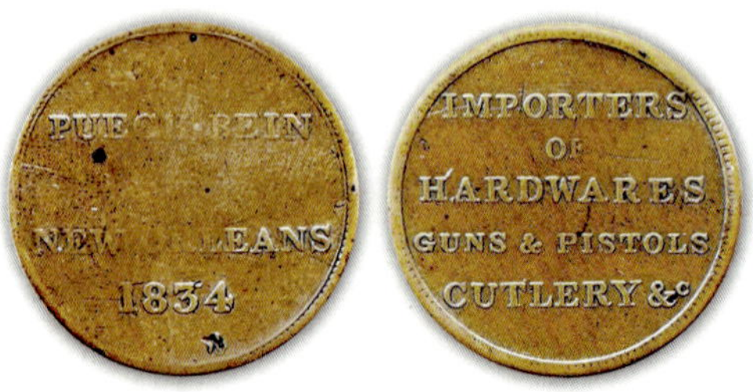

W-LA-200-10a • Low-82; HT-123. R-8. 25.5 mm. Copper. Two known: Don Partrick (ex Tilton, Gould, Fuld, Ford, Byrne, Presidential Coin and Antique Co., and Bowers) and American Numismatic Society collections, the last illustrated here.

Walton & Co.
New Orleans, LA
Hardware and chandlery
W-LA-240

Walton & Co. was another of several businesses conducted by John S. Walton and was active in the 1830s through the early 1840s, until it was dissolved in 1843. Walton was also involved in the McGehee Female Seminary that opened in New Orleans in 1838 under the direction of two ladies that had conducted a seminary in Huntsville, Alabama.

In 1841 at 17 New Levee, Walton announced:

> Phenix Foundry. The subscriber having hired the above named establishment is prepared to execute any order for iron or brass castings, copper and sheet iron, and blacksmiths' work, on reasonable terms.[13]

A skilled mechanic was on hand. Anyone calling on Walton at 18 New Levee could be taken to the foundry in "a comfortable and expeditious conveyance."

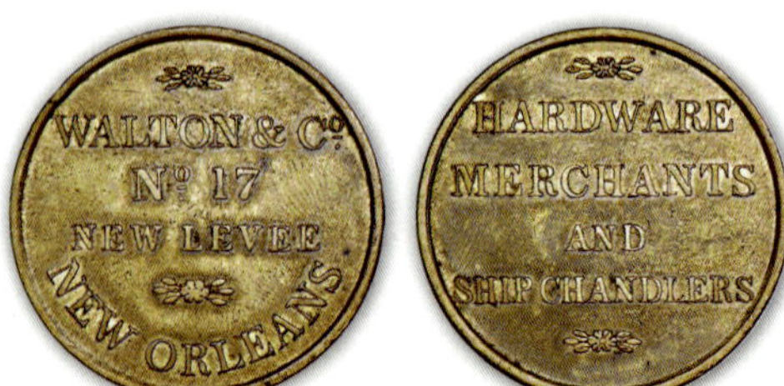

W-LA-240-10b • Rulau: "Low-288"; HT-128. R-7. 33 mm. Brass. Steinberg (Stack's 2002) holed VF with scratches $1,610. Sarah Hinckley Presidential Coin and Antique Co. Sale 122 (2006) EF with nicks and scratches $3,565. Presidential Coin and Antique Co. Sale 79 (2009) VF-EF with attempted puncture $2,300. Dice-Hicks (Stack's 2008) AU $9,775. Ford (SBG 2013) AU-58 $6,462, AU with spot on the reverse $15,275.

Walton, Walker & Co.
New Orleans, LA
Hardware and chandlery
W-LA-260

Walton, Walker & Co., iron mongers, was one of several businesses involving John S. Walton. In 1837 this business was located from 16 to 19 New Levee. Their 1836 token has the address of 16 New Levee. On July 17, 1837, when money was scarce, the firm advertised this in the *Arkansas Gazette:*

> Walton, Walker & Co., Nos. 17 and 18 New Levee, New Orleans, take this method of informing their friends and customers in Arkansas, that they will receive, in payment of notes and accounts due them, Mississippi, Alabama, and Tennessee paper at ten per cent discount, and all New Orleans paper at par. For specie, they will allow twenty per cent, premium, and on treasury warrants ten per cent, premium.

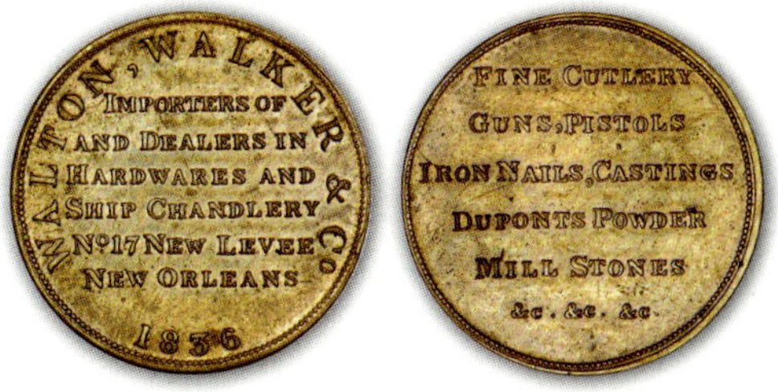

W-LA-260-10b • Low-106; HT-129. R-7. 34 mm. Brass. Russell Rulau lists this in white metal, unknown to Low and in modern times to Robert A. Schuman, so not given a separate entry here. EF and AU are the grades known to exist. Ford (Stack's 2004) Choice EF $48,875 to Dice-Hicks (Stack's 2008) Choice EF $63,250.

Maryland Hard Times Tokens

John L. Chapman
Baltimore, MD
Druggist
W-MD-020

According to Russell Rulau, John L. Chapman, born in 1813 at Fell's Point, Baltimore, began business as a druggist in 1834 at the southeast corner of Baltimore and South streets. In 1841 he moved to the other side of South Street.

After the Hard Times era, in 1846, he and his brother Jonathan acquired the glass manufacturing company formerly run by his uncle, George Chapman. He followed this business into the early 1860s. In 1862, 1864, and 1866 he was elected mayor of Baltimore. In 1869 President U.S. Grant appointed him as naval officer of the Port of Baltimore. Later he was superintendent of the bonded warehouse there. Chapman died on November 18, 1880.

Chapman's two tokens are soda checks from dies of good workmanship. "BALTI" (the left side of a BALTIMORE punch) was separately stamped below the eagle on such pieces.

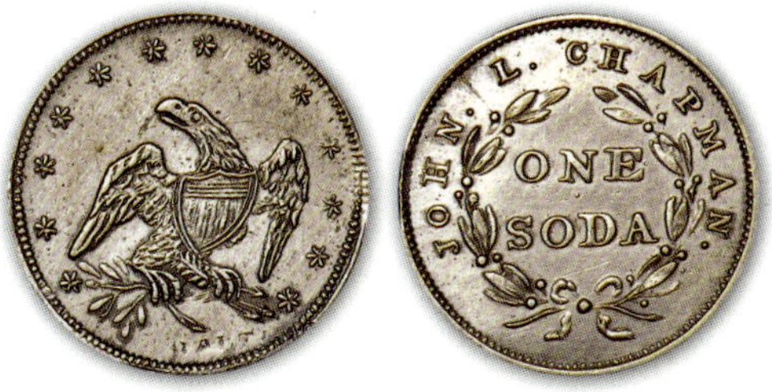

W-MD-020-10j • **Stars distant from eagle** • Rulau: "Low-378"; HT-132. R-7. 17 mm. German silver. On some (perhaps all?) a die crack on the reverse extends from the border after JOHN. to an outer berry. VF and EF are typical grades. • VF-20 $1,000; EF-40 $1,500; AU-50 $2,500.

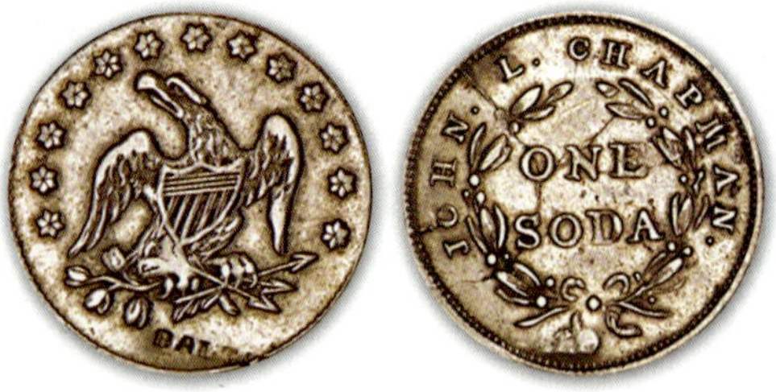

W-MD-020-15j • Stars close to eagle • Rulau: "Low-379"; HT-133. R-7. 17 mm. German silver. On the Dice-Hicks example (illustrated) the reverse die is shattered. VF and EF are typical grades. • VF-20 $900; EF-40 $1,350; AU-50 $2,000.

H. Herring / Fair Mount Gardens Baltimore, MD
Hotel Keeper
W-MD-040

This token was called to Lyman H. Low's attention shortly after the turn of the 20th century. He designated it as No. 173 and listed it in his 1906 supplement as follows:

> 173. *Obverse*, H. HERRING above FAIR MOUNT. An ornament above and below the issuer's name. *Reverse.* A continuous wreath enclosing the date 1834. Metal Wm. Size 35. R. 8.
>
> This token first came to my notice about four years ago, and from the best investigation I have been able to make it was unknown to collectors until then; I have never learned of its duplicate. Notwithstanding the fact that collectors of store-cards and tokens have been always with us, and the work in their special lines has been unceasing, this interesting piece seems to have evaded their watchful eyes.
>
> When we remember that such cabinets as those of Messrs. Groh, Levick, Geo. B. Mason, Benjamin Betts, Benjamin Tilton, Dr. James, Dr. Wright and others, contained many precious cards, the record prices of which in various sales show that they have brought from $10 to $50, it is remarkable that this piece should have escaped the notice of them all for nearly seventy years. The indefatigable labor and zeal of Mr. Duffield has traced this token to Baltimore, though at first sight it was his opinion—shared by Dr. Wright and myself,—that it originated in Philadelphia.

Mr. Herring was the proprietor of a hotel, promenade and pleasure ground at "Fair Mount," to which he appears to have given the name. Its site was formerly known as Hampstead Hill, in the eastern part of the city of Baltimore. His advertisement appears in the *Baltimore American and Commercial Advertiser* in May, 1834, when he announced that he was "erecting at great expense, a large and elegant House" etc. The resort was subsequently known as "Fair Mount Gardens." His name is found in the Baltimore directories from 1834 to 1845.

Just what purpose this piece served, it is very difficult to assert at this remote time, but the fact that it is dated would lead one to believe it was used in some detail of his conduct of the place, during the first year of its existence, and not as an advertising venture.

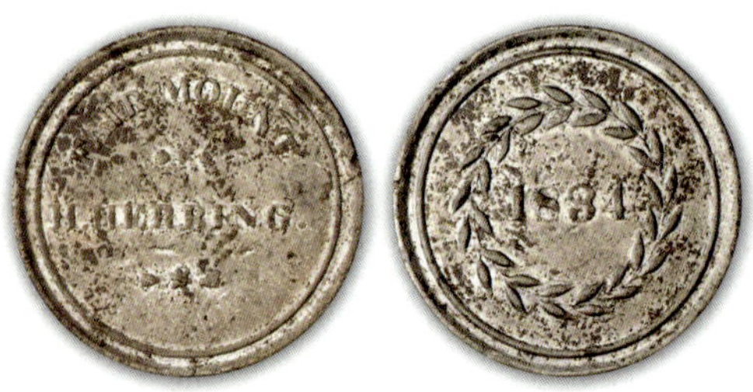

W-MD-040-10e • Low-173; HT-139. R-9. 35 mm. White metal. This unique token was given a price of $50,000 by Russell Rulau in the 4th edition of the *Standard Catalog of United States Tokens 1700–1900*, the highest of any Hard Times token. The runner up was Low-54A, AM I NOT A MAN & A BROTHER at $29,500 VF and $35,000 EF. In the Stephen L. Tanenbaum estate (the most highly valued Hard Times token in that holding), ex Benjamin P. Wright, F.C.C. Boyd, and John J. Ford Jr. collections, the last at $32,200.

Randall & Co.
Baltimore, MD
Mineral water
W-MD-080

Dudley A. Randall & Co. was in business circa 1840 to 1842 in the basement of Barnum's City Hotel on the southwest corner of Fayette and Calvert streets on Monument Square. After 1842, and until 1871, the "& Co." designation was not used. David Barnum was the lead partner among the owners. The hotel was constructed in 1826 and could accommodate 500 guests. In the mid-to-late 1830s Randall was a maker of mead liquor at 126 North Howard Street. He died on February 6, 1881, at age 75.

W-MD-080-10j PE • Rulau: "Low-403"; HT-147. Estimated R-8. 22 mm. German silver. Unverified. Not known to Robert A. Schuman or Steve Hayden. • VF-20 $300; EF-40 $400; AU-50 $550.

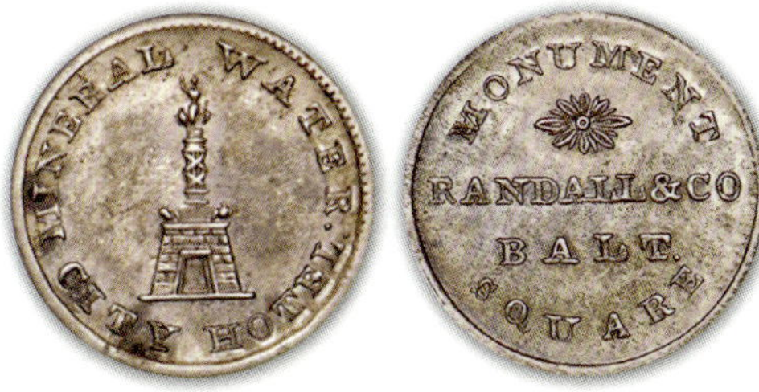

W-MD-080-10j RE • Rulau: "Low-403A"; HT-147A. R-5. 22 mm. German silver. Ford (1913) AU-55 $294, MS-62 spotted, two $305 and $352, MS-62 $499. • VF-20 $200; EF-40 $300; AU-50 $400.

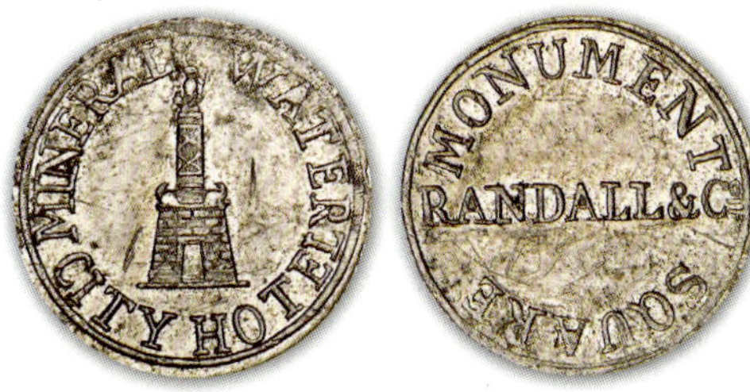

W-MD-080-15g PE • Rulau: "Low-403B"; HT-148. R-8. 22 mm. Lead or white metal. Two reported. Dice-Hicks (Stack's 2008) AU $7,475 (illustrated). Ford (SBG 2013) Fine-12 $822.50.

Massachusetts Hard Times Tokens

Hard Times tokens of Massachusetts are mostly the size of copper cents, exceptions being the smaller-diameter issues of the Roxbury Coaches and related Maverick Coach, both in Feuchtwanger Composition or similar alloy.

Robinson's, Jones & Co., token manufacturers of Attleboro, supplied many customers in the East. Most familiar of these tokens, perhaps, are those with the standing figure of Lafayette and the date of his death, May 20, 1834. Among the firm's Massachusetts issues are some non-related mulings using a die showing a planing machine, made for S.B. Schenck & Co. Likely, these were made just to turn out a quantity of tokens to be sold into the marketplace for various merchants who ordered miscellaneous tokens wholesale, not as commissions from the firms involved.

The tokens of William Rutter of Boston, with inscriptions relating to music on one side and junk metal on the other, reflecting his two simultaneous businesses, are rarities today—making him the most elusive merchant.

H.M. & E.I. Richards
Attleboro, MA
Jewelry trade
W-MA-010

Two young men, cousins Henry Manning Richards and Edmund Ira Richards, ages 18 and 15 respectively, formed their partnership in 1830, entering the jewelry business. Both had learned the trade from Henry's father Ira. The reverse die used on their tokens has them as manufacturers of jewelry near the Union House in Attleboro.

E.H. Richards, son of Henry M. Richards, was interviewed in the late 19th century by Lyman H. Low and stated that many thousands of the tokens were struck and wholesaled at 60¢ to 75¢ per hundred. Likely the comment about striking the tokens is incorrect—a result of passed-down memories of his father from years earlier. Russell Rulau's research calls into question the idea that they actually manufactured tokens, contrary to comments in the 1899 Low text. More likely they distributed tokens struck locally by Robinson's, Jones & Co.

Token distribution probably began in 1834 or 1835. In 1837 Henry moved to Philadelphia, where he continued in the jewelry trade for about six years. In Philadelphia Henry traded as H.M. Richards' Wholesale Jewelry Store at No. 9 North Fifth Street. Within the store was a branch display facility of Smith & Co., of Smith's Clock Establishment, whose home branch was located at 7-1/2 Bowery, New York City—this firm was also an issuer of Hard Times tokens. Edmund continued the business in Attleboro.

A variant history is given by John Daggett in *A Sketch of the History of Attleborough*, 1894:

> E. Ira Richards & Co. is the oldest firm in town, though it exists at present under a name of comparatively recent date. It began in 1833, when Hervey[14] M. and Edmund Ira Richards formed a partnership under the name of H.M. & E.I. Richards. In 1834 the name was changed to Ira Richards & Co. by the entrance of Ira Richards.
>
> In 1836 H. M. Richards retired, and George Morse and Virgil Draper became members, the name remaining unchanged. In 1841 the two last-named gentlemen withdrew, and Abiel Codding entered the firm. The original building erected by this firm not long after its establishment stood about where the present one stands. The second one was built on to the first about forty years ago, and the present one, probably not far from twenty years old, is as large as any, if not the largest, in town.

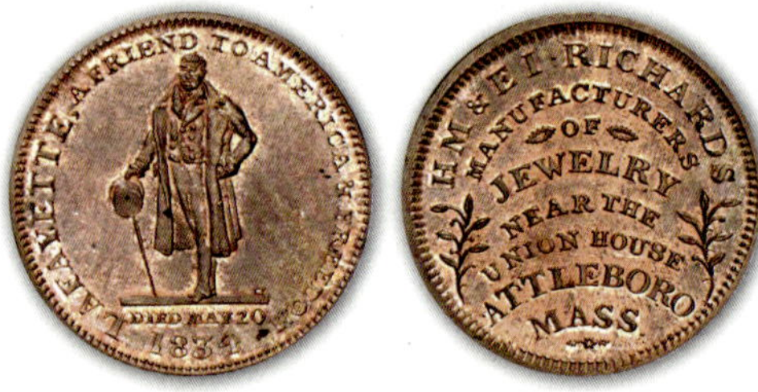

W-MA-010-10a • Low-83; HT-150. R-1. 28.5 mm. Copper. Obverse die features Lafayette and his 1834 death date. Lafayette, the French hero of the American Revolution, paid a return visit to the United States in 1824 and 1825 and visited each of the states. The Lafayette image on the token is after a popular engraving by Ary Scheffer that was also used on some bank notes. Although this token is seen with frequency in lower grades, AU pieces are slightly scarce and Mint State examples are rare. • VF-20 $30; EF-40 $50; AU-50 $85; MS-63 $250.

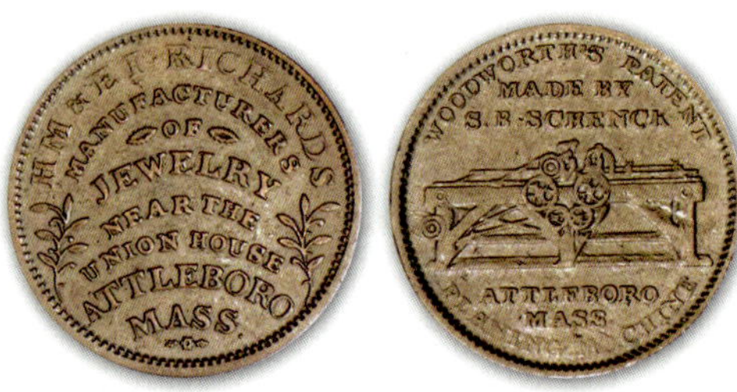

W-MA-010-15a • Low-164; HT-151 and 159 (inadvertent duplicate listing). R-3. 28.5

mm. Copper. Muling with unrelated die of S.B. Schenck & Co., likely made to create tokens for sale at a discount, without a commission from either merchant. No. 164 was the last entry in Lyman H. Low's 1899 *Hard Times Token* book. It was in no particular order in the listing, suggesting that it was a late discovery at the time. This token is usually seen in lower grades although there are scattered listings for rare AU or Mint State pieces. (Also listed under S.B. Schenck & Co., W-MA-040) • VF-20 $50; EF-40 $85; AU-50 $150; MS-63 $400.

Robinson's, Jones & Co.
Attleboro, MA
Button manufacturer
W-MA-020

The button-making industry commenced in Attleboro in 1823 when Richard Robinson, Virgil Blackinton, and Willard Robinson formed Richard Robinson & Co.[15] In 1836 the two Robinsons formed R. & W. Robinson (see listing for their Hard Times tokens). The machinery used by Richard Robinson & Co. was of their own invention and manufacture and was driven by horse power. Richard conducted the business on a small scale in the early years and encountered many challenges and difficulties. The other partners all played a minor role or eventually retired. In 1826 a new company was formed with the same name. Business was conducted in a shop measuring about 35 by 22 feet, enlarged to that size in 1826. Gilt buttons were introduced.

In 1827 the firm moved into a new brick factory 60 feet long, 25 feet wide, and two stories tall. In 1828 a 25-foot addition was made to the building's length. Power was from water carried from the Ten Mile River. The facility included a rolling mill to make brass sheets.

William Henry Jones, who apprenticed as a diecutter in England, joined the business in 1828, forming Robinson's, Jones & Co. The other partners were Richard and Willard Robinson, William Henry, and H.M. Draper. By 1832 the company had 75 employees, of whom 30 were women. Production was about 100 gross of buttons per day. These were used on military, sporting, and other clothing.

Edward Hulseman, who engraved many Hard Times token dies and signed some with his initial H, was a die sinker in Attleboro from about 1833 to 1836 and worked for Robinson's, Jones & Co., and its successor in 1836, R. & W. Robinson. From 1837 to 1849, he was at 80 Edward Street in New York City where he issued tokens and paper scrip notes. In July 1840 he was implicated in counterfeiting bank notes using plates and equipment formerly owned by Burton, Edmunds & Co. and fled to Canada.[16]

At the sixth annual Fair of the American Institute, held in New York City from October 16 to 19, 1843, the company received this honor: "Robinson, [*sic*] Jones & Co., Attleborough, Mass., for the best specimen of military, naval, and sporting buttons, and for the truth and finish of plain flat buttons, for sale at their store, No. 11 Cedar Street—silver medal." Including this, the firm had been awarded three silver medals and two diplomas at various exhibitions.

The company had capital of about $50,000. A contemporary account stated that making a typical gilt button involved more than 30 processes and handling 21 times. In 1835 the firm had about 100 employees. Thirteen tenements for employees had been erected earlier, and by 1834 several new building were complete. The cluster of housing was known locally as Robinsonville. This later became part of Attleborough Falls.

On November 24, 1834, Jones sold his interest in the partnership and soon after moved to Waterbury, Connecticut, where he formed W.H. Jones & Co., maker of buttons. The name Robinson's, Jones & Co. was subsequently changed to R. & W. Robinson (see next entry).

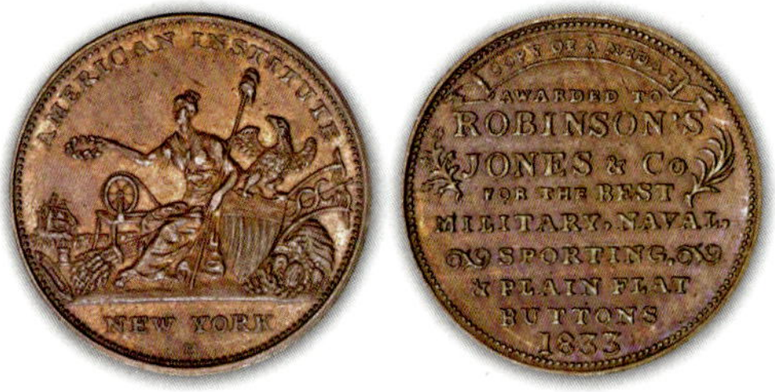

W-MA-020-10a • Low-75; HT-152. R-2. 28.5 mm. Copper. Obverse with American Institute, same die without hyphen in NEW YORK as used on two varieties of W-MA-030 tokens. Reverse die with normal 1 (1833) even with the top of the 8. H (THE BEST) leans slightly right. Bottom of stem at left is small. Readily available in higher grades such as AU and lower levels of Mint State. • VF-20 $30; EF-40 $45; AU-50 $85; MS-63 $275.

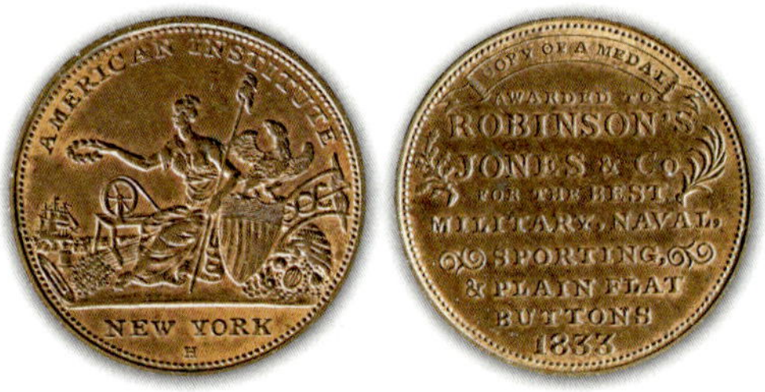

W-MA-020-15a • Low-76; HT-153. R-1. 28.5 mm. Copper. Obverse as preceding. The reverse is a close copy of the preceding, but with minute differences. Short 1 (1833) below the top of the 8. H (THE BEST) is vertical. Bottom of stem at left is larger than the preceding. Sometimes described as having a slanted 1 in the date, but this is not distinctive. Rulau lists a silver plated version as HT-153A (not listed here in the present text). Robert A. Schuman, long-time specialist in the series, commented: "I don't believe such a token is an original striking."[17] Readily available in higher grades such as AU and lower levels of Mint State. • VF-20 $25; EF-40 $40; AU-50 $65; MS-63 $225.

R. & W. Robinson
Attleboro, MA
Button manufacturer
W-MA-030

R. & W. Robinson was the successor in interest to Robinson's, Jones & Co. with the name change made in late 1834. The partners were Richard and Willard Robinson. The firm underwent bankruptcy soon after the Hard Times era ended and was succeeded in 1848 by D. Evans & Co., with Daniel Evans being numismatically remembered as the maker of a series of tokens with the Hope, anchor, and shield Rhode Island reverse die.[18] In 1840, for the William Henry Harrison presidential campaign, they struck tokens with a log cabin and the inscription, "Harrison and Reform."[19]

By 1843, button fashions changed, competition increased, and the firm was closed for a time. It soon reopened and concentrated on making buttons for the military and police. John Hatch, a staff mechanic, devised a machine to make suspender buttons. This machine was patented by Willard Robinson on February 20, 1845. Six such devices were made, one of which was sent to Germany. Each could make from tin plate 23 buttons a minute or 13,800 in a day. These buttons were profitable to produce and were made by the millions.

In October 1836, in Niblo's Garden, New York City, the American Institute held its 9th annual fair, and the official report of the event included this award: "R. & W. Robinson, Attleborough, Mass. for a most splendid specimen of buttons. *Gold Medal.*" This furnished the motif for the three varieties of tokens issued by the firm. They were made by the tens of thousands and widely distributed in their time.

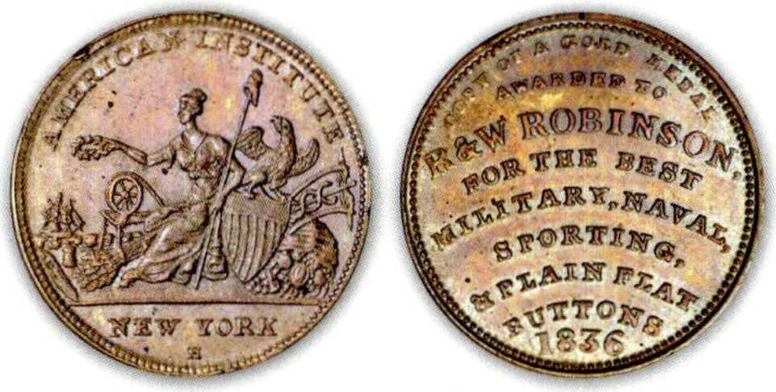

W-MA-030-10a • Low-103; HT-154. R-3. 28.5 mm. Copper. Obverse die with NEW YORK (no hyphen). Reverse die the same as W-MA-010-20a, but in a later state with E (MEDAL) filled. VF and EF are typical grades, AU tokens are elusive, and true Mint State examples are rarities. MITAD tokens were struck over some of these. • VF-20 $40; EF-40 $75; AU-50 $150; MS-63 $350.

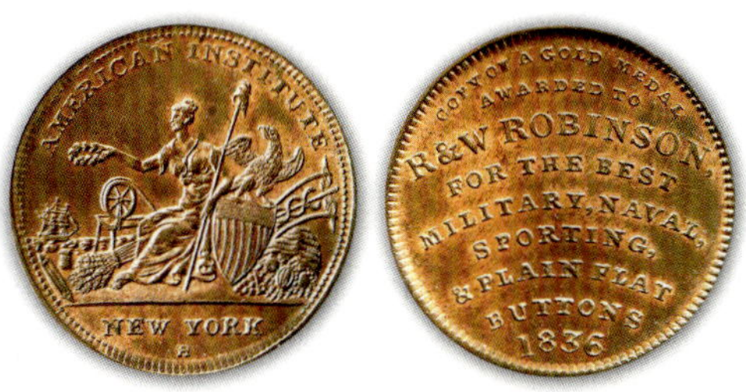

W-MA-030-15a • Low-104; HT-155. R-1. 28.5 mm. Copper. Obverse die as preceding with NEW YORK (no hyphen). Reverse with A (AWARDED) opposite Y (COPY). 1 (1836) distant from U (BUTTONS). Earlier reverse die state than W-MA-30-10a and therefore struck first. AU and lower Mint State tokens are easily found. • VF-20 $25; EF-40 $40; AU-50 $65; MS-63 $225.

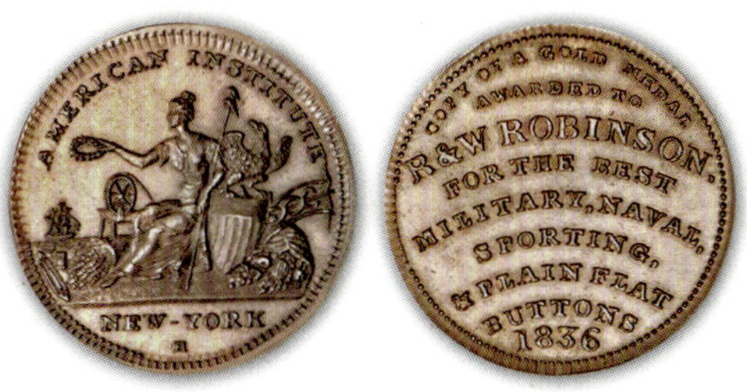

W-MA-030-20a • Low-105; HT-156. R-4. 28.5 mm. Copper. New obverse die with NEW-YORK (with hyphen). Reverse with A (AWARDED) opposite space between Y (COPY) and O (OF). 1 (1836) close to U (BUTTONS). EF and AU grades are typical in great collections auctioned in the past. • VF-20 $100; EF-40 $175; AU-50 $300; MS-63 $750.

S.B. Schenck
Attleboro, MA
Planing machine manufacturer
W-MA-040

Under the Woodward patent, Samuel B. Schenck manufactured machines that planed wood at a high speed. He advertised extensively in his time.

The 1850 Census lists Samuel (45), his wife Caroline (40), and their children Caroline B. (21), Sarah (20), Elaine (14), Henry (12), Angenette (11), and Samuel B. Jr. (3). Ellen Hardy (22), born in Ireland, was the live-in housekeeper. Schenck owned $26,000 in declared real estate. Samuel B. was born in New York, as was daughter Sarah. Other family members were all born in Massachusetts.

In the *Boston Traveler*, July 16, 1833, Samuel B. Schenck advertised:

> Patent Planing Machines. The subscriber, having been engaged in improving, building, and erecting Woodworth's Patent Planing Machines for the past three years, respectfully announces to the public that he is now building them upon the most improved construction, combining strength, convenience, durability and neatness with economy.
>
> His Machine Shop is in Attleborough, Mass. on the old Boston Road, half a mile from Hatch's Tavern, or the junction of the old Boston Road and Providence and Union Turnpike, where the above machines will be furnished at the shortest notice. Sam'l B. Schenck per Jas. W. Schenck, agent. N.B. Ten of the above machines nearly finished and will be ready for delivery in a few days.

In 1836 Schenck was on the first board of directors of the newly-formed Attleborough Bank. In 1837 the report of the annual Fair held by the Massachusetts Charitable Mechanic Association included this:

> S.B. Schenck, Attleboro'. Planing Machine. This is Woodworth's machine, improved. It is too well known to need any description. There have been several improvements which have added to the value of the machine; and we can only say it is a good machine, durable and strong; leaves a good surface, and works quickly.

In the *Boston Traveler*, November 1, 1839, Samuel B. Schenck advertised:

> Woodworth's & Emmons' Patent Planing, Tonguing & Grooving Machine. Warranted to plane 7,500 to 15,000 feet in 12 hours. The subscriber having had nine years' experience in building the above machines offers them for sale at his establishment in Foxborough, 5 miles from the Foxborough depot and 4 miles from the Mansfield depot of the Boston & Providence Rail-Road.
>
> Patent rights in North Carolina and several other states for sale on favorable terms. Applications post-paid will receive immediate attention. Samuel B. Schenck, Foxborough, Ms. N.B. Machines may be seen in operation at the Mill of Capt. Richard Mann, Boston, and in many other cities and towns in the United States.

The 1850 census lists his company with $25,000 capital, employing 47 men who earned a total average of $1,405 per month. They made 79 machines per year, with a value totaling $30,000. Power was provided by water.

In 1852 Schenck was listed as a machinist in Mansfield, Massachusetts.

Of the tokens, only W-MA-140-10a completely relates to Schenck's business. The other three are mulings with non-related reverses. Likely the tokens were struck by Robinson's, Jones & Co. of Attleboro.

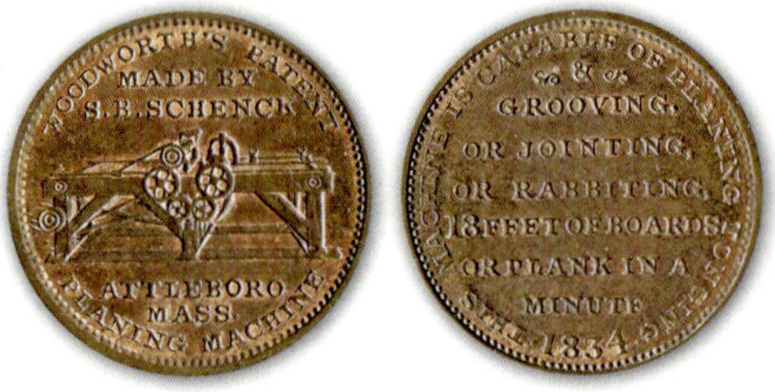

W-MA-040-10a • Low-84; HT-158. R-1. 28.5 mm. Copper. Schenck reverse die. These tokens were produced for Schenck to advertise his business, after which the die was used to make non-related mulings. Available in lower Mint State grades but slightly scarce as such. Most show evidence of having circulated for many years. • VF-20 $30; EF-40 $45; AU-50 $75; MS-63 $225.

(W-MA-010-15a) • Low-164; HT-151 and 159 (inadvertent duplicate listing). R-3. 28.5 mm. Copper. Muling with non-related H.M. & E.I. Richards die, likely made to create tokens for sale at a discount, without a commission from either merchant. Usually seen in lower grades. (Listed as W-MA-010-15a under H.M. & E.I. Richards.)

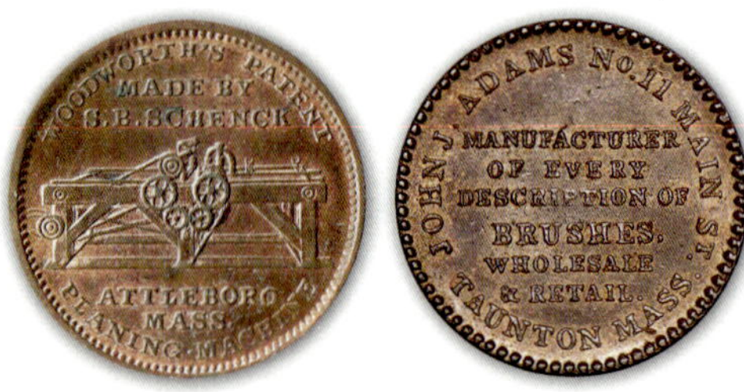

W-MA-040-20a • Rulau: "Low-326"; HT-160. R-2. 28.5 mm. Copper. Muling with a non-related Peck & Burnham die as used on W-MA-110. Made by Robinson's, Jones & Co. to create items for circulation, not on commission for either firm mentioned.

Typically seen VF or EF, but lower-range Mint State coins are occasionally offered. • VF-20 $35; EF-40 $70; AU-50 $175; MS-63 $400.

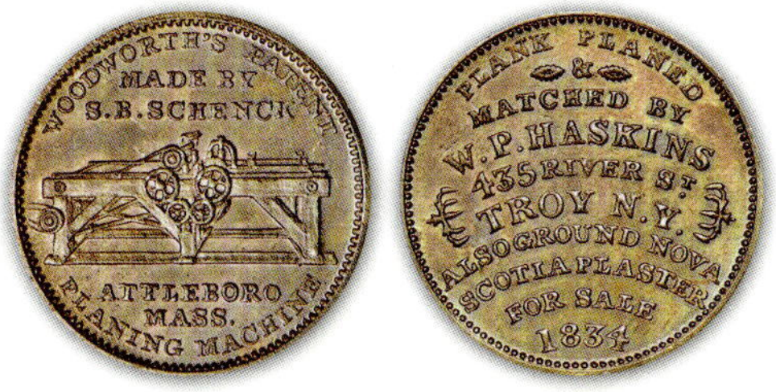

W-MA-040-25a • Low-80; HT-157 and 362. R-1. 28.5 mm. Copper. Muling with die for W.P. Haskins of Troy, New York, who among other services offered to plane planks. Likely made as a circulating token for Haskins. One is known struck over Low-83. (Also see listing under Haskins in Troy.) VF and EF grades are par for the course. At the AU level this otherwise common variety is very hard to find. • VF-20 $30; EF-40 $45; AU-50 $100.

Farnsworth, Phipps & Co.
Boston, MA
Dry goods dealers
W-MA-070

Walter Farnsworth and William Phipps formed Farnsworth, Phipps & Co. on September 2, 1819. Located at 14 Market Street, the company specialized in "European, India & American goods."

In August 1825, Phipps married Miss Elizabeth L. Young. The firm made the national news in 1826 when Charles Fisher was arrested for taking a newspaper from the door of the firm. In court he said he saw no harm in doing so. The judge disagreed and ordered him to pay a fine of $1 within 24 hours, or go to jail. Fisher had no money and was confined to jail for 10 days of labor.[20]

Walter Farnsworth, William Phipps, and William Munroe Jr. were partners in Farnsworth, Phipps & Co. In 1832 the company had premises on the corner of Kilby and State streets. Phipps was a director of the Hamilton Bank, capital $500,000, located at 53 State Street. On September 6, 1832, the company announced its move to 85 Kilby Street, the address on the token. The company seems to have ended its business in 1833. The tokens were struck by Wright & Bale of New York City. The comma was omitted from the company's name on the tokens.

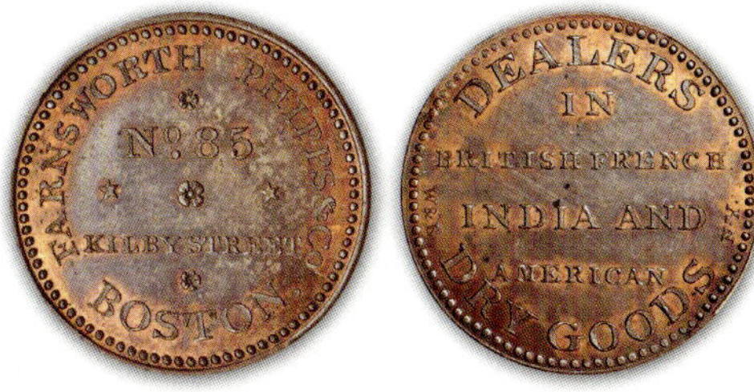

W-MA-070-10a • Rulau: "Low-314"; HT-162. R-5. 26.5 mm. Copper. The typical token is very well struck, this being true of most of the issues of Wright & Bale. VF and EF are the grades usually seen. Ford (SBG 2013) had AU-55 $88, MS-62 $329, and MS-64 $705. • VF-20 $80; EF-40 $150; AU-50 $250; MS-63 $500.

W.H. Milton
Boston, MA
Clothing
W-MA-090

William H. Milton's tokens give his address as Nos. 4 & 6 Faneuil Hall, Boston, "Faneuil Hall Clothes Warehouse." They advertise, "An extensive assortment of fashionable ready-made clothing," which included "cloths, cassimeres & vestings."

In 1829 and earlier times, the business was known as Pillsbury & Milton. From

1830 to 1834, the official trade style was Wm. M. Milton, Milton's Clothes Warehouse, but related trade styles were used, some mentioning the location of the business in Faneuil Hall. A 16-page *Catalogue of the Entire Stock of Ready-Made Clothing of Wm. H. Milton* described items to be sold at public auction on February 1 and 2, 1833, at his store in Faneuil Hall. Such merchandising techniques were unusual in their time and sometimes brought complaints from competitors.

Mr. Slocomb joined the firm a few years later, and by 1839 the name of the company was Milton & Slocomb.

The *Haverhill Gazette*, September 7, 1833, included this:

> Advertising Coin. We lately took a piece of money of the shape and size of a cent, having on one side the words, "Cloths, Cassimeres and Vestings, Wm. H. Milton, Merchant Tailor, Nos 4 & 6, Faneuil Hall, Boston." And on the other side, "Faneuil Hall clothes warehouse. An extensive assortment of fashionable ready-made clothing." This, we think, appears to be a novel mode of advertising and bids fair, if followed up, to interfere with us printers.

At the time No. 5 Faneuil Hall was also occupied by Reed & Ellis, booksellers and stationers. Later, Milton & Slocomb rented the premises.

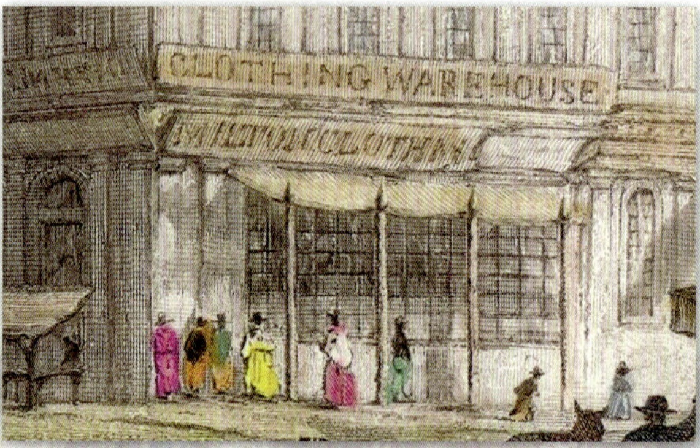

Milton's store as shown at the left corner of Faneuil Hall on an 1839 print by W.H. Bartlett and H. Griffiths, published in London. (Detail enlarged at right.)

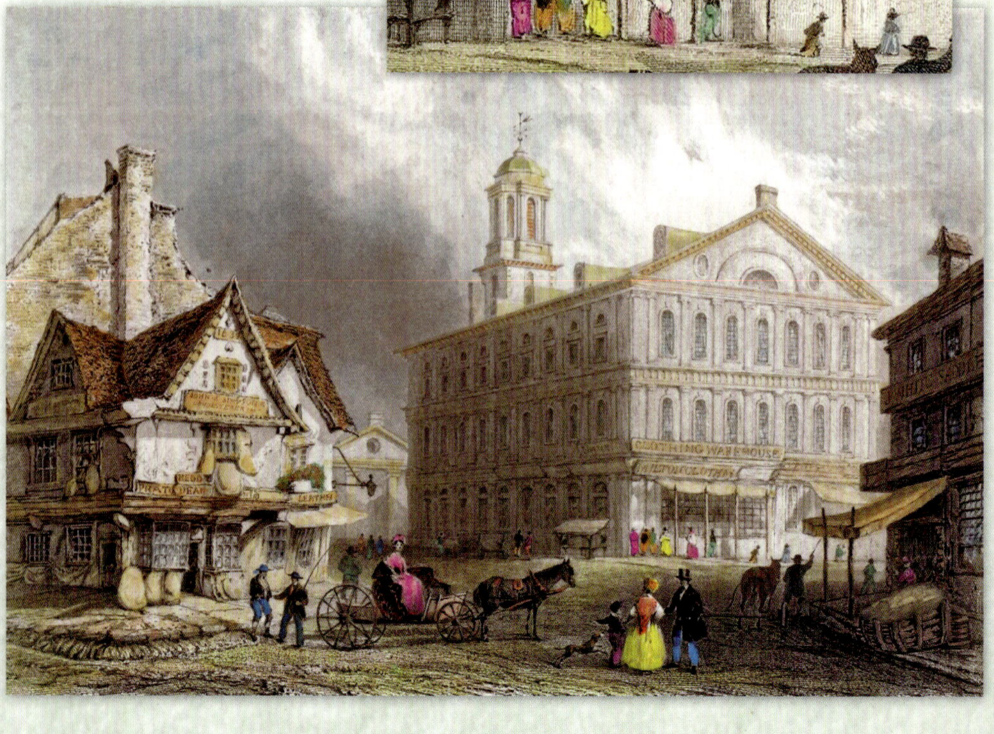

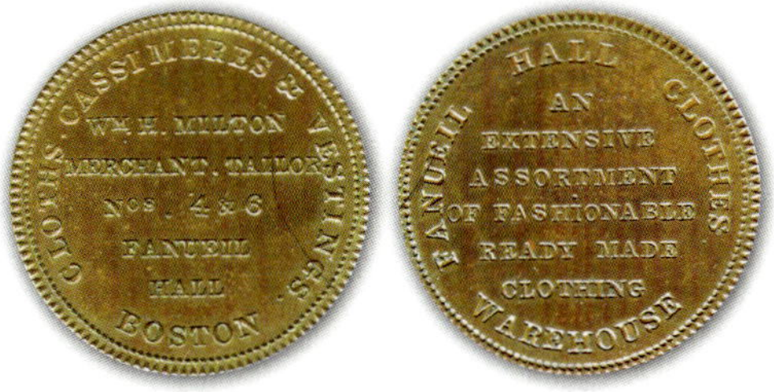

W-MA-090-10a • Rulau: "Low-265"; HT-163. R-3. 28.5 mm. Copper. FANUEIL misspelling on both sides (should be FANEUIL). Most are Fine to VF, but EF and AU examples appear now and again. • Fine-12 $15; VF-20 $30; EF-40 $65; AU-50 $150.

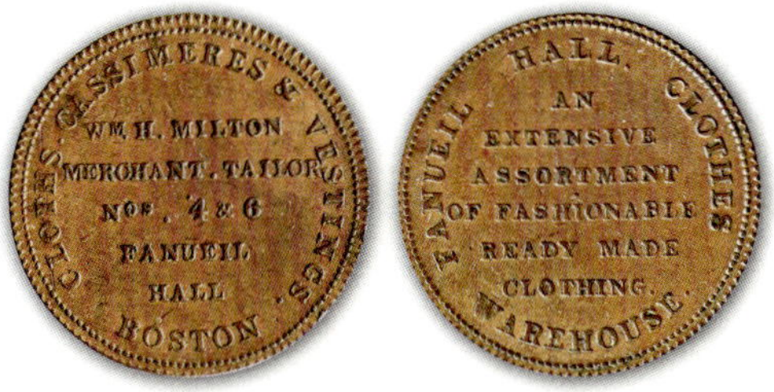

W-MA-090-15a • Rulau: "Low-265A"; HT-163A. R-5. 28.5 mm. Copper. Obverse die as preceding. Reverse from the same die but with periods added after HALL, CLOTHING, and WAREHOUSE. EF and AU are typical grades. • Fine-12 $30; VF-20 $60; EF-40 $110; AU-50 $225.

W.H. 5Milton & Co.
Boston, MA
Clothing
W-MA-100

W.H. Milton & Co. was the trade style used on this token, which was probably issued between 1834 and 1835, although facts are scarce.

In 1837 the store was heated by Fessenden's portable apparatus for warming apartments by steam and hot water. An invitation was given to the public to see the heater in use.[21]

From the *Boston Courier*, December 21, 1837:

> Who Began It. Mr. Milton, who keeps in Faneuil Hall, says that he did not commence the system of periodical sales of clothing, although it has been generally supposed that he did. The system is a bad one, and injurious to the regular business of a tailor, and was commenced when he was an apprentice to Mr. Whitemarsh a number of years ago. Last year he was obliged to have a sale of stock in self-defense, but did not hang out his flag until about ten days after a similar one had been hung out at Concert Hall. . . .

From the *Boston Courier*, May 16, 1839, letter to Hon. Daniel Webster dated May 6:

> Dear Sir, Having heard of your intention to visit Europe, we beg you to accept the accompanying suit of clothes, made from American cloth, manufactured by Messrs. W. & D.D. Farnum, Waterford, Mass., which we have no doubt you will be happy to wear as a specimen of American manufacture. Very respectfully, your obedient servants, Milton & Slocum.

Webster, writing from Summer Street, replied on the next day, stating in part, "I shall be proud to show them as proofs of the progress of American manufacturing skill." This was part of ongoing dialog in the country about the American System—the boosting of domestic products in contrast to imports.

From the *Boston Courier*, September 26, 1839, commenting on an exhibit which opened the day before at the Fair of the Mechanic Association held in Quincy Hall:

> These indefatigable and ever-active tailors, Messrs. Milton & Slocomb, have here some specimens of their handicraft, which, for style, comfort, and workmanship, might do honor to any graduate of Regent Street who ever crossed the 'salt sea ocean' for the benevolent purpose of enlightening us, ignorant Yankees, in the sublime mysteries of modes and fashions.

In the early 1840s, the firm occupied Nos. 4, 5, 6, and 7 Faneuil Hall and traded as the Faneuil Hall Wholesale Cloth and Clothing Warehouse. In 1840 the partnership declared real assets of $6,300, and Milton had personal assets of $3,500.

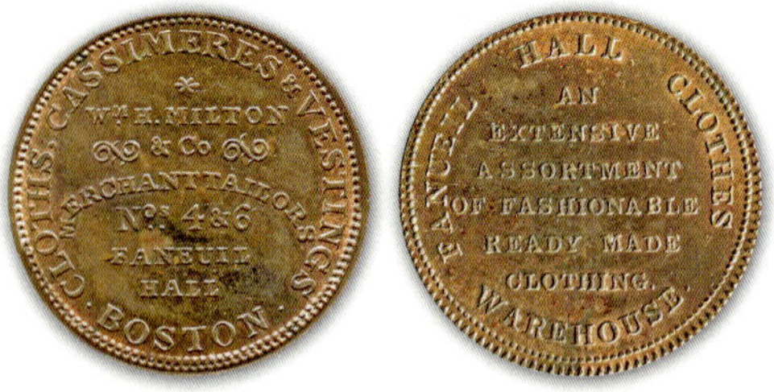

W-MA-100-05a • Rulau: "Low-266"; HT-164. R-2. 28.5 mm. Copper. New obverse, with FANEUIL spelled correctly. Reverse as preceding with FANUEIL misspelling and periods after HALL, CLOTHING, and WAREHOUSE. Rulau lists this in brass, but its existence is doubtful.[22] Most are VF or EF. • Fine-12 $10; VF-20 $25; EF-40 $50; AU-50 $90.

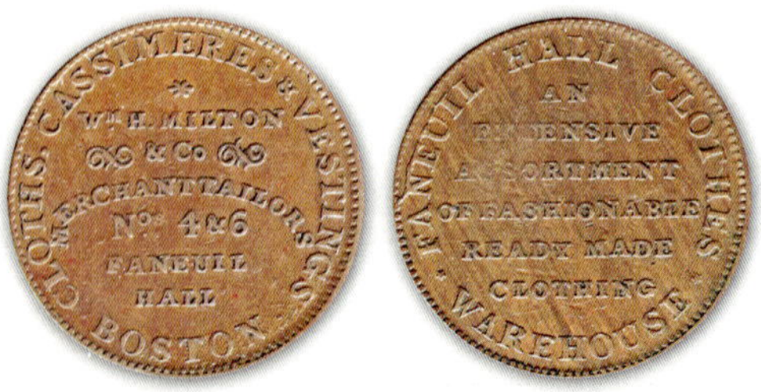

W-MA-100-10a • Rulau: "Low-267"; HT-165. R-4. 28.5 mm. Copper. Same obverse. New reverse die with similar inscriptions but with a five-pointed star before and after WAREHOUSE. FANEUIL spelled correctly on both sides. Considerably rarer than the R-2 rating assigned by Rulau. Three reverse die states exist: (1) perfect, (2) with linear crack, and (3) with crack and with cud covering NEU (FANEUIL). Brass and silver-plated brass listed by Rulau likely do not exist.[23] Most are VF or EF. • VF-20 $40; EF-40 $100; AU-50 $200.

Peck & Burnham
Boston, MA
Dry goods
W-MA-110

The firm of Peck & Burnham was located at 54 Hanover Street from 1832 to 1835. On May 1, 1832, an advertisement noted that the company was:

> Constantly receiving from the New-York and Boston auction shops and other cheap sources a general assortment of fancy goods consisting of silks, muslins, handkerchiefs, laces, hosiery, ribbons, perfumery, &c.—Together with, directly from the manufacturers, a prime assortment of wrought and plain tuck, curl, hound, neck, and side horn combs, fancy and shaving soaps, pocket books, jewelry, cutlery, &c.
>
> The prices of which cannot fail to please those who may wish to make purchases in greater or less quantities of the above or similar articles.

After the partnership ended, Abel Peck went to 15 Central Street and was associated with a dry goods company. Afterward the firm of Abel Peck & Co. was at 6 Kilby Street (1837 to 1845) then at 35 and 37 Kilby Street (1846 and 1847).

The firm's tokens were made by Robinson's, Jones & Co.

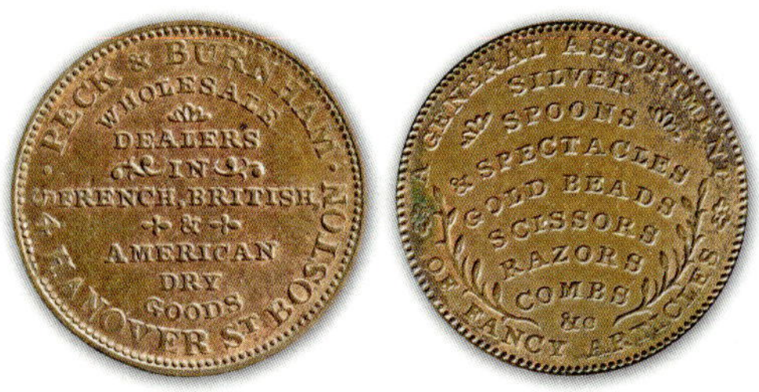

W-MA-110-10a • Rulau: "Low-325"; HT-167. R-2. 28.5 mm. Copper. VF and EF are typical grades. • Fine-12 $15; VF-20 $30; EF-40 $60; AU-50 $100.

(W-MA-040-20a) • Rulau: "Low-326"; HT-160. R-2. 28.5 mm. Copper. Muling with unrelated S.B. Schenck die. Made to create tokens for bulk circulation, not a commission from either firm mentioned. (Listed as W-MA-040-20a under W.B. Schenck.)

William Rutter
Boston, MA
Dealer in sheet music and scrap metal
W-MA-140

Born in Vermont around 1788, William Rutter became an interesting character in Boston in the early 19th century. His copper token advertises music on one side and junk on the other—seemingly unrelated lines of endeavor. For a long time this token has engendered a lot of interest and study, indeed excitement, among numismatists. It seems to have been unknown to Lyman H. Low when he finalized his version of *Hard Times Tokens* in 1899, nor did he add it to his 1906 supplement. The great rarity of the token plus its lack of a date to place it in the period of 1832 through 1844 were probably the reasons that motivated him to ignore it.

In the Scott & Co. sale of October 23 and 24, 1877, lot 337, "Store card, William Rutter, cash for rags, junk, iron, copper, brass, &c. Good" brought $1. In the same sale an 1874 Proof set with the cent, three-cent piece, and nickel brought 20¢; an 1875 set, 30¢; and a current 1877 set, 30¢.

An example also appeared in W. Elliot Woodward's sale of the Joseph N.T. Levick collection of tokens—the greatest collection of tokens publicly sold up to that time—held from May 26 to 28, 1884, where it sold for $2, a high price in an era in which cent-size copper tokens of the early 19th century often sold for 25¢ to 50¢.

One of the greatest scholars of his era, Howland Wood, tackled the situation in an article, "Some Notes on the Rutter Store Card," in *The Numismatist*, March 1913. He researched old directories and other sources, listed his various partnerships over the years, and concluded with this paragraph:

> Now let us look up Fulton St., the location that appears on his token. Before 1828 where this street is now, were wharves and water. In this year Fulton St. was platted on the recently filled in land, but the name Fulton was not given to the street until 1831. Therefore the token cannot be earlier than this date. Cross St. crosses Fulton, and we find that Rutter was on Cross St. near Commercial between 1830 and 1835. Commercial Street is the next street parallel to Fulton, and Rutter's shop was probably on the corner of Cross & Fulton streets. The token must therefore have been issued between the years 1831 and 1835, for after that date Rutter was nowhere near Fulton St. I therefore consider this card entitled to admission to the Hard Times series.

Thomas L. Elder in "A Plea for American Token Collecting," *The Numismatist*, April 1915, noted:

> William Rutter, a gentleman of Boston, seemed to be of a musical turn of mind and mixed business with pleasure and the sublime, and at the same time paid "cash for rags." This token Woodward listed as the rarest piece offered in one of his sales.

Rutter was a publisher of sheet music and songsters (booklets with the words but not the music to popular tunes). *What Are You About*, sung to the tune of *Yankee Doodle*, had as its first line, "Ye men and boys who rove the town" and was published in two columns on a small broadside sheet.[24] Another song was *The Yankee's Return from Camp*, 15 stanzas by Edward Bangs, also sung to *Yankee Doodle*, starting with "Father and I went down to camp along with Captain Gooding." Such sheets enjoyed a wide sale and were used by those who attended songfests, rallies, and other events.

Rutter also bought old rags and scrap metal—an enterprise he was engaged in for quite a few years, in which he employed itinerant men with carts to go around the city to look for such things. In light of confusing matters and directory listings, it is likely that he sometimes had more than one depot at the same time.

The story is told that Edward T. Taylor, born in Richmond, Virginia on December 25, 1793, went to sea at an early age. When he was 17 and in the port of Boston he visited several churches and determined to preach the word of God: "William Rutter, the proprietor of a junk store in Ann Street, was his first employer."[25]

The *Columbian Centinel*, Boston, May 25, 1822, included a notice that Wm. Rutter & Co., David Manley and William Rutter, dissolved their partnership on May 18, 1822. Further: "Wm. Rutter informs his former customers and the public that he continues business at No. 2, Town Dock, where is for sale paper of all kinds at the lowest prices. Likewise paper stock, scrap iron, &c., as usual." In 1827 and 1828, he was at 152 Ann Street. Afterward he moved to Fulton Street. The above-mentioned Howland Wood article lists other addresses.

Of the tokens, according to Malcolm Storer in *Numismatics of Massachusetts*, 1923, "Only 20 were struck and their use was prohibited after they had been in use for only an hour." This seems improbable, as nearly that number are known today, all showing circulation, often extensive and often with impairment. It would be interesting to know the source of the "only an hour" information. Both dies are hand-punched in an amateurish fashion, certainly not the work of an experienced die cutter.

Today the William Rutter token, although not a prime rarity, is the key to the Massachusetts Hard Times series.

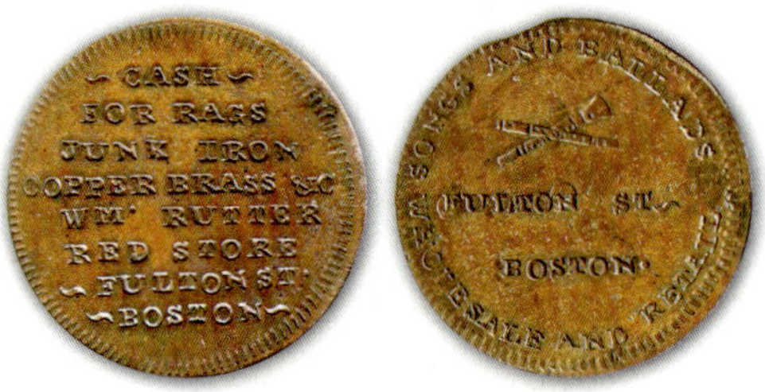

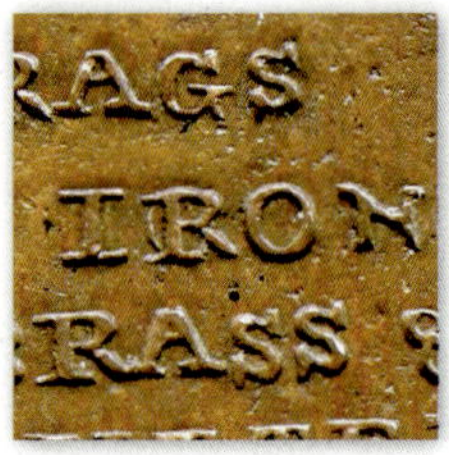

W-MA-140-10a • Rulau: "Low-327"; HT-170. R-6. 29 mm. Copper. Detail illustration shows some of the rustic lettering with R punched over O (IRON). John J. Ford Jr. owned four examples including three incredible Mint State pieces offered in 2013: MS-61 $558 and two MS-62 $822, generally thought to be well below market due to the surprise of so many. Normally seen VF or EF. • Fine-12 $350; VF-20 $650; EF-40 $1,000; AU-50 $1,500.

Alfred Willard
Boston, MA
Combs, cutlery, jewelry, etc.
W-MA-160

Alfred Willard conducted his business at 149 Washington Street in downtown Boston, billing himself on his copper token as an importer of jewelry, brushes, perfumery, combs, cutlery, fancy goods, etc., offering them retail and wholesale. His depot was well known in its time. He resided in Boston at 14 Carver Street.

On June 18, 1831, *Niles' Weekly Register* took notice of the trade in combs:

> This is not a small business. The combs manufactured in the United States are not worth less than two million a year. One comb valued at 25 dollars, has lately been made by Mr. Willard, of Boston, as a present to Gen. *Jackson*. It is surmounted by the Eagle, with portraits of Washington, Lafayette and the president, and has other highly finished ornaments.

More was said in *Niles'* a month later on July 16:

> *President's Comb:* We have already noticed a splendid shell comb, made at Mr. Willard's extensive manufactory at Boston, as a present to the president of the United States, and by him to be presented to some lady of his household. The letter of Mr. John Jones (the maker of the comb) to the president, and his reply, have been published—we give the following extracts from Mr. Jones' letter, and add the reply of the president at full length:
>
> "You will perceive that on each side of your own portrait are to be seen also the portraits of Washington and Lafayette. I was induced to place, as it were, the names of these great men in conjunction with your own conspicuously, upon the comb, because I believe the fame of the trio are inseparately connected, and fast bound up in the heart of the American people. The eagle which surmounts the comb and who holds in his beak a scroll with the words 'New Orleans' inscribed upon it, I hope speak for themselves.
>
> "This trifling present, sir, such, as it is, I now offer you, not as a practical illustration of the benefits flowing from the 'American System,' but as a token of my undiminished regard for the man who, in the cabinet and in the field, has shed an unfading lustre upon our national history, and who, in the memorable words of the illustrious Jefferson, 'has filled the measure of his country's glory.'"

President Jackson's reply:

> Washington City, June 16th, 1831
>
> Dear Sir:
>
> The beautiful shell comb which you have so kindly presented to me, and described in your letter of the 6th instant, has been received, and is most thankfully accepted. As a specimen of the success which is sure to attend American skill, wherever it meets on equal terms that of foreign competitors in the various departments of manufacture—this comb, sir, possesses a value far above that which it derives from its qualities as a mere product of mechanic labor—a value which cannot fail to have weight in confirming the wisdom of that policy which seeks to enlarge our home production of all the subjects of national wealth.
>
> It shall be highly prized also, sir, as a token of your partial regard for my own character, and of the undeserved honor which you have paid me, by placing my likeness by the side of those of Washington and Lafayette.
>
> It will be worn by my niece, Mrs. Donelson, who will take a pride in preserving it.
>
> Very respectfully, your obedient servant
>
> *Andrew Jackson*

At the annual Massachusetts Charitable Mechanic Fair in 1837, Alfred Willard & Co. was awarded a diploma for "Carved combs of very superior quality and some of original designs. Also some curious, ingenious, and creditable specimens of miniature shell work." In 1838 at the fair of the American Institute he was given a silver medal, "For the best specimen of combs." His address at the time was listed as 73 Maiden Lane, New York City. Throughout the decade, Willard, or agents selling his goods, were frequent exhibitors at fairs and related commercial events. A label on one of his boxes was lettered:

> Boston Comb Manufactory. Alfred Willard, 149, Washington-Street, (Opposite the Old South Meeting House) Boston. / Shell and Horn Comb Manufactory. / Viz.: Plain, Side, Dressing, Round, and Pocket COMBS. / Shell and Imitation / CARVED COMBS. / Carved and Plain Combs made and repaired at short notice. / Cash paid for shell and horns. / Importer of every description of hair work. / Viz.: Bunches of curls, Frizetts, Bands / Of Long Hair—Hair and Mohair Puffs, Netts, &c &c / All kinds of Morocco Goods, Silver Spoons, Gold Beads, Silver Thimbles, &c. / English, French, and American Perfumery. / Tooth, Nail, Comb, Shaving, Hair and Clothes Brushes / Constantly on hand a general assortment of / Fancy Articles, Cutlery &c &c/ Wholesale or retail—Low for cash.

Willard's copper tokens were made in quantity in the 1830s and are readily obtainable today. Most show circulation.

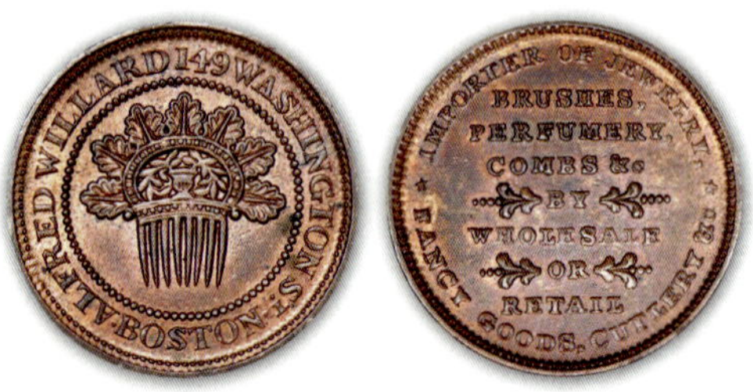

W-MA-160-10a • Rulau: "Low-328"; HT-171. R-1. 28.5 mm. Copper. Usually seen worn, but lower-range Mint State coins are offered now and again. • VF-20 $30; EF-40 $50; AU-50 $85; MS-63 $225.

Maverick Coach
East Boston, MA
Coach line
W-MA-200

The Maverick Coach was a horse-drawn stage or omnibus on the Roxbury Line (see W-MA-300 below) and in 1837 ran from the Norfolk House in Roxbury to Maverick Square in East Boston, a long stretch whose termination gave its name to the line. Likely there were specific names given to Maverick coaches, as were given to the Roxbury Coaches, and this token could be used on any one of them.

A token in German silver, described as "very fine and rare," sold for 13¢ (a typical price for a store card) in W. Elliot Woodward's sale of April 28 to May 1, 1863, which included items from the Brooks, Colburn, Finotti, Field, and Shurtleff collections.

The Chapman brothers' catalog of the Charles I. Bushnell Collection, 1882, lot 2230 was described: "Maverick Coach, 1837, East Boston. Silver. Very Good." This is assumed to have been German silver or Feuchtwanger's Composition and so is not listed as silver below. The Chapmans were somewhat careless in the preparation of their first major sale (after having gone into business in 1878).

The reverse die EAST / BOSTON / 1837 of this token was preserved and was used in late 1864 or early 1865 on the commission of the Rhode Island Numismatic Association and Albert V. Jencks in combination with new dies of Providence merchants to create rare varieties of Civil War tokens.

This appeared in *Niles' Register*, October 4, 1834:

> East Boston developed. A small island, beautifully located near the city of Boston, has been laid off in lots and is now in a rapid state of improvement. A number of pretty cottages have been built, with a magnificent hotel, etc., and the new town is called "East Boston." It will become a place of great resort in the summer season, and is an excellent site for certain manufacturers and mechanics.

In later years much of Boston Harbor was filled in, and East Boston was no longer an island.

In October 1920, *The Numismatist* included this:

> Low No. 116 Again in Circulation: When someone a few days ago dropped one of the old Maverick Coach tokens of 1837 into the prepayment box on the Boston Elevated road in payment of a fare, he probably thought he was putting one over on the company and getting a cheap ride. If he had known that it was worth to collectors the price of several rides, he would probably have realized on it to some collector or dealer.

The above incident was related in the *Boston Post* of August 30 as follows, and the obverse of the token was illustrated:

> There is nothing new or original about the metal tokens that are being used by the various street-car lines throughout the country today and which were in use on the Boston Elevated during 1918 and 1919.
>
> To prove this, the Boston Elevated officials have in their possession a metal token which was dropped into one of their prepayment boxes the other day. The token is about the size of a dime and is marked on the obverse side: 'Maverick Coach, 1837,' and on the reverse side, 'East Boston, 1837.' It was in use some time during the running of the old stage coach from Norfolk House, Roxbury, via the ferry to Maverick Square, East Boston.
>
> According to the Elevated officials, evidently some 'old-timer' is travelling around East Boston and has forgotten that the old Maverick stage coach has ceased to exist.

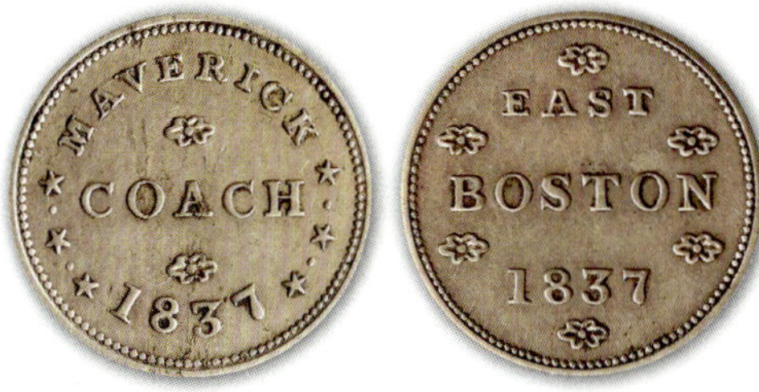

W-MA-200-10j • Low-116; HT-172. R-5. 18.7 mm. German silver. Known copper strikings, including the Ford example, have proved to be electrotypes.[26] Silver strikings are not confirmed and are probably miscataloged regular (German silver) pieces. In summary, other than regular strikings in German silver, none of the multiple other-metal listings have been confirmed, and those examined have proved to be electrotypes or in German silver. The typical example grades from Fine to Extremely Fine. • Fine-12 $225; VF-20 $400; EF-40 $550; AU-50 $800.

S.L. Wilkins
Lowell, MA
Dealer in shoes, caps, etc.
W-MA-240

Samuel L. Wilkins dealt in boots, shoes, caps, hats, and furs as described on his token. He was at the Town House next to the Post Office in 1830, and later moved to 22 Merrimack Street, the address on the token. After 1836 he was listed at 21 Merrimack Street. Before engaging in business on his own he was a clerk in the same trade with a Mr. Critchett. His wife was the former Sarah Ann Heald; the couple married in Westford, Massachusetts on June 7,

1831. S.L. Wilkins died at age 38 on August 31, 1843, at the McLean Asylum in Somerville, Massachusetts.

Only one variety is known, this with a stock obverse die featuring the standing figure of Lafayette and his death date of May 20, 1834—which places the issue of this token at least several months after that time. The tokens were struck by H.M. & E.I. Richards of Attleboro, Massachusetts. The obverse is signed H for engraver Edward Hulseman.

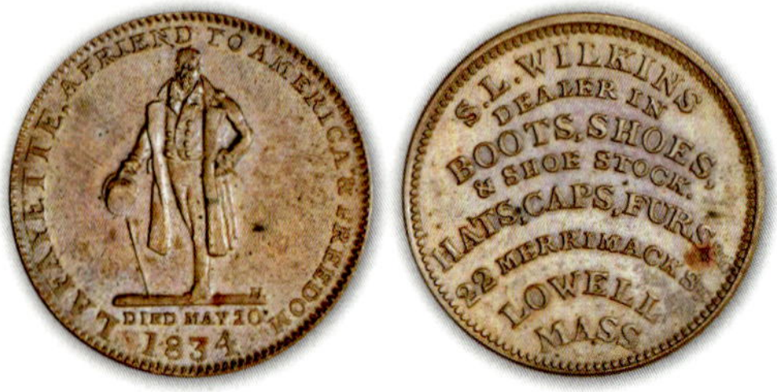

W-MA-240-10a • Low-86; HT-174. R-3. 28.5 mm. Copper. This token is usually seen worn. The Dice-Hicks token was EF. • VF-20 $70; EF-40 $135; AU-50 $250.

Francis L. Brigham
New Bedford, MA
Clothier
W-MA-280

In 1833, the date on both of his tokens, Francis L. Brigham operated two sales facilities. The main depot was at No. 1 Cheapside, New Bedford—premises in a long building that housed multiple shops and formed one side of Market Square. The other was in the Union Lodge Building at 94 Main Street on the island of Nantucket.

On December 12, 1833, and other days he ran this notice in the *Nantucket Inquirer*:

> New Store for Four Weeks. Francis L. Brigham, from No. 1 Cheapside, New Bedford, will on Tuesday next offer 36 packages of Dry Goods which were purchased at the lowest auction price and must be sold cheap—at the Union Lodge Building, Main Street.

Advertisements for clothing continued, such as this in the *New-Bedford Mercury*, January 16, 1835:

> F.L. Brigham will this day open one bale 6–4 @ English Merino, rich and desirable colors, at 3s. 9d. per yard; 500 pairs ladies kid gloves at 1s. per pair; 1 case wrought Thibet Hdffs at 4s. 6d.; broadclothes, cassimeres, flannels, Canton flannels, prints, silks, &c. &C. No. 1 Cheapside.

In the 1836 *New Bedford Directory*, he was listed as a dentist at 24 Purchase Street, which profession he continued to follow. In 1841 he was listed as a surgeon-dentist at the same location and boarded at the Mansion House, 87 Union Street. Brigham died on September 18, 1845, at the age of 42.

There are two varieties of the Brigham token, both from the same pair of dies. The first, W-MA-280-10a, was used to strike most of the pieces. After this was done, both dies were reworked by adding a circle of tiny beads, each touching, inside of the circle of large beads with spacing. On the obverse certain details of the Cheapside building were redone, including strengthening the walk in front and extending it to the right, and retouching certain window details. The rightmost window, weak on the early state of the die, is quite detailed on the later state. In its revised form, it seems that the obverse die failed at an early date. As Lyman H. Low commented, all seen have a large die crack.

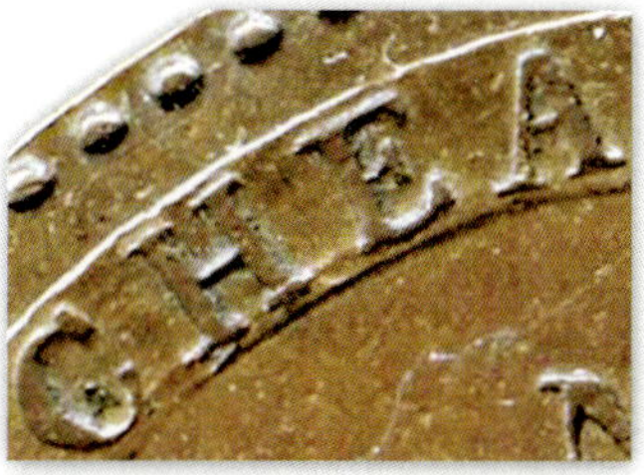

Detail of the obverse die in its early state as used for W-MA-280-10a.

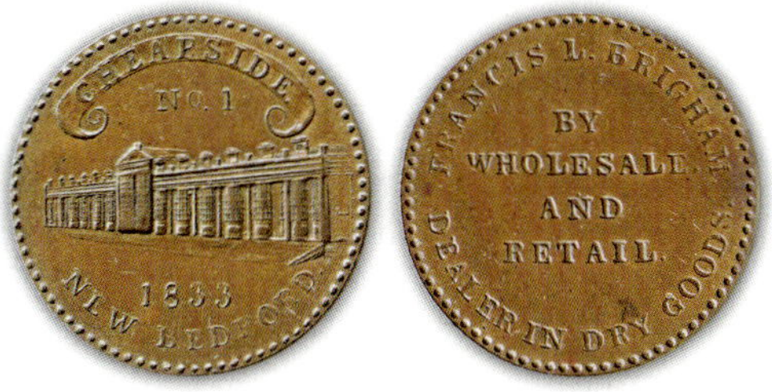

W-MA-280-10a • Low-73; HT-176. R-2. 28.5 mm. Copper. Typical grades are VF and EF. • VF-20 $135; EF-40 $250; AU-50 $400.

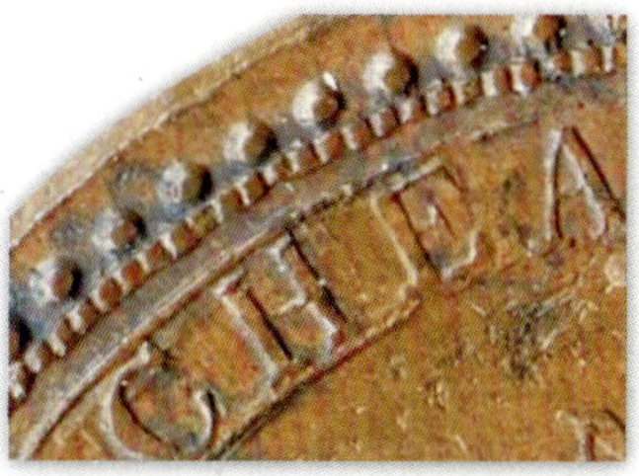

Detail of the obverse die in its late state as used for W-MA-280-15a.

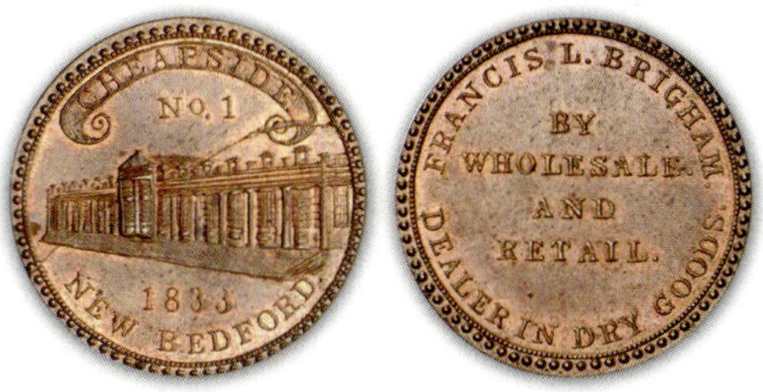

W-MA-280-15a • Low-72; HT-175. R-5. 28.5 mm or slightly larger. Copper. Low: "All I have seen of this variety show a long break in the obverse die." Most of these are in grades of VF and EF. The Ford example, Mint State, is illustrated; now in the Robert A. Schuman Collection. Rulau also includes the unique example struck over Low-51 (HT-70), listing it as HT-175A, in the Tanenbaum Collection. • VF-20 $350; EF-40 $600; AU-50 $1,200.

Roxbury Coaches
Roxbury, MA
Coach line
W-MA-300

Roxbury was a separate town in the 1830s, before it was annexed to Boston in 1868. In the 1820s, public transportation in Boston and to the outskirts consisted of horse-drawn carriages and coaches with no particular schedules. Pickups and stops were made at hotels, squares and other places. Connections to Roxbury were via a daily stagecoach accommodating 45 passengers and drawn by two horses. A post horn was blown to notify would-be passengers to be ready when the stagecoach arrived. On March 1, 1826, Brooks Bowman, trading as the Norfolk Company, initiated an hourly stagecoach from the Norfolk House in Roxbury to the historic Old South Church in Boston, with stops in between.[27] In 1832 the company was acquired by Horace King, who operated it until July 1, 1851, when he sold it to the partnership of Flagg & Estabrook.

The fare each way connecting Roxbury and Boston was one bit or 12-1/2¢, reduced to 6-1/4¢ in June 1838.

Likely the tokens of the line, dated 1837, were good for one fare. Most in existence today show wear, indicating use in their time. They are made of nickel composition similar to Feuchtwanger's Composition.

The *Boston Traveler*, November 18, 1838, included this advertisement:

> To the Public. Fare Reduced. The new and elegant line of Roxbury Coaches, the Regulator and the Conqueror, now run half hourly to and from Roxbury at the reduced price of six and a quarter cents each way, and stop for passengers anywhere on the route.

More common than federal coins in circulation were Spanish-American silver issues including the medio (6-1/4¢), bit (12-1/2¢), and, most popular of all, two bits (25¢).

The line featured a distinctive range of coaches, which were individually named. In *Romantic Days in Old Boston*, Mary Caroline Crawford, 1910, stated that "The *Governor Brooks*, an omnibus drawn by four horses and having seats for eighteen passengers inside and for six outside, began in 1835 to run regularly from Winnisimmet Ferry at the foot of Hanover Street to Roxbury, two and a half hours being allowed for the round trip. . . ." This was the first omnibus of its kind seen in Boston, and was an improvement in comfort over the earlier coaches. The daily schedule, excluding Sunday, had departures from Roxbury at 8 a.m., 10 a.m., noon, 2 p.m., 4 p.m., and 6 p.m. The trip from the North Church in Boston departed at 9 a.m., 11 a.m., 2 p.m., 5 p.m., and 7 p.m. It was well patronized, and the similar *Northender* was soon put into service in between times, giving hourly departures from both Roxbury and Boston.

Additional coaches were added to the line, including *Regulator*, *Conqueror*, and *Aurora*. The last coach with "a goddess in her cloud-borne chariot on its yellow sides made a great impression on the juvenile mind when it first appeared," Lyman H. Low commented. Additional routes were laid out. In 1852, under the ownership of Flagg & Estabrook, there were five routes in operation:

> Norfolk Line with 26 men, 100 horses, and 16 coaches.
>
> Mt. Pleasant Line with 7 men, 25 horses, and 4 coaches.
>
> Warren Street Line with 6 men, 25 horses, and 4 coaches.
>
> Oak Street Line with 7 men, 25 horses, and 4 coaches.
>
> Foot of Mt. Pleasant Line with 3 men, 13 horses, 2 coaches.

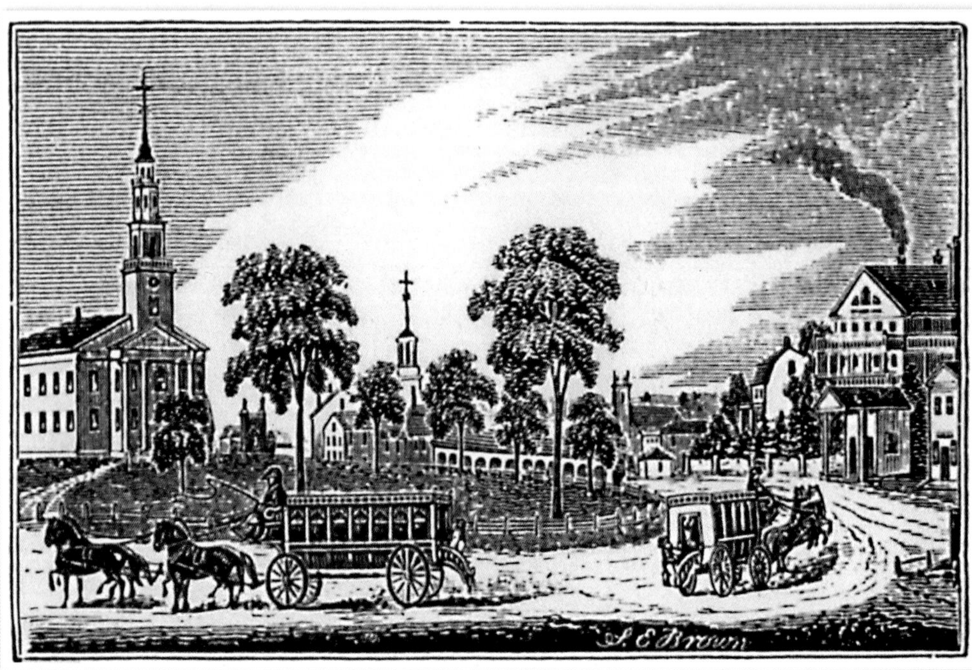

***The Old Norfolk House* (S.E. Brown sketch in *The Town of Roxbury: Its Memorable Persons and Places*, 1878).**

This totaled 64 men, 213 horses, and 34 coaches. Tickets were regularly 10¢ each or 16 tickets for $1, the last amounting to 6-1/4¢ per ticket. Activity was such that each day a coach crossed the line into Boston once every three and one-half minutes. Certain Sunday and evening coaches maintained their price of 12-1/2¢.

In the 1850s the Roxbury Line wound down its operations in face of competition from the more advanced horse-drawn rail car system.

In the *American Journal of Numismatics*, January 1905, in the article "Hard Times Tokens," the editor reflected upon a sale of such tokens from the J.B. Dunning Collection to be sold by Lyman H. Low in March:

> Still another token in the sale, though well known to collectors, is that used by the old Roxbury omnibuses, which belongs to Boston local issues as well as to the series under notice. These rare pieces revive in the hearts of Boston boys the memories of departed days. The long, lumbering coaches, with a flight of steps leading to the door in the rear, ran from the old Norfolk House in Roxbury, over "The Neck," through Washington street, into the business part of the city; and from the fact that they left the starting place once an hour, were known as "hourlies."
>
> They were drawn slowly along by four horses, and a single fare-taker, who entered, collected his fares, and then departed to meet the coach coming in the opposite direction, and repeat the operation; his entrances and exits were carefully watched by the urchins on the street, who found the steps at the rear a safe place to steal an unmolested ride; a bell, placed on the seat in the corner by the door, and rung by the nearest occupant, served to notify the driver when a passenger wished to alight. The coaches held perhaps twenty passengers, and, except in the early morning and late in the afternoon, there was no crowding of the seats. . . .
>
> Of the Roxbury Coaches of those quiet and peaceful days, these little copper tokens are all that are left to recall them. Similar coaches were long used in East Boston, for which tokens were issued, dated 1837 like those of Roxbury, but whether these pieces served as tickets, advertisements, or for making change, does not appear, but most probably they were accepted as currency.

Also see Maverick Coach W-MA-200, which was part of the Roxbury Line; that token has an East Boston address.

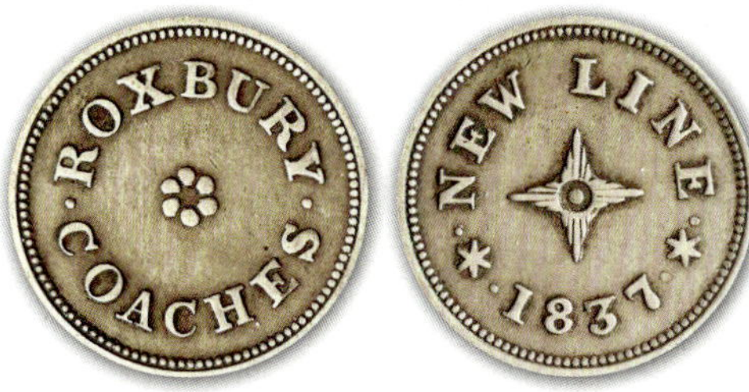

W-MA-300-10j • Low-129; HT-169. R-3. 18.7 mm. German silver. This variety has been popular for a long time. Scattered examples have appeared in auctions dating to the 1850s. The typical example grades from Very Fine to Extremely Fine. The Ford example in copper, 2004, was determined to be an electro and the sale negated.[28] Nearly all are in Fine to EF grades. Any higher example with mint luster is a rarity. • Fine-12 $100; VF-20 $225; EF-40 $375; AU-50 $600.

John J. Adams
Taunton and Boston, MA
Manufacturer of brushes
W-MA-320

John J. Adams, cousin of the president of the United States, was a highly regarded manufacturer of brushes in Medfield, Massachusetts. The business grew and was moved to Taunton. His factory was at 11 Main Street in Taunton during the 1830s, and he maintained an office in Boston at 12 Elm Street. Both addresses are given on his tokens. In the 1840s the firm was at 72 Washington Street in Boston, and a sales outlet was established in New York City.

The catalog of the Massachusetts Charitable Mechanic Association exhibition of 1844 reflects the company's products at the time:

> No. 1005. John J. Adams, Boston. The Committee has given a particular examination to a very general assortment of brushes presented under this number and invoice, embracing nearly all the most useful kinds of brushes that are manufactured in this country. They feel that Mr. Adams is deserving of much commendation for furnishing so good a representation of this branch of American manufacture, especially as it has not been so fully represented since the year 1841.
>
> Although these brushes are made in a thorough and workmanlike manner, yet we do not perceive any marked improvement as to workmanship, or utility over others that have been previously exhibited; excepting the few instances which we will mention. The Committee was happy to notice a decided improvement in the shaving brushes made in ebony and boxwood, they are so made that while they are full and strong, they are less heavy than those in bone, or metal sockets, and less liable to fail. A patent scrubbing brush, for floors, decks, halls, and so forth, is considered a great improvement. Also a double (banister) duster, and a cloth brush for ladies' dresses, bonnets, &c., were considered admirably adapted to the purposes for which they were intended.
>
> The Committee further noticed a beautiful duster, made of black ostrich feathers, the handle composed of peacock's quills, woven with silk and morocco, which evinced much taste and ingenuity in its manufacture. In view of the above consideration, the Committee think Mr. Adams deserving of a *Silver Medal.*

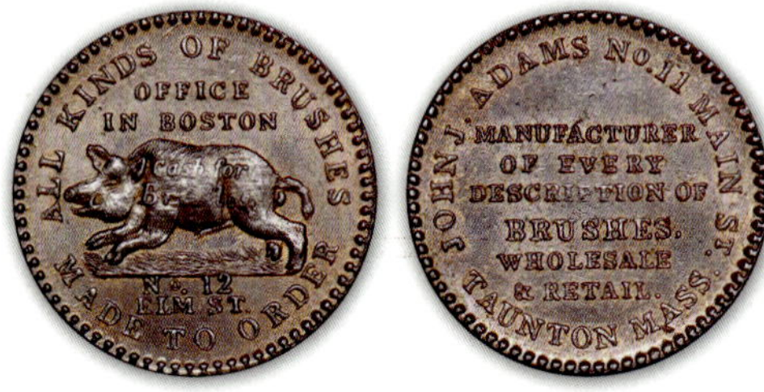

W-MA-320-10a • Rulau: "Low-300"; HT-181. R-1. 28.5 mm. Copper. This side of the token is in very high relief. Usually seen with the inscription on the boar incomplete due to striking on high-grade examples and wear on circulated pieces. Fine and VF grades are usual, although a handful of AU and low-range Mint State tokens exist. • VF-20 $30; EF-40 $55; AU-50 $100; MS-63 $275.

W-MA-320-10b • Rulau: "Low-301A"; HT-181A. R-8. 28.5 mm. Brass. 2 known. Ford (SBG 2013) MS-65 $6,462.50.

W-MA-320-10j • Rulau: "Low-301A"; HT-181B. R-9. 32.5 mm. German silver. Striking of the obverse die on the obverse of an 1811 federal half dollar.

Crocker Brothers & Co.
Taunton, MA
Manufacturer of metal goods
W-MA-360

In 1826, taking up an enterprise earlier conducted by their father, the three Crocker brothers—William Allen, George Augustus, and Samuel Leonard—formed Crocker Brothers to manufacture copper goods on the Watling River in Norton, to the northwest of Taunton.[29]

In 1831 the business was incorporated as Crocker Brothers & Co., capitalized at $200,000. The Norton factory was doubled in size. Workmen skilled in copper were brought from England to formulate alloys and to assist with manufacturing. An alloy called yellow metal was made, composed of 60 percent copper and 40 percent zinc. Among their customers was the Philadelphia Mint, to which tens of thousands of dollars' worth of finished planchets for copper cents were shipped. William Allen was in charge of planchet production. In 1832 he was one of the organizers of the Bristol County Bank of Taunton, and later, for a time, was its president.

In 1849 a large factory was erected at Weir Village for making and rolling copper, brass, and zinc. The company continued to expand, had its ups and downs, and went through transitions into the 20th century.

Russell Rulau states that the dies for the token were made by William H. Jones, who also struck them.

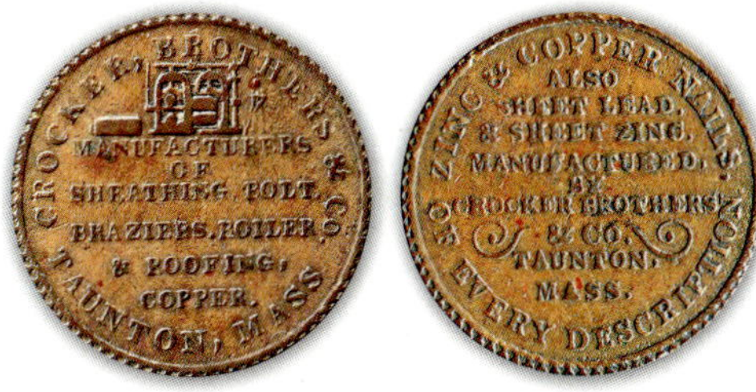

W-MA-360-10a • Rulau: "Low-234"; HT-182. R-5. 28.5 mm. Copper. Extraneous comma after 2nd R (CROCKER). The typical grade for this token is Very Fine, usually with some marks or problems. White metal strikings, including one ex Wayte Raymond consigned by John J. Ford Jr. to a Bowers and Merena sale in 1990, have proved to be casts.[30] VF to AU examples are usually seen. In 2013 Ford's two AU-55 pieces sold for $352 and $381. • VF-20 $200; EF-40 $350; AU-50 $600.

Missouri Hard Times Tokens

Huckel, Burrows & Jennings
St. Louis, MO
Chandlers and grocers
W-MO-020

Huckel, Burrows & Jennings were grocers and were also chandlers to steamships on the Missouri and Mississippi rivers. It seems that Huckel left the firm, after which his name was mostly but not completely erased from the die that struck the tokens.

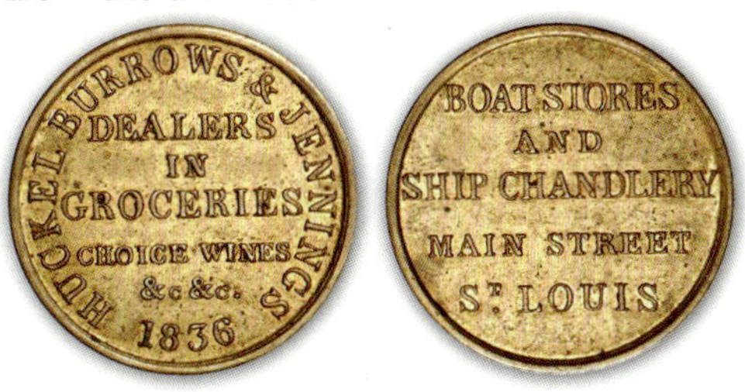

W-MO-020-10b • Low-102; HT-187. R-8. 29 mm. Brass. Plain edge. (Silvered, Low-177 and HT-187A, R-8.) Ford's AU at $60,375 in 2004 crossed the block for $80,500 in the Dice-Hicks sale in 2008.

W-MO-020-10e • Low-178; HT-187B. R-8. 29 mm. White metal. Plain edge. The American Numismatic Society has a memorable Mint State example.

W-MO-020-25b • **HUCKEL removed from die** • Rulau: "Low-102A"; HT-188. R-8. 29 mm. Brass. Plain edge. The American Numismatic Society has an example. Rulau lists a white metal example, but this has not been confirmed.

New Hampshire Hard Times Tokens

A complete collection of New Hampshire Hard Times tokens involves five different merchants. As four of them each shared different sides of the same token, this nets to just three necessary tokens. All were issued in 1837, per the dates, and were made in Attleboro, Massachusetts by R. & W. Robinson. Large quantities were made with the result that examples of each are easily enough found today.

Haselton & Palmer
Dover, NH
Crockery, cookware
W-NH-100

James Cutter Haselton was born in Portsmouth, New Hampshire, on May 6, 1817, to James and Susanna Haselton. On August 1, 1837, an announcement was made that J. Cutter Haselton and Ezra K. Palmer had formed a partnership, had acquired the stock recently owned by Haselton & Co., and were doing business at No. 2 Cocheco Block in Dover.[31] The firm sold dry goods, groceries, and other items. On October 15, 1839, in Dover, Haselton married Mary Hanson. On February 11, 1840, the Haselton & Palmer partnership was dissolved by mutual consent. Haselton continued in business and in that year had 11 people associated with his company. In 1884 Haselton was a registered voter in Alameda, California. Haselton died in New York on November 4, 1889. Funeral services were held two days later at the residence of his sister-in-law, Mrs. George W. Simpson, at 157 Oxford St. in Brooklyn.

Ezra K. Palmer was born in Dover in 1817, the son of William and Maria Palmer. In 1850 he lived in Boston. He died of Bright's disease in Boston on June 25, 1887. At the time he lived at 1 Bulfinch Place.

Their business was in the Cocheco Block, a large building constructed in 1832 as part of a manufacturing complex built by the Cochecho Co. The name is correctly spelled as *Cochecho*, after the Cochecho River (which in the early days was nearly always spelled *Cochecho*, not *Cocheco* as on the token).

A.M. Smith (see next listing) shared this token with Haselton & Palmer and advertised on the other side.

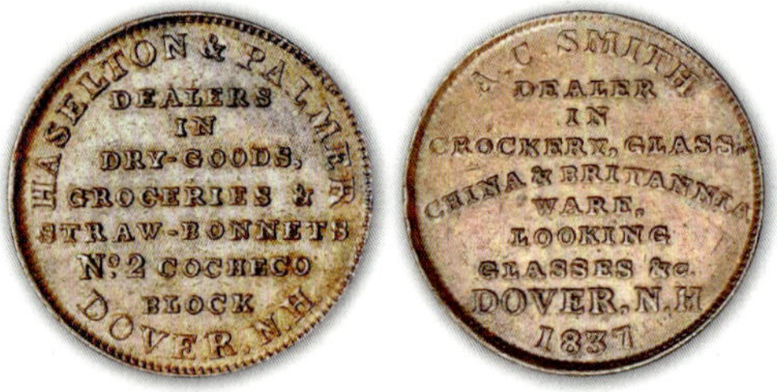

W-NH-100-10a • Low-131; HT-192. R-4. 28.5 mm. Copper. Low stated: "This token like that of Portsmouth (Smith and Simes, No. 124) seems to have been a joint venture, but I have not learned its history; probably it was suppressed for similar reasons." Apart from the Low comment the writer has not learned of any suppression. As such tokens are fairly common today, it can be presumed that they circulated widely in their time. Most are in grades of VF and EF, punctuated by occasional offerings of higher-level examples. • VF-20 $50; EF-40 $80; AU-50 $150; MS-63 $300.

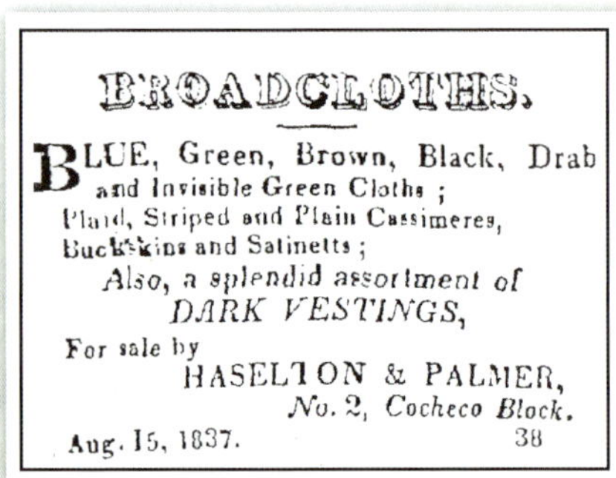

BROADCLOTHS.

BLUE, Green, Brown, Black, Drab and Invisible Green Cloths;
Plaid, Striped and Plain Cassimeres,
Buckskins and Satinetts;
Also, a splendid assortment of
DARK VESTINGS,
For sale by
HASELTON & PALMER,
No. 2, Cocheco Block.
Aug. 15, 1837. 38

Haselton & Palmer notice in the *Strafford Advertiser*, September 12, 1837.

A.C. Smith
Dover, NH
Crockery, cookware
W-NH-120

Abel C. Smith, dealer in crockery, glass, china, and Britannia ware (imitation silver) set up at No. 1 Cochecho Block, although the address is not given on the token. As noted earlier, his advertisement appears on the other side of the token representing Haselton & Palmer.

Abel C. Smith was born in Gilmanton, New Hampshire, circa 1793. He married Sarah Rice, two years his junior, in Framingham, Massachusetts, on October 1, 1823. The couple moved to Durham, New Hampshire, where Abel set up as a dealer in English and West India (Caribbean) imports, groceries, and other items of general stock.

On November 30, 1824, John Ingalls joined him in the business. The partnership was short-lived and was dissolved on October 17, 1825.

In 1828 he traded as the Dover Crockery Store. On December 4, 1837, he advertised from a store formerly occupied by one Benjamin Meegin and offered English and West India imports.

The 1850 census lists Abel and Sarah Smith as residing in Dover. Ann Gray, age 14 and from Ireland, lived with them. In 1859 Morrill Brothers, dealers in crockery, china, feathers, looking glasses, window shades, and fixtures, operating from the same address, advertised as "Successors to A.C. Smith." He died at the age of 73 in Lawrence, Massachusetts, on May 23, 1866.

Considering the 1837 date on the tokens, the maker was likely R. & W. Robinson of Attleboro, not H.M. & E.I. Richards as suggested by Low. This is not a criticism of Low, as he was first in the field. As is true in many other numismatic specialties, later scholarship found additional information.[32]

(W-NH-100-10a) • Low-131; HT-192. R-4. 28.5 mm. Copper. (The advertisement of Smith is on the reverse of W-NH-100-10a, listed under Haselton & Palmer.) • VF-20 $50; EF-40 $80; AU-50 $150; MS-63 $300.

Copartnership.

The subscribers respectfully inform the public that they have formed a connexion in business under the firm of

SMITH & INGALLS,

at the store recently occupied by A. C. Smith, in Durham. They have, and intend to keep on hand, a general assortment of

English & West-India Goods
& Groceries,

which they will sell very cheap for cash or country produce.

ABEL C. SMITH,
JOHN INGALLS,

Durham, Nov. 30, 1824.

A. C. Smith requests all persons indebted to him on note or account, to make payment by the middle of January next, otherwise their demands will be left with an attorney for collection.

Durham Nov. 30, 1824.

Smith & Ingalls partnership, *New Hampshire Republican*, January 3, 1825.

NEW ADDITIONS TO THE
Dover Crockery Store.

A. C. SMITH,

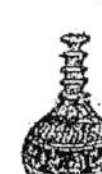

HAS Just Received many new and valuable Articles, which together with his former STOCK comprises an Elegant Assortment of

CROCKERY,
GLASS & CHINA
WARE.

LOOKING-GLASSES, &c.

A. C. Smith would inform his friends and the public generally, that as he intends making this his principal business, he is determined to sell as low as any one in the State, and hopes by paying strict attention to business, keeping a good assortment, and selling CHEAP, to merit and receive a share of the public patronage.

—*ON HAND*—
A few Elegant DINING SETTS, fashionable patterns and newest style.

March 25, 1828. tf

A.C. Smith, Dover Crockery Store, notice in the *Dover Gazette & Strafford Advertiser*, June 10, 1828.

NOTICE.

THE CO-PARTNERSHIP heretofore existing under the firm of HASELTON & PALMER is this day, (by mutual consent) dissolved. All persons indebted to us are requested to make immediate payment, and those having demands against us, will please present them for adjustment.

The business will hereafter be conducted by J. C. HASELTON.

J. CUTTER HASELTON,
EZRA K. PALMER.

Dover, Feb. 11, 1840. 6w12

The end of Haselton & Palmer, *Dover Gazette & Strafford Advertiser*, March 17, 1840.

Nathaniel March
Portsmouth, NH
Groceries, spirits
W-NH-140

This token, similar to the foregoing, mates two businesses in the same city—each on one side. Likely, the tokens were a cooperative venture between Nathaniel March and William Simes & Co., purely as a matter of convenience. Such tokens were inexpensive in their day, so there was no need for a cooperative venture. The maker of this token was W. & R. Robinson, as evidenced by the distinctive style, which features lettering arranged in curved rows.

Nathaniel March was born in Portsmouth on June 14, 1807. By 1827 he was a partner in Childs & March, stationers and booksellers in that city, and successors to Childs & Sparhawk. By 1831 he was at No. 7 Exchange Buildings, the address given on his token. Earlier the premises had been occupied by Harrison Gray & Co. They offered for sale books, stationery, small musical instruments, wallpaper, and other goods. Ruling, bookbinding, and printing could be done on short notice. Not long afterward, patent medicines were also offered.

March was prominent in civic affairs. In early summer 1833 he was a deputy marshal in a grand civic procession welcoming President Andrew Jackson, Vice President Martin Van Buren, and other officials to Portsmouth.[33] He was active in Democratic politics in New Hampshire throughout the decade. In the early 1840s he was secretary of the Portsmouth Mutual Fire Insurance Co. His local advertisements emphasized patent medicines, the most notable being Brandreth's Pills and Clackener's Sugar Coated Vegetable Pills. Nathaniel March died at age 39, on July 9, 1846, after which the business was continued by Samuel A. Badger.

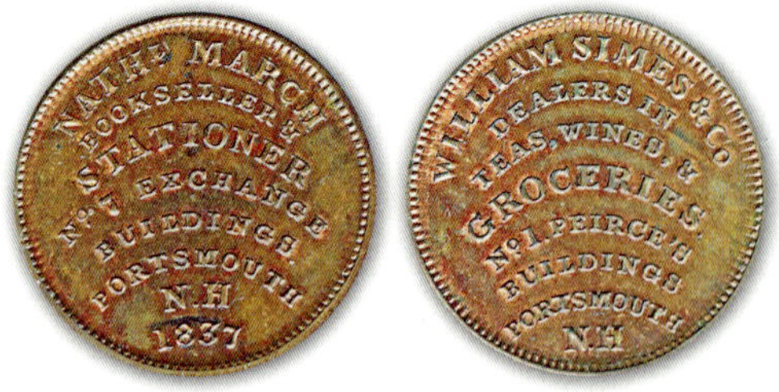

W-NH-140-10a • Low-124; HT-194. R-1. 28.5 mm. Copper. These tokens must have been made in large quantities, surely in the tens of thousands at least, as they are very plentiful today. Most are in higher grades such as EF and AU, and lower-range Mint State pieces are easily obtained. Lyman H. Low said these were deemed illegal and were suppressed, but the present writer has found no evidence to substantiate this. Low cited no source. • VF-20 $25; EF-40 $40; AU-50 $70; MS-63 $225.

William Simes & Co.
Portsmouth, NH
Groceries, spirits
W-NH-180

William Simes, a son of George Simes, was born in Portsmouth on April 9, 1806. He entered the retail trade as a young man and for many years did a good business combining the disposition of large wholesale quantities of food and smaller items for the retail trade. Selected advertisements from the era illustrate his activity.

The *Portsmouth Journal of Literature & Politics* included this advertisement on October 18, 1828:

> William Simes informs his friends and the public that he has taken Store No. 1 Peirce's Building (opposite the Court House) and intends keeping a general stock of West India goods & groceries by wholesale and retail. Families favoring him with their custom may depend on having articles of the first quality and as cheap as can be purchased elsewhere.

In the same paper, on April 2, 1831, he advertised that he had on hand 1,700 bushels of yellow corn, 24 barrels of Baltimore S.F. flour, 24 barrels of Baltimore fine flour, and 15 barrels of Baltimore Susquehanna flour. Purchases could be made from him or Joseph Walton Jr.

An advertisement of June 24, 1834:

> Gun Powder. 100 kegs gun powder (warranted of the first quality, or the money refunded) will be sold cheaper than can be bought in this town, to close a consignment. Purchasers will find it for their interest to call on William Simes opposite the Court House.

On February 28, 1835:

> Bacon, Lard & Cheese. 100 kegs lard, first quality; 4,000 pounds bacon, small hams, first quality. 8,000 pounds cheese. For sale by William Simes, No. 1 Peirce's Buildings.

On May 13, 1837, when the Panic of 1837 was barely getting underway:

> Bank Bills Wanted! Bank bills wanted in exchange for groceries at prices to conform to the times. Purchasers having any of the above articles on hand will find it to their advantage to call William Simes & Co.
>
> N.B. We should feel ourselves much accommodated at this time to exchange some of our standing old accounts for the above article.

Simes was elected mayor of Portsmouth in 1861 and 1862. His friends pressed him to run for a third term, but he declined. He died on May 15, 1880.

(W-NH-140-10a) • Low-124; HT-194. R-1. 28.5 mm. Copper. (The advertisement is on the reverse side of W-NH-140-10a, listed under Nathaniel March.) • VF-20 $25; EF-40 $40; AU-50 $70; MS-63 $225.

E.F. Sise & Co.
Portsmouth, NH
Commission merchant
W-NH-200

Edward F. Sise was born in Dover, New Hampshire, on September 19, 1799. His partner in Sise & Co. was John Walker. The company imported crockery, glassware, and other items, also trading in salt and coal. In 1837 (the date on his token) he was selling many varieties of merchandise and was also an agent for the Hartford Fire Insurance Co.

Goods were often wholesaled from Sheafe's Wharf. Sise retired about 1854, after which Walker continued the business with William H. Sise and Joseph Sise. Edward died on May 25, 1868. A later history told this:

> The firm of E.F. Sise & Co., coal and salt, was established in 1818, by E.F. Sise, the pioneer in the coal business in New Hampshire. The first coal shipped into the State was consigned to him in 1831, and consisted of thirty-five tons of Lehigh lump coal, and was part of the general cargo of the Portsmouth and Philadelphia packet schooner *Fawn*.
>
> In 1847 William H. and Joseph, sons of E F. Sise, entered the firm and continued until 1894, when Joseph died and William H. conducted the business until his death in 1896, when Charles W. Gray and Herbert O. Prime, clerks for Sise & Co., succeeded to the business. The old firm was largely interested in shipping, and in the office, on the walls, may be seen the best collection of old models of Portsmouth vessels to be found, and some of them historic.[34]

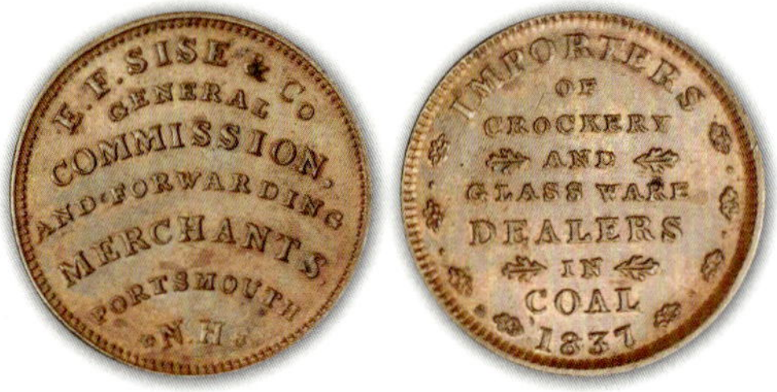

W-NH-200-10a • Low-132; HT-195. R-1. 28.5 mm. Copper. (Impressions of the obverse and reverse dies well centered on a well-worn 36 mm 1797 British Soho "cartwheel" penny; HT-132A; R-9, ex Robert Lindesmith Collection.[35]) This token completes the suite of three issued in the state of New Hampshire. Examples are easily enough obtained today. Most are in high circulated grades, although Mint State pieces appear in the marketplace at widely spaced intervals. • VF-20 $25; EF-40 $40; AU-50 $80; MS-63 $250.

New Jersey Hard Times Tokens

Howell Works Garden
Allaire Village, NJ
Iron works
W-NJ-100

James P. Allaire, was an important factor in the making of marine steam engines including for large ships.[36] As the fires of the Revolution were burning, his family of Loyalists who lived in New Rochelle, New York, fled to Nova Scotia. It was there that James was born in July 1785. The family returned to the United States not long afterward. James was educated in local schools. As a teenager he was apprenticed to a druggist, but he abandoned the pursuit and became a blacksmith.

In 1802 teenaged Allaire went to work in New York City for Francis Ellsworth, a brass founder. At age 18, with just twenty-five cents in his pocket, according to his own account, he married his cousin Frances Duncan. The couple had nine children, five of whom lived to adulthood. In 1806 he set up his own shop in New York City. Not long afterward, he received a commission from Robert Fulton to cast the air chamber for the steamship *Clermont*, which in 1807 had successful trials on the Hudson River. This established him in the making of marine steam engines and also ships, a field in which he soon became famous. The SS *Savannah*, built in 1818, with the 90-horsepower engine

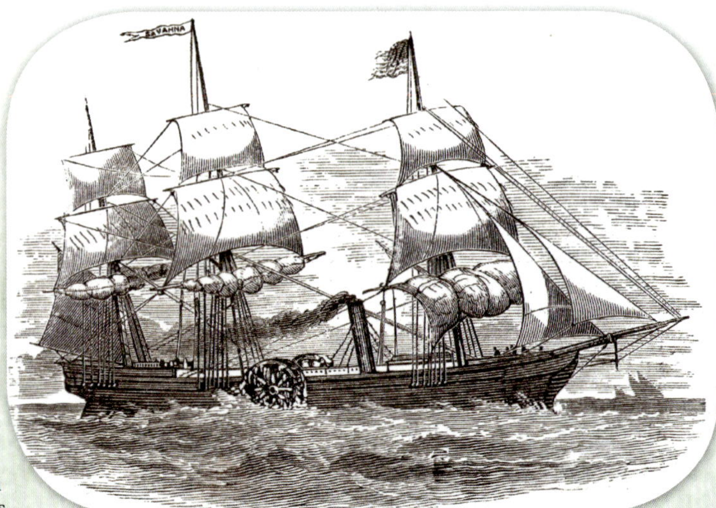

The SS *Savannah*. The wind is blowing the sails in one direction while the smoke streams the other way, common artistic license in 19th century nautical prints.

supplied by Allaire, crossed the Atlantic from May 24 to June 20, 1819—the first steamship to do so! Steam power was used for 41-1/2 hours of the 207-hour voyage. Otherwise, the extensive auxiliary sails provided the power.

In 1821 Benjamin B. Howell, then lessee of the Manasquan Furnace iron works in Monmouth County, called Allaire's attention to the facility and the bog iron ore found in quantity nearby as a source of material for his business. Such ore could be very rich and contain up to 50 percent iron. There were also abundant trees from which charcoal could be made to use in the smelting process. This was a labor-intensive business involving several dozen or more men. The molten metal was cast into ingots called pigs. Some pigs were processed with a trip hammer to make wrought iron. Various products including water pipe and household wares were made there. There is no record of the typical output of iron, but 20 to 30 tons per day has been estimated by historians.

In April 1822, Allaire acquired the 5,000-acre property for $19,000 and changed its name to the Howell Furnace, after which it transitioned to become the Howell Works. In 1828 the State Legislature authorized the formation of the Howell Works Company with a capital of $150,000, for the purpose of making iron, hollow ware, and brass castings. In 1831 Howell purchased the Allaire-built, ocean-going SS *Bellona*, from "Commodore" Vanderbilt. This replaced several old-fashioned sailing vessels, including the *Copheron*, *Anthrucopheron*, and *Cycripedium*, and shortened the time to deliver goods.

In a letter dated March 16, 1833, to Nicholas Biddle, president of the Bank of the United States, Allaire petitioned for a loan for $40,000 to expand the facility, noting, "the works have not been productive until recently. They are now in full operation and have the last year given a net income of $15,000."[37]

Buildings were erected, more than two dozen in all, the larger structures mostly of brick and some in the Federal style, to house various shops and facilities and to provide housing for 300 or so workers (other workers lived outside of the complex). During the 1830s, Allaire streamlined the transportation and maintained a regular wagon schedule to take goods to the Eatontown dock on the Shrewsbury River, where the company had a four-story stone warehouse, a railway, and wharf. From there they were put aboard steamships. Another route connected to an ocean dock on the Navesink River at Red Bank. Although most shipments were made to New York City in particular, and to other coastal ports, much iron was also shipped to England.

Allaire Village became a self-contained community with its own church (Episcopal, used as a school on weekdays), post office, carpenter and woodworking shop, grist mill, bakery, and apothecary shop. *Allaire's Lost Empire* describes the store in the village, which cost $7,000 to build as a replacement for an old store that was razed in 1834:

> Four stories high and of brick construction, the store was a marvel in its day. Because of the isolated location of the Works an enormous stock of various goods was carried, and the store was patronized both by Howell employees and by residents for miles around. Howell Works provided a ready market for much of the farm produce from the area, and the store and the green in front were reported to have been used as a market place by the farmers. As the last stop on the new stage route to Toms River it also had considerable transient trade. The business transacted at the store seemed enormous and phenomenal.
>
> Two unusual features of the store were a primitive soda fountain and a massive manually-operated hoist used

to lift supplies to the upper floor. Constructed with huge beams, the store was further strengthened with a series of brick archways on each floor, bisecting the building. At some time in the past a second roof with greater pitch was installed without removing the original. In the cellar of the building was a room where meat was packed and salted. On that floor were sold meats, fish, molasses, and coarse groceries. On the first floor, where the post office apparently was located, were divisions for the sale of dry goods, hardware, light groceries, wines and liquors, flour and meal, and heavier iron ware. The upper floors were crowded with furniture and unpacked merchandise, and on the third level were huge bins for grain.

Allaire frequently bought items in New York and sent them to his family at Howell, listing their prices so they might be added to the store's stock if not to the family's liking. Garden produce and milk from farms on the property were also sold at the store. Garden supplies were paid for by employees with copper tokens marked "Howell Works Garden." The store closed in 1849.

A retail and wholesale store for items made at the Works was maintained at 173 Water Street in New York City to sell various models of stoves, hollow-ware kitchen items, and the like. In May 1832, the facility was moved to 261 Front Street.

Allaire formed the Southern States Packet Service in 1832, to offer scheduled steamer service from New York City southward to Charleston. Tickets were sold at the 261 Front Street office and salesroom of the Howell Works. In the warmer months the company office sold tickets to ride the steamer *Frank* to various places in Monmouth County, including the popular Long Branch vacation town.

In 1834, the date on one of the tokens, a New York firm offered "An assortment of sheet lead, sheet zinc, brazier's copper, copper bolts, copper nails, copper rivets, anvils, vises, &c. and American hollow ware from the Howell Works"—illustrating the diversity of products beyond iron.

Dr. Peter J. Guthorn told of the peak of activity:

> 1836 was the most successful year of the Allaire works. The blast furnace was in continuous operation for 21 months,

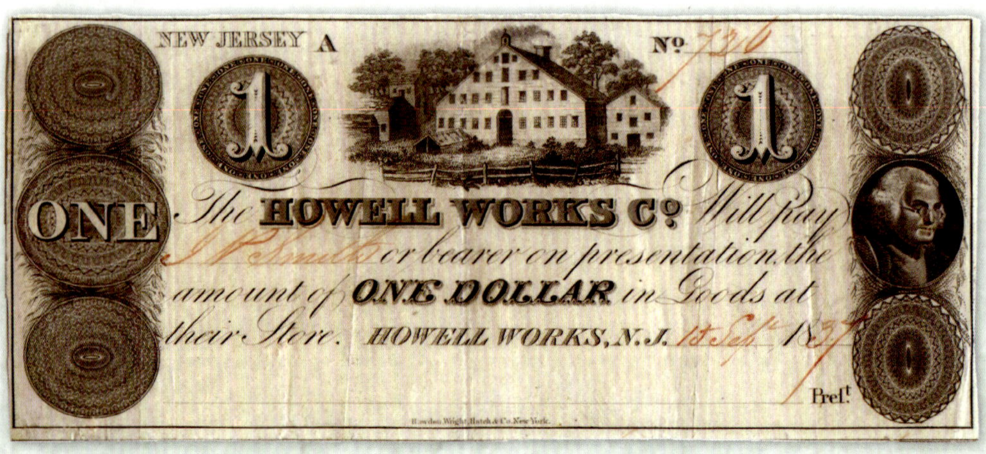

Scrip note of the Howell Works Co., 1837, printed by Rawdon, Wright, Hatch & Edson. Depicted is the main iron-works building for smelting, pouring, and molding. Issued notes bear the signature of James P. Allaire.

probably going out of blast about August 1837. This was a phenomenal record for furnaces and operations of this type. Smelting was discontinued in 1837 when the furnace blew out. . . .

The sawmill was completed in 1837, just about when the Works were going out of operation. The two cupolas in the furnace house continued in occasional operation. An attempt was made to rebuild the furnace in 1837, and intermittently into the 1850s. It is not known whether iron was smelted during this time.[38]

In the Panic of 1837, Allaire suffered further setbacks, but in time his shipbuilding business recovered. The Howell Works declined, as noted, and most workers left to find employment in other places. The hot-blast system of iron smelting was developed elsewhere, and the use of anthracite coal for heat proved to be economical. This sealed the fate for traditional charcoal furnaces such as the Howell Works, as they could not compete. The business closed in 1846, at which time there were 25 buildings in Allaire Village, which became a ghost town.

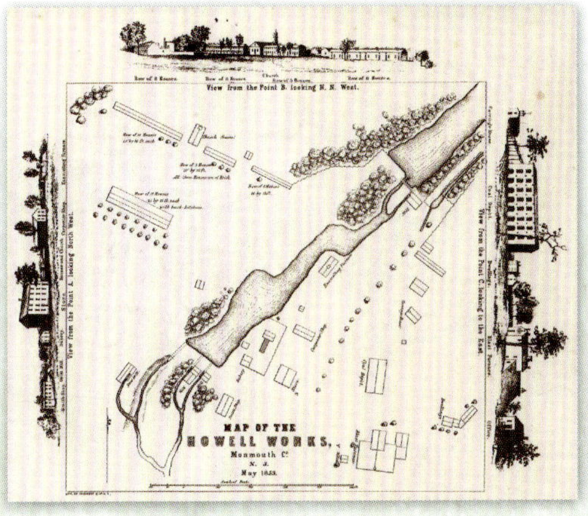

Map of the Works and sketches of buildings published in 1853 when the village and facilities were offered for sale. No buyer was found.

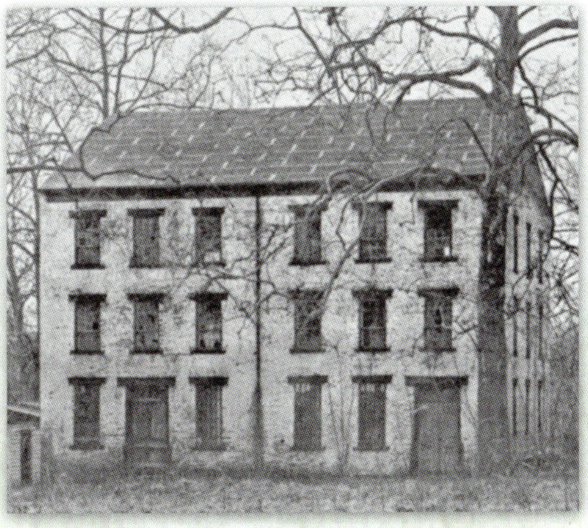

The derelict store as it appeared decades later (*Allaire's Lost Empire*).

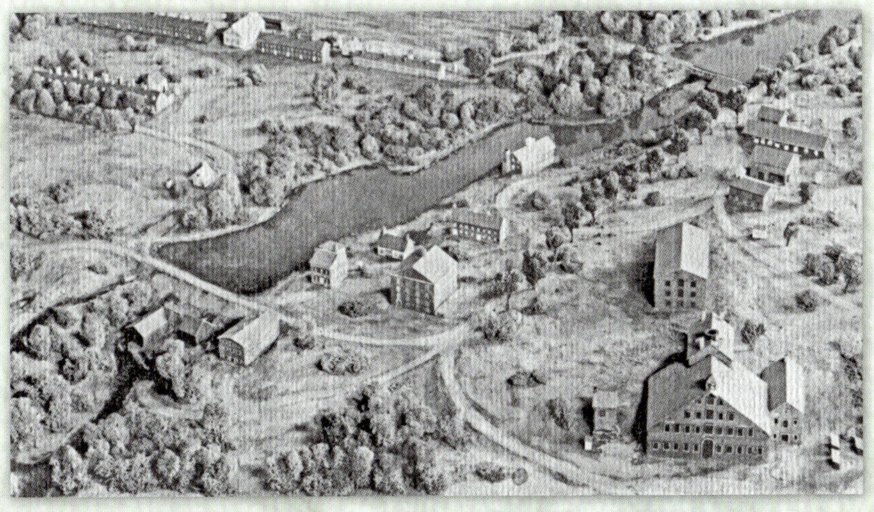

Model of the village constructed to show how it appeared at the height of its activity (New Jersey Department of Conservation and Development).

The Allaire Works that was based in New York City continued in business and became preeminent in the field of marine engines. The business continued and prospered in the era of ocean-going sidewheel steamers. Allaire served as president. He eventually lost control of the company and was dismissed from the office in 1850. Allaire resided for the rest of his life with his second wife Calicia in the Howell Works Big House. The couple had one son, Hal, born in 1847. The Howell Works property, by then comprising 7,000 acres with idle buildings, was improved by landscaping and was put up for sale, but with no buyers at the time. Allaire died on May 20, 1858.

Regarding the Howell Works Garden tokens, Lyman H. Low said this:

> Just what relation the Garden had to the Works does not appear, but that it was connected with them we have on good authority. From the device the token bears it was very likely a social resort for the workmen, under the control of the company.

Considering the extensive nature of Howell Works and the self-contained town, the "garden" tokens were probably used in the large store there.

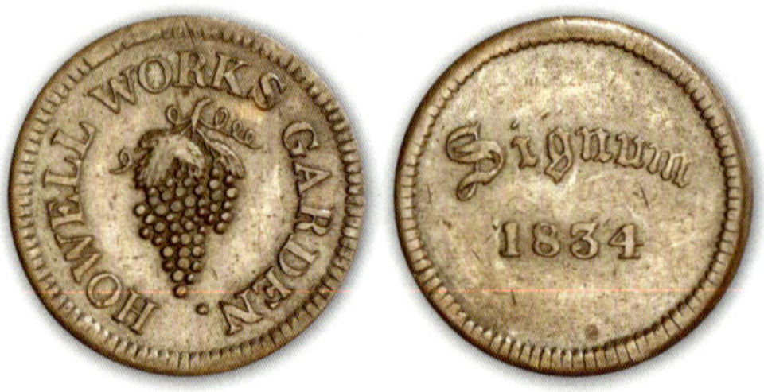

W-NJ-100-10a • Grapes / Signum 1834 • Low-81; HT-200. R-4. 22 mm. Copper. Typical grades are Fine to EF. The Tilden Collection example is probably the finest and was described by Don Miller in 1958: "Finest known Low-81. Sharp Uncirculated. Much red. From the Robert Bird Collection [in the 1910s]. Cost $30 at that time." The Ford token (2004) was later graded as AU-50 by NGC. • Fine-12 $175; VF-20 $350; EF-40 $700; AU-50 $1,350.

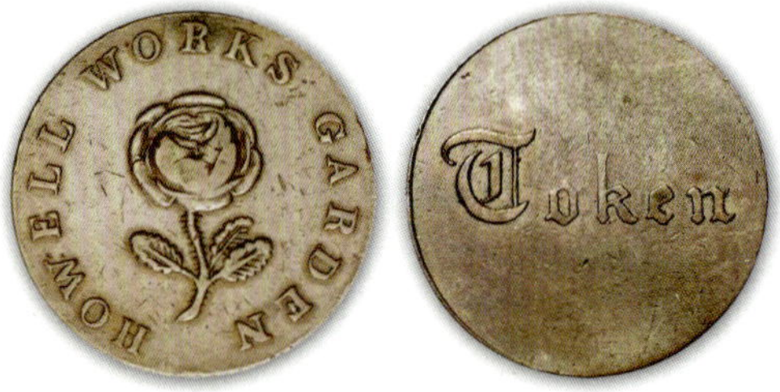

W-NJ-100-15a • Rose / Token • Low-163; HT-201. R-3. 26.5 mm. Copper. Typical grades are Fine and the occasional VF. EF examples are rarities, especially if well struck. The Tilden token was graded EF. The Ford token (2004) was later graded as EF-45 by NGC. When a Mr. Sherow exhibited a VF example at the May 30, 1922, meeting of the Pacific Coast Numismatic Society in San Francisco, special mention was made in *The Numismatist* (July 1922). Fine and VF are typical grades, with weak striking in areas. • Fine-12 $150; VF-20 $275; EF-40 $550.

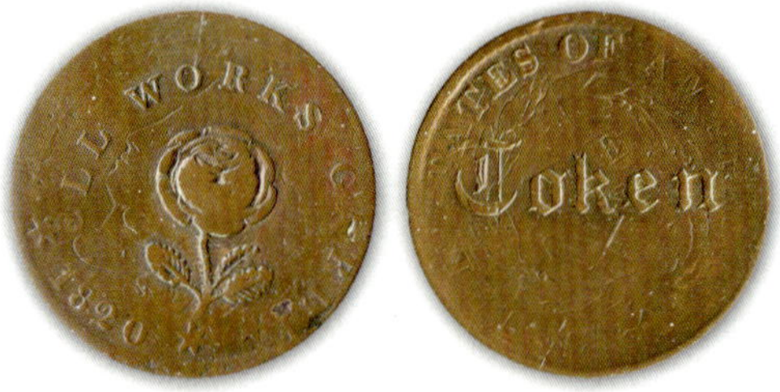

W-NJ-100-15a Over 1820 Cent • Low-Unlisted; HT-201A. R-9. 29 mm. Copper. Unique overstrike on an 1820 copper cent. The 1820 date is boldly visible at the lower left of the obverse.

John Gibbs
Belleville, NJ
Maker of tokens and medals
W-NJ-120

John Gibbs was born in Birmingham, England in 1809. Coincidentally, at the time that city was the main center for minting tokens in Great Britain. He came to America with his father and in time set up in Belleville, and with a partner, John

Gardner, he obtained space in a building occupied by Stephens, Thomas & Fuller, makers of sheet brass.[39] The men all became associated in the button business. John F. Thomas of the firm lived in nearby Newark and was an experienced die cutter, as was Stevens, who was trained in Birmingham, England.

The *Newark Daily Advertiser* printed this notice:

> The connection in the button manufacturing business heretofore existing between Arthur Nicholson, John Gibbs, and James Bishop, and Stephens, Thomas & Fuller is this day dissolved. . . .

Demands and claims were to be settled by Stephens, Thomas & Fuller. On March 5, 1833, the partnership of Gibbs, Gardner & Co. was dissolved by mutual consent.[40] John Gibbs was now on his own.[41]

The copper and brass industry was important to Belleville, and several companies were engaged in rolling out sheets from ingots. An 1835 notice stated:

> On Mill Street are erected a brass rolling mill, a woolen manufactory, paint manufactory, the American Cotton Print Works, 2 copper rolling mills, flour and saw mills, chemical manufactory in full operation and one now erecting, silk printing establishment, button and lamp factories, &c. employing 500 to 600 hands.[42]

What was later known as the Belleville Copper Rolling Mill, successor to the Soho Copper Co. established in 1812, was an especially prominent local mill, important in making copper sheeting to protect the hulls of seagoing vessels. It would have been a ready source for planchet stock, and there would have been multiple sources locally for obtaining stock from which to strike tokens.

In September 1834, John Gibbs joined several dozen others of Whig persuasion at the Mansion House in Belleville to form a Committee of Vigilance. This group and many others were against the actions of the Jackson administration.

The obverse of his token declares, "J. GIBBS MANUFACTURER / OF / MEDALS / AND / TOKENS / &c / NJ / BELLEVILLE." The reverse is lettered "AGRICULTURE AND COMMERCE" enclosing a fully rigged sailing ship, probably engraved by the same hand that cut the die for the 1841-dated Webster political tokens which were actually struck in 1837. Probably, the reverse die was intended for a Canadian token as the same lettering was used on certain other tokens, of the bouquet sou style.

Minting activities in Belleville took place into the early 1840s. The *Newark Daily Advertiser*, August 21, 1844, included this exchange item from the *New York Tribune:*

> Counterfeit Coppers. Samuel Beatty, of Toronto, Canada, who was sent to Belleville, N.J., to get made a large amount of counterfeit Canadian pennies, was arrested this morning on the charge of counterfeiting foreign coin. In his trunk was found a letter of instructions from his father, as also a bill and receipt for 324 pounds of copper from persons in Belleville, at 30 cents a pound; and those pennies were put up in boxes to be conveyed to Canada by the boy.

On September 2, the same paper told more:

> The *Newark Daily Advertiser* furnishes the following explanation of the paragraphs published in the papers of this city, relative to the seizure of a quantity of coin made in Belleville, N.J. alleged to be counterfeit Canadian coppers:
>
> There is neither mystery nor wrong in this case—much less are counterfeit pennies made at Belleville by the "persons" referred to. The facts, as we

> are informed, are simply these. The people of Canada have felt the want of some copper coin, and as the government furnishes none, the merchants and we believe the banks too, have long been in the habit of sending orders to the highly responsible house which carries on the copper business at Belleville, for a small copper token which is a little larger than our half cent.[43]
>
> They are probably used there in making change, but the manufacturers have nothing to do with that as they do not imitate any species of authorized currency and bear no date or description that could deceive anybody. They are simple medals or tokens,[44] sold by the pound, and the manufacturers did not enter into the business until after they had taken the advice of the most eminent legal counsel.

Thomas L. Elder, in "A Plea for American Token Collecting," *The Numismatist*, April 1915, commented:

> J. Gibbs of Belleville, N.J. was a well-known character and one of the best die sinkers of the Jackson period. Gibbs was born in England and so was his partner, Mr. Stevens. Curiously enough Gibbs at one time ran a line of stage coaches from Belleville to Newark and also to New York. Belleville is a little place three miles from Newark. This Belleville establishment did a considerable die-cutting business and doubtless engraved some of the bouquet sou tokens which appeared in such large numbers in Canada.
>
> William Gibbs issued a token, now quite rare, which bore a bouquet and a steer. At the same time this same Gibbs cultivated a large flower and vegetable garden on what is now Fifth Avenue and Seventy First Street.

Elder did not say anything further about John's father, William.

Lyman H. Low, who had done much research in New Jersey by the 1880s, wrote that he was told those who lived in that town referred to John Gibbs's establishment as the Belleville mint. Other cent-size tokens were made that today are collected as part of the Hard Times series, most famously that of T.D. Seaman, local butcher. So-called bouquet sous—coppers with flowers on one side—were made in large quantities for Canada. Certain copper issues of Brazil, Liberia, and San Domingo have also been attributed to the Belleville mint.

Conventional wisdom discarded, it is the writer's belief that John Gibbs maintained this business without any of his former partners from the late 1830s into the early 1840s. A similar ship to that featured on the obverse of this token is seen on the advance-dated 1841 Webster die on tokens issued in 1837. The ship obverse and reverse cow / FRIEND TO THE CONSTITUTION die is adrift regarding numismatic classification and is listed earlier as W-11-740a. It was also used on tokens advertising T.D. Seaman (W-NJ-160) and John Gibbs' father William (see New York listings).

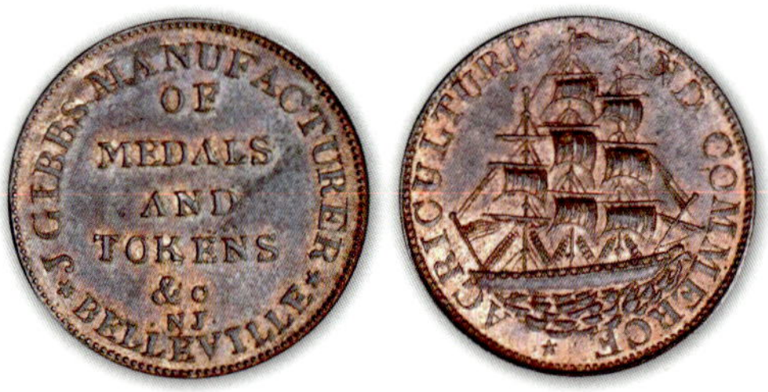

W-NJ-120-10a • Low-150; HT-202. R-6. 27.3 mm. Copper. Obverse with Gibbs advertisement. Reverse with sailing ship, AGRICULTURE AND COMMERCE. VF and EF are typical grades. Anything finer is a rarity. Ford (Stack's 2004) Choice Uncirculated $8,050. Dice-Hicks (Stack's 2008) Choice VF $1,495.

I. Gibbs / Belleville & New York U.S.M. Stage Belleville, NJ
Stagecoach
W-NJ-140

This token of I. Gibbs, a pseudonym of John Gibbs (W-NJ-140), was not listed by Lyman H. Low. It was illustrated and described by Edgar H. Adams under "Live American Numismatic Items" in *The Numismatist*, August 1912. He described Gibbs's token business, gave biographical notes concerning him, and then added this:

> Gibbs owned and ran a line of stage coaches from Belleville to Newark and also to New York. For use on these lines he struck a brass token which reads I. GIBBS (the top of the letter I spreads a little and suggests a T, but it is probably meant for a J. It is very rare.
>
> He removed from Belleville to New York in 1846, where he had a shop on Forsyth Street. In 1856 his home was in Williamsburgh, then a separate municipality, but later united to Brooklyn and now a part of "Greater New York." While living there he manufactured shade fixtures, buckles, lamp burners, &c. He was an ingenious mechanic, and while a resident of Belleville he invented a spring for a clock which required winding but once a year.
>
> So many of the Hard Times tokens came from Belleville that some further notes on the establishment there seem desirable to complete the history of these pieces.
>
> Belleville was a quiet little town in Essex County, N.J., on the Passaic River, three miles from Newark. Here, about 1830, was situated the factory in which was carried on the business—extensive for the period—to which reference is made above. . . .

Russell Rulau noted, "An advertisement in an 1831 newspaper publicized John Gibbs's Belleville to Newark (3 miles) and Belleville to New York (8 miles) stages."

In 1838 a daily mail stagecoach went into service between Belleville and New York City, quite possibly another key to the era of the token.[45] The Post Office in Belleville closed not long afterward. Commencing January 1, 1840, the Newark & Paterson Stage U.S. Mail Line passed through and stopped at Belleville on Monday, Wednesday, Friday, and Saturday. On November 19, 1840, the *Phoenix* coach of the Belleville & Newark Stage, operated by Thomas Mason, connected at Newark for trains bound for New York City.

"Gibbs may have operated the stage as late as 1846 when he relocated to Forsythe Street in Manhattan," George S. Cuhaj stated in a paper presented in 1994.[46]

Woodward's 1884 sale of the J.N.T. Levick Collection included this:

> Lot 438. Good for one ride to the bearer; rev., Belleville and New York U.S.M. Stage, I.G. Gibbs; brass, fine, and, so far as I can trace it, unique. Plate. [$14]

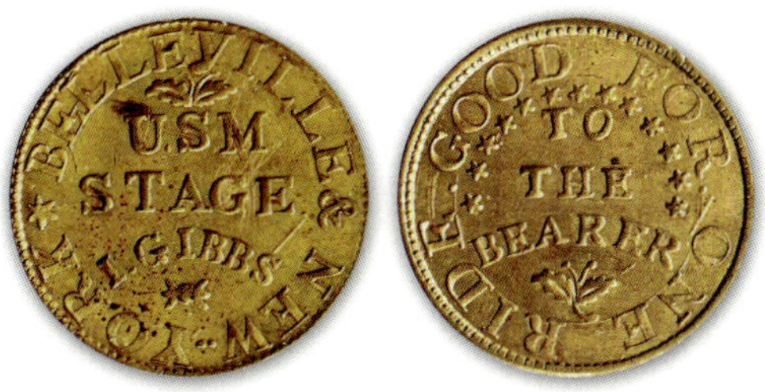

W-NJ-140-10b • Rulau: "Low-374"; HT-203. R-7. 23 mm. Brass. All examples studied have a die crack at the center left and upper left of the obverse. Likely, the die failed after it was in use for a short time, accounting for its rarity today. This is one of the great rarities among Hard Times tokens. The Dice-Hicks Collection, sold in 2008 and one of the most comprehensive offerings ever, lacked an example. John J.

Ford Jr. had two, one of which was described as EF-45, ex Robert A. Schuman, and auctioned for $7,050 in August 2013; the other, EF cleaned $4,406. Joseph Levine / Presidential Coin and Antique Co. auctioned a VG example in June 2012, noting it was the first specimen seen at auction since the Benjamin Betts Collection crossed the block in 1898. One is held by the American Numismatic Society, is pictured on its website, and grades VF. An About Good example is pictured on the exonumia.com website, no provenance given. The illustrated token is from the Max M. Schwartz Collection to Duane Feisel to Steve Tanenbaum and is the Atwood NY-630A plate token. In the Atwood catalog this has the highest value listing of any token.

T.D. Seaman / (T. Duseaman) Belleville, NJ

Butcher, tradesman

W-NJ-160

Tobias D. Seaman, who advertised as T.D. Seaman, butcher, on his token, also kept a public house in Belleville. Rulau states that he conducted the Mechanics Hotel, 188 Broad Street, Newark from about 1845 to 1850, and in 1851 he conducted the South Ward Hotel at 398 Broadway in the same city. The obverse of the token has his name and trade around the border and flowers of the style used on Canadian bouquet sous at the center.

A variant token, one of the most famous in the series, has "T. DUSEAMAN BUTCHER / BELLEVILLE" around the obverse border with a standing eagle holding a shield with a Rhode Island motif (fouled anchor) at the center; 13 stars surround the center. All examples seen have a prominent die crack from upper left across the die to the lower right. Low called the workmanship "wretched" and conjectures that when Seaman saw the die he rejected it, at which point the engraver added an extraneous U to create "Duseaman," after which it was put into circulation by the maker or sold to someone who took them to Canada. Inspection of the details reveals, however, that the workmanship is quite good. Readers can determine for themselves. This "error" token, or whatever it is, has created a lot of attention in numismatic circles for a long time. Certainly it is one of the more interesting pieces. As examples are easily encountered, they have been very popular.

The August 1867 issue of the *American Journal of Numismatics* included this:

> A recent letter from one of our Montreal subscribers, R. W. McLachlan, Esq., contains the following paragraph:
>
> "Availing myself of the opportunity offered in your column devoted to Queries and Replies, I would ask you concerning a coin described on page 60 of Bushnell's *Arrangement of Store Cards*, &c., as pertaining to Belleville, New Jersey, and one in my own collection, of which the obverse is an eagle with an oval in front, surrounded by thirteen stars; legend: T. DUSEAMAN, BUTCHER BELLEVILLE, and the reverse a bouquet similar to the Canadian 'Un Sou." AGRICULTURE AND COMMERCE, BAS CANADA. Both sides of the coin have a crack across the face. It is, though scarce, sometimes met with in circulation, and is decidedly a Canadian coin. Is the coin mentioned by Bushnell not Canadian also?"
>
> To this Query our friend Mr. Groh has furnished the following reply, adverse both to the inquirer's opinion about the one coin, and to his surmise in regard to the other:
>
> "The token of T. Duseaman, Butcher, Belleville, which many collectors believe to be Canadian, on account of its reverse bearing the words 'Bas Canada' and there being a Belleville in Canada, is of New Jersey origin. The following description of

three cards, struck in and for Belleville, N. J., will show their relationship to the above piece:

“1. Obv.: T.D. Seaman Butcher Belleville. A bunch of roses, thistles and spears of grain tied by ribbon. Rev.: A Cow. ‘A Friend to the Constitution.’

“2. Obv.: W. Gibbs Agriculturist, N. York. A bunch of Roses, Thistles and Grain as in last. Rev.: A Cow. “A Friend to the Constitution.’

“3. Obv.: ‘J. Gibbs, Manufacturer of Medals and Tokens &c. Belleville, N. J.’ Rev.: A Ship. ‘Agriculture and Commerce.’

“They are all of exactly the same size and style of workmanship; and the difference in the names on the first two mentioned is evidently owing to a mistake made by the die-sinker. Some years ago there was a T.D. Seaman doing business at Newark, N.J., about three miles south of Belleville, and he is probably the same party for whom these tokens were made.

“The eagle, with anchor in an oval, and surrounded by a circle of 13 stars, is additional proof of the coin’s belonging to the United States.

“As there was a copper rolling mill in operation at Belleville, N.J., some twenty or thirty years ago, and a die-sinker at the same place, there can be no doubt, that many of the Un Sou and other tokens of Canada were extensively manufactured in that village.”

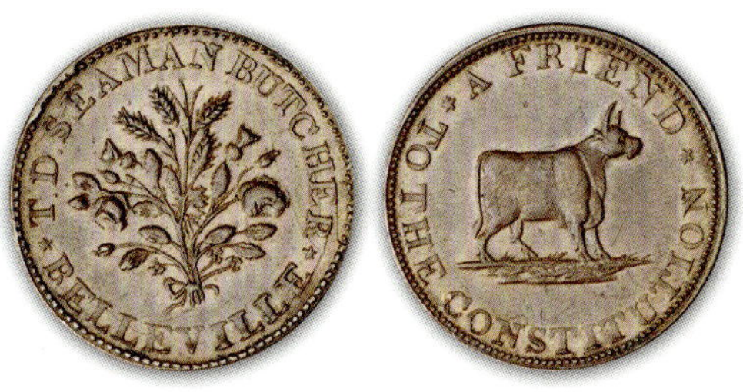

W-NJ-160-10a • T.D. Seaman • Low-155; HT-204B. R-5. 27.5 mm. Copper. Obverse with T.D. Seaman and bouquet; reverse with cow and “A FRIEND TO THE CONSTITUTION.” If the reverse die is from the late 1830s as speculated under W-NJ-120 above, then this token would date from that period. This would be consistent with the thought that Gibbs was a major manufacturer of Canadian bouquet sous in the early 1840s. The finer pieces in collections are usually EF or AU. Very few higher-grade pieces have ever come on the market. Ford (Stack’s 2004) AU $978. Dice-Hicks (Stack’s 2008) AU $1,380, Choice Unc $1,955.

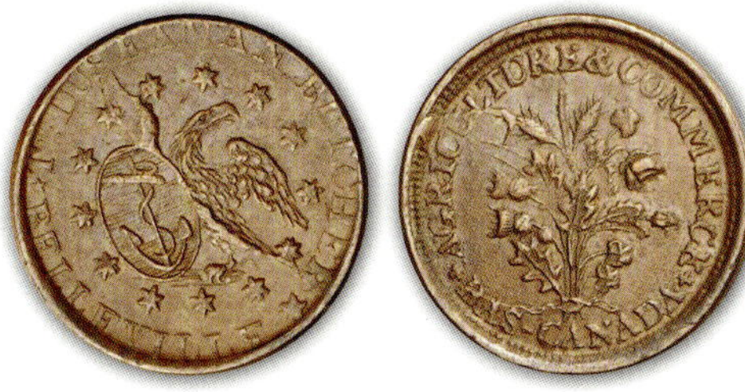

W-NJ-160-15a • T. Duseaman • Low-148; HT-204. R-2. 28.0 mm. Copper. Breton-670 as a Canadian token. Obverse with erroneous “T. DUSEAMAN,” always seen somewhat lightly impressed due to the crack and impending failure of the dies. Eagle, shield, and 13 stars at the center. Reverse with “AGRICULTURE & COMMERCE / BAS CANADA” around a bouquet. A die specifically made for Southern Canada. This curious token is a favorite for just about everybody. EF and AU are typical higher grades seen in the marketplace. • VF-20 $45; EF-40 $100; AU-50 $225; MS-63 $550.

Bergen Iron Works
Lakewood, NJ
Iron works
W-NJ-180

The Bergen Iron Works, located in what is now Lakewood Township, was an operation similar to that of the Howell Works. Regionally abundant bog iron ore was smelted, using charcoal as fuel and oyster shells as flux. Later in the decade that this

1840 token was issued, new refining processes and the use of anthracite coal from Pennsylvania rendered this process obsolete. The mill continued operations into the 1850s. The factory was located at about four miles from the north end of Barnegat Bay where the railroad crossed the Metedeconk River.

Joseph Woolston Brick purchased the Washington Furnace on the south branch of the Metedeconk River and renamed it the Bergen Iron Works, a name selected as at the time much of the ore came from Bergen. Iron from the smelted ore was used to cast water pipes, architectural columns, and other products, mostly for industrial rather than consumer products.

Residences were erected in a village at the works, including, in 1835, one on Madison Avenue for Joseph and Margaret Brick and their five children—Caroline, Riley, George, Sarah, and Josephine. Parts of the girls' names were adapted more or less to name Lake Carasaljo adjacent to the factory. With the much smaller Lake Manetta, this was one of two created by damming up the Metedeconk River to provide water power to drive machinery in the factory.

By 1844 there were 200 people living in the Bergen Iron Works Village. By this time, the earlier-discussed Howell Works was inactive. There were 14 buildings, including a company store that used the tokens studied here. Joseph Brick died on February 1, 1847, leaving an estate of $47,000, not including land. The business was willed to his young children, of whom Caroline, age 12, was the oldest.

The Bergen Iron Works Post Office opened on June 22, 1848. Widow Margaret Campbell remarried in 1848. The business was continued under others, including Benjamin Snyder, the agent (a term for general manager and sales agent), and John L. Snyder, who conducted the company store and may have been connected with the tokens of the 1830s. In the early 1850s, the smelting operation was moved to Perth Amboy, while casting continued to be done at the Bergen Iron Works.

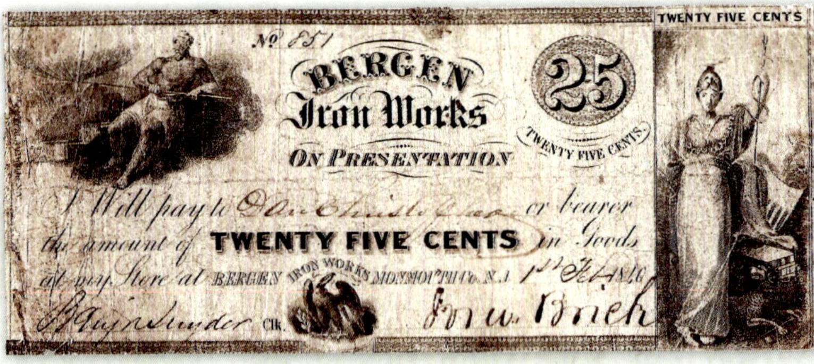

Scrip note for twenty-five cents issued by the Bergen Iron Works in 1840 and redeemable at the company store.

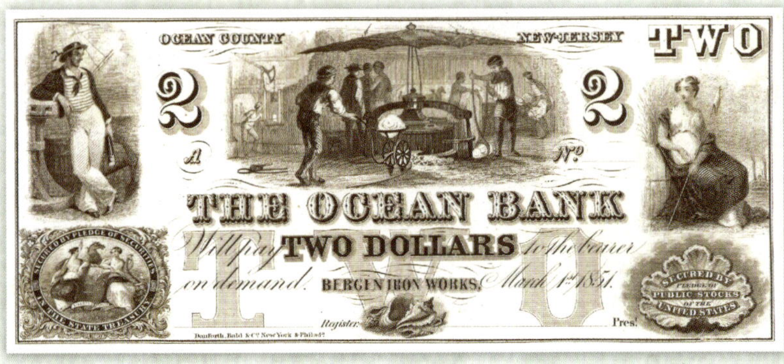

Iron foundry activity as shown on a $2 note issued by the Ocean Bank of Bergen Iron Works.

The Snyders, who were important in the affairs of the Iron Works after the death of Brick, became involved in a banking scheme. The state of New Jersey enacted its General Banking Law that permitted groups of entrepreneurs to raise capital and obtain banking charters, simplifying the old process of having the right political connections with the State Legislatures. This led to immediate abuse, as banks were formed simply to issue paper money and sell it at a discount to agents who put the notes into circulation in distant places.

William H. Dillistin, in *Bank Note Reporters and Counterfeit Detectors 1826–1866*, 1949, gave much information on this caper:

> The Union Bank at Toms River had an authorized capital stock of 20,000 shares of a par value of $25 each, of which 19,993 shares were subscribed for by one Benjamin Snyder of Bergen Iron Works. The Ocean Bank at Bergen Iron Works had the same authorized capital stock of which 19,993 shares were subscribed for by one John L. Snyder of Bergen Iron Works.

Banker's Magazine, August 1852, took up the subject:

> There is a small locality in New Jersey, under the name of Toms River, within about a day's journey from New York, which has been selected as the nominal place of issue of two Wall Street banks, in addition to one in the immediate neighborhood—at the Bergen Iron Works. From this circumstance, the place derives some interest to us of New York, and it seems desirable to make known that the town or village contains four stores, one public house, and *two banks*, besides the one in the neighborhood. . . .
>
> This out-of-the-way place presents several difficulties in the way of the redemption of the bills. The bills are mostly issued in Wall Street, and sold largely to brokers at a discount, to put them in circulation. Leaving the city at an early hour in the morning, and

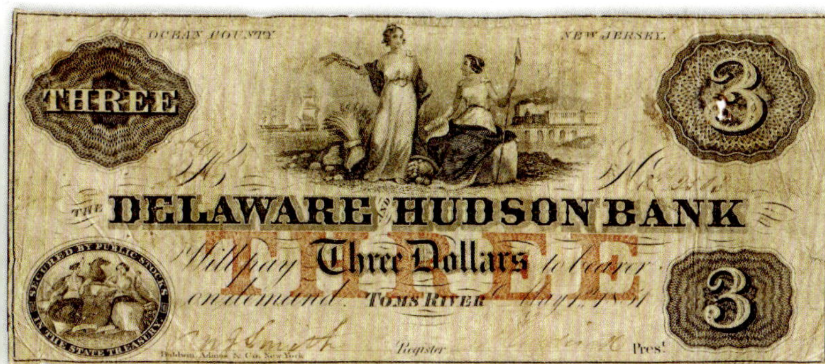

Notes from the disreputable banks at Toms River and Bergen Iron Works.

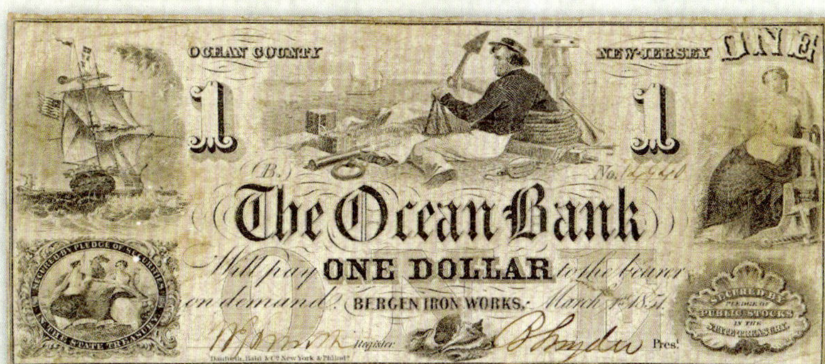

> taking the train by the Amboy Railroad, the locality cannot be reached before six o'clock in the evening—after banking hours. To present them for payment, it is necessary to remain a day there, as the train passes before banking business commences, and a third day must pass before New York can be again reached. By the banking law of New Jersey, banks are entitled to three days' grace in redeeming their notes, after presentation; which enables the officers to send to New York for specie, if any large amount of bills is presented for payment. In this manner is working the trade in a depreciated currency, which is on the increase, and which it behooves the State of New Jersey to remedy.

By 1854 the Snyder's bogus banks were no longer in operation. In the 1860s, Joseph's children renamed the village Bricksburg. In 1892 the village detached itself from Brick Township and was named Lakewood.[47]

W-NJ-180-10a • Low-180; HT-205. R-4. 20.9 mm. Copper. Obverse with eagle perched on braided wire, BERGEN IRON / WORKS surrounding; 5-pointed star to each side of STORE. Reverse with BONÆ FIDEI SIGNUM ["a good common bond"]. / 1840 around the border. Two clasped hands at the center with glory of rays surrounding. VF and EF are typical grades, but several higher-grade pieces exist. • VF-20 $150; EF-40 $250; AU-50 $350; MS-63 $750.

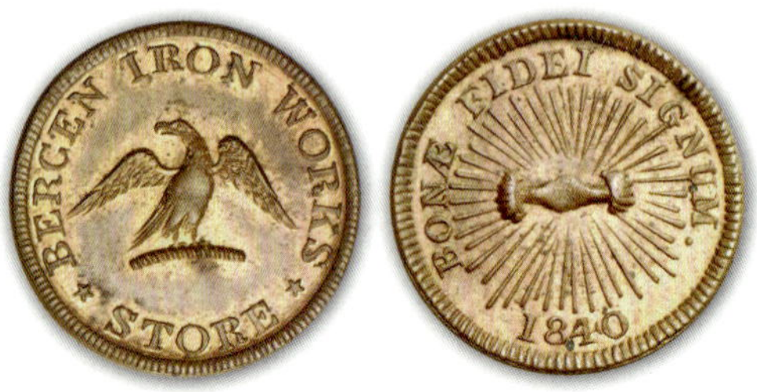

W-NJ-180-10b • 5-pointed star to each side of STORE • Low-142; HT-205A. R-2. 20.9 mm. Brass. Most are VF to AU, although Mint State examples appear when great collections are sold. • VF-20 $100; EF-40 $150; AU-50 $250; MS-63 $450.

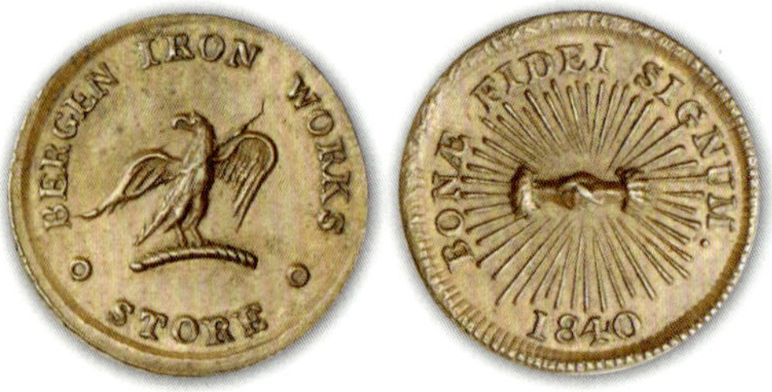

W-NJ-180-15a • Circle to each side of STORE • Low-143; HT-206. R-3. 20.8 mm. Copper. Obverse with eagle perched on braided wire, BERGEN IRON / WORKS surrounding in a different font from the preceding; tiny circle to each side of STORE. The die cracked early in its use (Robert A. Schuman has never seen a perfect die example) and continued to fail, eventually having massive cracks. Reverse die as preceding. Most are EF or AU, although Mint State coins are occasionally offered; Ford had two, one cleaned at $403 and the other pristine for $891. • VF-20 $125; EF-40 $200; AU-50 $450; MS-63 $1,250.

W-NJ-180-15b • Low-144; HT-Unlisted. Estimated R-8. 21 mm. Brass. Listed by Low. Robert A. Schuman: "Unknown today."

E. & I. Bragaw
Newark, NJ / Mobile, AL
Hat manufacturers
W-NJ-200

These undated tokens, from dies cut by Wright & Bale in New York City, were issued sometime during that shop's 1829 to 1833 existence. The token lists New Jersey and Alabama addresses. As New Jersey was listed first in the inscription, the token is featured here under New Jersey and cross-referenced earlier in the Alabama section.

In Newark, Elias and John Bragaw were listed as wholesale hatters with premises at 348 Broad Street, as well as in Alabama. In 1836 their partnership was dissolved. Elias Bragaw continued the business on his own in Newark and John Bragaw independently conducted the facility in Alabama.

On December 28, 1832, Elias Bragaw posted a notice of a runaway:

> An indented apprentice to the hatting business named Randolph Tuttle, about 18 years of age, 5 feet 6 or 7 inches high, of slender make—had on when he went away a dark olive coat and pantaloons, black vest and black fur hat. He ran off with a small black and white cow. Whoever will return them both shall receive one dollar and six cents, or if returned separately, one dollar for the cow and six cents for the boy. All persons are forbid trusting the boy or harboring either.[48]

Rulau told this about Bragaw:

> Elias Brevoort Bragaw was born June 15, 1800 at Newton, Sussex County, New Jersey, the son of Richard Bragaw and Elizabeth Painter, his wife. He married Alethea Williams on Dec. 24, 1824 at Newark, Essex County, N.J.

The *Newark Daily Advertiser*, December 13, 1834, included a notice of an auction of properties owned by the estate of Luther Goble to be held on the 20th of various properties including "1 lot with shop thereon, in Harrison St., 40 by 140, at present occupied by Mr. E. Bragaw as a hatter's shop."

W-NJ-200-10a • Rulau: "Low-302"; HT-207. R-7 per Rulau. 26.6 mm. Copper.

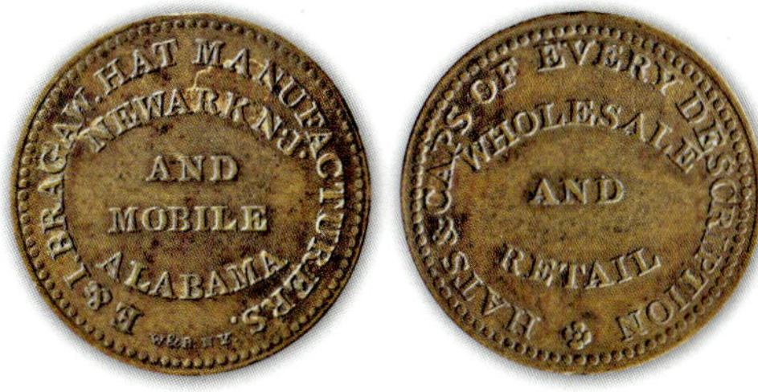

W-NJ-200-10b • Rulau: "Low-303"; HT-207A. High R-7. 26.6 mm. Brass. An example in W.E. Woodward's Sale No. 67, May 26 to 28, 1884, brought $3, a high price for the time. VF and EF grades are typical. Rulau could only find a holed example to illustrate. Dice-Hicks (Stack's 2008) VF $3,450.

W-NJ-200-10e • Rulau: "Low-304"; HT-207B. R-7. 26.6 mm. White metal.

W-NJ-200-15b • Low-Unlisted; HT-207AA (assigned by Steve Tanenbaum). R-8. 26.6 mm. Brass. The reverse is similar to the preceding but with slightly different letter spacing. Two known per Steve Hayden. Russell Rulau had never seen and could not describe this token (but he mentioned it in passing under HT-207A).

New York Hard Times Tokens

N. Safford / Temperance House
Albany, NY
Hotel for temperance advocates
W-NY-050

During the Hard Times era (as defined by Low) there were two great social movements in America. One was the abolition of slavery, and the other was abstinence from drinking alcohol, or temperance. By the early 1830s there were several thousand temperance clubs and societies in America. Many of these were connected to Christian churches. To accommodate devotees of this movement, many restaurants and hotels advertised that they were temperance establishments. Such was the hotel maintained by N. Safford.

The *Religious Messenger*, published in Norwich, Connecticut, printed this on May 12, 1832, "We take much pleasure in stating that an excellent Temperance House of Entertainment is kept in Albany by Mr. N. Safford."

The establishment was new at the time, per this advertisement in the *Albany Argus*, July 24, 1832:

> Albany Temperance House—N. Safford, late of Oneida Temperance House, Utica, has taken the spacious and convenient building in the city of Albany, known as the Albany Temperance House, and belonging to E.C. Delavan, Esq., situation on the corner of North Market and Steuben streets, a short distance north of the Post Office.

In the third edition of *The Temperance Text Book*, 1836, Safford advertised with a different address (the one used on the token):

> Temperance Hotel and Grocery, Albany, N.Y. Temperance House. No. 280 Market Street, Albany, by N. Safford. This establishment has been greatly enlarged, and the whole thoroughly repaired. The proprietor, grateful for the patronage that seemed to warrant this improvement, solicits a continuance of past favours. Warm baths at short notice, every day (Sunday excepted) from 9 A.M. to 11 P.M.

The Albany Temperance House was mentioned favorably in many notices. On August 2, 1842, this appeared in the *Albany Argus:*

> Delavan House. Mr. George T. Hill, the estimable and enterprising proprietor of the Temperance House, corner of Broadway and Steuben Street, Albany, after a thorough renovation of his establishment has given it the above name, in order to distinguish it from the Temperance Houses that, we are happy to say, abound here and elsewhere. The new name, however appropriate, was unnecessary. It will still be known as *The* Temperance House, and it is sufficient to say that it will continue to be all that it was under Mr. Safford, the former proprietor, and that it has since been under its present management.

The token under study was listed as No. 930 by Benjamin P. Wright in "American Store or Business Cards," in *The Numismatist,* June 1899. Certainly Lyman H. Low was aware of this listing, but he did not pick it up, perhaps as the date of issue was not given. The tokens were struck by James Bale in New York City.

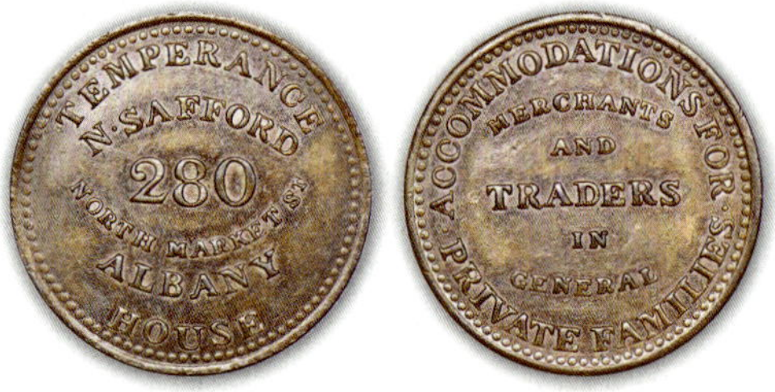

W-NY-050-10a • Rulau: "Low-348"; HT-210. R-5. 26.6 mm. Copper. VF and EF are typical grades. • VF-20 $175; EF-40 $300; AU-50 $450.

W-NY-050-10e • Rulau: "Low-349"; HT-210A. R-7. 26.6 mm. White metal. VF and EF are typical grades. • VF-20 $300; EF-40 $450; AU-50 $750.

J. Cochran Batavia, NY *Bell founder* W-NY-080

The J. Cochran token is one of the most famous in the series. The obverse is an adaptation of the Liberty Head with beaded hair cords, as used on federal copper cents of the late 1830s. J. COCHRAN BELLFOUNDER is at the top border, groups of three stars are at the lower left and right, and BATAVIA is below.

The reverse has a wreath loosely adapted from the federal cent, with AN ARMY FOR DEFENCE and 1844 at the border. Within the wreath is NOT / ONE / CENT / FOR TRIBUTE, a unique variation on the usual "Millions for defence, not one cent for tribute," inscription.

Each of the known examples shows extensive wear.

In his 1899 book Lyman H. Low listed this token as No. 161, noting more information in his 1906 supplement, as shown above:

> James H. Cochran was a bell founder in Batavia, N. Y., early in the "forties." His foundry and place of residence were both on Bank Street. He cast the bell now in the First Presbyterian Church. It has been stated by an old resident, who knew Cochran when residing there, that he made these tokens on each Saturday. Very few people now living recollect the piece. It is improbable that he struck more than a few of them.
>
> No other has been learned of since the one that appeared in 1896. There was no Directory published in the town in those early days. His name appears on the records at the County Clerk's office. It is believed that he died in Batavia.[49]

The Numismatist printed this in July 1912:

The following very interesting information in regard to the unique Hard Times Token, issued by J. Cochran, Bell Founder, of Batavia, N. Y., popularly known as Low 161, has been communicated by E. Hallenback of Schenectady, N.Y.:

"When Mr. Low was preparing his supplement of Hard Times Tokens I obtained for him the additional information in regard to 161—J. Cochran, see supplement. I now find an additional item of interest in the *Antiquarian and General Review*, edited by Rev. Wm. Arthur, father of ex-President Arthur, published at Schenectady, and later at Lansingburgh, the number containing this being Vol. III., No. 1, March, 1847, which I quote verbatim:

"'James Cochran, a bell founder, and very ingenious mechanic, died lately at the age of 83, in Batavia, N. Y. He invented cut nails, and claimed to have made the first cent coined in the United States. He was born in Philadelphia, where he worked in brass and fine metals. Franklin, it is said, often visited his shop.'"

It is understood that there is one other specimen of this interesting piece, and that is in the collection of Mr. [Virgil] Brand of Chicago. Dr. Hetrich is the possessor of several other splendid Hard Times tokens

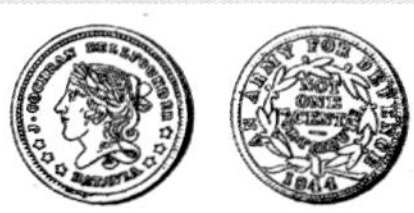

161. *Obv.* J. COCHRAN BELLFOUNDER above, and below, completing the circle, ★★★ BATAVIA ★★★ surrounding a female head, laureated, in profile to left. *Rev.* AN ARMY FOR DEFENCE outside of an unfinished wreath of olive leaves and berries formed by a single branch tied at the base with a bow of ribbon, between the end of which and the stem is the date 1844; within the wreath the inscription NOT | ONE | CENT | — | FOR - TRIBUTE the last line curving upward. Borders 4. Edge 1. Metal Æ. Size 28.

I believe that the first knowledge of this piece by collectors, certainly the first mention of it which has been found on record, so far as I have been able to discover, dates from its appearance in a public sale held in New York, on December 1, 1896. The motto "Millions for Defence" had ceased to be a popular cry; the era of peace and good feeling, save for the growing opposition to slavery, was regnant; the war with Mexico had not begun, and the special signification of the reverse legend is therefore difficult to discover; it is doubtful if it be anything more than a modification of the earlier motto. I attribute it to Batavia, now a wealthy city in Genesee County, N. Y., then a prosperous town. No other specimen is known to me.

Lyman H. Low's description of L-161.

LIVE AMERICAN NUMISMATIC ITEMS.

BY EDGAR H. ADAMS.

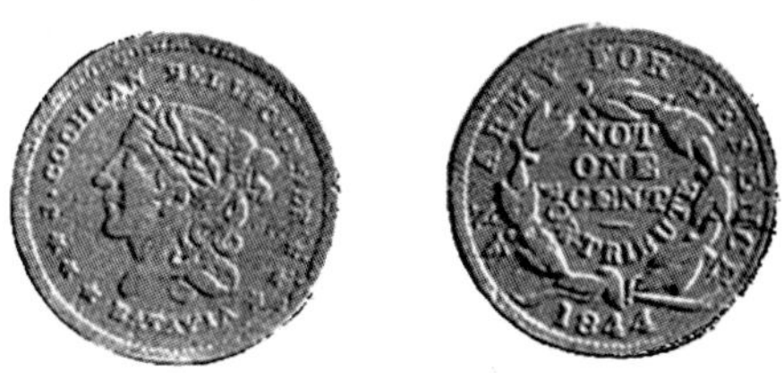

Low 161.

The Edgar H. Adams illustrations, the first photographs published.

> which are equally as rare as the Cochran token. He shows in his collection a specimen in brass, Uncirculated, and a specimen in white metal, Uncirculated, of Low No. 7 showing the radiated liberty cap and the ship, with the inscription of "The Glorious Whig Victory of 1834," etc. It is not known where other specimens of these excessively rare varieties are located.

Under "Live American Numismatic Items," in *The Numismatist*, October 1912, Edgar H. Adams illustrated the token that George Hetrich had recently acquired. He began:

> We are especially pleased to be able this month to show an illustration of one of the rarest of the series of Hard Times tokens, popularly known to the advanced collector as Low 161. This piece illustrated above is in copper, and the one formerly in the collection of the late Charles Morris of Chicago, and was purchased by its present owner, Dr. George Hetrich, of Birdsboro, Pa., and the sale recently held by Mr. Green of Chicago. Dr. Hetrich has kindly permitted us to reproduce the rare token for *The Numismatist*, and we are sure there will be many who will view it with interest. . . .

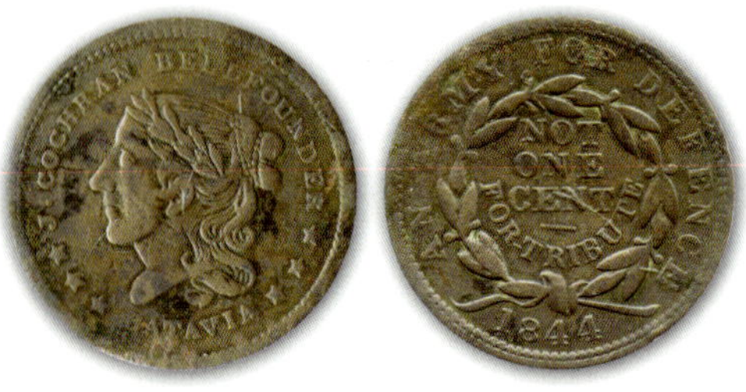

W-NY-080-10a • Low-161; HT-211. High R-7. 27.4 mm. Copper. 4 known. This census was prepared by Robert A. Schuman in 2014:

> 1. David U. Proskey; Ed. Frossard's 142nd sale, December 1896, lot 486; Ben Green sale July 1912; Dr. George Hetrich; Donald M. Miller; Q. David Bowers; Rossa & Tanenbaum; Donald G. Partrick. Plated by E.H. Adams in *The Numismatist*, October 1912; plated by Q. David Bowers in *High Profits from Coin Investment*, 1981, p. 120. Overstruck on another token, not identified. In his notes John J. Ford, Jr. graded this as VF-20.
>
> 2. Chili Coin Co. 1974; Stephen L. Tanenbaum; Q. David Bowers. VF-30, some surface roughness.
>
> 3. Virgil M. Brand; Jane Brand Allen (Brand estate) to F.C.C. Boyd February 28, 1955; Boyd estate (Helen Boyd) privately to John J. Ford, Jr.; Ford sale, Stack's 2004 lot 302; dealer; Robert A. Schuman. Ford called this Fine-12; "NOT" on reverse scraped off.
>
> 4. Emanuel Wertman Sale (Henry Chapman, December 10, 1910, lot 651); Virgil M. Brand; unknown connection to John J. Ford, Jr.; Ford offered this to Rossa & Tanenbaum and to Stack's but no agreement was made; came back to Ford; sold to Robert A. Schuman; consigned to H. Joseph Levine; purchased by James E. Dice and M. Lamar Hicks for $15,525; sold in the Dice-Hicks sale of July 2008. About Fine, filed at the center obverse, edge damage $11,500.

Patterson Brothers
Brooklyn, NY
Hardware
W-NY-100

In 1832 the firm advertising on the token was known as Patterson & Brothers. It resided at 6 Cheapside, Main Street, and was affiliated with Gardiner & Patterson, importers, at 208 Main Street. On November 19 of that year, a large fire ravaged a section of the business district, including

Patterson & Brothers. Their loss was given as $20,000, of which $9,000 was insured.[50] In 1833 the firm advertised as Patterson, Brothers (with a comma separating the words), no address given. Gardiner & Patterson continued at the address used earlier.

Patterson Brothers in the late 1830s and early 1840s advertised as a "cheap hardware establishment" at 170 Main Street, the address on the token. Incoming shipments were advertised now and again, as were seasonal goods. John and James Patterson were the owners, with John seemingly the more important partner. By 1844 John led the business and James clerked there. John lived at 350 Washington Street, and James was a boarder there.

W-NY-100-10a EE • Rulau: "Low-324A"; HT-212A. R-2. 28.5 mm. Copper. Engrailed edge. Same grade comment as preceding. • F-12 $20; VF-20 $45; EF-40 $150; AU-50 $400.

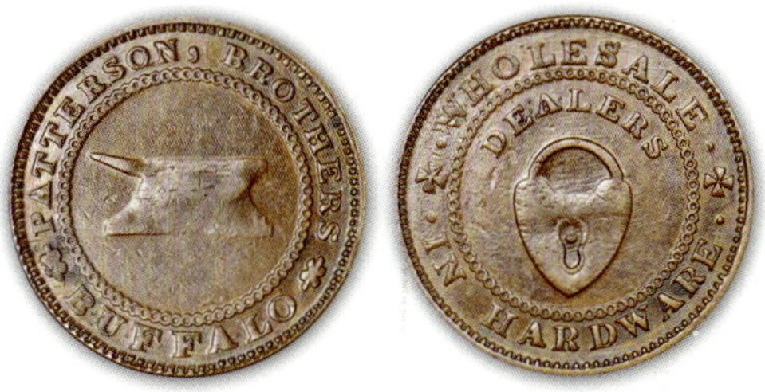

W-NY-100-10a PE • Rulau: "Low-324"; HT-212. R-5. 28.5 mm. Copper. Plain edge. VF and EF are typical grades, but higher examples are occasionally seen. • F-12 $25; VF-20 $75; EF-40 $175; AU-50 $400.

W-NY-100-15a • Low-Unlisted; HT-212B. R-9. Small 24 mm. Copper. Blank reverse with dentils, lines later scored on the reverse. Ex Byron White, Larry Dzuibek, Presidential Coin and Antique Co., SLT estate (listed at $1,250).

W.A. Thomson
Buffalo, NY
Hardware
W-NY-120

William A. Thomson was in the hardware business in the 1830s and 1840s. In 1838 he was a clerk for Patterson Brothers (see entry). By 1839 he was in business on his own at No. 9 Webster Buildings (also listed as Webster Block) on Main Street, sometimes listed as No. 6 as well.

In the *Jamestown Journal*, April 18, 1839, Thomson—then at No. 9 Webster Buildings—advertised that he was importing large quantities of cutlery, bar iron, and English hardware, via the Erie Canal boats *Virginia*, *Siddons*, *Roscoe*, *Europe*, and *Westminster*, that "will be offered for sale as soon as the canal will permit." Traffic was beginning to commence after the winter freezing.

In 1844 he was at Nos. 7 and 9 Webster Buildings. Robert H. Thomson was a clerk at the same address, and Thomas Thomson was also listed there, with no specialty given. John S. Hamlin was Thomson's bookkeeper. Later Thomson admitted his brother Hugh to the business, and the name was changed to Thomson Brothers.

Tools were an important part of Thomson's trade. He marked his name on many that he sold, with the result that his identified tools are seen with some frequency among offerings of antiques today.

Probably because the Thomson tokens are not the size of copper cents and bear no date, they attracted little notice in the 19th century when Hard Times tokens began to be collected with a passion. In *The Coin Collector's Journal*, December 1885, both tokens are listed, the smaller as No. 366 and the larger as No. 367, but neither is identified with any period in time.

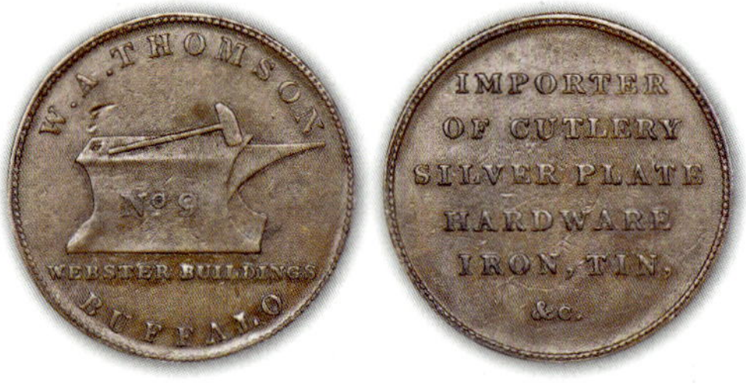

W-NY-120-10a • Low-Unlisted; HT-213. R-5. 38 mm. Copper. No. 9 Webster Buildings address is on the token. Typically VF or EF. • VF-20 $150; EF-40 $300; AU-50 $600.

W-NY-120-15a • Low-Unlisted; HT-214. R-4. 33 mm. Copper. Typically VF or EF. Dice-Hicks (Stack's 2008) AU $863. • VF-20 $100; EF-40 $200; AU-50 $400.

Walsh's General Store
Lansingburgh, NY
General store
W-NY-150

The tokens of Walsh's General Store, Lansingburgh, New York, have been popular ever since they were first published by Charles I. Bushnell in 1858. Since that time, examples of the three varieties have appeared in countless auctions and other offerings. Lansingburgh, sometimes spelled as Lansingburg, was established in 1807 on land that was part of the towns of Troy and Peterborough. Today, although Lansingburgh is back as a part of Troy, it has its own school district and post office.

The establishment was conducted by Alexander Walsh, a prominent citizen of the state, who had been the keeper of the General Store since early in the century. For the grand ceremony opening the Erie Canal in 1825, he rode with Governor DeWitt Clinton on the first boat, the *Seneca Chief*, and received one of the silver medals struck from dies engraved by Charles Cushing Wright. In 1839 he raised silkworms, part of a general interest in the Northeast that saw several related projects established, in Connecticut in particular. In October of that year, at the annual Fair of the American Institute in New York City the catalog listed this: "No. 933. Specimens of cocoons from the garden of Alexander Walsh, Lansingburg; also teasles from the same establishment." For the New York State Horticultural Fair of 1844 he built a "temple" 26 feet long and 12 feet high decorated with thousands of flowers.[51] Walsh was active in agriculture and was cited in many articles over a long period of time.

Illustrating the diversity of his goods, an advertisement in the *Saratoga Sentinel*, January 11, 1831, offered items from 71 packages of dry goods recently received, plus other stock including India sewing twist, Prussian shawls, Levantine satins, ribbons, gloves, Russian sheeting, bandannas, silk flags, and more. "In short, the contents of the store as now furnished cannot be stated in one advertisement, nor yet in any handbill of moderate size. Indeed, where every article of usual consumption, and even those so rare as seldom to be called for, can be found, to particularize may be deemed superfluous." Locals sometimes called the store Walsh's Museum.

Walsh admired Lafayette and may have met him in 1824 when the French hero of the American Revolution was given a special reception in Troy. The plan was for Lafayette to go by boat from Albany across the Hudson River and north to Troy, then by land to Lansingburgh and Waterford, then to Cohoose Falls to board a boat. However, the ceremony ran late into the day and he was not able to go to Lansingburgh. Instead he boarded a boat and returned to Albany. Lafayette was featured on certain of Walsh's 1835-dated tokens. In 1839 Henry Clay called upon Walsh in Lansingburgh. Alexander Walsh retired in 1846 and died on August 3, 1849.

The tokens were made by R. & W. Robinson of Attleboro, Massachusetts. The Lafayette reverse was used on the tokens of several merchants. Each of the three varieties is common, making a complete collection feasible for almost anyone to acquire.

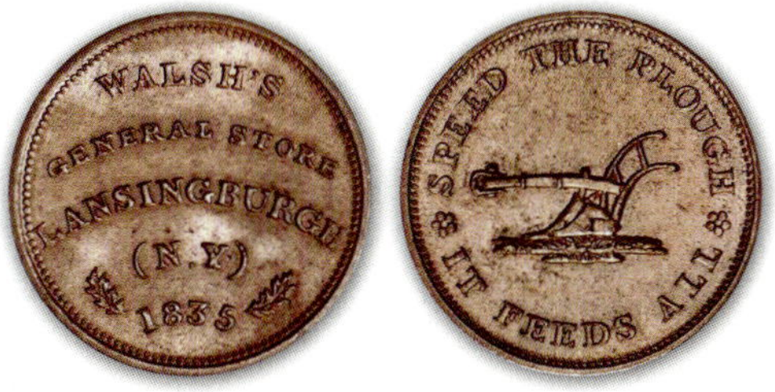

W-NY-150-10a • Lansingburgh / Speed the Plough • Low-99; HT-216. R-1. 28.5 mm. Copper. The term used on the reverse may have come from the title of a 17th century English play, *Speed the Plough*, by Thomas Morton. It has earlier use as well, as in an observance called Plow Monday in England in the 14th century, with a poem beginning "God spede the plow." Tokens finer than AU are rarities. • VF-20 $25; EF-40 $45; AU-50 $85; MS-63 $250.

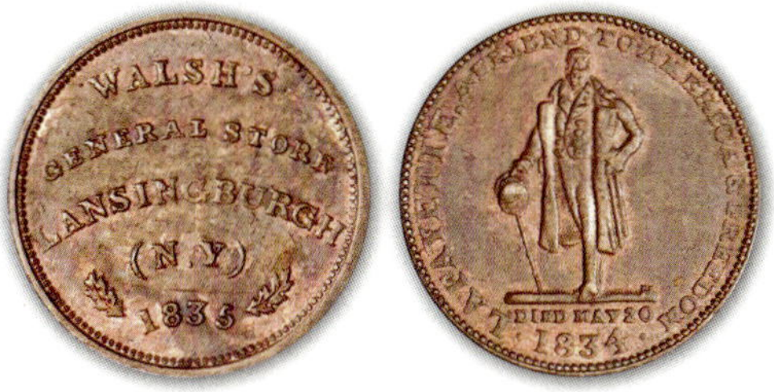

W-NY-150-15a • Lansingburg / Lafayette • Low-100; HT-217. R-2. 28.5 mm. Copper. AU and lower Mint State grades are typically seen in fine collections. • VF-20 $30; EF-40 $60; AU-50 $100; MS-63 $350.

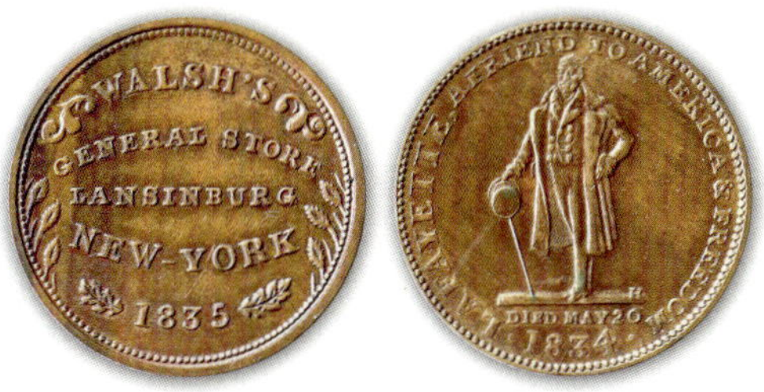

W-NY-150-20a • Lansinburg / Lafayette • Low-101; HT-218. R-2. 28.5 mm. Copper. Town name misspelled. VF to AU grades are typical. Mint State tokens are very elusive. • VF-20 $30; EF-40 $60; AU-50 $100; MS-63 $400.

Henry Anderson
New York, NY
Boots and shoes
W-NY-180

The single token variety issued by Henry Anderson, featuring the "Mammoth Boot" sign in Chatham Square, New York City, with its iconic boot on the obverse, has been a favorite for a long time. In 1858 it was listed as No. 28 in Charles I. Bushnell's pioneering book, *An Arrangement of Tradesmen's Cards, Political Tokens, also Election Medals, Medalets, &c.* This study had a section listing dozens of New York City tokens, many not in the Hard Times series, that set the scene for succeeding generations of numismatists who endeavored to acquire as many tokens from that city as possible. Such names as F.C.C. Boyd, Wayte Raymond, John J. Ford Jr., and Stephen L. Tanenbaum come to mind.

In 1837 Anderson's store was at 158 Chatham Square. He lived at 88 Bayard Street. In the same era he was also listed at 149 Chatham Square. P.B. & S. Deveau, who were in the same business and also issued tokens, were at 156 Chatham Square in 1837. Henry Anderson seems to have been in business for a relatively short time.

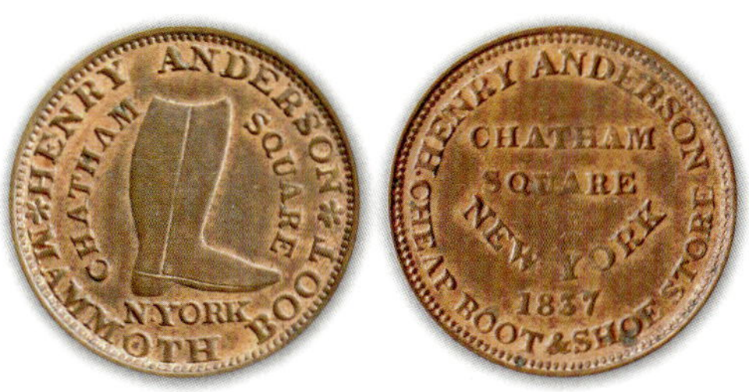

W-NY-180-10a • Low-107; HT-219. R-1. 28.5 mm. Copper. AU and lower-range Mint State examples are readily available. Some MITAD tokens were struck over these. • VF-20 $25; EF-40 $45; AU-50 $70; MS-63 $225.

Atwood's Railroad Hotel
New York, NY
Hotel
W-NY-200

This token is lettered, CARRY ME TO / ATWOOD'S / RAILROAD HOTEL / 243 BOWERY / AND MY FACE / IS GOOD FOR / 3 CENTS. The token provided coach fare to Atwood's. The hotel was kept by Henry C. Atwood, known as Harry to his friends. The location had been the first downtown stop of the New York & Harlem Railroad when it opened for service in 1832.

On December 11, 1832, D.P. Hall, of 17 Hanover Street, posted this advertisement: "Bowery Property for Sale—The corner house and lot at 245 Bowery—directly opposite the termination of the Harlem Rail-Road and known as the Rail-Road Hotel House, very substantially built of brick, lot 27 feet 7 inches front by about 120 feet on Stanton Street. The above would be a first rate stand for a large grocery or hotel." The notice was continued through early 1833.

It seems that no buyer came forward. On January 21 this was announced:

> Peremptory Sale of Bowery Property—James Bleecker & Sons will sell at auction, Friday 25th instant, at 12 o'clock at the [Merchants] Exchange the 3 story brick house and lot, 245 Bowery, corner of Stanton Street, directly opposite the termination of the *Harlaem Rail Road*, known as the Rail Road Hotel—lot 25 feet 7 inches front by 120 feet deep on Stanton Street. The above property offers a very eligible opportunity for an investment as the house at a trifling expense can be yours so as to produce a handsome interest.

The New York *Commercial Advertiser*, January 21, 1836, published this notice relative to the great fire that consumed more than 600 buildings in the downtown district on the preceding December 16, which began: "Eleventh Ward Meeting for relief of sufferers by the fire. At a meeting of inhabitants of the Eleventh Ward, held at the house of Mr. Henry C. Atwood, Rail Road Hotel, Bowery, on the evening of the 19th instant, Charles A. Clinton, presiding. . . ."

At a later date, Atwood turned to other activities. In 1845 and 1846, he was a gauger in the New York Custom House. He also served as Grand Master of the St. John's Grand Masonic Lodge.

As to the property, which had been renumbered 243, on February 1, 1843, an advertisement by William H. Franklin, auctioneer, stated that on Friday, February 10, the house and grounds would be offered for sale. It was put up for auction again on February 7, 1844. On July 2, 1850, a notice stated: "Foundling—a fine female child about two or three weeks old and well-dressed was found last night in the hall of No. 243 Bowery."

This is one of the most famous tokens of its era, combining the appeal of a transportation token plus a George Washington token. Lyman H. Low did not list it as a Hard Times token, seemingly unaware of its era, in the absence of a striken date. Russell Rulau did additional research and placed the token as circa 1835 to 1838, with no citations given. The reverse die (Washington side) was also used by Bale & Smith for their own token (W-NY-240-10).

In 1858 Charles I. Bushnell listed the token as No. 116 in his study. At the Bangs, Merwin & Co. sale of the Benjamin Haines Collection, January 19 to 23, 1863, lot 908 was described as: "George Washington, equestrian figure. Reverse, Carry Me to Atwood's. etc. Very fine, very rare." It sold for $9, a very high price at the time. In the same sale an 1859 Proof set from the cent to the dollar sold for $4.50, an Uncirculated 1793 half cent realized $8.75, an AU 1793 Wreath cent went to $7.75, a Proof 1856 Flying Eagle cent fetched $1, a Proof 1829 half dime brought 75¢, an "unusually fine" 1796 quarter commanded $3, and a Proof 1824 half dollar fetched $3.75.

In 1864, *Coins, Medals, and Seals*, by W.C. Prime, a popular book on the hobby, called the Atwood's token "highly prized" and suggested a valuation of $5. At the sale of the J.C. Brevoort Collection in June 1886, a similar token sold for $11. Over time the Carry Me to Atwood's token only increased in recognition.

In the 20th century and into the 21st, this token was considered to be of great rarity, rated as R-7 by Russell Rulau (4 to 12 known). Since circa 1950 John J. Ford Jr. had quietly bought every one he could find. What surprise! When tokens in his estate were examined, in a shipment received from his heirs in 2013, *11 pieces* were found! These were auctioned by Stack's Bowers Galleries at the American Numismatic Association Convention in August of that year, lots 22176 to 22186, graded by NGC as MS-64BN (3), MS-63BN (1), AU-58 (2), AU-50 (2), AU-50 later gilt on obverse (1), VF-30 (1), and Fine-12 (1).

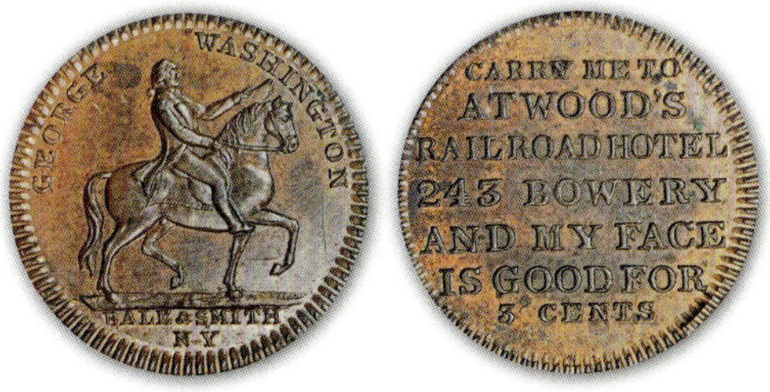

W-NY-200-10a • Rulau: "Low-201"; HT-221; Baker-510. R-6. 25 mm. Copper. All bets regarding rarity were off when 12 from the Ford Collection were auctioned in 2013, ranging in grade from Fine to *three* MS-64—a shock and surprise. It seems that these were hoarded by Ford for many years, including from the holdings of F.C.C. Boyd and Wayte Raymond. Illustrated is the finest of the Ford pieces. The MS-64 pieces realized $3,055 for one and $3,535 for three others. It was speculated that if such had been offered singly the price would have been much higher. As these are dispersed into the marketplace the rarity will of course remain the same, but the *availability* will sharply decrease. The same obverse die was used for W-NY-200 and W-NY-240. Typical grades not including Ford are VF and EF. • VF-20 $600; EF-40 $1,000; AU-50 $1,650.

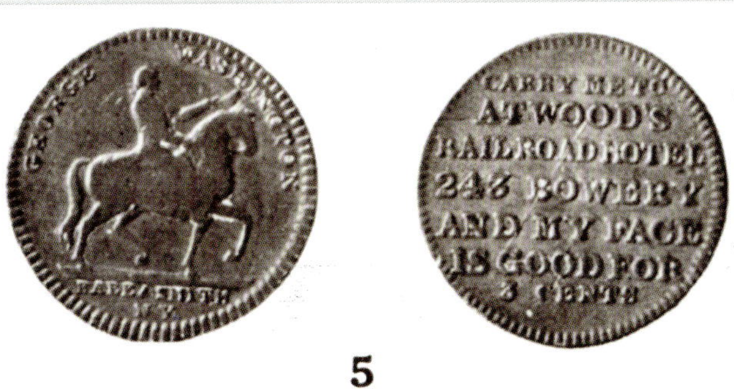

5

ATWOODS' RAILROAD HOTEL. 243 Broadway (1835-44) Three Cent Token. By Bale and Smith. Copper, brass or white metal. All rare.

It seems that the finest illustration of the Atwood's Rail Road Hotel token Wayte Raymond could secure for the 1941 edition of the *Standard Catalogue of United States Coins and Tokens* was of a well-worn example.

W-NY-200-12a Fire Gilt • Rulau: "Low-202"; HT-222. R-9. Small 20.5 mm. Copper. Striking from the center of the dies. Ex J.N.T. Levick (who probably had it struck to his order), Benjamin Betts (1898), Richard Picker, George Fuld, B&M (June 31, 1981, lot 12), Dr. Robert Shalowitz, Robert A. Schuman (August 1983), SLT estate.

W-NY-200-12b • Low-Unlisted; HT-Unlisted. R-9. Brass. Lot 241 in the Levick Sale was a smaller size (14/16 of an inch or 22.5 mm), was struck in *brass*, and was described: "Brass. Uncirculated, *extremely rare*. Small planchet being only size 14." Sold for $10.75, one of the most expensive tokens in the sale. Not traced today.

W-NY-200-10f • Low-Unlisted; HT-Unlisted. R-9. 25 mm. Silver. Unique. Ford Collection 2023 VF-30 $5,581.

W-NY-200-10g • Low-Unlisted; HT-221. R-7. 24 mm, smaller planchet. Lead. Uniface obverse trial strike, "virtually as struck." Ford 22187, August 2013, $2,232. (White metal listed by Rulau but not known.)

Bailly, Ward & Co.
New York, NY
Importers, fancy goods
W-NY-220

The firm of Bailly, Ward & Co. was formed on February 1, 1829, successor to S. Bailly & Co. The partnership had been planned the previous autumn. An agreement was signed on November 29, 1828, by S. Bailly, who was in Paris at the time, and Augustus H. Ward, signed on January 15, 1829, in New York City. Shipping and import notices relating to the company appeared regularly in the newspapers.

An advertisement in the New York *Evening Post*, January 3, 1833, noted:

> Paris Articles, Toys, &c.—Bailly, Ward & Co., No. 41 Maiden Lane and 96 William Street have received by the late Havre packets a supply of articles in them, such as ladies' work boxes furnished with silver, pearl and bone instruments with and without music, toilet boxes, gentlemen's dressing cases, portable desks, fancy boxes, glove boxes, fine Paris-made stands, tables, and screws, bead reticules and purses, velvet and cashmere purses embroidered, carved ivory, pearl, and shell cases, fine pocket books and wallets, bronze and plated candlesticks, screw pincushions and reels, alabaster and China vases, fine snuff boxes, music boxes, necklaces and guard chains, fancy cards, whips and umbrellas, earrings, breast pins, finer rings and shirt studs, neck chains, bracelets, spectacles, opera glasses, gold and silver pencil cases, waist buckles, thimbles, perfumery, soaps, toilet and smelling bottles, brushes, combs, carved shell and imitations combs, boxes of paints, bronze, plated and China inkstands, pearl and ivory folders, engravings and lithographic prints, chessmen, backgammon boards, dominos, batteldores, games of Greece, paper toys, harmonicas, toy watches, small china tea sets, barking dogs, dolls, &c.

In the early 1840s the partnership was succeeded by A.H. Ward & Co. at the same address.

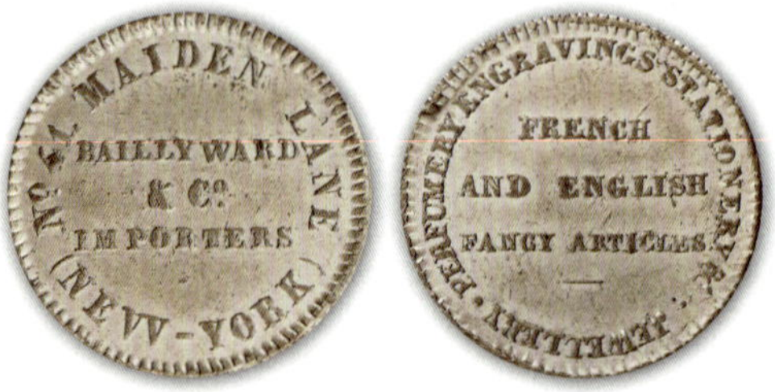

W-NY-220-10e • Rulau: "Low-206"; HT-226. R-7. 25 mm. White metal. The token die omits the comma between Bailly and Ward. White metal. Ford (SBG 2013) AU-55 $3,290, AU-58 $2,467.50.

W-NY-220-10f • Rulau: "Low-206A"; HT-226A. R-8. 25 mm. Silver. Ford (SBG 2013) EF-40 $4,700.

Bale & Smith
New York, NY
Engravers and minters
W-NY-240

The partnership of James Bale and Frederick B. Smith, known as Bale & Smith, was formed circa 1834. The shop was at 16 Maiden Lane, where Bale's previous partnership with Charles Cushing Wright, Wright & Bale, had been located, and where Bale had been working on his own since 1832. From about 1835 to 1838, Bale & Smith was at 68 Nassau Street; then circa, 1839 to 1847, at 95 Fulton Street. Punches and other tools were on hand from their antecedent Wright & Bale.

Their products were often signed B&S or BALE & SMITH. From circa 1834 to 1844, certain dies were signed BALE, BALE NY, or JAMES BALE, although the partnership was still in effect. George W. May, an engraver, was with Bale & Smith from 1843 to 1848. In the latter year Bale formed a new partnership with him, Bale & May. May transitioned to May & Glaubrecht in 1851 and remained in that firm until 1854.[52] After Bale & Smith was dissolved, F.B. Smith formed Smith & Hartmann.

The tokens of Bale & Smith are as a rule well lettered and boldly struck—among the finest workmanship of the era.

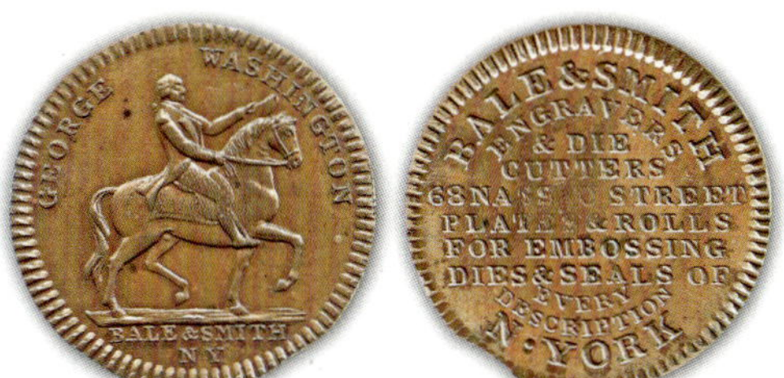

W-NY-240-10a • Bale & Smith • Rulau: "Low-207"; HT-227. R-7. 28.5 mm. Copper. Obverse with BALE & SMITH / N-Y signature. The same obverse die was used for W-NY-200 and W-NY-240. An example sold for $10.10 in W. Elliot Woodward's 49th Sale in July 1882. Dice-Hicks (Stack's 2008) VF $1,725. Ford (SBG 2013) AU-58 $5,875. The typical grade for the variety is VF.

W-NY-240-10e • Bale & Smith • Rulau: "Low-208"; HT-227A. R-8. 28.5 mm. White metal. Ford (SBG 2013) AU with scratches $4,400. Americana Sale (SBG 2013) EF rough and damaged $1,410.

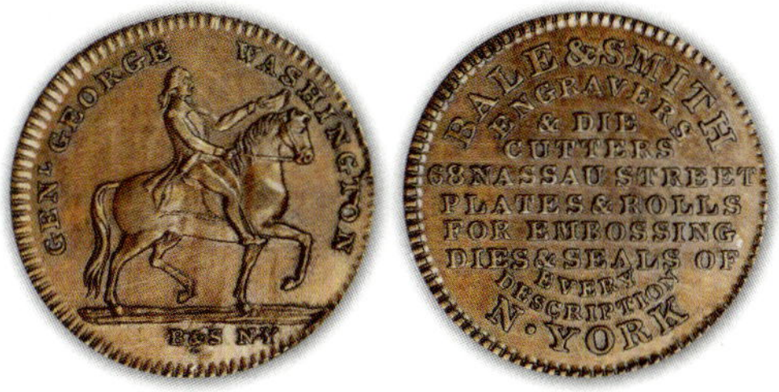

W-NY-240-15a • B&S • Rulau: "Low-209"; HT-228. R-7. 28.5 mm. Copper. Obverse with B&S N-Y signature. Ford (SBG 2013) AU-50 $4,406, MS-63 $5,581.

W-NY-240-15e • B&S • Rulau: "Low-210"; HT-228A. R-8. 28.5 mm. White metal.

John Barker / American Repository of Fine Arts
New York, NY
Music, prints, stationery
W-NY-260

This 19 mm token, with a small portrait of Washington on the obverse, is in the style that Wright & Bale and its successor, Bale & Smith, did for certain other tokens, most notably the Henderson & Lossing token of Poughkeepsie, New York (see listing).

An advertisement in the New York *American*, July 30, 1830, sets the time of John Barker's move to the address given on his token:

> A Card. J. Barker having removed his Fancy Stationary [*sic*], Print and Music Store from No. 5 Arcade to 16 Maiden Lane, begs to tender his grateful acknowledgment to the public for

> their liberal patronage, and solicits a continuance of their favors.
>
> J.B. has just added to his catalogue a number of very beautiful songs and pieces of music; also a great variety of scraps and engravings. His store being connected with Messrs. Wright & Bale's extensive engraving, medaling, and die-cutting establishment, all orders for cards, diplomas, bills of exchange; college, school, and other medals; notarial, counting-house, and private seals; music, and other punches; stamps, bookbinders' tools, door-plates, brand, &c., &c., attended to with promptness and dispatch. Also copperplate printing executed in all its branches and in the finest style.

In his 1884 catalog of the J.N.T. Levick Collection, W. Elliot Woodward offered the discovery token:

> Lot 243. Barker, John. "Music, prints," etc., small head of Washington within a wreath, "American Repository of Fine Arts." Doubtless the work of Wright. I found this piece in a collection nearly twenty years ago and sold it in the McCoy Sale, No. 2638, for $8, and believe that no other is known; brass, very fine. Plate. [Sold for $8.25]

Russell Rulau states that Barker was in business from 1829 to 1833, possibly taking this from the period that Wright and Bale was in business. The present writer has not found any of his advertisements after 1830.

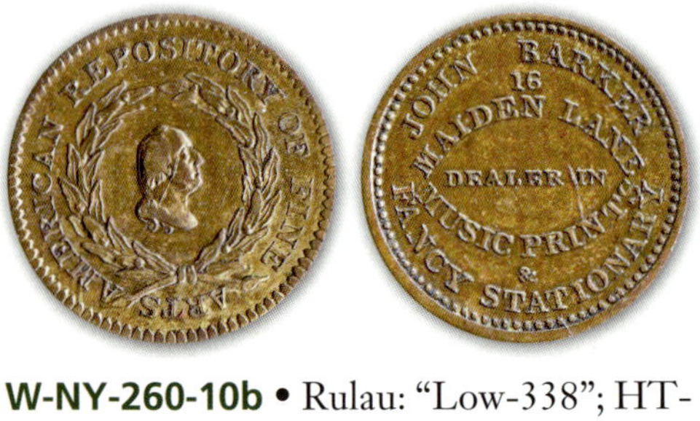

W-NY-260-10b • Rulau: "Low-338"; HT-230. R-7. 19 mm. Brass. It seems that Russell Rulau was unable to find an image of this token to illustrate in his *Standard Catalog of United States Tokens 1700–1900*. Ford (SBG 2013) had three: EF-45 $4,112, EF with scratches $2,115, and EF with graffiti $2,585. Glenn Firestone to Steve Tanenbaum, AU is the highest grade known (illustrated).

J. & L. Brewster
New York, NY / New Orleans, LA
Hat manufacturer
W-NY-280

Joseph and Lemuel were the proprietors of this partnership. In 1820 the business was at 102 Broadway. Russell Rulau states that it was at 166 Water Street, the address on their token, in 1835 and 1836. In 1840 and 1841 they were at 176 Water Street. As one of the tokens is signed W&B (Wright and Bale), a partnership that operated from 1829 to 1833, the Brewsters must have been at 166 Water Street even earlier than Rulau's research suggests.

In the late 1820s into the 1830s, they were active in distributing tens of thousands of religious leaflets for the American Tract Society. Both partners were public-minded individuals and contributed often to various charities and relief efforts. They contributed to the American Bible Society as well—shipping large quantities of bibles to Africa, for example. The partners were also active in the temperance movement. On October 6, 1839, a large fire ravaged nearly all of the buildings in an area bounded by Water, Fulton, Front, and Stirling streets, the most destructive conflagration since December 16, 1835. The flames could be seen from 100 miles out to sea.[53] The Brewster facility was destroyed. Fortunately it was fully insured.

There are two different die varieties, the first listed by Rulau as HT-235 and the other from HT-235A to 335A. These tokens have had little recognition in early numismatic history, Benjamin Wright's 1898 listing in "American Business Tokens" being an exception.

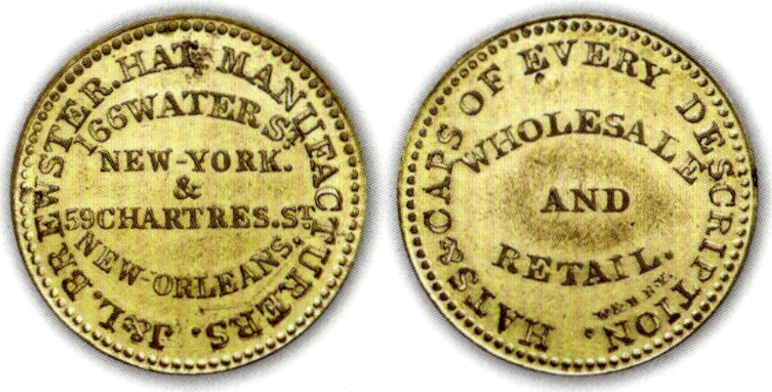

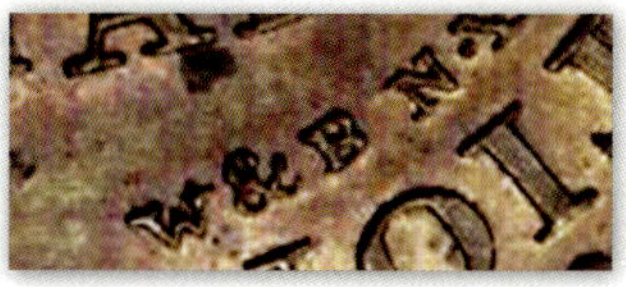

W-NY-280-10a • W&B N.Y. • Rulau: "Low-220"; HT-235. R-6. 26.5 mm. Copper. Rulau lists only as gilt. B (W&B) is defective. Rulau dates this as 1832–1833. Ford (SBG 2013) damaged Mint State with spots $1,292, MS-62 $4,700. Typically VF to EF.

W-NY-280-10b • W&B N.Y. • Rulau: "Low-221"; HT-235A. R-7. 26.5 mm. Brass.

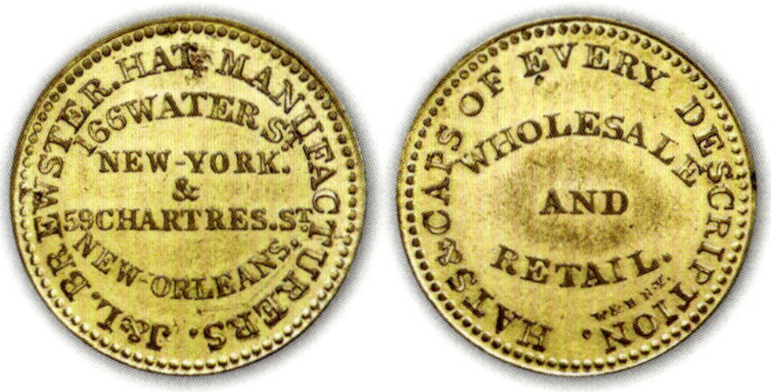

W-NY-280-20a • BALE N.Y. • Rulau: "Low-222"; HT-236. R-7. 26.5 mm. Copper. Rulau lists only as gilt. Typically VF to EF.

W-NY-280-20b • BALE N.Y. • Rulau: "Low-223"; HT-236A. R-7. 26.5 mm. Brass. Typically VF to EF.

David L. Buchan
New York, NY
Chair manufacturer
W-NY-290

David L. Buchan was a manufacturer of chairs from the late 1820s to at least 1841. He was at the corner of North Moore and Greenwich streets, also listed as 80 North Moore Street. Russell Rulau states that his tokens were made by Thomas Halliday in Birmingham, England. The first state of the reverse die has North Moore as NORTHMORE and the second has it expertly reworked (but still without a space) as NORTHMOORE, without a trace of the earlier error.

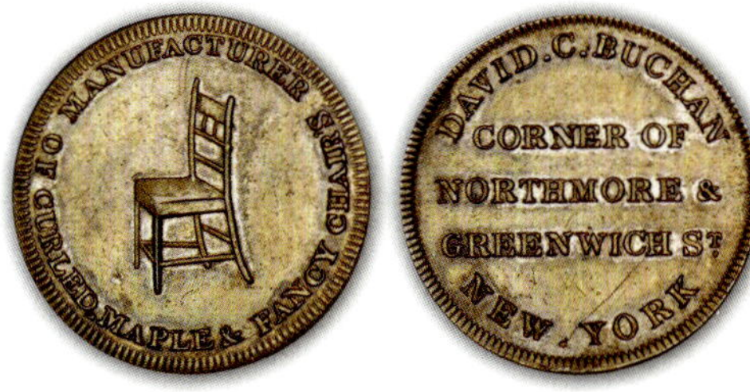

W-NY-290-10b • Northmore • Rulau: "Low-225"; HT-237. R-6. 27 mm. Brass. (Some were lightly silvered; R-7.) • VF-20 $350; EF-40 $450; AU-50 $800.

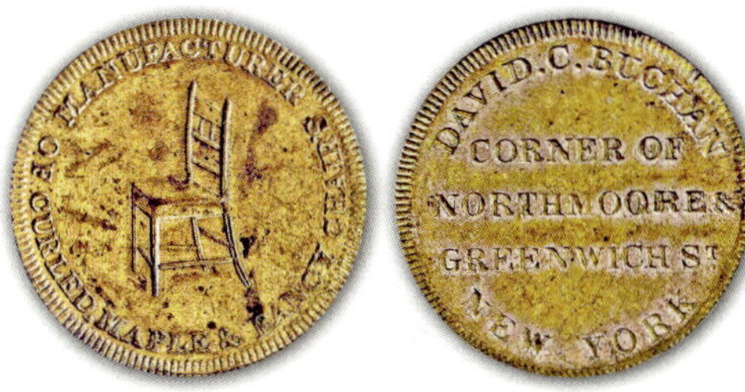

W-NY-290-15b • Northmoore • Rulau: "Low-226"; HT-238. R-7. 27 mm. Brass. • VF-20 $350; EF-40 $450; AU-50 $800.

Centre Market
New York, NY
Public market
W-NY-300

The Centre Market was on Centre Street in downtown Manhattan. These public markets were open daily except on Sunday. Stalls could be rented, payable quarterly in advance. In 1835 application was made for the expansion of the market on the grounds that the quarters were cramped and decayed and the accommodations inadequate. The Common Council endorsed the idea, but the State Assembly denied it on February 11—one reason being that acquiring land 300 feet on only one side would cost no less than $200,000.

The stall holders were listed in directories together with stall numbers, such as Cornelius M. Cregier, butcher, at stall No. 6. Representative stall designations included clams, huckster, crockery, porterhouse, poultry, hostler, shoemaker, grocer, brewer, fishmonger, merchandise, refectory, and laborer. In the mid-1830s, there were many complaints that the market was too small to accommodate the needs of the area. One proposal was to construct a new separate building for the butchers. Another was to make special accommodations for grocers who needed to have wagons nearby.

This proposal to build a new market was eventually passed, and in 1839 construction was underway to replace the building shown on the tokens.

In 1839 the public markets were Catherine Market, Centre Market, Clinton Market, Essex Market, Franklin Market, Fulton Market, Gouverneur Market, Monroe Market, Greenwich Market, Jefferson Market, Tompkins Market, and Washington Market.

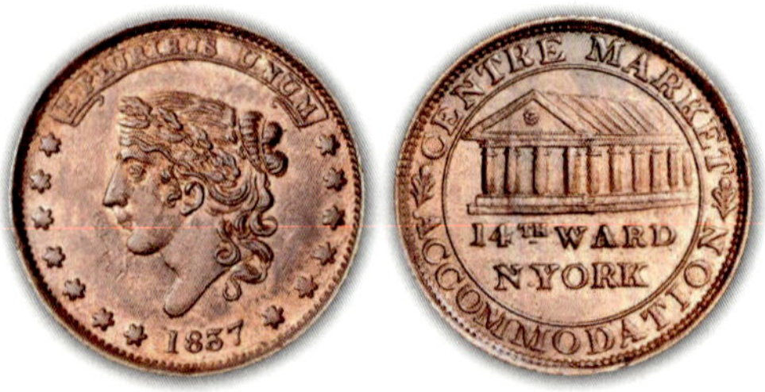

W-NY-300-10a • Scroll ends under 2nd U (UNUM) • Low-110; HT-239. R-1. 28 mm. Copper. The obverse die was also used on Low-34 to 40. Some MITAD tokens were struck over these. VF to AU are standard grades, but lower-range Mint State pieces are readily available. • VF-20 $20; EF-40 $35; AU-50 $60; MS-63 $225.

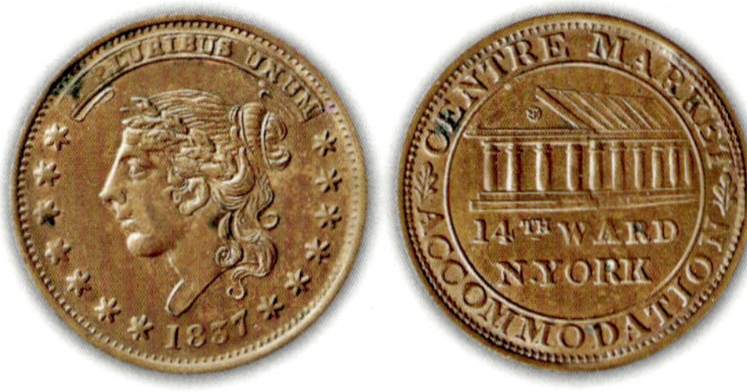

W-NY-300-15a • Scroll ends under N (UNUM) • Low-111; HT-240. R-1. 28 mm. Copper. This obverse die was also used on Low-32 and 33. VF to AU are standard grades, but lower-range Mint State pieces are readily available. • VF-20 $20; EF-40 $35; AU-50 $60; MS-63 $225.

Clinton Lunch
New York, NY
Restaurant
W-NY-320

This small brass token has been widely known for a long time and was listed in 19th-century catalogs. It has not been included among Hard Times tokens in the past, as it was thought that it was issued post-1844. However, a search of contemporary sources reveals that it was indeed in business during that era.

Advertisement in the New York *Evening Post*, May 19, 1832:

> Clinton Lunch. Corner of Liberty Street and Broadway. This well-known establishment, which now has a frontage of one hundred and ten feet, having been considerably enlarged, and fitted up in a style of splendor, it is presumed, not surpassed by any similar establishment in the United States, will be open for the examination of the public on Tuesday the 22d of May.
>
> The proprietor rests his claim to public patronage on his solemn pledge that no pains or expense shall be spared in procuring and keeping con-

> stantly on hand every article in season, of the best quality; and a degree of confidence is indulged that the various dishes furnished will at all times gratify and please the palate of the most fastidious epicure. With his own personal attention, and the assistance of other branches of his family of considerable experience, with attentive and obliging servants, it is confidently hoped this establishment will be rendered second to none in the United States.
>
> Open every day (Sunday excepted) from 12 to 3 o'clock. Refreshments of any kind may be had in handsome style at a few minutes' notice, at all times. Parties can be accommodated with dinners and suppers of the choicest delicacies to be found in the markets.
>
> Especial care will be taken that the bar be supplied with the best liquors and wines; and in the larger will be found at all times a supply of choice relishes. Oysters of the best quality will be served up in all their variety. The proprietor will at all times exercise his best efforts to please and hopes to meet the patronage he respectfully solicits.

In 1833, Goold & Atkins, proprietors of Clinton Lunch, opened Ladies' Ordinary at 71 Liberty Street, in two houses opposite the Lunch, to serve lunch and dinner to ladies. Mrs. Goold was the manager.

On Wednesday, January 29, 1834, Thomas Asten was to conduct this:

> Assignee's Sale. At 10 o'clock will be sold by assignees the whole of the establishment known as Clinton Lunch, corner Liberty Street and Broadway. Also furniture of a dwelling house 71 Liberty Street.[54]

The sale was rescheduled for Friday, January 31. A revised notice included:

> At 10 o'clock will be sold by order of the sheriff the whole of the establishment known as the Clinton Lunch. Also the furniture of a dwelling house 71 Liberty Street. This establishment comprises every article for carrying on an extensive eating house, from the well-furnished kitchen to the eating room. There are also 5 kegs or firkins of the finest pickles, preserved in the London style and fit for the table, consisting of cucumbers, onions, beans, cabbages, &c. Also, 40 quarts of superior made currant jelly, will worthy the attention of families or confectioners. Also the liquors consisting of brandy, wine, gin, and rum, all of the best quality, and about 20 barrels of ale.
>
> In addition to the furniture is a superior fine toned piano forte, a valuable double case patent lever watch, carpets, sideboard, dressing bureau, glassware, &c. Also furniture at 71 Liberty Street consisting of carpets, room and store beds, mattresses, patent bedsteads, sofa, chairs, dressing bureaus, dining and tea tables, cut glass, china, crockery, &c.

The sale was postponed again, to February 7, 1834.

On March 27, 1834, Abner Joy was in possession of the business and reopened it to the public, serving dinner every day from noon until 4 p.m. In the autumn of 1835, the restaurant advertised, "Splendid Nantastick chowder served up on Monday, Wednesday, and Saturday at the Clinton Lunch, corner of Broadway and Liberty Street. None other genuine."

On December 16, 1835, much of the Financial District was ravaged by a fire, destroying hundreds of businesses. This was a short distance from Clinton Lunch. No advertisements have been seen after this time, possibly as most of the establishment's trade had been drawn from businesses in the burned-out area.

On December 26, 1835, this was advertised, "Unclaimed goods. A parcel of goods taken from the late fire are in possession of the subscriber at Clinton Lunch, Broadway & Liberty Street. Joseph H. Havens."

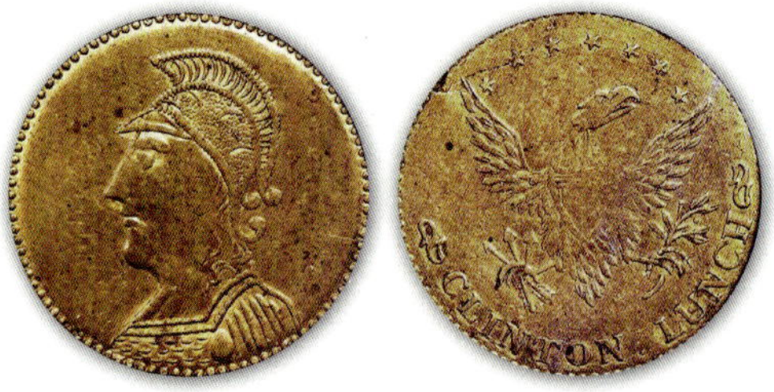

W-NY-320-10b • Low-Unlisted; HT-A240. R-6. 19.5 mm. Brass. Centola (Presidential Coin and Antique Co. 1999) AU $1,045. Sara Hinckley (Presidential Coin and Antique Co. 2006) VF-EF $759. Troy Wiseman (Heritage 2006) SU-55 $863. Dice-Hicks (Stack's 2008) EF $920.

W-NY-320-10j • Low-Unlisted; HT-B240. R-6. 19.7 mm. German silver, sometimes described as "silver" in old catalogs. Litman, Sullivan & Dreyfuss (Presidential Coin and Antique Co. 2004) Unc $978. Dice-Hicks (Stack's 2008) $575.

Collins Ready Made Linen & Fancy Store New York, NY

Linen and fancy goods

W-NY-340

Although it is one of the most important in the series, until recent years little was published about this very rare token, and consequently little is known.

The obverse die, with a dock and ship, was also used by engraver Robert Lovett Sr. for his own store card.

William Collins, maker and seller of linen, and a manufacturer of spectacles, was listed at 67 Maiden Lane from the mid-1830s to 1840. The address comprised both his business and home. In 1833 he was secretary of the New York Amateur Music Fund and sold concert tickets from his home. The dies are by Robert Lovett Sr.

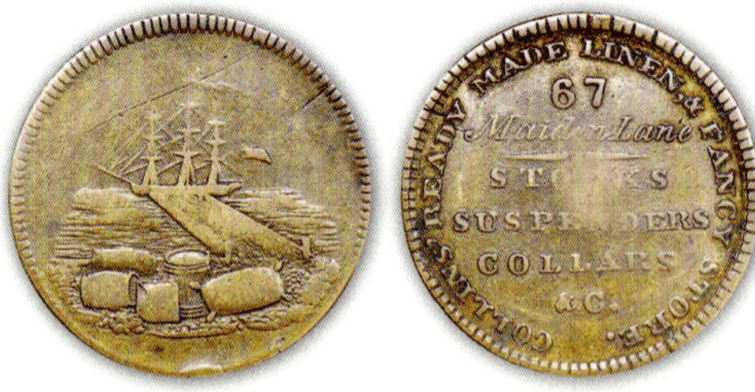

W-NY-340-10b • Rulau: "Low-233"; HT-241. R-7. 25.5 mm. Brass. The Dice-Hicks token (illustrated), VG on one side and VF on the other, sold for $2,530; this came from Litman, Sullivan & Dreyfuss (Presidential Coin and Antique Co. 2004). It was sold again in August 2013 and brought $2,145. The finest known by far, an MS-64 from the John J. Ford, Jr. Collection, earlier from F.C.C. Boyd, was sold in November 2013 for $11,162. Americana Sale (SBG 2013) VF with scratches and abrasions $2,115.

H. Crossman New York, NY

Umbrella manufacturer

W-NY-360

Henry Crossman manufactured umbrellas at 92-1/2 Chatham Street, the address on his tokens, from 1830 to 1841. Later he was at other addresses. The trade style was changed to H. Crossman & Co. in 1857.

There are two types of Crossman tokens, each cent size, each with a different obverse.

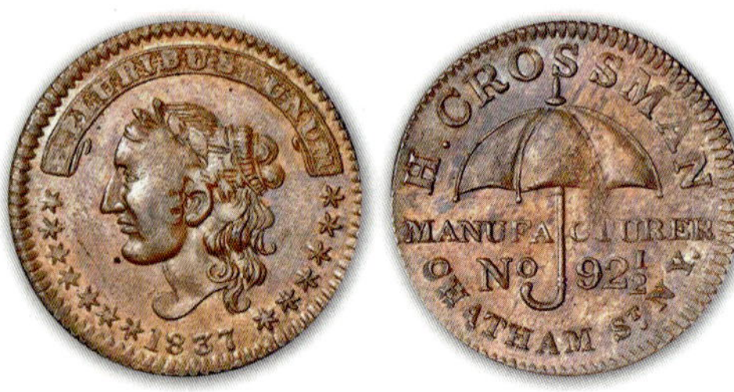

W-NY-360-10a • 1837 Liberty Head / Umbrella • Low-112; HT-243. R-1. 28.5 mm. Copper. The same obverse die was used on W-11-100a (Low-29). Due to the deep recess in the Liberty Head on the obverse and the umbrella on the reverse, the typical example is lightly struck at the centers. The illustrated Ford Collection example shows this. VF to AU are standard grades, but lower-range Mint State pieces are readily available. • VF-20 $35; EF-40 $60; AU-50 $110; MS-63 $300.

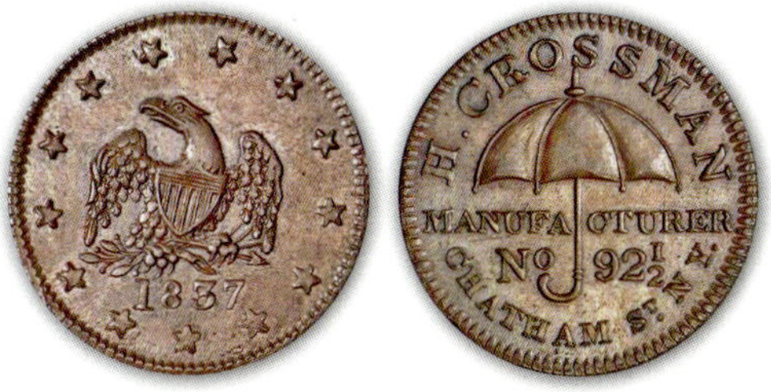

W-NY-360-15a • 1837 Eagle / Umbrella • Low-113; HT-244. R-2. 28.5 mm. Copper. The neck of the eagle typically shows light striking. This is one of the most appealing die combinations in the series, per the opinion of some specialists. VF to AU are standard grades. Lower-range Mint State examples are slightly scarce. • VF-20 $50; EF-40 $75; AU-50 $150; MS-63 $450.

James Crumbie
New York, NY
Pharmacist
W-NY-370

James Crumbie was born circa 1810. He was practicing the pharmaceutical trade by the mid-1830s. In 1835 he was a signatory to a petition to the Common Council protesting the expansion of the New York & Harlem Rail Road in the Bowery. By 1836 he was a trustee of the College of Pharmacy of the City of New York, which awarded degrees to students. In that year, and afterward, he had a pharmacy at the corner of the Bowery and 4th Street, the address on his token. In 1837 Robert Crumbie was a printer at the same location. Later, he worked with James as a druggist.

The inscription reads: CRUMBIE / COR BOWERY & FOURTH ST around the border, enclosing SODA / WATER. The attribution to *James* Crumbie is from directory listings and many advertisements.

In 1837 and 1838 James Crumbie advertised Yeast Powder, Beckwith's Anti-Dyspeptic Pills, and other patent medicines for sale. By that time, and through the 1850s, he gave his address as 363 Bowery, corner of 4th Street. In 1848 he lived at 381 4th Street, and William D. Crumbie (see next listing) lived at 383 4th Street. By 1850 he owned $50,000 worth of property, an immense sum at the time. In December 1879, he died of pneumonia in Clarkstown, New York.

The business seems to have passed to John W. Shedden in the 1860s, as per contemporary listings and also this obituary in *The Pharmaceutical Record*, February 1, 1884:

> Mr. John W. Shedden died January 19, from hemorrhage of the lungs, at his residence in this city. Born in Stamford, Conn., in 1826, he came to this city in 1838, and entered a drug store in the employ of Mr. Crumbie, at the corner of Bowery and Fourth Street, and, passing through the stages of boy, clerk, and proprietor, he retained his connection with the same store until some five years since, when he disposed of it to one of his clerks.

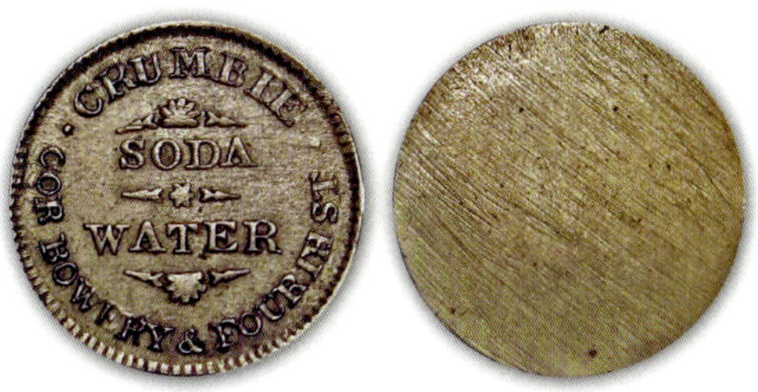

W-NY-370-10j • Low-Unlisted; HT-Unlisted. R-8, Steve Hayden estimates 2 known. 19 mm. German silver. Uniface; the reverse is ground off. The only example seen is from the Tanenbaum estate.

William D. Crumbie
New York, NY
Pharmacist
W-NY-375

William D. Crumbie was in business as a pharmacist by 1844, qualifying his token as a Hard Times issue. In that year he was at the corner of the Bowery and Houston Street. In 1850 his address was 286 Broadway. He resided with or close to James Crumbie (see preceding listing). The 1850 census gives his age as 28 years and his occupation as a druggist. His wife Sarah Marie, née Dunning, was 23; they were married on August 25, 1849. Margaret A. Jackson, age 16, born in Ireland, was a member of the household. In 1852 William D. Crumbie had two drugstores: 318 Bowery and 862 Broadway.

In "The Medals, Jetons, and Tokens Illustrative of the Science of Medicine," *American Journal of Numismatics*, April 1894, Dr. Horatio R. Storer listed a German silver example of William D. Crumbie's token as No. 722 and noted that it was owned by Frank W. Doughty. The diameter was given as 25 mm, which may have been an error.

The die work from both the James and William D. Crumbie tokens is from the same hand.

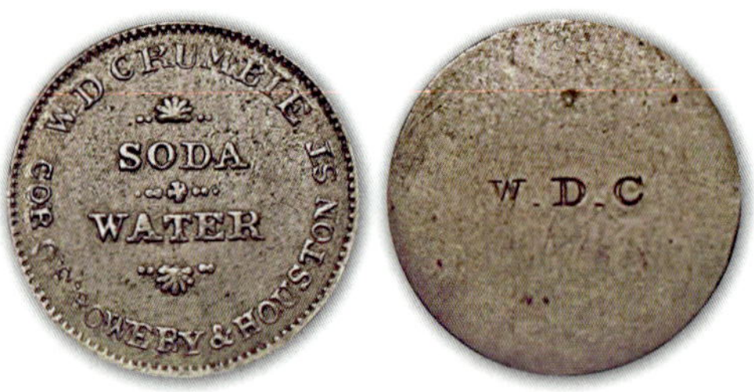

W-NY-375-10j • Low-Unlisted; HT-245A. R-8. 19 mm. German silver. Reverse stamped W.D.C. Gilbert Steinberg Collection (Stack's 2002) VF $2,300.

Day, Newell & Day
New York, NY
Manufacturers
W-NY-380

Day, Newell & Day, manufacturers of locks, bolts, and hinges and makers of brass, copper, and iron castings, were located at 389 Broadway. Most directory and other listings list them as *locksmiths*. The undated tokens are imprinted W&B, for Wright & Bale, engravers in business circa 1829 to 1833.

The firm exhibited at the annual American Institute Fairs. A gold medal was given in 1838. The citation for the October 1840 event: "Day, Newell & Day, 589 Broadway, N. Y., for the best of bank, store, and dwelling house locks, combining safety, simplicity, and exquisite workmanship. The present being superior to any heretofore exhibited. (A gold medal having been before awarded), *Diploma.*" At the Massachusetts Charitable Mechanic Fair in 1837 the firm was awarded a gold medal. The Franklin Institute bestowed a silver medal in 1839.

In 1834 the congressional Committee on Finance acknowledged and referred to study a petition signed by several thousand New York City merchants, traders, and others stating that times were difficult in the city and that sound finances and money could not be restored unless the charter of the Bank of the United States was renewed or a new federal bank set up in its place. Day, Newell & Day was listed as a petitioner.

In court testimony in 1834 William Day discussed problems arising from tools made by convicts in the Auburn State Prison, and also told of his firm:

> William Day, being duly sworn, and examined, deposed, that deponent[55] carries on the business of lock making

in the city of New-York, and is one of the firm of Day, Newell & Day; that he has been employed in this business in this city for about 10 years past, and the whole number of men and boys in their employ is 44; there are in the city establishments, where locksmithing business is carried on; and there are about 50 journeymen in the city; some of whom are out of employ and waiting for work; journeymen's wages are from 12 shillings to 16 shillings per day, according to their skill and execution.

Deponent's firm employed 80 to 90 hands some two or three years ago, but since the locks made by the state in the prisons, have come into the market, their business has decreased; since then deponents have introduced machinery in their business, and reduced their prices, to enable them to compete with the State Prison manufacturers, but the State Prison manufactures are again reduced and sold lower than deponent's firm can afford to sell.

The average profit of the business at the present prices of their shop, is about 15 percent; the prices in the city shops are pretty uniform, but the prison prices are lower than those of any of the shops in the city; deponent knows of three men, locksmiths, from one shop in this city, now in State Prison; he is not aware of but one locksmith being discharged from prison.

A locksmith, by looking at the keys of ordinary locks, can make skeleton keys that will enable him to go through an ordinary house, unlocking all the doors without difficulty. Locks can be made and are made complicated, but expensive, so that it is difficult to make skeleton keys to fit them; one skeleton key is calculated to open many locks; they are so constructed as to pass all the wards and yet operate on the bolt. Deponent thinks it a dangerous business for rouges to understand; with the facilities which a locksmith has, he could, deponent believes, open half the stores in this city, that is on the present general construction of locks in use in the city; many locks made in the State Prison are used on stores here, and they have also locks made here for patterns in the prison; the locks made in this country are now chiefly used in the city, many imported locks are used in the country; the imported locks are very inferior to those made here.

The business of deponent's firm amounts to about $30,000 a year in locks, and the whole amount made in the city probably amount to about $100,000 a year. Deponent often has calls from individuals, who offer them less than their regular prices, and state their preference for locks not made in the prison, but state that the prison locks are offered so much lower than deponent's prices that they must buy them, unless deponent will afford them lower than they do, or can afford to. His firm has lost the orders for a good many houses in this way, because they stated they could get the prison made locks cheaper.[56]

On May 10, 1837, the firm was one of 23 merchants, traders, and others at a hastily called meeting at the Merchants' Exchange to discuss the suspension of specie payments that day.[57]

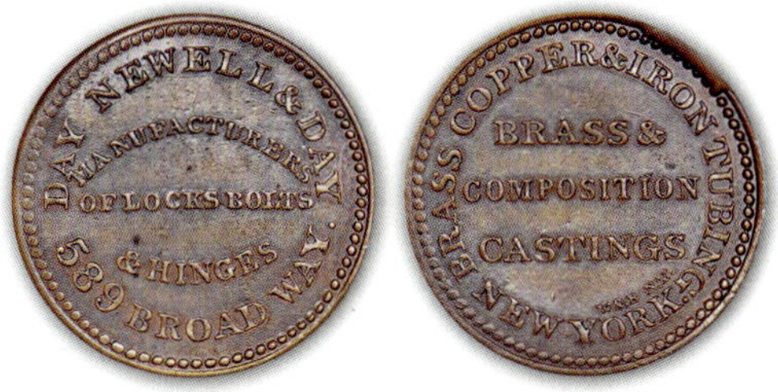

W-NY-380-10a • Rulau: "Low-239"; HT-247. R-6. 26.5 mm. Copper. Dice-Hicks (Stack's 2008) Unc $747.50. Five of the six pieces in the John J. Ford Jr. sale of August 2113 had a cud break on the reverse rim opposite IRO (IRON). A sixth example was of an advanced die state; on the obverse a massive cud break took away the rim above AY NEWELL and 9 BRO, and on the reverse there were cud breaks on the rim opposite YOR (YORK) and IRO (IRON). Ford enjoyed hoarding these, absorbing more than anyone knew.

W-NY-380-10b • Rulau: "Low-240"; HT-247A. R-8. 27 mm. Brass. An EF-40 copy in the Tanenbaum Collection was sold by Presidential Coin and Antique Co. in 1985.

W-NY-380-10j • Rulau: "Low-241"; HT-248. R-7. 26.5 mm. German silver. Centola (Presidential Coin and Antique Co. 1999) EF with edge clip $1,375. Sara Hinckley (Presidential Coin and Antique Co. 2006) EF $1.092.50. The four examples in the John J. Ford Jr. sale of August 2013, and four more pieces sold in September 2013, each had a cud break on the reverse rim opposite IRO (IRON).

J.H. Dayton / Union Steam Washing Establishment
New York, NY
Steam washing service
W-NY-400

John H. Dayton's Union Steam Washing Establishment was on 17th Street near Fifth Avenue in 1837, the date on the token.

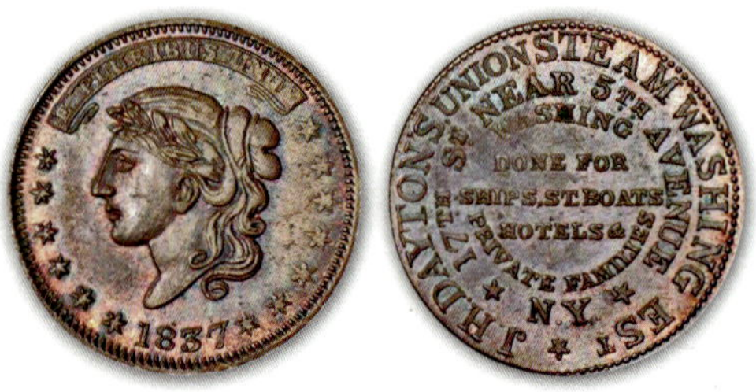

W-NY-400-10a • Low-114; HT-249. R-3. 28.5 mm. Copper. This obverse die was also used on Low-28 and Low-170. Most are well circulated. • VF-20 $75; EF-40 $125; AU-50 $200; MS-63 $400.

P.B. & S. Deveau
New York, NY
Boots and shoes
W-NY-420

The shoe store of Peter & Shepherd Deveau was at 156 Chatham Square from circa 1831 to the early 1850s, encompassing the entire Hard Times token era plus additional years. Henry Anderson's similar business (W-NY-180) was also located in Chatham Square. In 1837, the year of the tokens, Peter resided at 2-1/2 Division Street and Shepherd at 74 Forsyth Street.

Their basic store card token with the 1837 Liberty Head obverse was issued in quantity and is readily collectible today. The other die combinations was unknown to Low and is a great rarity today.

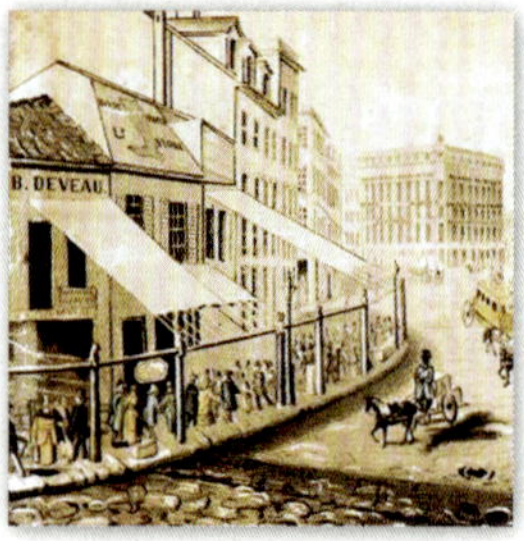

The Deveau store at one of the entrances to Chatham Square.

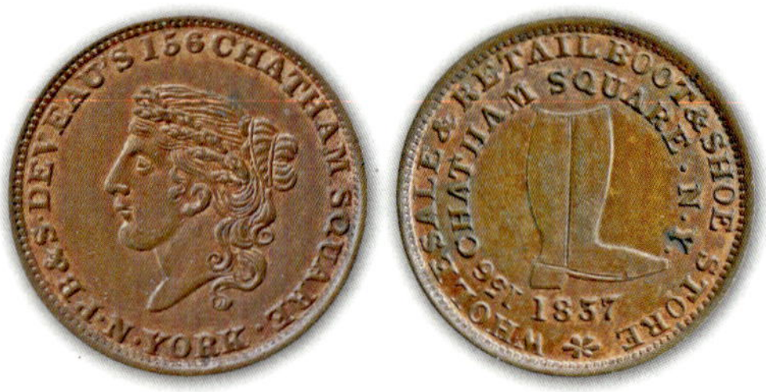

W-NY-420-10a • 1837 Deveau Liberty Head / Boot • Low-115; HT-250. R-2. 28.5 mm. Copper. AU and lower-range Mint State are typical grades in finer collections, but most tokens are VF to EF.[58] • VF-20 $30; EF-40 $50; AU-50 $85; MS-63 $275.

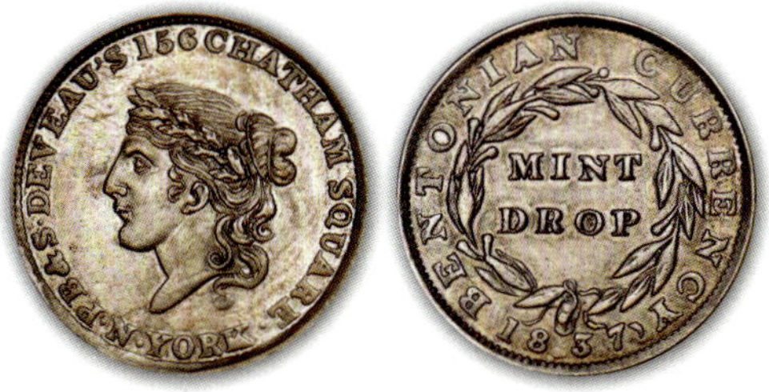

W-NY-420-20a • 1837 Deveau Liberty Head / Mint Drop • Rulau: "Low-335"; HT-251. High R-7. 28.5 mm. Copper. Reverse HT-61: BENTONIAN CURRENCY 1837 around border, wreath, with MINT / DROP at the center. Rulau: "There are only three known specimens of HT-251. Discovered and sold by Presidential Coin and Antique Co. in 1981, VG/Fine $3,000. One in Very Good realized $3,520 in the Presidential Coin and Antique Co. November 1999 sale, lot 66, ex Krause collection. A VG/F example fetched $3,000 in 1981, and a VF/EF specimen brought $5,280 in the Presidential Coin and Antique Co. 1986 Leidman sale." To that can be added the illustrated MS-60 Dice-Hicks token, ex Tilden, Dupont, Miller, and Litman collections at $34,500 to Robert A. Schuman, making four known.

Doremus, Suydam & Nixon
New York, NY
Dry goods
W-NY-440

The firm of Doremus, Suydam & Nixon was formed in 1829 as the successor to Doremus, Suydam & Co. The firm was located at 171 Broadway, at the corner of Courtlandt Street. The partners were Thomas C. Doremus, Rynier Suydam, and John M. Nixon. They advertised their business extensively, including the sale of imported goods from England, Russia, and elsewhere. Their Navarino Stock Manufactory at the same address made silk goods, clothing items, and other products for local sale and for the "country trade." In 1831 the store and factory were relocated to the first floor of a five-story brick building at 209 Pearl Street, four doors from Maiden Lane. The firm also advertised in South Carolina, Virginia, and other places and did a good business shipping to distant customers.

On the morning of Tuesday, July 8, 1834, a fire destroyed most of the company's store and factory. Temporary facilities were set up at 52 William Street near Pine Street, while the Pearl Street structure was being rebuilt. In late 1834, a new partner, Cornelius R. Suydam, was admitted and the company name, now with two Suydams, was changed to Doremus, Suydams & Nixon. Business was conducted at 50 and 52 William Street between Wall and Pine Streets. By the summer of 1835, the name was back to Doremus, Suydam & Nixon. On January 1, 1836, the firm moved to 37 and 39 Nassau Street. Baker, Johnson & Co., wholesale clothiers, moved into the old premises. In the early 1840s the company became Doremus & Nixon at the Nassau Street address.

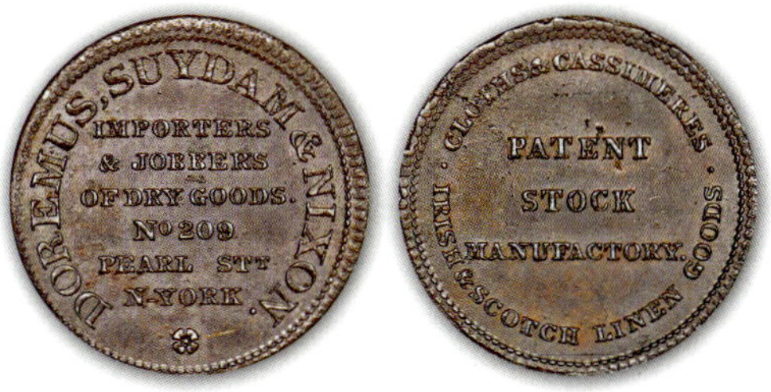

W-NY-440-10a • Rulau: "Low-306"; HT-901. R-6. 26.5 mm. Copper. Obverse with period after GOODS and after NIXON. No dash under o (No) or t (STt). N-YORK. Reverse with period after MANUFACTORY. M nearly touches H (IRISH). At right, period distant from S and S. VF and EF grades are typical. • VF-20 $250; EF-40 $450; AU-50 $800.

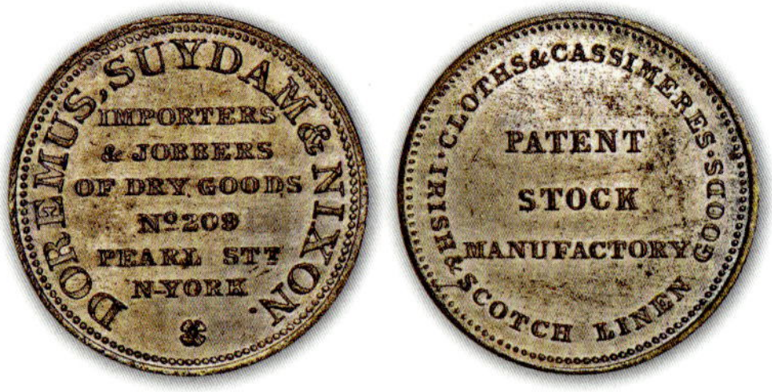

W-NY-440-15b • Rulau: "Low-307"; HT-901A. R-5. 26.5 mm. Brass. Obverse with no period after GOODS. Period after NIXON. Dash under o (No) as t (STt). N-YORK. Reverse with no period after MANUFACTORY. M nearly touches &. At right, period close between S and S. Some silvered, called HT-901B by Steve Tanenbaum. EF tokens are seen with some frequency. • VF-20 $125; EF-40 $200; AU-50 $350.

W-NY-440-20a • Rulau: "Low-308"; HT-902. R-7. 26.5 mm. Copper. No period after NIXON. N. YORK. M nearly touches H (IRISH). At right, period distant from S and S. VF and EF grades are typical. • VF-20 $400; EF-40 $600; AU-50 $1,000.

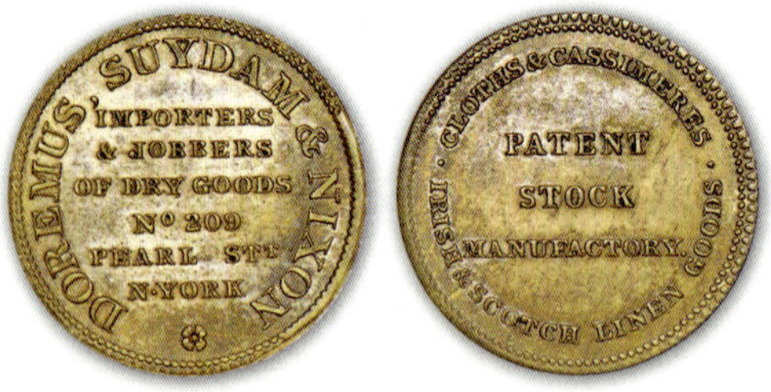

W-NY-440-20b PE • Rulau: "Low-309"; HT-902A. R-7. 26.5 mm. Brass. Obverse with no period after NIXON. No dash under o (No) or t (STt). N. YORK. Reverse, same die as used for W-NY-440-10a. M nearly touches H (IRISH). At right, period distant from S and S. VF and EF grades are typical. • VF-20 $250; EF-40 $450; AU-50 $800.

W-NY-440-20b RE • Rulau: "Low-309A"; HT-902B. R-7. 26.5 mm. Brass. Reeded edge. VF and EF grades are typical. • VF-20 $250; EF-40 $450; AU-50 $800.

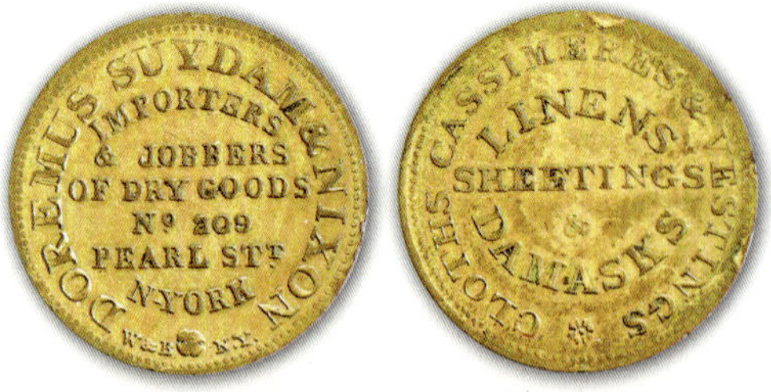

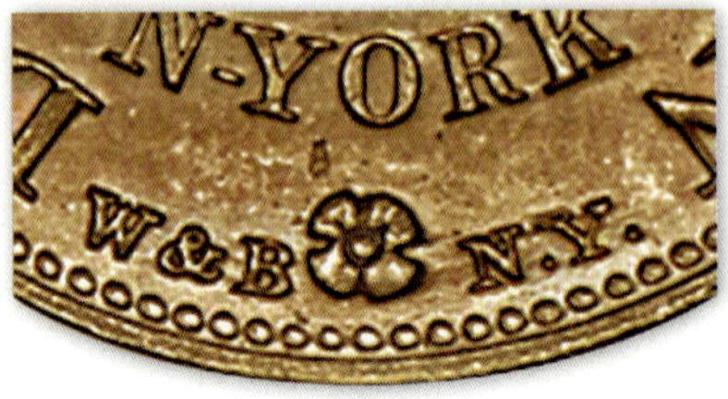

W-NY-440-30a • **209 Pearl St. W&B N.Y.** • Rulau: "Low-310"; HT-253. R-6. 26.5 mm. Copper. Most were gilt. With W&B N.Y. on obverse. N-YORK curved. VF and EF grades are typical. Americana Sale (SBG 2013) MS-65BN $1,645. • VF-20 $125; EF-40 $250; AU-50 $450.

W-NY-440-30b • Rulau: "Low-311"; HT-254. R-6. 26.5 mm. Brass. (Also HT-254A; silvered brass. HT-254B; gilt brass.) VF and EF grades are typical. • VF-20 $125; EF-40 $250; AU-50 $450.

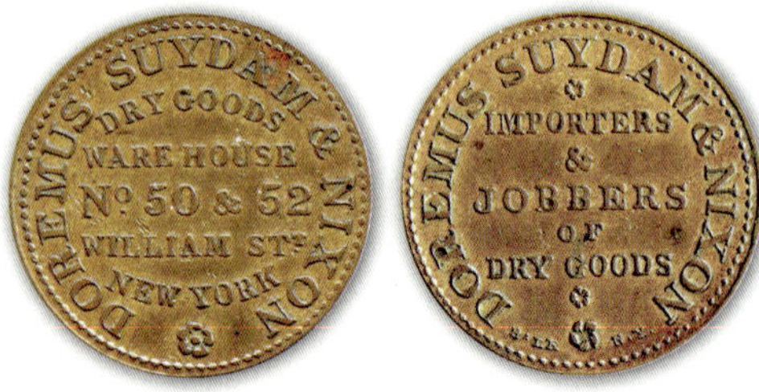

W-NY-440-40a • **50 & 52 William St. BALE NY** • Rulau: "Low-242"; HT-255. R-6. 26.5 mm. Copper. Typically seen in VF and EF grades. • VF-20 $175; EF-40 $300; AU-50 $550.

W-NY-440-45a • **50 & 52 William St. BALE N-Y** • Rulau: "Low-243"; HT-256. R-6. 26.5 mm. Copper. Typically seen in VF and EF grades. • VF-20 $175; EF-40 $300; AU-50 $550.

W-NY-440-50a RE • "SUYDAMS" 37 & 39 Nassau St. B&S N.Y. • Rulau: "Low-245A"; HT-258A. R-6. 26.5 mm. Copper. Reeded edge. Company name on both sides. Typically seen in VF and EF grades. • VF-20 $125; EF-40 $150; AU-50 $250.

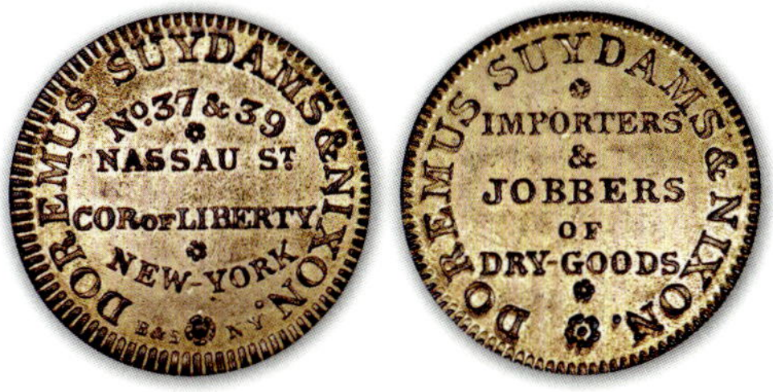

W-NY-440-50b PE • Rulau: "Low-245"; HT-258. R-5. 26.5 mm. Brass. Plain edge. Typically seen in VF and EF grades. • VF-20 $125; EF-40 $150; AU-50 $250; MS-63 $450.

W-NY-440-50b PE • Rulau: "Low-245var"; HT-258B. R-7. 28 mm. Larger diameter. Brass. Reeded edge. • VF-20 $175; EF-40 $225; AU-50 $350.

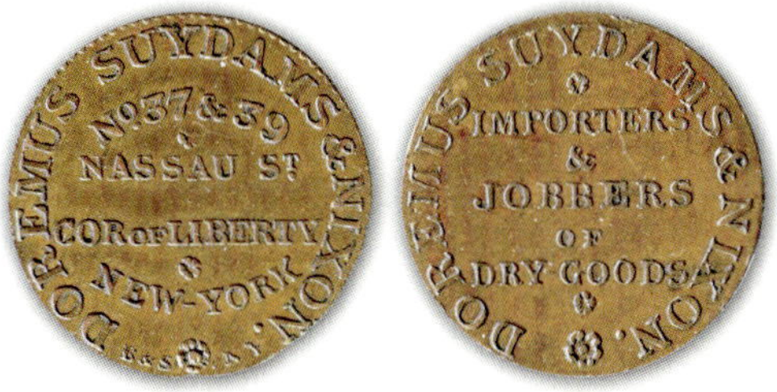

W-NY-440-50a RE • Rulau: "Low-245var"; HT-258AA. R-9. 24.7 mm. Small diameter. Copper. Reeded edge. Unique. Regular dies, but long dentils now very abbreviated, regular strike (not an error on an accidental small planchet). Tanenbaum Collection ex Werner Mayer, 1988.

W-NY-440-50b RE • Rulau: "Low-245var"; HT-258C. R-7. 28 mm. Larger diameter. Brass. Reeded edge.

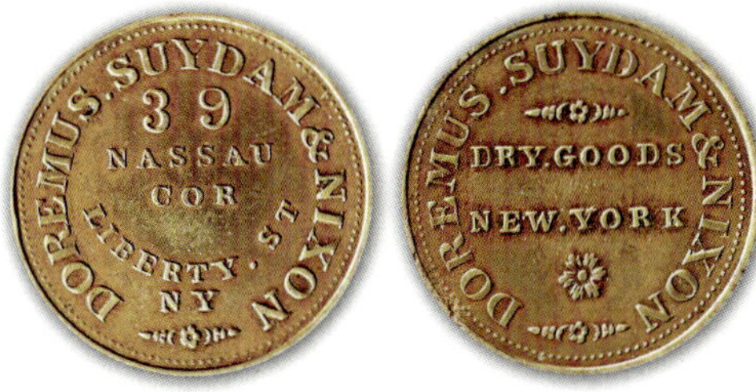

W-NY-440-60b • 39 Nassau St. / Periods after DRY and NEW • Rulau: "Low-245C"; HT-259A. R-5. 26.5 mm. Smaller diameter. Brass. Border of separated dots. VF and EF grades are typical. • VF-20 $125; EF-40 $175; AU-50 $300.

W-NY-440-65b • 39 Nassau St. • Rulau: "Low-245B"; HT-259. R-6. 27.3 mm. Larger diameter. Brass. Gilt. • VF-20 $150; EF-40 $200; AU-50 $300.

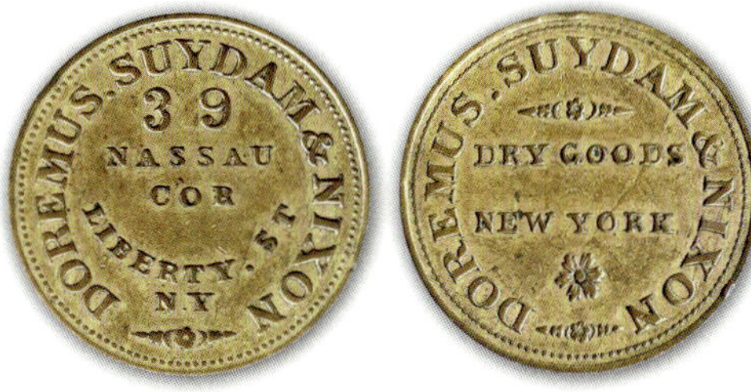

W-NY-440-80b • 39 Nassau St. / No periods after DRY and NEW • Rulau: "Low-245var"; HT-259B. R-9. 27.3 mm. Brass. Different reverse die with letters aligned very slightly differently and without periods after DRY and GOODS. Border of connected dots. Crack from border through M (SUYDAM), through D, O (YORK), to ornament and slightly beyond. Tanenbaum Collection. Unique.

Dr. Lewis Feuchtwanger
New York, NY
Chemist, metallurgist
W-NY-480

Of all issuers of Hard Times tokens, Dr. Lewis Feuchtwanger was the most prominent of his era and is one of the more widely studied today.[59] Born in Fürth, Bavaria, Germany, January 11, 1805, the son of a mineralogist,[60] he developed an interest in science at an early age. In 1827 he graduated as a medical doctor from the University of Jena, Germany, an institution with which he kept in contact for years thereafter. Seeking expanded opportunities, Lewis Feuchtwanger emigrated to America in 1829 and settled in New York City, where in time he opened the first German pharmacy. From this time onward, he imported medicines, apparatus, chemicals, and other items from the German states.

In the year of his arrival in the United States, Lewis Feuchtwanger introduced an alloy he had compounded, later widely known as Feuchtwanger's Composition, a version of German silver, intended to imitate silver through an alloy of other metals, typically nickel, copper, and tin, sometimes with a trace of silver. To differentiate his alloy from the German silver of others—a common alloy at the time—and to build a trade for it, he called his compound not only Feuchtwanger's Composition, but also suggested that it be referred to as American Silver. This alloy was recommended as being an ideal substitute for silver in many uses and for copper in coinage.

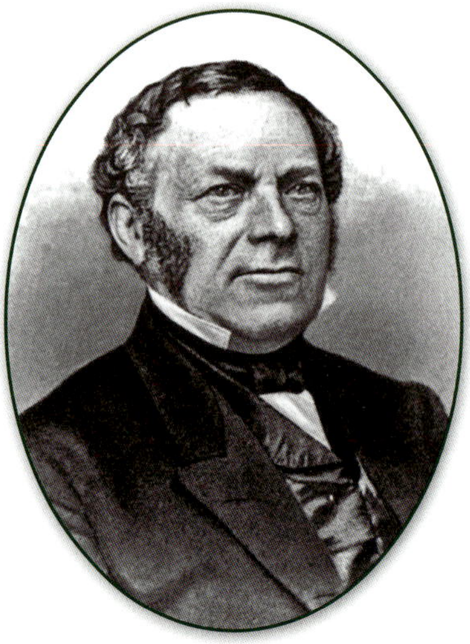

Dr. Lewis Feuchtwanger.

By 1831 he set up a drugstore, curiosity shop, and museum at 377 Broadway, near the corner of White Street,[61] where he would remain until 1837. In addition to his business as a druggist and chemist, he also sold natural curiosities, such as rare minerals, gems, preserved reptiles, etc., a large collection of which he placed on exhibition at Peale's Museum and Gallery of Fine Arts at 252 Broadway,[62] and at a later time (in the 1850s) at the New York Lyceum of Natural History. At his Broadway store, 'one door below White Street,' he advertised 'Nuremburgh Salve' and 'Kreosote . . . a recent German discovery for preventing toothache.' These nostrums seem to have been highly esteemed in their time.[63] In 1834 Feuchtwanger was proprietor of a German drug and chemical store and laboratory, 377 Broadway, with dentist Jacob Feuchtwanger listed with the same information as in 1833.[64 65]

At the annual fair of the American Institute in 1834, Lewis Feuchtwanger was awarded a silver medal for the display of his special alloy, Feuchtwanger's Composition, and products made from it. Likely, the medal was from dies cut by James Bogardus, possibly from a master by Moritz Fürst. Another silver medal was given to Feuchtwanger by the American Institute in 1835 and a third in 1836. Apparently, his displays were different each time.[66]

In 1836 Lewis Feuchtwanger is listed as a partner in Feuchtwanger & Senff, apothecaries, 377 Broadway. A partner, Henry Senff, M.D., lived at 344 Greenwich Street, just a short distance away.[67] The arrangement must have lasted for but a short time, for Senff is listed separately in later directories. In 1837 Feuchtwanger commissioned Bale & Smith to strike a large quantity of small-diameter, reeded-edge tokens. The obverse had an eagle killing a rattlesnake and the date 1837 below. The reverse had FEUCHTWANGER'S COMPOSITION and ONE CENT. These circulated widely in their time, as evidenced by the fact that they are common today and nearly all show wear, sometimes extensive. Not long thereafter, by April 1837, Feuchtwanger moved his business a short distance to 2 Cortlandt (also spelled Courtlandt) Street, setting the scene for his popular "silver penny" and other issues.

In 1837 Feuchtwanger also issued three-cent pieces in his composition. These were larger, about the size of a quarter dollar, and had two different obverses: an eagle and the State Arms of New York, each with the date 1837 below.

In late summer and autumn of 1837, Dr. Lewis Feuchtwanger spent much time and effort in trying to interest Congress in adapting his alloy to make coins. The new metal was said to have been "clean, while a durable material, of specific value, from which coins and all articles can be advantageously manufactured as are now wrought out of silver."[68] His ideas were outlined in a petition dated September 13, bearing the heading, 25th Congress, Document No. 7, House of Representatives, 1st Session, titled "Substitute for Copper. Memorial Lewis Feuchtwanger." The text noted:

> That your memorialist after repeated labors, has succeeded in making and perfecting a metallic composition, known as German silver, of clean, white, and durable material, of specific value, from which coins and all articles can be advantageously manufactured, as are now wrought out of pure silver. Your memorialist proposes to your honorable body to substitute this composition for the copper currency of the country, by striking off pieces of the size of a dime, and of the value of one cent, specimens of which he has prepared for inspection.
>
> Your memorialist proposes to furnish this substitute for copper as cheaply as copper is now furnished to the Mint, and is confident that the "silver cent" thus proposed as a substitute for the cent pieces will be more acceptable, more portable, and would be more generally used in making up the fractional parts of a dollar. Your memorialist prays your honorable body to take the subject under your consideration, and, as in duty bound, will ever pray.

In Congress on September 13, Senator Thomas Hart Benton, of Missouri, presented Feuchtwanger's proposal "accompanied by specimens" for distribution to fellow legislators.[69]

To advance his proposal, the inventor prepared a "Circular," as it was titled, enclosing an example of a "silver penny" made of his American Silver, and with this text:[70]

> I submit for your consideration a specimen of a one-cent piece made of American Composition, known by the name of German Silver, equivalent in value to One Cent in Copper, which I propose with the authority of Congress, to substitute for the existing unclean and unhealthy Copper Currency by which a handsome current coin may be obtained answerable for the fractional parts of a Dollar, and acceptable in the operations of trade and local purchases.
>
> If this "Silver Penny" as I wish to have it designated shall be approved by Congress as a substitute for the one Cent pieces, I shall in that case, propose to remunerate the Mint for any loss sustained by the United States by the withdrawal of the Copper Coin. I am ready to contract for the delivery at the Mint of any amount of the Composition which Congress may authorize to be coined.
>
> *Dr. Lewis Feuchtwanger,*
> *New-York City*

This proposal stirred up a lot of interest, and many notices were published in newspapers. The *U.S. Gazette*, Philadelphia, September 11, 1837, liked the idea:

> One Cent Pieces: Dr. Lewis Feuchtwanger, of New York, has issued a German silver penny, milled at the edge, on one side a fine bold eagle, and the reverse a wreath, with the words, "one cent," with his name on the circle. It is of the intrinsic value of one cent, and about the size of a dime. They are a first rate substitute for small change. One hundred makes a dollar.

On the next day the *Gazette* said more:

> The Cent: A friend called on us yesterday, with a sample of M. Feuchtwanger's coin of 'one cent' to which we referred to in our morning's paper. It was a beautiful piece of money, if it may be allowed such a title, much more convenient in every way than the copper coin; and should silver and gold ever come again in fashion, we think this kind of "cent" would be a very excellent attendant.

Mint Director Robert M. Patterson rejected it for a variety of stated reasons, including that the right of coinage belonged to the government and that German silver was hard to analyze and deal with. He conveniently overlooked what was really its fatal flaw: at the time the Mint charged only nominal fees for converting depositors' silver and gold to coins. In contrast the Mint bought copper on the open market, coined cents from the metal, and issued them at face value—earning a profit on each one. If Feuchtwanger's metal had been adopted, this source of profit—the only one the Mint had—would have ended.

These cents attracted the attention of numismatists. Augustus B. Sage, writing in the *New-York Dispatch*, August 16, 1857, discussed the following, a very early numismatic reference:

> *Feuchtwanger Cent.* In 1837 Dr. Feuchtwanger, of this city, submitted a cent; to Congress for their examination, wishing them to adopt it for general circulation. It was refused. It was composed of lead and tin, I believe. On the obverse there is an eagle standing in a very hostile position upon a snake, and underneath the date 1837. On the reverse there is "one cent" on the field surrounded by a wreath, and around the coin, "Feuchtwanger's Composition." The edge is nicely grained. Take it all in all, it is a very fair sample of work, and if Congress can accept such a piece of work as the 'new cent,'[71] why didn't they accept that? It was exactly the *size of the present issue*, and has a white color.

Likely, millions of these tokens were issued in their time. Today all of the Feuchtwanger Composition tokens are highly desired, and nearly all are collectible. The cents exist in various die combinations as listed below. All are 18.5 mm diameter.

Store cards of two varieties were issued early in the 1830s followed by 1837-dated three-cent pieces with the State Arms of New York and with an eagle facing left (opposite direction from that on the cents). All of these are scarce today.

In 1864, additional three-cent pieces were issued by Feuchtwanger. These are part of the Civil War token series and are beyond the purview of the present study. Around this time some 1837-dated tokens were restruck (see following entries).

Feuchtwanger Cents

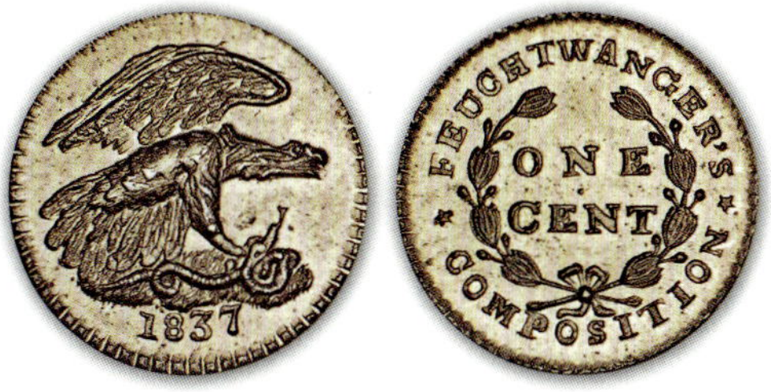

W-NY-480 Dies 1-A RE • Low-120; HT-268. R-5. 18.5 mm. Feuchtwanger's Composition. *Obverse 1:* Coarse dentils. Large date close to ground above, the 3 exceptionally large, the 7 very high. Snake's tongue slightly to the right of vertical. Seven tail feathers, four of them touching the ground. Known combinations: 1-A. *Reverse A:* ONE very widely spaced. Small O's in COMPOSITION. A and P recut. Known combinations: 1-A, 2-A. VF and EF grades are usual; AU is very elusive. • VF-20 $125; EF-40 $225; AU-50 $400.

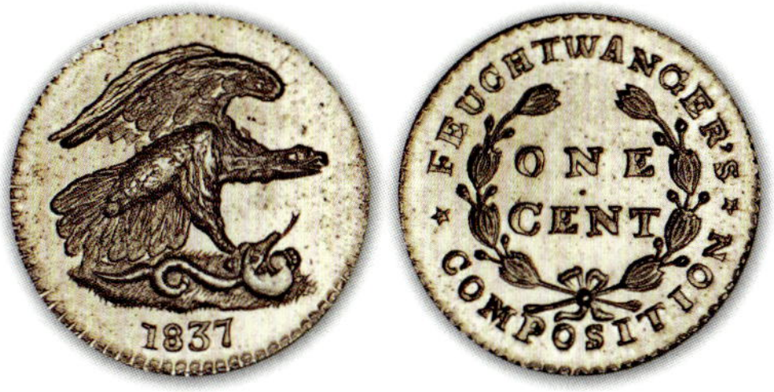

W-NY-480 Dies 2-A RE • Low-120; HT-268. R-5. 18.5 mm. Feuchtwanger's Composition. *Obverse 2:* Similar treatment of the eagle to obverse 1. In date 18 low, small, closely spaced; 37 much larger, higher, also closely spaced. Eight tail feathers, five touching ground. Grass is wavy or billowy and generally slants upward to the right. On the eagle's neck there are two raised bars, slanting down to the left and extending slightly into the field. Of the tail feathers, four large feathers are delineated with their tips touching the ground, after which the 5th feather is not as well formed and may consist of two smaller feathers touching ground. In back below wing, four feathers, the lowest being somewhat indistinct. Back loop of snake: More or less circular in shape; above 8. *Reverse A.* Known combination: 2-A. VF and EF grades are usual; AU is very rare. • VF-20 $125; EF-40 $225; AU-50 $350.

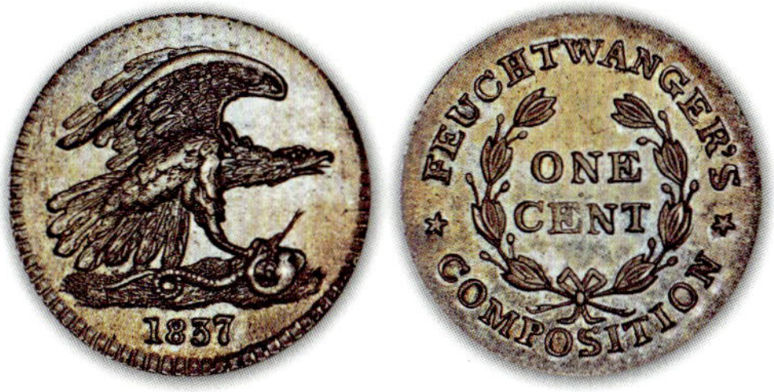

W-NY-480 Dies 3-B RE • Low-120; HT-268. R-5. 18.5 mm. Feuchtwanger's Composition. *Obverse 3:* Date closely spaced, from smaller punches as on all to follow, and in a straight line on top. Seven tail feathers, first two and fourth (latter recut) touching ground. Ground resembles pine branches. Known combinations: 3-B, 3-C, 3-D, 3-E, 3-G. *Reverse B:* Stems end in marked claws. 1st left inside berry has two stems. S in COMPOSITION very defective at top. Upright of F recut. N in COMPOSITION recut. Known combination: 3-B. VF and EF grades are usual grades seen; AU is very rare. • VF-20 $125; EF-40 $225; AU-50 $400.

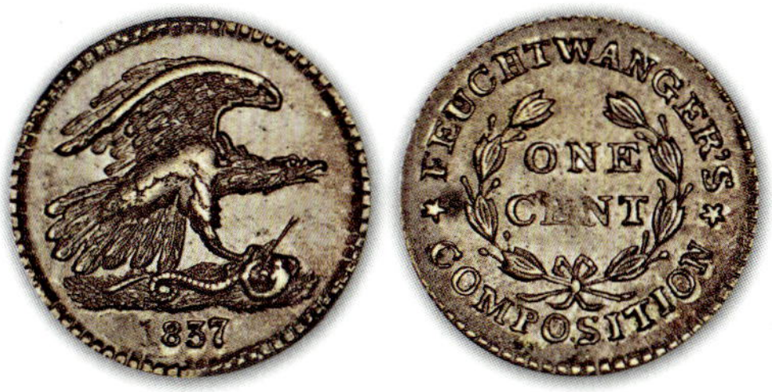

W-NY-480 Dies 3-C RE • Low-120; HT-268. R-8. 18.5 mm. Feuchtwanger's Composition. *Obverse 3. Reverse C:* Star close to final S in FEUCHTWANGER'S (the only reverse die used with obverse 3 for which this is true). Stems of the two upper inside berries of the right branch arise from innermost leaves almost at tips. Known combination: 3-C. This and the 4-F are the Holy Grail varieties among circulation strikes of Feuchtwanger cents.

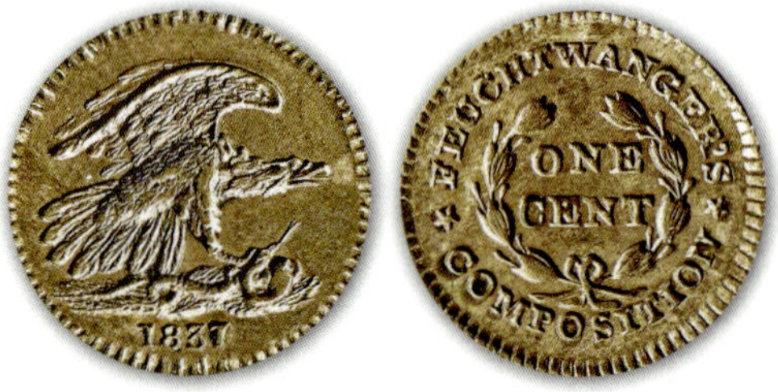

W-NY-480 Dies 3-D RE • Low-120; HT-268. R-7. 18.5 mm. Feuchtwanger's Composition. *Obverse 3. Reverse D:* O in ONE too low. Right bow plainly overlaps left one. Right ribbon almost touches both S and I. The 7 shows crumbling between horizontal and upright; rim breaks down at lower right. This is a slightly later state than seen on 3-E. Known combination: 3-D. Coin Galleries (2005) Mint State $2,900. SBG (2011) EF $6,900. • VF-20 $2,500; EF-40 $3,500; AU-50 $5,000.

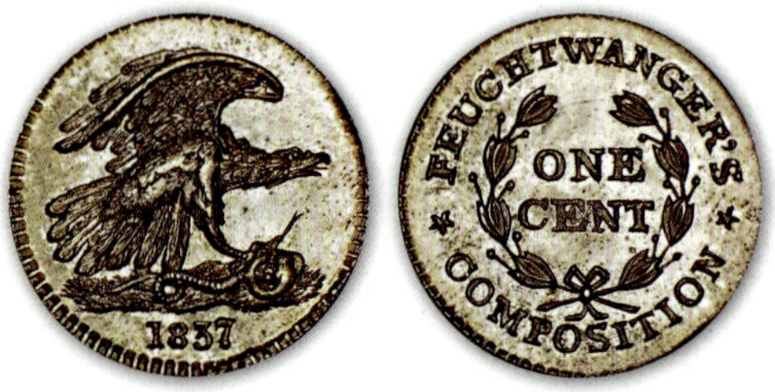

W-NY-480 Dies 3-E RE • Low-120; HT-268. R-3. 18.5 mm. Feuchtwanger's Composition. *Obverse 3. Reverse E:* IT about touch. E in ONE, T in CENT (left top) and P in COMPOSITION clearly recut N's in ONE CENT crumble. Known combinations: 3-E (struck first), 4-E (struck last). On this combination 7 begins to crumble between horizontal and upright; rim breaks down at lower right. VF and EF grades are usual grades encountered in the marketplace; AU is very rare. • VF-20 $100; EF-40 $150; AU-50 $225.

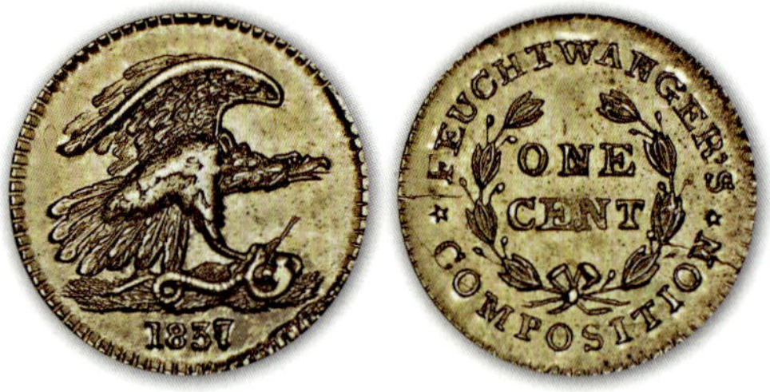

W-NY-480 Dies 3-G RE • Low-120; HT-268. R-6. 18.5 mm. Feuchtwanger's Composition. *Obverse 3. Reverse G:* 13 berries, the extra one just right of bow. Berry near base of T in CENT attached to a leaf. Star too close to final N in COMPOSITION. Stems end in claws though not too distinctly. M P O spaced apart. The 7 shows crumbling between horizontal and upright; rim breaks down at lower right. N in ONE crumbles at base (this die is found perfect only on the 6-G combination). Known combinations: 3-G, 5-G, 6-G. VF and EF grades are usual grades seen; AU is exceedingly rare. • VF-20 $250; EF-40 $400; AU-50 $900.

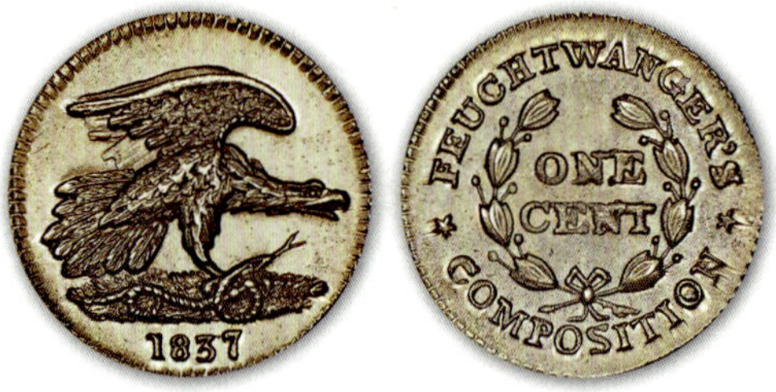

W-NY-480 Dies 4-E RE • Low-120; HT-268. R-5. 18.5 mm. Feuchtwanger's Composition. *Obverse 4:* In date 3 low, rather distant from 7 and often joined to it at top by a line. Loop in snake's tail left of date; in all other dies loop is above 18. Snake's tongue very long, very deeply forked. Back loop of snake: somewhat flattened; centered above the top of the flag on 1; a very distinctive diagnostic feature. Eagle's head droops. Eight tail feathers, three touching ground. *Reverse E.* Known combinations: 4-E, 4-F. 4-E as here is the latest die state of the reverse. EF and AU are typical grades found in a leading auction, but Mint State pieces exist and are notable rarities. • VF-20 $125; EF-40 $200; AU-50 $300; MS-63 $600.

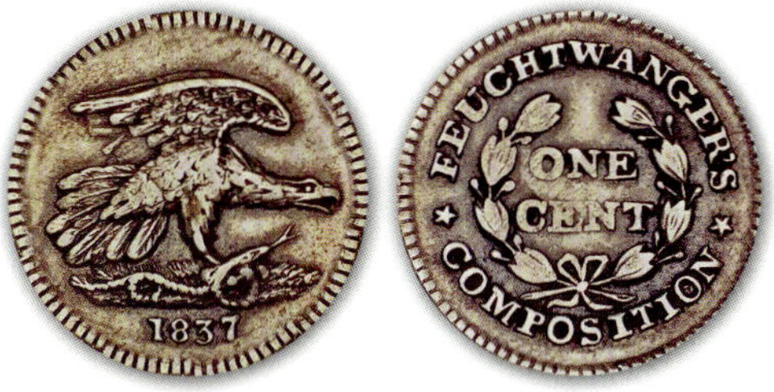

W-NY-480 Dies 4-F RE • Low-120; HT-268. R-8. 18.5 mm. Feuchtwanger's Composition. *Obverse 4. Reverse F:* ER joined at bases. Left stem, divided like a pen point, is close to top or right vertical of M. Known combination: 4-F. This and the 3-C are the Holy Grail varieties among circulation strikes of Feuchtwanger cents.

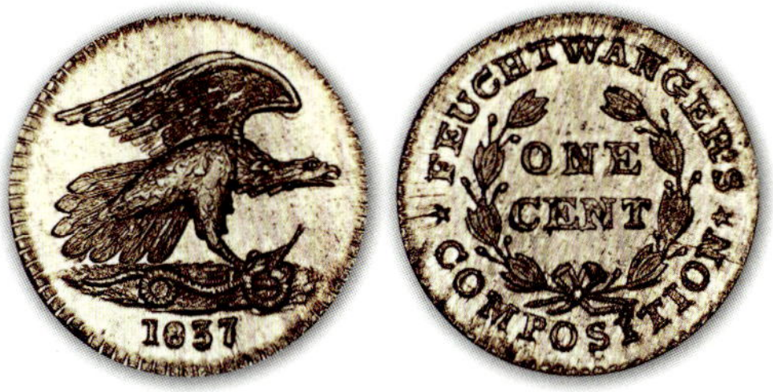

W-NY-480 Dies 5-G RE • Low-120; HT-268. R-2. 18.5 mm. Feuchtwanger's Composition. *Obverse 5:* Date widely and evenly spaced; slightly curved bar in ground directly above 83. Seven tail feathers, only the second barely touching ground; fourth recut at tip. Ground resembles pine branches, but not as closely as Obverse 3. 1st feather very close to ground above coil of snake, no vegetation in this area. In back below wing, six feathers with more or less rectangular ends; some slight vane details on feathers 2, 3, and 4. Small curved line extends below bottom of leading edge of eagle's wing on right. Back loop of snake: more or less circular, prominent beadlike segments evident; centered over space between 1 and 8, and closer to 1. *Reverse E.* Reverse Die State I: Perfect die. Reverse Die State II: Crack from wreath through left upright of N (COMPOSITION) to edge; this on about half of the extant pieces seen. On this die state a raised curved line develops at lower right of O (ONE), resembling a repunching. Reverse Die State III: Latest state seen. Lowest-inside-left and second-lowest inside-right berries repunched to make them larger; lowest inside left now has a hook or thorn projecting from it. Die crack from stem above 1st O (COMPOSITION) through tops of POSI. Known combinations: 5-G, 5-H. EF and AU are typical grades found in a leading auction, but Mint State pieces exist and are notable rarities. • VF-20 $100; EF-40 $150; AU-50 $225; MS-63 $450.

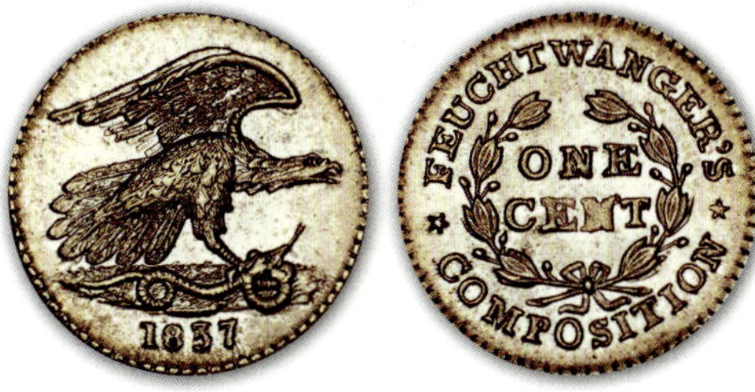

W-NY-480 Dies 5-H RE • Low-120; HT-268. R-3. 18.5 mm. Feuchtwanger's Composition. *Obverse 5. Reverse H:* 13 berries, extra one just left of bow. E in ONE top high at top and base. Crude recutting NE CEN; crumbling develops on these letters. Known combination: 5-H. Most range from VF to EF, but a handful of higher grades exist. • VF-20 $100; EF-40 $150; AU-50 $225; MS-63 $450.

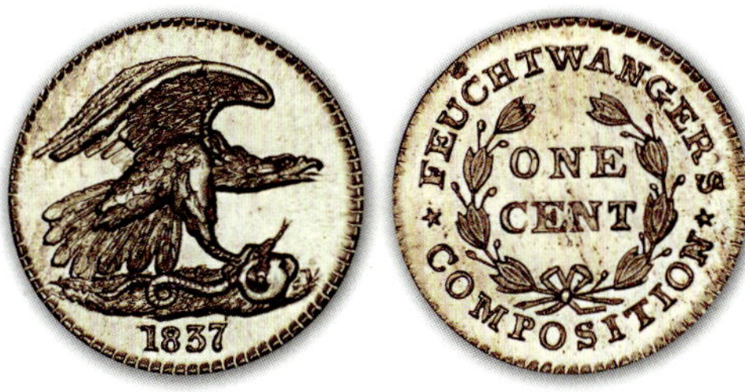

W-NY-480 Dies 6-G RE • Low-120; HT-268. R-5. 18.5 mm. Feuchtwanger's Composition. *Obverse 6:* Closely spaced date, bottoms in a straight line; 83 a little apart. Dash to left from upper serif of 1. Base of eagle's neck smooth. Seven tail feathers, four of them touching ground. *Reverse G.* Known combinations: 6-G, 6-I, 6-RER (Russell). EF and AU are typical grades, and Mint State is a prime rarity. • VF-20 $100; EF-40 $150; AU-50 $250; MS-63 $550.

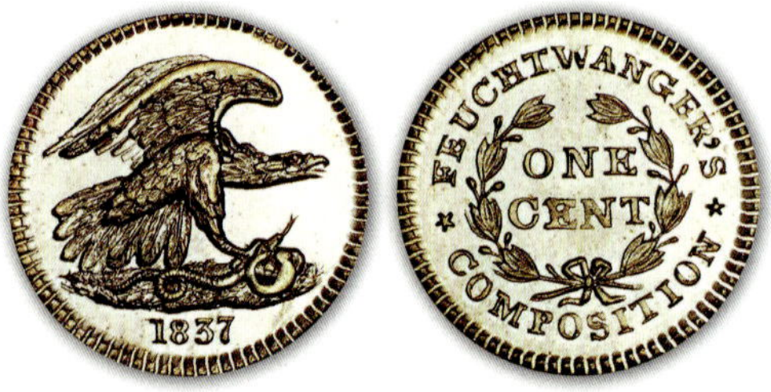

W-NY-480 Dies 6-I RE • Low-120; HT-268. R-1. 18.5 mm. Feuchtwanger's Composition. *Obverse 6. Reverse I:* 13 berries, extra one just left of bow, and looking more like an extra stem. E in CENT heavily recut. E in ONE high at base but in line with N at top. EU widely spaced; base of W significantly lower than left foot of A; R weak at top. Known combination: 6-I. Notes: The most plentiful variety, probably at several times as populous as the next contender. When high-grade Feuchtwanger cents are offered they are usually of this variety. More Mint State examples of this variety exist than of all earlier varieties combined *times 10.* This is the affordable "type" variety. He also has a plain edge example thought to be a striking error. • VF-20 $100; EF-40 $150; AU-50 $200; MS-63 $400.

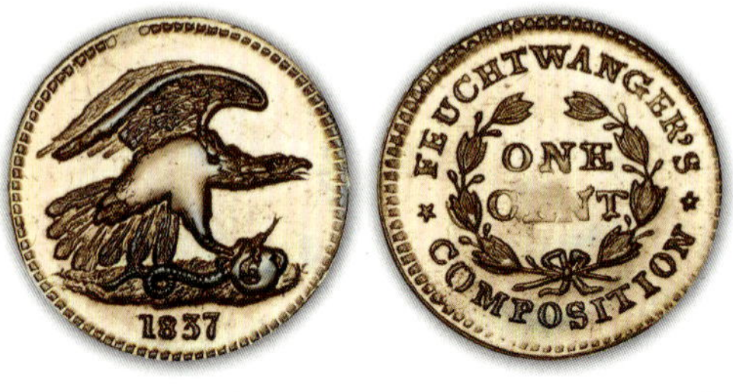

W-NY-480 Dies 6-I RE, Copper • Struck in copper, not Feuchtwanger's Composition • Low-Unlisted; HT-Unlisted. R-9. 18.5 mm. Copper. *Obverse 6. Reverse I.* Unique. Robert A. Schuman Collection. All other "copper" Feuchtwanger cents have proved to be electrotypes.

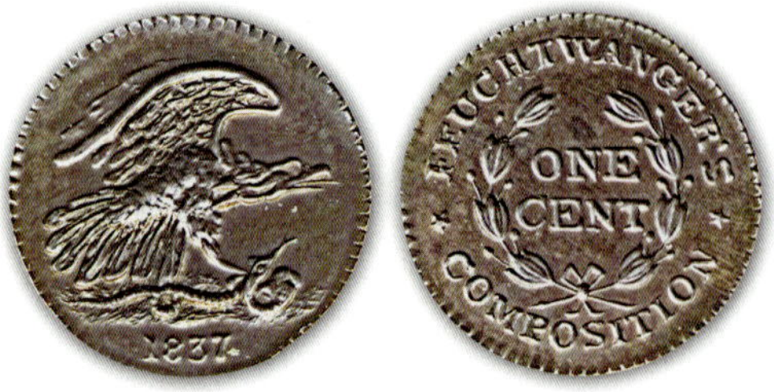

W-NY-480 Dies 7-J Pattern PE • Low-120; HT-268A. R-9. 18.5 mm. Feuchtwanger's Composition. Pattern struck in silver, plain edge. Perfect dies. *Obverse 7:* 18 (1837) low, 3 high, 7 highest. Snake's tongue very short. Tail feather 1 embedded in top of coil of snake, feathers 2 and 3 touch ground, 3 close but with small plain space intervening. In back below wing, three feathers with vane details (superficially resembling these details in Obverse 3, but with differences). Details of back wing (above top edge of front wing) incomplete. Eagle with very long tongue. Back loop of snake: more or less circular, prominent beadlike segments evident, centered over space between 1 and 8, closer to 8; somewhat similar to Obverse 3, but with important differences. A very distinctive die. Known combination: 7-J. *Reverse J:* A carefully made die, wide spacing of border letters, good alignment, and with delicate features. Berry positions: Left outside berries opposite: Center of C / right side of upright of F / left of C. Right outside berries opposite: Left upright of N / center of S / space between GE and slightly closer to E. Known combination: 7-J.

FEUCHTWANGER STORE CARDS

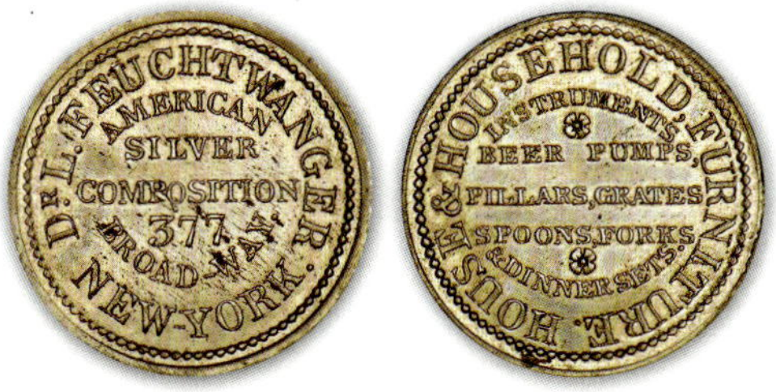

W-NY-480-50j PE • 377 Broadway • Rulau: "Low-247"; HT-260. R-7. 27 mm. Feuchtwanger's Caomposition. 377 Broadway address, his location until autumn 1836. The Garrett Choice Mint State piece sold for $3,000 to Ford in 1981 and was resold for $6,600 in the Ford Sale. The Choice Mint State Dice-Hicks token sold for $5,750 in 2008 and was resold by Stack's Bowers Galleries in 2011 for $6,900. VF and EF are typical grades.

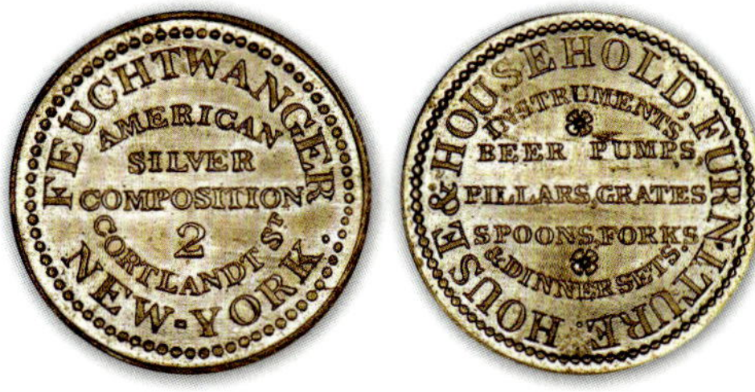

W-NY-480-55j PE • 2 Cortlandt St. • Rulau: "Low-248"; HT-261. R-7. 27 mm. Feuchtwanger's Composition. 2 Cortlandt Street address used beginning late in 1836. The street name was sometimes spelled Courtlandt in other venues (not on the tokens). Most are VF to AU. The Dice-Hicks Mint State token sold for $8,625 in 2008. Stack's Bowers Galleries sold a similar piece in 2010 for $17,250.

FEUCHTWANGER THREE-CENT PIECES

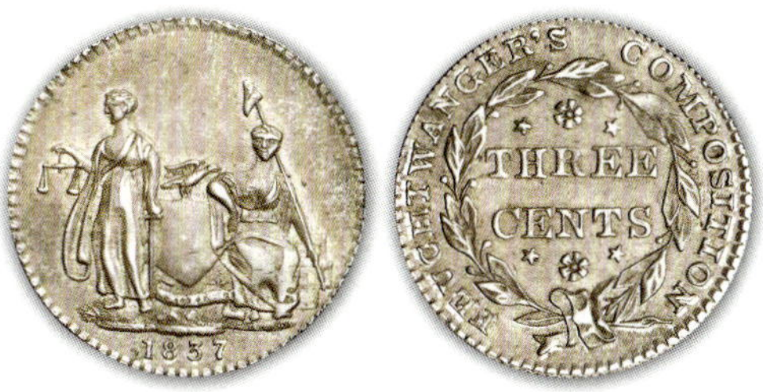

W-NY-480-60j RE • 1837 N.Y. Arms • Low-117; HT-262. R-3. 25 mm. Feuchtwanger's Composition. Circulating issue valued at three cents. Obverse die rather amateurishly cut, upon close inspection. Left-side figure is of Justice standing, holding balance scales and a sword; the balance scales are supported slightly to the left of center. On top of the shield is a perched eagle facing right. To the right is a seated figure with a scythe and a pole with liberty cap, with bales of merchandise in the background. Date numerals widely spaced; 3 slightly double punched.[72] Ford (Stack's 2004) AU $1,840, Choice AU $2,990, Unc $3,450. Dice-Hicks (Stack's 2008) Unc $7,475. Most of these circulated extensively, yielding grades of VF and EF in collections today. AU pieces are available with patience and a number of Mint State pieces have crossed the auction block in recent decades.[73]

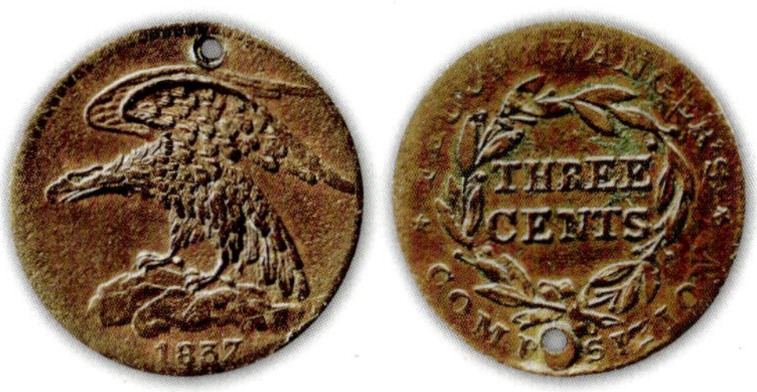

W-NY-480-65a • 1837 Eagle / Three Cents PE • Low-179; HT-264. R-9. 25 mm. Copper. Obverse: Eagle perched on rocks or ledge, facing left. Date 1837 below. Date in small numerals, closely spaced. Eagle with feather tips separated. Reverse: FEUCHTWANGER'S / COMPOSITION around border, five-pointed star at each side. Within, endless wreath tied with smaller and somewhat loose ribbon, enclosing: THREE / CENTS. Unique. VF, holed. Ex Lorin G. Parmelee (June 25,

1890, lot 264); Charles Morris (Henry Chapman June 30, 1911); Dr. French Collection; Collection by Pennypacker, to Don Miller, John J. Ford (1904 $17,200), Dice-Hicks (Stack's 2008 $9,000), Steve Tanenbaum, and David M. Sundman collections.

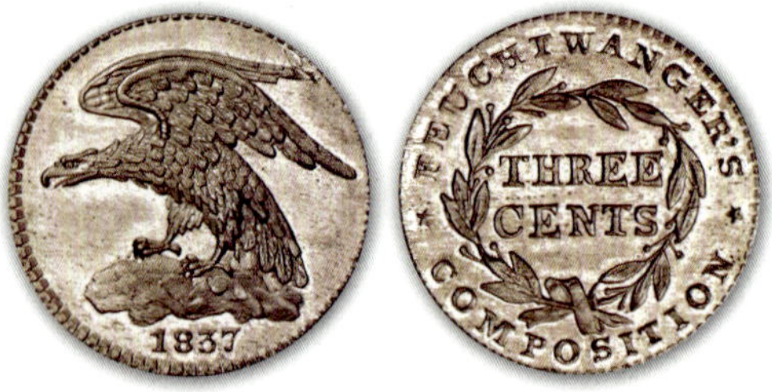

W-NY-480-65j RE • 1837 Eagle / Three Cents • Low-118; HT-263. R-4. 25 mm. Feuchtwanger's Composition. Same dies as the preceding. Circulating issue valued at three cents. Some are hallmarked "JMP" on the reverse, for an unknown reason. In *An Arrangement of Tradesmen's Cards, Political Tokens, also, Election Medals, Medalets, &c.*, 1858, Charles I. Bushnell described this variety: "No. 100. Ob: An Eagle, with expanded wings, facing to the left, standing upon a ledge of rocks. Below, the date '1837.' Rev: Same as last. Edge, milled. Metal, German silver. Size, 6½. Very few were struck of this variety." Typical grades range from VF to EF or so, but Mint State pieces exist, including two in the 2004 Ford Collection, Choice and Gem Mint State, each at $25,300. Dice-Hicks (Stack's 2008) Gem Prooflike Unc $29,900.

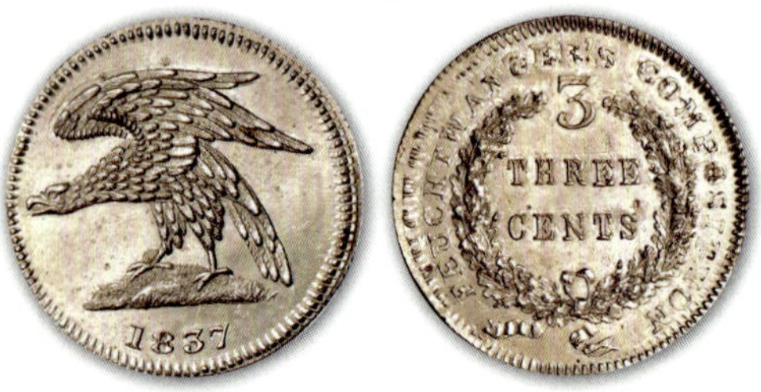

W-NY-480-70j Novodel RE • 1837 Eagle / 3 Cents • Low-119; HT-265A. R-7. 24.2 mm. Feuchtwanger's Composition. Probably struck after 1858, likely in the early 1860s. A novodel, not a restrike, as none from these dies were made in 1837 and thus there are no originals. This variety was *not* included by Bushnell in his 1858 study, probably as this issue had not been struck yet. He only listed the two basic circulation styles, one with the State Arms of New York and the other with an eagle, both with a reverse utilizing a wreath. Most have been offered as Mint State, often highly Prooflike. Ford (Stack's 2004) Gem Prooflike Unc $13,800. Dice-Hicks (Stack's 2008) Gem Prooflike Unc $32,200.

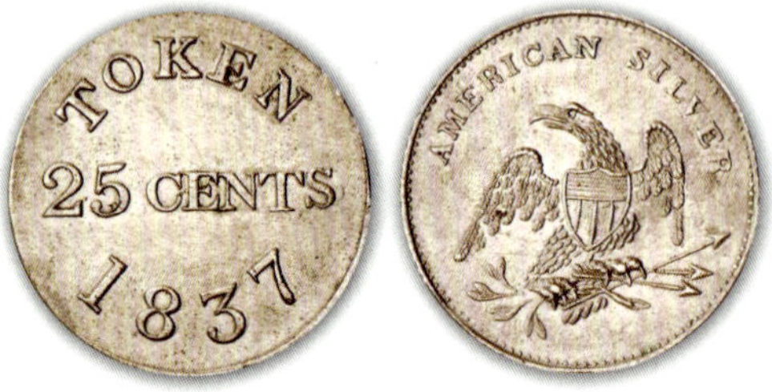

W-NY-480-80j • American Silver / 1837 25 Cents Token • Low-50; HT-74. R-8. 26 mm. Feuchtwanger's Composition. One is Miller to Bowers to Partrick, and the second is the Ford Collection example sold in 2004 to Robert A. Schuman for

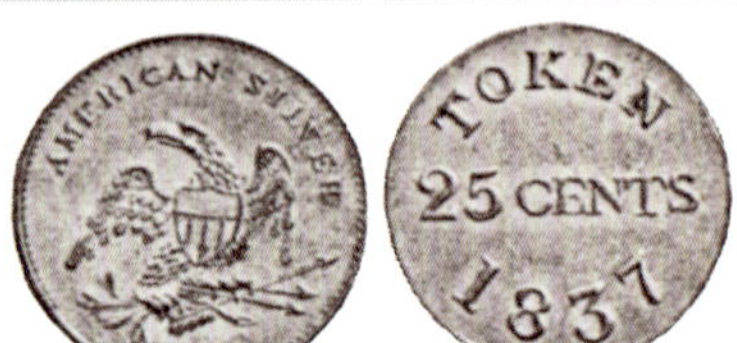

50 American Silver 25 Cents. Feuchtwanger metal.

Mr. Low's libel on this token is entirely uncalled for as it bears no resemblance to the other so-called Bushnell tokens—24, 25, 26, 27, 41, 42, 43. The piece is undoubtedly a product of Feuchtwanger the originator of the "American Silver Composition." Furthermore it is not in silver but in Feuchtwanger's metal. Now in the collection of Wayte Raymond.

In the 1941 edition of *The Standard Catalogue of U.S. Coins and Tokens* publisher Wayte Raymond showcased the American Silver token. By this time he had ceased collecting federal coins (his cabinet of these was later auctioned by the Numismatic Gallery) and devoted most of his time to tokens and colonial coins.

$126,500, setting a Hard Times token record (illustrated). In *An Arrangement of Tradesmen's Cards, Political Tokens, also, Election Medals, Medalets, &c.*, 1858 Charles I. Bushnell seems to have introduced this variety; at least, no earlier mention of it has been found: "No. 24, Ob: An Eagle, with expanded wings, facing to the left, holding an olive branch in one talon, and three barbed arrows in the other. The shield of the United States upon his breast. '*American Silver.*' Rev: '*Token. 25 Cents. 1837.*' Edge, milled. Metal, Silver. Size, 7." This listing would seem to indicate that Bushnell did not associate the token with Feuchtwanger, nor did he seem to be aware that "American Silver" was Feuchtwanger's term for his compound of German silver (although "American Silver" could have had other meanings as well). Bushnell does not seem to have paid it much notice in his 1858 listing, whereas he could have called it "very rare," etc. The writer considers it to have been a legitimate Feuchtwanger issue. Low did not hold a high opinion of this piece:

> *Obv.* Token I 25 Cents I 1837 in large letters and figures. *Rev.* American Silver in small letters above an eagle, type of 49; the shield has three pales. This piece was first introduced to the public by the late Charles I. Bushnell in his work published in 1858. It next appeared in his collection of coins, which was dispersed by auction in 1881 [*sic*, should be 1882]. I purchased the piece for a collector who still retains it; no other is known to me, and I have no hesitancy in stating that my conclusions are, that it is unique and was struck from dies made by Bushnell's order. I hold a similar unfavorable opinion of Nos. 24, 25, 26, 27, 41, 42 and 43, but in these latter I think a partner was admitted, and a very limited number of each was struck, but probably only single specimens in silver.

Early Feuchtwanger Auction Listings

From the 1850s to the present day, listings of Feuchtwanger cents and three-cent pieces have been featured in many auctions. Here are a few 19th-century offerings:

W. Elliot Woodward, who had been gaining prominence since his first auction in 1860, from November 11 to 14, 1864, presented his *Catalogue of Selected Specimens from the American Portion of the Finotti Collection of Coins and Medals*, which he had purchased outright. Included were these items:

> Lot 1626: 1837 Feuchtwanger's Composition, three cents; rev. arms of New York; nearly proof, very rare. [sold for $1.25]

> Lot 1627: 1837 Obv. Resembling the last; rev. Eagle on a rock. Very few of this variety struck, much rarer than the preceding, very fine. [$6.50]

> Lot 1628: 1837 Feuchtwanger's Composition, "one cent" on both sides; fine and very rare. [40¢][74]

> Lot 1629: 1837 Feuchtwanger's Composition, one cent; five different varieties, all very fine and scarce. [12¢ each]

Woodward bought the collection of Joseph J. Mickley in 1867, sold the United States gold coins to William Sumner Appleton, and auctioned most of the rest at the Book Trade Sale Rooms of Messrs. Leavitt, Strebeigh & Co., Clinton Hall, New York City, in a multi-day event that began at 5:30 in the afternoon of October 28, 1867. These Feuchtwanger items were included:

> Lot 2153: Feuchtwanger's Three Cent Piece, 1837, eagle on a rock; very fine indeed, and extremely rare. [$7.50 to Crawford]

> Lot 2154: Feuchtwanger's Three Cent Piece, 1837, arms of New York; very fine, almost proof, scarce. [$1.50 to Crosby]
>
> Lot 2155: Feuchtwanger's Cents, 1837, five piece, all fine, different varieties. [25¢ each to Fellows]
>
> Lot 2156: Feuchtwanger's Cent, struck from two reverse dies, "One Cent" on both sides; very fine, rare. [$1.45 to Cohen][75]
>
> Lot 2587: Feuchtwanger, Dr. L. "American Silver Composition, 377 Broadway, N.Y."; rev. "Household furniture," &c.; German s., nearly p. This and the following are amongst the rarest of American Store Cards. [$4 to Bushnell[76]]
>
> Lot 2588: Feuchtwanger, Dr. L. "American Silver Composition, 2 Cortlandt St., N.Y."; rev. "Instruments," &c., German s., nearly p. [$4 to Levick]

On May 27, 1881, Édouard Frossard's *Catalogue of Ancient and Modern Silver and Copper Coins* noted on the title page that "Feuchtwanger Currency" was included, these items being presented on page 21 as follows:

> The following coins were the property of Dr. Feuchtwanger's family, and comprise the entire lot until lately in their possession.
>
> Lot 536: 1837 Eagle on a rock. Rev., FEUCHTWANGER'S COMPOSITION; wreath of oak, within which 3 THREE CENTS. Fine proof, and extremely rare. Size 16. [$19.50 to Lowe][77]
>
> Lot 537: 1837 Coat of Arms of New York. Rev., Same inscription, but THREE CENTS, four stars, and two mullets within wreath of olive. Uncirculated and scarce. [$5 to C, presumably Chapman]
>
> Lot 538: Duplicate of last number. Very fine. [$1.75]
>
> Lot 539: Another. Same condition as last. [$1.62½][78]
>
> Lot 540: 1837 Eagle on a serpent. Rev., ONE CENT in wreath of laurel. Eight feathers to tail and serpent in large coils. Uncirculated. [$1.87½ to Lowe]
>
> Lot 541: Duplicate of last. Uncirculated. [75¢]
>
> Lot 542: Another. Very fine. [50¢ to H, presumably Haseltine]
>
> Lot 543: From different dies. Eagle with seven feathers and pointed left wing. Uncirculated. [$1.50 to C]
>
> Lot 544: Another Cent from still different dies. Eagle with seven feathers and blunt left wing. Uncirculated. [$1.12½ to C]
>
> Lot 545: Duplicates of last. Very fine. 2 pieces. [25¢ each to H]
>
> Lot 546: The same obv., but reverse with delicate wreath; evidently from another die. Uncirculated. [$2.12½]
>
> Lot 547: 1864 Eagle displayed, grasping a serpent. Rev., the same as reverse of No. 536. Nearly proof and rare. [$4.25]
>
> Lot 548: Duplicate of last. Fine and rare. [$4.25 to Lowe]

It seems reasonable to assume that the preceding pieces were issued by or under the auspices of Dr. Feuchtwanger, including the 1837– and 1864–dated three-cent pieces with the "3 / THREE CENTS" used in both instances. Later, Frossard gave a report of the event:[79]

The bidding on the Feuchtwanger currency was extremely spirited and the several pieces brought extraordinary high figures. An 1837 Eagle on a rock, three cent piece, in poor condition, sold at $19.50; 1837, Coat of Arms of New York, three cents, $5; the 1837 cents, nearly all from different dies averaged $1.25 each; the 1864, Eagle displayed, three cents, $4.25.

Beside the pieces represented at this sale Dr. Feuchtwanger issued two or three store cards, all of the highest degree of rarity, and none of which have been in the possession of his family since his death. The Feuchtwanger currency will form the subject of an article which will appear in a future number of *Numisma.*

The collection of coins and tokens formed by J.N.T. Levick, cataloged by Woodward, crossed the block at Bangs & Co., New York, from May 26 to 29, 1884. Levick was one of the grand 19th-century figures in the field of token collecting, making these his first love, though he achieved considerable success in other series (most notably large copper cents).

Lot 413: 1837 Eagle standing; rev., Feuchtwanger's Composition, 3 Cents; almost proof, *extremely rare.* This and all the other pieces in this series are of Feuchtwanger's metal. Plate. [$3.50]

Lot 414: 1837 Arms of New York; rev., like the last; equally fine, equally fine, *rare.* Plate. [$1.90]

Lot 415: 1864 Eagle and serpent; rev., Feuchtwanger, etc., three cents; nearly proof, *rare.* Plate. [$2.90]

Lot 416: Feuchtwanger American Silver Composition, 2 Courtland St.; rev., Household Furniture, etc.; perfect, *very rare.* [$4][80]

Lot 417: The same, on thicker planchet; finer than the last and *equally rare.* Plate. [$8.25]

Lot 418: Feuchtwanger, Dr. L., 377 Broadway; rev., like the preceding; perfect, *extremely rare.* [$8]

Lot 419: 1837 Feuchtwanger Cents. A series, believed to be complete; all different, and all very fine. 14 pieces. [16¢ each]

Lot 420: Feuchtwanger Cent. One Cent on both sides; fine, *very rare.* [$3]

Lot 421: 1837 Obv. Of Feuchtwanger's Cent; rev., R.E. Russell, I.O.U. 12½c., fine, *extremely rare.* [$6.50]

W. Field
New York, NY
Manufacturer of hats, caps, and furs
W-NY-500

W. Field was a hatter at 148 Chatham Street, corner of Mulberry Street in a building that had street floor premises and several lofts to accommodate businesses. Russell Rulau states that Field was active in 1835. Charles Watson, hat manufacturer, was upstairs at 148 Chatham Street in 1842. In 1835 continuing into the early 1840s George C. Howe was a watchmaker at the same address. In 1844 the jewelry firm of Freeman & Wallin was there.

Field's tokens have been listed for a long time, including by Bushnell in 1858, but in the absence of being dated they were not connected to the Hard Times series until the 20th century. In his article, "A Plea for American Token Collecting," in *The Numismatist*, April 1915, Thomas L. Elder listed this among the various tokens that he felt to be worthy of investigation.

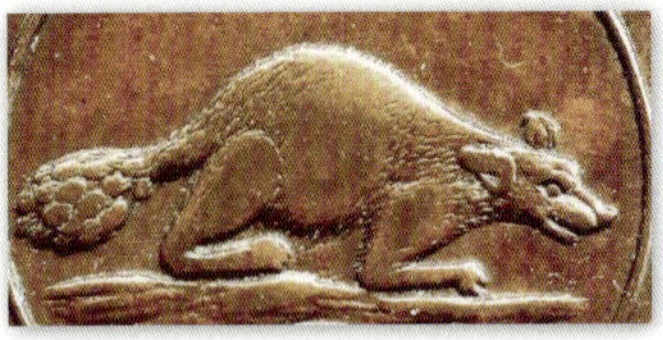

The "beaver" on the reverse of Field's token has the head of a dog and a tail resembling a pineapple.

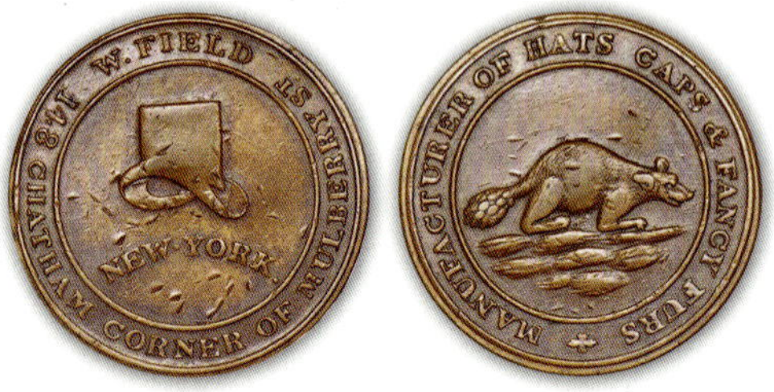

W-NY-500-10a • Rulau: "Low-249"; HT-269. R-7. 28 mm. Copper. The beaver seems to have the head of a dog and a tail resembling a pineapple! Seen in worn grades. Rulau lists HT-270, 39 mm, R-7. Several EF sales in the $4,000 to $7,000 range took place in the early 21st century. Steve Tanenbaum marked his "finest known."

W. Gibbs
New York, NY
Agriculturist
W-NY-520

William Gibbs, the father of John Gibbs of Belleville, New Jersey (see listing), came to America in the mid-1830s, after his son had become established. Low informs us that by the early 1840s William had a house at what was later Fifth Avenue on the corner of 71st Street. He raised vegetables and flowers. His token, with a motif reminiscent of a bouquet sou on the obverse and a cow and A FRIEND TO THE CONSTITUTION reverse, was minted by John Gibbs, likely in the late 1830s. These seem to have been made in limited numbers and to have circulated extensively. The rarity of this token is generally unappreciated. Most major collections have either lacked an example or have had a low-level example.

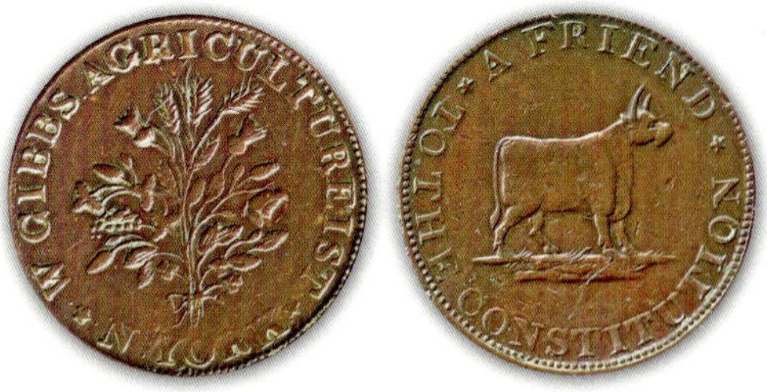

W-NY-520-10a • Low-151; HT-272. R-6. 27.6 mm. Copper. Typical grades are Fine and VF, often with problems. Any finer token is a rarity. The Ford token, cleaned VF, sold for $346. • Fine-12 $300; VF-20 $500; EF-40 $900.

Hallock & Bates
New York, NY
Dry goods
W-NY-540

Hallock & Bates seems to have been in business for just a short time and was succeeded by Hallock, Dolson & Bates (see next listing).

On February 2, 1835, notices were prepared and subsequently inserted in New York City and regional papers. This was published in the *Norwich Courier*, February 25, 1835:

Notice

> Charles Hallock, of the late firm of Hallock & Moore, and Gilbert Bates, of the late firm of Bates & Valentine, case dry goods dealers, have associated themselves for the prosecution of the same business under the firm of Hallock & Bates, No. 134 Pearl Street, corner of Burling Slip.
>
> The commodious store which they occupy affords them ample room for continuing to keep an extensive stock of staple and fancy dry goods comprising an assortment which, if equaled, will probably not be surpassed by any in the city. They respectfully invite country merchants generally to call and examine their

goods when they visit the city, and they will find the variety, &c. taken in connection with the prices at which they are offered render inducements to purchasers not usually found.

In late 1835 or early 1836, a man named John Williams opened his business as a merchant tailor at 45 John Street. In December 1836 he was arrested and was found to have obtained large quantities of goods under false pretenses. Hallock & Bates were included among a group of merchants defrauded by up to several thousand dollars.[81]

On January 4, 1837, the firm's principals were among many in the city who sent a petition to the Senate and House of Representatives pleading that a new Bank of the United States be established. This token was made by the Scovill Manufacturing Co.

The undated token of Hallock & Bates was not noticed by Low, but in 1898 was No. 414 in Benjamin Wright's "American Business Cards." Low did not make a careful study of undated early tokens and thus missed many opportunities.

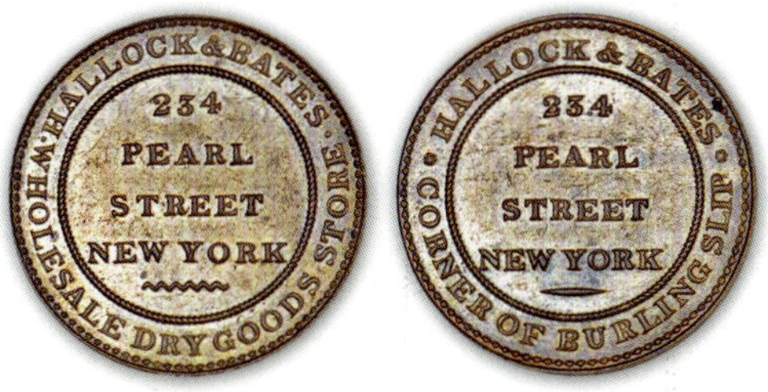

W-NY-540-10b • Rulau: "Low-251"; HT-275. R-4. 29.8 mm. Brass. Reeded edge. This is one of the most desired varieties in the entire Hard Times token series. Rulau lists a uniface brass striking as HT-276 and a copper striking as HT-A276, but notes "May not exist." VF and EF are the grades usually seen of this variety. AU and Mint State examples have been in some of the greatest collections. • VF-20 $40; EF-40 $75; AU-50 $150; MS-63 $350.

Hallock, Dolson & Bates
New York, NY
Dry goods
W-NY-560

The firm of Hallock, Dolson & Bates was located at 41 William Street, fifth door south of Wall Street, New York City. The partners were Charles Hallock, Henry W. Dolson, and Gilbert Bates. The firm was in the wholesale dry goods business as the successor to Hallock & Bates.

Brass tokens were issued, probably in a modest quantity. On the reverse die the street name is misspelled as WILLAM. There is no comma between Hallock and Dolson. The company was in business from at least 1836 to 1839, overlapping with the preceding company. Both firms signed the 1837 petition for a National Bank.

Similar to the preceding, this undated token was not noticed by Low. In 1898 it was No. 416 in Benjamin Wright's "American Business Cards." In Edward Cogan's Sale of January 13 and 14, 1878, this token, listed with a 40 William Street address (presumably an error), was called "very scarce." Both tokens were made by the Scovill Manufacturing Co.

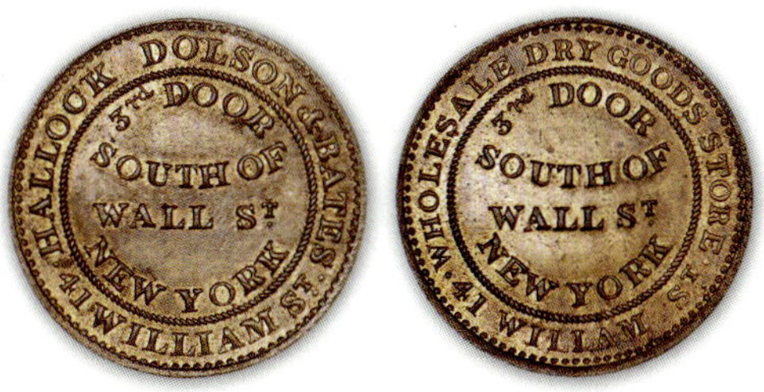

W-NY-560-10b • Rulau: "Low-253"; HT-277. R-5. 29.8 mm. Brass. VF and EF are typical grades. • VF-20 $75; EF-40 $150; AU-50 $250.

Dr. J.G. Hewett
New York, NY
Bone setter
W-NY-580

Dr. Jonas G. Hewitt, surgeon, whose token states he is a bone setter, was at 68 Prince Street, the address on the token, in the late 1830s. The reverse of the token lists multiple specialties in what today would be called orthopedics.

In 1836 he advertised that he was permanently established in New York City at 55 Franklin Street five doors from Broadway. "He has in his employment Dr. J. Sweet, bone setter, of Rhode Island, and one of the celebrated Sweets of Rhode Island and Lebanon, Connecticut." The notice included endorsements from his brother, Dr. S.C. Hewett, as well as W.W. Fairbanks, George Baker, and Captain Abner Hall, all of Providence, Rhode Island.[82]

On May 5, 1837, he announced:

> **Removal**
>
> Dr. J.G. Hewett, bone setter (brother of Dr. S.C. Hewett of Boston), informs the public that he has removed to No. 68 Prince St., near Niblo's Garden, where he has fitted more commodious rooms to enable him to accommodate the increased number of his patients. His attention if mostly confined to diseases of the limbs, such as dislocations, fractures, hip disease, sprains, contractions, deformities—to curvative of the spine, paralyzed limbs, rheumatism, white swelling, weakness of the limbs, nervous affections, &c., &c.
>
> His system of practice (originated by the late Dr. Job Sweet of Boston) is essentially different and distinct from that of ordinary surgery. For testimony as to the signal efficacy and success of this mode of treatment he will be happy to refer those who wish to consult him to patients who have been or are now under his care.
>
> Dr. Hewett will continue to attend at their own residences such persons who are unable or find it inconvenient to attend at his rooms.

The height of his practice seems to have been in 1837 and 1838, when he advertised extensively. By 1841 Hewett was at 141 Spring Street in the same practice. In 1845 he was at 111 MacDougal Street, one door above Bleecker Street, and was advertising Dr. J.G. Hewett's Improved Liniment for various pains of the limbs. In 1860 he was at 128 Greene Street receiving patients.

Restrikes from the dies were made in the 19th century. These are on thin planchets, show rust on the dies, and are seen in higher grades today.

W-NY-580-10a • Original (thick planchet) • Rulau: "Low-255"; HT-278. R-5. 29 mm. Copper. Thick planchet. Scarcer than the following and usually seen in circulated grades. • VF-20 $150; EF-40 $250; AU-50 $400.

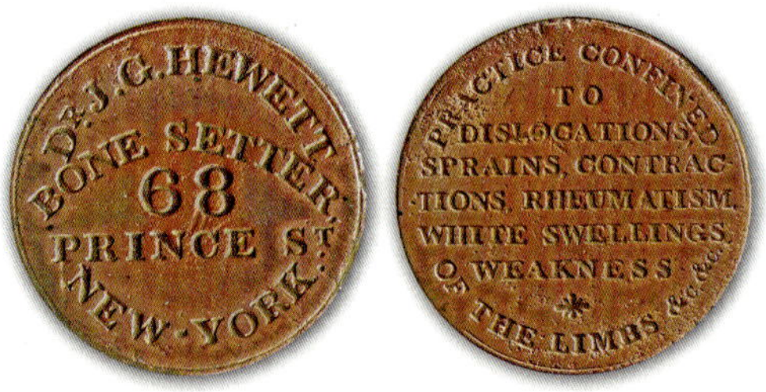

W-NY-580-10a • Restrike (thin planchet) • Rulau: "Low-256"; HT-279. R-4. 29 mm. Copper. Thin common in Mint State. Both dies extensively rusted. Restrike issue but hardly ever described as such, due to lack of knowledge. Americana Sale (SBG 2013) MS-66RB $1,116.25. • AU-50 $150; MS-60 $300; MS-63RB $500.

Benjamin Hooks
New York, NY
Hatter
W-NY-600

The small token of B. Hooks, 276 Broome Street, corner of Allen Street, was listed as

No. 76 by Bushnell in 1858. The obverse depicts the bust of Franklin wearing a fur hat, with BALE below, indicating that the die was made by Bale & Smith. Benjamin Hooks was listed as a hatter at this address in 1841 and 1842, some years after other tokens marked only BALE were issued. By the 1840s Bale was a partner in Bale & Smith. Perhaps the Franklin obverse was made earlier and was used by Bale as a stock die even after the formation of Bale & Smith. The small diameter, the striking of some in silver, and the existence of obverse-only strikes (without mentioning Hooks) suggest a numismatic production of uncertain date for these . In the opinion of the author, the *uniface* pieces of this merchant are die trials with no connection to a merchant, and thus there is no reason to designate *them* as Hard Times tokens. That said, the address and Hooks's dates of residence there would seem to indicate that copper pieces with Hook's name, HT-280, were circulated and can certainly be considered Hard Times tokens.

In a program he gave to the New York Numismatic Club on January 8, 1915, Thomas L. Elder commented, "A most interesting card, one of which I have with me this evening, was one by Bale, bearing a bust of Franklin, issued by B. Hooks, of Broome Street. This token is mentioned by Woodward as a great rarity."[83]

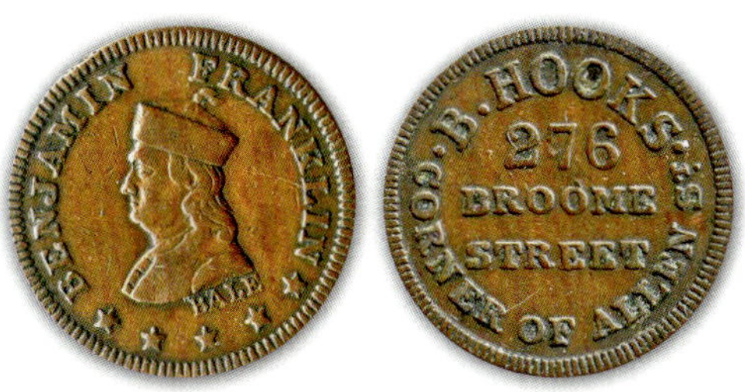

W-NY-600-10a • Rulau: "Low-360"; HT-280. R-7. 19 mm. Copper. XXVI in William Sumner Appleton's "Medals of Franklin" list in the *American Journal of Numismatics*, January 1873. Two were in the John J. Ford, Jr. Collection sale by Stack's Bowers Galleries, August 2013: AU-55 $6,452.50 and Fine-12 $1,527.50. The American Numismatic Society has one. HT-281, Appleton XXVII, has the obverse only with a blank reverse (and thus no mention of Hooks) and is counterstamped with the image of a dog. One sold in the 1855 J.W. Kline sale for $1.50. The August 2013 Ford sale had three: AU-58 $1,116.25, MS-62BN $1,527.50, and MS-62RB $3,055.

W-NY-600-10f • Rulau: "Low-361"; HT-280A. R-8. 19 mm. Silver. Not seen.

L.G. Irving / J.S. Pease & Co. New York, NY / St. Louis, MO

Hardware, etc.

W-NY-620

J.S. Pease & Co. was established in St. Louis and operated there for a long time. One of the partners, Lewis G. Irving, was in New York City. The curious token of the firm bears the Pease name on both sides and lists L.G. Irving separately on the obverse. It could just as well be attributed to St. Louis.

In 1837, in *The Western Address Directory*, J.S. Pease & Co. advertised as "importers and wholesale dealers in British and American hardware, cutlery, and heavy goods, No. 20 Main Street, St. Louis. J.S. Pease, L.G. Irving."

Although Irving is listed as a partner in St. Louis, he resided in New York City and conducted a business there. In 1827 he was at 70 Maiden Lane and resided at 335 Washington Street. In 1834 he was in the hardware business at 233 Pearl Street.

In a petition against Lewis G. Irving of Yonkers, New York, Merchant, "and as one of the late firm of J.S. Pease & Co.," he was declared bankrupt in an action of the United States District Court, City

Hall, New York, on February 11, 1843, at 11 a.m.[84] This places the token squarely in Low's definition of the Hard Times series. By 1845 Irving was representing the American Mutual Insurance Co. at No. 2, Merchants' Exchange and living on 19th Street near 3rd Avenue. Still later he was in the storage business.

There was one pair of dies made for this token. The obverse has around the border, HE WHO LIVES BY THE SWEAT OF HIS BROW SELDOM LIVES IN RUIN. This sentiment was later altered on the die by punching VA over RU (RUIN), changing it to HE WHO LIVES BY THE SWEAT OF HIS BROW SELDOM LIVES IN VAIN.

The nature of this token was not widely known at the time. As the piece is undated it was not attributed to the Hard Times series until Russell Rulau included it. He listed "two varieties" indicating there were two different obverse dies. The "VAIN" die state is a great rarity.

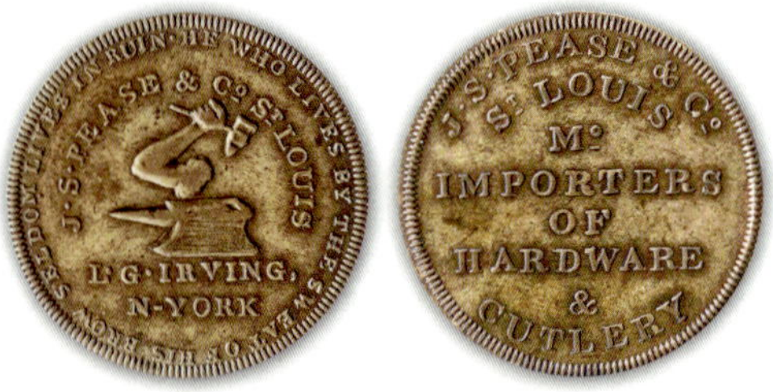

W-NY-620-10b • "Ruin" • Rulau: "Low-257"; HT-282. R-7. 27 mm. Brass. Many were silvered. In the Chapman Brothers sale of March 20, 1883, described in a slim catalog of 20 pages, an example brought $15.25, an extremely strong price for the time. The die state was not mentioned. Ford (SBG 2013) VF scratched $940, scratched Fine $705, silvered AU $4,406.25. The Dice-Hicks (Stack's 2008) silvered AU $5,462.50. Americana Sale (SBG 2013) AU-58 $4,406.25.

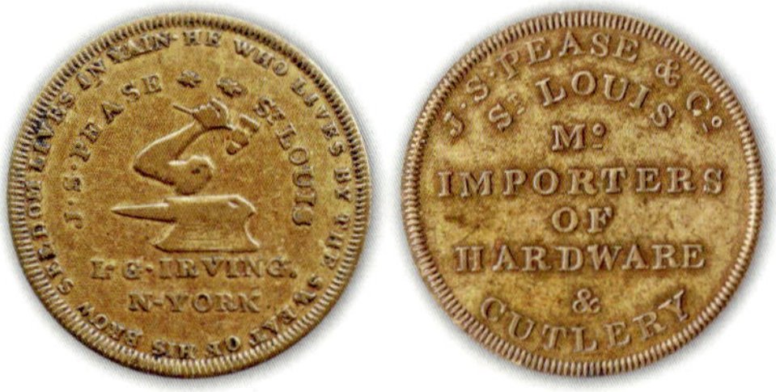

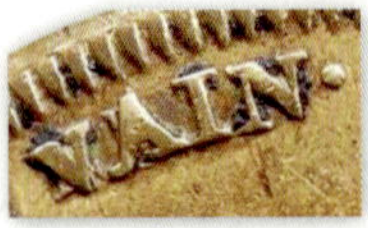

W-NY-620-11b • "Vain" • Low-Unlisted; HT-A282. R-8. 27 mm. Brass. Very few have ever been offered, resulting in little publicity being given to this variety. Ford (SBG 2013) VF-30 $822.50.

George A. Jarvis
New York, NY
Wine and tea
W-NY-640

George A. Jarvis, a partner in Peckwell & Jarvis at 150 Grand Street, went into business on his own in 1829. In 1830 he moved to 142 Grand Street at the corner of Elm Street, where he advertised wine and tea. In 1839 Jarvis moved to 81 Front Street, where he remained until at least 1858.

His token was issued in two varieties, one sharing a common 1837, Liberty Head, obverse die also used on Low-32, and the second using the Liberty Head die used on Low-30. These attractive pieces are easily enough acquired and have been very popular for a long time.

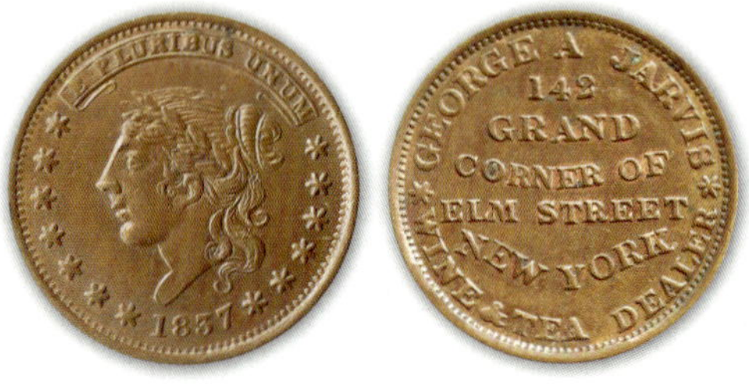

W-NY-640-10a • 2 stars at the reverse border • Low-122; HT-283. R-2. 28.5 mm.

Copper. Obverse die also used on Low-32. Although most grade VF or EF, AU and lower-range Mint State tokens are readily available. • VF-20 $30; EF-40 $50; AU-50 $75; MS-63 $250.

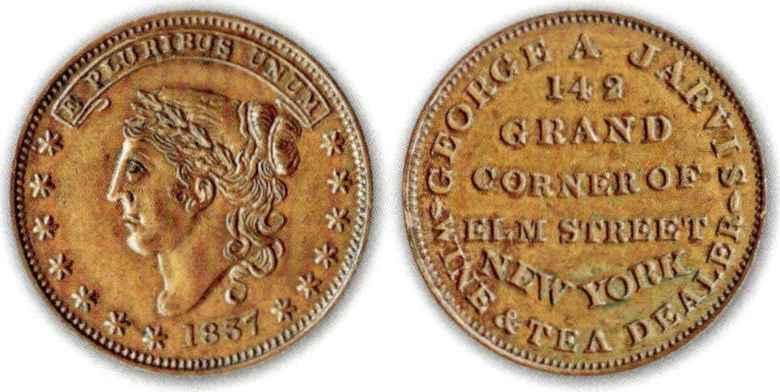

W-NY-640-15a • 2 leaves at the reverse border • Low-123; HT-284. R-1. 28.5 mm. Copper. Obverse die also used on Low-30. Same grading comment as preceding. • VF-20 $30; EF-40 $50; AU-50 $75; MS-63 $250.

W.G. Jones / Union Coal Yard
New York, NY
Coal dealer
W-NY-660

William G. Jones operated the Union Coal Yard and Coal Office from 1829 to 1838. The tokens were probably issued before 1837. By 1838 the trade name was Wm. Jones & Son. The Yard was at the foot of Chambers and Warren Streets, and the Coal Office, the address on the token, was at the corner of Chambers and Washington streets. He specialized in anthracite coal from Pennsylvania, much of it brought on barges on the Delaware & Hudson Canal or by sea on sloops, but coal imported from Liverpool and Newcastle was sold as well. In 1834 Lackawanna coal was priced at from $4.50 to $6.50 per ton, depending on the size of the pieces. Cleaned egg-size at $6.50 per ton was recommended for use in stoves. William G. Jones was born in 1787 and died on June 5, 1870.

W-NY-660-10a PE • Rulau: "Low-259"; HT-285. R-7. 26.5 mm. Copper. Plain edge. "LACKAWANA" misspelling on token. Presidential Coin and Antique Co. (1989) Good $165. Dice-Hicks (Stack's 2008) VG/Abt. Good ex Gilbert Steinberg $170. VG-8 brought $161 at the Stack's Bowers Galleries 2011 sale.

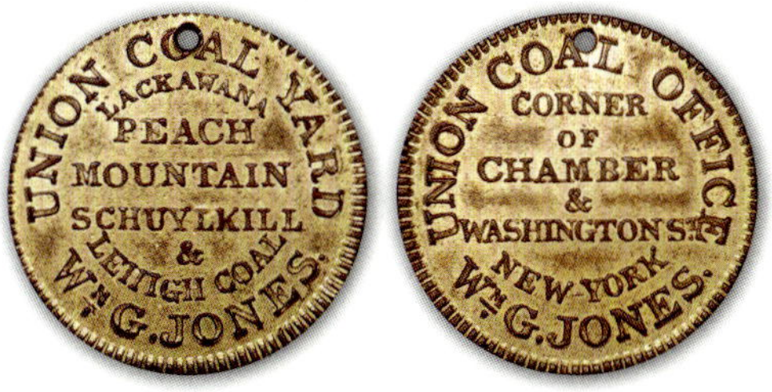

W-NY-660-10b RE • Rulau: "Low-260"; HT-285A. R-6. 26.5 mm. Brass. Reeded edge. Some brass pieces were gilt. Mostly seen in high grades, EF and AU. Hayden (2011) MS-63 $1,500. • EF-40 $600; AU-50 $800; MS-63 $1,250.

Henry Law
New York, NY
Baker
W-NY-680

Henry Law was a baker at 187 Canal Street from circa 1834 to 1837.

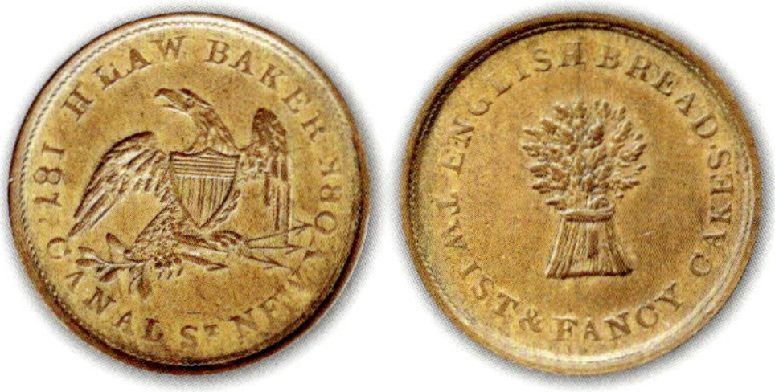

W-NY-680-10a • Rulau: "Low-261"; HT-286. R-2. 28.5 mm. Copper. Most are well worn, but a few AU and lower-range Mint State pieces have appeared in sales. • VF-20 $90; EF-40 $200; AU-50 $450; MS-63 $1,000.

Leverett & Thomas
New York, NY
Hardware, cutlery
W-NY-700

The company of Leverett & Thomas imported hardware and other goods and acted as an agent for the Scovill Manufacturing Co. of Waterbury. The depot of Josiah H. Leverett and Edward I. Thomas was at 235 Pearl Street. On February 18, 1833, they sent this advertisement to the city papers:

> **Leverett & Thomas**
>
> Importers of hardware and cutlery, No. 235 Pearl Street, New York, have been receiving, by recent arrivals from Europe, and are now opening an entire new stock comprising a general assortment of hardware, viz.—
>
> Knives and forks, pocket and pen-knives, scissors, razors, mill, cross-cut and circular saws, edge tools, anvils, vices, traces, steel nails, hollow ware, &c., &c. including every variety of foreign and domestic hardware. Also an assortment of best London emery.
>
> This stock of goods has been selected more particularly for the Eastern market, and at prices unusually low, owing to the unprecedented small demand for goods the past year. Those visiting New York for the purpose of purchasing goods will do well to call and examine before they purchase.

In late 1835, the firm moved to its "new store" at 13 Broad Street and opened for business there on January 1, 1836. On January 2, 1836, it advertised, "We remove our present stock of goods from No. 235 Pearl St. and close them off at reduced prices." In 1838 the firm gained a diploma at the annual Fair of the American Institute for "good specimens of brads and tacks."

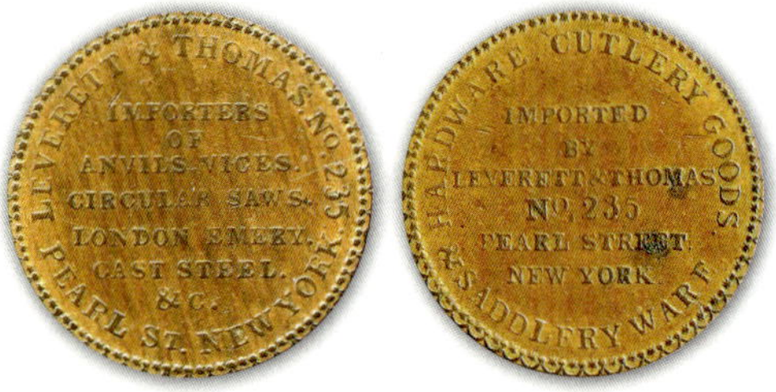

W-NY-700-10a • Rulau: "Low-262"; HT-287. R-5. 28.5 mm. Copper. The borders of the dies are unusual with dots, stars, and arabesques. VISES is misspelled VICES. HT-387A in brass is unconfirmed. Fine and VF are typical grades. • VF-20 $175; EF-40 $300; AU-50 $600.

Robert Lovett Sr. / Lovett Seal Engravers
New York, NY
Engraver
W-NY-720

Robert Lovett Sr., one of America's best known die engravers, was at 67 Maiden Lane in 1833 and 1834, when he issued the token studied here. Lovett was the father of three die sinkers who were prominent in their own right: George Hampden Lovett, Robert Lovett Jr., and John D. Lovett.

Robert Lovett was born on March 19, 1796, on Cherry Street in New York City.[85] His family moved into the City Hotel in 1802. In 1807 his mother and his sister Harriet died of yellow fever. His father died in 1809, and Robert moved in with his older brother, John. In 1813 he apprenticed to Thomas Brown, a seal engraver.[86] In the next year he married Anna Doubleday. In the War of 1812 he served as a captain in Shatterton's Company, New York Militia.

In 1816 he relocated to Philadelphia, where he was an engraver of metal and stone. There the couple had several children: Robert Jr. (1818), George (date unknown, died in infancy), John Doubleday (1819), Thomas (1820), Anna (date unknown), Maria Augusta (date unknown), and George Hampden (1824). In 1824 the family moved back to New York City and set up a shop at 259 Broadway. His family lived at 414 Broome St., and later at 63 Church St. In 1829 and 1830, he was listed at 297 Broadway. In 1831 he was at 8 Grove St. and by 1832, had relocated to 67 Maiden Lane, the address on the token. He lived at 362 Hudson St. at the time.

In 1835 he lived at 43 Second St. In 1836, continuing into the 1840s, his shop was at 183 Broadway. In 1847 he served as a manager of the American Institute. In later years he was at several addresses. Robert Lovett died in New York City on December 31, 1874, six hours after the death of his wife. The two were buried in Greenwood Cemetery in Brooklyn.

Lovett's tokens are quite elusive. They have always been in strong demand, not only as Hard Times tokens, but also as part of the class of tokens in which die sinkers advertised their own work. One token appearing in Woodward's 1884 sale of the Levick Collection was described as:

> Lot 318. Lovett, 67 Maiden Lane. Coat of arms, seals, etc.; rev., ship at a wharf; brass, very fine and the only one I have seen. [$3]

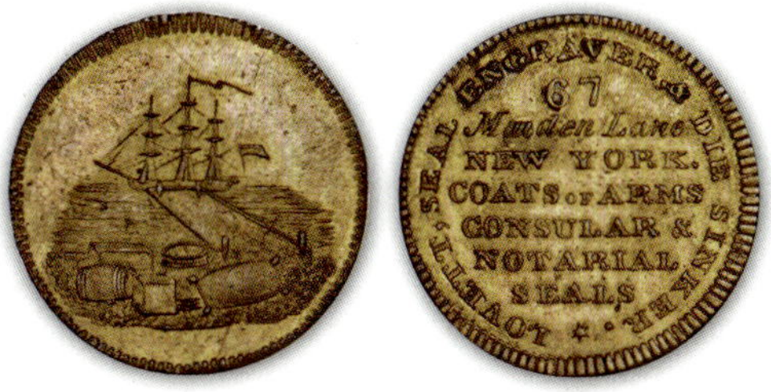

W-NY-720-10b • Rulau: "Low-263"; HT-288. R-7. 25 mm. Brass. The same obverse die was used for the Collins Ready Made Linen & Fancy Store token, W-NY-340. Michael Brand Zeddies (B&M 1990) AU $3,900. Presidential Coin and Antique Co. Sale 73 (2004) EF $5,520. (Stack's 2008) AU $16,100. Ford (SBG 2013) MS-61 $10,575.

S. Maycock & Co.
New York, NY
Pencil case manufacturer
W-NY-740

S. Maycock & Co., Everpointed Pencil case manufacturer, was operated by Samuel Maycock and John Hague at 35 City Hall Place, as lettered on its tokens.

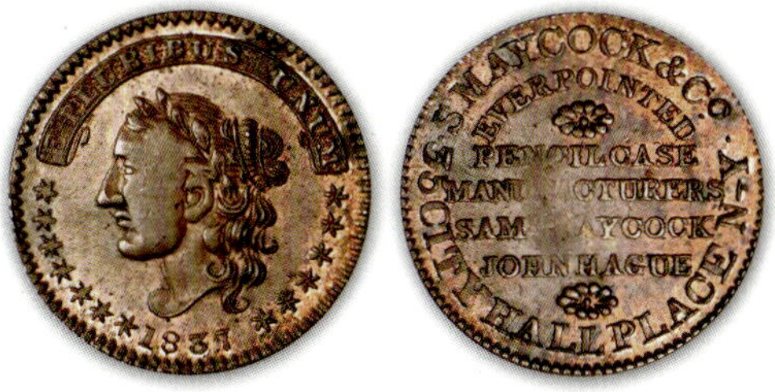

W-NY-740-10a • **Maycock / 1837 Liberty Head** • Low-125; HT-289. R-2. 28.5 mm. Copper. This obverse was also used on Low-29. The relief of the Liberty Head is such that the higher parts are always lightly struck, as is the corresponding opposite area of the reverse. Most of the finer cabinets have an AU or Mint State example. • VF-20 $40; EF-40 $70; AU-50 $150; MS-63 $350.

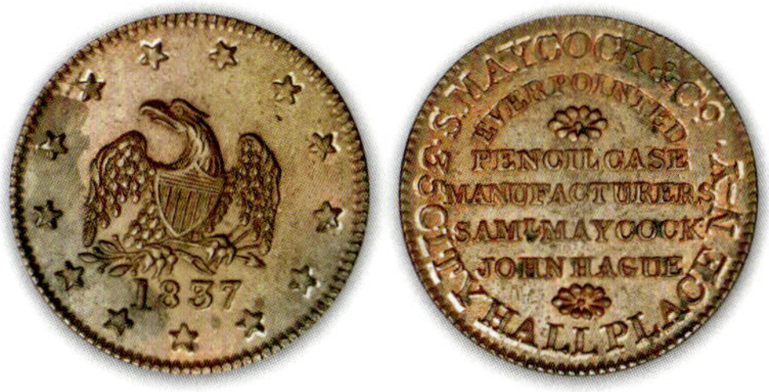

W-NY-740-15a • **Maycock / 1837 Eagle** • Low-126; HT-290. R-1. 27.7 mm. Copper. This obverse was also used on Low-113. Most are VF and EF, but AU and Mint State tokens are easily enough found. • VF-20 $30; EF-40 $55; AU-50 $110; MS-63 $250.

Merchants' Exchange (old)
New York, NY
Exchange and offices
W-NY-760

The Merchants' Exchange was a center of commerce from its opening in 1827 until its destruction by fire in 1835. Its demise was memorialized on three varieties of Hard Times tokens, each sharing a common obverse with a different reverse.

New York As It Is, 1833 edition, described the structure:

> **The Merchants Exchange**
>
> The Merchants Exchange extends southward 150 feet to Exchange-street. It has a front on Wall-street of 115 feet, and is three stories high, exclusive of the basement, which is considerably elevated. Its southwest front in Exchange-street, is 114 feet long, and three stories high, including the basement, which is only one step above the pavement. The Wall Street front is the principal one, and is built entirely of white Westchester marble. The first and second stories are of the Ionic order, from the temple of Minerva Polias, at Priene, in Ionia. A recessed elliptical portico of about 40 feet wide has been introduced in front, with great convenience and beauty. A screen of four columns and two antx [*sic*], each column being thirty feet high, and three feet four inches in diameter above the base, composed of a single block of marble, extends across the front of the portico, nearly in a line with the front of the building. The columns support an entablature of about six feet in height, upon which rests the third story, making a height of about 60 feet from the ground. On each side of the portico is a passage through the basement story to the Post Office and Exchange Street.
>
> The principal entrance to the Exchange Room is by a flight of nine or ten marble steps, with a pedestal at each end. On ascending to the portico, three doors open to the vestibule in front, while one on either hand opens into Insurance Offices, &c. The vestibule is of the Ionic order,

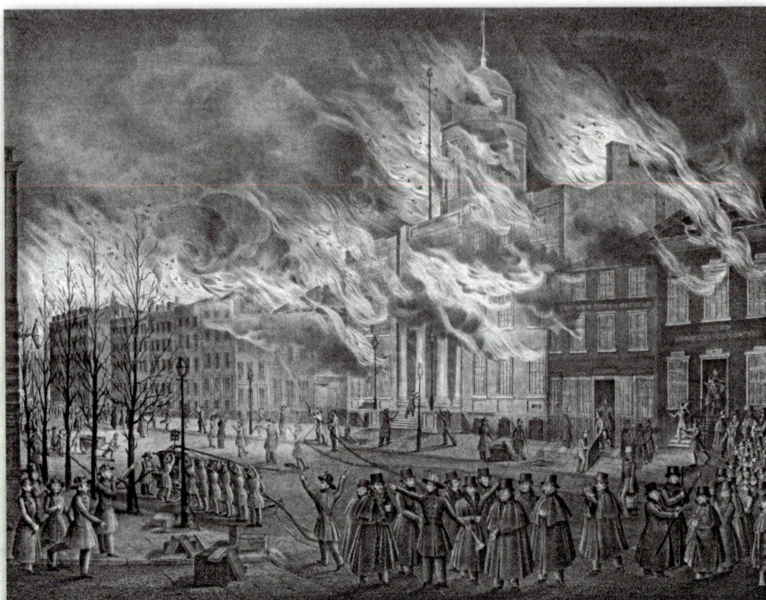

The Merchants' Exchange in flames.

from the little Ionic temple of Illyssus. The Exchange Room is 85 feet long, 55 wide, and 45 high; adjacent to it are the offices of the *Daily Advertiser* and the *Atlas* to which latter establishment is attached an extensive Reading Room of newspapers. The office of the *Journal of Commerce* is in the basement. In the rear of the Exchange Room is a place for auction sales, and in the second story are rooms for the Board of Brokers, and the Chamber of Commerce. The building was begun on the first of April 1825, and completed in July 1827. The plan was wholly that of Martin Euclid Thompson, the architect of the edifice.

In the evening of December 16, 1835, fire broke out in a warehouse at the corner of Pearl and Exchange streets. It expanded rapidly, could not be checked, and soon included the south side of Wall Street. Eventually, about 650 buildings were destroyed. The Merchants' Exchange caught fire about three in the morning, and the tower fell about a half hour later. Many businesses were totally destroyed, including Rawdon, Wright, Hatch & Edson, America's leading bank-note printer.

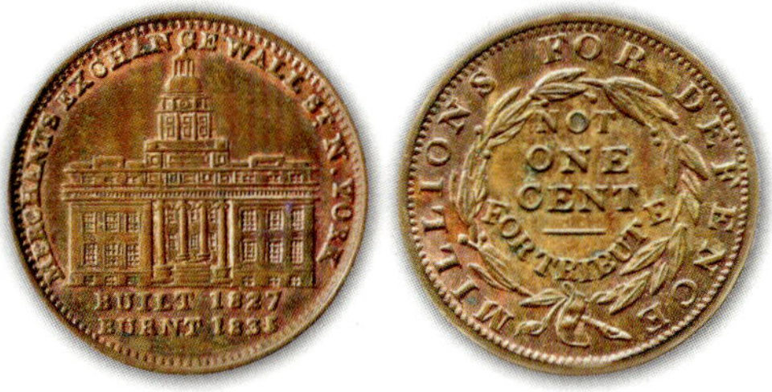

W-NY-760-10a • 6 berries within wreath, 4 outside, dash under CENT • Low-95; HT-291. R-1. 28.1 mm. Copper. One of these was used as an undertype or planchet to strike a token issued by A. Loomis of Cleveland, Ohio (see listing). Readily available in low Mint State grades. • VF-20 $25; EF-40 $40; AU-50 $65; MS-63 $225.

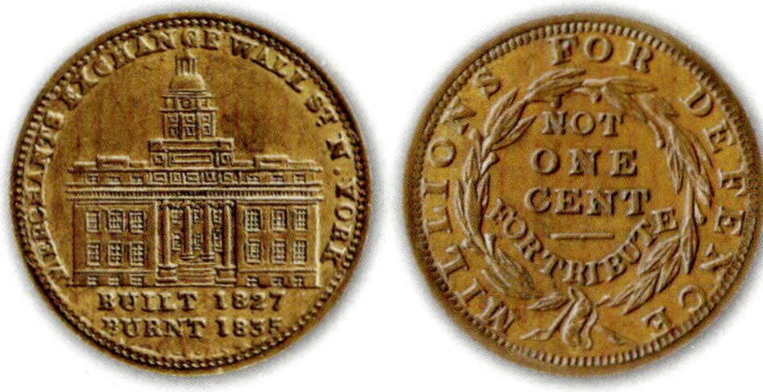

W-NY-760-15a • 5 berries within wreath, 3 outside, dash under CENT • Low-96; HT-292. R-6. 28.1 mm. Copper. This has been a well-known rarity for a long time. Probably about 20 or so are known today. Typical grades are VF and EF, although some AU and lower-range Mint State pieces exist. It is particularly popular as the key to this set of three tokens, with the other two being common. • VF-20 $1,500; EF-40 $2,250; AU-50 $3,500.

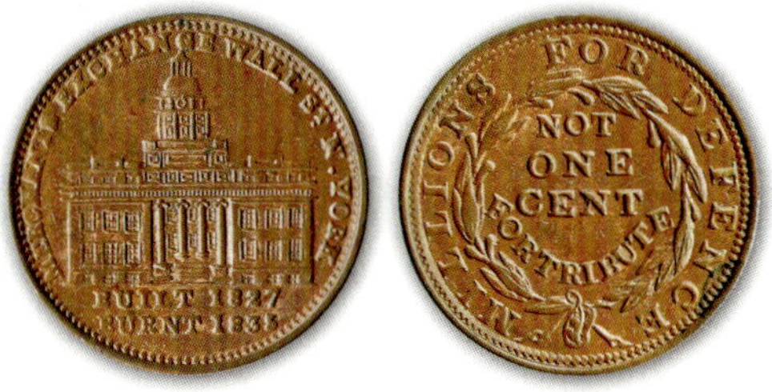

W-NY-760-20a • Dash under CENT • Low-97; HT-293. R-1. 28.1 mm. Copper. This was the final use of the obverse die. Some of the letters are filled, as at the end of MERCHANTS. AU and lower Mint State grade examples are easily found. Some South American MITAD tokens were struck over these. • VF-20 $20; EF-40 $35; AU-50 $55; MS-63 $200.

Merchants' Exchange (new)
New York, NY
Exchange and offices
W-NY-780

The new Merchants' Exchange, 55 Wall Street, occupying the entire block between William and Hanover streets, was designed in the Greek Revival style by Boston architect Isaiah Rogers in 1836, and it was opened in 1842. The façade was dominated by 12 large Ionic columns, and the top was domed over a rotunda. Within there were three floors, which housed various businesses, including in finance, commodities, shipping, auctioneering, and sales.

The New York Custom House relocated there in 1862. In 1899 the structure was remodeled and extended in height by the National City Bank. In January 2000. the building was reopened as the Regent Wall Street Hotel, but it was later converted into condominiums.

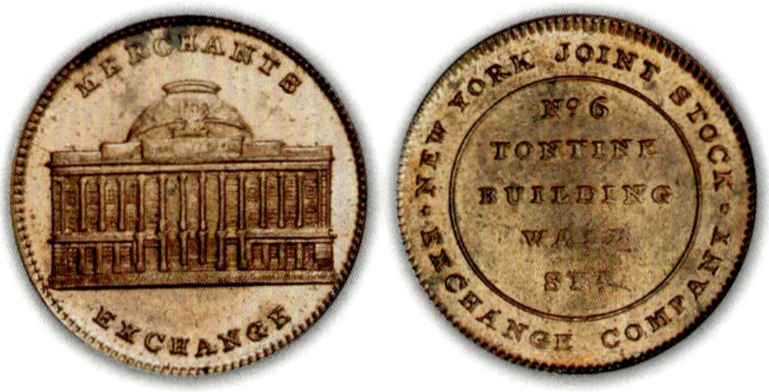

W-NY-780-20a • Low-98; HT-294. R-1. 28.8 mm. Copper. Often slightly weakly struck at the center. Mint State examples are easily found. • VF-20 $20; EF-40 $35; AU-50 $55; MS-63 $200.

James G. Moffett
New York, NY
Metal products
W-NY-800

James G. Moffet's tokens advertise his business as a brass founder and worker in other metal. The token, describing his business as being located at 121 Prince Street in New York City, was issued in the 1830s. He lived at 156 Spring St. He rolled sheet brass using a sweep powered by yoked oxen. He also plated metal, made railings, and fashioned other products. Russell Rulau states he was a minter of tokens, including his own and those of S. Maycock & Co., as well as Henry Crossman. If this is so, he was probably associated with still more tokens with a Liberty Head motif.

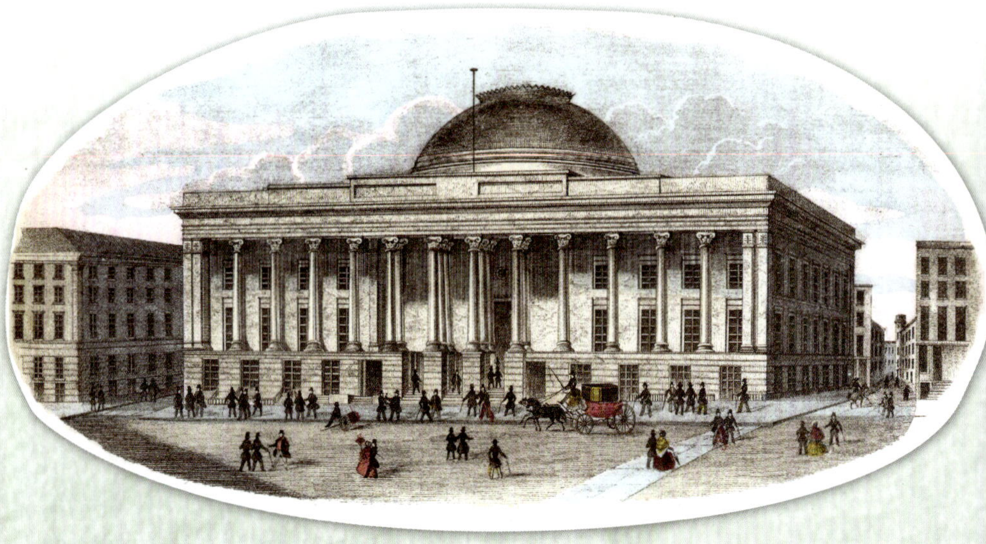

The new Merchants' Exchange.

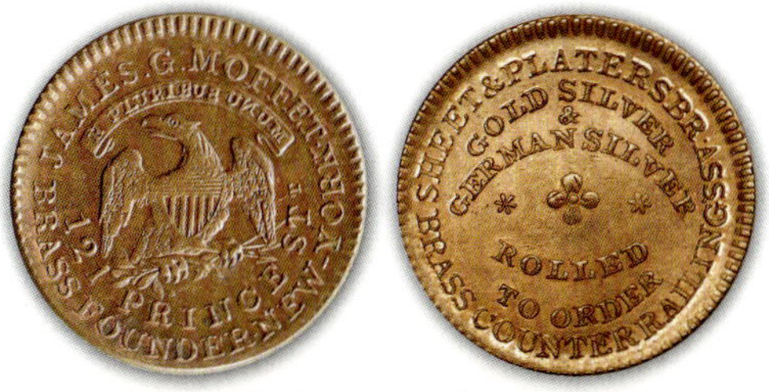

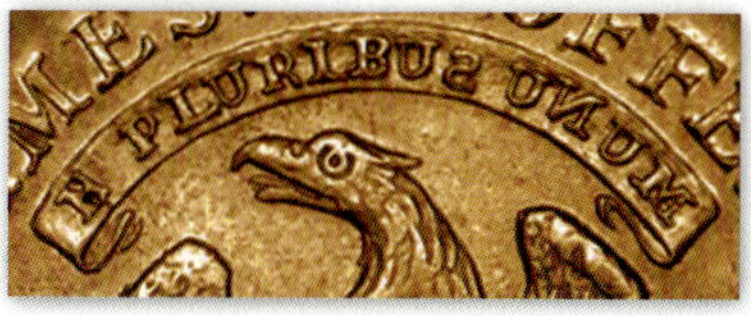

W-NY-800-10a • PLURIBUS • Rulau: "Low-321"; HT-295. R-2. 28.5 mm. Copper. Backward S in PLURIBUS, backward N in UNUM. Quatrefoil at center of the reverse, a five-pointed star to each side. Although most are in lower grades, AU and lower-range Mint State coins are available. • VF-20 $35; EF-40 $75; AU-50 $125; MS-63 $250.

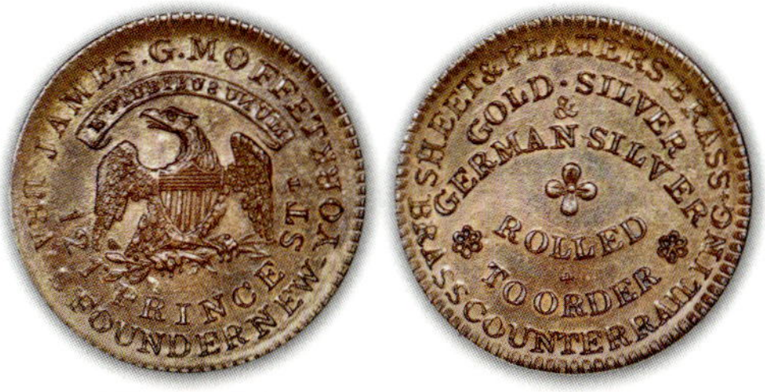

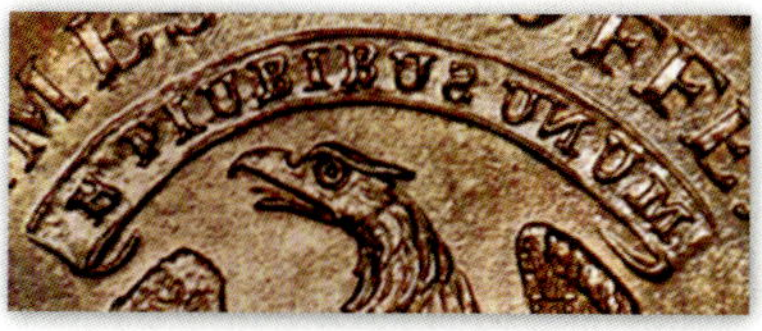

W-NY-800-15a • PLUBIBUS • Rulau: "Low-323"; HT-297. R-2. 28.5 mm. Copper. Backward S in PLUBIBUS (and also misspelled), backward N in UNUM. Different die from the preceding. Quatrefoil at center of the reverse, rosette to each side of TO ORDER. Most are VF or EF. Scarce at higher levels. • VF-20 $45; EF-40 $125; AU-50 $225; MS-63 $450.

Motts
New York, NY
Jewelry, clocks, etc.
W-NY-820

For many years the 1789-dated Mott token, as it is called, with Mott singular instead of Motts, has been attributed as a very early American store card. In 1859 Charles I. Bushnell, in *An Historical Account of the First Three Business Tokens Issued in the City of New York*, included it as one of three tokens of that genre, the other two being the Talbot, Allum & Lee issues of 1794 and 1795. This earned the Mott token a seemingly secure niche as one of just a handful of pre-1800 American store cards.

The obverse shows a regulator-type shelf clock with an eagle at the top of the crest. Around the border is this inscription starting at the center left: MOTTS, N.Y. IMPORTERS, DEALERS, MANUFACTURERS, inside of which it continues with OF GOLD & SILVER WARES. There are crude dentils around the outside of the border on both sides.

The reverse has a perched eagle at the center, copied from John Reich's motif, first used on the $5 half eagle of 1807. Above is the date 1789. Around the border is a series of words separated by commas. Starting at the top: WATCHES, JEWELRY, SILVER WARE, CHRONOMETERS, CLOCKS.

The name Motts, without a possessive, indicated a business with more than one Mott. Bushnell said this relating to the history of the family:

> The firm of Motts was composed of William and John Mott, and their place of business was at No. 240 Water street—a location at which they continued for a number of years,

> and which was at the time a most fashionable business part of the city. Some of the immediate descendants of the firm were engaged in the same pursuit until within a few years past.
>
> The firm of Motts was well known in its day and generation. Their store was the resort of the rich and the great, and of the gay belles and beaux of the time. The learned judge who wished a pair of spectacles to aid his failing sight, the lovely maid who craved a splendid ring to deck her tapering hand, their wants supplied with hearts' content from Motts' extensive stock. More than one venerable dame now living can yet produce, in the shape of a watch of somewhat antique style, but still faithful to its early mission, her bridal gift, purchased in her days of youth and beauty from their well-furnished establishment.
>
> Many a venerable time-piece, solid and substantial as the maker, and bearing upon the face the name of "Motts," has outlived a host of modern abortions, and still graces the dining rooms of some of our oldest and most respectable, though not, perhaps, our most fashionable citizens, and still chronicles the days of man, and re-echoes still, the steps of passing time.

Quite a few years ago I questioned the 1789 date on the token, suggesting it might have commemorated the year of founding for the Motts business or some other event in family history. The eagle on the reverse is a close copy of that which John Reich created for use on the 1807 $5 gold piece. The rustic nature of the dies suggested a production in the Hard Times era, much like the tokens of William Rutter (Boston) and Bucklin's (Troy and West Troy, New York), but not from the hands that made them.

Others also pondered the anachronism, including Eric P. Newman and Dr. Angel Pietri. Some years later, Russell Rulau and Wesley Cox spent two months studying the tokens and their characteristics. In "The 1789 Mott Token Likely from the 1830s," *Numismatic News*, July 23, 2002, Rulau summarized his thoughts after giving many paragraphs of detail:

> Our conclusion: Robert Lovett Sr. of New York City struck the Mott tokens, most likely in the years 1833–1834 but possibly a bit later. . . .
>
> The famous clock and jewelry firm, Mott's of New York—as it was always known—was probably founded in 1795 by Jeremiah Mott, but it was headed 1796–1836 by Jordan Mott. . . . Jordan Mott was part of Mitchell & Mott 1797–1801 at 247 Pearl Street, yet he had separate watchmaker directory listings along at 104 Gold Street in 1798; "near Alms House" 1799–1800; 39 Frankfort Street 1802–1803. Mott & Morrell was organized in 1804 at 247 Pearl Street, but William Morrell died in 1808. Mott's of New York then appears in directories every year 1809–1831, when it became J.S. & J. Mott (James Striker and Jordan Mott, son and father) but this partnership ended in 1834. The firm then became J.H. & J. Mott 1835–1840, but Jordan Mott retired in 1836 and died in 1840. . . . Mott's was not ready to abandon its position as New York's premier jeweler, a precursor to the later Tiffany's of New York. Mott Brothers were listed until 1850, reigning supreme for some 55 years. . . .
>
> Enter Robert Lovett Sr. In the process of matching letter-for-letter die punches, Wesley Cox discovered that Robert Lovett Sr. had also cut the dies for several Hard Times tokens honoring Andrew Jackson.

These are HT-5, 6, 7, 8 and 14 (or, if you prefer, Low-3, 4, 5, 5A and 6). In addition, Lovett cut his own store card (HT-288) and that of William Collins (HT-241). Several students of medallic art consider Robert Lovett Sr., who began working in New York in 1824, a caricaturist rather than an artist when it came to portraying human features. His ships and other inanimate objects are just fine, but his treatment of Jackson on HT-7 exhibits his lack of portraiture talent. . . .

One of the illustrations accompanying this article shows that the "6" punch in "6" Maiden Lane" on Lovett Sr.'s store card, HT-288, was merely inverted to create the "9" in the 1789 Mott token. The 10-times-actual size photos show this; any small differences are probably due to die wear. Also the 7s in both "67" and "1789" are very alike. To illustrate Cox's point that Robert Lovett Sr. cut HT-7 (1833) and the Mott copper, he numbered each letter on each side of each token, then used horizontal comparison lines at 10-times size to demonstrate, graphically, the letter-punch similarities. . . .

The above article in full form, plus a few other comments, was repeated in the fourth (2004) edition of the *Standard Catalog of United States Tokens 1700–1900.*

Russell Rulau's article parallels in some way my thoughts, except that I feel that the die work on the token, with its amateurish dentils and other crude characteristics, is too unaccomplished to have been done by Robert Lovett Sr. Common sets of letter punches were used by various jewelers and engravers, which could explain the superficial similarity to Lovett's work.

In his 1884 sale of the Levick Collection, W. Elliot Woodward offered this remarkable group:

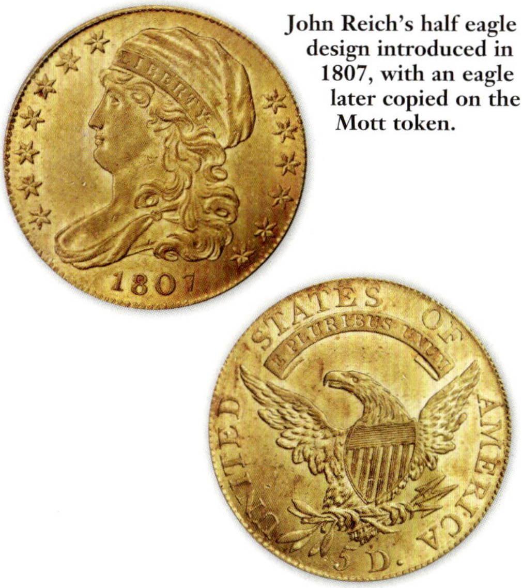

John Reich's half eagle design introduced in 1807, with an eagle later copied on the Mott token.

Lot 326. Mott's token, 1789. A set comprising probably all known varieties, originals; restrikes, thick and thin planchets, engrailed and lettered; all in copper, and some of the originals are nearly proof; planchets vary two or three numbers in size. It is probably that a duplicate set can be produced. 8 pieces. [$80]

Many thousands must have been struck, considering that hundreds survive today. Die states vary from perfect to bulged with a massive break obliterating part of the clock. Weights and planchet thickness varies. Perhaps they were struck on the Mott premises over a period of time. Who knows?

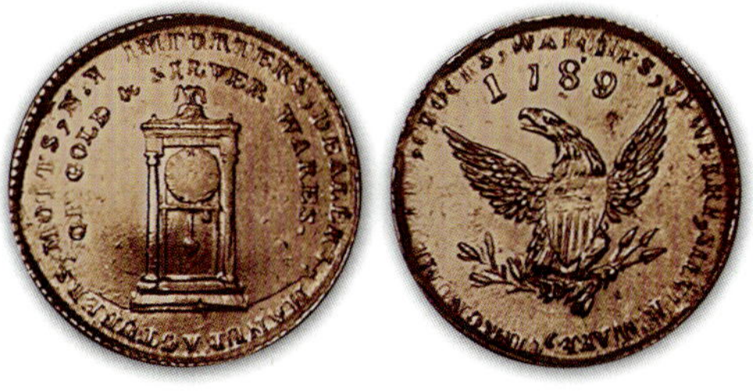

W-NY-820-10a • Low-Unlisted; Listed by Rulau in 2004 in the *Standard Catalog of United States Tokens 1700–1900* under early

American tokens (not Hard Times tokens), as Rulau NY-610 to 613 in several die states, etc. R-4. 28 mm. Copper. Typical grades are VF and EF with irregular surfaces. • VF-20 $400; EF-40 $550; AU-50 $900.

New York & Harlaem Railroad Co.
New York, NY
Railroad
W-NY-840

Among the earliest of American transportation tokens are the little octagonal pieces bearing on one side a coach on wheels and on the other an inscription. These trace their origin to the New York & Harlem Railroad, or *Harlaem* as it is spelled on the token. More properly it could be called a street railway. The railroad was not powered by a steam engine, at least not at first, but by horsepower in the literal sense of the word. Each coach was drawn by two trusty steeds hitched to the front. Running on steel rails, it was certainly the first such line in New York state and one of the earliest in America, possibly the world.

The enterprise was incorporated as the New-York & Harlem Railroad on April 25, 1831, to link Harlem, a fine farming and residential district, with the lower reaches of Manhattan. Among the incorporators was John Mason, the president of the Chemical Bank and a well-to-do land owner, whose name was lettered on the side of the first car put into service. Mordecai Noah, a journalist, playwright, and diplomat was another principal. Others involved were engaged in such pursuits as law and sales, and some owned land in Harlem and stood to benefit from the connection.

A route was chosen along the eastern side of Manhattan—it was thought that the rise of steamship commerce on the Hudson River on the western side might present unfavorable competition. It was planned that in Harlem passengers could connect with the New York & Albany Railroad to go farther north, but this arrangement never materialized.

The coaches were designed by John Stephenson. Ground breaking took place on February 23, 1832, in the Murray Hill district near 4th Avenue. Progress was made in stages. The first section was

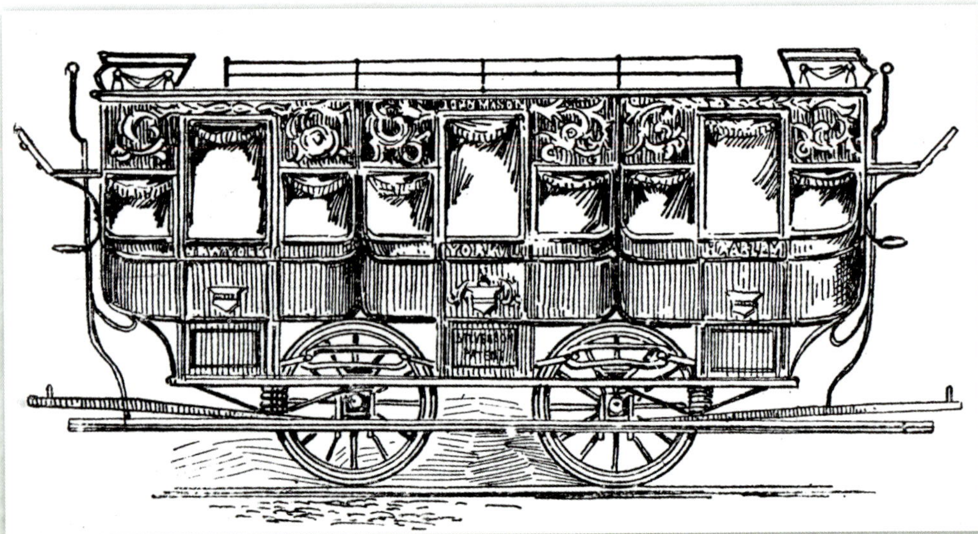

The earliest type of New York & Harlem Railroad car.

opened on November 26, 1832, and carried passengers along the Bowery—the main area in the city for entertainment—from Prince Street north to 14th Street. Construction proceeded apace, and on June 10, 1833, it was opened to the north along Fourth Avenue up to 32nd Street. On May 9, 1834, the line was opened north to Yorkville, including through the Murray Hill Tunnel. Next came development continuing on Fourth Avenue to Harlem, including via the Yorkville Tunnel, opened to passengers on October 27, 1837. In that year, steam locomotives burning wood were introduced, but these were limited to operating only on the northern section of the tracks above 23rd Street, as they were forbidden in the Manhattan commercial district. Then followed the opening on May 4, 1839, of tracks farther south through the Bowery, Broome Street, to City Hall and Park Row.

Tokens good for a ride were ordered from Bale & Smith, who signed them B & S on the obverse.

The expansion of the railroad was not without difficulty, including lawsuits. Not everyone agreed that it was a good idea to have coaches on rails running along routes traveled by pedestrians and other horse-drawn vehicles. This was overcome in part by recessing the rails slightly below the level of the street, so as not to interfere with other traffic. In later years the line was blended into others. In one form or another the Harlem name was used for decades afterward.

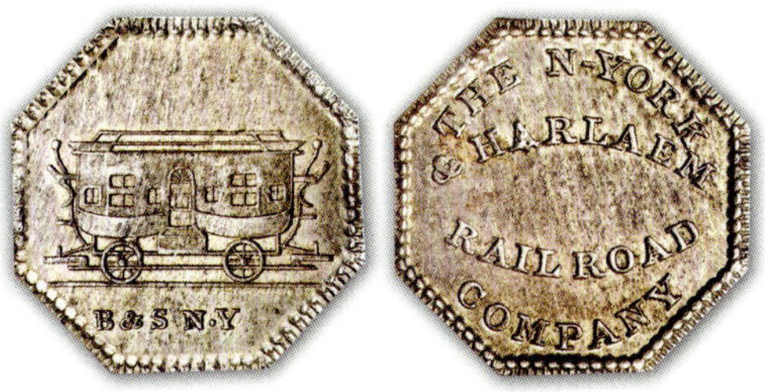

W-NY-840-10j • Rulau: "Low-370"; HT-298. R-5. 18 mm octagonal. German silver. Nearly all known today are VF or EF.

These tokens seem to have been used intensely. Quietly since circa 1950 John J. Ford Jr. bought every one he could find, similar to the Atwood's Railroad Hotel tokens listed above. When tokens in his estate were examined in a shipment received from his heirs in 2013, a hoard of 14 pieces was found! These were auctioned by Stack's Bowers Galleries at the American Numismatic Association Convention in August of that year, lots 2281 to 2294, graded by NGC as MS-64 (2), MS-62, AU-55 (2), AU-58 (2), AU-53, AU-50 (2), AU (2; damaged), EF-45, VF-20. Most were weakly struck at the obverse center. • VF-20 $800; EF-40 $1,100; AU-50 $1,350; MS-63 $2,500.

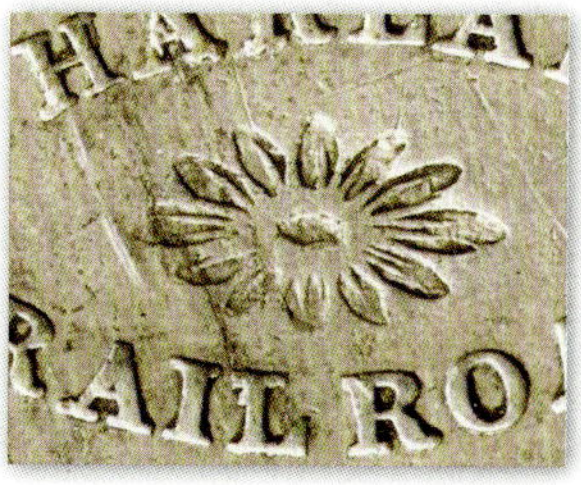

W-NY-840-10j • Counterstamped with a rosette • Rulau: "Low-371"; HT-299. R-6. 18 mm octagonal. German silver.

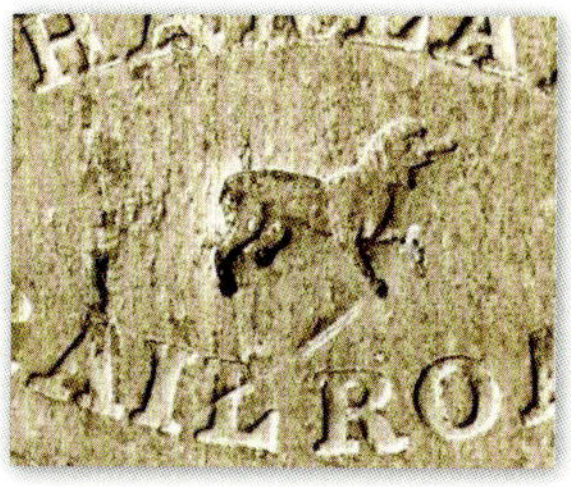

W-NY-840-10j • Counterstamped with a dog • Rulau: "Low-372"; HT-300. R-8. 18 mm octagonal. German silver. Ford (SBG 2013) EF-45 $2,232.50.

W-NY-840-10a • Counterstamped with a leaf • Low-Unlisted; HT-301. R-7. 18 mm octagonal. Copper. Sometimes called a feather. Americana Sale (SBG 2013) AU-55 granular $1,645.

W-NY-840-10e • Counterstamped with a leaf • Low-Unlisted; HT-A300. R-8. 18 mm octagonal. White metal.

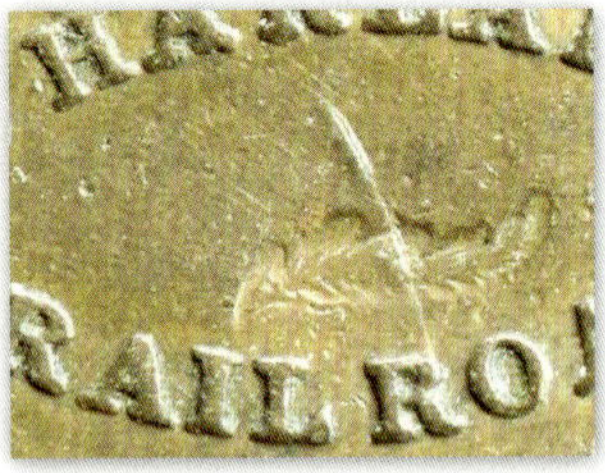

W-NY-840-10j • Counterstamped with a leaf • Low-Unlisted; HT-Unlisted. R-8. 18 mm octagonal. German silver. Dice-Hicks (Stack's 2008) VF $748, AU $1,955. Ford (SBG 2013) EF-45 $1,293, MS-62 $2,703.

Edwin Parmele
New York, NY
Bowling saloon
W-NY-860

Edwin Parmele kept a tavern and a bowling hall at 340 Pearl St., corner of Dover St., circa 1834 to 1839. He is QUITE COMFORTABLE holding his wine glass—one of the most appealing and sought-after tokens in the Hard Times series. In 1842 he was at the Bowery Cottage, 298 Bowery.

At the Bangs, Merwin & Co. sale of the Benjamin Haines Collection, January 19 to 23, 1863, lot 1658 was described as:

> Edwin Parmele, 340 Pearl St., N.Y. Obv. man holding up a glass of ale, "Quite comfortable." This is the only specimen known to collectors. Brass, fine, size 11.

In his 1884 sale of the Levick Collection, W. Elliot Woodward offered this without notation regarding its pedigree:

> Lot 344. Parmele, Edwin, 340 Pearl St. Bust of a jolly old fellow in ruffled shirt, with a glass of wine in his hand, "quite comfortable"; brass, fine, *excessively rare*, perhaps unique. Plate. [$5.75]

In January 1898, when Lyman H. Low auctioned the Benjamin Betts Collection, he described an example as:

> A rare and unique token is that issued by Edwin Parmele, keeper of a bowling saloon at 340 Pearl Street, in the period of 1834–8. On the face are stamped the name and address, and on the reverse a picture of a jolly toper with the words "Quite Comfortable."

Low must have forgotten this when he did his *Hard Times Token* text shortly thereafter.

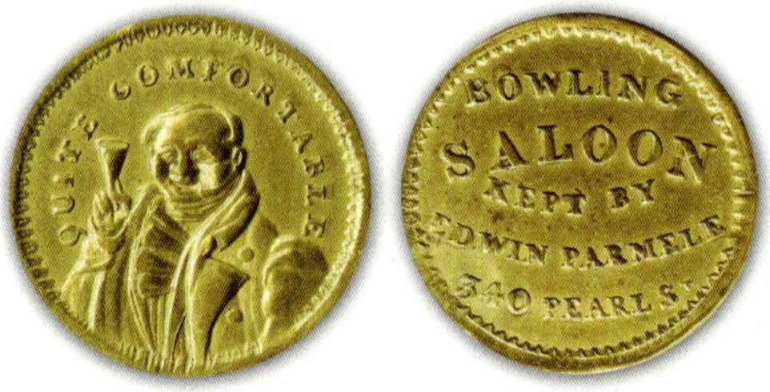

W-NY-860-10b • Rulau: "Low-268"; HT-302. High R-7. 18.5 mm. Brass. In 1886 an American Art Association Anderson Galleries offered lot 335, a Fine example, plated, that was described as "excessively rare." The American Numismatic Society has one in its cabinet, high grade, perhaps AU, listed as one of five known. In 1976 Otto Sghia's VF with planchet cracks realized $1,200. A damaged VF example in the June 1996 PCAC sale brought $4,400. Ford (SBG 2013) AU coin holed at the top $2,350, AU with obverse spotting $9,400.

Phalon's Hair Cutting
New York, NY
Hair cutting
W-NY-880

Edward Phalon began his trade as a hairdresser in the 1830s. In 1837 he was listed in directories as a hairdresser at 37 Broadway, probably a slightly variant address for the same location as 35 Broadway, as lettered on his 1837-dated token. He either moved frequently, or else had multiple salons, as Low found at least 11 different addresses for him from 1834 to 1860. Low also suggested that he began his business in 1834 at 161 Chatham Street. That was the home of his mother Mary, who died that year.

In 1841 he was given a silver medal at the annual Fair of the American Institute, and in 1842 he earned first premium at the next event. In addition to hairdressing he also sold hair lotions, preparations, and toupees. His most famous stand was as a society hairdresser in the prestigious St. Nicholas Hotel after the Hard Times era. At that time many notices and illustrations of his parlor appeared in popular magazines.

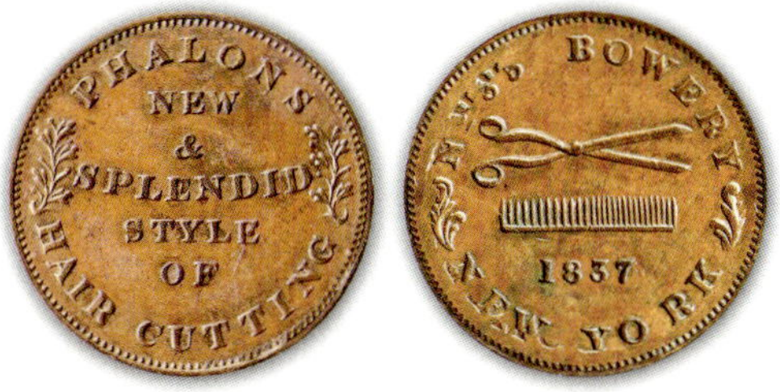

W-NY-880-10a • Low-127; HT-304. R-2. 28.5 mm. Copper. Which side is the obverse is a matter of opinion. Here the side with his name is used. VF and EF grades are par, AU tokens are easily enough available, but true Mint State pieces are rare. • VF-20 $60; EF-40 $125; AU-50 $225; MS-63 $450.

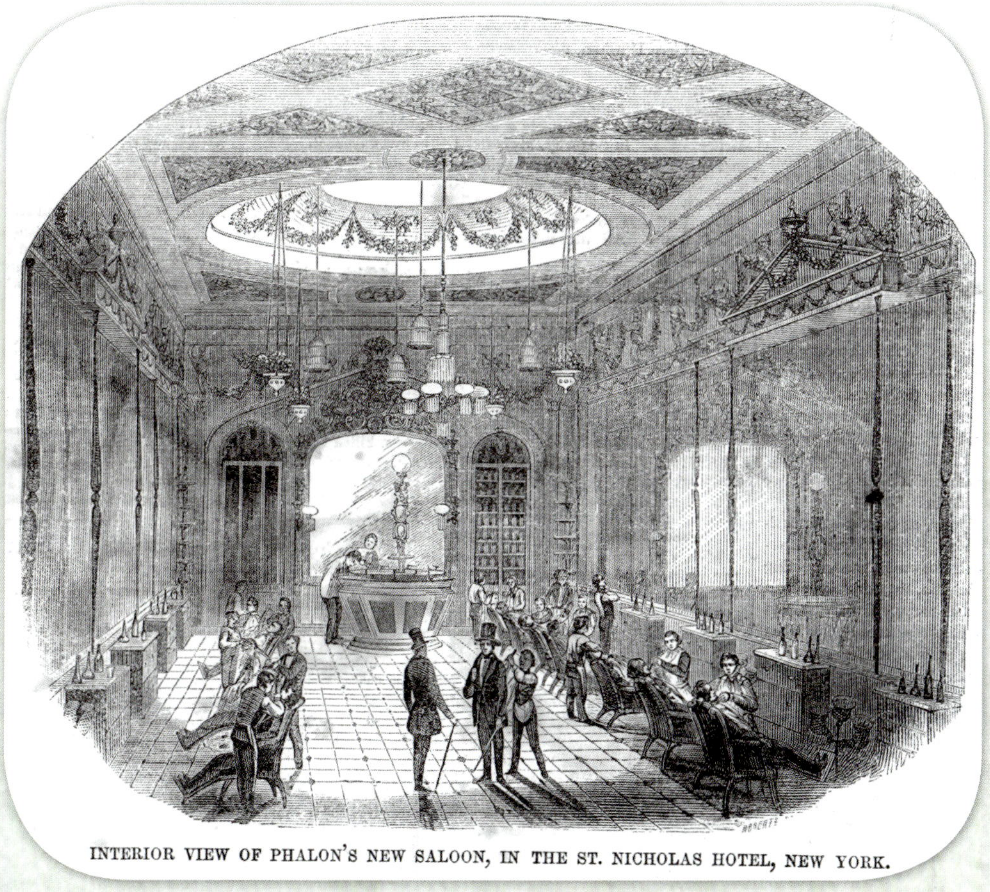

INTERIOR VIEW OF PHALON'S NEW SALOON, IN THE ST. NICHOLAS HOTEL, NEW YORK.

Phalon's new saloon in the St. Nicholas Hotel in 1853.

Abraham Riker
New York, NY
Boots and shoes
W-NY-900

Abraham Riker was a dealer in boots and shoes at 131 Division Street, opposite Allen Street in lower Manhattan. Apparently he was well known in his time. He was a Millerite who anticipated the coming of Jesus Christ in October 1844 and is said to have closed his shop and made other preparations of the Second Coming. Mention of him is made in *Advent*, a periodical devoted to the cause. One tale, later debunked, had it that in 1844 he scattered boots and shoes to crowds who gathered nightly at his door, until his son had him committed to an asylum.[87] In 1849, reflecting on this, he published a notice, "Not Dead Yet."

As is true of a number of other shops that issued Hard Times tokens, the Riker business was local with walk-in customers. There was no need to do much advertising or issue catalogs. Hence the "paper trail" of Riker and certain other token issuers of the 1830s is sparse today.

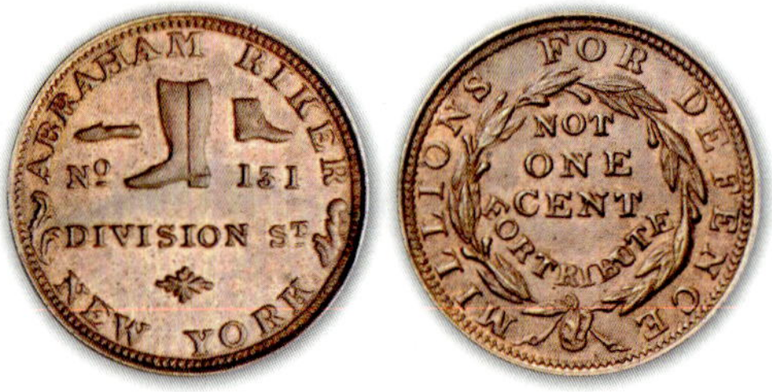

W-NY-900-10a • 3 berries on outside of wreath, 5 berries on inside • Low-153; HT-305. R-2. 28.5 mm. Copper. Reverse die is the same as used for Low-97. Although this is a common issue, Mint State examples are elusive. Most are VF or EF complemented by the occasional AU or rare Mint State example. • VF-20 $35; EF-40 $75; AU-50 $150; MS-63 $300.

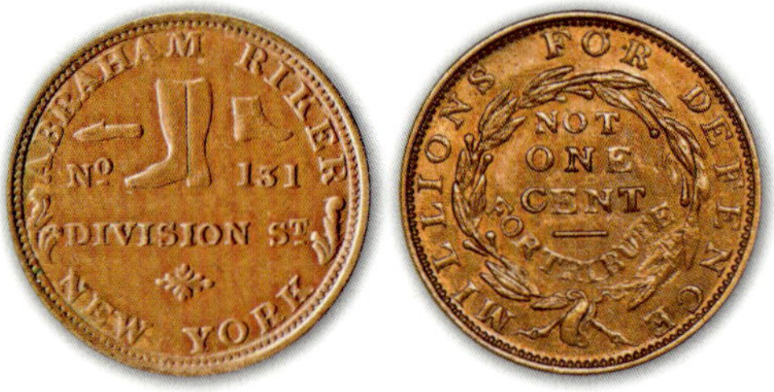

W-NY-900-15a • 2 berries on outside of wreath, 6 berries on inside • Low-154; HT-306. R-3. 28.3 mm. Copper. Reverse die is the same as used for Low-36. • VF-20 $100; EF-40 $175; AU-50 $250; MS-63 $500.

Robert B. Ruggles
New York, NY
Gold beater
W-NY-920

Robert B. Ruggles was a gold beater at 225 Canal St. He produced thin sheets and foil in various metals. In 1852 publicity was given to a mechanical gold beater that he had invented and patented. He was prominent in this specialty for a long time.

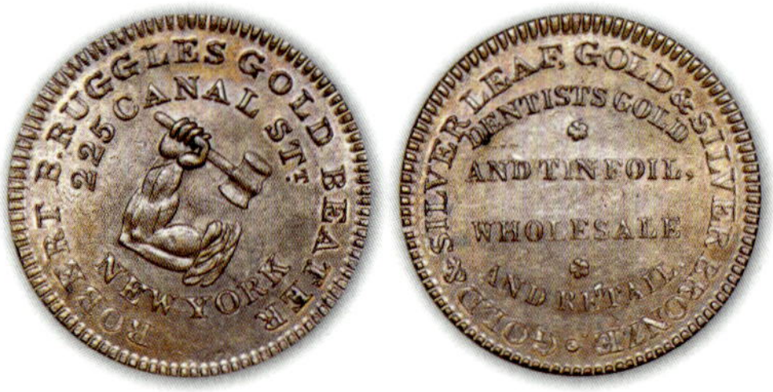

W-NY-920-10a PE • Rulau: "Low-273"; HT-307. R-2. 28.5 mm. Copper. Prominent dentils around the borders on both sides. No Bale signature. AU is typical for a high-grade piece. • VF-20 $30; EF-40 $50; AU-50 $100; MS-63 $300.

W-NY-920-10a RE • Rulau: "Low-273A"; HT-307A. R-4. 27.9 mm. Copper. Struck in a reeded collar. A variant, HT-307B, is on a very thick planchet and rated unique by Rulau. (HT-307D brass is unverified). EF is a typical grade. • VF-20 $70; EF-40 $110; AU-50 $200; MS-63 $400.

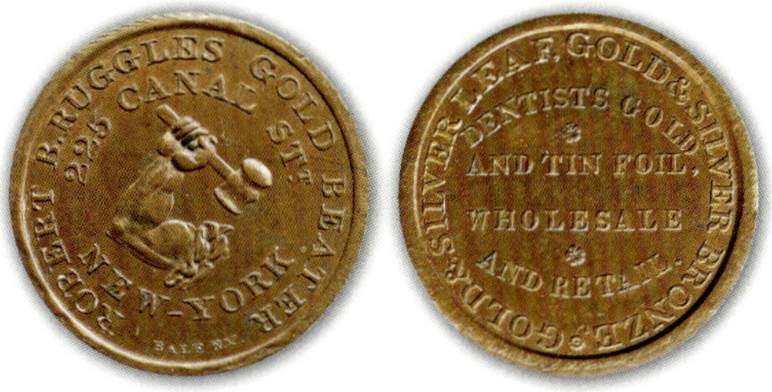

W-NY-920-15a PE • BALE N.Y. • Rulau: "Low-274"; HT-308. R-4. 28.5 mm. Copper. Plain borders on both sides. Different dies from the preceding, but with the same inscriptions plus name of coiner added. EF and AU examples have appeared in various sales, although in the marketplace most are in lower grades. • VF-20 $35; EF-40 $75; AU-50 $125; MS-63 $300.

W-NY-920-15a RE • BALE N.Y. • Rulau: "Low-274A"; HT-308A. R-6. 28.5 mm. Copper. Rare in higher grades. • VF-20 $100; EF-40 $200; AU-50 $300; MS-63 $600.

W-NY-920-15a Diagonally RE • BALE N.Y. • Low-Unlisted; HT-308B. R-7. 28.5 mm. Copper.

W-NY-920-20a Diagonally RE • Low-Unlisted; HT-Unlisted. R-8. 26 mm. Copper. From the same original dies as "Low-274" but with dentils now added around the entire obverse and reverse borders. Small-diameter planchet. A VF example was in the Robert Vlack Sale, Bowers & Merena, November 1996.

Sans Souci
New York, NY
Hotel
W-NY-930

From at least 1839 to 1842, and perhaps longer, Asa Hinckley operated the Sans Souci Hotel at 61 Broadway, New York City. This attribution is in the Rulau *Standard Catalog*. The French term *sans souci* means *without care* and was used for a number of American places of pleasure.

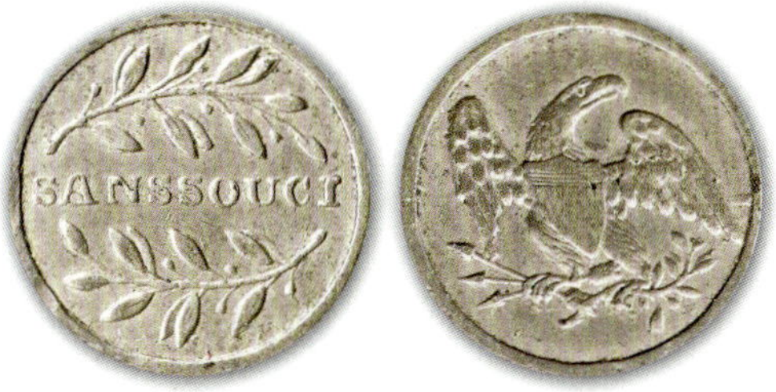

W-NY-930-10e • Low-Unlisted; HT-310. R-7. 18.5 mm. Lead or white metal. Saccone (B&M 1989) 1989 VF, dig $962.50. Presidential Coin and Antique Co. Sale 73 (2001) VF $1,725. Dice-Hicks (Stack's 2008) VF $2,185. Ford (SBG 2013) AU-55 $2,115.

Smith's Clock Establishment
New York, NY
Clocks
W-NY-940

Smith's Clock Establishment, the issuer of several varieties of Hard Times tokens, seems to have had an ephemeral existence under this particular name. The proprietor, Andrew B. Smith, advertised in 1837 that his business was at the corner of the Bowery and Division Street, "upstairs, third story, 7½ Bowery." It must have been a hike up the stairs. An advertisement:

> Clocks & Time-Pieces Large and Small. For banks, churches, and public buildings generally. Manufactured and warranted at Smith's Clock Establishment, Cor. Bowery & Division Sts.

T.L.P. Wiley, who did gilding and lettering on glass for the firm, was awarded a first premium by the American Institute.

In autumn 1838, the trade style was changed to A.B. Smith & Co., although other names were used. The *Philadelphia Inquirer*, November 27, 1839, included this notice:

> The *New York Express* states that Smith & Brothers, proprietors of the large Clock Establishment, corner of the

> Bowery and Division Street, lost all their stock and expensive tools for the manufacturing of steeple clocks and fine regulators by the fire in Elizabeth Street on Sunday morning last, together with a large quantity of lumber, veneers, and machinery, for carrying on every branch of their extensive concern.
>
> Not disheartened, however, they have already commenced putting up new machinery and are now ready to contract for clocks of all kinds and in any quantity.

By 1840 a branch of Smith & Brothers had been opened in cooperation with H.M. Richards's wholesale jewelry store at 9 North Fifth Street in Philadelphia. A notice in the Philadelphia *Public Ledger*, March 20, 1840, stated that a special sale of "500 clocks and time pieces of various patterns, consisting of brass and wood, eight-day and thirty-hour clocks, alarm ditto, &c.," was being held at both the New York City office at 7-1/2 Bowery and at the Philadelphia store. In 1841 the Philadelphia branch was moved to 201 Market Street, where steam-powered machinery was set up "for the purpose of manufacturing clocks of all kinds."[88]

Among the larger clocks made by the firm in the 1840s and early 1850s were those in the Connecticut State House in Hartford; the Center Church in the same city; the First Presbyterian Church in Natchez, Mississippi; the Court House in Canandaigua, New York; and the Court House in Reading, Pennsylvania. Most of Smith's clocks were of the regulator type, for household use on a shelf or mantel.

The tokens can be attributed by the position of the hour and minute hands on the obverse, the alignment of ESTABLISHMENT on the reverse (straight or curved), and certain other details as given below. These must have circulated by the hundreds of thousands in their time.

Today, assembling a set of the five different varieties is an interesting pursuit. The grades of typical issues range from VF to AU.[89] At the center of the face the winding post is surrounded with a small flat circle, except on W-NY-940-30a, which has a beaded circle.

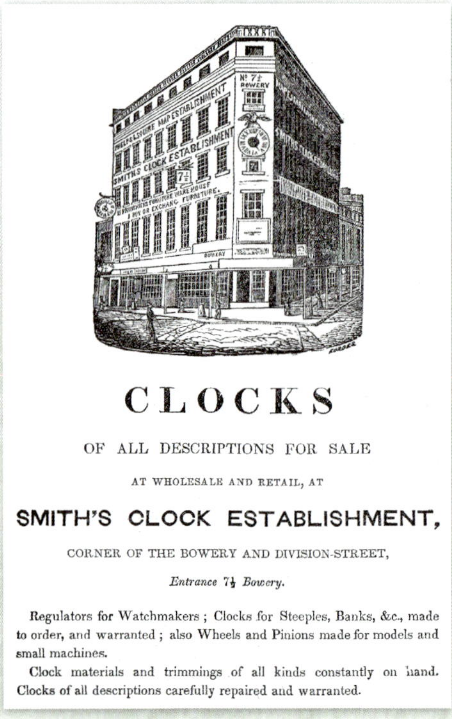

Advertisement for Smith's Clock Establishment.

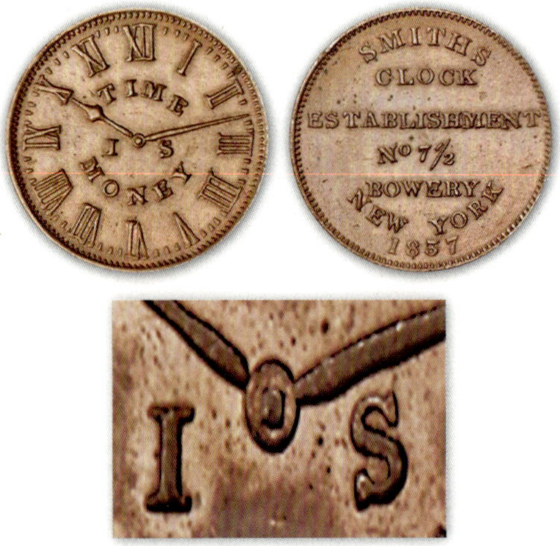

W-NY-940-10a • Low-134; HT-313. R-4. 28.5 mm. Copper. Hour hand: *Center of X*, *the only token with this feature;* Minute hand: *Obscures central triangle;* Establishment: *Straight;* the first struck of two varieties with this reverse die. Hayden 2013 MS-63 $1,300. • VF-20 $125; EF-40 $200; AU-50 $325.

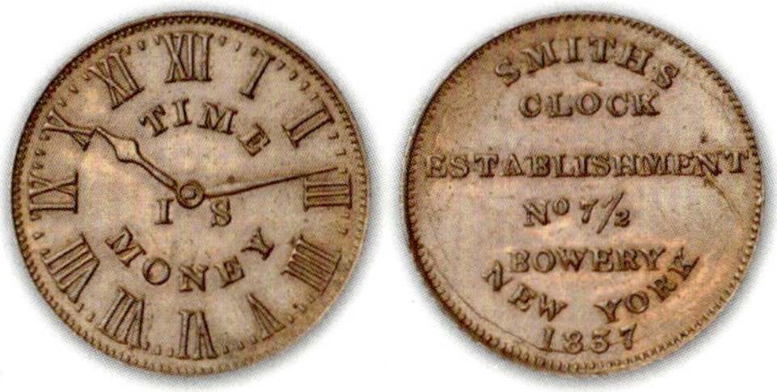

W-NY-940-15a • Low-133; HT-311. R-4. 28.5 mm. Copper. Hour hand: *Below right tip of right foot of X;* Minute hand: *Slightly above the tip of the triangle:* Establishment: *Straight;* second and last struck of two varieties with this reverse die. In the meantime W-NY-940-20a, from the same obverse die, was struck. The reverse die develops a crack from 8 o'clock close above the dentils, through 1837, extending to the right of 7. Another is through the top of MITH'S to the border down to the right. HT-312B is this die pair with silvering, R-7. VF and EF are typical grades. Mint State is very rare. • VF-20 $125; EF-40 $200; AU-50 $325.

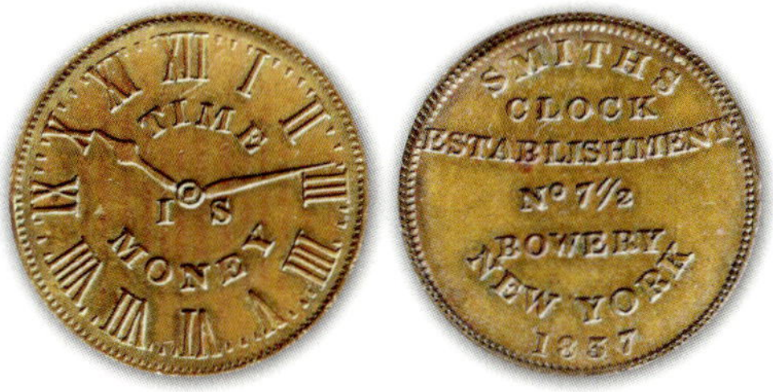

W-NY-940-20a • Low-135; HT-314. R-2. 28.5 mm. Copper. Obverse as preceding. Establishment: *Curved; No ornaments on reverse die.* Struck after W-NY-940-10a and before W-NY-940-20a. AU pieces are encountered now and again and Mint State pieces sometimes appear when collections are sold. • VF-20 $60; EF-40 $110; AU-50 $200; MS-63 $400.

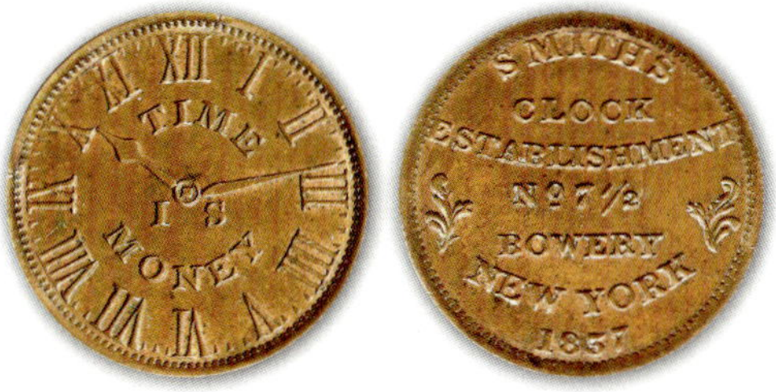

W-NY-940-25a • Low-136; HT-315. R-1. 28.5 mm. Copper. Hour hand: *Partially right of X;* Minute hand: *Opposite the tip of the triangle.* Establishment: *Curved; Small ornaments at left and right border on the reverse.* Some were silvered (unlisted). Most range from VF to AU. A few Mint State pieces exist. • VF-20 $50; EF-40 $90; AU-50 $175; MS-63 $350.

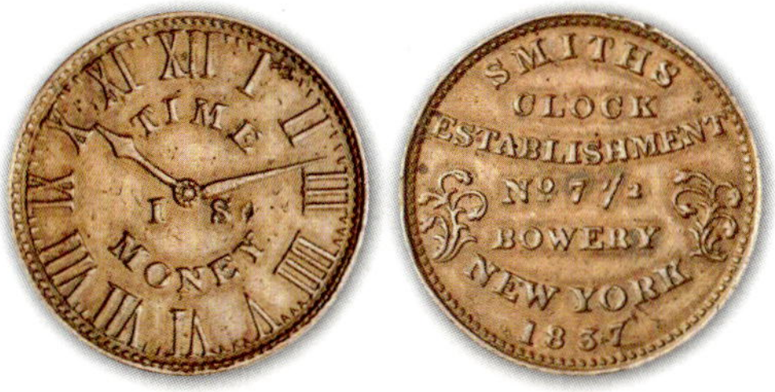

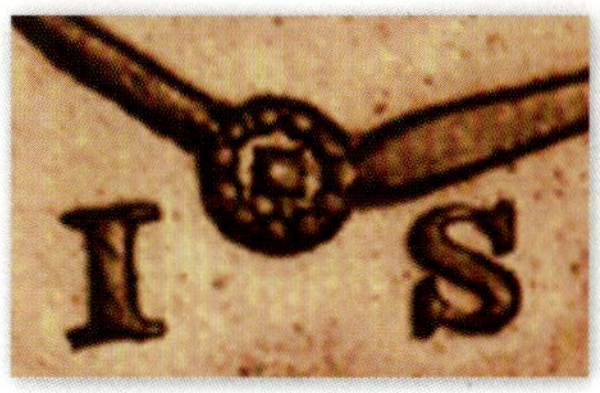

W-NY-940-30a • Low-138; HT-317. R-4. 28.5 mm. Copper. Obverse: *Circle at center is formed of beads; definitive.* Establishment: *Curved; Large ornaments at left and right border on the reverse.* "HT-317A" seemingly originally gilt is R-7 or R-8. Usually seen VF or EF. AU examples are rarities. • VF-20 $75; EF-40 $125; AU-50 $250.

Squire & Merritt
New York, NY
Ship chandlers
W-NY-960

The firm of Squire & Merritt, ship chandlers, was at 175 South Street, corner of Roosevelt Street, from circa 1831 to 1837. The partners were Lewis L. Squire and Jacob T. Merritt.

Court testimony made by Squire in 1834 stated that, from among other sources, the firm bought tools made by T.J. McMasters & Co., who used convict labor at the Auburn State Prison, which caused some controversy in the trade, especially from firms that could not buy as cheaply. Most sales were made to New Orleans and the Southern market, with limited trade in the East. Discounts made to buyers and various retailers were typically 40 percent from the list. Hardly any retail business was done. In 1833 the sales total was $10,097.22, of which only $97.10 was retained in New York City.[90]

The company was succeeded by Lewis L. Squire & Son, who issued tokens beginning in the mid-1840s. This company, and also Lewis L. Squire individually, counterstamped many thousands of silver coins in the 1830s and 1840s, to the extent that such pieces are frequently encountered today.

The Round Table, April 23, 1864, told of the organization of the New York Numismatic Society and of coin collecting, including this comment:

> It is worthwhile to note the singular fact that while this desire for the possession of rare American store cards was raging in this country there was little or no interest in ancient coins. The result was that, while such cards as that of Tilly Haines & Co., or Long, or Squire & Merritt were sold for $1.50 or $2 each, a denarius of Trajan or of Hadrian would not bring fifty cents. . . .

The Hard Times tokens are known from three obverse dies and two reverses:

> Obverse 1: Small letters. S (STt) over space between O and R; no period after STt. Beaded border.
>
> Obverse 2: Small letters. S (STt) over R; period after STt. Beaded border.
>
> Obverse 3: Large letters. Dentils around border.
>
> Reverse A: Small letters. N (NAILS) over I (IMPORTERS). Beaded border.
>
> Reverse B: Large letters. N over M. Dentils around border.

Many, if not most, have 175 counterstamped above the street name.

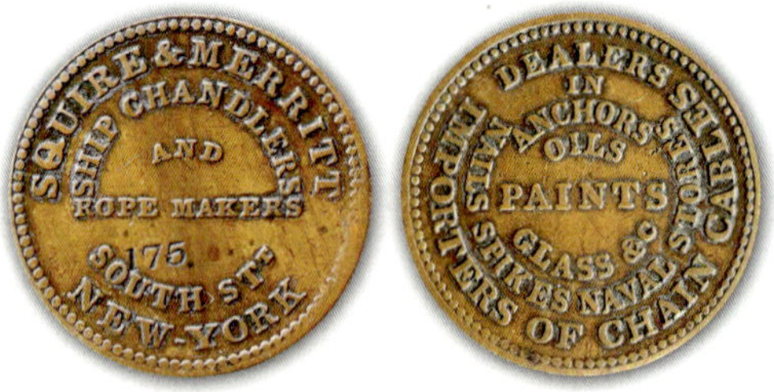

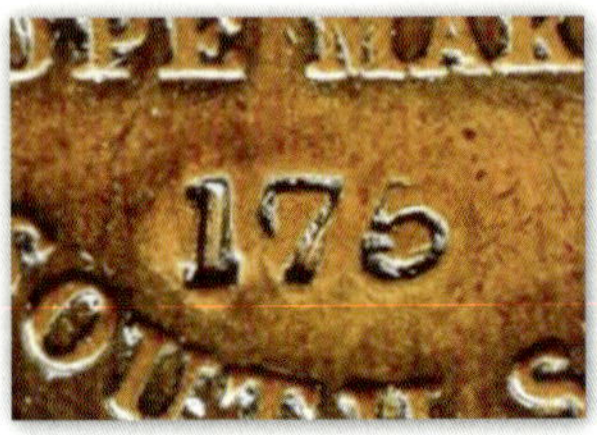

W-NY-960-10a PE • Dies 1-A • Rulau: "Low-279"; HT-318. R-6. 27 mm. Copper. Regular planchets. With 175 counterstamp HT-318A, R-4 (illustrated). This is the usually seen and readily collectible variety. • VF-20 $125; EF-40 $250; AU-50 $400.

W-NY-960-10b RE • Dies 1-A • Low-Unlisted; HT-319. R-7. 27 mm. Brass. Thick planchet.

W-NY-960-10f RE • Dies 1-A • Rulau: "Low-280"; HT-320. R-8. 27 mm. Silver. (HT-320AA; over English shilling of the 1816–1820 type; reeded edge; 175 counterstamp; R-9, 25 mm. Abt. Good.)

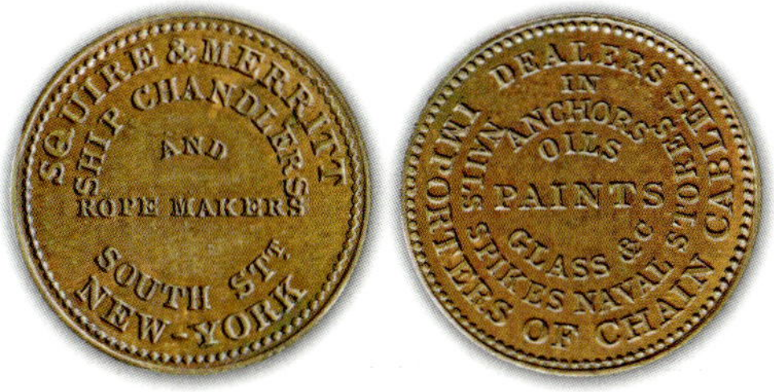

W-NY-960-15a PE • Dies 2-A • Rulau: "Low-281"; HT-321 (thin planchet R-6) and 322 (thick planchet R-6). 27 mm. Copper. This is the scarcest of the three die combinations. • VF-20 $200; EF-40 $300; AU-50 $500.

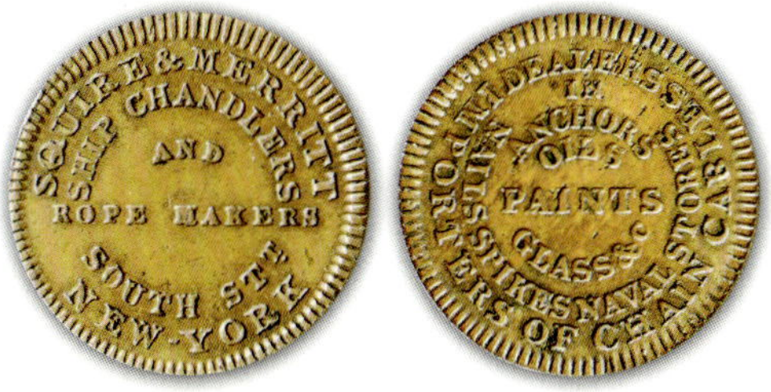

W-NY-960-20a PE • Dies 3-B • Rulau: "Low-282A"; HT-323. R-6. 27 mm. Copper. Thin planchet. • VF-20 $150; EF-40 $275; AU-50 $450.

W-NY-960-20a RE • Dies 3-B • Rulau: "Low-283"; HT-324. R-5. 27 mm. Copper. Usually seen with 175 stamped (HT-325, R-4). • VF-20 $150; EF-40 $275; AU-50 $450.

Furman B. Stage
New York, NY
Wine and liquor
W-NY-970

Furman B. Stage, born about 1818, was in the wine and liquor business at 71 Fulton Street, in 1842. He continued this trade into the late 1840s. He resided at 128 William Street. He and his wife Rebecca, both of the same age, were born in New York City. It is likely that his store, which may have been called No. 1 (the inverted inscription on his token), had a brief existence. By 1850 he was a police officer. In 1856 he lived at 524 Greenwich Street. It is likely that the same maker produced the W-NY-1120-10a token for W.W. Young. Both seem to have been kept together for a long time, and both are from the estate of Norman Stack.

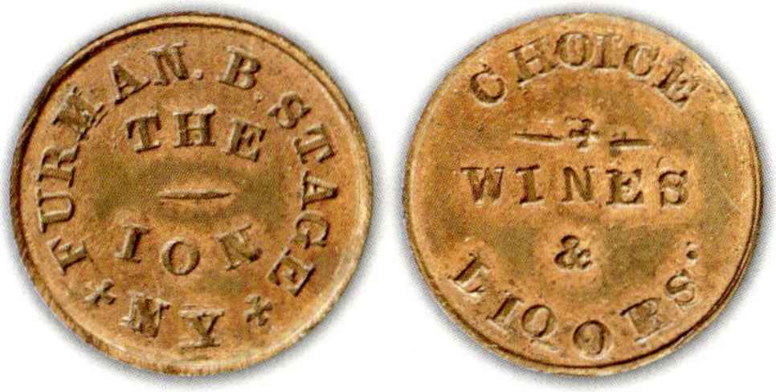

W-NY-970-10a • Low-Unlisted; HT-Unlisted. R-9. 19.2 mm. Copper. Unique. Mint State. From the Norman Stack estate, earlier in an R.M. Smythe sale.

Suydam & Boyd
New York, NY
Dry goods, clothes
W-NY-980

The firm of Suydam & Boyd has traditions dating back to the first decade of the 19th century.[91] Various members of the Suydam family, who were from old Dutch stock, were active in business in the city for many years and figure prominently in historical accounts. In the 1810s the name of Boyd & Suydam was used by the firm.

In 1829 Suydam & Boyd were at 286 Broadway, opposite Washington Hall. In March of that year, they moved to 183 Broadway opposite John Street and between Courtlandt and Dey streets. The address of 187 Broadway was sometimes used for the same location. Henry Suydam and William Boyd were the proprietors. In autumn 1830, they advertised the premises for rent and moved to 187 Pearl Street, on the corner of Cedar Street, an address used on tokens. In 1834 they moved to 157 Pearl Street, an address also used on tokens. Later in the decade, they were succeeded by Suydam, Sage & Co.

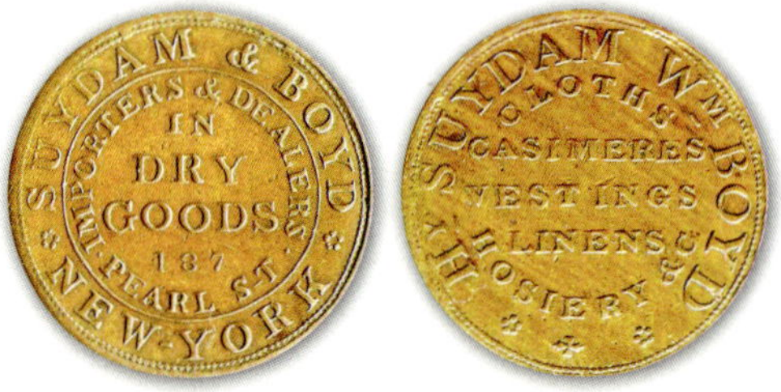

W-NY-980-10a • 187 Pearl St. • Rulau: "Low-285"; HT-332. R-5. 26.1 mm. Copper. Same reverse die as used on W-NY-980-15b but in a *later* state (as evidenced from tiny rim cuds). VF is the typical grade seen. • VF-20 $175; EF-40 $300; AU-50 $550.

W-NY-980-10b • 187 Pearl St. • Low-Unlisted; HT-332A. R-8. 26.1 mm. Brass. Steve Tanenbaum: "2 known."

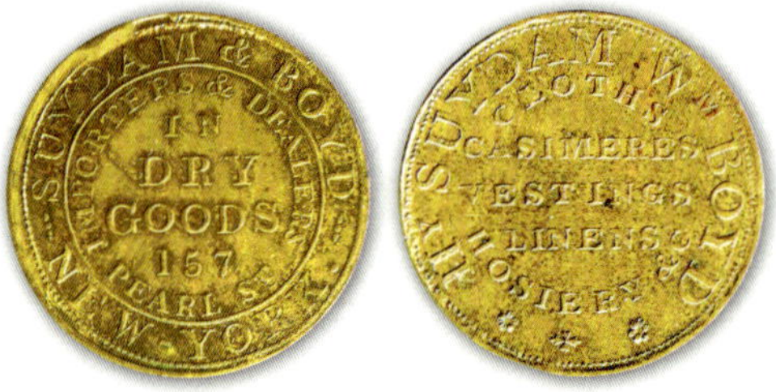

W-NY-980-15b • 157 Pearl St. • Rulau: "Low-286"; HT-333. Low R-6. 26.5 mm. Brass. Same reverse die as used on W-NY-980-10b but in an *earlier* state (as evidenced from tiny rim cuds). VF is about par for the variety. • VF-20 $175; EF-40 $300; AU-50 $550.

Ezra B. Sweet
New York, NY
Kitchen goods, roofing, etc.
W-NY-1000

Ezra B. Sweet sold stoves, kitchen furniture, and roofing, per the inscription on this token. He moved frequently, and from 1825 to 1852 he was at 12 different addresses. From 1836 to 1839, he was at 200 Canal Street, the address on his token. In 1840 he operated a bell foundry at 249 Water Street between Peck Slip and Beekman Street. In 1841 he was at 177 Hudson Street. His business card also advertised that he was a plumber. In 1845 he bid an unsuccessful run for the office of alderman in the 8th Ward.

The obverse has LIBERTY on the headband and is the closest imitation of a federal cent found in the Hard Times tokens.

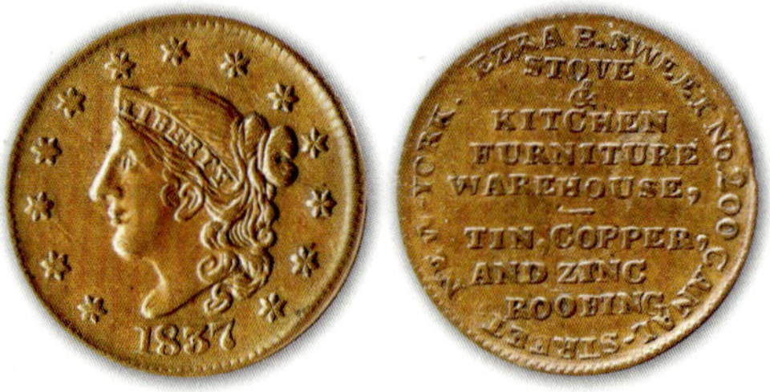

W-NY-1000-10a • Low-140; HT-334. R-4. 27.5 mm. Copper. Small planchet. VF and EF are typical grades. Finer examples are very scarce. • VF-20 $125; EF-40 $200; AU-50 $325.

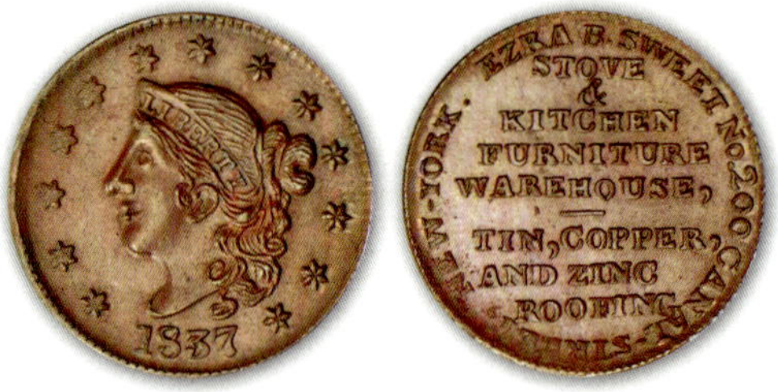

W-NY-1000-11a • Low-141; HT-335. R-3. 28.5 mm. Copper. Larger thick planchet. VF and EF are typical grades. Finer examples are rare. • VF-20 $125; EF-40 $200; AU-50 $325.

Tisdale & Richmond
New York, NY
Hardware, metal products
W-NY-1020

Located in New York City, the firm was at 250 Water St., the address on its token, in 1833 and 1834. They were listed in directories at 210 Water St. in 1834 and 1835 and 218 Water Street in 1835 and 1836. They imported much merchandise made in Taunton, Massachusetts, via sailing ships.

> *Obverse:* TISDALE & RICHMOND around the top border, No. 250 WATER ST., NEW YORK around the bottom border, KEEP / CONSTANTLY / ON HAND / SHOVELS. NAILS. / HOLLOW WARE / PIG. & BAR IRON / &c &c &c.
>
> *Reverse:* TACK & BRAD PLATES around the border above NAIL RODS. HOOP IRON & C. around the border below. In the center in lines, SHEATHING. / & BOLT, COPPER. / TACKS. BRADS. / & SPARABILLS. / SUGAR KETTLES / ROLLING MILL, / ROLLS. &c. / &c. &c. at center.

The die work is somewhat rustic and has periods instead of commas in several places.

In 1833 the company was given a silver medal at the American Institute's annual Fair, October 16 to 19, for exhibiting one of the items they offered for sale:

> Hollow ware cast by Crocker & Richmond of Taunton, tinned by Mr. Nabbet same place. . . . First ever manufactured in the United States—a very valuable article.

W-NY-1020-10a • Low-Unlisted; HT-A335. R-8. 2 known. 28 mm. Copper. This token was unknown until the 1980s when Charles Kirtley, who conducted mail auctions of tokens, discovered it. H. Joseph Levine of Presidential Coin and Antique Co. verified it. Robert A. Schuman announced it in an article, "Rescued from Obscurity," in *Rare Coin Review* No. 75. The token is lightly struck and is in VG or finer grade. A second example was later reported by Schuman.

Van Nostrand & Dwight
New York, NY
Book sellers and publishers
W-NY-1040

Van Nostrand & Dwight, book sellers and publishers, had a retail store situated in the American Tract Society House at 146 Nassau St., the address on their token, from 1835 to 1837. William Dwight and David Van Nostrand were the partners.

Most of their titles were of a religious nature. A few were illustrated by W.L. Ormsby, an engraver who later became prominent in the bank note business.[92] The firm operated for about three years. David Van Nostrand went on to fame and fortune as a publisher of popular as well as historical and technical books. Their token was struck by Bale & Smith, New York.

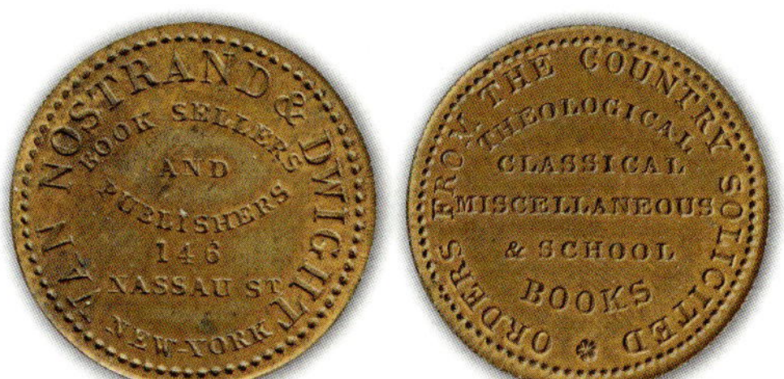

W-NY-1040-10a • Rulau: "Low-287"; HT-336. R-4. 26.5 mm. Copper. All are with reeded edge. AU and lower-range Mint State pieces have appeared in various sales, but the typical token in the marketplace is apt to be VF or EF. • VF-20 $60; EF-40 $100; AU-50 $175; MS-63 $400.

C.H. Webb / Congress Hall Hotel
New York, NY
Hotel
W-NY-1060

On October 20, 1832, this notice was published in the New York *Evening Post*, by which time the hotel was considerably delayed in its opening.

Webb's Congress Hall

142 Broadway between Liberty and Cedar streets. The subscriber respectfully announces that tomorrow he will be able to redeem the pledge which he gave to the public in March last, by opening for the accommodation of merchants, private families, and guests in general this spacious house (belonging to the estate of the late James Anderson, Esq.) which has been fitted up in superior style for a hotel of the first class.

The arrangement, completion, and furnishing of its numerous apartments have been governed by a liberal regard for the convenience and enjoyment of the guests, and the same principle will at all times regulate the conduct of the subscriber and his assistants in its management.

Its situation is in the most attractive part of Broadway, at a short distance from the principal places of amusement on the one hand, and within a few steps of the centre of mercantile business in Maiden Lane, Cedar, Wall, and Pearl streets on the other, and enjoying a fine circulation of air so desirable to persons accustomed to the fresh atmosphere of the country, combines all the advantages, while it is subject to none of the causes of complaint which would be in a house of entertainment located in the narrow and confined streets of the commercial parts of the city.

The subscriber observes that during his summer attendance at the Catskill Mountain House, another person has applied the name of Congress Hall to the house in Broadway lately known as the National Hotel, whether through ignorance of the subscriber's intentions (so long and in so many ways before the public) or for a cause less justifiable he will not presume to determine, but he takes this occasion to remark that having as early as March last announced this as the name of the house which he intended to establish and having sent to Europe at great expense for plate, cutlery, &c., marked "Congress Hall," he cannot consistently or conveniently adopt another name.

It is not therefore with feelings of hostility towards his neighbor or with a wish to injure him, but from a necessity that he has determined to retain the name fixed on at first, and he wishes the public to understand that the name of the establishment placed at the head of this advertisement is the CONGRESS HALL formerly announced by him, but to distinguish it as far as is practicable from that of his neighbor, it will be known as WEBB'S CONGRESS HALL.

The subscriber tenders his grateful acknowledgments to his friends and the public for their very liberal support of the Pearl Street house and the Catskill Mountain House, and indulges a confident hope that if every advantage which a place of fashionable entertainment can boast in situation and interior comfort, in connection with prompt attention and long experience of patronage, these advantages will be found, and that patronage bestowed at his new establishment.

N.B. Boarders can be taken on Monday after 4 o'clock P.M.

Charles H. Webb

From *Views of New York and Its Environs*, 1831, which anticipated the opening of the hotel:

Webb's Congress Hall

This spacious and elegant hotel is now open for the reception of guests. Its situation is one of the most pleasant and eligible in the city, being on the east side of Broadway, between Cedar and Liberty streets. The buildings which have here been converted into an establishment for the accommodation of travelers and others, belong to the estate of the late James Anderson, and have been fitted up in very superior style.

The upper parts of the four dwellings on Broadway have been thrown into one, and the sleeping and other apartments are well adapted to their several purposes—in fact, from an examination of the premises, we are free to confess that the *tout ensemble* exhibits a rare combination of the useful and ornamental. There are

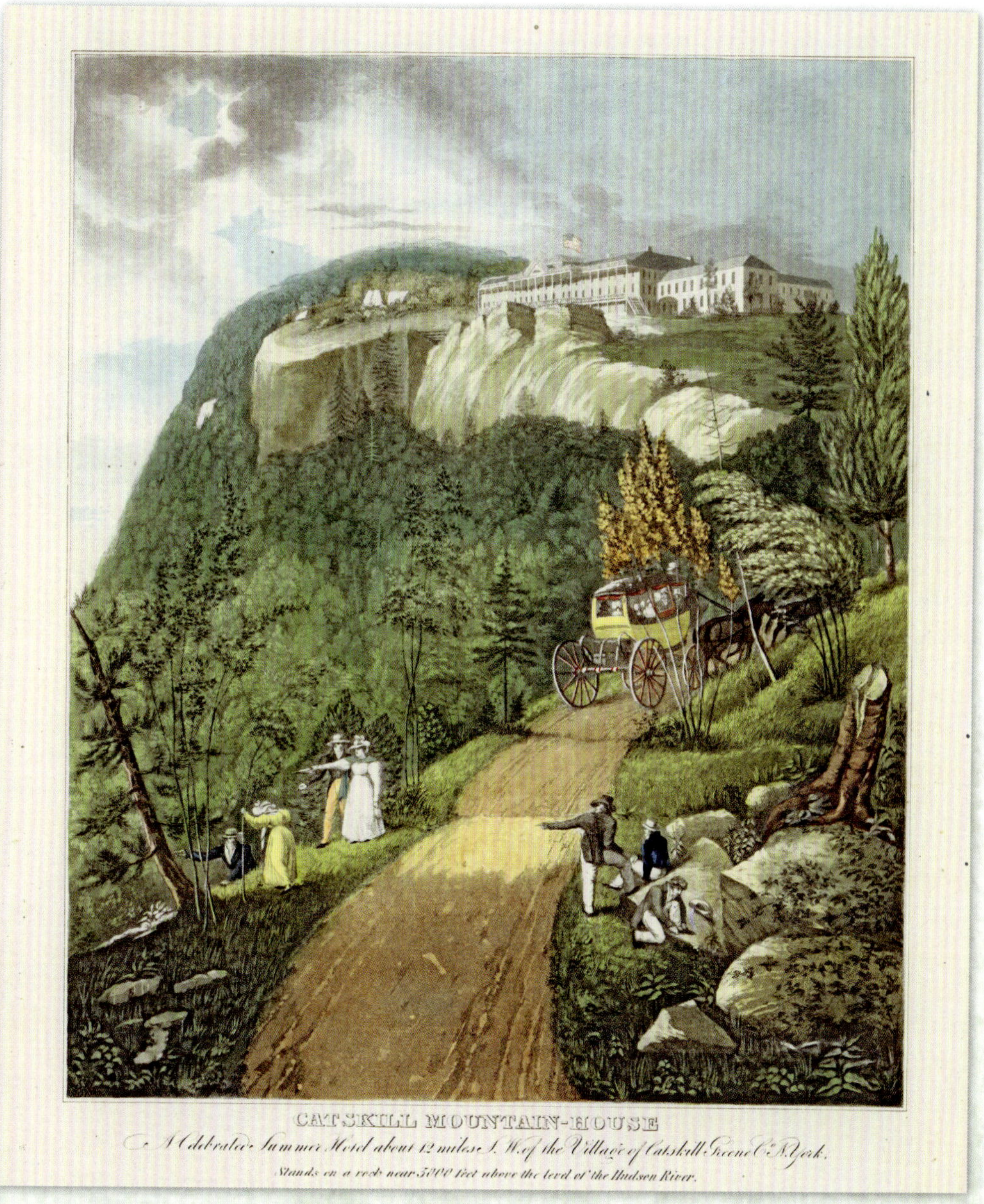

Charles H. Webb's Mountain House was 140 long, 24 feet deep, and of four stories. It was perched on a rocky ledge about 3,000 feet above the Hudson River (John Rubens Smith, 1775–1849).

> twelve parlors for the accommodation of private families, to each of which a bed-room is attached—a convenience that cannot be too highly appreciated.
>
> A large four-story building has been erected in the rear, the first floor of which is occupied by the dining-room, than which there is not a more elegant one in the city. One hundred and fifty persons can here dine, without the slightest inconvenience, or fear of being crowded. The upper part is entirely occupied as sleeping apartments, most of which are single rooms, and all neatly furnished. In addition to this description, it is only necessary to say, that this fine hotel is conducted by Mr. Charles H. Webb, too long and extensively known as one of the most intelligent, gentlemanly, and capable persons of his calling in this country to need any compliment from us. We have more than once had "a taste of his quality" as host of the Mountain House, and have therefore reason to know with what liberality, ability, and address he presides over an extensive establishment.

By 1835 Webb was listed at 438 Greenwich Street, this isolating the time of issue of his tokens to the early 1830s. His tokens were struck by James Bale. The dating of the imprints of Wright & Bale, Bale on his own, and Bale & Smith does not conform in some instances to the dates in which various trade styles were listed in contemporary directories.

Charles H. Webb was born in 1795 and died on February 24, 1867.

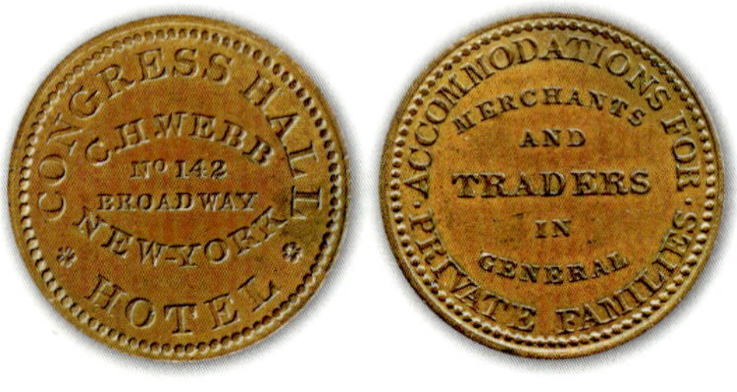

W-NY-1060-10a • Rulau: "Low-392"; HT-337. R-3. 26.2 mm. Copper. VF and EF are typical grades. • VF-20 $90; EF-40 $150; AU-50 $250; MS-63 $450.

W-NY-1060-10b • Rulau: "Low-392A"; HT-337. R-5. 26.2 mm. Brass. VF and EF are typical grades. • VF-20 $125; EF-40 $225; AU-50 $350; MS-63 $750.

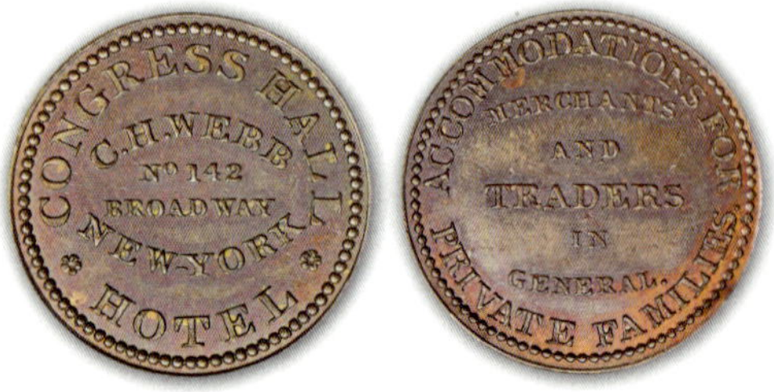

W-NY-1060-15a • Rulau: "Low-392B"; HT-338. R-7. 26.2 mm. Copper. Obverse die as preceding. Different reverse die; period after GENERAL. VF and EF are typical grades. • VF-20 $200; EF-40 $300; AU-50 $550.

Richard Williams / Union Hall
New York, NY
Refreshments
W-NY-1080

Richard Williams operated the Union Hall, a source for refreshments at the corner of Henry and Oliver streets. Russell Rulau gives the date range as 1833 through 1835. The heart in hand symbol is associated with the Independent Order of Odd Fellows, a charitable fraternity.

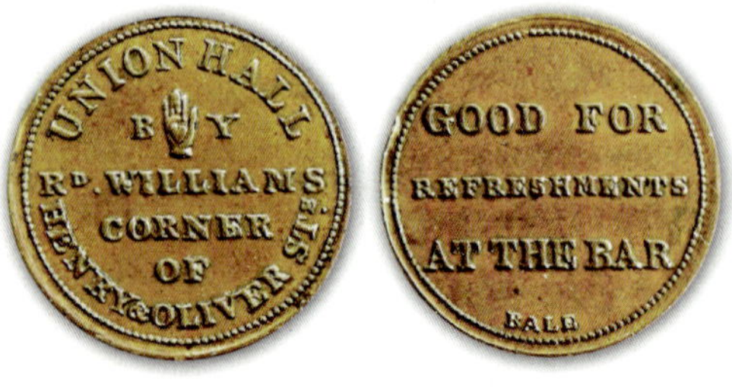

W-NY-1080-10a • Rulau: "Low-365"; HT-339. R-7+. 19.5 mm. Copper. Die signed BALE. Dice-Hicks (Stack's 2008) EF $8,050. Ford (SBG 2013) EF-45 $3,055, AU-58 $9,400.

Wright & Bale
New York, NY
Token manufacturers
W-NY-1100

The firm of Wright and Bale was a partnership between two engravers—Charles Cushing Wright and James Bale. The arrangement began in May 1829 and continued until late 1833. James Bale was in business independently for several years beginning in 1833. Certain dies signed by the partnership were in use after its dissolution, reflecting the opportunistic use of older dies still on hand, or other procedures of convenience and necessity.

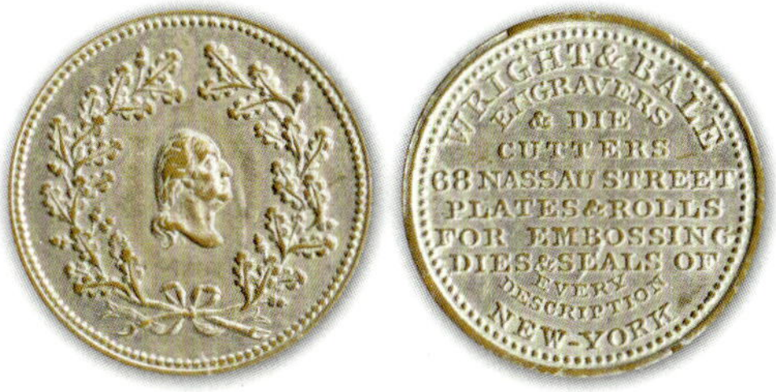

W-NY-1100-10a • Rulau: "Low-331"; HT-341 (thick planchet) and 342 (thin planchet as usually seen). R-5. 18 mm. Copper. Some were silver plated (as illustrated). The same Washington portrait obverse die was used on the Henderson & Lossing token (W-NY-1200-10a). VF and EF are typical grades. • VF-20 $225; EF-40 $350; AU-50 $500.

W.W. Young
New York, NY
Gold watch case maker
W-NY-1120

William W. Young operated a gold watch case factory on Broadway, opposite Union Street. The business began about 1836 and lasted into the early 1840s. In 1836 he lived at 25 Jay Street.

The New York *Commercial Advertiser*, April 15, 1840, included this:

> The fire last evening was in No. 187 Broadway,[93] occupied by Derby & Farnham, tailors; Egbert Scudder, watch maker; W.W. Young, watch-case maker, and others. The roof and fourth story were partially damaged by fire, and a considerable amount of damage was done by the water used in extinguishing it. The loss was principally covered by insurance.

His Hard Times token would have been issued sometime between the mid-1830s and early 1840. In 1842 Young's business was at 12 Maiden Lane. He resided in New Jersey. It is likely that the same maker produced the W-NY-510-10a token for Furman B. Stage No. 1.

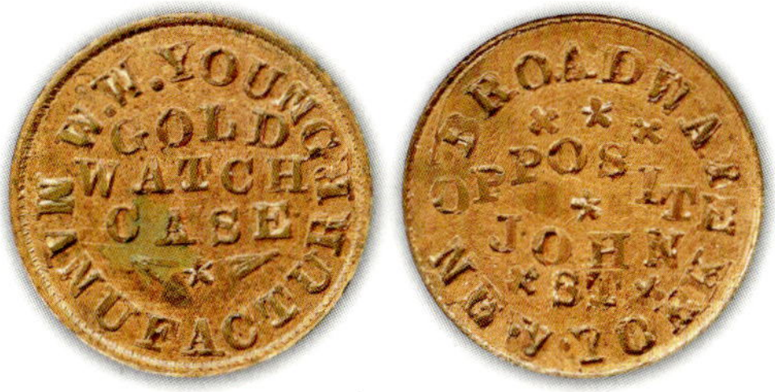

W-NY-1120-10a • Low-Unlisted; HT-Unlisted. R-8. 19 mm. Copper. Obverse: W.W. YOUNG / GOLD / WATCH / CASE / MANUFACTURER. Reverse: BROADWAY / OPPOSITE / JOHN / ST. / NEW YORK. Letters and numbers on both sides are of the same size and font. At the bottom of the obverse is MANUFACTURR. Mint State red and brown, mostly red. From the Norman Stack estate, at one time included in an R.M. Smythe sale.

Henderson & Lossing
Poughkeepsie, NY
Jewelry, clocks, and watches
W-NY-1200

Benson John Lossing was born on February 12, 1813, in Beekman, New York. In 1824 he was orphaned and moved to Poughkeepsie.

In 1826 watchmaker Adam Henderson took orphan Benson John Lossing, age 13, as an apprentice. In 1833, when Benson was 20, he joined as a partner in Henderson & Lossing, which made and sold timepieces and jewelry. Silverware with their hallmark was produced as well. Their token uses the Washington obverse employed by Wright & Bale on their own store card (see entry). Lossing resigned in 1835 to become a writer, editor, and part owner of the *Poughkeepsie Telegraph.* In 1838 he moved to New York City, and in the next year he became editor of the *Family Weekly.* In time he became one of America's most popular historians, covering American history in narratives that were interesting and informative. These were illustrated with his own engravings. Many coins and medals were pictured in various volumes. In 1853, following serialization in a magazine, his two-volume *Pictorial Field Book of the Revolution* was published. Sales were excellent, and it was reprinted in 1855.

On June 17, 1858, the American Numismatic Society elected Lossing as its first honorary member. Benson replied to ANS founder Augustus B. Sage on July 2, stating in part:

> I have the pleasure to acknowledge the receipt of your letter of the 24th ultimo. (forwarded to me by Harper & Bros.) announcing my election to honorary membership in the American Numismatic Society.
>
> My limited knowledge of the interesting and highly important subject which forms the object of your association would not entitle me to active membership. Therein, I assure you that I feel a deep concern in such investigations, so kindred to those in which I have been engaged. In that interest you have perceived a reason for enabling me [to] arrange yours. As a fellow delver I most cheerfully accept the profound honor, and beg you to receive my cordial thanks, and my earnest wishes for the success of your enterprise. It is the hand-made and worker with history, and is one of its most reliable aids in discovering truths and errors in the chronicles of the race. . . .

Lossing went from one success to another and became a national figure. He died at his home in Dover, New York, on June 3, 1891.

In his article, "A Plea for American Token Collecting," in *The Numismatist*, April 1915, Thomas L. Elder included this:

> Many of the Wright & Bale and Bale & Smith cards bore the heads of Washington or Franklin, and all are now rare, that of Henderson & Lossing being exceptionally so. A year or so ago a citizen of Poughkeepsie

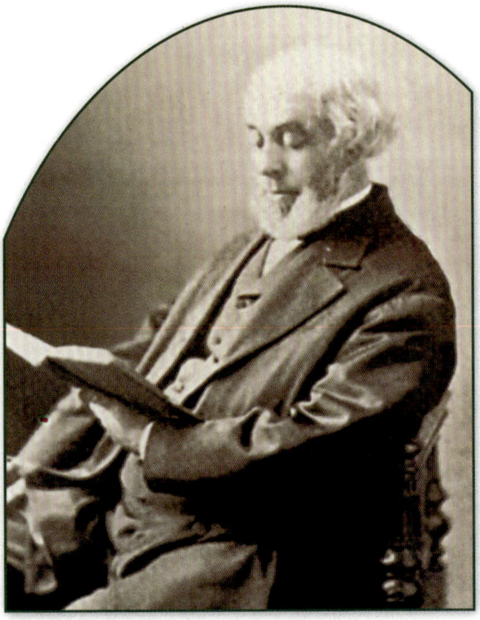

Benson J. Lossing.

showed me a holed example of this token. He claimed to have the full history of its issue and said that only 16 specimens were struck before the die broke and it was cast aside.

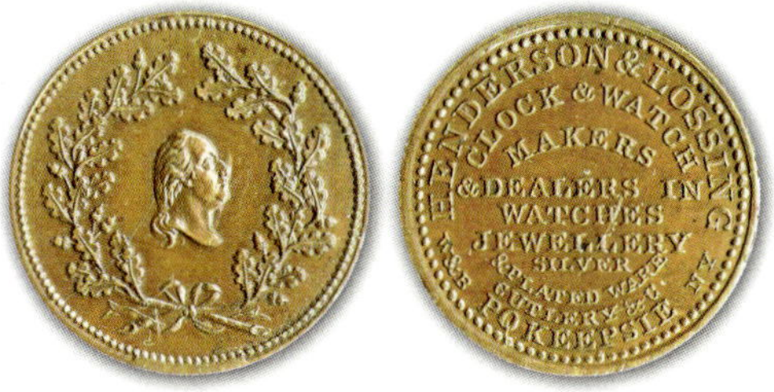

W-NY-1200-10a • Rulau: "Low-317"; HT-344 (thick planchet) and 344A (thin planchet). High R-6. 19 mm. Copper. The Ford Collection sold in August 2013 had two: MS-62BN $764; MS-62 some silvering remaining $1,058. Coin Galleries, July 2011 VG $273.[94] Most are seen in lower grades, often with problems. Choice EF or finer examples are rarities. • VF-20 $250; EF-40 $400; AU-50 $750; MS-63 $1,500.

Hiram Judson
Syracuse, NY
Silversmith, jewelry, music
W-NY-1600

Hiram Judson's token states that he was a watchmaker, silversmith, and jeweler and also offered military goods, pianofortes, musical instruments, and sheet music. He also counterstamped coins. Judson was a justice of the peace, a town officer involved in civic affairs, and a respected member of the community in Syracuse.

Hiram Judson was in business from the 1820s through the early 1850s, including during all of the Hard Times token period. He lived over his store in the location where the Wieting Block was later built. His tokens were made by Bale & Smith and are signed B&S NY.

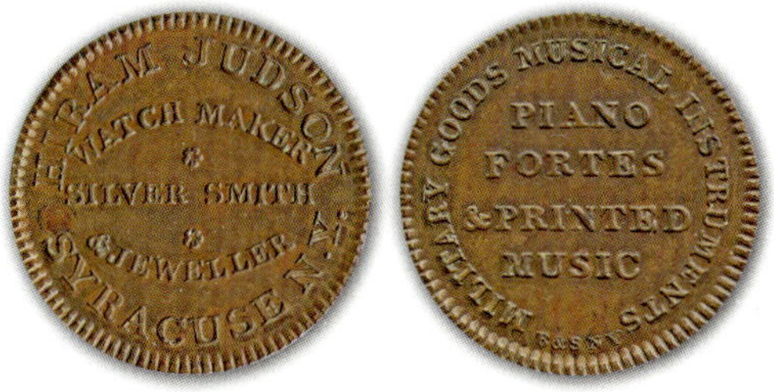

W-NY-1600-10a PE • Rulau: "Low-318A"; HT-346. R-4. 28.5 mm. Copper. Thicker planchet than the following. VF and EF are typical grades. • VF-20 $75; EF-40 $175; AU-50 $350.

W-NY-1600-10a RE • Rulau: "Low-318"; HT-345. R-5. 28.5 mm. Copper. VF and EF are typical grades. • VF-20 $75; EF-40 $175; AU-50 $350.

O. & P. Boutwell
Troy, NY
Bakers and confectioners
W-NY-1640

Brothers Oliver and Phardice Boutwell conducted this partnership from 1835 (the date on the token) to 1837. Beginning in 1831, Oliver had been a baker at 314 River Street in Troy, in a wooden building opposite Washington Hall. On May 13, 1833, it was destroyed by fire. The nearby premises of Carpenter & Mosher (also token issuers; see listing) barely escaped. Boutwell had only $400 in insurance, amounting to only a fraction of his loss. He subsequently set up at 7 Grand Division Street, the address given on the token.[95]

In 1837 Phardice set up his own milling business near the Sloop Lock on the Hydraulic Canal and remained in the trade until after the Civil War. In 1837 Oliver established his own business as O. Boutwell at the Sloop Lock and erected a two-story mill that was later expanded. In that trade he was a very prolific issuer of brass

Civil War tokens, which seem to have been circulated by the hundreds of thousands. In 1866 his son Charles A. became a partner, after which the trade style was O. Boutwell and Son. Oliver died on November 13, 1888. The business was continued by his son.

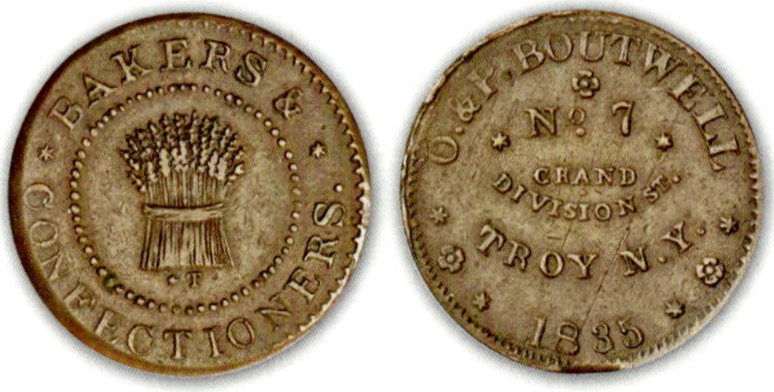

W-NY-1640-10a • Low-87; HT-347. R-7. 28.5 mm. Copper. Rulau lists a unique example struck over a large cent as HT-347A and a unique overstrike on a 1774 silver two-real piece as HT-347B. Melvin and George Fuld, 1952: "This is one of the very early tokens cut by True of Albany, and is of very crude workmanship, and very few were issued." The initial T on the obverse suggests one of the True die cutters of the area. Ford (Stack's 2004) EF $6,613 to Robert A. Schuman (illustrated). Dice-Hicks (Stack's 2008) EF cleaned $7,475. Grades generally range from Good to VF.

W-NY-1640-10f • Low-174; HT-347B. R-9. Silver. Struck over a Spanish-American two-real piece. Unique. American Numismatic Society.

Bucklin's Interest Tables
Troy, NY
Interest tables
W-NY-1660

Bucklin's Interest Tables, a guide to calculating and bookkeeping, were published by Isaac B. Bucklin, a Troy schoolteacher in the 1830s. He lived in West Troy, a district that later became part of Troy. In 1833 he published *Bucklin's Counting House Journal.* Other guides were issued as described on his tokens.

In 1835 he was involved with Marshall S. Mead and Ammon Hammond in the West Troy India Rubber Manufacturing Co., (earlier proposed as the West Troy Caoutchouc Manufacturing Co.) which was capitalized for $200,000 and chartered "for the purpose of manufacturing rubber coating and rubber covering and other articles incident thereto, in the village of Watervliet in the county of Albany, and not elsewhere." On February 29, 1836, he applied to Congress for a grant of land in the Oregon Territory, which at the time was largely unoccupied. The petition was withdrawn.

Bucklin invented the Improved Railway Cooking Stove (patented by him on July 9, 1838), described here:

> The stove is so constructed that the part which contains the fuel is movable on rollers and may be made to slide under that portion of it which contains the oven, thus decreasing the size of the whole according to the use intended to be made of it.

From 1839 onward, Isaac Bucklin was a dealer in stoves, including those of his own patent, at 221 River Street in Troy, while continuing to live in West Troy.

The first token listed, W-NY-1660-10a, is dated 1834 and has the reverse die signed BALE N.Y. It consists entirely of minute lettering that gives details:

> *Obverse:* 1834. BUCKLIN'S BOOK KEEPING SIMPLYFIED MAY BE USED BY EVERY ONE. / SHOWS AT / ONE VIEW THE / EXACT STATE OF / YOUR BUSINESS. / SECOND EDITION / IMPROVED, PRICE / ONE DOLLAR. / TROY. N.Y.

Reverse: BUCKLIN'S INTEREST TABLES. 100 DOLLARS FOR DETECTING AN ERROR OF 1 CENT. / SHOWS THE / INTEREST AT A / GLANCE OF ANY SUM, / FOR ANY TIME, / AT 6 AND 7 PER CENT / PRICE / FROM 25 CENTS TO / 2 DOLLARS. / BALE N-Y. [smaller letters] TROY, N-Y.

This token was not listed by Low, even though it is obviously dated 1834.

Certain of his later tokens with a Liberty Head obverse (with TROY on the coronet) and wreath reverse, are the epitome of rustic or naïve die cutting by True, a local engraver. All were irregularly struck. These were widely circulated for a long time. That together with low relief on the dies resulted in the typical example seen today being VG or Fine with parts indistinctly struck. The latest tokens listed are dated 1835 from dies signed by True, which have lettering on both sides. These are less crude than the Liberty Head types. As no example of Low-91 (HT-352) has been verified to exist, it is thought that it is an erroneous listing in the Low text. All of the following tokens have the obverse head facing right except for the last-listed variety.

(Also see Bucklin's Bookkeeping tokens issued with a West Troy address and listed under that location.)

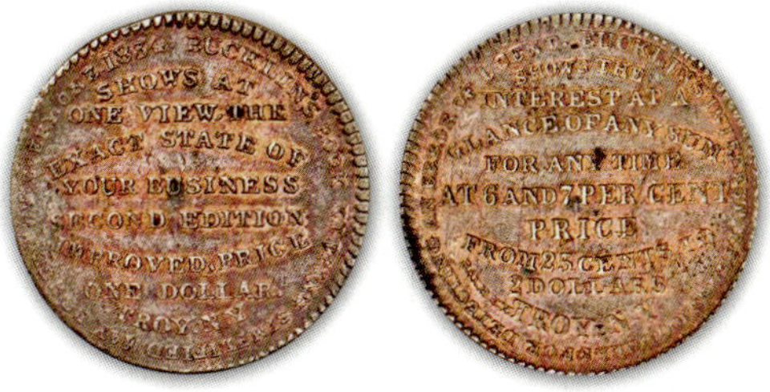

W-NY-1660-10a • 1834. Lettering on both sides • Low-77; HT-348. R-5. 28.2 mm. 1834 issue. Copper. Reverse die signed BALE N.Y. Typical grades are Fine and VF. Striking is nearly always weak in some border areas. Scarcer than generally realized and rare in any grade if well struck. Americana Sale (SBG 2013) EF $1,352.25. Fine and VF are typical grades. • VF-20 $500; EF-40 $1,000; AU-50 $2,000.

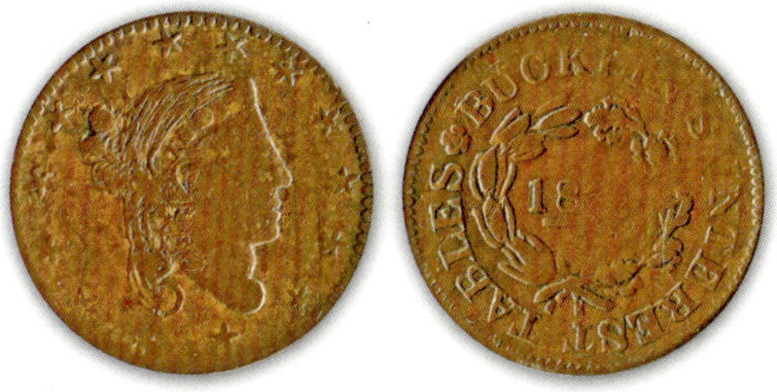

W-NY-1660-15a • Star left of and close to neck tip / 1835 • Low-89; HT-349. R-5. 28.2 mm. Copper. Two stars under head, but the one close to the neck tip is visible on many examples while the other star is not. Due to low-die-relief examples that were in circulation for just a short time, these tokens usually have the appearance of being well worn. Good and VG are typical grades, but with patience a VF example can be found. • F-12 $150; VF-20 $500; EF-40 $1,500.

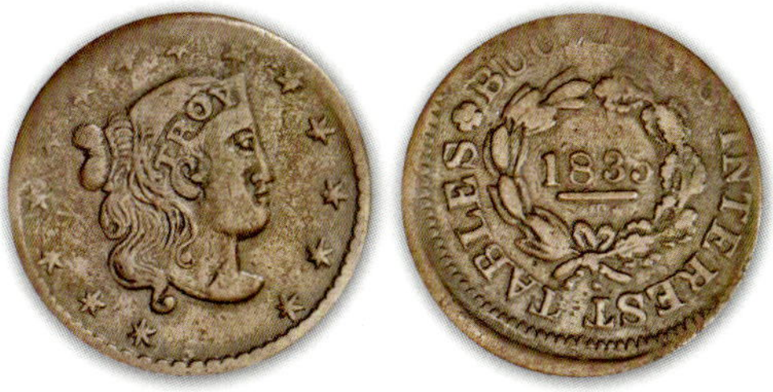

W-NY-1660-20a • No stars under head / 1835 T and star under 1835 • Low-88; HT-350. R-7. 27.5 mm. Copper. Ford (Stack's 2004) EF $6,325. Dice-Hicks (Stack's 2008) Fine, unsold. Typical grades range from About Good to Good or so, punctuated by a few exceptions. The relief of the dies was very shallow to begin with, so even a lightly circulated example appears to be well worn. Often, most of the details of the reverse center are gone.

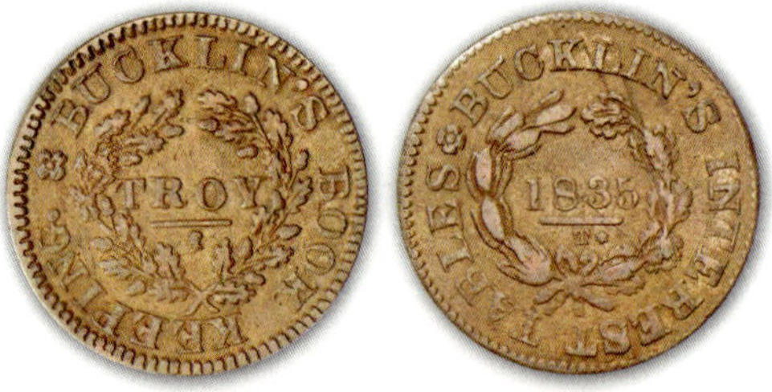

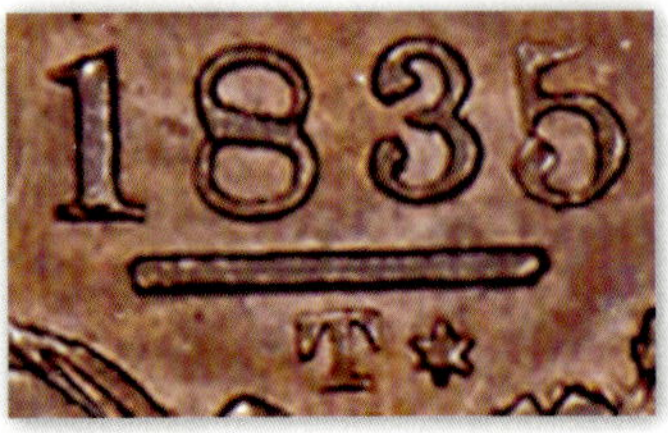

W-NY-1660-35a • Tiny head under TROY / T and star under 1835 • Low-92; HT-353 (28.5 mm) and 354 (27 mm). R-1. Copper. Reverse as preceding. Two planchet sizes with 28.5 mm being more plentiful. High-grade examples are VF, but a few finer ones exist and are rare. • VF-20 $40; EF-40 $100; AU-50 $250; MS-63 $750.

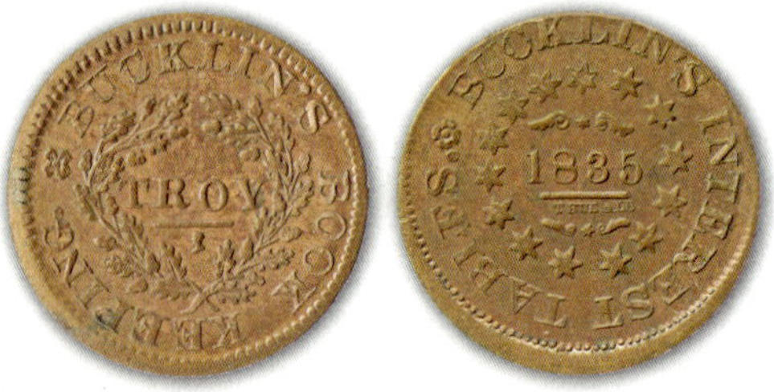

W-NY-1660-40a • Tiny head under TROY / TRUE ALB under 1835 • Low-93; HT-355. R-5. 28.5 mm. Copper. Obverse die as preceding. On the reverse engraver True signed with an Albany address. Known in various die states. Fine to VF grades are typical. In EF or higher preservation the variety is a major rarity. By far the finest is the MS-64 once owned by Steve Tanenbaum. • VF-20 $400; EF-40 $800; AU-50 $2,000.

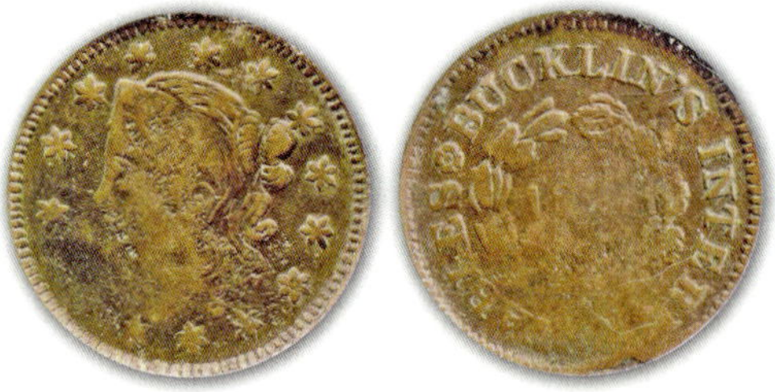

W-NY-1660-50a • Head Facing Left • Low-Unlisted; HT-Unlisted. R-9. 28.5 mm. Copper. Head left—definitive as all other issues for Bucklin's Interest Tables have the head facing right. This obverse was also used with Low-145 (Bucklin's Bookkeeping, West Troy) and 146 and 147 (both Carpenter & Mosher, Troy, see listing). The reverse was used on Low-88, 89, and 92. This variety was discovered by the late Stephen L. Tanenbaum, who spent time trying to find a citation or other information about it.

Carpenter & Mosher
Troy, NY
Dry goods
W-NY-1680

Carpenter & Mosher were in the dry goods business from 1829 to 1831 at 404 River Street, then at 325 River Street, and from 1835 to 1841 at 310 River Street, the last address being that used on the token. In 1841 the partnership ended when James Mosher withdrew.

A listing of tokens in *The Coin Collector's Journal*, January 1886, included this:

> No. 402. *Carpenter & Mosher.* Obv. A most disreputable head of Liberty, left. Upon the coronet, "Troy." Fourteen stars. Rev. "Carpenter & Mosher River St." Within a laurel wreath: "Dry / Goods" 310. Size 18. Copper.

The obverse die used on both of the tokens issued by the firm was by True of Albany and was also used on Bucklin's Book Keeping Tables tokens (see listing below under West Troy). The reverse die on both tokens is the same, with 310 added on the later die state.

These tokens have been recognized as rarities for a long time. In *The Numismatist*, August 1913, a Very Fine example of Low-146 recently obtained by W.W.C. Wilson of Montreal was illustrated for the benefit of readers.

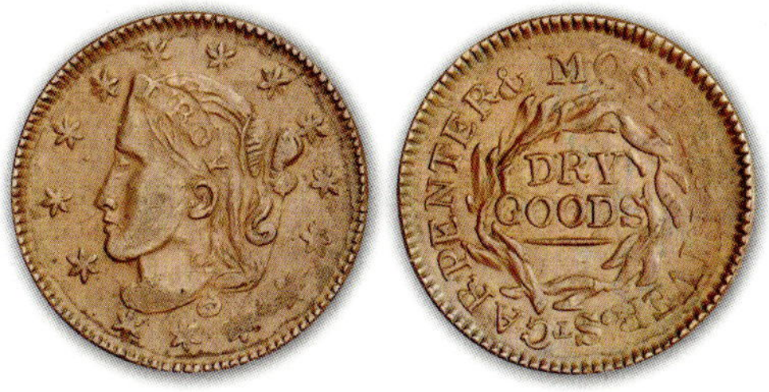

W-NY-1680-10a • Low-146; HT-359. High R-7. Robert A. Schuman traced four different. 28.5 mm. Copper. In 2008 the Dice-Hicks example was described in part: "Rarity-7. Very Fine. Plain edge. 128.6 gns. 27.6 mm. Struck coin turn offset right. . . . The obverse about as poorly struck as when used to make Bucklin's Book Keeping token, the die broken behind Liberty's head, the quality control about as absent as laudable, this piece struck through on obverse with a depression between TR on the coronet. Reverse always soft at right but nicely here MOSHER is fully legible (it wasn't all there on the finest known $35,000 hammer Ford specimen). The die work on this side is very crude and the cataloger would not be surprised to learn that the reverse die of Low-145 had been planed down to make a surface suitable for engraving the reverse of Low-146." It sold for $40,250 to Robert A. Schuman (illustrated). VF and EF are typical grades and have some areas of light striking.

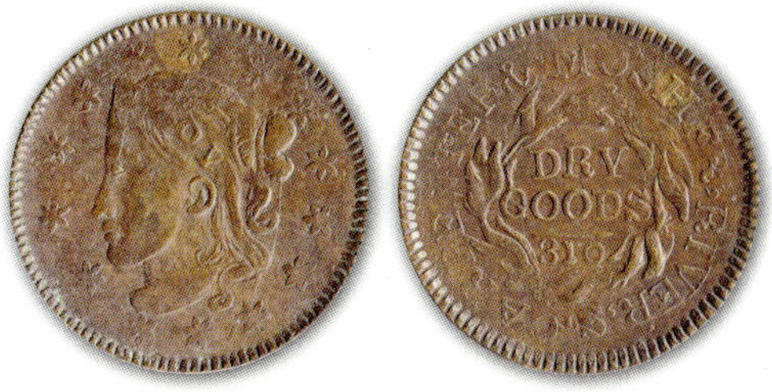

W-NY-1680-11a • 310 added to the same reverse die • Low-147; HT-360. R-7. 28.5 mm. Copper. Later die state of the preceding. The street address was added to the die. In *The Numismatist*, August 1913, a comment from Low was added, to the effect that this variety is "somewhat rarer than No. 146." Fine or VF with areas of light striking describes most. Presidential Coin and Antique Co. archives note that in a span of a century only five auction appearances were found. For a long time Low-147 was thought to be rarer than 146, but modern research has established the opposite is true. Robert A. Schuman has traced eight different. Dice-Hicks (Stack's 2008) VF $10,350 to Schuman (illustrated).

W.P. Haskins
Troy, NY
Planer of planks, etc.
W-NY-1700

W.P. Haskins planed wood planks and sold ground Nova Scotia plaster at 435 River Street in Troy, according to the inscription on his tokens. One shows Lafayette and the other depicts a Woodworth patent planing machine as manufactured by S.B. Schenck of Attleboro, Massachusetts.

An 1840 notice in the *Troy Daily Whig:*

> Plank Planing Mill, Saw Mill, Machine Shop, &c. for sale or to let. The above establishment which is the same heretofore carried on by William P.

> Haskins is very conveniently and favorably located in this city for business. Everything necessary to carry on the mill is now in the same, and in good order, and will be sold or let with it. The machine shop is also well furnished with lathes and all kinds of tools. The terms will be liberal. . . .

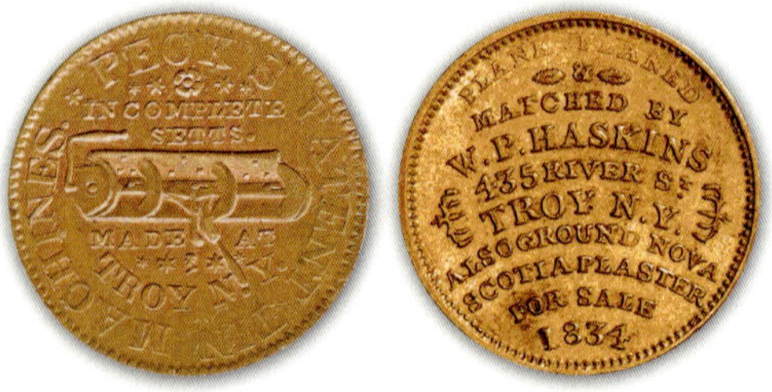

W-NY-1700-10a • Lafayette • Low-79; HT-361. R-4. 28.5 mm. Copper. VF and EF are typical grades. Rare at the AU level. The Garrett Collection example (1981) was VF with problems. This seems to be a token of only medium scarcity until a search is mounted for a high-grade example. • VF-20 $125; EF-40 $225; AU-50 $450.

(W-MA-040-25a) • Low-80; HT-157 and 362. R-1. 28.5 mm. Copper. Muling with die for W.P. Haskins of Troy, New York, who among other services offered to plane planks. Likely made as a circulating token for Haskins. One is known struck over Low-83. This token was listed twice by Rulau—as HT-157 and HT-362—with slightly different information in each place. (Also see listing under S.B. Schenck, Attleboro, MA.) VF and EF grades are par for the course. At the AU level this otherwise common variety is very hard to find. • VF-20 $30; EF-40 $45; AU-50 $100.

J. & C. Peck
Troy, NY
Machinists
W-NY-1720

J. & C. Peck, machinists, manufactured equipment for the processing of cotton, wool, and other products. Peck's Patent Tin Machine was illustrated on the obverse of their token.

The listing for this merchant introduces the curious blacksmith's tokens, also associated with N. Starbuck & Son of Troy (see listing). These combine Hard Times token dies with crude hand-made dies said to have been created by a Montreal blacksmith. R.W. McLachlan, Howland Wood, Warren Baker, John J. Ford Jr., and others have studied these over a long period of time.

McLachlan wrote in the *American Journal of Numismatics*, volume XIX, 1884:

> Previous to 1837 when the lack of specie caused copper change to be accepted in bulk, there lived in Montreal a blacksmith of dissipated habits. He prepared a die for himself, and when he wished to have a 'good time' he struck two or three dollars in these coppers and thereby supplied himself with sufficient change with which to gratify his habits.

McLachlan heard the story from his mother, who grew up in Montreal, knew the blacksmith, and visited his shop in the 1830s. As this was a first-hand account it has never been challenged by numismatists. Otherwise, their creation would be deep in mystery, as no contemporary record is known to have survived.

In *The Numismatist*, April 1910, "The Canadian Blacksmith Coppers," by Howland Wood, explored the tokens in depth and illustrated many of them with line drawings, which are the source of the illustrations used here. There were only two United States store card dies used by the blacksmith—Peck and Starbuck, as noted. Each die seems to have been ground down so as to remove most of the detail.[96] The dies may have found their way to Canada as scrap iron.

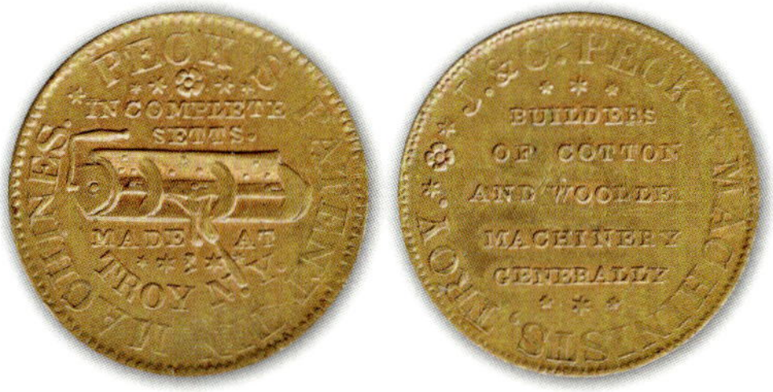

W-NY-1720-10a • Rulau: "Low-271"; HT-363. R-2. 28.5 mm. Copper. This is the only "regular" store card of the firm. VF and EF grades are typical. Higher grades are very elusive. • VF-20 $45; EF-40 $85; AU-50 $225; MS-63 $600.

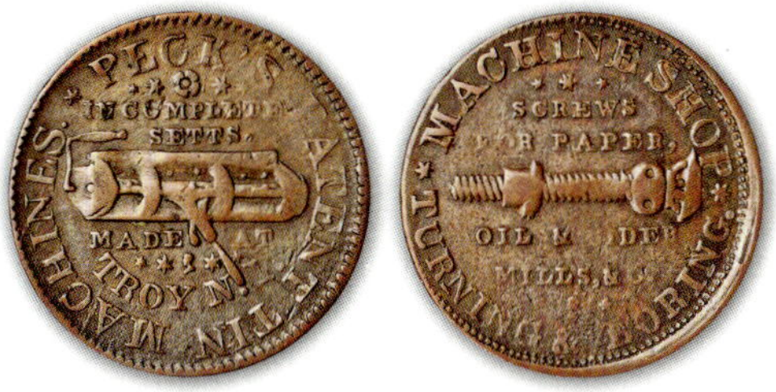

W-NY-1720-20a • Peck die / Starbuck die • Rulau: "Low-284C"; HT-371. R-5. 28.5 mm. Copper. Muling of the obverse of the Peck die with the reverse of the Starbuck die. Listed by Rulau under Starbuck. As this token seems to have circulated by the thousands, and as the dies were made locally, probably the token was a cooperative venture between the two firms. Most are well-worn. • F-12 $150; VF-20 $300; EF-40 $600.

W-NY-1720-30a • Blacksmith token with eagle • Rulau: "Low-272"; HT-364. R-7. 28.5 mm. Copper. Struck from the mostly defaced Peck obverse die. Absent from most collections. Dice-Hicks (Stack's 2008) Fine $1,840.

W-NY-1720-35a • Blacksmith token with seated figure • Rulau: "Low-272A"; HT-365. R-7. 28.5 mm. Copper. See the upper left sketch on the Howland Wood plate. Struck from the mostly defaced Peck obverse die. Absent from most collections.

N. Starbuck & Son
Troy, NY
Manufacturers
W-NY-1740

In 1818 Nathaniel and Charles Starbuck established a plow factory in Troy on the west side of River Street south of the old Fulton Market.[97] Ephraim Gurley became a partner in April 1821, bringing with him his Troy Air Furnace—which in 1818 became the first air furnace in the city—to be manufactured in a foundry on the southeast corner of Fifth and Grand Division streets.[98] The Starbuck & Gurley facility was also known as the Troy Plough Factory at the time. In 1825 they made castings for steamboats on Lake Champlain, the *General Greene*, *Buffalo*, and *Black Rock*.

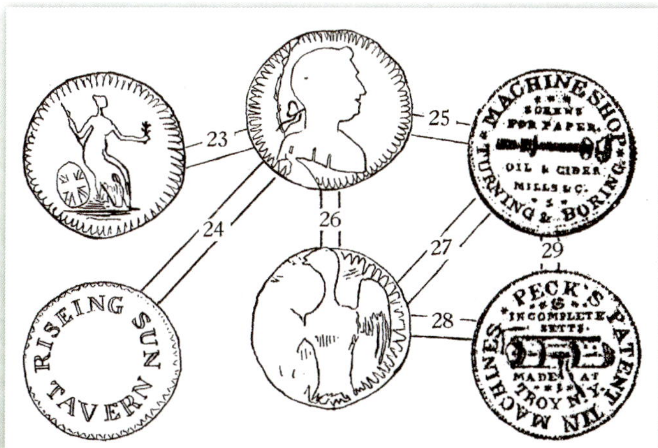

Selected blacksmith tokens as illustrated by Howland Wood in 1910. At the upper right is the reverse of the N. Starbuck & Son token as it appeared on a token of the firm, not after it was partly defaced for use on blacksmith tokens. At the lower right is a drawing of the Peck token obverse die in its earlier form.

The *Troy Directory* of 1830 included this:

> Troy Air Furnace, owned by N. Starbuck & Sons, melts about 600 tons of iron annually. In connection with this establishment the proprietors have also a machine shop, for making steam engines, and boilers, for turning and boring iron, for cutting screws, &c. They have a plough factory, which turns out annually 500 ploughs; they employ about thirty men constantly.

Charles Starbuck died in 1823. By 1830 the firm became known as N. Starbuck & Son.

The company continued in business into the 1840s. A 16-page booklet, *Things Requiring Special Attention*, described cast iron products of the firm. In a state document dated September 30, 1838, N. Starbuck & Son, which owed $409.84, was listed as "shoemakers." In the 1840s into at least 1850 the company exhibited various plows and other items at fairs.

A muling of a J. & C. Peck die with the common Starbuck reverse die is also listed under J. & C. Peck. These are the two dies that were partly defaced and used to strike blacksmith tokens.

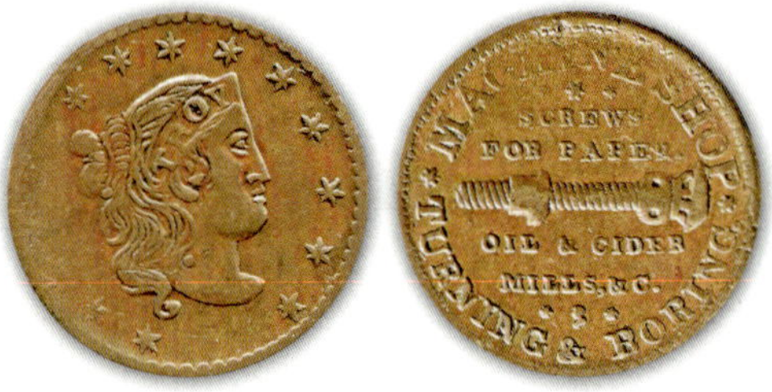

W-NY-1740-10a • 14 stars, no stars under head • Low-156; HT-366. High R-5. 27.5 to 28.5 mm. Copper. Obverse die also used on W-NY-1660-30a. All have areas of light striking. Dice-Hicks (Stack's 2008) AU $2,300. Americana Sale (SBG 2013) AU $1,880. VF is the median grade; at the AU level this variety is a rarity. Grading opinions vary widely due to the irregular striking. • F-12 $200; VF-20 $450; EF-40 $800.

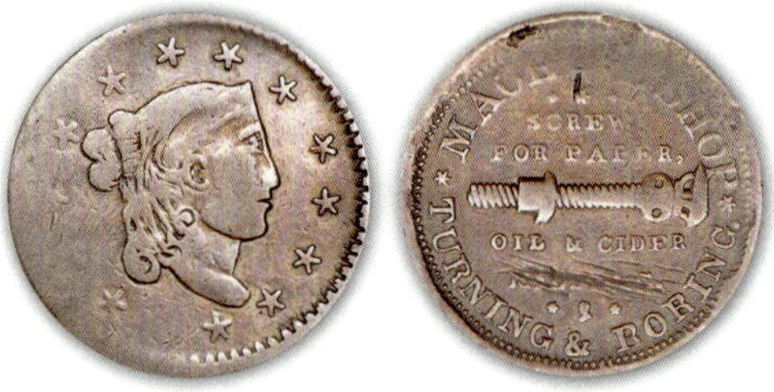

W-NY-1740-15a • 13 stars, 2 stars under head • Low-157; HT-367. R-8. 28.5 mm. Copper. Obverse with "Shapely Head." Reverse die as preceding. Michael Brand Zeddies told Rulau in 1995 that he had sold Virgil Brand's VF specimen privately for $19,000. VG to Fine grades. The "Shapely Head" designation refers to the portrait being closer in appearance to contemporary federal cents than are most in the series. Dice-Hicks (Stack's 2008) VG/Fine scratched reverse $16,100.

Edgar H. Adams in "The Starbuck Store Cards," *The Numismatist*, October 1913, stated that in many years of studying the series, he had only located one example of Low-157 and went on to state this:

> There has always been considerable doubt in the minds of the majority of the collectors of Hard Times Tokens as to the exact difference between Low 156 and 157. Now, through the courtesy of Mr. Virgil M. Brand of Chicago, who kindly loaned us his specimen of the latter variety, we are enabled to illustrate it, in all probability this being the very first time the variety has been reproduced in any publication. It will be noted that there is a wide difference between the position of the stars around the head of Liberty, one being distinctly under the bust on No. 157, while on No. 156 the star is at the point of the bust. The rest of the obverse design is not greatly dissimilar to No. 156, except that on the diadem of Liberty, where the word TROY appears, it will be noted that the space is left blank on No. 157, and there is no evidence that

the word ever was intended to appear on the latter variety. The reverses on all three varieties are from the same die. The dies of the three varieties, according to Mr. Low, were cut by Engraver True, of Troy, and it is remarkable that a perfect specimen of neither variety is known. Indeed it is quite probable that such a specimen never was made. All of the True productions are noted for their imperfect workmanship.

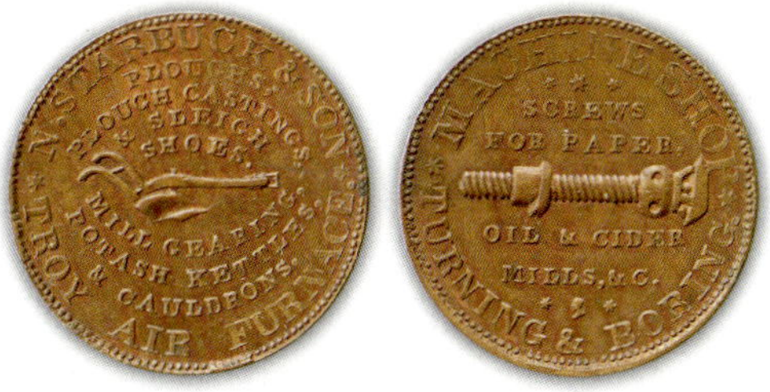

W-NY-1740-20a • Plow on obverse • Rulau: "Low-284"; HT-368. R-2. 28.5 mm. Copper. Reverse die as preceding. VG to VF grades are typical. At the AU level this is a rarity. • VF-20 $60; EF-40 $125; AU-50 $250.

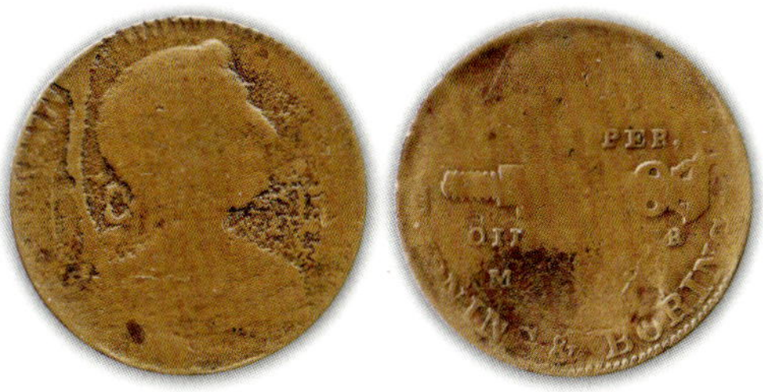

W-NY-1740-40a • Blacksmith token with portrait • Rulau: "Low-284A"; HT-369. R-7. 28.5 mm. Copper. Struck from the mostly defaced Starbuck reverse die, consequently weak in areas. The portrait is non-specific but has been said by some to be of George III. Good to VG examples bring around $2,000.

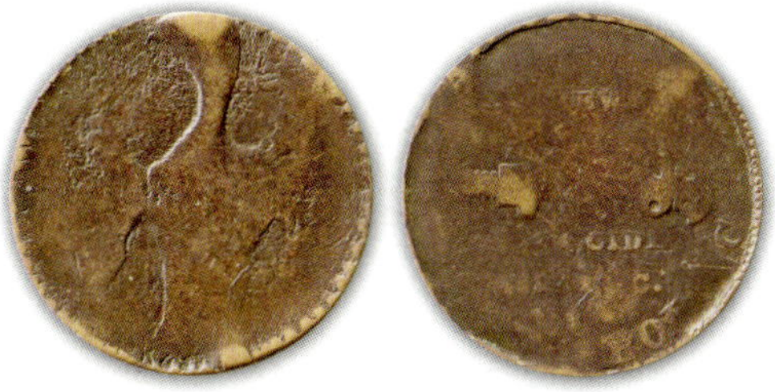

W-NY-1740-45a • Blacksmith token with eagle • Rulau: "Low-284B"; HT-370. R-7. 28.5 mm. Copper. Struck from the mostly defaced Starbuck reverse die, consequently weak in areas. Absent from most leading collections. Good to VG examples bring around $2,000.

Bucklin's Book Keeping West Troy, NY

Bookkeeping system

W-NY-1780

Isaac B. Bucklin is described under W-NY-1660 in connection with Bucklin's Interest Tables. Bucklin lived in Albany, not West Troy, the address on the present tokens, nor in Troy as his Interest Tables tokens suggest.

Low commented:

> This piece is found struck on both thick and thin planchets; the latter are more common. The dies were cut by *True;* the striking is faulty, and the piece is perhaps the most wretched example, both in the die cutting and the striking, of all his work.
>
> There were two die-cutters in Troy named True—Benjamin C. and Daniel. Judging by the appearance of their names in the directories, the first was the elder, but whether relatives or not, I have not found. Benjamin C. was a "letter cutter," having a shop at

7 Beaver Street, and residence at 134 Lydius Street, as early as 1832; in 1834 he is called a gunsmith, and in 1835 a die-cutter, at 7 Beaver Street, "up-stairs."; in 1840 he added to his business as a die-cutter that of a "military store keeper,"—perhaps making military buttons,—and his store was 88 North Market Street, if the notes furnished me are correct. In 1842–4 he was in business with J. Roseboom & Co., on Church and Division streets, but I have not been able to trace him further.

Daniel True was a die-cutter at 48 Union Street as early as 1837, and continued to do business as such at various locations, in time adding that of seal engraving, until 1856, when he seems to have been the senior partner in the firm of True & Pilkington, and his address was "Bleecker Hall." In 1858 he was at the same location, alone; in 1868, the same name,—presumably the same person—appears as a die-cutter and steel engraver, on Hudson Street, and afterwards at 396 Broadway until 1879. The work of this engraver (whether Benjamin or Daniel is uncertain), as shown on these tokens, is not of a very high order.

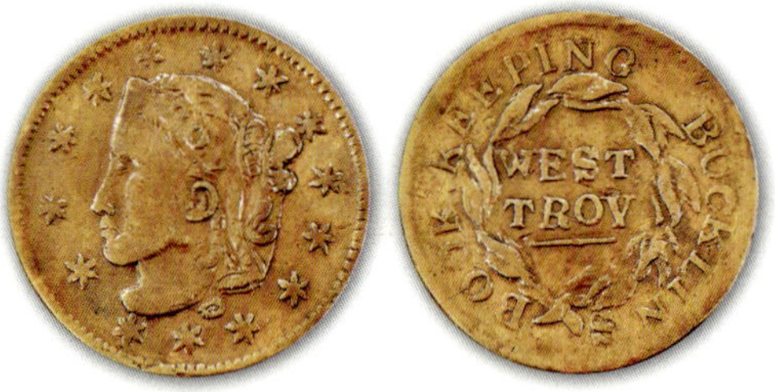

W-NY-1780-10a • Low-145; HT-356. R-2. 28.5 mm. Copper. Rulau adds "large thin flan" as HT-357, "smaller thin flan" as HT-357A, and "thick flan" as HT-357B. HT-358 is unconfirmed. VF and EF are typical high grades for this variety. • VF-20 $125; EF-40 $250; AU-50 $500.

Ohio Hard Times Tokens

Platt Evens
Cincinnati, OH
Draper and tailor
W-OH-020

During the Hard Times token era Platt Whitman Evens, or P. Evens, as styled on his tokens, was a draper and tailor at 149 Main Street in Cincinnati.[99] His advertisements noted that, besides this specialty, he sold fancy goods such as lamps. He began advertising extensively in 1835.

Evens came to Cincinnati from New York circa 1815 and set up in business as a merchant tailor at 138 Main Street. He tailored custom clothes and also sold hats, coats, and other furnishings, which he purchased in New York City, Philadelphia, and other locations. There was no clothing industry in Cincinnati at the time. From the outset his attractive store with its large show room attracted the attention of passersby and garnered mentions of the institution in various articles. Among his famous customers over the years were the Marquis de Lafayette and President Zachary Taylor.

On February 26, 1836, beginning at 7:30 in the evening, a "grand illumination" was held to celebrate the granting of a charter by the Legislature of Kentucky to the Louisville, Cincinnati & Charleston Railroad. Many stores, offices, and other buildings in Cincinnati and across the Ohio River in Newport and Covington, Kentucky, had back-lighted scenes for the public to view.

At P. Evens's there was a view of Covington and the mouth of the Licking River with a splendid temple on the river bank, representing, we suppose, the future capital of the United States.[100]

The Western Directory, 1837, had a section about Cincinnati that included this:

> *Main Street* is to Cincinnati what Broadway is to New York: but this city also has a Broadway. The former extends from the Ohio river at right angles until it intersects the canal in the northern suburbs. Warehouses, stores, manufactories, and pork houses, are to be found on Main Street; and, as in every other city, there is a point more attracting than another—in this it is Mr. Platt Evens' lot to be distinguished—and the front of his store, with his large plates of French glass, through which may be viewed every article almost, of fancy, continues to attract crowds of men, women and boys, from morning till night—when the day is pleasant, much to the annoyance of foot passengers.

In 1838 he was chairman of the committee organizing the Fair of the Ohio Mechanics Institute. When railroad connections reached Cincinnati, Evens would make buying trips to the East and advertise his purchases upon his return. In the early 1840s, the business evolved to become Platt Evens & Farnum, drapers and tailors, on Main Street between Third and Fourth streets.

By 1845 he had reduced his advertising presence or abandoned merchandising and set up as a horticulturist at Spring Place farm, where he raised strawberries, melons, pumpkins, corn, potatoes, cabbage, and other products—with great success according to an account published that year.[101] Evens died in the summer of 1873, was widely mourned, and was given a Masonic funeral. He was survived by his wife Eliza Ann and several children. In May 19, 1874, his "fine 2-story brick mansion and 22 acres of ground at the corner of Spring Grove Avenue and Winton Road" was sold at auction on behalf of his estate and brought $50,521. He had occupied it for 25 years. In the autumn of 1874 the mansion and seven acres of land were offered for sale as being ideal for a hotel. His widow died on May 20, 1878.

Evens's son, Platt Evens Jr., was an engraver and sewing machine manufacturer in Cincinnati, upstairs at 64 West 4th Street, during the Civil War. He was an issuer of Civil War tokens that are rare today.

W-OH-020-10a • BALE. NY. • Rulau: "Low-313A"; HT-375B and 376A. R-7. 24 mm. Copper. Some gilt. VF and EF grades are typical.

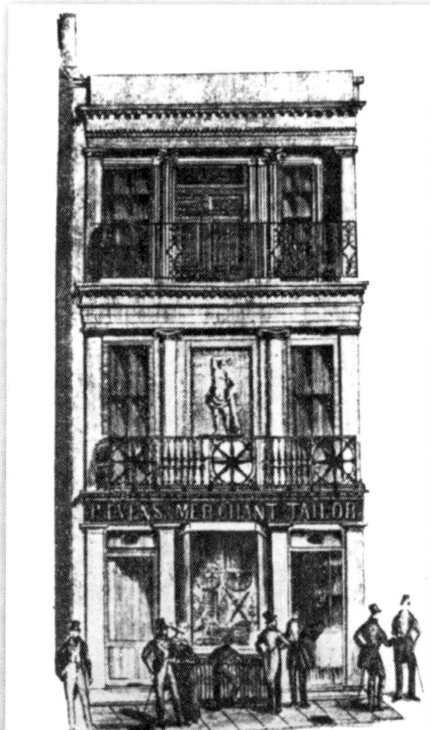

The Platt Evens store in the 1830s.

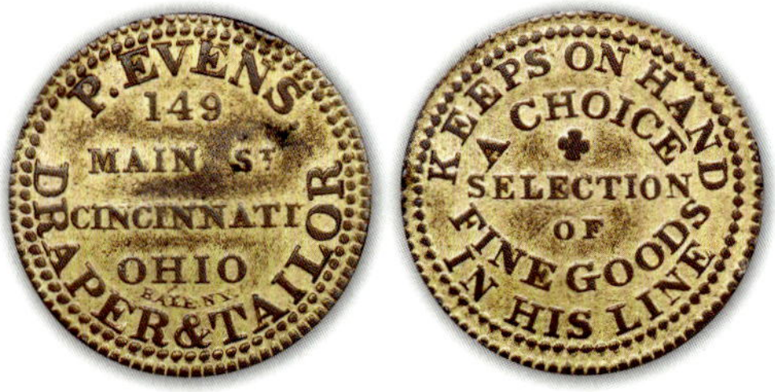

W-OH-020-10b • BALE. NY. • Rulau: "Low-318"; HT-376. High R-6. 24 mm. Brass. Some gilt. Dice-Hicks (Stack's 2008) AU $1,955. Ford (SBG 2013) MS-63 $822.50, MS-64 $2,467.50.

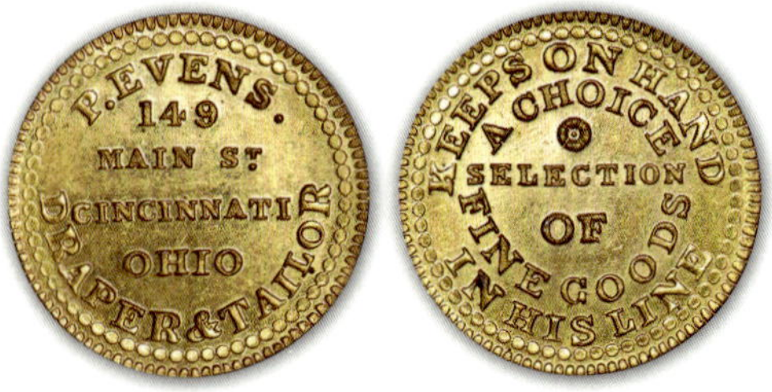

W-OH-020-15b • Rulau: "Low-312A"; HT-375A. R-7. 24 mm. Brass. Some gilt. Dice-Hicks (Stack's 2008) Choice Unc $3,738. Ford (SBG 2013) MS-64 $2,233, MS-66 $3,290.

W-OH-020-15j • Rulau: "Low-312"; HT-375. R-6. 24 mm. German silver.

A. Loomis
Cleveland, OH
Groceries and liquor
W-OH-040

The Hard Times tokens of Anson L. Loomis, grocer and dealer in liquor, have been widely known to numismatists for a long time.[102] These were made in the early to mid-1840s on the latter cusp of the Hard Times period.

Loomis was born in Sangerfield, New York, on April 6, 1812. He and his wife, the former Charlotte Brown, came to Cleveland from St. Louis in 1836. In Cleveland, he set up as G. & A. Loomis, grocer, at 14 Dock Street. Anson L. Loomis resided at the Cleveland House and G. Loomis at Lawton's at 15 Dock Street.

In the *Cleveland Daily Herald*, May 26, 1841, he advertised:

> Fresh groceries. The subscriber would respectfully inform the citizens of Cleveland and vicinity that he has just received from New York a fresh supply of groceries, ship chandlery, oils, etc., which he will sell cheap for cash. Anson Loomis, No. 24 Cor. Dock & River St.

From 1843 to 1847 he traded as A.L. Loomis & Co. at 34 Merwin Street, this being the address on certain of his tokens. He is not listed in city directories after this time. His tokens have three interlocked rings as part of the motif, in the eagle's beak or below the eagle. On the tokens the state is spelled as OIHO, which resulted either from an error or from the deliberate decision to place the lettering upside down as part of the border inscription. The tokens are crudely engraved.

It seems likely that Loomis himself, or someone located near him, produced these tokens strictly as advertisements. Had they been produced in order to realize profit from the discount of the price of copper from the trade value of one cent, there would have been no advantage on striking them over federal copper cents of the era or other Hard Times tokens. As such, the overstruck Loomis tokens are of special interest.

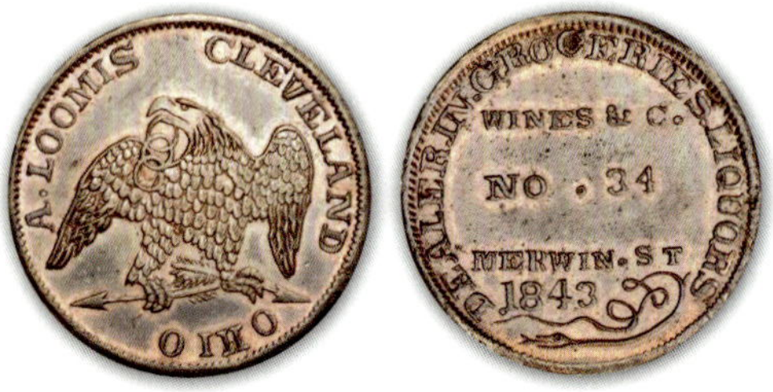

W-OH-040-10a • Rings in beak, 2 arrows, one pointing right, one left /

1843 • Low-158; HT-377. R-7. 28.2 mm. Copper. (HT-377A struck on a cent.) The meaning of the three rings is unknown. It is essentially the same as the Independent Order of Odd Fellows (founded in the United States in 1819) linkage, but Loomis, a Mason, is not known to have been an Odd Fellow. The reverse die in particular is very rustic. At the bottom is a very long and thin serpent, the significance of which is unknown. Ford (Stack's 2004) VF initials for $3,737, AU $20,700 to Robert A. Schuman (illustrated). Dice-Hicks (Stack's 2008) Fine $4,313. Fine and VF grades are typical.

W-OH-040-20a • Rings in beak, 2 arrows pointing right / 1843 • Low-159; HT-378. R-8. 28 mm. Copper. Reverse die as preceding.

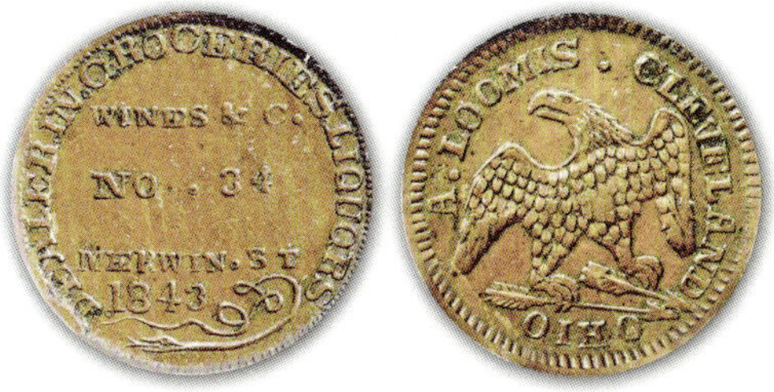

W-OH-040-25a • No rings in beak, 2 arrows pointing right / 1843 • Low-160; HT-379. R-8. 28 mm. Copper. (HT-379A silvered copper.) Reverse die as preceding. (HT-379C on a large cent.) ANA Museum. Hayden (2011) Fine with hole $13,450.

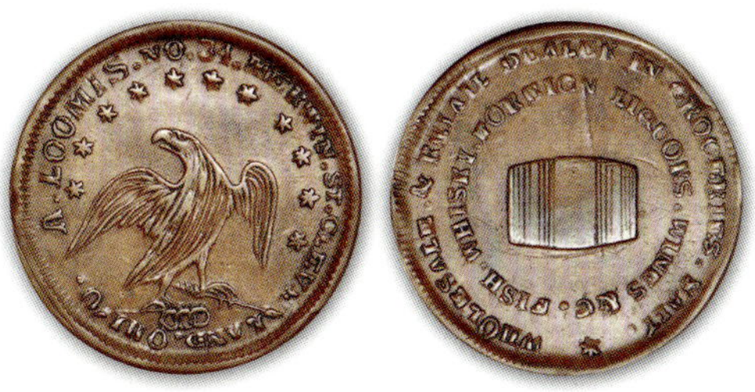

W-OH-040-30a • 11 stars above eagle • Rulau: "Low-319"; HT-380. R-6. 28.5 mm. Copper. VF and EF are typical grades. • VF-20 $500; EF-40 $800; AU-50 $1,500.

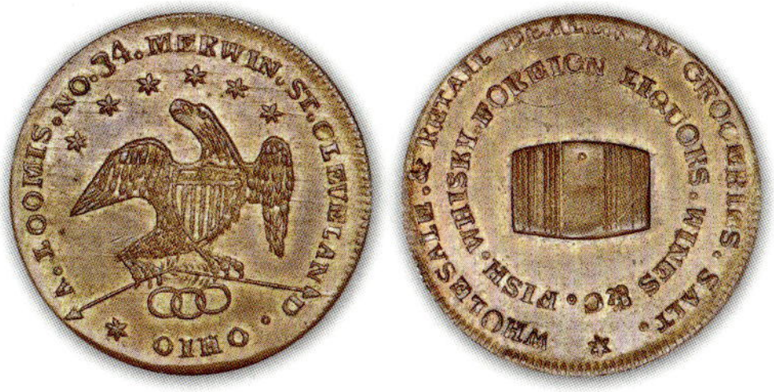

W-OH-040-40a PE • 6 stars above eagle • Rulau: "Low-320"; HT-381. R-5. 30 to 30.7 mm. Copper. Edge mostly plain but with traces of reeding. (HT-381A double struck.) • VF-20 $400; EF-40 $650; AU-50 $1,250.

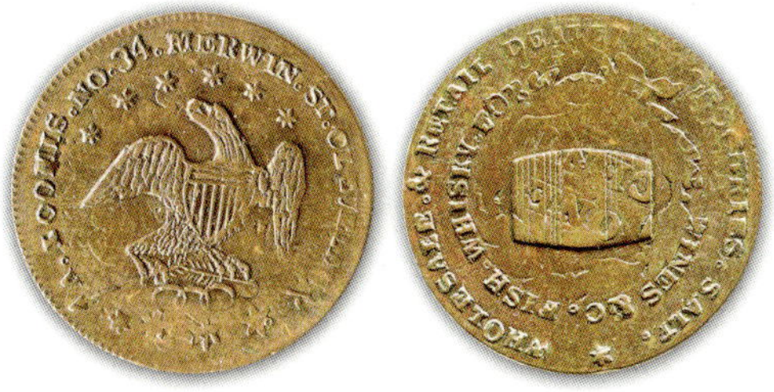

W-OH-040-40a Over 1837 Cent PE • Low-Unlisted; HT-381C struck on an 1837 cent with date and certain details of the undertype clear. R-9. Copper. Ex Chesterfield (B&M 1981) and Tanenbaum collections.

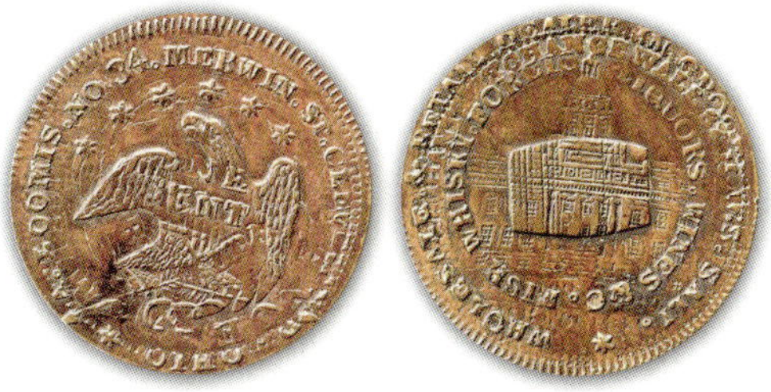

W-OH-040-40a Over Low-95 PE • Low-Unlisted; HT-Unlisted. R-9. Copper. Boldly overstruck on Low-95, W-NY-760-10a Merchants' Exchange token with many undertype features very clear. Ex Mike Ringo and Tanenbaum collections.

W-OH-040-40a RE • 6 stars above eagle • Rulau: "Low-320B"; HT-381B. R-8. 30.7 mm. Copper. Edge reeding prominent.

Pennsylvania Hard Times Tokens

Isaac Barton & Co.
Philadelphia, PA
Dry goods
W-PA-040

Isaac Barton & Co. was located at 30 South 2nd Street in 1833. In 1837 he was at 27 South Second Street, the address on the token. By 1841 the address was given as 29 South 2nd Street, which was possibly in the same building.

Barton was born in Philadelphia on March 13, 1795. He was the senior partner in his company, with Redman Cooper being the junior partner. Cooper at one time was a director of the Philadelphia Insurance Co. Cooper died on November 12, 1892.

Isaac Barton never married. He died in Philadelphia on April 24, 1868. He had a large estate, mostly given to charities including the Woman's Medical College, Woman's Hospital, Pennsylvania Hospital, and the Institute for Colored Youth.

W-PA-040-10b PE • Rulau: "Low-398"; HT-385. R-5. 27 mm. Gilt brass. EF and AU are typical grades. • VF-20 $150; EF-40 $275; AU-50 $500.

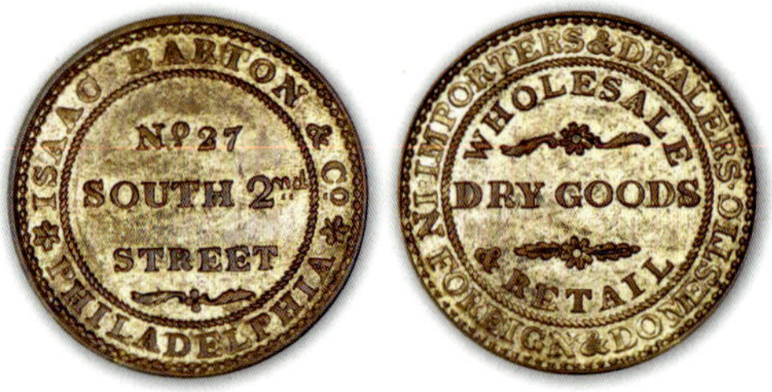

W-PA-040-10b RE • Rulau: "Low-398A"; HT-385A. R-6. 27 mm. Gilt brass. EF and AU are typical grades.

C.W.B.(ender) /
Bender's Star Hotel
Philadelphia, PA
Hotel
W-PA-050

Charles W. Bender conducted the Star Hotel at 71 Dock Street from 1842 to 1848. The hotel name is represented by a five-pointed star. At another time he owned an eating saloon at 3rd and Chestnut Streets. Bender was in business at various addresses for many years.

W-PA-050-10f • Low-182; HT-399A. R-7. 14 mm. Silver. Uniface. Wide planchet with beads not as close to the rim as on the following. Dated 1843 with "43" being inverted and mirror-image. These tokens and the following were struck without a collar. Thus, diameters can vary. Dice-Hicks (Stack's 2008) Choice EF $4,888 and EF $3,450.

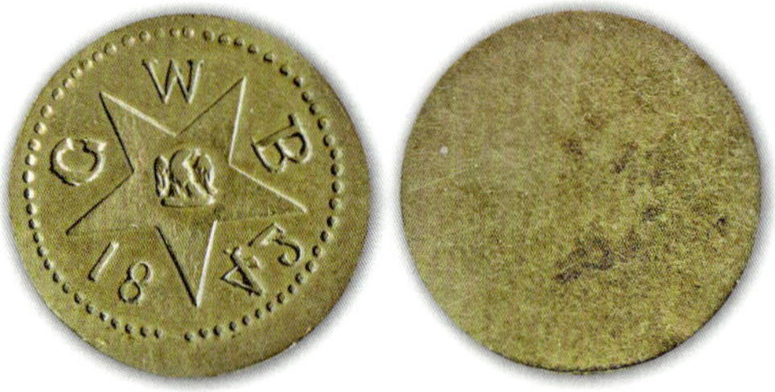

W-PA-050-10j • Low-181; HT-399. High R-6. 16 mm. German silver. Uniface. Same die as preceding. Typical grades are VF and EF, with several known higher. Ford (Stack's 2004) had three: VF $2,400, Choice VF $3,910, Choice EF $2,760. The Marcus Collection (Presidential Coin and Antique Co. 2001) had a VF with weakness at $3,795.

Buehler's & Smith
Philadelphia, PA
Hardware
W-PA-060

The three partners in Buehler's and Smith are spelled out on the token: Martin Buehler, William Buehler, and Edward Smith. Their tokens are the first of several look-alike issues made for hardware dealers on Market Street—an unusual cluster in the context of the Hard Times series.

The address on the token is 192 Market Street. *McElroy's Philadelphia City Directory*, 1837, and certain other listings give the address as 192 High Street. At the time the High Street and Market Street names were interchangeable. Some listings appear as Market (High) Street or High (Market) Street.

On November 29, 1838, the partnership was dissolved by mutual consent. On January 1, 1839, George Handy & Co., 98 Market Street, announced that it had purchased the stock of Henry Bird & Co. and had formed George Handy & Co., the partners being George Handy, William Buehler, and Edward Smith.

W-PA-060-10a • Rulau: "Low-405"; HT-402A. R-9. 29 mm. Copper. Reeded edge. The apostrophe in Buehler's on the token is an error. Steve Hayden reported that he had never seen an example.

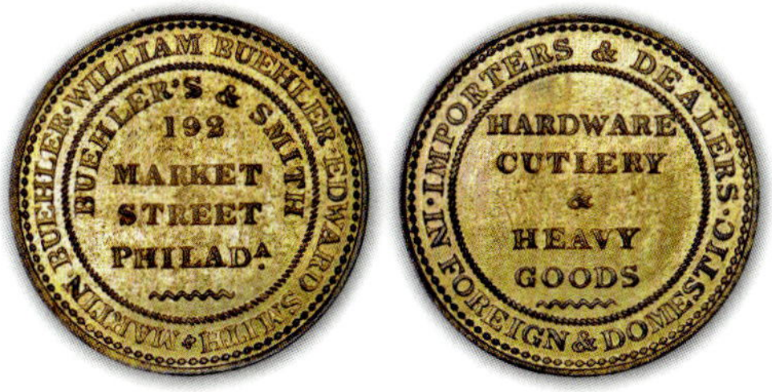

W-PA-060-10b • Rulau: "Low-404"; HT-402. R-6. 29 mm. Brass. Reeded edge. (HT-402B gilt; R-7.) EF is a typical grade. • VF-20 $150; EF-40 $300; AU-50 $700.

Dickson, White & Co.
Philadelphia, PA
Jewelers, importers
W-PA-100

Dickson, White & Co. opened for business with a "New Establishment" announcement dated July 15, 1836. The company advertised as importers and manufacturers of watches, jewelry, plated ware, and fancy goods at 129 Market Street, on the north side, above Third Street.

The partners were John Dickson, William M. White, and John M. Harper, as listed on the tokens. The business was succeeded by Dixon & Harper at the corner of Fifth and Commerce streets, which was discontinued in 1840 and succeeded by Dickson & Co. at the same address.

The existence of off-metal strikings suggests that some of these, white metal in particular, were probably restruck at a later time.

W-PA-100-10a • Low-Unlisted; HT-485. R-7. 30 mm. Copper.

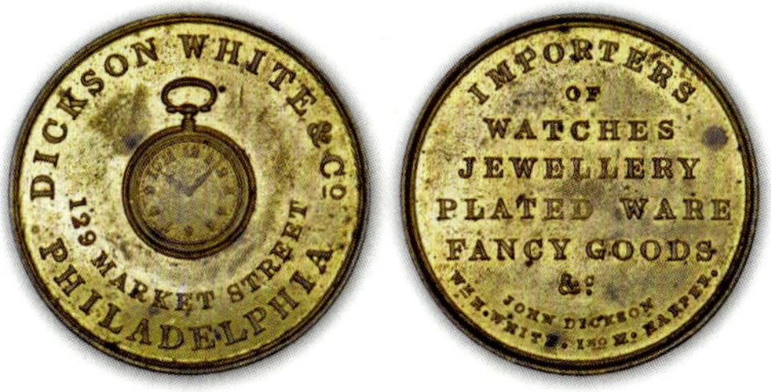

W-PA-100-10b • Low-Unlisted; HT-488. R-6. 30 mm. Brass. Edward Cogan's sale of April 7 and 8, 1863, offered lot 297, "Dickson, White & Co., Philadelphia, brass, very scarce," which sold for 75¢. An example was listed as lot 1389 a few weeks later in W. Elliot Woodward's April 28 to May 1, 1863, sale of the Brooks, Colburn, Finotti, and Field collections, as "Dickson, White & Co., Phila., brass, almost proof and exceedingly rare." It sold for 25¢. Presidential Coin and Antique Co. Sale 67

(2000) Mint State $1,100. Presidential Coin and Antique Co. Sale 72 (2004) Mint State $851. Presidential Coin and Antique Co. Sale 74 (2005) VF/EF $207. Hayden (2005) MS-63 $1,133.

W-PA-100-10e • Low-Unlisted; HT-487. R7. 30 mm. White metal.

W-PA-100-10j • Low-Unlisted; HT-486. R-7. 30 mm. German silver.

A. Goodyear & Son
Philadelphia, PA
Hardware
W-PA-130

A. Goodyear & Son, founded by Amasa J. Goodyear, was in business through 1831 under the management of Amasa's son Charles, though it continued under the same name for some years after Charles gave up the management. Although the token says Sons, the singular, A. Goodyear & Son, is found in contemporary accounts. Whether this token was struck during the Hard Times era has been a matter of discussion. H. Joseph Levine commented:

> The fact that the Goodyear token was crafted with punches first belonged to Richard Trested, does not necessarily mean that it was Richard Trested who did the work. Trested's business was purchased from his widow by Wright and Bale after his death and so it is quite possible, even probable, that they continued using his letter punches. Since the A. Goodyear and Son firm appears in the Philadelphia directories through 1833, it is entirely possible that the token was indeed struck by Wright and Bale, who themselves were in business until October of 1833.

This is one of the most intricately engraved tokens in the series.

Amasa Goodyear was born in New Haven, Connecticut, on June 1, 1772. In the early 19th century, he established a manufacturing business in Naugatuck, Connecticut, where he made buttons, agricultural implements, and other goods. In 1821 he took a son, Charles, into the business. In 1826 Charles moved to Philadelphia, the address on the tokens, where he set up a store to sell products made in Connecticut. A shop was rented on Church Alley connecting Second and Third streets. Goods included pitchforks, knife sharpeners, and other products, many associated with agriculture, plus some products of other firms. The last included buttons from the Scovills, ivory combs from Ezra Williams, wood combs from Howard Pratt, plated tableware by L.P. Lee, scythe stones from the Globe Company, Britannia metal spoons by Mix, shaving brushes from D.B. Thompson, and augurs by N.C. Sanford. The firm was very prosperous by the end of the decade.

In 1830 Charles ran into financial difficulties with creditors and on more than one occasion was sent to debtors' prison for a short time. The company also ran into financial difficulties in the early 1830s, although it still held valuable patents. The shop was moved into smaller premises on Church Alley. Accounts vary as to what happened next. One stated that the firm under that name continued in business for some years afterward:

> A. Goodyear & Son, having failed through speculations of the junior partner in real estate, the business, in January 1831, passed into the possession of Messrs. Curtis & Hand by whom it is still conducted and who exerted themselves to give currency to various articles of home manufacture.[103]

Goodyear's Philadelphia hay forks continued to be advertised into the mid-1830s at least. In the next several years Charles struggled, in the meantime experimenting with India rubber, which was often gooey and messy. Eventually this led to a nitric acid process, then with sulfur, creating the vulcanizing process. Charles went on to see the process be a great success, but patent suits, infringements, and other difficulties took away most potential profit.

Amasa, son Amasa Jr., and Junior's wife and child moved to Florida to raise fruit. Amasa Goodyear died on August 19, 1841, at Indian Keys, FL, succumbing to yellow fever, which in the same year claimed his other family members.

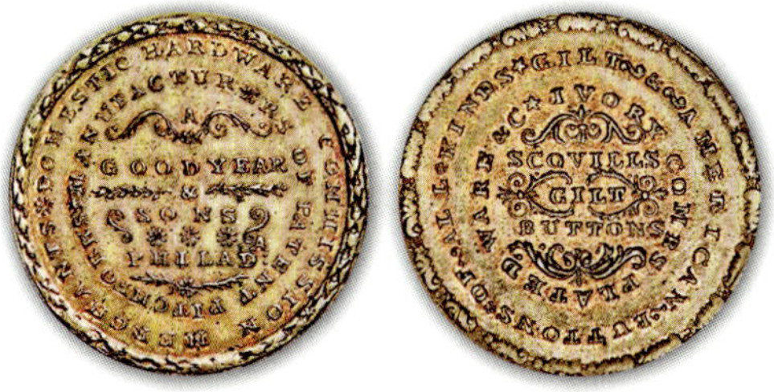

W-PA-130-10b • Low-Unlisted; HT-409. R-8. 29.2 mm. Brass. Two known. One in the American Numismatic Society Collection. The other, in EF grade, was sold in Presidential Coin and Antique Co. Sale 73 (2004) to Steve Tanenbaum for $14,950.

Samuel & Joseph Harvey
Philadelphia, PA
Hardware
W-PA-140

The partnership of Samuel & Joseph Harvey was located at 62 North Front Street in the early 1830s. In 1837 the company is listed at 195 High Street, this the same as the 195 Market Street address on the tokens. Earlier the premises had been occupied by George Spackman, wholesale agent for various button manufacturers.

W-PA-140-10a • Rulau: "Low-383A"; HT-410A. R-7. 27 mm. Copper. Reeded edge. • VF-20 $100; EF-40 $175; AU-50 $300.

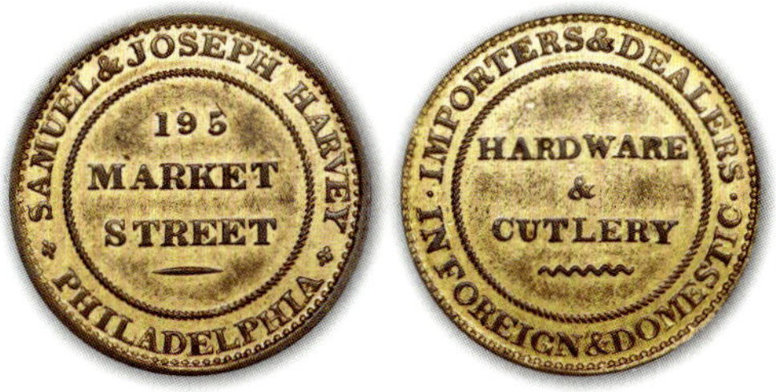

W-PA-140-10b • Rulau: "Low-383"; HT-410. R-5. 27 mm. Brass. Reeded edge. Some or most were gilt (unofficially HT-410B, R-6). EF and AU examples have been in several sales. • VF-20 $80; EF-40 $135; AU-50 $225.

Hooper, Martin & Smith
Philadelphia, PA
Hardware
W-PA-160

The principals of Hooper, Martin & Smith, 113 High Street, seem to have been the successors to Martin, Craven & Smith, hardware dealers at the same address in 1833. The Hooper, Martin & Smith partnership was listed there in 1839. In the early 1840s John Hooper was listed at this location on his own.

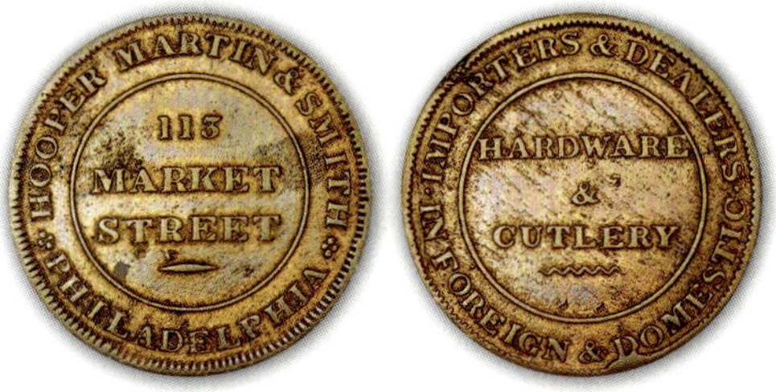

W-PA-160-10b • Rulau: "Low-385"; HT-411. R-6. 27 mm. Brass. Reeded edge. Some were gilt. Usually seen well worn. • VF-20 $175; EF-40 $275; AU-50 $450.

Corporation of Philadelphia
Philadelphia, PA
State arms
W-PA-180

The obverse of this token has the arms of the State of Pennsylvania (not of Philadelphia) but no lettering, although the original seal has VIRTUE LIBERTY AND INDEPENDENCE. This adds to the mystery of these tokens. These tokens exist with two reverse varieties, one lettered as CORPORATION OF PHILADELPHIA / ONE / SHILLING / TOKEN and the other as 50 CENTS F.S. Both are the same size. At the time a shilling was worth 24¢ or 25¢, so one has a value of twice the other. The meaning of F.S. is unknown, although it might be for Feuchtwanger Silver. Lyman H. Low related this regarding No. 152:

> The striking of this token is approximately fixed by an incident in the life of Mr. William Bellamy, of New York, who wrote to Mr. Geo. B. Mason, June 28, 1863, that he found one of these pieces "in Washington Park or Parade Ground about the year 1835 or 1836." Mr. Bellamy in his letter, the original of which is now before me, says he is able to fix the date by the fact that he was on his way to visit the lady who shortly after became his wife.

Woodward described the J.N.T. Levick examples in his 1884 sale:

> Lot 1167. Arms of the city of Phila., rev., "Corporation of Phila.; one shilling token," white copper or Feuchtwanger's metal. I sold a similar piece many years ago for a large price. The same was recently sold in the Bushnell sale and was supposed to be unique. It is certainly of extreme rarity, but two are known to exist. I think it is of the 1837 period and ought to be classed with the coins of the time. The specimen in the Mickley Sale brought $30; at the Bushnell sale the same piece sold for $41. Very fine indeed. [$28.50]
>
> Lot 1168. Obverse like the last; rev., within a wreath F.S., 50 cents. The material of this piece is the same as the last, the obverse from the same die, hence its origin must be the same; unique without doubt; very fine indeed. [$28.50]

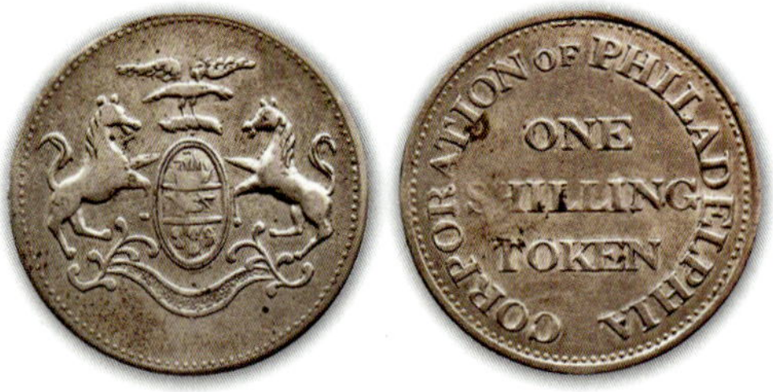

W-PA-180-10j • One shilling • Low-152; HT-412. R-8. 26.4 mm. German silver. Illustrated is the example in the collection of the American Numismatic Society. The other of two verified is in the cabinet of Donald G. Partrick. Perfect obverse die.

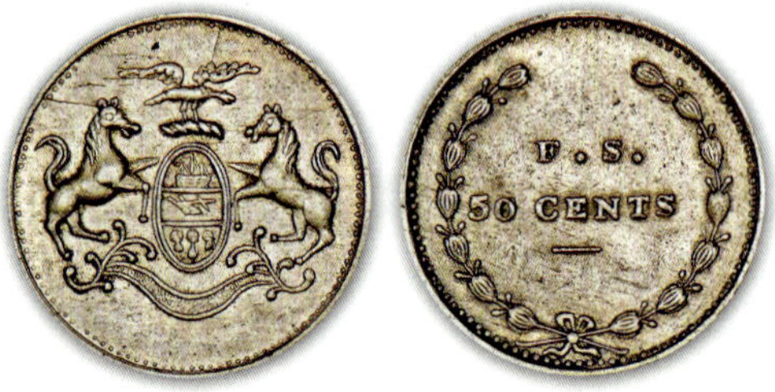

W-PA-180-15j • 50 cents • Low-149; HT-413. R-7. 26.4 mm. German silver. F.S. on the reverse may stand for Feuchtwanger Silver. The wreath and especially the ribbon and bow are the same in style as on the Feuchtwanger cents of 1837. The obverse die is close to shattering, with cracks in from the border at 10 o'clock, half past 12 o'clock, and 2 o'clock, indicating this variety was struck later than the preceding. Dice-Hicks (Stack's 2008) EF $10,350 to Robert A. Schuman (illustrated). Fine and VF are typical grades. Many show scratches or other problems.

Smith & Brothers Philadelphia, PA

Hardware

W-PA-220

Smith & Brothers imported and sold hardware and cutlery at 188 Market Street. Their token is somewhat similar to those issued by certain other hardware merchants nearby on the same street. The same trade style was used after 1837 by the unrelated Smith & Brothers, proprietors of Smith's Clock Establishment at 7-1/2 Bowery, New York City.

A copartnership notice in the *Philadelphia Inquirer*, January 6, 1837:

> T.W. Smith and Clifford Smith (late of Smith & Brothers) associated with John R. Penrose and John H. Ritchie as Smith, Brothers & Co., hardware merchants, 188 Market Street.

In November 1838, under the name of Smith & Brothers, the firm received a certificate for a display at the Franklin Institute Exhibition of edge tools made by William Beatty & Co., Springfield, Pennsylvania. The *Philadelphia Inquirer*, on January 2, 1840, stated that Smith, Brothers & Co. had been dissolved by limitation (the charter expired).

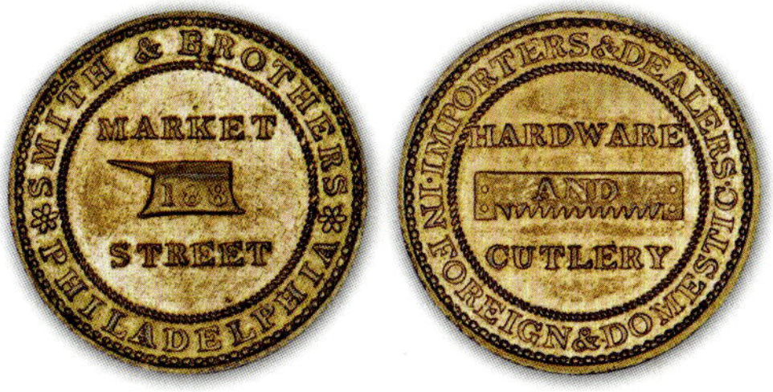

W-PA-220-10b • Rulau: "Low-386"; HT-417. R-5. 27 mm. Brass. Reeded edge. Some silvered (HT-417A, R-6) or gilt (HT-427B, R-7). VF and EF are typical grades. Gilt pieces average slightly higher in grade. • VF-20 $125; EF-40 $200; AU-50 $350.

Snyder & Shankland Philadelphia, PA

Drapers and tailors

W-PA-240

As first noted by H. Joseph Levine, Jacob A. Snyder and John R. Shankland conducted Snyder and Shankland, drapers and tailors, at 102 South Fifth Street in the early 1840s. A notice in the Philadelphia *Public Ledger*, October 8, 1840, stated this:

> Snyder & Shankland, drapers and tailors, 102 South Fifth Street, corner of Powell, having received the fashions established in London for the ensuing season together with a fashionable assortment of French cloths, cassimeres, vestings, &c., including English, respectfully invite their customers to call and see them.

A notice in the Philadelphia *Public Ledger*, March 4, 1843, informed the public that the partnership "is this day dissolved by mutual consent."

The obverse die features Cupid with a bow and arrow. The initial B is on the ground below.

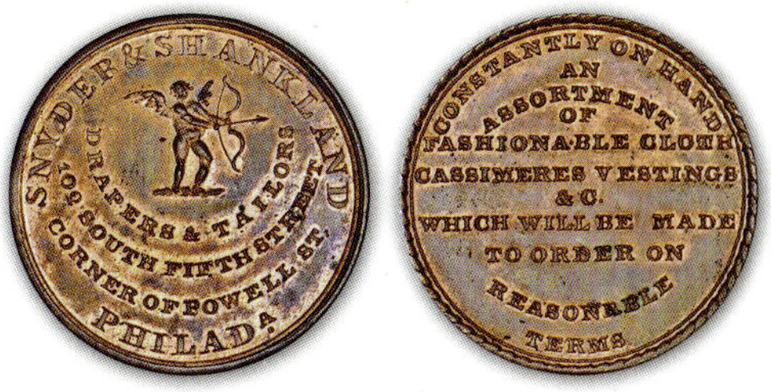

W-PA-240-10a • Low-Unlisted; HT-A417. R-7. 33 mm. Copper. Dice-Hicks (Stack's 2008) $3,738. Americana Sale (SBG 2013) MS-63RB $3,055.

W-PA-240-10b • Low-Unlisted; HT-B417. R-7. 33 mm. Brass. Dice-Hicks (Stack's 2008) Choice Unc $3,738. Hayden (2005) MS-62 $2,805.

W-PA-240-10e • Low-Unlisted; HT-C417. R-7. 33 mm. White metal. Dice-Hicks (Stack's 2008) EF $2,530.

Spering, Mixsell & Innes
Philadelphia, PA
Dry goods
W-PA-260

Spering, Mixsell & Innes conducted business in dry goods at 138 Market Street. The partnership was formed circa 1837 by William Spering and Francis B. Innes (who had formerly owned Spering, Innes & Co. at the same address) and Edmund B. Mixsell, who had earlier been a partner in Mixsell, Wilson & Co., at 206 Market Street. Francis B. Innes died on July 27, 1839, ending the business. At that time the partners were Innes, Spering, and Lewis LaForgue.

In 1832 Spering and Mixsell both served on a commission appointed by the State Legislature to investigate the affairs of the Girard Bank in Philadelphia.

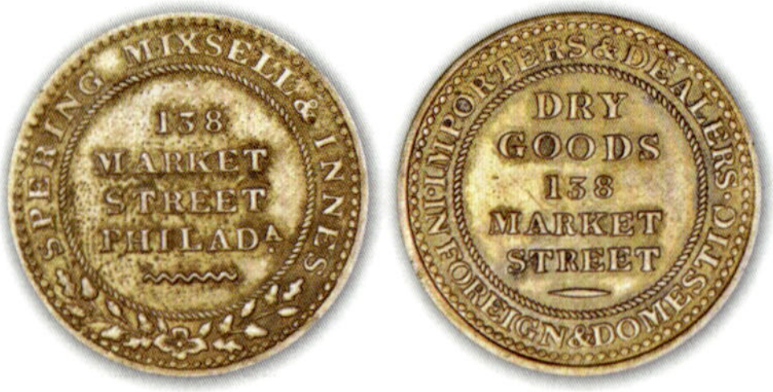

W-PA-260-10b • Rulau: "Low-358"; HT-418. R-5. 28 mm. Brass. Also silvered as HT-418A, R-6. VF and EF are typical grades. • VF-20 $250; EF-40 $400; AU-50 $800.

Spering, Good & Co.
Philadelphia, PA
Dry goods
W-PA-280

Spering, Good & Co. at 138 Market Street, the successor to Spering, Mixsell & Innes, conducted business starting on July 23, 1839, a few days before the expiration of its predecessor due to the death of Francis B. Innes. The partners in Spering, Good & Co. were William Spering, Cyrus J. Good, and Lewis LaForgue. The tokens are of a different style than those of its predecessor. The business was continued until about 1844.

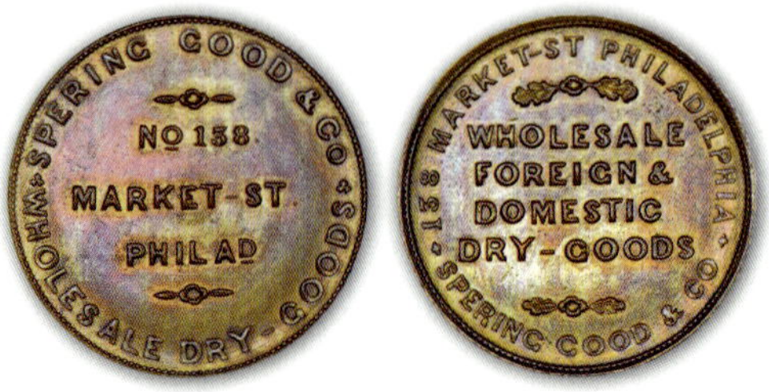

W-PA-280-10b PE • Rulau: "Low-356"; HT-419. R-5. 32 mm. Brass. Also silvered, R-8 per Steve Tanenbaum. VF and EF are typical grades. • VF-20 $200; EF-40 $350; AU-50 $700.

W-PA-280-10b RE • Rulau: "Low-357"; HT-419A. R-8. 32 mm. Brass. The edge is crudely reeded. • VF-20 $300; EF-40 $450; AU-50 $1,000.

James Watson
Philadelphia, PA
Hardware and cutlery
W-PA-320

James Watson was in the hardware and cutlery importing and merchandising business at 11 North Fourth Street. He became the sole owner in May 1838, following the dissolution by mutual consent of the partnership of Watson & Reed, with Henry H. Reed, which had operated at the same address. Russell Rulau related that the Scovill Manufacturing Co. received an order for "gilt counters" from James Watson on March 2, 1835. Watson was a graduate of Jefferson College and received an honorary AM degree from that institution in October 1843.

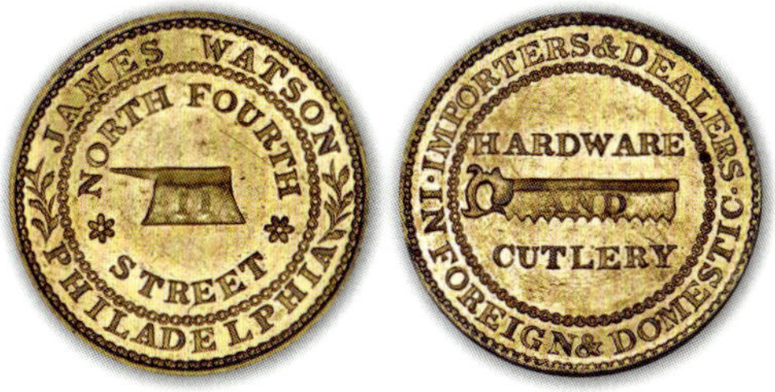

W-PA-320-10b • Stars to lower left and right of anvil • Rulau: "Low-384"; HT-421. R-6. 27 mm. Brass. Reeded edge. Most are gilt (HT-421A). Higher-grade examples are AU and Mint State. • VF-20 $125; EF-40 $200; AU-50 $350; MS-63 $750.

W-PA-320-15b • Dots to lower left and right of anvil • Rulau: "Low-384B"; HT-422. R-5. 27 mm. Brass. Reeded edge. Higher-grade examples are AU and Mint State. • VF-20 $150; EF-40 $250; AU-50 $400; MS-63 $850.

W.H. White & Co.
Philadelphia, PA
Jewelry and watches
W-PA-340

William H. White was in business as W.H. White & Co., importers and sellers of watches and jewelry, at 129 Market Street. The business was formed under this name in 1835 when White, long established in the trade, admitted Benjamin H. Smith. The company transitioned in 1838 to become B.H. Smith & Co. with Benjamin H. Smith, William K. Smith, and William H. White. White died in 1859.

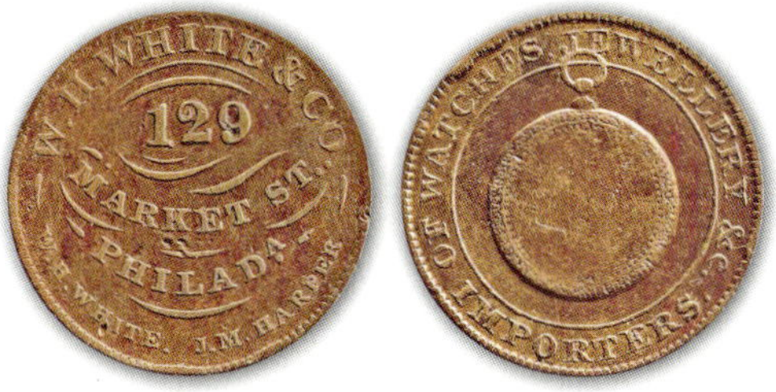

W-PA-340-10a • Low-Unlisted; HT-423. R-8. 26 mm. Copper. Steve Tanenbaum: "Only one auctioned in modern times," Miller Collection to Presidential Coin and Antique Co. December 4, 2004, Fine at $679 (illustrated). Earlier rarity ratings were incorrect.

Rhode Island Hard Times Tokens

Clark & Anthony
Providence, RI
Jewelers and watchmakers
W-RI-020

The partnership of Clark & Anthony was located at 25 and 27 Cheapside in Providence from 1827 to 1837, at which latter time it was discontinued. According to information given to Low by Lorenzo D. Anthony, the company ordered 36,000 tokens through H.M. & E.I. Richards of Attleboro, Massachusetts (see listing) for a cost of $270. Lorenzo D. Anthony was the only surviving principal of a Hard Times token issuing entity that Low was able to interview.

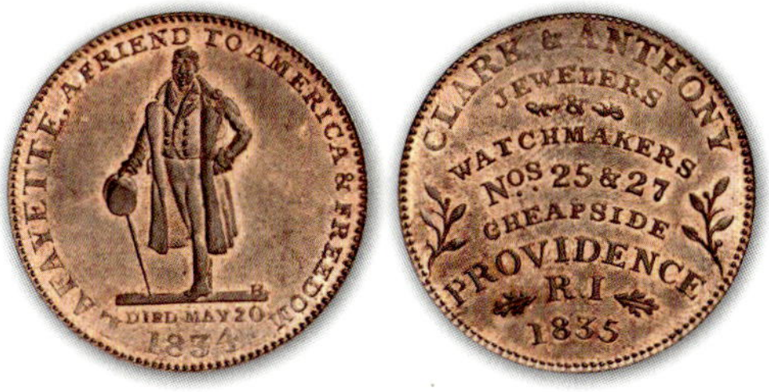

W-RI-020-10a • Low-94; HT-425. R-1. 28.5 mm. Copper. Some were silver plated.[104] AU and lower Mint State grades are easily available. • VF-20 $25; EF-40 $45; AU-50 $75; MS-63 $225.

W.A. Handy
Providence, RI
Merchant tailor and clothier
W-RI-040

In November 1831, E.C. & T. Wells advertised their rental, Store No. 1 Washington Row, "an excellent stand for any kind of business." This attracted the notice of Willard A. Handy who set up in the premises as a merchant tailor and clothier. Later, he issued copper tokens with this address.

In December 1832, he advertised that as "the comet having passed the track of our Earth without having done any serious injury, save for frightening a few old women into hysterics and affording some speculation for fanatics," it was time to settle accounts by the first of the year or else delinquents "will not be entitled to any grace after that time."[105]

In January 1833, at 1 Washington Row (the address on his tokens), Handy advertised that he wanted to acquire a tenement "within five minutes' walk of the Bridge."[106] At that time he advertised his supply of any kind of clothes anyone could want to buy. Into early 1834, Handy advertised large stocks of clothing available and a custom tailoring service for any items desired.

In May 1834, Handy closed his store and the City Baths opened for business there. For the next several months Handy liquidated his stock at that location and also requested that past customers pay their overdue bills. In the autumn the City Baths advertised it would stay open, with heat provided by a Nott's stove.

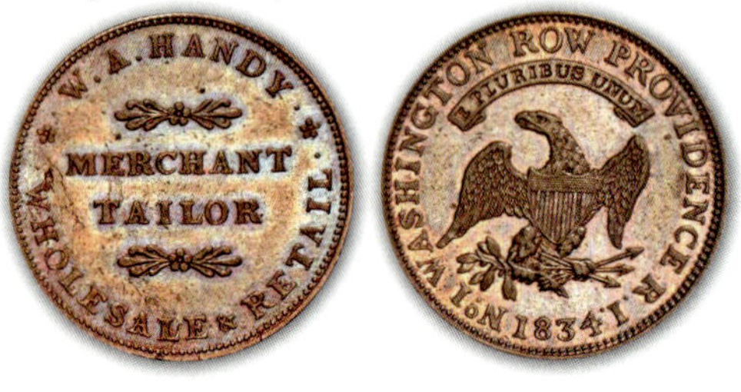

W-RI-040-10a • Low-78; HT-427. R-1. 28.5 mm. Copper. Some are silvered. The reverse motif is a close copy of federal silver coins of the era. VF and EF are typical grades, with AU being top of the line or close to it. • VF-20 $35; EF-40 $60; AU-50 $125.

Ephraim A. Hathaway / City Coal Yard
Providence, RI
Dealer in coal
W-RI-060

In the late 1820s, Ephraim A. Hathaway was the official inspector, gauger, weigher, and marker for the Port of Dighton, MA, a town on an inlet of Narragansett Bay. On December 11, 1819 (or February 3, 1820, early records differ), he married Sarah Ann Williams there. In 1831 he was postmaster of Dighton. On February 12, 1833, President Jackson nominated him as the collector of the customs for the district and inspector of revenue for the Port of Dighton, replacing William Wood, deceased.

In 1833 he became a dealer in anthracite, or hard coal, mined in Pennsylvania. This was brought by ship from Philadelphia to Providence. On August 8, 1833, in the *Manufacturers' and Farmers' Journal*, he advertised:

> New Coal Yard: The subscriber has obtained a lease of Butler's new wharf (recently occupied by the Lackawanna Coal Co.) for the purpose of establishing a yard for our sale of anthracite coal. He will keep constantly on hand the celebrated *Peacock Vein* and *Mann's Gate Vein*, two varieties which are said to be superior to any other for parlor grates and culinary purposes.
>
> His prices *throughout the season* will be governed by those of the Philadelphia Market, and any persons wishing to test the quality of the coal will be furnished specimens for trial. Orders left with Mr. Adam Foster, No. 49 Westminster St., or with the subscriber at his Counting Room on the

Wharf will be promptly attended to. E.A. Hathaway.

On October 12, 1833, in the *Newport Mercury*, Hathaway advertised this:

> City Coal Yard: Real Peach Orchard mined this season. The subscriber is now daily receiving cargoes of this very celebrated coal, the increased demand for which is the surest proof of its superiority.
>
> It is taken from the *Spohn Vein*, the *Peacock Vein*, and *Mann's Gate Vein*, three of the best in what is called the Peach Orchard District, and *not* from the *Centreville* tract owned by the North American Coal Co.
>
> This coal produces heavy red ashes, is easily ignited, burns freely, and is preferred to any other for parlor grates and culinary purpose. . . . Prices as low as any in the City. E.A. Hathaway.

In addition, he sold coal through John Sterne on Banister's Wharf in Newport, Rhode Island.

In 1834, the date on Hathaway's token, the above advertisement was rerun. In 1835 he emphasized Gate Vein coal from the Peach Orchard District in the vicinity of Pottsville, Pennsylvania, that yielded red ashes, and Broad Mountain coal from the district of that name that produced white ashes. These notices were continued in 1836 and through early 1837. His main depot was in Providence. In Newport he sold through George Knowles and George Bowen.

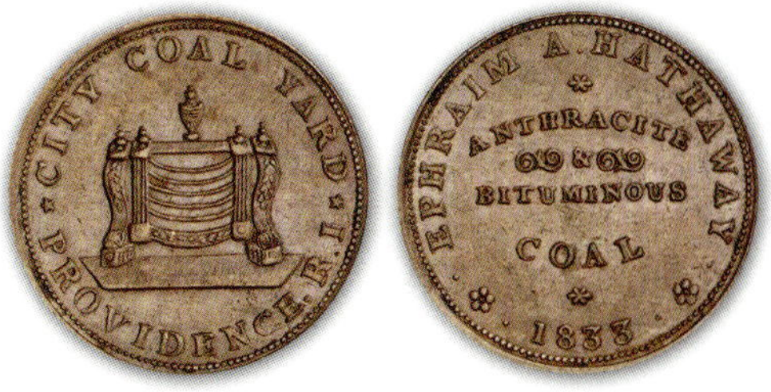

W-RI-080-10a • Low-74; HT-428. R-1. 28.5 mm. Copper. Some are silvered (HT-28A, R-3). AU and lower Mint State specimens are not difficult to locate. • VF-20 $25; EF-40 $50; AU-50 $90; MS-63 $250.

South Carolina Hard Times Tokens

R.L. Baker
Charleston, SC
Soda water
W-SC-020

R.L. Baker was a druggist in Charleston with premises on the ground floor of a building at the corner of Broad and East Bay streets until 1837. The *Charleston Courier* published this notice of change on September 26, 1837:

> Removal—The subscriber respectfully announces to his city and country friends that he has removed his Drug and Soda Water Establishment from the corner of East Bay and Broad streets to one door from the corner, in Broad Street No. 2, opposite the office of the Fire and Marine Insurance Company.
>
> On entering his new establishment he cannot but feel sensibly grateful to the public for their liberal supports, and with pleasing recollections he reverts to the generous patronage extended to him by his city and country friends and ardently hopes to cherish and retain their support and confidence, by a zealous desire to please and an honorable determination to discharge his duty toward the public, by furnishing to them, at all times, the most choice and genuine drugs, chemicals, &c. and every article usually kept in the Medical Department, upon the most reasonable terms.
>
> His Mineral Water Establishment having undergone a thorough repair, his patrons will be furnished with that cooling and grateful draught, equal if

not superior perfection to any other establishment in the city. It is the object of the subscriber to keep supplies of the most choice English and French garden seeds, for which he as at present orders in Europe, which are daily expected; also, at seasonable periods he will furnish nurseries and orchards with bearing fruit trees, green house exotic plants, and the most rare selections of new rose trees. City and country orders will be punctually and faithfully executed. The public are respectively invited to call at his new establishment, No. 3 Broad Street, one door from his former stand. Rob't L. Baker.

Advertised the same month were many patent medicines, including Cosby's Compound Dyspeptic Bitters; Bernard's Remedy for Asiatic Cholera Morbus, diarrhea, &c.; Butler's Apeirent Magnesia; Dr. Blackwell's Antincid Tincture for all stages of venereal disorder; Mrs. E. Kidder's Cholera Morbus, Dysentery and Diarrhea Cordial; Dean's Rheumatic Pills cure for rheumatism; Godfrey's Head Ache Drops cure for nervous headache; Coster & Coxe Southern Tonic for the cure of fever and ague; Dr. John T. Hamilton's Lisbon Anti-Venereal Tincture; and Roche's Embrocation, a certain cure for hooping [*sic*] cough. Further, Baker had "been appointed agent for this city of H. Gregory's Celebrated Vanilla Cream Candy, by wholesale and retail."

Baker was a heavy advertiser locally, usually extolling the virtues of patent medicines. He was also important in the affairs of the Agricultural Society of South Carolina. In 1840, Gallighan's Vegetable Fever and Ague Pills were showcased in lengthy notices, as were other cure-alls. His extensive advertising ended in that year.

J.W. Haseltine, in his 82nd Sale, November 1884, stated that just three specimens of Baker's token were known. Over a long period of years, this token has been showcased whenever offered at auction.

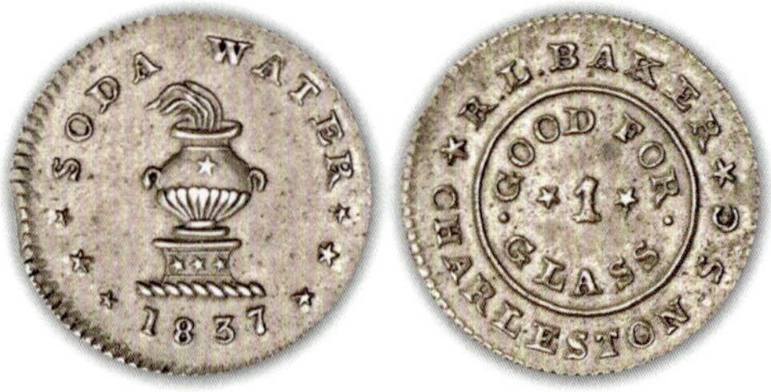

W-SC-020-10j • Low-108; HT-430. High R-6. 19 mm. German silver. Reeded edge. Russell Rulau stated that only 7 pieces were in public hands. VF and EF are typical grades. Hayden (2008) Choice EF with small stains $6,655. Rulau's report of a copper striking cannot be verified.

R.E. Russell
Columbia, SC
Public bath
W-SC-040

The R.E. Russell token has the obverse side with Feuchtwanger die 6, also used to strike Feuchtwanger Composition one-cent pieces. While it is proper form to assign the advertising side as the obverse, tradition has it that the date side with the eagle and rattlesnake is the obverse—the procedure followed for the various Feuchtwanger cents.

The reverse die has R.E. RUSSELL at top border. At top center, there are three rosettes (the center one larger; two smaller ones punched over stars) below which is I • O • U. Near the bottom border is 12½ c, with three stars below (the center one being larger). In the fraction, the denominator "2" is punched over an erroneous "1". From the left center border continuing to the bottom border and ending at the center right border are nine stars with stars two, five, and eight being considerably larger than the others.

For generations, this token, although it bears no location, has been attributed to New York because of the Feuchtwanger obverse. Aaron M. Packard changed that assumption in 2013, when he located advertisements by Robert E. Russell, a Charleston botanist and the conductor of a popular tourist attraction, the Botany Garden. Included among the features of his establishment was a public bath.[107] This service fits in nicely with the 12-1/2 cents denomination of the token. This value was popular at the time and was equal to one Spanish real or "bit."

Packard's research has revealed that Robert E. Russell was born in 1795. He spent most of his life in Columbia, the state capital. He began business as a tailor. On August 1, 1816, his partnership with Samuel Treadwell in the tailoring firm of Treadwell & Russell was dissolved, after which Robert pursued the trade on his own. In 1819 he advertised that he had "employed" a number of first-rate tailors in London, Liverpool, and Glasgow who would furnish him with high-quality goods. In the 1820s, certain of his property was sold at sheriff's sale on several occasions. He later became a furniture salesman. He traveled widely in the East, often mentioning his destinations, including New York City, in his advertising. Perhaps he made contact in that city with Dr. Lewis Feuchtwanger. Still later he pursued botany, and in time he was a prolific advertiser of products such as plants and seeds. His Botany Garden was established in downtown Columbia. A later writer recalled:

> Opposite the State House Robert E. Russell, formerly a tailor, had somewhat later, a flower garden of an acre in extent, where he received a handsome income from the sale of roses and other plants. In 1839 he was deeply involved in buying and reselling mulberry trees, a popular pursuit in the East at the time (Alexander Walsh, issuer of Hard Times tokens in Lansingburgh, New York, was similarly involved). An article in the *Fayette Observer*, August 21, 1839, stated that he was set to purchase 100,000 of the trees! Russell lived at the northwest corner of Washington and Assembly streets. . . .[108]

He opened a new bath on the grounds in 1842, charging 25¢ (two bits) for a cold bath and 37-1/2¢ (three bits) for a warm bath. His 1837-dated tokens would have been useful in such transactions. The assumption is made that these were struck in New York City, slightly later than the year indicated. In the early 1850s, Russell opened the Palmetto House hotel nearby his establishment.

Robert E. Russell died in March 1854 at the age of 59. He was survived by his wife Sarah and at least five young children. His earlier marriage to another woman, Martha Taylor, who was later described as "notorious," ended when she ran off with a Mr. Durang, a performer at Young's Theatre.

The R.E. Russell token has been a well-known rarity for a long time. At the Thomas Birch & Sons sale of the S.W. Chubbuck Collection, on February 27 and 28, 1868, one brought $10.25—twice the price of a 1796 quarter in Good grade that sold for $5 at the same event. When the collection of Matthew A. Stickney was auctioned by Henry Chapman, in New York City, on June 26 to 29, 1907, a Russell token brought $105, or about 10 times the typical price for an 1856, Flying Eagle, cent in the marketplace! This was in an era of great passion for Hard Times and related tokens, when such pieces were widely publicized in *The Numismatist*, in dealers' catalogs, and elsewhere.

Today, several dozen examples are known. The token is especially popular due to its use of an 1837 Feuchtwanger cent obverse.

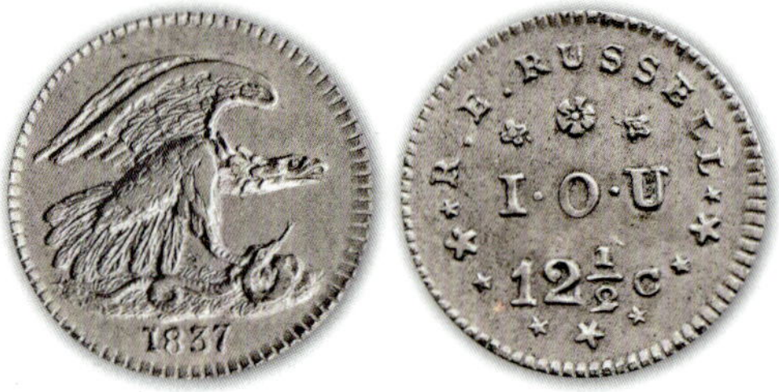

W-SC-040-10j • Low-128; HT-309. High R-5. 19 mm. German silver. Reeded edge. Ford (Stack's 2004) VF $776, another VF $920, AU $2,300, Choice Unc $6,038. Dice-Hicks (Stack's 2008) EF $1,495. Hayden (2011) VF $2,112. VF and EF are typical grades, but higher level pieces are seen at wide intervals.

Tennessee Hard Times Tokens

Yeatman & Armistead
Nashville, TN
Merchandise
W-TN-020

William B. Armistead was born in Nashville in 1811. Henry T. Yeatman married Sarah Ann West in Nashville on December 8, 1834.

The Yeatman and Armistead business was located in Nashville, and both principals lived there.[109] They had a store and a warehouse with a steamer landing on the Cumberland River, which connected to the Mississippi. In the late 1830s, the firm did importing and shipping through the Port of New Orleans. Tobacco was an important product, and the company dealt in cotton as well.[110]

In the 1837–1838 edition of *Longworth's American Almanac: New-York Registry and City Directory*, a branch of Yeatman & Armistead's dry goods store was listed at 34 Cedar Street, but it does not seem to have lasted long. No home addresses were given for the principals, as they lived in Nashville. In the 1850s, there was the court case of Yeatman v. Armistead. Later each went into a separate business.

This token, unknown to Low and Rulau, was discovered by Stephen L. Tanenbaum.

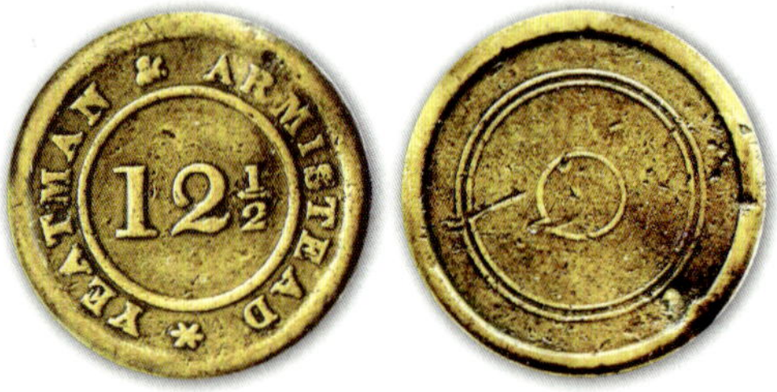

W-TN-020-10b • 12½ (one real or bit) • Low-Unlisted; HT-Unlisted. R-9. 23 mm. Brass. Unique. Steve Tanenbaum Collection. EF.

Vermont Hard Times Tokens

Gustin & Blake
Chelsea, VT
Metal workers
W-VT-010

The partnership of Gustin & Blake, metal workers and tinware manufacturers in Chelsea, Vermont, produced the token that Lyman H. Low called, "probably the crudest workmanship of any contained in the series"—a numismatic compliment, sort of, as rusticity among Hard Times tokens trumps precision and uniformity, at least in the eyes of most enthusiasts. If there are cruder pieces, they are probably certain Troy, New York, tokens from dies that made their way to Montreal to become one side of the curious "blacksmith's tokens."

Sebre Gustin Jr. was born in Chelsea on January 18, 1808. Amos S. Blake was born in Brookfield, Vermont, on January 18, 1812. The indefatigable Low interviewed Sebre

Gustin's daughter in Chelsea sometime after 1900, when his book did not list such tokens, and before 1906, when his supplement did. She had the token dies in her possession. He learned that the Gustin & Blake partnership was of short duration. Blake went to Waterbury, Connecticut, where he made various goods, including percussion caps for the government. When he retired he was a wealthy man. In Chelsea, Gustin remained in the metal goods and hardware business for several years, then took up the practice of dentistry, which at the time required no license. He remained in that profession until his death on September 7, 1883.

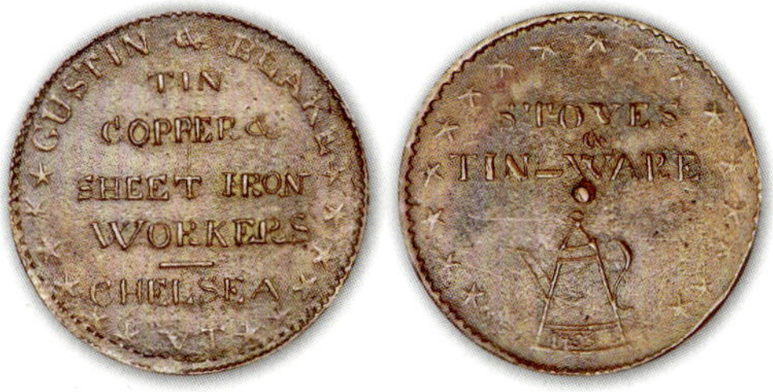

W-VT-010-10a • Low-175; HT-433. R-5. 28.5 mm. Copper. Typical grades are VF and EF with indistinct areas due to striking and poor planchets. Worth a premium if the 1835 date on the pot is full and clear. • VF-20 $1,000; EF-40 $2,500; AU-50 $5,000.

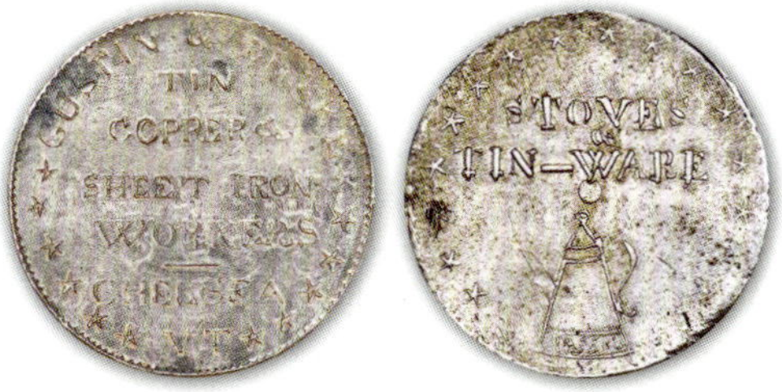

W-VT-010-11a • Low-176; HT-434. R-5. 28.5 mm. Copper. Reverse die very slightly reworked to strengthen features. Rulau lists silvered copper as HT-434A, R-7. Americana Sale (SBG 2013) silvered AU-55 $3,525. Typical grades are VF and EF with indistinct areas due to striking and poor planchets. The top areas are usually clearer than the bottom areas. Worth a premium if the 1835 date on the pot is full and clear. • VF-20 $700; EF-40 $1,500; AU-50 $3,000.

Virginia Hard Times Tokens

S.N. Botsford
Norfolk, VA
Maker of clocks and watches
W-VA-020

S.N. Botsford opened his business as a maker of watches and clocks in Norfolk in early 1839 and continued through 1842.[111] In the mid-to-late 1840s he went back to Bristol, Connecticut, the city of his birth and formed S.N. & H.C. Botsford in order to engage in the watch and clock trade. He was involved in various companies and ventures.

Samuel Norman Botsford was born in October 1815 in Bristol, Connecticut, according to the research of Russell Rulau. He had two younger brothers, Henry and Hobart. When Botsford moved to Norfolk he took along Hobart, who, as a teenager, died in Norfolk on August 9, 1840. Botsford was also involved in surveying the telegraph line route from Pittsburgh to Cincinnati and later experimented with detonating explosive charges by using electric wires.

Botsford married twice. On September 1, 1834, he wed Clarissa M. Beebe, who died in 1836 along with their infant daughter Ellen. His second wife was Caroline Beebe, possibly Clarissa's sister, with whom he had six children. Botsford committed suicide by drowning in the East River in New York City in 1864.

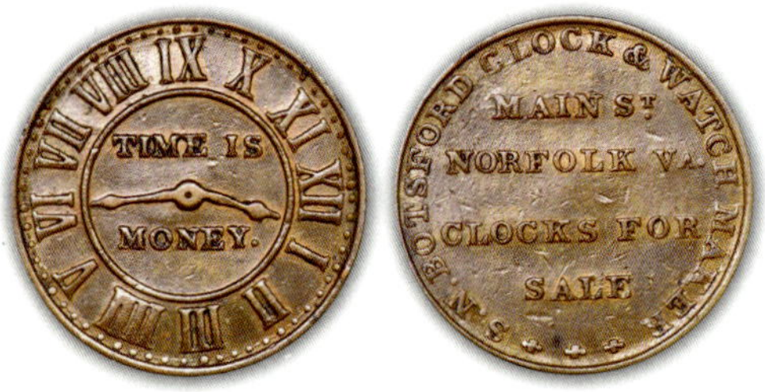

W-VA-020-10a • Rulau: "Low-293"; HT-440. R-5. 28.5 mm. Copper. VF and EF are typical grades. • VF-20 $300; EF-40 $450; AU-50 $900.

W-VA-020-10b • Rulau: "Low-294"; HT-440A. R-7. 28.5 mm. Copper. VF and EF are typical grades. • VF-20 $350; EF-40 $550; AU-50 $1,100.

Beck's Public Baths
Norfolk, VA
Public baths
W-VA-040

In the Hard Times era—throughout which Charles Beck distributed his Beck's Public Baths tokens in Richmond, Virginia—bathing was an occasional experience at best.[112] Houses did not have indoor plumbing, and for most people in the city the closest thing to a bath was wiping with a soapy wet cloth. Across the country, some academies and boarding schools made it an offense to bathe in the colder months, the practice being deemed unhealthy.

For those who desired to bathe, public baths were operated in most of the larger cities. Under the listing for W.A. Handy of Providence, Rhode Island, it is noted that by 1834 City Baths occupied the premises earlier used by Handy for his tailoring and clothing business. Records show that in 1832 Charles Beck was a confectioner and the operator of a bathing facility. The baths were in operation until at least 1844. These tokens, about the size of a quarter dollar, may have circulated locally as currency, or, more likely, they were used as admission checks. The dies are by James Bale or Bale & Smith of New York City.

With its somewhat risqué depiction of a nude woman, this token is a favorite today, just as it was with collectors of the mid-19th century.[113]

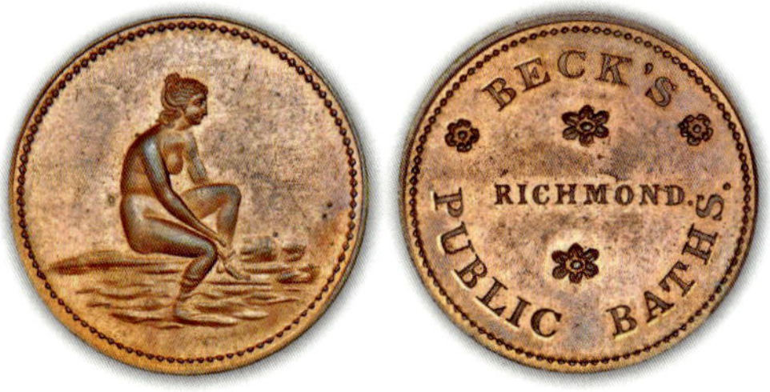

W-VA-040-10a • Rulau: "Low-275"; HT-441. R-4. 28.5 mm. Copper. • VF-20 $1,100; EF-40 $1,750; AU-50 $2,500; MS-63 $6,000.

W-VA-040-10e • Rulau: "Low-276"; HT-441A. R-8. 28.5 mm. White metal.

W-VA-040-10j • Rulau: "Low-277"; HT-441B. R-8. 28.5 mm. German silver.

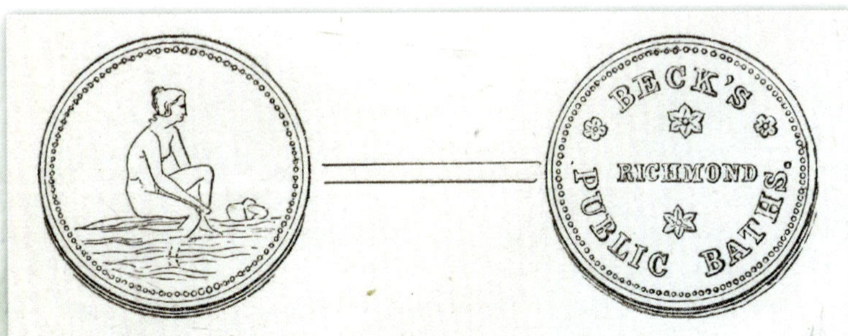

Bushnell's illustration of the Beck's Public Baths token.

Non-Local Hard Times Tokens

S.S.B. 1837
Non Local
Trade unknown
W-NL-140

The identity of the issuer and the location are both unknown. This token has been widely known for a long time and was listed by Lyman H. Low, who was unable to learn anything about it.

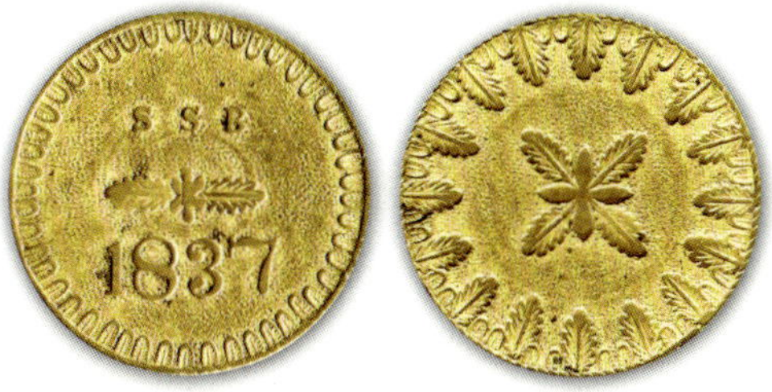

W-NL-140-10b • Low-139; HT-464. R-6. 19.5 mm. Brass. Obverse with S.S.B. above center, 1837 below, and an ornament with two leaves at the center. The border is composed of leaves. Reverse with large and small leaves. Stippled fields, unlike any other in the Hard Times token series. Dice-Hicks (Stack's 2008) AU $1,940. Americana Sale (SBG 2013) AU-58 $2,350. Most are VF or EF with a few at the AU level. This variety usually attracts more attention in auctions than do other R-6 tokens.

14

Fantasy Hard Times Tokens

A Unique Series

Sometime in the late 19th century, an unknown person created fantasy Hard Times tokens by having new dies made with motifs used in the 1830s. Impressions were made in copper and, for some, in silver. The copper pieces were aged or distressed to give them the appearance of having been circulated. These were presented as extreme rarities. It is not known when they first appeared or to whose order they were made. In *Hard Times Tokens*, 1899, Lyman H. Low incorrectly attributed an American Silver token to Charles I. Bushnell, and then continued to describe what today are known as fantasies:

> I hold a similar unfavorable opinion of Nos. 24, 25, 26, 27, 41, 42 and 43, but in these latter I think a partner was admitted, and a very limited number of each was struck, but probably only single specimens in silver.

Chapter 2 also discusses their background. Joseph N.T. Levick is the likely candidate, but nothing relating to his specific involvement is known to have appeared in print in his lifetime.

In April 1870 Joseph N.T. Levick's pioneer listing of Hard Times tokens in the *American Journal of Numismatics* included 56 varieties and the numbers he assigned to them (given in full in appendix II). These fantasy tokens were not listed. The 1882 catalog of the sale of the Charles I. Bushnell Collection by the Chapman brothers had two such pieces. The other Hard Times tokens in the Bushnell Collection were very average in condition, and apart from a handful of pieces the offering was in no way memorable. In the 1884 sale of the Levick Collection by W. Elliot Woodward, seven of these were listed, but without any mention of their origin. The catalog pages are shown here.

After Levick's collection was sold in 1884 it seems he continued to acquire interesting pieces in the series. Alternatively, perhaps Woodward offered only a part of Levick's collection in the first sale. In 1907, a year before Levick's death, Thomas L. Elder auctioned many of his tokens and related items, including a record *nine* fantasy Hard Times pieces. This places Levick as the most likely person to have commissioned these fantasy pieces.

26 THE HARD TIMES TOKENS.

497 1841 Design the same, but die differing from the last: rev., wrecked ship without lightning; very fine, scarce. (53)

498 1841 Similar to the last, but ship has a jib sail set; rev., like the last; perfect, nearly proof, and struck before the die was cracked; *rare.* (54)

499 Bust of Martin Van Buren. "The sober second thoughts of the people are O. K."; rev., a safe; pierced as all are; fine. Hardly of this series, but relates wholly to the subject which gave rise to it. (55)

The preceding comprise all of this series described in the list referred to, with the exception of four pieces, in two of which Mr. Levick expresses his disbelief. The seven following I do not find described in any of the recognized lists, and so far as I know but two of them exist in any other collection; the remainder, catalogued under this heading, are coins of the time, and though their significance is not political, their use as currency at the period grew out of the dearth of small change. In my Catalogue, No. 46, will be found a plate illustrating this interesting series.

500 1837 Female head facing left, wearing a chaplet of laurel leaves, the crown of the head high, the back hair worn low and bound with a beaded cord, seven stars to left, six to the right, E Pluribus Unum on the field above, the date below; rev., "Millions for defence, not one cent for tribute," the five last words surrounded by a wreath of laurel; bronze, nearly proof. Both obv. and rev. of this piece, so far as I know, are undescribed, and I have no doubt whatever that it is unique. See plate.

501 1837 In general appearance like the last, except that the stars are placed nearer together, and the motto above is on a label; rev., "Millions for defence; Not One Cent for tribute"; a large star before and after for, a dash under cent, a laurel wreath surrounding the last five words. The wreath comprises thirty-two leaves, and bears fourteen berries; the end does not meet the stem. In very fine condition, and like the preceding, without doubt, unique. See plate.

502 1837 Laureated female head, seven stars in front, six back, E Pluribus Unum in plain field above the head; rev., "Millions for defense; Not Onf Cent for tribute"; no dash under the word Cent; laurel wreath with thirty leaves and eleven berries. I think this is like No. 3208, Bushnell Catalogue, though the female head on that piece is described as *laureated* with a wreath

Offering of fantasy Hard Times tokens in the 1884 catalog of the J.N.T. Levick Collection by W. Elliot Woodward.

THE HARD TIMES TOKENS. 27

of *vine* leaves. As I have never observed a laurel wreath made of vine leaves, I presume there is a mistake in the description, and that this is really the duplicate of the piece there described; brought in that sale $39, which sufficiently indicates its rarity; extremely fine, almost proof. See plate.

503 1837 Obv. like the last; rev., the same in general design, but One is correctly spelled; the laurel wreath bears more leaves and berries; bronze, nearly proof; presumed to be a duplicate of Bushnell 2209. It was stated in that catalogue to be unique, and it sold for $38. See plate.

504 1841 Female head, facing left, at each side a spray of roses, the date below, E Pluribus Unum on a label above; rev., "Millions for defense; Not One Cent for tribute"; to the right and left of *for*, a small star; under the Cent a dash; the laurel wreath comprises twenty-eight leaves, and bears eight berries, all but one of which are remarkable for size. In the inscription, the word *not* is in larger type than the other words. This piece, like the last, both obv. and rev. unique; in condition it is perfect. See plate.

505 1837 Dismasted ship Experiment drifting on the rocks; Van Buren metallic currency; no lightning about the ship; rev., "Millions for defense," etc.; no dash below Cent, open laurel wreath, twenty-one leaves, nine berries; bronze, about proof; planchet one size larger than ordinary; unique beyond doubt. See plate.

506 1837 Closely resembles the last, but the ship is encompassed by lightning, and tops of the three masts are represented as detached and falling; rev., similar design, and inscription; dash under the word Cent; the wreath has twenty-eight leaves, and bears fourteen berries; planchet size of the last; nearly proof, unique. See plate.

The following Store Cards, etc., include a few duplicates of the preceding pieces. I print them here merely for the sake of preserving the sequence. Some of them are included in the original list, and many of them, by the adoption of similar devices, seem to claim a place there.

507 Riker, Abraham, Division St.; rev., "Not One Cent," etc., no dash under Cent; very fine.

508 The same; rev. has no dash under Cent; fine.

509 1837 Jarvis, George A.; rev., laureated head; uncirculated, nearly proof.

Today the fantasies are still appreciated as rarities, and when examples cross the auction block they usually bring strong prices with strong bidder competition. The Miller, Ford, and Dice-Hicks collections each had examples. The copper pieces are oxidized or distressed, as noted earlier.[1] The dies were boldly impressed, and the Liberty Head on certain varieties is in fairly high relief.

Catalog of Fantasies

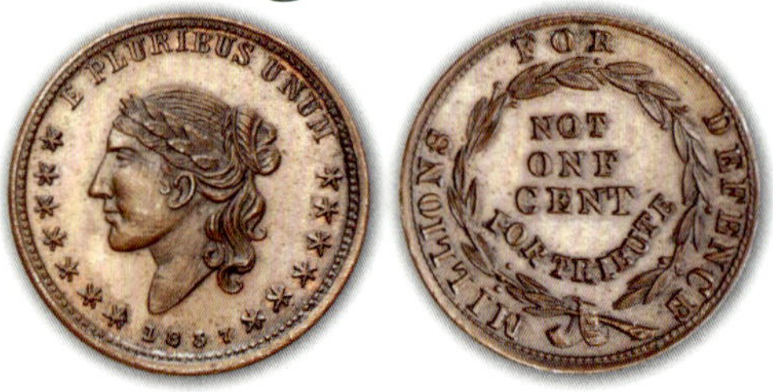

W-X-100a • 1837 13 stars E PLURIBUS UNUM • Low-24; HT-38. R-7. 28 mm. Copper. Plain edge. Obverse with tiara of olive leaves, plain hair cords, E PLURIBUS UNUM above, 7 stars left, 6 stars right, small widely-spaced 1837 date below. Reverse without line below CENT, error ONF, large space to each side of FOR. Wreath not continuous; space at end of farthest leaf to the right. The status of this variety was questioned by Low in 1899.

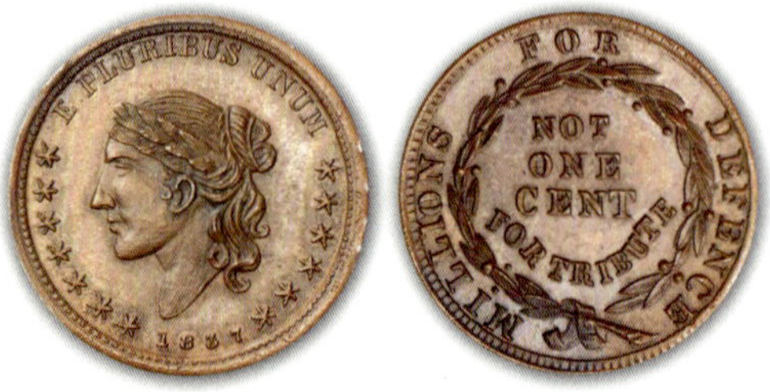

W-X-200a • 1837, stars 7x6, E PLURIBUS UNUM in field • Low-25; HT-39. R-7. 28 mm. Copper. Plain edge. Obverse die as preceding. Reverse from the same die as preceding, but ONF corrected to ONE and extra berries added to the wreath. The status of this variety was questioned by Low in 1899.

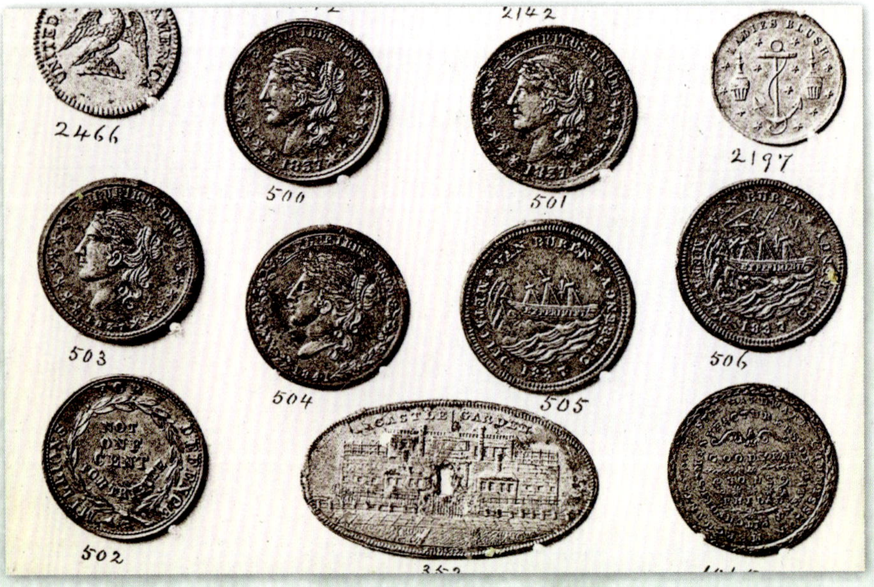

Detail of the first plate showing several fantasy Hard Times tokens (500 series numbers).

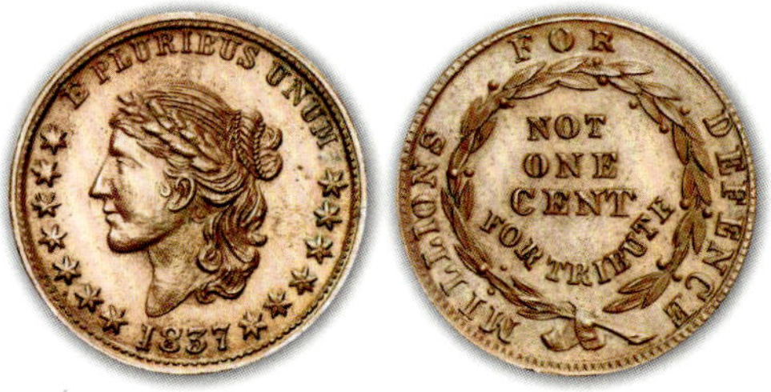

W-X-300a • 1837, stars 7x6, E PLURIBUS UNUM in field • Low-26; HT-40. R-7. 28 mm. Copper. Plain edge. Obverse with tiara of olive leaves, beaded hair cords, E PLURIBUS UNUM above, 7 stars left, 6 stars right, large 1837 date below. Star 5 repunched. Reverse without line below CENT, large space to each side of FOR. Wreath not continuous; prominent berries in wreath; space at end of farthest leaf to the right. Some are overstruck on other tokens, perhaps reflecting that they were struck under makeshift arrangements. The status of this variety was questioned by Low in 1899.

W-X-300b • Dies as preceding • Low-Unlisted; HT-Unlisted. R-9. 28 mm. Brass. Plain edge. Unique. Reported by Robert A. Schuman. The report of a silver striking cannot be verified.

W-X-400a • 1837, stars 7x6, E PLURIBUS UNUM on scroll • Low-27; HT-41. R-7. 27.9 mm. Copper. Plain edge. Obverse with tiara of olive leaves, beaded hair cords, E PLURIBUS UNUM on scroll above, 7 stars left, 6 stars right, large 1837 date below. Reverse die altered from the preceding, now with line below CENT and a six-pointed star to each side of FOR. The status of this variety was questioned by Low in 1899.

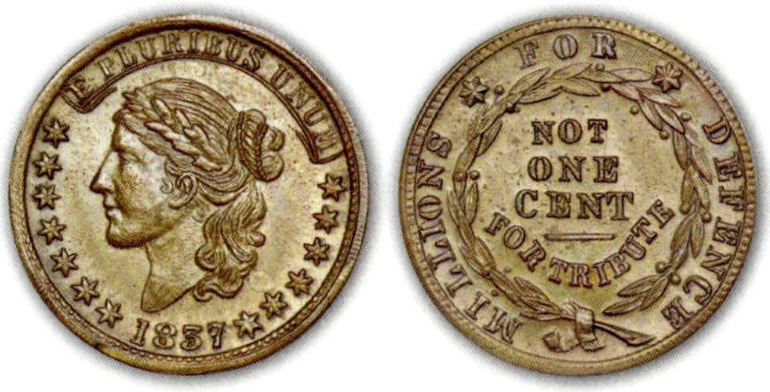

W-X-400b • Dies as preceding • Low-27; HT-Unlisted. R-9. 27.9 mm. Brass. Plain edge. Unique. Ford to Dice-Hicks to Robert A. Schuman. The report of a silver striking cannot be verified.

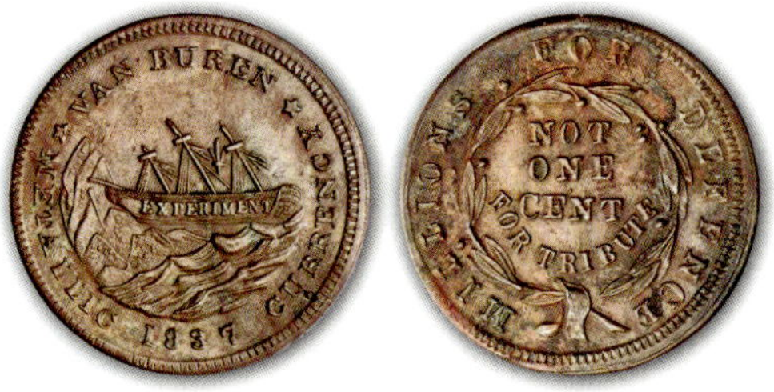

W-X-500a • 1837 Van Buren • Low-41; HT-53. R-7. 29 mm. Copper. Plain edge. Obverse with ship *Experiment* wrecked on rocky shore. VAN BUREN / METALLIC 1837 CURRENCY in small letters around. Reverse with MILLIONS FOR DEFENCE around wreath that ends near ribbon. Outside berries below first L, space between S and F, and D. Within wreath NOT / ONE / CENT / FOR TRIBUTE. No line below CENT. Two berries distant to right of T (NOT). The status of this variety was questioned by Low in 1899.

W-X-500f • Dies as preceding • Low-Unlisted; HT-53A. R-8. 29 mm. Silver. Plain edge.

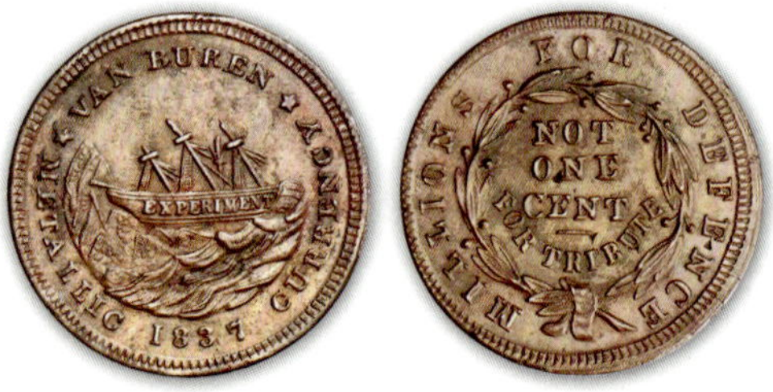

W-X-600a • 1837 Van Buren • Low-42; HT-54. High R-7. 29 mm. Copper. Plain edge. Obverse as preceding. Reverse with MILLIONS FOR DEFENCE around wreath that ends near ribbon. Outside berries below first L, first N, space between S and F, under O, before D, under D, and under second E. Line below CENT. The status of this variety was questioned by Low in 1899.

W-X-600f • Dies as preceding • Low-42; HT-54A. R-8. 29 mm. Silver. Plain edge. Called "believed unique" by Low.

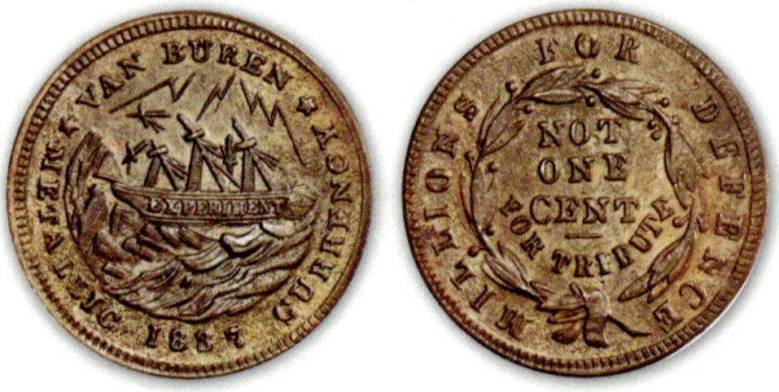

W-X-700a • 1837 Van Buren • Low-43; HT-55. R-7. 28.3 mm. Copper. Plain edge. Obverse die is a later state of the preceding, retouched and with lightning bolts added above the ship. Reverse die as preceding. The status of this variety was questioned by Low in 1899.

W-X-700f • Dies as preceding • Low-43; HT-55A. R-8. 28.3 mm. Silver. Plain edge. Called "doubtless unique" by Low. Dice-Hicks (Stack's 2008) Unc $17,250.

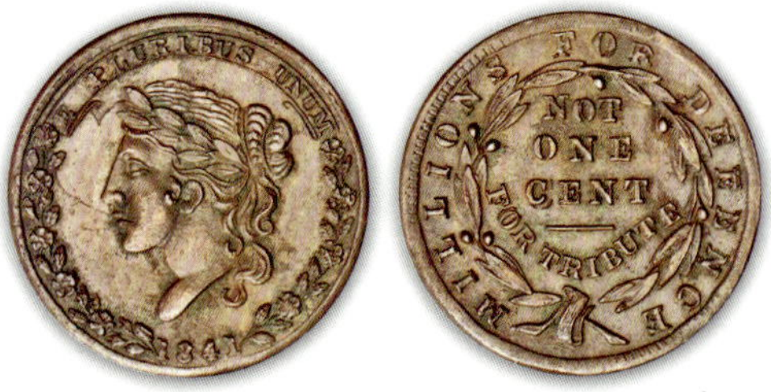

W-X-800a • 1841 Liberty Head • Low-70; HT-59. R-7. 28 mm. Copper. Plain edge. Obverse with Liberty Head, plain hair cords, E PLURIBUS UNUM on scroll above, wreath to left and right, date 1841 below. Portrait with great detail in the hair. Reverse from the die used on W-X-300. One is struck over a Draped Bust copper cent (ex Virgil M. Brand Collection).

W-X-800f • Dies as preceding • Low-70; HT-59A. R-8. 28 mm. Silver. Plain edge. Low: "I believe it to be unique."

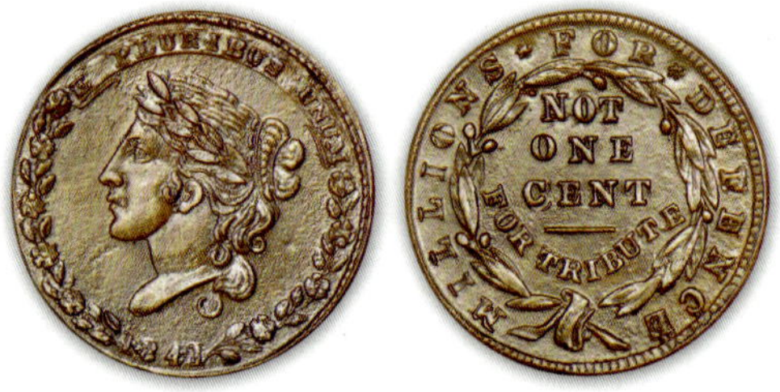

W-X-900a • 1841 Liberty Head • Low-71; HT-60. R-7. 27.8 mm. Copper. Plain edge. Obverse from the die as preceding. Reverse from the die used on W-X-400, altered from the preceding.

W-X-900b • Dies as preceding • Low-Unlisted; HT-Unlisted. R-9. 27.8 mm. Brass. Plain edge. Unique. Reported by Robert A. Schuman.

W-X-900f • Dies as preceding • Low-71; HT-60A. R-8. 27.8 mm. Silver. Plain edge. Low: "I believe it to be unique."

APPENDIX I

Selected Biographies

Henry Davenport

A Pioneer Numismatist

In an article, "Early Collections of Coins," published in the *American Journal of Numismatics* in July 1874, Jeremiah Colburn of Boston included a mention of John Davenport:

> Mr. Joseph J. Mickley, of Philadelphia, had a small collection of coins as early as 1818. He continued the pursuit until 1867, when he sold his collection to W. Elliot Woodward, of Roxbury, Mass., for $12,000, who sold it at auction at Messrs. Leavitt, Strebeigh, & Co.'s, New York, in October, 1867. It contained the rarest and finest specimens of American Coins then known.
>
> James Hall, of Allentown, and Jacob Wolle, of Bethlehem, Penn., had collections as early as 1820. They bought the Cabinet of Medals and Coins belonging to Bishop Hüffel, of Bethlehem, who had made up the collection in Germany, and divided it between themselves. Bishop Hüffel left this country in 1836, on a visit to the Moravian Congregations in the West Indies; from there he went to Herrnhut, in Saxony, where he died.
>
> Hon. Henry A. Muhlenberg, of Reading, Penn., had a collection as early as 1835 or 1836. After his decease, it was sold by Bangs, Merwin, & Co., New York, June 9 and 11, 1863. The late William G. Stearns, of Cambridge, Matthew A. Stickney, of Salem, Henry Davenport, of this city, and the writer, had formed collections as early as 1830; of these, Mr. Stickney's is the largest, and has constantly increased to the present time. Mr. W.S. Appleton's collection is, without doubt, the largest and most valuable in this country. J.C.

Of the above pioneers, Henry Davenport is the only numismatist known to have collected Hard Times tokens in the era in which they were issued. He had special silver strikings made to his order by the original manufacturers and may have commissioned other pieces as well.

INVOLVEMENT IN NUMISMATICS

Born in Boston, Henry Davenport spent most of his life in the area with addresses in Boston and Roxbury. He was an executive of Pacific Mills, a prominent textile firm, where he remained until his retirement in the late 1880s. Davenport was also active in the Massachusetts Horticultural Society. He had begun pursuing numismatics by the time he was age 21, and he continued in the field for most of the rest of his life, although many of his Hard Times tokens were sold through W. Elliot Woodward in the 1860s.

When, on March 3, 1860, the Boston Numismatic Society was founded, the roster included veteran collectors such as Winslow Lewis, Joseph M. Finotti, John Kimball Wiggin, Jeremiah Colburn, Henry Davenport, William Eliot Lamb, Augustine Shurtleff, Henry Dearborn Fowle, George Williams Pratt, and William Sumner Appleton, some being prominent, others obscure. Meetings were held on the first Saturday of each month at 13 Bromfield Street.

In 1866 Davenport was appointed by President Andrew Johnson to serve on the Assay Commission in Philadelphia. While there he bought an 1866 minor and silver Proof set and donated it to the Boston Numismatic Society, of which he was treasurer for several years. At the time Boston was the main American center for numismatic study and research, while Philadelphia and especially New York City were more important in coin auctions. He attended meetings regularly and showed many items from his collection. When S.S. Crosby's *Early Coins of America* was published in 1875, Davenport's name was listed among 140 individual subscribers, reflecting his status as a leading numismatist of the era. In the 1880s he served as vice-president of the Boston Numismatic Society and curator of its cabinet.

On January 24, 1898, at age 87, Henry Davenport died of heart disease in New York City, where he had been residing with the family of Dr. Clement Cleveland, his son-in-law. He was survived by his widow, two sons, and a married daughter.[1]

Joseph N.T. Levick

LEVICK AND HIS TOKENS

Joseph N.T. Levick, who lived in Philadelphia, was one of the most active collectors of tokens in the 1850s. His "collection" seemed to be continuous, lightened now and again by selling many pieces and also consigning them to auction. On December 19 and 20, 1859, W.C. Cook, an auctioneer in Philadelphia, offered a sale of 976 lots cataloged by Edward D. Cogan under the title of *The Extensive Collection of Choice and Valuable American Coins, Comprising Many Extremely Fine and Rare Specimens Together With A Very Large and Complete Collection of Store Cards, Medalets, Political Tokens, Etc. From The Cabinet of Jos. N. T. Levick*. Cogan, an English immigrant who was mainly in the business of selling art, frames, and related objects, had been involved in commercial numismatics for about a year. "My sale

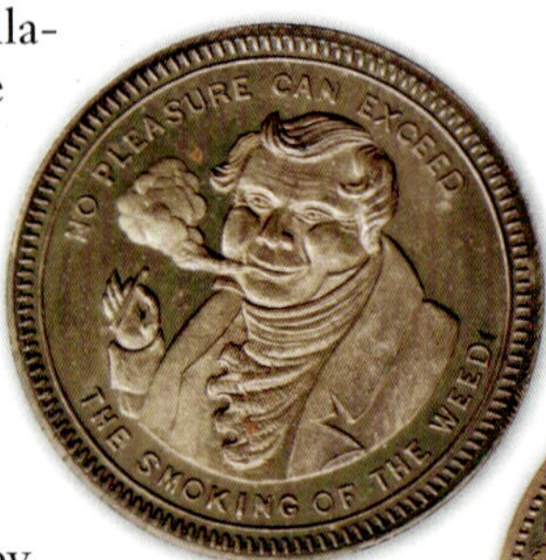

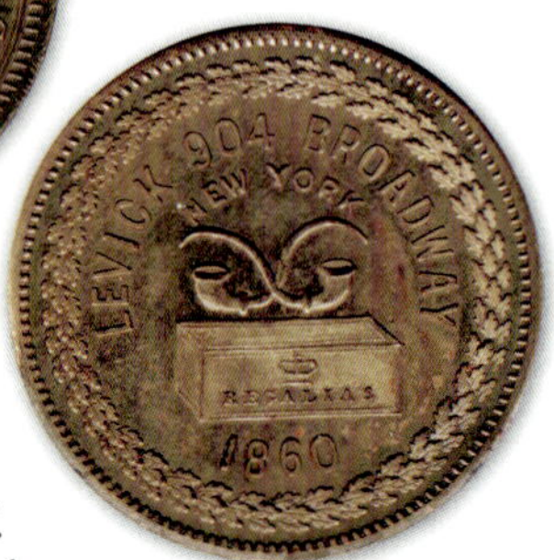

"The Smoker" token issued by Levick in 1860.

was the first printed catalogue collection which Mr. Cogan had the charge of, and it was the first in this country reprinted with prices," Levick recalled.[2]

In 1860 Levick moved to New York City, and while at 904 Broadway he issued tokens, including the famous "The Smoker," as collectors designate it. As might be expected from Levick, the distinctive "old duffer" obverse was muled with other reverses as well. Creating numismatic rarities and unusual varieties was his specialty. During the Civil War he served with the Army of the Potomac and eventually rose to the level of captain.

After leaving military service in 1864, Levick set up an office on Wall Street where he was a banker, broker in government securities, and dealer in specie, stocks, and bonds. In the same year he was a founder of the New York Numismatic Society, which was short-lived and expired on October 25, 1866, transferring its assets to the American Numismatic and Archaeological Society, also established in 1864, which was the group to succeed the interests of the American Numismatic Society of 1858 and 1859. He joined that society on December 14, 1865, and soon immersed himself in its activities.

In 1870 he advertised:

> Banker & broker, No. 54 Wall Street, New York, dealer in government securities, foreign and domestic specie, stocks, bonds, and gold bought and sold, strictly on commission. Dividends and coupons collected, with prompt returns. Rare coins bought and sold. Collections sold on commission. Orders for the purchase of coins executed at sales.[3]

In the *American Journal of Numismatics*, April 1870, Levick's article, "Description of the 'Hard Times Tokens' of '37," described in detail 56 numbered varieties of this year, as discussed in chapter 2 and delineated in full in appendix II. This served as the standard reference until the 1886 study by Lyman H. Low.

He continued to be immersed in the acquisition and study of tokens. Collections and groups of coins and tokens bearing his name on their catalog covers were sold by various dealers over a long span of years. The most memorable sales were held by Bangs, Merwin & Company—one in 1865, and a second, later offering featuring his token collection. He was also a devoted student of 1793 large cents. He contributed the photographic plate to Sylvester S. Crosby's *American Journal of Numismatics* article on the subject which appeared in April 1869. The Levick pedigree on a large cent is at once distinguished and elusive.[4] Pedigrees attached to his tokens are even harder to find, as few such pieces were illustrated in catalogs, and there were no imprinted envelopes at the time.

From May 26 to 28, 1884, W. Elliot Woodward's 67th Sale was held with the title, *Coins and Tokens. The Levick Collection.* The offering of 2,535 lots realized $2,591.74. The listing included a large offering of Hard Times tokens, largely from his 1870 listing. This was part of a much larger offering of 19th-century store cards highlighted by Civil War tokens that Levick had commissioned in the 1860s, including some in silver and other non-standard metals.

In July 1885, *The Coin Collector's Journal*, then edited by David U. Proskey, described some 38 varieties of Levick's Civil War and other mulings, after which it was speculated that others, especially silver pieces, would appear in due course. They quipped, "As to the actual number of varieties struck by Mr. Levick, we can say in the language of the immortal Dundreary, 'That's—that's—something no feller can find out.'"

In *Numisgraphics* in 1886 Emmanuel Attinelli described the collector.

> Mr. Levick is a gentleman, well known among collectors and to the readers of the [*American Journal of Numismatics*]. To those who have not read his carefully prepared articles

relative to some of the issues of this country, it need only be said that they have missed a treat. He is a painstaking and thorough seeker after numismatic knowledge, devoting himself principally to American store cards, tokens, and political pieces.

His knowledge relative to the first of these is probably unequaled; delighting to surprise his friends with a view of some new or rare pieces, after he has had them quietly put away for a time in his cabinet. Time or distance trouble him but little, if he but gets the idea that he will be rewarded, by turning up something new or unknown, and it is this ambition, which has led him sometimes into the not to be admired practice of "muling."[5]

In July 1906, he was listed as No. 815, a new member of the American Numismatic Association. Thomas L. Elder sold many of Levick's tokens at auction in 1907, including nine different Hard Times fantasies from antedated dies. Levick died in 1908. His library was given to the American Numismatic Society, which had just moved into its new building on Audubon Terrace, Broadway and 155th Street.

Lyman H. Low

DEALER, GENTLEMAN, SCHOLAR

Lyman Haynes Low was among the most respected figures in numismatics in his lifetime, and history has been kind to him ever since. A dealer by profession, he also found time to do much excellent research, including, of course, on Hard Times tokens. For his books on the subject he consulted *contemporary material*, rather than building upon numismatic theories.[6] This was a rare benefit to later students of the Hard Times series inasmuch as his definitive 1899 *Hard Times Tokens* book and the 1906 *Supplement* are just as useful today as they were when first published.

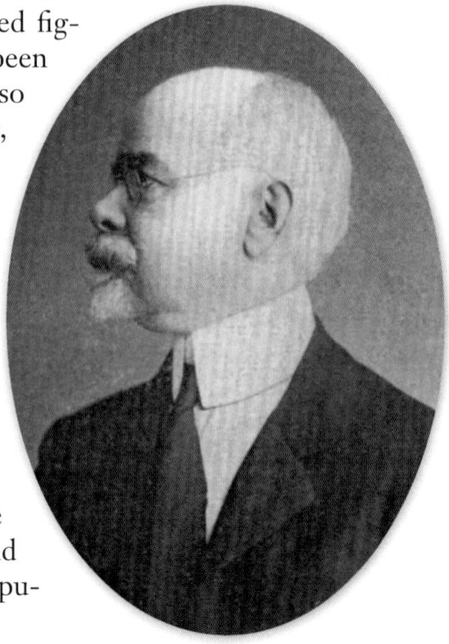

Lyman H. Low portrait published in 1908.

Lyman Low was born in Boston in 1844. At the age of 12 he became interested in coin collecting, just in time to see the old copper "large cents" be replaced by their small copper-nickel successors, and just in time to catch the wave of coin-collecting popularity, which began in a large way in 1857.

On January 28, 1861, the House of Representatives recorded that Low was among thousands of Boston residents who signed a petition urging Congress to find a "pacific settlement for our present difficulties" with the South. During the Civil War he was a soldier for three years. He enlisted on April 22, 1861, very early in the conflict, and served with Company B, 13th Massachusetts Volunteers.

After the war, Low traveled widely in the United States and Canada to sell dry goods and other merchandise, operating from his home, which, beginning in 1870, was in New York. In 1874 he and Ella Mordaunt Peshine married, starting a relationship that endured for decades.

In the meantime, his numismatic interest had been at a minimal level. No mention of him has been found in connection with any of the great sales of the 1860s or early 1870s, nor does he appear in the early issues of the *American Journal of Numismatics*.

About the year 1878, his coin-collecting activity resumed in a significant way, and he began reading the many auction catalogs that were being published, this being a time of intense growth in the hobby.

Dealing in Coins

In 1880 he became a rare-coin dealer in New York City, at first by mail, then in 1881 from an office at 44 West 27th Street. On February 28, 1882, Édouard Frossard conducted a sale described in a 40-page catalog that included the *Collection of American and English Copper Tokens of Lyman H. Low of New York.* This would seem to indicate that Frossard and Low were friends, a situation that changed in the 1890s when they ended up sprawled on the floor in a fight in an auction room—a most memorable scene. The nature of this arrangement is not known, for Low issued his own catalog for a sale held in December 1881. From then until June 1887 he produced 17 auction catalogs, or 18 if you include the R.E. Kingsford Collection, cataloged in November 1885, but sold privately before the catalog was released.[7]

Meanwhile, he joined the firm of B. Westermann & Co., advertising in October 1883:

> Lyman H. Low of B. Westermann & Co. Coins, medals, and tokens. No. 838 Broadway, New York. Coins, medals and tokens, ancient, mediaeval, and modern. Also numismatic publications. Our line of books treating upon the various classes will always be found large. An obscure coin accurately described, free of charge. Coins sent upon approval to parties furnishing satisfactory references. Correspondence solicited, to which we pledge our prompt attention. Collectors, and those interested in the subject, are invited to call when visiting our city.

In 1886 he wrote for and sold subscriptions to *The Stamp and Coin Gazette*, published in Altoona, Pennsylvania, by Edwin C. Mann and Edward E. Kendig. Low managed the numismatic content, resigning his commitment after December 1886, the year he published his pioneering 18-page *Descriptive Catalogue of Hard Times Tokens Issued For and Against the United States Bank, and with References to the Financial Troubles of 1834–1841.* At the time he had an office at 853 Broadway and was no longer with Westermann.

In April 1887, his "Numismatic Notes" column began in the *American Journal of Numismatics.*

With Scott Stamp & Coin

On September 1, 1887, Low joined the staff of the Scott Stamp & Coin Co., 721 Broadway, which had been sold to the Calman brothers by its founder, J.W. Scott, and which was primarily a merchandiser of low-value stamps and coins.[8] Low was in charge of the Coin Department of the Scott enterprise, but he could not have had much to do with the several editions and versions of the *Standard Catalogue*, which described coins and paper money in an amateurish manner, evincing little—if any—scholarship. He did write the Scott auction catalogs, taking over the reins from David U. Proskey, who did most of the catalogs circa 1877 through 1886.

In 1888 Low went to Europe in the late summer and autumn, visiting dealers, museums, and others, buying on behalf of Scott. In December 1894, *The Numismatist* printed this:

> When we place Lyman H. Low as the best known numismatist in this country, we only utter the consensus of opinion of the guild. By those who personally are acquainted with him he is pronounced genial, cultured and affable. At the head of the numismatic branch of the Scott Stamp and Coin Company he reigns supreme; as a numismatist in general information regards our science, he is among the leaders. . . .[9]

From 1891 through 1907 he was co-editor of *The American Journal of Numismatics*, truly a labor of love. In 1894 he was co-editor with W.T.R. Marvin of C. Wyllys Betts's book, *American Colonial History Illustrated by Contemporary Medals*—another immense contribution to the art and science of numismatics.

In January 1892, *The Numismatist* recognized his contributions, and this was *before* his editing of C. Wyllys Betts's book on early medals; the production of his own expanded study, *Hard Times Tokens;* and certain other notable accomplishments, and at a time when his editorship of the *AJN* had barely started. They extolled:

> His knowledge of this important branch of historical research is generally and deservedly recognized, few of our American collectors having larger experience or putting it to better service. He has twice crossed the ocean, and visited principal cities of Europe, and enjoys the personal acquaintance of prominent numismatists abroad.

IN LATER YEARS

In 1896 Lyman Low left J.W. Scott & Co. and reactivated his own business. From that time until 1909 he produced more than 100 catalogs.

In 1900, Low gave this credo, which is still applicable today:

> The foundation of a library should always accompany the collection of a cabinet of coins. To fully enjoy your treasures, books are necessary; coin study cannot be conducted intelligently without them. If we wish to learn the particulars in detail of any coin, just make a specialty of it for a time, and you will find much that is new and entertaining. Gather every specimen possible that comes to your notice.

In 1902, Thomas L. Elder, an up-and-coming dealer in Pittsburgh, went to New York City and saw Low in action. He reminisced about it years later:

> The courtly old gentleman Lyman H. Low, a florid faced, bespectacled man wearing a goatee, his hair even then snow white. . . . He was an aristocratic old gentleman [who] attended his sales dressed in a long Prince Albert coat and white vest, dressed to kill. . . . Low joked as he went along, paused during the session to look up bids at times, smoked a cigar while working, got into an occasional argument in the auction room over a lot, and otherwise helped to enliven auctions. . . . At the time, Low sat at the podium and tended to the bid book, while the sale was called by auctioneer Henry C. Merry.[10]

In 1904 Low's office was in New York City at 4th Avenue and East 23rd Street in the United Charities Building. About this time, Thomas L. Elder set up in New York City as a competitor to Low. Decades later, in another reminiscence, Elder told more of Low's activities of the era:

> A ruddy-faced, bald-headed old gentleman, with snow-white goatee, with an unusual air of dignity and ceremony about him. Always neat and well dressed, his shoes well-polished, one cannot recall Mr. Low as a man of careless or slipshod habits of life. Even his dog, Major, of whom he and his wife, were very fond, was a white French poodle, kept immaculately trimmed and garbed. I say garbed, for he wore the latest things in collar and harness. He usually held a lighted cigar in his hand as he conducted his sales. . . . A cold bottle of liquor was kept on hand to serve clients who requested such; this encouraged bidding.
>
> At that time Mr. Low, our respected dean of American coin cataloguers, lived in a cute little house, a detached house, a bit above 125th Street, in Harlem, in a section then populated by people of very good taste and position. . . .[11]

In New Rochelle

In February 1909, Lyman H. Low contacted the American Numismatic Society, which had recently set up in its beautiful new building at 155th Street and Broadway. He explained that he was going to leave the coin business, and offered his full-time services to the Society for $3,000. The Society declined, as it could not afford the sum. The proposal was made that he be librarian and devote his evenings to this office, for $1,200 per year, but this was not accepted either.[12]

Afterward, in 1911, Low moved to the fashionable community of New Rochelle and did business from his home at 28 Clinton Place. He enjoyed New Rochelle, and his home was open to collectors and friends who wanted to stop by to visit. On Sunday afternoon, June 11, 1921, his 205th public auction sale was held there.

Low died at his home on February 10, 1924, having been predeceased, five years earlier, by his wife Ella. The catalog upon which he was working was undone, and Part II of the J. Coolidge Hills Collection was left unsold for the time being, Part I having been sold on December 1, 1923.[13]

Russell Rulau

A New Numbering System

Beginning in the late 20th century, Russell Rulau of Iola, Wisconsin, developed a strong interest in Hard Times tokens. For Krause Publications in Iola, he created new arrangement of the series, completely departing from the Low numbering system. First, he updated Low by adding many new varieties, and then he rearranged the order, giving them "new" Low numbers.

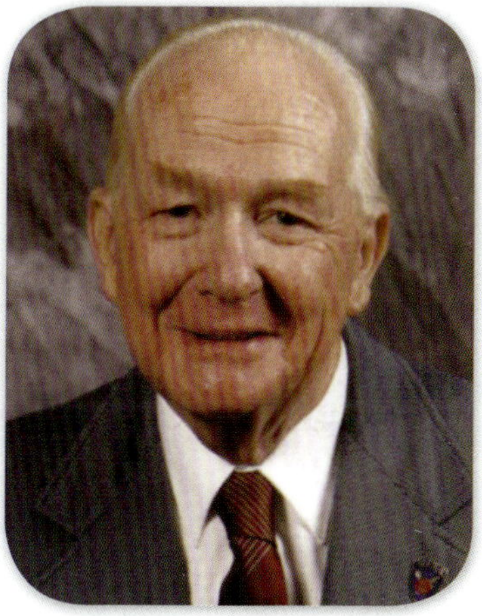

Russell Rulau.

Eventually he added counterstamped coins, tickets, and scrip notes from the 1832–1844 Hard Times era (as defined by Low), dropped the new Low numbers, and ceased referencing Low's 1899 numbers. In their place he used a new system, of somewhat erratic arrangement, though easy enough to follow with his illustrated book in hand. The last iteration of his study appeared in the fourth edition of his *Standard Catalog of United States Tokens 1700–1900.* This is well indexed by merchant names. A fifth edition was planned, but Rulau's passing on November 12, 2012, prevented this from being published.

A Lifetime of Collecting

Born in 1926, by 1939 Russell Alphonse Rulau was a collector. He later recalled:

> Your author acquired his first Civil War token, an 1863-dated Indian Head / OUR ARMY copper, in the summer of 1939 while residing on a turkey ranch in what is now El Cajon, California. I had no clear idea then what it was, but it had been taken in trade as a cent during the 1930s by the Hansen Grain and Feed Mill in El Cajon by my grand-aunt's late husband. My grandaunt Rose Hansen sold the feed mill, but I obtained from her all the "odd" coins her husband had put aside the many years he ran the business. These were mostly old U.S. coins like an 1822 half dollar, 1865 two-cent piece, a number

> of Indian Head cents, and a rather large number of Philippine centavos and 5-centavo pieces (many seamen brought these to ranches in the area).
>
> I learned the term Civil War token only in 1940, from a sale catalogue of the old Tatham Stamp & Coin Co. of Springfield, Massachusetts which advertised in comic books. It took a long time to learn more about CWT's. The first numismatic article I ever had published was in 1958. It listed some Civil War tokens which others had either overlooked or ignored.[14]

In the 1960s Russ and his wife Darlene lived in Sidney, Ohio, where he worked as a writer and editor for the Sidney Printing & Publishing Co., publishers of *Coin World* and, for a time, the *Numismatic Scrapbook Magazine.* The couple moved to Iola, Wisconsin, where Russ wrote for and helped edit *Numismatic News, World Coin News*, and *Bank Note Reporter.* He wrote several books, mostly on tokens. Most of these were later combined into his *Standard Catalog of United States Tokens 1700–1900*, which became the hobby standard for rarity and pricing information on the title subject.

Russ was the recipient of many honors, including the Clemy Award from the Numismatic Literary Guild and induction into the American Numismatic Association Hall of Fame in 2000. In July 2008 he announced a new venture:

> New Iola Coin Shop Opens: One of the world's 10 best known numismatists, Russell Rulau, a recent widower, announced today the opening of Coin & Curio Shop at 125 No. Main Street in downtown Iola, Waupaca County, Wis.
>
> Having begun collecting coins in July 1939 in California, he has amassed an enormous collection of tokens, "good fors", mirror cards, wooden nickels, encased Lincoln cents, Depression tax tokens and scrip, etc., which he abandoned plans recently to sell at auction or private treaty sale. Thus no middleman's commission will be included.
>
> His collection includes U.S. and foreign coins; Latin American, Spanish and world tokens; U.S. and world paper money; medals in silver and bronze; U.S. and world gold coins; stocks and bonds; scrip; numismatic books; and a previously undisclosed collection of hallmarked British, Norwegian, Irish and American silver objects, including spoons, tea sets, etc.
>
> Rulau is best known as a coin magazine editor, coin newspaper editor, author of catalogs and books, but he served as North American broker for England's Pobjoy Mint 1985–98 and freelance writer 1999 to date. His biography and works may be found in Wikipedia, Google and *Who's Who in America.* He was employed as an editor with Amos Press 1962–74 and Krause Publications 1974–84; self-employed 1984 to present.
>
> Among the curios to be offered is a giant Coca-Cola sign; swords; Arisaka rifle of Japan (no bullets); upscale ladies' and men's clothing; pewter imitations of ancient coins; bank bags; old documents; etc. The building, foreclosed by a bank, was purchased by Rulau from the bank for about 50 cents on the dollar. Distressed properties are losing value every day, he says. Grand opening date is set to coincide with the 100,000-person Iola Old Car Show July 9–12.

The above reflects the diversity of Russ's interests, numismatic and otherwise. He is fondly remembered as a great researcher and scholar with indefatigable energy, always willing to share with others.

APPENDIX

II

THE LEVICK 1870 STUDY

In April 1870, Joseph N.T. Levick's pioneer listing of Hard Times tokens in the *American Journal of Numismatics* included 56 varieties and the numbers he assigned to them.

Description of the "Hard Times Tokens" of '37

Furnished by J.N.T. Levick from His Own Collection

1. Obv.: A full length figure of Jackson in citizen's dress, holding out a well-filled purse in left hand, and defending it with a drawn sword in the other hand; around the margin or base "A Plain System Void of Pomp." Rev.: A jackass drawing or shying back, on his side the letters "LL.D" above the animal "Roman Firmness," below him the date "1834," legend "The Constitution As I Understand It." Edge, plain; metal, copper. Size 18.

2. Obv.: A military bust of Jackson, three quarter face, "My | Experiment | My | Currency | My Glory" | in six lines across the field; around the base "My Substitute For The U.S. Bank. Rev.: A boar running at full speed, upon his side "My Third Heat," above him "My Victory," and below him "Down with the Bank"; around the base, "Perish Credit" "Perish Commerce" "1834." The boar's nostril nearly opposite C of the word "Credit." Edge, plain; metal, copper, also brass. Size 18.

3. Obv.: Same in character as No. 2, but of another die, well known as the "Broad-shouldered Jackson." Rev.: Same as No. 2, but of another die; the boar's nostril opposite the space between P in "Perish" and C of "Credit. Edge, plain; metal, copper, also brass. Size 18.

4. Obv.: Jackson in a General's uniform, inside of an iron safe, three-quarter view, holding up a sword with the right hand as if defending the bag of coin grasped in his left; a small letter "H" under the safe; the whole surrounded by the quotation "I Take The Responsibility. Rev.: A mule facing to the left, across his side are the letters "LL.D"; above the mule "Roman Firmness"; below the mule the word "Veto"; on the border, "The Constitution As I Understand It. Edge, plain; metals, copper, and brass. Size 18.

5. Obv.: Same die as No. 4. Rev.: A wrecked ship striking against rocks; the word "Experiment" the whole length of the side of the vessel; around the border, "*Van Buren* Metallic Currency" "1837." Edge, plain; metal, copper. Size 18.

6. Obv.: and Rev.: Same as No. 5 in design, though not in execution; known as the "big bellied Donkey" variety. Edge, plain; metal, copper. Size 18.

7. Obv.: A jackass heading left, running at full speed; "I follow In the Steps of my Illustrious Predecessor. Rev.: A turtle walking off with an iron chest on its back, marked "Sub Treasury"; the date "1837" and "Fiscal Agent" below the turtle; "Executive Financiering" in the exergue. Edge, plain; metal, copper. Size 18.

8. Obv.: Same as 7 in character or design, though not the same die. Rev.: Same as 7 but another die, and the words "Executive Experiment" substituted for "Executive Financiering." Edge, plain; metal, copper. Size 18.

9. Obv.: and Rev.: Same as 8, with the exception of being another pair of dies. The marked difference between 7 and 8 and 9 is in the word "Financiering" instead of "Experiment." The difference between 8 and 9 is somewhat difficult to point out, but in comparing the two together can be readily seen. In 8 the donkey's right ear points in the direction of the second L in "Illustrious"; the letter I in "I follow" comes almost under the space between L and U in "Illustrious." In 9 the donkey's ear is under the first L of "Illustrious"; "I" in "I follow," under second L in "Illustrious."

Of 8 or 9 there exists a piece struck in silver, which, it is said, was originally from the "Davenport" Collection, was sold at the "McCoy" Sale to F. I. Illsley for $8.50, and resold in Woodward's Fifth Semi-Annual Sale for $7 to John Bailey.

10. Obv.: A ship under full sail, on her side "Constitution"; legend, "Webster * Credit Currency*" "1841." Rev.: Same die as reverse of No. 5. Edge, plain; metal, copper. Size 18.

11. Obv.: Same as 10 in design, but a different die, noticeable specially in the riggings of the vessel, as all the sails are not set. Rev.: Same die as reverse of 5 and 10. Edge, plain; metal, copper. Size 18.

12. Obv.: Ship under full sail, similar to 10 and 11, but still another die; legend, "Webster Credit Current," "1841." Rev.: A wrecked vessel—broken masts, parts falling, a portion of the hull on rocks, on her side "Experiment" running the extreme length, flashes of lightning—legend, "Van Buren Metallic Current," "1837." Edge, plain; metal, copper. Size 18.

Note:—This is the only variety which has the word "Current" on both sides; there exists one specimen of it in silver, sold in the McCoy sale for $10, resold in the 5th S. A. sale for $9.

13. Obv.: Similar to No. 12, but a different die of inferior execution. Rev.: Wreck of the "Experiment" striking against rocks, flashes of lightning; legend "Van Buren Metallic Currency" 1837. Edge, plain; metal, copper. Size 18.

14. Obv.: Same die as 13. Rev.: Similar to 13, but another die and different in execution, the word "Experiment" being straight and not curved as in the preceding two. Edge, plain; metal, copper. Size 18.

15. Obv.: Same die as 13. Rev.: "Millions for Defence" around the border; "Not | One | Cent | For Tribute" inside of a wreath of twenty-five leaves and nine berries or buds. The reverses of the following Nos. are from the same die as this: 33, 36, 37 and 43. Edge, plain; metal, copper. Size 18.

16. Obv.: Same die as 13. Rev.: "Millions for Defence" around the outside; "Not | One | Cent I For | Tribute "in four lines surrounded by a circle of twenty-seven stars. This die was also used on No. 27. Edge, plain; metal, copper. Size 18.

17. Obv.: Same design as 13 but another die, with difference in execution, the distinguishing feature being the small leaf before and after the name "Webster" in the legend "Webster Credit Current," instead of the small star as in 10 to 16 inclusive. Rev.: A laureated female head facing left; above the head a ribbon inscribed, "E Pluribus Unum"; under the head, the date "1837"; six stars on right, and seven stars on left of head. The laurel wreath consists of ten leaves. This reverse and the obverse of 34 are the same; and they are also familiar to card-collectors as the head on one of the two varieties of the George A. Jarvis card; see No. 50. Edge, plain; metal, copper. Size 18.

18. Obv.: A Phoenix rising from the flames; "Substitute For Shin Plasters" "Novr 1837." Rev.: "Specie Payments Suspended" on the outside of a wreath; "May Tenth 1837" within the wreath, which is of oak leaves and acorns. This reverse is different for the reverses of Nos. 19, 22, and 23. Edge, plain; metal, copper. Size 18.

19. Obv.: Same die as 18. Rev.: Similar to No. 18, but not the same die; slight difference in execution, see reverses of 22 and 23 for this variety. Edge, plain; metal, copper. Size 18.

20. Obv.: Same die as 18. Rev.: "Millions For Defence" on the outside of wreath, within the wreath "Not One Cent" "For Tribute. This reverse is not the same die as that of 15, although but slightly differing, and they must be compared to observe it. Same die as that of 35, 39, and 44. Edge, plain; metal, copper. Size 18.

21. Obv.: Same die as 18. Rev.: Similar to reverse of 20, though a different die, with a slight variation in execution; same as reverse of 38; wreath composed of twenty-two or twenty-three leaves and eight berries. Edge, plain; metal, copper. Size 18.

22. Obv.: Laureate head to left, above the head a ribbon inscribed "E Pluribus Unum", under the head, "1837"; seven stars on left side or front of face, six stars on right side or behind the head. The laurel wreath consists of twelve leaves, same as 24, 27, 37, 38, and 40. Rev.: Same die as reverse of 19. Edge, plain; metal, copper. Size 18.

23. Obv.: Laureate head to left, above the head a ribbon inscribed "E Pluribus Unum", below the head the date "1841," on either side of date extending up to the ribbon, are quarter wreaths or sprigs of flowers and leaves. The laurel wreath consists of twelve leaves, same as 25 and 39. Rev.: Same die as reverses of Nos. 19 and 22. Edge, plain; metal, copper. Size 18.

24. Obv.: Same die as that of 22, 27, 37, 38, and 40. Rev.: "Bentonian Currency" "1837" surrounding a wreath, inside of which "Mint" | "Drop"; same as 25. Edge, plain; metal, copper. Size 18.

25. Obv.: Same die as that of 23 and 39. Rev.: Same die as the reverse of 24. Edge, plain; metal, copper. Size 18.

26. Obv.: An idiotic female head to left, with a band or frontlet, inscribed "Loco Foco"; the date, "1838," below the head, thirteen stars surrounding the head. Rev.: "Benton Experiment" around the border or margin, "Mint Drop" within a wreath. Edge, plain; metal, copper. Size little over 18.

27. Obv.: The same die as the obverses of 22, 24, 37, 38, and 40. Rev.: "Millions For Defence," &c.; the same die as reverse of 16. Edge, plain; metal, copper. Size 18.

28. Obv.: Liberty head to left. A fillet around the head inscribed "United," twelve stars around the border, below the head the date, "1837," in large figures. Rev.: "Millions For Defence" around the border; inside of a wreath, "Not One Cent for Tribute." Edge, plain; metal, copper. Size 18.

29. Obv.: Laureate head to left surrounded by thirteen stars; date "1837" under the head; laurel wreath of seven leaves and three berries. Rev.: "Millions For Defence" on the outside of wreath; "Not One Cent For Tribute" within the wreath, the words "Not" and "For Tribute" being smaller than all others of this series. This and the one following are a pair of themselves, being so unlike the others, and somewhat scarce. Edge, plain; metal, copper. Size 18.

30. Obv.: Same in character with 29, but a smaller and more homely head; and, in addition to the thirteen stars which surround the head, there are two very small stars before and after the date "1837." The laurel wreath consists of seven leaves, and no berries as in preceding. Rev.: The same die as preceding. Nos. 26, 28, 29, and 30 are the only varieties which have no legend or inscription around the head, which is surrounded by stars. Edge, plain; metal, copper. Size 18.

31. Obv.: Laureate head to left; laurel wreath of eight leaves. May be recognized by card-collectors as the J.H. Dayton's card-die (see No. 49). Above the head a ribbon inscribed "E Pluribus Unum"; below the head the date "1837"; six and seven stars. This is the only variety which has no curl in front of the ear, the head facing six stars, instead of seven as in all others. Rev.: "Millions for Defence" around the margin; within a wreath of twenty six leaves and twelve or thirteen berries, "Not One Cent" "For Tribute." Edge, plain; metal, copper. Size 18.

32. Obv.: Laureate female head to left, known to many collectors of cards as the head on the Crossman and Maycock cards (see Nos. 47 and 48), and next to the Loco Foco head the ugliest of this series; should be called "Thick Head." Above the head a ribbon inscribed "E Pluribus Unum," the letters of which are larger than in any others. The date, "1837," below the head; thirteen stars—seven stars facing—the stars being unusually close, almost touching each other. The laurel wreath composed of nine leaves. Rev.: "Millions For Defence" around the base; "Not One Cent For Tribute" within a wreath of twenty-four leaves and eight berries, all the letters being large. Edge, plain; metal, copper. Size 12.

33. Obv.: Laureate head to left, the laurel wreath of twelve leaves, the head resembling that of 22, but superior in execution, the bottom curl twisting or curved to the right; in the 22 die the curl turns to the left. Rev.: The same die as those of Nos. 15, 36, 37 and 43. Edge, plain; metal, copper. Size 18.

34. Obv.: The same die as 1 7 and 50. Rev.: "Millions For Defence" around the base; "Not One Cent For Tribute" within a wreath of twenty-nine leaves and nine berries. The dash below the word "Cent" is omitted. A scarce variety. Edge, plain; metal, copper. Size 18.

35. Obv.: Laureate head to left, laurel wreath of nine leaves. Same die as 36 and 41. Card collectors can readily trace this variety to the second variety of George A. Jarvis' card (No. 51). Rev.: Same die as 20. Edge, plain; metal, copper. Size 18.

36. Obv.: Same die as 35 and 41; but examine the latter for guiding you as to the variety. Edge, plain; metal, copper. Size 18.

37. Obv.: Same die as Nos. 22, 24, 27, 38, and 40. Rev.: Same die as 1 5, 33, 36, 37, and 43. Edge, plain; metal, copper. Size 18.

38. Obv.: Same die as Nos. 22, 24, 27, 37, and 40. Rev.: Same die as No. 21. Edge, plain; metal, copper. Size 18.

39. Same die as 23 and 25. Rev.: Same die as 20. Edge, plain; metal, copper. Size 18.

40. Obv.: Same die as 22. Rev.: A market house; below it, "14th Ward N. York"; around the base, "Centre Market Accommodation." Edge, plain; metal, copper. Size 18.

41. Obv.: Same die as 35. Rev.: Same die as 40. Edge, plain; metal, copper. Size 18.

42. Obv.: View of Merchants' Exchange; "Merchants' Exchange Wall St. N. York Built 1827 Burnt 1835." Rev.: "Millions for Defence"; around the base, "Not One Cent For Tribute" within a wreath of twenty-four leaves and eight berries; like 34 it has no dash after the word cent, though not the same die as 34. Edge, plain; metal, copper. Size 18.

43. Obv.: Same die as No. 42. Rev.: Same die as 15. Edge, plain; metal, copper. Size 18.

44. Obv.: Same die as No. 42. Rev.: Same die as No. 20. Edge, plain; metal, copper. Size 18.

The following described pieces are by some collectors classed with this series; while others disregard them: the same remarks may be applied to 40, 41, 42, 43. and 44.

45. Obv.: View of the Exchange; "Merchants' Exchange." Rev.: "New York Joint Stock Exchange Company No. 6 Tontine Building Wall St." Edge, plain; metal, copper. Size 18.

46. Obv.: A cow facing to right; "A Friend to the Constitution." Rev.: A ship under full sail; "Agriculture and Commerce." Edge, plain; metal, copper Size 18.

47. Obv.: Same die as 32. Rev.: "H. Crossman, Manufacturer No. 92} Chatham St. N.Y." Edge, plain; metal, copper, Size 18.

48. Obv.: Same die as 32. Rev.: "S. Maycock & Co., No. 35 City Hall Place, N.Y." etc., etc. Edge, plain; metal, copper. Size 18.

49. Obv.: Same head, though not the same die as 31. Rev.: "J. H. Dayton Union Steam Washing Est." etc. Edge, plain; metal, copper. Size 18.

50. Obv.: Same die as 17 and 34. Rev.: "George A. Jarvis Wine and Tea Dealer" 142 Grand corner of Elm street New York a small leaf before and after the name "George A. Jarvis." Edge, plain; metal, copper. Size 18.

51. Obv.: Same as 35, 36, and 42. Rev.: Same as 50 but a different die. Instead of a leaf there is a small star before and after the "George A. Jarvis." Edge, plain; metal, copper. Size 18.

52. Obv.: Same die as reverse of No. 21. Rev.: Abraham Riker's card. Edge, plain; metal, copper. Size 18.

53. Obv.: Same die as reverse of 42. Rev.: Same die as 52. Edge, plain; metal, copper. Size 18.

54. Obv.: Same die as 46. Rev.: T.D. Seaman's card. Edge, plain; metal, copper. Size 18.

55. Obv.: Same die as 46 and 54. Rev.: W, Gibbs's card. Edge, plain; metal, copper. Size 18.

56. Obv.: A spread Eagle, "U. S. Standard Weight and Value 1837" around the eagle. Rev.: "Half Cent Worth of Pure Copper" thirteen stars. Edge, plain; metal, copper. Size 18.

Many collectors regard this piece as a pattern; why so I cannot explain; I should more readily assume it to be a satirical piece. Other collectors place it among their half cents of that year, there being no half cents issued in 1837, '8 and '9.

J.N.T. Levick

Notes

Chapter 2

1. R.W. McLachlan, "Fifty Years a Coin Collector," *The Numismatist*, September 1911.
2. Per the date on the monument over his grave in Greenwood Cemetery in Brooklyn (as visited by Katherine (Jaeger) de Silva, who sent the author photographs). Beneath his life dates is "Be just and fear not." His wife Abby Jane (January 4, 1834 to October 11, 1903) is interred there as well, as is their only son, Giles F. Bushnell (1858–1906).
3. The Bangs name is associated with New York City coin sales at least since 1841 (see Attinelli, p. 6) with the sale of one coin lot as part of an auction, March 17, 1841, by Bangs, Richards & Platt. Circa 1853–1856 the trade style was Bangs Brother [or Bro.] & Co., changing to Bangs, Merwin & Co. in the latter year. In the 1880s the firm was generally known as Messrs. Bangs & Co. Later it was succeeded by Merwin-Clayton Sales Co., which never became numismatically important. Still later the company became a part of the Anderson-American Art Association (with whom coin dealer Wayte Raymond did a great deal of business), which evolved into Parke-Bernet Galleries, later Sotheby Parke-Bernet, presently trading as Sotheby's.
4. George Parish Jr., *American Journal of Numismatics*, August 1866. Attinelli, *Numisgraphics*, 1876, stated the offering brought $733.62 and, further: "This catalogue was, I believe, also issued with date of April 28."
5. Suggestion and information from Karl Moulton, letter, May 19, 1997.
6. *American Journal of Numismatics*, March 1868. Why Bushnell did not participate in the activities of the Society remains an interesting question; he did belong to multiple *historical* societies in various states.
7. Identified at the time as "acting for the British Museum." However, many of these purchases went into the Bushnell Collection and were later sold by the Chapman brothers in the 1882 offering of his estate. (Information from Karl Moulton, letter, May 19, 1997; also see the note by the Chapman brothers in the 1882 sale of the Bushnell Collection, lot 184, where he is mentioned as "Stevens.")
8. Karl Moulton has analyzed Bushnell's unpublicized participation in the Mickley Collection sale and concluded that he was the "biggest buyer."
9. This comment does not seem to have applied to Bushnell's Hard Times tokens which, save for just a few pieces, were very ordinary in condition and rarity—as evidenced by the 1882 sale of the Bushnell Collection by the Chapman brothers. This collection was consigned by Lorin G. Parmelee, who extracted coins of interest before giving it to the Chapmans. Parmelee is not known to have had an interest in Hard Times tokens.
10. His place in history is irreparably tarnished by his actions as secretary of state in the Jackson administration, being the main person to implement the Indian Removal Act of 1830, leading to the "Trail of Tears" in which thousands of Cherokees and other tribal members were killed and driven from their land in the South.
11. Perhaps a reference to the manuscript (no printed catalog was published; thus Ledyard did not send one to Brock) sale of the W.C. Tripler Collection in Edward D. Cogan's store, 48 North 10th Street, Philadelphia, October 28, 1859. His cabinet, which he had sold to Edward D. Cogan, was called by local auctioneer W.C. Cook. At the event, 161 pieces brought a total of $403.29, an exceptionally high realization per lot for the time. The sale commenced at 8 a.m., and was finished by 9:30 a.m. (see *American Journal of Numismatics*, April 1867). Tripler had been a buyer from Cogan for some time and had participated in Cogan's November 1, 1858, sale "by private biddings" of cents.

12. Edward D. Cogan's sale in Philadelphia of items from local collector J.N.T. Levick (who was soon to move to New York City), December 19–20, 1859.
13. The reference is to the Philadelphia Numismatic Society, formed several months prior to the organization of the American Numismatic Society.
14. Over a period of time Taylor's name appeared on the cover of several auction catalogs written by his fellow townsman Edward D. Cogan. Taylor was also a prolific issuer of tokens in the early 1860s; advertised were his apothecary shop at the corner of Walnut and Ninth streets as well as two of his compounds: Denticrete and Orilote for the teeth (see the Civil War token known as Fuld PA-750-U-1c). In 1867 his address was 1015 Chestnut Street, Philadelphia. Taylor remained active in numismatics until at least the early 1870s.
15 *American Journal of Numismatics*, July 1874. Access per Jeremiah Colburn.
16. Life dates: August 1, 1913 to April 18, 1995.
17. Mehl died in 1957. Certain of this information came to light in later years through his friend and colleague Abe Kosoff (who handled Mehl's numismatic estate), Garrett correspondence preserved by The Johns Hopkins University (certain extracts from which are printed in *The History of United States Coins as Illustrated by the Garrett Collection*, 1979), and discussions between the author and Donald M. Miller, among other sources.
18. From Mehl's introduction: "The major portion of this great collection of Hard Times tokens was originally formed, over a period of many years, by the eminent numismatist, Carl Wurtzbach, of Lee, Massachusetts, from whom Mr. Dunham purchased the collection. . . ." In addition, Dunham bought widely elsewhere, including from Raymond's 1925 sale of the W.W.C. Wilson Collection.
19. Michael Hodder was the primary cataloger.
20. David T. Alexander was the primary cataloger.

Chapter 3

1. William G. Sumner, *A History of American Currency*, pp. 122–123; adapted from Condy Raguet, *Money and Banking*, plus the annual report of the Secretary of the Treasury.
2. *International Monetary Conference Held . . . in Paris, in August 1878*. Senate Executive Document No. 48, Forty-fifth Congress, Third Session, study by John White, cashier of the Bank of the U.S., Baltimore branch; "Statement of the Price of Specie During the Suspension of Specie Payments," p. 646.
3. Francis Parsons, *A History of Banking in Connecticut*, 1935, pp. 11, 12.
4. *American State Papers, Class III, Finance*, volume III, 1834, pp. 57 ff. M. St. Clair Clarke and D.A. Hall, *Legislative and Documentary History of the Bank of the United States including the Original Bank of North America*, 1832, *passim.*
5. *Ibid.*, May 14, 1817.
6. *Ibid.*, July 18, 1817.
7. *Ibid.*, March 7, 1818; many other notices.
8. *Ibid.*, June 20, 1818.
9. The history of this controversial branch can be found in Wendell Wolka, *A History of Nineteenth Century Ohio Obsolete Bank Notes and Scrip*, 2004, p. 95.
10. Bray Hammond, *Banks and Politics in America from the Revolution to the Civil War*, 1957, p. 256; American State Papers – Finance. Other sources.
    Throughout this era, *deposite* was used, in this book changed to *deposit*.

Chapter 4

1. *International Monetary Conference Held . . . in Paris, in August 1878.* Senate Executive Document No. 48, Forty-fifth Congress, Third Session, Table H ("Rates of Exchange in Philadelphia. . . .").
2. Horace White, *Money and Banking Illustrated by American History*, p. 366.
3. Ralph C.H. Catterall, *The Second Bank of the United States*, p. 171, dismisses Hill as "a pettifogging politician and newspaper editor," apparently with little information as to the importance and achievements of Hill in the state (at least, these are not discussed by Catterall).
4. Although earlier the Supreme Court, in the case of *McCulloch v. Maryland*, had held that the charter of the Bank of the United States was indeed acceptable under the Constitution.
5. Ronald E. Shaw, *Andrew Jackson 1767–1845*, 1969, pp. 23–28, text of message.
6. It is seen that Jackson continued to adhere to the alleged unconstitutionality of the Bank of the United States.
7. Ronald E. Shaw, *Andrew Jackson 1767–1845*, 1969, pp. 33–40, text of message. This would seem to be an excellent synopsis of Jackson's feelings at the time: He favored a government bank as an agency of the Treasury Department, not as a private institution with directors, etc. It would not issue paper money in competition with the state banks, but would relinquish this as the sole province of the state institutions. It would not give private loans in competition with state banks, but would work with them in certain mutually beneficial matters.

   The majority of popular historians of the 20th century who have written about the Jacksonian era seem to have had very little understanding of Jackson's sentiments and the workings of state banks *vis-à-vis* his proposed government bank. For this reason, such popular texts have been of relatively little use here, and 19th-century sources, including contemporary documents, have been consulted. as have transcripts of his speeches and his letters.
8. Also cited as the Franklin Hotel (in particular) and Franklin Inn in contemporary mentions. In June 1821, O'Neale advertised that he wanted to rent the Franklin House, 20 rooms up to all 70 rooms. This did not happen, and O'Neale remodeled and continued operating it. On May 23, 1823, the property was to be sold at auction to satisfy debts due to the Bank of the Metropolis. O'Neale stated that this was not his fault at all, but involved $10,000 to $12,000 in debt he had guaranteed for another person (*National Daily Intelligencer*, May 12, 1823, two advertising notices). However, for a time the O'Neale family continued its operation. Within a year John Gadsby became proprietor, and it was afterward known as Gadsby's Franklin House. In Parton's *Life of Andrew Jackson*, p. 184, he had the title subject coming to Washington as a senator in 1823 and staying with O'Neale. William O'Neale died at age 86 on October 25, 1837, following a long illness. At the time of his passing he was an inspector at the District Penitentiary.
9. If Jackson actually composed this letter it contradicts any statement that he was less than literate!
10. The "petticoat affair" tag was used in newspaper accounts by the summer of 1831. In 1932 *The Autobiography of Peggy Eaton* was published, with a preface by Charles F. Deems, her pastor after she moved to New York City and became involved in religion. The text was dictated by her in 1873 and, per her wishes, was withheld from publication at the time. Peggy claimed to have been virtuous at all times and

to have been the victim of many calumnies, including in 1861 by James Parton in his biography of Jackson.

11. Kendall (1789–1869) was postmaster general in the Jackson administration. He became prominent as editor-in-chief of the influential *Argus of Western America*, published in Frankfort, the capital of Kentucky, and widely read in what was then the American West. He was perhaps the most influential person in building the Democratic Party. After returning to private life he was a major investor in Samuel F.B. Morse's new telegraph.
12. Multiple modern histories of the Jackson era, presidential scandals, etc., 1990s to date, one source seemingly picking up from another. No contemporary citation has been seen. Today it is virtually impossible to sort fact from fiction in accounts, contemporary and modern, of the life and conduct of Mrs. Eaton.

Chapter 5

1. Ronald E. Shaw, *Andrew Jackson 1767–1845*, 1969, pp. 45–53, for text of message. James Parton, *Life of Andrew Jackson*, volume III, 1861, pp. 407, 408, for analysis by the numbers.
2. Parton, p. 421.
3. As a general rule, biographers of Jackson and popular historians writing of the 1830s introduced many errors regarding coins, tokens, and other aspects of money.
4. *Ibid.*, p. 430.
5. *Ibid.*, p. 431.
6. Ronald E. Shaw, *Andrew Jackson 1767–1845*, 1969, pp. 74–79, text of message read to the Cabinet, September 18, 1833, outlining the procedure. James Parton, *Life of Andrew Jackson*, volume III, 1861, p. 528.
7. *Niles' Weekly Register*, January 7, 1833, p. 297, showed a report from Secretary of the Treasury Levi Woodbury, January 1, indicating the amounts to be transferred to each of the states during the coming year.

   John M. McFaul, *The Politics of Jacksonian Finance*, 1972, devotes a chapter to "Domesticated Pets." Sample entry (p. 146): "The Treasury had carried a nominal deposit with the Albany [New York] Regency Bank of $25 through 1833 and 1834, but in 1835 it was appointed a full-time pet, and the government balance swelled to more than $100,000 by the end of the year. At the same time, however, $5,500,000 in federal funds were on deposit in the three Wall Street pets."
8. Ronald E. Shaw, *Andrew Jackson 1767–1845*, 1969, pp. 80–83, text of message. John Jay Knox, *United States Notes*, 1885, p. 172.
9. Reginald Charles McGrane, *The Correspondence of Nicholas Biddle Dealing with National Affairs*, 1919.

Chapter 6

1. James Parton, *Life of Andrew Jackson*, volume III, 1861, p. 590; other sources.
2. Ronald E. Shaw, *Andrew Jackson 1767–1845*, 1969, pp. 84–90, text of protest, including additional comment sent by Jackson to the Senate on April 21, 1834.
3. Ronald E. Shaw, *Andrew Jackson 1767–1845*, 1969, pp. 84–97, text of message.
4. A report of Secretary of the Treasury Levi Woodbury, December 6, 1836, printed in *Niles' Weekly Register*, December 17, 1836.
5. During the 1820s and early 1830s he claimed his senatorial salary in gold coins at face value, as congressmen had the right to do. Most sold them at a profit to bullion exchanges, after which nearly all were melted. Quarter eagles ($2.50 gold), not popular for export, were mostly coined for congressional salaries.

6. For example, in an advertisement in the New York *Evening Chronicle*, June 13, 1837: "Benton's mint drops, Mexican dollars, American halves, and sovereigns, bought and sold by Thomas D. Carpenter, No. 13 Wall Street."
7. Not true. Earlier coins did not return to circulation and continued to sell at a premium, listed as "old tenor" in prices current tables. Moreover, virtually no gold coins had been available at par (in terms of silver) since 1821, and even before that in terms of paper money. If anyone had a "chest" of old-tenor gold coins, there was absolutely no reason why they would cash it in after the Act of June 28, 1834.
8. *International Monetary Conference Held . . . in Paris, in August 1878.* Senate Executive Document No. 48, Forty-fifth Congress, Third Session, pp. 696–697; review of past coinage legislation and its effects.
9. As quoted in *Niles' Register*, February 8, 1834.

Chapter 7

1. Also known as Gadsby's Franklin House, this was the later name for William O'Neale's Franklin House. In the 1810s John Gadsby had operated the Indian Queen hotel, which in 1820 was opened under the ownership of D. Barnum of Boston, late keeper of the Exchange Coffee House in Boston.
2. Much information concerning the financial distress of the time has been quoted or adapted from *Niles' Weekly Register*, May 13, 1837, and other issues of the time.
3. DEFENCE, not DEFENSE as the later style, was used on these tokens.
4. Quoted in *Niles' National Register*, November 25, 1837. The 1841 date on the numerous tokens of this character has led quite a few numismatists to attribute them to having been issued in that year.

Chapter 8

1. *Niles' National Register*, May 23, 1840.
2. For an overview of this and related proposals see "Centennial Address of the Hon. E.G. Spaulding at the Meeting of the Bankers' Association at the International Exposition, Philadelphia, May 30, 1876," published in *Bankers' Magazine*, July 1876.
3. Printed in *Niles' National Register*, December 25, 1841.
4. Senator Benton's autobiography, *Thirty Years in the U.S. Senate*, also called *Thirty Years' View*, presents an interesting window on many aspects of 19-century finance and was consulted by the author of the present text. In 1856 Frémont ran for president for the newly formed Republican Party. One of the campaign tokens was lettered JESSIE'S CHOICE.

Chapter 10

1. Adams's diary entry, June 18, 1833, after receiving the invitation.

Chapter 11

1. Dispatch from Washington, January 21, 1837, quoted in the *Portland Weekly Advertiser*, January 31, 1837.
2. Robert A. Schuman, communication, January 25, 2014.
3. *Commercial Advertiser*, (New York City), September 23, 1837.
4. Justin D. Fulton, *Memoir of Timothy Gilbert*, 1866, p. 94.
5. From "The Promotion and Suppression of Hard Times Tokens," Eric P. Newman, Coinage of the Americas Conference, American Numismatic Society, 1994.

Chapter 13

1. From research by Cindy Wibker and H. Joseph Levine as cited by Russell Rulau.

2. *Commercial Advertiser*, (New York City), September 8, 1836.
3. Warren K. Tice, *Uniform Buttons of the United States 1776–1865*. p. 47. Henry Bronson, a doctor, did research on cholera and also published the first history of Waterbury.
4. Edgar H. Adams, in "Benedict & Burnham," in *The Numismatist*, November 1912 gives additional information.
5. A history of the enterprise would fill a large volume. Over the years there have been many articles published on the firm—enough that to read them all would take many hours. University professor Theodore Marburg spent time at the Scovill plant in the early 1940s and created an information-filled doctoral thesis which has been used by other scholars since that time.
6. However, in the early 1860s, during the Civil War, such inscriptions were widely used by various token manufacturers.
7. *The Parish Will Case*, volume III (of VI), 1864, pp. 712, 713. Other entries detail real estate owned by the former firm, dividends paid, etc.
8. *Baltimore Sun*, June 28, 1838.
9. Ellen Gerth, of Odyssey Marine Exploration, Tampa, Florida, prepared a paper, "(Site BA02): the Ceramic Assemblage," 2011, which told of the finding in 2003 of a china-laden coastwise vessel, called the "Blue China wreck," 70 miles offshore of Jacksonville. The wreck contained a large amount of ceramic goods, providing the occasion for a detailed essay on such imports destined for New Orleans and mention of certain firms there, including Henderson & Gaines (of an earlier era).
10. Amy C. Earls and George L. Miller, "Painted Wares from a New Orleans Importer," Chipstone Foundation, 2008, describes in detail certain of the company's wares. In 2014 Kolbe & Fanning, numismatic booksellers, offered this for $250: "New Orleans: December 30, 1834. 20 by 16.5 cm. Printed invoice, filled out by hand, for china and various kitchen wares purchased by J. Lee. Docketed on verso and signed by Lee and one Mathieson."
11. The descriptions were minimal in this sale and the contents quite ordinary, except for a remarkable offering of early auction catalogs.
12. Russell Rulau: "Scovill Mfg. Co., Waterbury, Conn., correspondence dated March 30, 1835, refers to 'brass medals (like J. A. Merle & Co. of New Orleans) one side Kohn Daron & Co.—other, Good For One load.' (Research by H. Joseph Levine) Since 1920 and its attribution to Memphis by Edgar H. Adams, these tokens have been considered Tennessee issues. Due to research by Ray W. Brown published in the *TAMS Journal* for October, 1996, they are repositioned as New Orleans tokens."
13. *Times-Picayune*, September 25, 1841.
14. U.S. Census information gives his first name as Henry.
15. Sources include John Daggett, *A Sketch of the History of Attleborough*, 1894. This book was compiled from his notes by his daughter. Certain dates in the book are inaccurate, but the general information is good.
16. *New York Journal of Commerce*, July 29, 1840.
17. Letter to the author, December 5, 2013.
18. Russell Rulau, *Standard Catalog of United States Tokens 1700–1900*, p. 144.
19. *Boston Courier*, April 6, 1840.
20. *Centinel of Freedom*, Newark, New Jersey, July 4, 1826.
21. *New England Farmer*, February 2, 1837.
22. Robert A. Schuman, letter, December 5, 2013.

23. Robert A. Schuman, letter, December 5, 2013.
24. Brown University Digital Depository.
25. Rev. Gilbert Haven and Hon. Thomas Russell, Rev. Edward T. Taylor, *Incidents and Anecdotes of Rev. Edward T. Taylor, for over Forty Years Pastor of the Seaman's Bethel, Boston*, 1872.
26. The Ford example was later verified as such by Michael Hodder (of Stack's) and Robert A. Schuman, and the sale was negated.
27. Francis S. Drake, *The Town of Roxbury: Its Memorable Persons and Places*, October 1878; Lyman H. Low, *Hard Times Tokens*, 1899.
28. Robert A. Schuman, letter, December 5, 2013.
29. Certain information is from Samuel Hopkins Emery, *History of Taunton, Massachusetts*, 1893.
30. Robert A. Schuman, letter, December 5, 2013.
31. Strafford Advertiser, Dover, September 12, 1837, and other issues.
32. Certain information concerning the merchants listed on both sides of this token was furnished by Wesley Balla, curator, New Hampshire Historical Society.
33. *New-Hampshire Gazette*, June, 25, 1833.
34. Caleb Stevens Gurney, *Portsmouth, Historic and Picturesque*, 1902.
35. This large-diameter penny obviously circulated for many years after the Sise dies were impressed on it, as the inscriptions are now well worn. What trade value did this oversize token have?
36. *American Notes and Queries*, September 21, 1889, included an inquiry from Theodore W. Reath, the answer to which provided much information given here. Other information can be found in James S. Brown, *Allaire's Lost Empire: A Story of the Forges and Furnaces of the Manasquan*, Transcript House, 1958; *The Howell Works Restoration: The Deserted Village of Allaire*, The Trustees, The Historic Howell Works, 1971; Morton Sitkus, *Images of America: Allaire*, Arcadia Publishing, 2002. Today the remains of the village to which new structures have been added are a popular tourist attraction.
37. Charles S. Boyer, *Early Forges and Furnaces in New Jersey*, University of Pennsylvania Press, 1931.
38. *The Howell Works Restoration: The Deserted Village of Allaire*, p. 30.
39. Stephens is misspelled as "Stevens" in many numismatic accounts. Contemporary listings give the name as Stephens.
40. In June 1835, accounts in the regional papers told of the arrest of Joseph Gardner and his alleged accomplice John Campbell on charges of counterfeiting. In the cellar they found "a complete and efficient die sinking establishment, tools, presses and metals," in a nearby barn were found two dies for Spanish dollars, and elsewhere they found other dies and counterfeit coins. (Information found by Wesley S. Cox, distributed by Russell Rulau.)
41. Regarding a former associate, the *Newark Daily Advertiser*, January 2, 1835, included this notice: "J.F. Thomas, Die Sinker, Letter Cutter and Engraver, Mechanic St., near Broad. Dies cut for coins, medals, etc."
42. *Newark Daily Advertiser*, November 4, 1835.
43. The Canadian government first issued copper coins in 1858; these were struck in England.
44. "Medals and tokens" is part of the inscription on the Gibbs token.
45. *Centinel of Freedom*, Newark, NJ, January 23, 1838.

46. "Early Transportation Tokens and Tickets of New York City," Coinage of the Americas Conference at the American Numismatic Society, New York, October 29, 1994.
47. "Who is Joseph Woolston Brick?" Gene Donatiello, Brick Township Historical Society, 2003, was the source of certain information.
48. *Newark Daily Advertiser.*
49. This is in response to a letter (now owned by Robert A. Schuman) from John H. Ward, cashier of the Farmers Bank of Batavia, to E. Hallenbeck, 27 Grove Place, Schenectady, NY, July 24, 1905, who had written inquiring about Cochran (spelled Cochrane in the letter).
50. *Albany Argus*, November 20, 1832, from several dispatches.
51. *Albany Argus*, October 4, 1844.
52. Gene Hessler, *The Engraver's Line*, 1993.
53. *New York Journal of Commerce*, October 7, 1839.
54. *Commercial Advertiser*, (New York City), January 25, 1834.
55. A deponent is a witness testifying under sworn oath.
56. Court testimony of Lewis L. Squire, on November 15, 1834, "Examinations and Evidence Accompanying [New York State] Assembly Document No. 135, made to the Legislature, January 29, 1835," pp. 70–71.
57. *Niles' Weekly Register*, May 13, 1837. Gulian C. Verplanck (see Hard Times token listing) was another of those present.
58. Rulau lists HT-252 muling with a Millions for Defence die (reverse of Low-39), but Robert Schulman reports that no such token has ever been seen in an auction or verified in the literature. Hence it is omitted here.
59. For a much more extensive biography of Feuchtwanger see the author's *More Adventures With Rare Coins*, 2002, chapter 17. Special thanks to Robert A. Schuman for the present study of Feuchtwanger.
60. Certain information is from *Appleton's Cyclopaedia of American Biography*, volume II, 1888, pp. 444–445.
61. *Longworth's American Almanac, New-York Register, and City Directory*, New York, Thomas Longworth, 1831, p. 272; "druggist." This is the earliest directory entry located for Feuchtwanger. For other information: *Longworth's American Almanac, New-York Register, and City Directory*, New York, Thomas Longworth, 1832 and later editions.
62. A well-known token relating to this attraction bears the inscriptions: PARTHENON / NEW-YORK 1825 on obverse; ADMIT THE BEARER/ PEALE'S MUSEUM & GALLERY OF THE FINE ARTS. The museum opened in a building known as the Parthenon, in late October of that year; earlier, Montaigne's Garden was on the site, and the Sons of Liberty held meetings there in the days prior to the American Revolution. Late in 1840 the name was officially changed to the New York Museum, by an act of the State Legislature, although it had been called that earlier. The lessees, Rathbone & Fitch, issued an oval pass or identification badge, from dies by Richard Trested, depicting the facility on one side, and engraved with the name of the holder of the badge. In time, these became highly sought numismatic items, especially after Wayte Raymond gave special notice to an example in his extensive catalog of the W.W.C. Wilson Collection, November 1925.

    In 1831 the New York facility, managed by Rembrandt Peale (whose father named each of his children after artists, including Rubens, Titian, and Vandyke) charged $10 for a family membership for one year; $5 for a gentleman's membership (at any time he had the privilege of bringing a lady with him); general admission 25¢; and children's tickets, 12-1/2¢. In 1831 the Siamese twins, Chang and Eng, were featured for a time.

63. Quoted, slightly revised, from *Hard Times Tokens*, Lyman H. Low, 1900, p. 49.
64. *New-York As It Is, In 1834; and Citizens' Advertising Directory*. J. Disturnell, New York, 1834, p. 230.
65. Thomas Longworth, *Longworth's American Almanac, New-York Register, and City Directory*, New York, 1834, p. 282.
66. In 1837 the Institute's library included more than 5,000 books. Premises were upstairs at 187 Broadway. Later, the Institute was in a four-story building at 351 Broadway.
67. Thomas Longworth, *Longworth's American Almanac, New-York Register, and City Directory*, New York, 1836, pp. 247, 594.
68. "Substitute for Copper. Memorial Lewis Feuchtwanger, September 13, 1837," 25th Congress, Document No. 7, House of Representatives, 1st Session.
69. *Niles' National Register*, September 16, 1837, p. 41.
70. Copy furnished by Kenneth E. Bressett.
71. Reference to the new 1857, Flying Eagle, cent, which Sage seems to have disliked.
72. In 1953 in a visit to the Scovill Manufacturing Co., Waterbury, Connecticut, Dr. George J. Fuld saw a *copy* of this token in lead. However, elsewhere at least one *authentic* lead example exists (Fuld, note to author, 2001).
73. All white metal and lead strikings of this combination are believed to be casts, per the research of Robert A. Schuman.
74. Probably the token described by Judd, *U.S. Pattern Coins*, 10th edition, appendix C, p. 265.
75. Probably the earlier-noted piece described by Judd, appendix C, p. 265.
76. Bidding under the pseudonym of "Stevens."
77. Francis Campbell, librarian at the American Numismatic Society, furnished prices realized and buyers' names for this sale, here adapted.
78. Advances were in increments of 2-1/2¢, but in price lists these were either rounded to the lower or higher even cent amount, there being no particular consistency in this regard.
79. *Numisma*, supplement, July 1881.
80. Apparently lot 2588 from the 1867 Mickley sale; see earlier citation.
81. *Spectator*, (New York), December 26, 1836.
82. *Newark Daily Advertiser*, November 25, 1836.
83. His narrative in his article, "A Plea for American Token Collecting," *The Numismatist*, April 1915.
84. *Hudson River Chronicle*, Sing-Sing, NY, January 31, 1843.
85. Certain biographical notes were provided by Katherine (Jaeger) de Silva, a Lovett descendant.
86. Source: Charles McSorley sent me a photocopy of the September 27, 1813 receipt for Albert Gallatin's personal seal, furnished by Brown. Payment was received by Robert Lovett, who signed the receipt for his master. This may be the same seal Gallatin placed beside his name on the Treaty of Ghent.
87. Francis D. Nichol, *The Midnight Cry*, 1944, p. 517.
88. *Public Ledger*, (Philadelphia), January 4, 1842.
89. Low-137 was described by Low in 1899: "The minute hand points at the space between the second and third mark after II. The circle around the pivot at which the hands turn is composed of eleven dots. Rev. Same as No. 135." In his 1906

supplement he stated that the information had been taken from unclear rubbings in an old book, and such a token probably did not exist.

90. Court testimony of Lewis L. Squire, on November 15, 1834, "Examinations and Evidence Accompanying [New York State] Assembly Document No. 135, made to the Legislature, January 29, 1835," pp. 70–71.
91. William Barrett, *The Old Merchants of New York City*, volume II, 1885, p. 273; also contemporary advertisements.
92. For example, *Lives of the Principal Reformers of the Sixteenth Century*, 1835, with 24 portraits engraved on steel.
93. Suydam & Boyd (see listing) were at this address until 1830.
94. For what might otherwise be the next listing in this text, Russell Rulau lists his HT-567, made for Ettenheimer's, a Rochester jewelry store, but we omit it here. It has a blank reverse on which a number is stamped as a watch check, not a circulating token.
95. Melvin and George Fuld, "The Tokens of the Boutwells of Troy, New York," *The Numismatist*, April 1952.
96. In instances in which multiple examples are known of a single variety the lack of detail on the Peck and Starbuck dies is the same—indicating that this reflects the state of the dies when used, not peculiarities of striking.
97. Edgar H. Adams, "The Starbuck Store Cards," *The Numismatist*, October 1913, included much information.
98. Arthur J. Weise, *Troy's One Hundred Years 1789–1889*, 1891; "Troy and the Making of Stoves," *Hardware Dealers' Magazine*, January 1913.
99. Among the sources for this entry was "P. Evens, Tailor," Waldo C. Moore, *The Numismatist*, May 1917.
100. Contemporary account from the *Daily Evening Post* reprinted in a reminiscence published in the *Cincinnati Daily Gazette*, February 27, 1880.
101. Article from the *Cincinnati Gazette* reprinted in the *Albany Evening Journal*, Albany, NY, November 33, 1845.
102. Certain information is from "A. Loomis and His Store Cards," Waldo C. Moore, *The Numismatist*, February 1913. See the article for an extensive commentary on the owners of Loomis tokens at the time and comments concerning their rarity.
103. J. Leander Bishop, *A History of American Manufactures 1608 to 1860*, volume II, 1864.
104. Horatio R. Storer, M.D., "The Medals and Tokens of Rhode Island." This paper was read before the Newport Historical Society, February 18, 1895. Storer also reported silver-plated copper examples of the Handy and Hathaway, the other two Hard Times token issuers of Rhode Island.
105. *Rhode Island American*, December 18, 1832.
106. *Rhode Island American*, January 11, 1833.
107. Correspondence with the author, November 29, 2013. Also see his NovaNumis.com website which has many advertisements and other contemporary notices about Russell.
108. Edwin J. Scott, *Reminiscences of a Long Life*, 1884, as cited by Aaron M. Packard.
109. *Tennessee Telegraph*, November 21, 1840, p. 3.
110. Typical tobacco notice from New Orleans: *Commercial Advertiser*, (New York City), August 6, 1832.

111. Rulau credited research by Chris H. Bailey, horologist, American Clock & Watch Museum; Robert B. Hitchings, archivist, Kim Memorial Library, Norfolk; and Wesley S. Cox.
112. Russell Rulau, *Standard Catalogue of United States Tokens 1700–1900*, 4th edition, p. 203.
113. See related letter from J. Ledyard Hodge, 1859, given in chapter 2.

Chapter 14

1. John J. Ford Jr. in conversations with the author in the 1970s stated that he had learned from F.C.C. Boyd that these pieces had been aged by placing them outdoors in horse manure for a period of time. Either Boyd was conjecturing or he had some undisclosed earlier source for this information.

Appendix I

1. *American Journal of Numismatics*, January 1897.
2. *American Journal of Numismatics*, October 1868.
3. *American Journal of Numismatics*, January 1870.
4. From the Bowers and Ruddy catalog of the John W. Adams Cents, 1982.
5. Attinelli, *Numisgraphics*, 1876, pp. 15-16.
6. The research of Sylvester S. Crosby (*Early American Coins*, published in 1875) and Edgar H. Adams (multiple books and articles, generally 1905–1915) involved the same methodology, and other early scholars could be mentioned as well.
7. John W. Adams, *United States Numismatic Literature*, volume I, p. 127.
8. *American Journal of Numismatics*, October 1887.
9. For extra reading: In January 1895 *The Numismatist* published a lively account of a fight (on the floor of an auction) between Low and Frossard after Low called Frossard a liar.
10. *Hobbies*, December 1934.
11. *Hobbies*, June 1936.
12. Howard L. Adelson, *The American Numismatic Society 1858–1958*, 1958, p. 160.
13. The catalog of Part II was completed by F.C.C. Boyd, and the sale was held on April 4, 1924.
14. From page 323 of Rulau's *Standard Catalog of United States Tokens: 1700–1900.*

Selected Bibliography

Abbott, John S.C. *Lives of the Presidents of the United States of America from Washington to the Present Time.* Boston, MA: B.B. Russell & Co.; San Francisco, CA: H.H. Bancroft & Co., 1867.

Adams, Edgar H. *United States Store Cards.* New York, NY: Edgar H. Adams and Wayte Raymond, 1920.

Bushnell, Charles I. *An Arrangement of Tradesmen's Cards, Political Tokens, also Election Medals, Medalets, &c. Current in the United States of America for the Last Sixty Years, Described from the Originals, Chiefly in the Collection of the Author.* Published by the author, 1858.

Catterall, Ralph C.H. *The Second Bank of the United States.* Chicago, IL: University of Chicago Press, 1902.

DeWitt, J. Doyle. *A Century of Campaign Buttons, 1789–1889.* Hartford, CT: Published by the author, 1959.

Eastwood, Sidney K. "The Ante-Bellum Tokens of New Orleans," *TAMS Journal*, August-October 1966.

Eaton, John Henry. *The Life of Andrew Jackson.* Philadelphia, PA: Samuel F. Bradford, 1824.

Fisher, Alan S. "Hard Times Tokens: The Legacy of Jackson and Van Buren." *The Numismatist*, August 1978.

Ford, John J. *John J. Ford, Jr. Collection*, Part IV, Stack's, New York City, NY. June 23, 2004.

Hammond, Bray. "Jackson, Biddle, and the Bank of the United States," *Journal of Economic History.* May 1947.

Jaeger, Katherine. *A Guide Book of United States Tokens and Medals.* Atlanta, GA: Whitman Publishing, 2008.

Mackenzie, William Lyon. *The Life and Times of Martin Van Buren: The Correspondence of His Friends, Family, and Pupils.* Boston, MA: Cooke & Co., 1846.

Marzalek, John F. *The Petticoat Affair: Manners, Mutiny, and Sex in Andrew Jackson's White House.* The Free Press, 1997.

Meacham, John. *American Lion: Andrew Jackson in the White House.* Random House, Inc., 1998.

Memoirs of John Quincy Adams Comprising Portions of his Diary from 1795 to 1848, volume V, ed. Charles Francis Adams. Philadelphia, PA.: J.B. Lippincott Co., 1875.

Minnigerode, Meade. *Some American Ladies: Seven Informal Biographies.* NY, New York: G.P. Putnam's Sons, 1926.

Newman, Eric P. "The Promotion and Suppression of Hard Times Tokens," Coinage of the Americas Conference at the American Numismatic Society, New York, October 29, 1994. Published in *The Token: America's Other Money*, 1995.

Parton, James. *Life of Andrew Jackson.* volumes I to III. New York, NY: Mason Brothers, 1861.

Quincy, Josiah. *A Memoir of the Life of John Quincy Adams.* Boston, MA: Crosby, Nichols, Lee and Company, 1860.

Raymond, Wayte "List of New York City Store Cards Struck in the Hard Times Period," *The Numismatist.* December 1928.

Reed, Alfred Z. "Guide to Hard Times Token Varieties," *The Numismatist.* January 1940.

Reed, Alfred Z. "The Trues, Die Cutters in Albany and Cincinnati," *The Numismatist.* December 1942.

Rulau, Russell. "The 1789 Mott Token Likely from the 1830s," *Numismatic News.* July 23, 2002.

Rulau, Russell. *Hard Times Tokens: A Complete Revision and Enlargement of Lyman H. Low's 1899 Classic Reference.* Iola, WI: Krause Publications, 1987.

Rulau, Russell. *Standard Catalog of United States Tokens, 1700–1900.* Fourth Edition. Iola, WI: Krause Publications, 2004.

Satterlee, Alfred H. *An Arrangement of The Medals and Tokens Struck in Honor of the Presidents of the United States and of the Presidential Candidates From the Administration of John Adams to That of Abraham Lincoln, Inclusive.* New York, NY: Printed for the author, 1862.

Schlesinger, Arthur M., Jr. *The Age of Jackson.* Boston, MA: Brown and Company, 1946.

Schuman, Robert A., M.D. *The True Hard Times Tokens.* M&G Publications, 2000.

Sullivan, Edmund. *American Political Badges & Medals.* Lawrence, MA: Quarterman Publications, 1981.

Tice, Warren K. *Uniform Buttons of the United States 1776–1865.* Gettysburg, PA: Thomas Publications, 1997.

Wurtzbach, Carl. "New Varieties of Hard Times Tokens," *The Numismatist.* March 1910.

Credits and Acknowledgements

American Antiquarian Society for source material • **Wes Balla** for historical information • **Charles Davis** for providing a plated copy of W. Elliot Woodward's 1884 catalog of the J.N.T. Levick Collection sale • **Katherine (Jaeger) de Silva** for biographical notes on the Lovett family of engravers • **David Fanning** for an illustration • **Francis (Frank) A. Ferland** for comments and suggestions • **George J. Fuld** for a lifetime of sharing information since the late 1950s • **David Gladfelter** for information dating back many years • **Elizabeth Hahn of the American Numismatic Society** for helping with images and historical catalogs • **Steven Hayden** as an associate in handling the Tanenbaum estate tokens, for sharing images, for rarity information, for pricing information, and many more things; he was one of the most important contributors to this book • **Michael Hodder** for his superb cataloging of the John J. Ford, Jr. (2004) and Dice-Hicks (2008) collections of Hard Times tokens • **Christine Karstedt** for assistance in many areas • **Paul Koppenhaver** as a source for rare varieties in the late 20th century • **Frank Leone** for assistance with some images • **Robert J. Lindesmith** for research information • **H. Joseph Levine** for sharing information gathered over a long period of time, including listings of examples that have appeared in his Presidential Coin and Antique Co. (PCAC) auctions and descriptions thereof • **Library of Congress** for many images • **Massachusetts Historical Society** for printed source material • **Charles McSorley** for historical information, biographical data, and ephemera • **Donald M. Miller** for sharing information • **Ernie Nagy** for sharing information on Hard Times political sayings • **Aaron M. Packard** for providing information on R.E. Baker of Charleston, SC • **Richard Rossa** for information and tokens over a long period of years • **Russell Rulau** for extensive discussions over a long period of years and for the work he did on this series in monographs on Hard Times tokens as well as in the *Standard Catalog of United States Tokens 1700–1900* • **David Schenkman** for historical and technical information over a long period of time • **Fred Schornstein** for images from his collection of satirical scrip notes • **Robert A. Schuman** for extensive information, particularly regarding Feuchtwanger tokens, and for images of several tokens, especially rare Feuchtwanger tokens and fantasy tokens • **Stephen L. Tanenbaum** for being a constant correspondent, advisor, mentor, and research associate from the early 1970s onward • **Warren K. Tice** corresponded regarding the history of buttons and their manufacturers • **Cindy Wibker** provided illustrations of a rare token • **Matthew Wittmann of the American Numismatic Society** provided illustrations of a rare token • **Evelyn R. Mishkin** was a copyeditor and helped in other ways as well.

About the Author

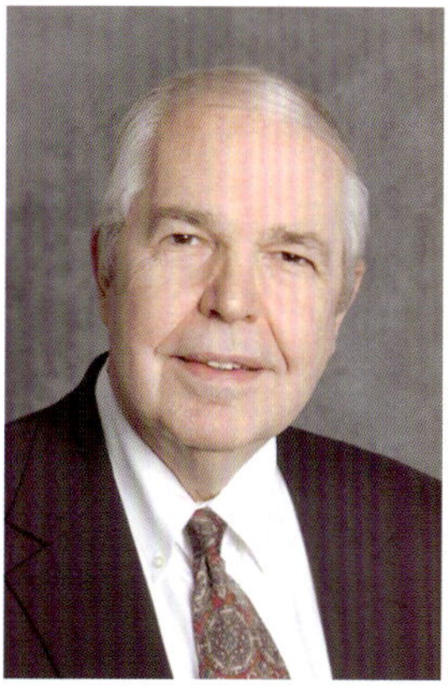

Q. David Bowers has been in the rare coin business since he was a teenager in 1953. He is chairman emeritus of Stack's Bowers Galleries and is numismatic director of Whitman Publishing, LLC. He is a recipient of the Pennsylvania State University College of Business Administration's Alumni Achievement Award (1976); he has served as president of the American Numismatic Association (1983–1985) and president of the Professional Numismatists Guild (1977–1979); he is a recipient of the highest honor bestowed by the ANA (the Farran Zerbe Award); he was the first ANA member to be named Numismatist of the Year (1995); and he has been inducted into the ANA Numismatic Hall of Fame, one of only 12 living members and the only professional numismatist among these. He has also won the highest honors given by the Professional Numismatists Guild. In July 1999, in a poll published in *COINage*, "Numismatists of the Century," Dave was recognized in this list of just 18 names. He is the author of over 50 books, including several on gold coins; hundreds of auction and other catalogs; and several thousand articles, including columns in *Coin World* (now the longest-running by any author in numismatic history), *The Numismatist*, and other publications. His books have earned more "Book of the Year Award" honors bestowed by the Numismatic Literary Guild than have those of any other author. Of the most valuable collections ever sold at auction—the Ambassador and Mrs. R. Henry Norweb Collection ($24 million), the Garrett Collection for The Johns Hopkins University ($25 million), the John J. Pittman Collection ($31 million), the Harry W. Bass, Jr. Collection ($45 million), the Eliasberg Collection ($55+ million), and the John J. Ford, Jr. Collection (nearly $60 million), he has been important in all but one (the Pittman Collection by the late David Akers). When the all-time high record for any rare coin ever sold at auction was achieved, a gem 1794 dollar in 2013, he cataloged it and his firm sold it. Dave is a trustee of the New Hampshire Historical Society and a fellow of the American Antiquarian Society, the American Numismatic Society, and the Massachusetts Historical Society. He has been a consultant for the Smithsonian Institution, the Treasury Department, and the U.S. Mint, and is research editor of *A Guide Book of United States Coins* (the annual best-selling book in numismatics, the standard guide to prices). In Wolfeboro, New Hampshire, he is on the Board of Selectmen and is the town historian. This is a short list of his honors and accomplishments.

Index of Low-to-Whitman Numbers

Low Number	Whitman Number
Low-1	W-09-10a
Low-1A	W-09-15a
Low-1B	W-09-20a
Low-2	W-09-30b
Low-3	W-09-35b
Low-4	W-09-25b
Low-5	W-09-40b PE; W-09-40b RE
Low-5A	W-09-45b RE
Low-6	W-10-10b PE; W-10-10b RE
"Low-6B"	W-10-10j RE
"Low-6C"	W-10-10f RE
Low-7	W-10-20a RE
Low-7D	W-10-30e RE
Low-8	W-10-210a
Low-9	W-10-210b
Low-10	W-10-230a
Low-11	W-10-220b
Low-12	W-10-310a
Low-13	W-10-120b
Low-14	W-10-130b
Low-15	W-10-112b
Low-15A	W-10-114b
Low-16	W-10-160b
Low-17	W-11-510a
Low-18	W-11-520a
Low-19	W-11-530a; W-11-530f
Low-20	W-11-540a
Low-21	W-11-10a
Low-22	W-11-20a
Low-23	W-11-30a
Low-24	W-X-100a
Low-25	W-X-200a
Low-26	W-X-300a
Low-27	W-X-400a; W-X-400b
Low-28	W-11-80a
Low-29	W-11-100a
Low-30	W-11-110a
Low-31	W-11-120a
Low-32	W-11-130a
Low-33	W-11-140a
Low-34	W-11-150a
Low-35	W-11-155a
Low-36	W-11-160a
Low-37	W-11-410a
Low-38	W-11-420a
Low-39	W-11-170a
Low-40	W-11-310a
Low-41	W-X-500a
Low-42	W-X-600a; W-X-600f
Low-43	W-X-700a; W-X-700f
Low-44	W-10-330a
Low-45	W-11-260a
Low-46	W-11-270a
Low-47	W-11-320a
Low-48	W-11-330a
Low-49	W-11-710a
Low-50	W-NY-480-80j
Low-51	W-10-320a
Low-52	W-10-320b
Low-53	W-10-330a
Low-54	W-11-720a
Low-54A	W-11-725a
Low-55	W-11-430a
Low-56	W-12-10a
Low-57	W-12-20b
Low-58	W-11-280a PE
Low-59	W-11-290a PE
Low-60	W-11-610a
Low-61	W-11-620a
Low-62	W-11-630a; W-11-630f
Low-63	W-11-640a
Low-64	W-11-650a
Low-65	W-11-660a
Low-66	W-11-740a
Low-67	W-11-340a
Low-68	W-11-440a
Low-69	W-11-300a PE
Low-70	W-X-800a; W-X-800f
Low-71	W-X-900a; W-X-900f
Low-72	W-MA-280-15a
Low-73	W-MA-280-10a
Low-74	W-RI-080-10a
Low-75	W-MA-020-10a
Low-76	W-MA-020-15a
Low-77	W-NY-1660-10a
Low-78	W-RI-040-10a
Low-79	W-NY-1700-10a
Low-80	W-MA-040-25a

Low Number	Whitman Number
Low-81	W-NJ-100-10a
Low-82	W-LA-200-10a
Low-83	W-MA-010-10a
Low-84	W-MA-040-10a
Low-85	W-LA-140-10b
"Low-85A"	W-LA-140-10e
Low-86	W-MA-240-10a
Low-87	W-NY-1640-10a
Low-88	W-NY-1660-20a
Low-89	W-NY-1660-15a
Low-92	W-NY-1660-35a
Low-93	W-NY-1660-40a
Low-94	W-RI-020-10a
Low-95	W-NY-760-10a
Low-96	W-NY-760-15a
Low-97	W-NY-760-20a
Low-98	W-NY-780-20a
Low-99	W-NY-150-10a
Low-100	W-NY-150-15a
Low-101	W-NY-150-20a
Low-102	W-MO-020-10b
"Low-102A"	W-MO-020-25b
Low-103	W-MA-030-10a
Low-104	W-MA-030-15a
Low-105	W-MA-030-20a
Low-106	W-LA-260-10b
Low-107	W-NY-180-10a
Low-108	W-SC-020-10j
Low-109	W-CT-080-10a
Low-110	W-NY-300-10a
Low-111	W-NY-300-15a
Low-112	W-NY-360-10a
Low-113	W-NY-360-15a
Low-114	W-NY-400-10a
Low-115	W-NY-420-10a
Low-116	W-MA-200-10j
Low-117	W-NY-480-60j RE
Low-118	W-NY-480-65j RE
Low-119	W-NY-480-70j Novodel RE
Low-120	W-NY-480 Dies 1-A RE through W-NY-480 Dies 7-J Pattern PE
Low-121	W-LA-040-10b
Low-122	W-NY-640-10a
Low-123	W-NY-640-15a
Low-124	W-NH-140-10a
Low-125	W-NY-740-10a
Low-126	W-NY-740-15a
Low-127	W-NY-880-10a
Low-128	W-SC-040-10j
Low-129	W-MA-300-10j
Low-130	W-CT-100-10a
Low-130A	W-CT-100-15b
Low-131	W-NH-100-10a
Low-132	W-NH-200-10a
Low-133	W-NY-940-15a
Low-134	W-NY-940-10a
Low-135	W-NY-940-20a
Low-136	W-NY-940-25a
Low-138	W-NY-940-30a
Low-139	W-NL-140-10b
Low-140	W-NY-1000-10a
Low-141	W-NY-1000-11a
Low-142	W-NJ-180-10b
Low-143	W-NJ-180-15a
Low-144	W-NJ-180-15b
Low-145	W-NY-1780-10a
Low-146	W-NY-1680-10a
Low-147	W-NY-1680-11a
Low-148	W-NJ-160-15a
Low-149	W-PA-180-15j
Low-150	W-NJ-120-10a
Low-151	W-NY-520-10a
Low-152	W-PA-180-10j
Low-153	W-NY-900-10a
Low-154	W-NY-900-15a
Low-155	W-NJ-160-10a
Low-156	W-NY-1740-10a
Low-157	W-NY-1740-15a
Low-158	W-OH-040-10a
Low-159	W-OH-040-20a
Low-160	W-OH-040-25a
Low-161	W-NY-080-10a
Low-162	W-12-30a
Low-163	W-NJ-100-15a
Low-164	W-MA-010-15a
Low-165	W-09-15e
Low-166	W-09-10b
Low-167	W-09-10f
Low-168	W-10-220a
Low-169	W-10-110b
Low-169A	W-10-114b
Low-170	W-11-90a
Low-171	W-10-320a

Low Number	Whitman Number
Low-172	W-12-10b
Low-173	W-MD-040-10e
Low-174	W-NY-1640-10f
Low-175	W-VT-010-10a
Low-176	W-VT-010-11a
Low-177	W-MO-020-10b
Low-178	W-MO-020-10e
Low-179	W-NY-480-65a
Low-180	W-NJ-180-10a
Low-181	W-PA-050-10j
Low-182	W-PA-050-10f
Low-183	W-12-30b
"Low-201"	W-NY-200-10a
"Low-202"	W-NY-200-12a Fire Gilt
"Low-206"	W-NY-220-10e
"Low-206A"	W-NY-220-10f
"Low-207"	W-NY-240-10a
"Low-208"	W-NY-240-10e
"Low-209"	W-NY-240-15a
"Low-210"	W-NY-240-15e
"Low-220"	W-NY-280-10a
"Low-221"	W-NY-280-10b
"Low-222"	W-NY-280-20a
"Low-223"	W-NY-280-20b
"Low-225"	W-NY-290-10b
"Low-226"	W-NY-290-15b
"Low-233"	W-NY-340-10b
"Low-234"	W-MA-360-10a
"Low-236"	W-LA-020-10b
"Low-236A"	W-LA-020-15g
"Low-237"	W-LA-020-20b
"Low-239"	W-NY-380-10a
"Low-240"	W-NY-380-10b
"Low-241"	W-NY-380-10j
"Low-242"	W-NY-440-40a
"Low-243"	W-NY-440-45a
"Low-245"	W-NY-440-50b PE
"Low-245A"	W-NY-440-50a RE
"Low-245B"	W-NY-440-65b
"Low-245C"	W-NY-440-60b
"Low-245var"	W-NY-440-50b PE
"Low-245var"	W-NY-440-50a RE
"Low-245var"	W-NY-440-50b RE
"Low-245var"	W-NY-440-80b
"Low-247"	W-NY-480-50j PE
"Low-248"	W-NY-480-55j PE

Low Number	Whitman Number
"Low-249"	W-NY-500-10a
"Low-251"	W-NY-540-10b
"Low-253"	W-NY-560-10b
"Low-254"	W-LA-100-10b
"Low-254A"	W-LA-020-80b
"Low-254B"	W-LA-020-80e
"Low-255"	W-NY-580-10a
"Low-256"	W-NY-580-10a Restrike
"Low-257"	W-NY-620-10b
"Low-259"	W-NY-660-10a PE
"Low-260"	W-NY-660-10b RE
"Low-261"	W-NY-680-10a
"Low-262"	W-NY-700-10a
"Low-263"	W-NY-720-10b
"Low-264"	W-LA-180-10b
"Low-265"	W-MA-098-10a
"Low-265A"	W-MA-098-15a
"Low-266"	W-MA-100-05a
"Low-267"	W-MA-100-10a
"Low-268"	W-NY-860-10b
"Low-271"	W-NY-1720-10a
"Low-272"	W-NY-1720-30a
"Low-272A"	W-NY-1720-35a
"Low-273"	W-NY-920-10a PE
"Low-273A"	W-NY-920-10a RE
"Low-274"	W-NY-920-15a PE
"Low-274A"	W-NY-920-15a RE
"Low-275"	W-VA-040-10a
"Low-276"	W-VA-040-10e
"Low-277"	W-VA-040-10j
"Low-279"	W-NY-960-10a PE
"Low-280"	W-NY-960-10f RE
"Low-281"	W-NY-960-15a PE
"Low-282A"	W-NY-960-20a PE
"Low-283"	W-NY-960-20a RE
"Low-284"	W-NY-1740-20a
"Low-284A"	W-NY-1740-40a
"Low-284B"	W-NY-1740-45a
"Low-284C"	W-NY-1720-20a
"Low-285"	W-NY-980-10a
"Low-286"	W-NY-980-15b
"Low-287"	W-NY-1040-10a
"Low-288"	W-LA-240-10b
"Low-291"	W-CT-060-10a
"Low-293"	W-VA-020-10a
"Low-294"	W-VA-020-10b

Low Number	Whitman Number
"Low-300"	W-MA-320-10a
"Low-301A"	W-MA-320-10b; W-MA-320-10j
"Low-302"	W-NJ-200-10a
"Low-303"	W-NJ-200-10b
"Low-304.	W-NJ-200-10e
"Low-305"	W-CT-040-10a
"Low-306"	W-NY-440-10a
"Low-307"	W-NY-440-15b
"Low-308"	W-NY-440-20a
"Low-309"	W-NY-440-20b PE
"Low-309A"	W-NY-440-20b RE
"Low-310"	W-NY-440-30a
"Low-311"	W-NY-440-30b
"Low-312"	W-OH-020-15j
"Low-312A"	W-OH-020-15b
"Low-313A"	W-OH-020-10a
"Low-314"	W-MA-070-10a
"Low-317"	W-NY-1200-10a
"Low-318"	W-NY-1600-10a RE
"Low-318A"	W-NY-1600-10a PE
"Low-318"	W-OH-020-10b
"Low-319"	W-OH-040-30a
"Low-320"	W-OH-040-40a PE
"Low-320B"	W-OH-040-40a RE
"Low-321"	W-NY-800-10a
"Low-323"	W-NY-800-15a
"Low-324"	W-NY-100-10a PE
"Low-324A"	W-NY-100-10a EE
"Low-325"	W-MA-110-10a
"Low-326"	W-MA-040-20a
"Low-327"	W-MA-140-10a
"Low-328"	W-MA-160-10a
"Low-331"	W-NY-1100-10a
"Low-335"	W-NY-420-20a
"Low-338"	W-NY-260-10b
"Low-344"	W-LA-020-60b
"Low-348"	W-NY-050-10a
"Low-349"	W-NY-050-10e
"Low-356"	W-PA-280 -10b PE
"Low-357"	W-PA-280 -10b RE
"Low-358"	W-PA-260 -10b
"Low-360"	W-NY-600-10a
"Low-361"	W-NY-600-10f
"Low-365"	W-NY-1080-10a
"Low-370"	W-NY-840-10j
"Low-371"	W-NY-840-10j Counterstamped with a rosette
"Low-372"	W-NY-840-10j Counterstamped with a dog
"Low-374"	W-NJ-140-10b
"Low-378"	W-MD-020-10j
"Low-379"	W-MD-020-15j
"Low-383"	W-PA-140-10b
"Low-383A"	W-PA-140-10a
"Low-384"	W-PA-320 -10b
"Low-384B"	W-PA-320 -15b
"Low-385"	W-PA-160-10b
"Low-386"	W-PA-220 -10b
"Low-392"	W-NY-1060-10a
"Low-392A"	W-NY-1060-10b
"Low-392B"	W-NY-1060-15a
"Low-398"	W-PA-040-10b PE
"Low-398A"	W-PA-040-10b RE
"Low-403"	W-MD-080-10j PE
"Low-403A"	W-MD-080-10j RE
"Low-403B"	W-MD-080-15g PE
"Low-404"	W-PA-060-10b
"Low-405"	W-PA-060-10a

Index of Rulau-to-Whitman Numbers

Rulau Number	Whitman Number
HT-1	W-09-10a
HT-1A	W-09-10b
HT-2	W-09-15a
HT-2A	W-09-15e
HT-3	W-09-20a
HT-3A	W-09-10f
HT-4	W-09-30b
HT-5	W-09-35b
HT-6	W-09-25b
HT-7	W-09-40b RE
HT-7A	W-09-40b PE
HT-8	W-09-45b RE
HT-9	W-10-210a
HT-10	W-10-210b
HT-11	W-10-230a
HT-12	W-10-220b
HT-13	W-10-220a
HT-14	W-10-10b RE
HT-14A	W-10-10b PE
HT-14B	W-10-10j RE
HT-14C	W-10-10f RE
HT-15	W-10-20a RE
HT-15E	W-10-30b PE
HT-15D	W-10-30e RE
HT-16	W-11-280a PE
HT-17	W-11-290a PE
HT-18	W-11-610a
HT-19	W-11-620a
HT-20	W-11-630a
HT-20A	W-11-630f
HT-21	W-11-640a
HT-22	W-11-650a
HT-23	W-11-660a
HT-24	W-11-740a
HT-25	W-10-310a
HT-26	W-10-120b
HT-27	W-10-130b
HT-28	W-10-112b
HT-29	W-10-112b; W-10-110b
HT-29A	W-10-110b; W-10-114b
HT-30	W-10-160b
HT-30B	W-10-160b
HT-31	W-11-510a
HT-32	W-11-520a
HT-33	W-11-530a
HT-33A	W-11-530f
HT-34	W-11-540a
HT-35	W-11-10a
HT-36	W-11-20a
HT-37	W-11-30a
HT-38	W-X-100a
HT-39	W-X-200a
HT-40	W-X-300a
HT-41	W-X-400a
HT-42	W-11-80a
HT-43	W-11-90a
HT-44	W-11-100a
HT-45	W-11-110a
HT-46	W-11-120a
HT-46A	W-11-120a
HT-46R	W-11-120a
HT-47	W-11-130a
HT-48	W-11-140a
HT-49	W-11-150a
HT-50	W-11-155a
HT-51	W-11-160a
HT-52	W-11-170a
HT-53	W-X-500a
HT-53A	W-X-500f
HT-54	W-X-600a
HT-54A	W-X-600f
HT-55	W-X-700a
HT-55A	W-X-700f
HT-56	W-11-260a
HT-57	W-11-270a
HT-58	W-11-300a PE
HT-59	W-X-800a
HT-59A	W-X-800f
HT-60	W-X-900a
HT-60A	W-X-900f
HT-61	W-11-410a
HT-62	W-11-420a
HT-63	W-11-430a
HT-64	W-11-440a
HT-65	W-11-310a
HT-66	W-11-320a
HT-66A	W-11-320a
HT-67	W-11-330a
HT-68	W-11-340a
HT-69	W-10-330a

Rulau Number	Whitman Number
HT-70	W-10-320a
HT-70A	W-10-320a
HT-71	W-10-320b
HT-72	W-10-330a
HT-73	W-11-710a
HT-74	W-NY-480-80j
HT-75A	W-12-10a; W-12-10b
HT-75B	W-12-10b
HT-76	W-12-20b
HT-77	W-12-30a
HT-77A	W-12-30b
HT-77B	W-12-30a
HT-81	W-11-720a
HT-81A	W-11-720a
HT-82	W-11-725a
HT-98	W-AL-040-10b
HT-99	W-AL-060-10b
HT-101	W-CT-040-10a
HT-102	W-CT-060-10a
HT-104	W-CT-080-10a
HT-105	W-CT-100-10a
HT-107	W-CT-100-15b
HT-115	W-LA-020-10b; W-LA-020-10g
HT-115A	W-LA-020-15g
HT-116	W-LA-020-20b
HT-117	W-LA-040-10b
HT-118	W-LA-020-60b
HT-119	W-LA-020-80b
HT-119A	W-LA-020-80e
HT-120	W-LA-100-10b
HT-121	W-LA-140-10b
HT-121A	W-LA-140-10e
HT-122	W-LA-180-10b
HT-123	W-LA-200-10a
HT-128	W-LA-240-10b
HT-129	W-LA-260-10b
HT-132	W-MD-020-10j
HT-133	W-MD-020-15j
HT-139	W-MD-040-10e
HT-147	W-MD-080-10j PE
HT-147A	W-MD-080-10j RE
HT-148	W-MD-080-15g PE
HT-150	W-MA-010-10a
HT-151	W-MA-010-15a
HT-152	W-MA-020-10a
HT-153	W-MA-020-15a
HT-153A	W-MA-020-15a

Rulau Number	Whitman Number
HT-154	W-MA-030-10a
HT-155	W-MA-030-15a
HT-156	W-MA-030-20a
HT-157	W-MA-040-25a
HT-158	W-MA-040-10a
HT-159	W-MA-010-15a
HT-160	W-MA-040-20a
HT-162	W-MA-070-10a
HT-163	W-MA-098-10a
HT-163A	W-MA-098-15a
HT-164	W-MA-100-05a
HT-165	W-MA-100-10a
HT-167	W-MA-110-10a
HT-169	W-MA-300-10j
HT-170	W-MA-140-10a
HT-171	W-MA-160-10a
HT-172	W-MA-200-10j
HT-174	W-MA-240-10a
HT-175	W-MA-280-15a
HT-176	W-MA-280-10a
HT-181	W-MA-320-10a
HT-181A	W-MA-320-10b
HT-181B	W-MA-320-10j
HT-182	W-MA-360-10a
HT-187	W-MO-020-10b
HT-187A	W-MO-020-10b
HT-187B	W-MO-020-10e
HT-188	W-MO-020-25b
HT-192	W-NH-100-10a
HT-194	W-NH-140-10a
HT-195	W-NH-200-10a
HT-200	W-NJ-100-10a
HT-201	W-NJ-100-15a
HT-201A	W-NJ-100-15a
HT-202	W-NJ-120-10a
HT-203	W-NJ-140-10b
HT-204	W-NJ-160-15a
HT-204B	W-NJ-160-10a
HT-205	W-NJ-180-10a
HT-205A	W-NJ-180-10b
HT-206	W-NJ-180-15a
HT-207	W-NJ-200-10a
HT-207A	W-NJ-200-10b
HT-207B	W-NJ-200-10e
HT-207AA	W-NJ-200-15b
HT-210	W-NY-050-10a
HT-210A	W-NY-050-10e
HT-211	W-NY-080-10a

Rulau Number	Whitman Number
HT-212	W-NY-100-10a PE
HT-212A	W-NY-100-10a EE
HT-212B	W-NY-100-15a
HT-213	W-NY-120-10a
HT-214	W-NY-120-15a
HT-216	W-NY-150-10a
HT-217	W-NY-150-15a
HT-218	W-NY-150-20a
HT-219	W-NY-180-10a
HT-221	W-NY-200-10a; W-NY-200-10g
HT-222	W-NY-200-12a Fire Gilt
HT-226	W-NY-220-10e
HT-226A	W-NY-220-10f
HT-227	W-NY-240-10a
HT-227A	W-NY-240-10e
HT-228	W-NY-240-15a
HT-228A	W-NY-240-15e
HT-230	W-NY-260-10b
HT-235	W-NY-280-10a
HT-235A	W-NY-280-10b
HT-236	W-NY-280-20a
HT-236A	W-NY-280-20b
HT-237	W-NY-290-10b
HT-238	W-NY-290-15b
HT-239	W-NY-300-10a
HT-240	W-NY-300-15a
HT-A240	W-NY-320-10b
HT-B240	W-NY-320-10j
HT-241	W-NY-340-10b
HT-243	W-NY-360-10a
HT-244	W-NY-360-15a
HT-245A	W-NY-375-10j
HT-247	W-NY-380-10a
HT-247A	W-NY-380-10b
HT-248	W-NY-380-10j
HT-249	W-NY-400-10a
HT-250	W-NY-420-10a
HT-251	W-NY-420-20a
HT-253	W-NY-440-30a
HT-254	W-NY-440-30b
HT-255	W-NY-440-40a
HT-256	W-NY-440-45a
HT-258	W-NY-440-50b PE
HT-258A	W-NY-440-50a RE
HT-258AA	W-NY-440-50a RE
HT-258B	W-NY-440-50b PE
HT-258C	W-NY-440-50b RE
HT-259	W-NY-440-65b
HT-259A	W-NY-440-60b
HT-259B	W-NY-440-80b
HT-260	W-NY-480-50j PE
HT-261	W-NY-480-55j PE
HT-262	W-NY-480-60j RE
HT-263	W-NY-480-65j RE
HT-264	W-NY-480-65a
HT-265A	W-NY-480-70j Novodel RE
HT-268	W-NY-480 Dies 1-A RE through W-NY-480 Dies 6-I RE
HT-268A	W-NY-480 Dies 7-J Pattern PE
HT-269	W-NY-500-10a
HT-272	W-NY-520-10a
HT-275	W-NY-540-10b
HT-276	W-NY-540-10b
HT-A276	W-NY-540-10b
HT-277	W-NY-560-10b
HT-278	W-NY-580-10a
HT-279	W-NY-580-10a Restrike
HT-280	W-NY-600-10a
HT-280A	W-NY-600-10f
HT-281	W-NY-600-10a
HT-282	W-NY-620-10b
HT-A282	W-NY-620-11b
HT-283	W-NY-640-10a
HT-284	W-NY-640-15a
HT-285	W-NY-660-10a PE
HT-285A	W-NY-660-10b RE
HT-286	W-NY-680-10a
HT-287	W-NY-700-10a
HT-288	W-NY-720-10b
HT-289	W-NY-740-10a
HT-290	W-NY-740-15a
HT-291	W-NY-760-10a
HT-292	W-NY-760-15a
HT-293	W-NY-760-20a
HT-294	W-NY-780-20a
HT-295	W-NY-800-10a
HT-297	W-NY-800-15a
HT-298	W-NY-840-10j

Rulau Number	Whitman Number
HT-299	W-NY-840-10j Counterstamped with a rosette
HT-300	W-NY-840-10j Counterstamped with a dog
HT-A300	W-NY-840-10e Counterstamped with a leaf
HT-301	W-NY-840-10a Counterstamped with a leaf
HT-302	W-NY-860-10b
HT-304	W-NY-880-10a
HT-305	W-NY-900-10a
HT-306	W-NY-900-15a
HT-307	W-NY-920-10a PE
HT-307A	W-NY-920-10a RE
HT-308	W-NY-920-15a PE
HT-308A	W-NY-920-15a RE
HT-308B	W-NY-920-15a Diagonally RE
HT-308E	W-NY-920-20a Diagonally RE
HT-309	W-SC-040-10j
HT-310	W-NY-930-10e
HT-311	W-NY-940-15a
HT-313	W-NY-940-10a
HT-314	W-NY-940-20a
HT-315	W-NY-940-25a
HT-317	W-NY-940-30a
HT-317A	W-NY-940-30a
HT-318	W-NY-960-10a PE
HT-318A	W-NY-960-10a PE
HT-319	W-NY-960-10b RE
HT-320	W-NY-960-10f RE
HT-320AA	W-NY-960-10f RE
HT-321	W-NY-960-15a PE
HT-322	W-NY-960-15a PE
HT-323	W-NY-960-20a PE
HT-324	W-NY-960-20a RE
HT-325	W-NY-960-20a RE
HT-332	W-NY-980-10a
HT-332A	W-NY-980-10b
HT-333	W-NY-980-15b
HT-334	W-NY-1000-10a
HT-335	W-NY-1000-11a
HT-A335	W-NY-1020-10a
HT-336	W-NY-1040-10a
HT-337	W-NY-1060-10a; W-NY-1060-10b
HT-338	W-NY-1060-15a
HT-339	W-NY-1080-10a
HT-341	W-NY-1100-10a
HT-342	W-NY-1100-10a
HT-344	W-NY-1200-10a
HT-345	W-NY-1600-10a RE
HT-346	W-NY-1600-10a PE
HT-347	W-NY-1640-10a
HT-347B	W-NY-1640-10f
HT-348	W-NY-1660-10a
HT-349	W-NY-1660-15a
HT-350	W-NY-1660-20a
HT-353	W-NY-1660-35a
HT-354	W-NY-1660-35a
HT-355	W-NY-1660-40a
HT-356	W-NY-1780-10a
HT-357	W-NY-1780-10a
HT-357A	W-NY-1780-10a
HT-357B	W-NY-1780-10a
HT-359	W-NY-1680-10a
HT-360	W-NY-1680-11a
HT-361	W-NY-1700-10a
HT-362	W-MA-040-25a
HT-363	W-NY-1720-10a
HT-364	W-NY-1720-30a
HT-365	W-NY-1720-35a
HT-366	W-NY-1740-10a
HT-367	W-NY-1740-15a
HT-368	W-NY-1740-20a
HT-369	W-NY-1740-40a
HT-370	W-NY-1740-45a
HT-371	W-NY-1720-20a
HT-375	W-OH-020-15j
HT-375A	W-OH-020-10a; W-OH-020-15b
HT-376	W-OH-020-10b
HT-376A	W-OH-020-10a
HT-377	W-OH-040-10a
HT-377A	W-OH-040-10a
HT-378	W-OH-040-20a
HT-379	W-OH-040-25a
HT-379A	W-OH-040-25a
HT-379C	W-OH-040-25a
HT-380	W-OH-040-30a
HT-381	W-OH-040-40a PE

Rulau Number	Whitman Number
HT-381B	W-OH-040-40a RE
HT-381C Overstrike	W-OH-040-40a Over 1837 Cent PE
HT-381C Overstrike	W-OH-040-40a Over Low-95 PE
HT-385	W-PA-040-10b PE
HT-385A	W-PA-040-10b RE
HT-399	W-PA-050-10j
HT-399A	W-PA-050-10f
HT-402	W-PA-060-10b
HT-402A	W-PA-060-10a
HT-402B	W-PA-060-10b
HT-409	W-PA-130-10b
HT-410	W-PA-140-10b
HT-410A	W-PA-140-10a
HT-410B	W-PA-140-10b
HT-411	W-PA-160-10b
HT-412	W-PA-180-10j
HT-413	W-PA-180-15j
HT-417	W-PA-220 -10b
HT-A417	W-PA-240 -10a
HT-B417	W-PA-240 -10b
HT-C417	W-PA-240 -10e
HT-417A	W-PA-220 -10b
HT-418	W-PA-260 -10b
HT-418A	W-PA-260 -10b
HT-419	W-PA-280 -10b PE
HT-419A	W-PA-280 -10b RE
HT-421	W-PA-320 -10b
HT-421A	W-PA-320 -10b

Rulau Number	Whitman Number
HT-422	W-PA-320 -15b
HT-423	W-PA-340-10a
HT-425	W-RI-020-10a
HT-427	W-RI-040-10a
HT-428	W-RI-080-10a
HT-428A	W-RI-080-10a
HT-430	W-SC-020-10j
HT-431	W-LA-160-10b PE
HT-431A	W-LA-160-10b RE
HT-433	W-VT-010-10a
HT-434	W-VT-010-11a
HT-434A	W-VT-010-11a
HT-440	W-VA-020-10a
HT-440A	W-VA-020-10b
HT-441	W-VA-040-10a
HT-441A	W-VA-040-10e
HT-441B	W-VA-040-10j
HT-464	W-NL-140-10b
HT-485	W-PA-100-10a
HT-487	W-PA-100-10e
HT-486	W-PA-100-10j
HT-488	W-PA-100-10b
HT-580	W-CT-020-10b PE
HT-580A	W-CT-020-10b RE
HT-901	W-NY-440-10a
HT-901A	W-NY-440-15b
HT-902	W-NY-440-20a
HT-902A	W-NY-440-20b PE
HT-902B	W-NY-440-20b RE

INDEX

1789 Mott token, 219
1834 Running Boar tokens, 99
1834 Seward and Verplanck tokens, 95
1837 Van Buren / 1841 Webster Ship tokens, 82, 113
1841 Webster Ship tokens, 82, 113
1841-dated tokens, 82
1914 ANA Convention, 24
"a plain system, void of pomp", 60
Adams, Edgar H., 23, 25, 93, 127, 175
Adams, John Quincy, 43, 44, 45, 88, 101
Alabama Hard Times tokens, 121
Allaire, James P., 160
Am I Not a Woman & a Sister token, 83, 116
American Numismatic and Archaeological Society, 20, 275
American Numismatic Association, 5, 24
American Numismatic Society, 9, 20, 238
American Silver, 196, 197
American System, 44, 143, 147
An Arrangement of Tradesmen's Cards, Political Tokens, also Election Medals, Medalets, &c., 9, 11, 179
Atwood's Rail Road Hotel, 2, 180
Bale & Smith, 7, 180, 183, 211, 238
Bank of the United States (1st), 36, 37
Bank of the United States (2nd), 40, 44, 45, 47, 48, 55, 57, 58, 59, 60, 63–64, 67, 87, 99
Beck's Public Baths token, 13, 266
Benton, Thomas Hart, 61, 62, 79, 88, 109
Benton's Mint Drops, 62, 109, 193
Bergen Iron Works banking scheme, 171
Bergen Iron Works, 169
Biddle, Nicholas, 41, 47, 48, 58, 59, 67, 83, 87
blacksmith's tokens, 244, 245, 246, 247
Bushnell fantasies, 18, 20, 22, 205, 206, 268
Bushnell, Charles I., 9, 10–11, 12, 17–18, 22, 268
Calhoun, John C., 43, 44, 45, 50, 53
Cherokee, 49–50, 63
Clay, Henry, 43, 46, 49, 51–52, 55, 57, 63, 85, 90
Cochran, J., 90, 174
Cogan, Edward D., 274
Connecticut Hard Times tokens, 122
Davenport, Henry, 14, 15, 18, 273–274
Democratic Party, 43, 61–62
Descriptive Catalogue of Hard Times Tokens Issued For and Against the United States Bank, and with References to the Financial Troubles of 1834–1841, 21, 23
Dunham, William Forrester, 23, 28
Eaton, John H., 47, 50, 51–53, 53, 54
Eaton, Peggy, 50–54
Elder, Thomas L., 278
Embargo Act, 37
Erie Canal, 33, 178
"executive financiering", 113
Fantasy tokens, 18, 20, 22, 205, 206, 267–272
Feuchtwanger Cents, 22, 79,199–202, 262
Feuchtwanger Composition, 4, 18, 79, 196–198
Feuchtwanger, Lewis, 18, 22, 79, 196–207
Ford, John J., Jr., iv, 7, 28, 29, 31
German silver, 4, 79, 196
Gibbs, John, 118, 164, 167
Gustin & Blake, 7, 25, 264
Hard Times era, 8
Hard Times Tokens. An Arrangement of Jackson Cents Issued for and Against the United States Bank., 21, 23, 25, 90, 268
Harrison, William Henry, 67, 85, 86–87, 119, 138
Hermitage, 42, 43, 57
Hetrich, George, 28, 29
Hill, Isaac, 47, 53
Hodge, J. Ledyard, 11, 12–13
Howell Works, 160–164, 169
"Illustrious Predecessor" tokens, 111
Indian Removal Act, 49
Ingham, Samuel D., 47, 53, 54
Jackass with LL.D. tokens 1834–1837, 101
Jackson cents, 14, 17
Jackson, Andrew, 1–2, 39, 42–43, 45–46, 48, 50, 51–53, 53, 55–56, 58, 60, 66, 83, 91–93, 99, 101, 147
Jackson, Rachel, 45–46, 53
James E. Dice & M. Lamar Hicks sale, 31–32
Jefferson, Thomas, 37
Kitchen Cabinet, 53
Levick fanatasies, 18, 20
Levick, Joseph N.T., v, 14, 18, 18–20, 126, 268–270, 274–276
Liberty Head, 75, 79, 103, 125
Loco Foco, 110–111
Louisiana Hard Times tokens, 127
Lovett, George H., 10, 214, 215
Lovett, Robert, Sr., 64, 214

Low numbers, 4, 30
Low, Lyman H., 1–2, 3, 4, 8, 20–23, 23, 24, 30, 276–279
Maryland Hard Times tokens, 133
Mason, Jeremiah, 47–48, 49
Massachusetts Hard Times tokens, 135
Maverick Coach, 148
"May Tenth 1837" tokens, 108
McCoy Collection, 14–15
Mehl, B. Max, 28
Merchants' Exchange, New York, 65, 191, 216–218
Miller, Donald M., 28–30, 31
"Mint Drop" tokens, 109
Mint Drops, 62, 109, 193
Missouri Hard Times tokens, 155
Moffett, James G., 218
Monroe, James, 42
"My Third Heat", 64, 99
New Hampshire Hard Times tokens, 156
New Jersey Hard Times tokens, 160
New York & Harlaem Rail Road tokens, 75, 222
New York Hard Times tokens, 173
Niles' Register, 36
Non Intercourse Act, 37
Non-Local Hard Times tokens, 267
"Not One Cent", 75, 103, 125
"Not One Cent" tokens, 75, 103, 107, 125
Numismatic Guaranty Corporation of America (NGC), 5, 32
Numismatist, The, 23, 24
O'Neal, Peggy, 50–54
obverse, 2–3
Ohio Hard Times tokens, 248
Panic of 1837, 1–2, 8, 74, 75
Pennsylvania Hard Times tokens, 252
"pet" banks, 58–59
Petticoat Affair, 53–54
Philadelphia Mint, 34, 67, 74
Philadelphia Numismatic Society, 11
Professional Coin Grading Service (PCGS), 5, 32
pseudo-Low numbers, 30
R.E. Russell token, 262
Raymond, Wayte, 25, 204
reverse, 2–3
Rhode Island Hard Times tokens, 259
Richards, H.M. & E.I., 136
Roxbury Coaches, 148, 151
Rulau numbers, 4, 30
Rulau, Russell, 4, 30, 279–280
Sage, Augustus B., 9
Scovill Manufacturing Company, 17, 75–78, 124–126
Seward, Wiliam H., 95–97
sharpness, 6–7
shinplasters, 78
slavery, 42, 44, 46, 63, 82, 83, 87, 88, 116–117
Smith's Clock Establishment, 136, 227
South Carolina Hard Times tokens, 261
specie, 34
Specie Circular, 66, 71, 82
Standard Catalog of United States Tokens 1700–1900, 4, 30, 279
state-chartered banks, 1, 34–36, 45, 47–48, 58–59
striking, 6–7
Sub-Treasury Bill, 79–82
T. Duseaman token, 168
Tariff of 1828, 44–45
temperance, 87, 173, 184
Tennessee Hard Times tokens, 264
"The Constitution as I understand it", 56
Tilden Collection, 28–29
Token and Medal Society, 30
Trail of Tears, 50, 63
True, 6–7, 247–248
Tyler, John, 86–87, 88
United States Bank of Pennsylvania, 67
USS *Constitution*, 38, 51, 82
Van Buren Campaign tokens, 119–120
Van Buren, Martin, 2, 50, 53–54, 67–68, 70–72, 81, 82, 83, 85, 86, 111, 113, 119–120
Vermont Hard Times tokens, 264
Verplanck, Gulian C., 95, 97
Virginia Hard Times tokens, 265
War of 1812, 38–39
Webster, Daniel, 47, 49, 55, 62, 64, 67, 82, 88, 107, 113, 143
Whig Party, 43, 62, 64, 67–68, 85, 94–95, 96, 98–99, 165
Whig Victory tokens, 94–95
Woodbury, Levi, 47, 55, 73–74
Woodward, W. Elliot, 13–17, 18–20, 268–269
Wright & Bale, 183, 184, 237
Wright, Benjamin P., 23